CW01113213

# Construction Project Management
## Planning, Scheduling and Controlling

# Construction Project Management
## Planning, Scheduling and Controlling

**K K Chitkara**
*Institute of Construction Project Management*
*Gurgaon, Haryana, India*

**Tata McGraw Hill Education Private Limited**
NEW DELHI

McGraw-Hill Offices
**New Delhi** New York St Louis San Francisco Auckland Bogotá Caracas
Kuala Lumpur Lisbon London Madrid Mexico City Milan Montreal
San Juan Santiago Singapore Sydney Tokyo Toronto

**Tata McGraw-Hill**

© 1998, Tata McGraw Hill Education Private Limited

Nineteenth reprint 2009
**RZCQCRYFDRBLB**

No part of this publication may be reproduced or distributed in any form or by any means, without the prior written permission of the publishers.

This edition can be exported from India only by the publishers,
Tata McGraw Hill Education Private Limited

**ISBN-13:** 978-0-07-462062-5
**ISBN-10:** 0-07-462062-2

Published by Tata McGraw Hill Education Private Limited,
7 West Patel Nagar, New Delhi 110 008, printed at Sai Printo Pack Pvt. Ltd.,
New Delhi 110 020

The **McGraw-Hill** Companies

# Dedication

## *On the 50th Year of India's Independence*

*Dedicated to the martyrs
who sacrificed their lives to free the Indian sub-continent*

# Preface

*Construction Project Management*, in its present form, is the end product of my over 25 years experience at senior level of planning and managing major construction projects, both in India and the Middle East; and imparting instructions on the subject to practicing professionals, engineers and engineering students.

Project is a mission, undertaken to create a unique facility, product or service within the specified scope, quality, time, and costs. With the emerging global opportunities, projects cross geographical boundaries, corporate channels, traditional systems and cultural diversities. The knowledge areas needed to manage such projects comprise project management techniques, general management practices and technology-related subjects. The project management techniques of planning, scheduling and controlling are the tools and devices that bind the subject's knowledge areas. These techniques can be applied to all types of projects. This book covers their application in the field of construction.

The construction industry accounts for 6–9% of the Gross Domestic Product (GDP) of many countries. The value of annual construction activity in the world exceeds one trillion dollars. Unfortunately, due to the secretive nature of construction business, knowledge gained in planning, scheduling and controlling construction process is rarely disseminated. Consequently, the cost of inefficiency is being incurred as a recurring cost. Moreover, in various businesses, the rate of business failure of construction contractors is one of the highest. One of the reasons for this high rate of failures is the lack of knowledge.

There is a vast scope for improving performance through knowledge in the construction industry, where men, materials, machinery, money and management work together to build a facility. Perhaps, it is one of the rare industries in the world that can provide such a vast scope for cost and time reduction at micro-level.

This book describes the planning, scheduling and controlling of time and cost in construction projects. Though vital for performance improvement, this subject is often neglected. The subject covered in this book is divided into four parts spanning eighteen chapters and the text is illustrated with real life cases:

- **Construction Project Management Overview** Chapters 1 and 2 provide an introduction to the subject. They cover the nature of construction industry, describe construction project concepts and characteristics, and outline project development process. While highlighting salient features of the project management process, they explain the causes for project failures, outline approach and importance of planning, scheduling and controlling in construction projects, including the functions and role of the chief planner.
- **Time Planning** Chapter 3 describes the methodology for breaking down project work into activities and for activity duration estimation. Chapters 4 and 5 cover the methodology for modelling and time analysis of CPM, PERT and Precedence networks.

Preparation of time-limited and resources-limited schedules are described in Chapter 6.

- **Resource Planning** This part containing six chapters is devoted to the strategy for planning manpower, construction materials, plant and machinery, production costs and project budget.
- **Planning Control System** This part containing six chapters deals with organization of control system; techniques for controlling resource productivity, costs and time; codification of planning system; and management of project information system using computers.

Each chapter of Construction Project Management can be expanded into a volume, but its scope has been restricted to the present size by making trade-offs between technique elaboration and their application coverage. A comprehensive bibliography has been included to supplement information on each topic. A CD-ROM covering lesson plans and self-test exercises for on-line study of the subject covered in the book is being prepared, and is likely to be available by the end of 1999

This book is designed for use by:

- Project managers and their team members
- Managers in corporate office dealing with the managment and execution of construction projects
- Academician, trainers and trainees connected with project management
- Consultants and specialists like architects, engineers, quantity-surveyors, accountants and other managers associated with projects
- Practicing engineers and students studying construction management and those new to the concept and techniques used in Project Management

The subjects covered mainly deal with contractor-oriented Project Management, as well as client-directed Project Management. This book presupposes fundamental engineering knowledge and familiarity with construction process and practices.

My interest in project management knowledge areas started in the early seventies, when as Commander Works Engineer of a Cantonment Construction Project, I conducted a number of project management courses to train the staff and engineer officers of the Military Engineering Services in India. Since then, I have been teaching and practising management of construction projects.

Despite best efforts, the possibility of some errors in the book cannot be ruled out. I welcome readers' comments to make improvements in this book. My e-mail addresses are:
chitkara@icpm.com
chitkara@nda.vsnl.net.in

It is hoped that the subject covered in this book will stimulate wider discussions and enable further development of **project management techniques.**

K K CHITKARA

# Acknowledgements

This book would not have been possible without the construction and academic experiences gained from the many organizations, both in India and the Middle East, where I had the privilege to serve. In gratitude, I salute my superiors, colleagues and subordinates for their direct and indirect contribution in developing this book. I am thankful to my friends who read the manuscript and made useful suggestions.

In particular, I am grateful to the following:

- Lt Gen. S N Sharma, PVSM, AVSM, retired Engineer-in-Chief of the Indian Army, for launching me into the field of project management.
- Dr R A Maker, Managing Director of Maker's Development Services, for permitting me to include case illustrations from 2000 Housing Units Project at Baghdad, Iraq.
- Col R N Kanwar, for his interest and sound counsel.
- Mr K S Kharb, Executive Director, Som Dutt Builders, for allowing me to reproduce a table from his book.
- Mr Mohammad Yusuff Khan, for word processing the major part of the manuscript.
- Management, staff and students of the National Institute of Construction Management and Research, India, for their contribution.
- Tata Consultancy Services Ltd and KLG Systel Ltd for providing computer software support.

Last but not the least, I am thankful to my family for their understanding and continuing support which saw me through the extended working hours.

# Contents

*Preface* vii
*Acknowledgements* ix

## PART I

## CONSTRUCTION PROJECT MANAGEMENT: AN OVERVIEW

**Chapter 1** The Construction Project Management Framework

- 1.1 Construction Industry — 3
- 1.2 Construction Projects — 8
- 1.3 Project Development Process — 14
- 1.4 Project Management — 21
- 1.5 Main Causes of Project Failure — 31

Exhibits

- *Typical Housing Project* 27

**Chapter 2** Project Planning Scope

- 2.1 Plan Development Process — 35
- 2.2 Time Planning Process — 39
- 2.3 Work Scheduling Process — 43
- 2.4 Resource Planning Process — 46
- 2.5 Project Control Process — 55
- 2.6 Importance of Planning, Scheduling and Controlling Projects — 60
- 2.7 Functions and Role of Chief Planner — 63

Exhibits

- *2000 Housing Units Project, Baghdad, Scope of Work* 40
- *2000 Housing Units Project, Summary Schedule of Construction Tasks* 44

xii Contents

- *2000 Housing Units Project: Man-month Requirement and Earned Value Forecasts* 48
- *2000 Housing Units Project: Extracts from Workers' Requirements for Crash Program* 50
- *Residential Buildings with Precast Concrete Superstructure: Main Materials Required* 51
- *2000 Housing Units Project: Major Plant & Equipment Planned* 53
- *Foundation Construction Sub-Project: Activity-wise Workers' Requirement Estimate for One Foundation Module Construction* 54
- *Foundation Construction Sub-Project: Major Materials Requirement Estimate for One Foundation Module* 56
- *2000 Housing Units Project: Responsibility Centres* 57

# PART II

# TIME PLANNING

## Chapter 3 Project Work Breakdown

| | | |
|---|---|---:|
| ❏ 3.1 | Project Work-breakdown Levels | 71 |
| ❏ 3.2 | Determining Activities Involved | 77 |
| ❏ 3.3 | Assessing Activity Duration | 86 |
| ❏ 3.4 | Activity Costs and Earned Value | 92 |
| ❏ 3.5 | Work Breakdown of a New Cantonment Project | 95 |

### Exhibits

- *2000 Housing Units Project: Sub-project and Task Level Work Breakdown* 74
- *Construction of Residential Building: Work-breakdown Structure* 75
- *Pumping Station Project: Work-breakdown Structure* 80
- *Planning of a Factory Project during Feasibility Stage: Task Matrix* 82
- *Primary School Construction: Work-breakdown Structure* 83
- *Construction of Education Buildings: Activities Matrix with Duration* 84
- *Sector-wise Location of Zones in a Cantonment Construction Project* 99
- *Inter-sector Construction Project External Services* 100
- *Cantonment Construction Project: Work-breakdown Structure* 101

## Chapter 4 Project CPM/PERT Network Analysis

| | | |
|---|---|---:|
| ❏ 4.1 | CPM Network Analysis Fundamentals | 104 |
| ❏ 4.2 | CPM Network Analysis Procedure | 120 |
| ❏ 4.3 | PERT Network Analysis | 130 |
| ❏ 4.4 | PERT *versus* CPM | 146 |

Exhibits

❑ *Pumping Station Project: Time Analysis CPM Network  105*
❑ *Activities of Pumping Station Project  122*
❑ *PERT Network of Pumping Station Project  133*

## Chapter 5  Precedence Network Analysis

| | | |
|---|---|---:|
| ❑ | 5.1  Precedence Network Analysis (PNA) Fundamentals | 147 |
| ❑ | 5.2  Case Illustrations | 157 |
| ❑ | 5.3  Classification of Networks | 169 |
| ❑ | 5.4  Guidelines for Drawing Project Network | 170 |
| ❑ | 5.5  PNA *versus* CPM | 173 |

Exhibits

❑ *Precedence Network of Raft Foundation Construction  148*
❑ *Repetitive Works Project: Precedence Network of Four Rafts Foundation Construction  156*
❑ *Primary School Structure Construction Precedence Network  162*
❑ *Summary Precedence Network of Primary School  163*
❑ *Summary Precedence Network of Educational Buildings  164*
❑ *Raw Water Treatment Clarifier  165*
❑ *Raw Water Clarifier Tank Construction Precedence Network and Schedule  167*
❑ *Site Development Project CPM and PNA Networks  174*
❑ *Factory Construction Project Conversion of CPM into PNA Network  175*

## Chapter 6  Project Work Scheduling

| | | |
|---|---|---:|
| ❑ | 6.1  Purpose of Work Scheduling | 181 |
| ❑ | 6.2  Bar Chart Method of Work Scheduling | 181 |
| ❑ | 6.3  Scheduling the Network Plan | 182 |
| ❑ | 6.4  Line-of-Balance Method of Scheduling Repetitive Projects | 195 |
| ❑ | 6.5  Factors Affecting Work Scheduling | 208 |
| ❑ | 6.6  Forecasting Inputs and Outputs | 211 |
| ❑ | 6.7  Schedule Hierarchy | 216 |

Exhibits

❑ *Site Development Project: Work Programme  183*
❑ *Site Development Project: CPM Network  190*
❑ *Site Development Project: Time Limited Optimum Resources Schedule  193*
❑ *Site Development Project: Resources Limited Schedule  196*
❑ *2000 Housing Units Project: Summary Schedule of Education Buildings  197*

- *Residential Buildings Foundations Work Packages Construction Cyclograph 204*
- *Residential Building Finishes Plan: Derived Using Line-of-Balance Technique 205*
- *Residential Building Finishes Control: Derived Using Line-of-Balance Technique 207*
- *2000 Housing Units Project: Residential Building Monthly Target Tracking Chart 209*
- *Site Development Project : Input-Output Cost Data 214*
- *Site Development Project: Forecasts of Input Costs and Workdone Value 216*

# PART III

# RESOURCE PLANNING

## Chapter 7 Planning Construction Manpower

| | | |
|---|---|---:|
| 7.1 | Establishing Workers' Productivity Standards | 222 |
| 7.2 | Scheduling Construction Site Workers | 232 |
| 7.3 | Project Manpower Grouping | 236 |
| 7.4 | Designing Workers Financial Incentive Scheme | 243 |

### Exhibits

- *2000 Housing Units Project: Extract from Workers' Requirement Forecast 235*
- *Typical Housing Project 237*

## Chapter 8 Planning Construction Materials

| | | |
|---|---|---:|
| 8.1 | ABC Classification of Construction Materials | 246 |
| 8.2 | Materials Usage Standard | 253 |
| 8.3 | Materials Provisioning Process | 254 |
| 8.4 | Planning Materials Inventory | 259 |
| 8.5 | Use of Operations Research in Materials Planning | 273 |

### Exhibits

- *Residential Building's Sub-Project: ABC Classification of Direct Materials 249*
- *Minor Materials Mobilisation Stock 270*

## Chapter 9 Project Construction Equipment

| | | |
|---|---|---:|
| 9.1 | Classification of Major Equipment | 276 |
| 9.2 | Earth Factor in Earthwork | 276 |

| | | | |
|---|---|---|---|
| ❑ | 9.3 | Earth Excavating Equipment | 280 |
| ❑ | 9.4 | Earth Cutting and Hauling Equipment | 285 |
| ❑ | 9.5 | Earth Compacting and Grading Equipment | 292 |
| ❑ | 9.6 | Concreting Plant and Equipment | 298 |
| ❑ | 9.7 | Cranes for Materials Hoisting | 305 |

### Exhibits

- ❑ *Functional Classification of Construction Equipment 277*
- ❑ *Earth Excavating and Lifting Equipment 281*
- ❑ *Excavator Output Adjustment Factors for Secondary Tasks 283*
- ❑ *Earth Cutting and Hauling Equipment 286*
- ❑ *Common Earth Compacting Equipment 293*
- ❑ *Typical Major Compacting Equipment: Salient Features 299*
- ❑ *Major Concreting Equipment 301*
- ❑ *Materials Handling Equipment 306*

## Chapter 10  Selecting Construction Equipment

| | | | |
|---|---|---|---|
| ❑ | 10.1 | Task Considerations | 316 |
| ❑ | 10.2 | Cost Considerations | 320 |
| ❑ | 10.3 | Equipment Engineering Considerations | 329 |
| ❑ | 10.4 | Equipment Acquisition Options | 331 |
| ❑ | 10.5 | Summary of Equipment Selection Considerations | 337 |

### Exhibits

- ❑ *Housing Construction Project: Major Plant and Equipment owned by Contractors 315*
- ❑ *Standard Methods of Determining Depreciation 322*
- ❑ *Construction Equipment Costing: Hourly Owning and Operating Cost Estimate 328*
- ❑ *Plant Leasing Offer of a Concrete Pump 335*
- ❑ *Equipment Replacement Decisions Data 338*

## Chapter 11  Planning Construction Costs

| | | | |
|---|---|---|---|
| ❑ | 11.1 | Classification of Construction Costs | 341 |
| ❑ | 11.2 | Unit Rate Costing Standards of Resources | 349 |
| ❑ | 11.3 | Work-package Standard Cost | 357 |
| ❑ | 11.4 | Standard 'S' Curve Forecasting Tool | 363 |

### Exhibits

- ❑ *Typical Indirect Costs Classification of a Multi-national Company 347*
- ❑ *Indirect Costs: Functional Breakdown 348*

## Chapter 12 Planning Construction Budgets

- **12.1** Structuring Responsibility Centres — 367
- **12.2** Sales Revenue Budget — 370
- **12.3** Operating Expenses Budget — 373
- **12.4** Costs Inflation, Escalation and Contingencies — 380
- **12.5** Budgetary Forecasts — 382
- **12.6** Project Master Budget — 388
- **12.7** Importance of Project Budget — 389

### Exhibits

- *2000 Housing Units Project: Organisation Chart 368*
- *2000 Housing Units Project: Task Responsibility Centres 369*
- *2000 Housing Units Project: Budgeting Data Source 375*

# PART IV

## PLANNING CONTROL SYSTEM

## Chapter 13 Project Control Methodology

- **13.1** Control System Framework — 394
- **13.2** Performance Parameters to be Controlled — 397
- **13.3** Performance Base Lines — 398
- **13.4** Performance Accounting Process — 400
- **13.5** Monitoring Performance — 405
- **13.6** Information Communication — 411
- **13.7** Control Benefits — 415
- **13.8** Prerequisites of Control Effectiveness — 417

### Exhibits

- *Project Control System 395*
- *2000 Housing Units Project Typical Responsibility Centre Performance Reports 403*
- *Foundation Construction Sub-project 406*
- *Formats for Reporting Selected Project Parameters Performance 414*
- *Site Staff Mobilisation Status Forecasts 415*
- *Typical Performance Control Responsibility Matrix 418*

## Chapter 14 Resources Productivity Control

- **14.1** Labour Productivity Control — 420

Contents **xvii**

- **14.2** Equipment Productivity Control — 427
- **14.3** Materials Productivity Control — 431
- **14.4** Role of Construction Managers in Improving Productivity — 436

Exhibits

- *Labour Productivity Control Chart 426*

## Chapter 15 Project Cost Control

- **15.1** Cost Control Preliminaries — 440
- **15.2** Revenue or Sales Control — 445
- **15.3** Direct Cost Control — 448
- **15.4** Indirect Cost Control — 457
- **15.5** Project Budgetary Control — 457
- **15.6** Risk Cost Management — 466

## Chapter 16 Project Time Control

- **16.1** Time Progress Monitoring Methodology — 470
- **16.2** What-if Analysis — 485
- **16.3** Time Reduction Techniques — 486
- **16.4** Work Progress Reviewing Procedure — 498

Exhibits

- *Primary School Construction: Updated Summary Precedence Network 478*
- *Updated Line-of-Balance Chart 479*
- *Updated Bar Chart Schedules 481*
- *Master Network of Pumping Station Project 483*
- *Pumping Station Project: Modified Network Incorporating Changes 484*
- *Pumping Station Project Original and Time Compressed Network 488*

## Chapter 17 Codification of the Planning System

- **17.1** Codification Approach — 502
- **17.2** Work Package and Activities Identification Code — 507
- **17.3** Resources Codes — 511
- **17.4** Cost and Finance Accounting Codes — 520
- **17.5** Technical Documents Codes — 523
- **17.6** Codification Effectiveness Criteria — 528

Exhibits

- *2000 Housing Units Project Work Codes 507*
- *Work Packages and Activity Identification Codes 512*
- *Labelled List of Drawings for a Health Centre Building 526*

## Chapter 18  Project Management Information System

- **18.1** PMIS Concept — 530
- **18.2** PMIS Framework — 534
- **18.3** Information System Computerisation — 537
- **18.4** User's System Specifications Development — 541
- **18.5** Acquiring a System — 542
- **18.6** Problems in Information System Management — 548
- **18.7** Benefits of Computerised Information System — 550

*Bibliography* — 552

*Index* — 554

# PART 1

# Construction Project Management: An Overview

- The Construction Project Management Framework
- Project Planning Scope

**CHAPTER 1**

# The Construction Project Management Framework

## ❑ 1.1 CONSTRUCTION INDUSTRY

### 1.1.1 Construction Scope

Ever since the dawn of civilisation, man has indulged in some form of construction activity. Even in ancient times, man created architectural marvels which came to be regarded as the wonders of the world, for example, the Pyramids of Egypt, the Great Wall of China, the Angkor temples of Cambodia, and the Tower of Babel. The pyramid of Giza in Egypt contains more than 2,000,000 blocks, with an average weight of about 2.3 tons each. About 100,000 persons worked on the pyramids for three to four months a year to build it in about 20 years. The Great Wall of China, built to provide protection against surprise enemy raids, is about 6400 km long and its height and width at the top varies from 5 to 10 m. It has 20 m high towers placed every few hundred metres. The medieval times witnessed the construction of world-famous landmarks like Taj Mahal in India and the Leaning Tower of Pisa in Italy. A more recent example of man's achievement in this direction is the Eiffel Tower in Paris.

In the present day world, technical breakthroughs have revolutionized construction activity. Modern construction areas include high-rise buildings, dams and irrigation networks, energy conversion and industrial plants, environmental protection works, infrastructural facilities like roads, bridges, railways, airports and seaports, satellite launching stations, onshore and offshore oil terminals, etc.

In the mid-eighties, the assessed annual construction in USA was to the tune of 350 billion dollars. During the same period, the annual value of construction works in western Europe was around 300–400 billion dollars per annum. The total annual value of construction works in the world ranges from 1–1.5 trillion dollars.

The market of the construction business is both domestic as well as global.

**4** Construction Project Management

**Home market** Construction is an everlasting activity across the globe. Its profitability, like of any other business, fluctuates according to the law of demand and supply. In most countries, construction activity constitutes 6–9% of the gross domestic product (GDP) and constitutes more than half of the fixed capital formation as infrastructure and public utilities capital works required for economic development. (Table 1.1) GDP is a measure of the level of income enjoyed by a country.

Table 1.1

**Construction Activity in Selected Countries: Year 1980**

| Sl. No. | Countries | Value added to Gross Domestic Product Percentage | Share of Gross Fixed Capital Formation Percentage |
|---|---|---|---|
|  | **Developed countries** |  |  |
| 1. | France | 5 | 56 |
| 2. | Italy | 6 | 57 |
| 3. | Japan | 8 | 67 |
| 4. | United Kingdom | 6 | 48 |
| 5. | USA | 4 | 55 |
|  | **Developing countries** |  |  |
| 6. | Kenya | 5 | 48 |
| 7. | South Korea | 6 | 63 |
| 8. | Mexico | 5 | 57 |
| 9. | Pakistan | 5 | 60 |
| 10. | India (approximate) | 5 | 44 |

Construction activity contributes to the economic development of a country. The GDP per capital and the investment in the construction per capita generally follow a straight line relationship, that is, construction activity increases with the increase in per capita income. In some of the developing countries, the growth rate of construction activity outstrips that of population and of GDP.

In case of India, for example, during the last ten years, the total capital formation by construction was about 44% of the total investment and the contribution of construction in GDP was 5% (Table 1.2). With the expected annual increase of GDP from 5% in 1995–96 to around 8% in 2004–05, the total investment in construction up to 2004–05 at 1995–96 prices works out to Rs 17,506,59 crore. Assuming an annual inflation rate at 8%, the total investment up to 2004–05 may reach a net amount of Rs 26,906,94 crore (Table 1.3).

Construction accelerates economic growth of a nation. In India, for example, during the plan period 1980–85 for every rupee of investment, construction added 78 paise to GDP as compared with 20 paise per rupee of investment in agriculture.

Construction is an employment spinner. It generates more employment than most of the sectors. In India, during the eighties, the overall annual employment increased by 2%, whereas increase of employment in the construction sector during the same period recorded an annual growth of about 7%. Further, in India, the number of persons employed in the

## Table 1.2

**India: Component of Construction in Capital Formation**

| Year | Capital all Sectors | Formation Construction | Construction of all Sectors |
|---|---|---|---|
| 1980–81 | 28453 | 13649 | 47.97 |
| 1986–87 | 71443 | 30573 | 42.79 |
| 1987–88 | 74882 | 34787 | 46.46 |
| 1988–89 | 97054 | 41445 | 42.70 |
| 1989–90 | 110791 | 47892 | 43.23 |
| 1990–91 | 137391 | 58363 | 42.48 |
| 1991–92 | 140864 | 67205 | 47.71 |
| 1992–93 | 163756 | 73403 | 44.82 |
| 1993–94 | 167553 | 79373 | 47.37 |

## Table 1.3

**India: Estimated GDP and Investment on New Construction**

(Rs. in crores)

| Year | Estimated GDP | Annual % Increase (assumed) | Construction Contribution to GDP | % Share of Const. in GDP (assumed) | Investment on New Construction @ 1995–96 Prices | Investment on New Construction @ 8% Inflation |
|---|---|---|---|---|---|---|
| 1995–1996 | 919289 | — | 55157 | 6 | 110315 | 110515 |
| 1996–1997 | 972607 | 5.8 | 60302 | 6.2 | 120603 | 130252 |
| 1997–1998 | 1031936 | 6.1 | 66044 | 6.4 | 132088 | 154067 |
| 1998–1999 | 1097980 | 6.4 | 72466 | 6.6 | 144933 | 182574 |
| 1999–2000 | 1171545 | 6.7 | 79665 | 6.8 | 159330 | 216767 |
| 2000–2001 | 1253553 | 7.0 | 87749 | 7 | 175497 | 257863 |
| 2001–2002 | 1345062 | 7.3 | 96844 | 7.2 | 193689 | 307360 |
| 2002–2003 | 1447287 | 7.6 | 107099 | 7.4 | 214198 | 367099 |
| 2003–2004 | 1560176 | 7.8 | 118573 | 7.6 | 237147 | 438942 |
| 2004–2005 | 168499 | 8.0 | 131429 | 7.8 | 26258 | 525455 |
| Total | | | | | 1750659 | 2690694 |

construction industry in 1995–96 was estimated at 14.6 million. According to studies conducted by the National Institute of Construction Management and Research, the work force in construction is expected to go up to 32.5 million in the years 2004–05.

**International market** Since the early eighties, the international construction market has risen to 120–180 billion dollars per annum. There are about 250 top international companies competing with each other for the global construction tenders.

During 1984–86, the Middle East accounted for over one-third of the global construction market, while Asia and Africa each held a 22% share. The developed countries, however, bagged the lion's share. They have dominated the construction of power and process plants, which require a high degree of sophisticated technology, while the developing countries like South Korea and India have concentrated more on the repetitive and routine types of works like building construction.

Table 1.4 shows the international export market in the year 1992.

Table 1.4

**Global Construction Activity Share of 225 International Construction Companies in Global Construction Export Market in the Year 1992**

| Company's Nationality | Number of Firms | Total Award $ Million | Percentage |
|---|---|---|---|
| USA/Canada | 80 | 72600 | 50 |
| Japanese | 27 | 12373 | 8 |
| British | 10 | 13791 | 9 |
| French | 7 | 11206 | 8 |
| German | 13 | 8190 | 6 |
| Italian | 24 | 11304 | 8 |
| Other European | 26 | 7795 | 5 |
| All others | 38 | 9271 | 6 |
| Total | 225 | 146530 | 100 |

*Source:* Engineering News Record (ENR), Special Report.

## 1.1.2 Construction Participants

The agencies supporting the construction industry include but are not limited to the following:

(a) Construction business promoters like government bodies, public and private enterprises for real estate and industrial development, and other similar agencies.
(b) Construction management consultant firms.
(c) Architect-engineering associates.
(d) Construction manpower recruitment and training agencies.
(e) Construction materials developing, manufacturing, stocking, transportation and trading firms.
(f) Construction plant and machinery manufacturing, distributing, and repair and maintenance organizations.
(g) Banking and finance institutions.
(h) Risk insurance and legal services companies.
(i) Construction quality assurance, and research and development establishment.
(j) Contractors and contracting firms.

There are five main agencies actively associated with the execution of major works. These are: business promoters, construction management consultants, architects-engineering associates, input suppliers and the contractors.

**Business promoter** Also called the client, he is the potential owner of the construction facility. He sponsors the construction works and ultimately utilizes them. A client can be a government body, a public or private enterprises, or some private individual. It is he who sponsors the works, finances their construction, and utilizes the facility constructed. It is on his demand that the market forces react. Thus, in reality, it is the client who is the promoter of the construction business.

The construction works can be executed through the client's own organization, that is, departmentally, or through contractors, or through a combination of both.

**Construction management consultants** The emerging trend these days among the clients, is to hire the construction management consultants for rendering certain services on contract basis for the entire life of the project. The nature of tasks assigned to this group by the clients vary, but it generally includes the following:

(a) Project feasibility, including cost estimates.
(b) Site survey and soil investigations.
(c) Scrutiny and coordination of designs and drawing work.
(d) Estimating, initial planning, and budgeting costs.
(e) Processing prequalification of construction agencies, tendering, and awarding contracts to the successful bidders.
(f) Designing project organizations for executing works and developing standard operating procedures and systems.
(g) Developing detailed construction plans, project schedules and performance measuring standards.
(h) Supervising works, including administration of contracts and controlling of project time, cost and quality objectives.

**Architect-engineering associates** An architect is an individual who designs the buildings, landscapes and other artistic features. The engineers associated with architects develop structural, electrical, mechanical and other specialist systems and designs. Architect-engineering associates are the firms employing both architects as well as engineers to provide complete design services under one roof. Some of these firms also provide construction management services.

The architect-engineering firms, when engaged, are frequently required to coordinate with the construction management consultant/manager, who knows the project needs, and to scrutinize designs and drawings from the construction point of view. Construction consultants, with all their construction expertise, can render valuable guidance and advice to the design team, especially when the latter has to finally approach them for approval.

**Input suppliers** Construction process needs resources input. Construction inputs exist in the form of men, materials, machinery and money. The workforce connected with construction includes architects, engineers, managers, technical and non-technical staff, highly skilled operators, and skilled and unskilled manpower. Construction activity requires a wide variety of materials, which from a substantial part of the entire construction cost. Induction of construction plant and machinery has revolutionized construction practices by adding the speed factor and reducing the need for difficult-to-manage manpower.

Money is at the core of all business activities and construction being a capital intensive business, generally also operates under money constraints. Construction input resources are converted into construction facilities by using the standard construction practices and management methodologies. This process of input procurement, conversion and management of resources covers a wide spectrum of the construction business activity.

**Contractors** Construction contractors form the backbone of the construction business as they execute most of the construction works. In the competitive construction business, which requires special resources for different types of construction work, the contractors generally tend to specialize in a particular area of construction. From this functional angle, the contractors can be classified into the following categories:

(a) General contractors.
(b) Building contractors.
(c) Specialist contractors for various types of heavy infrastructure construction work such as highways, bridges, dams, marine works etc.
(d) Specialist (mostly turnkey) contractors for various categories of industrial works like power plants, process industries, and so on.
(e) Specialist utility services contractors. These include electrical contractors, water supply and sewage disposal contractors, HVAC (heating, ventilation and air-conditioning) contractors, and so on.

Moreover depending upon their resource capability to handle construction work and their financial position and past performance, the contractors are further categorized by the various government bodies into workload capability divisions (like S, A, B and C class) for the purposes of awarding contracts.

## ❑ 1.2 CONSTRUCTION PROJECTS

### 1.2.1 Concept

A client, be it a government body, a public or private agency, an entrepreneur, or a builder, undertakes developmental facilities like housing, roads and power plants with certain motives or long-term aims. For example, the typical motives or the strategic aims of the government in developing infrastructure may include economic growth. A corporate body may aim at making a profit on its investments, providing service facilities to its employees, meeting growth needs of the organisation, diversifying corporate activities, engaging idle resources, staying in business, earning goodwill, projecting corporate image, or rendering social service to the society. These developmental facilities can be low-value minor works or high-value major works.

In general, major construction works are time bound and employ huge resources of men, materials and machines. They involve heavy investments, of million to billions of dollars. They require a high level of technology, and need an effective management of resources. The execution of major construction capital works is undertaken by projecting them, that is, by organizing them into one or more construction projects for implementation.

The term 'construction project' refers to a high-value, time bound, special construction mission with predetermined performance objectives. The project mission is accomplished within complex project environments, by putting together human and non-human resources into a temporary organisation (like a special mission task force in the army), headed by a project manager.

The project manager aims to achieve its mission by:

| | |
|---|---|
| *Managing* | • Time and progress |
| | • Cost and cash flow |
| | • Quality and performance |
| | • Organization behaviour |
| *With* | • Organization resources |
| *By* | • Planning resources |
| | • Scheduling resources |
| | • Organizing resources |
| | • Directing resources |
| | • Monitoring resources |
| | • Controlling resources |
| *Within* | • Quality constraints |
| | • Time constraints |
| | • Cost constraints |
| | • Environment constraints |

## 1.2.2 Project Categories

Broadly, the major construction projects can be grouped into 'Building Construction', 'Infrastructure Construction', 'Industrial Construction' and 'Special-purpose projects'.

**Building construction** Building works include residential and commercial complexes, educational and recreational facilities, hospitals & hotels, warehouse and marketing facilities. 'Buildings' constitute the largest segment of construction business. The building business serves mankind by providing shelter and services for its habitation, educational, recreational, social and commercial needs. The building works are mostly designed by the Architect/Engineering firms, and are financed by public and private sector and individuals.

**Infrastructure construction** These are capital intensive and heavy-equipment oriented works which involve movement of large quantity of bulk materials like earth, steel and concrete. These works include dams and canals, highways and airports, railways and bridges, oil/gas pipelines and transmission lines, large water supply and sewage disposal networks, docks and harbours. nuclear and thermal power plants, and other specialist construction activities which build-up the infrastructure for the growth of the economy. These works are designed by the specialist engineering firms and are mostly financed by the Government/ public sector.

**Industrial construction** These works include construction of manufacturing, processing and industrial plants like steel mills, petroleum refineries and consumer-goods factories. Industrial works also include connected utility services, environmental works and human needs facilities. These works involve heavy investment and are highly specialized. Industrial Constructions are financed by government, public and private enterprises.

**Special-purpose projects** These include environmental works, emergencies, remedial works, installation and commissioning of equipment, and complex key operations.

**Project classification** Based on the completion time and value of works, various types of construction projects can be further classified as under:

- Project completion time basis
  - Long duration projects (over 10 years)
  - Medium duration projects (3 to 10 years)
  - Short duration projects (few months to 3 years)
  - Special short-term projects (less than 1 year)
- Project value basis
  - Mega value projects (say over $1000 million)
  - Large value projects ($100 million to $1000 million)
  - Medium value projects ($10 million to $100 million)
  - Small value project (less than $10 million)

### 1.2.3 Project Mission

Each project has a specified mission or a purpose to be achieved. A construction project mission is to create a desired facility like a housing complex or a fertilizer plant. It is not a routine activity like the regular maintenance of buildings or roads.

Each project mission is unique in itself, and no two projects are ever alike. Projects differ from each other in one or more influencing factors such as client and contractors, quality specifications, resources employed, responsibilities delegated and the project environments. Each one of these factors may have decisive effect on the development of the project.

In general, construction projects are high value and they employ huge resources of men, materials and machines. Major works involve heavy investments, say from a million dollar to a few billion dollars, require high level of technology and need effective management of resources.

Construction projects are time bound. Each project has a predetermined duration with definable beginning and identifiable end. Its start point is the time when the client decides to undertake construction and commit his financial resources. It is completed as soon as the mission is accomplished. The time span between the start and the completion of a project represents the project life cycle. The completion period or the life of the project varies from few months to few years.

Each project is assigned predetermined objectives. These objectives quantify the measurable results to be achieved for accomplishing the mission. Generally, construction projects objectives are stated in terms of project completion time, budgeted cost and stipulated quality specifications.

### 1.2.4 Project Objectives

There are many factors that determine the outcome of a project but the six main parameters that can sufficiently define a construction project are size, complexity, quality, productivity, completion time and cost.

- Size denotes the number of tasks to be executed in a project and each task is measured in terms of quantities of work involved.
- Complexity is a measure of variety in the nature of tasks to be executed i.s. complexity increases as the number of dissimilar task increase and it decreases if the tasks are repetitive (or similar in nature.
- Quality to be achieved in accomplishing tasks is stated in terms of standard specifications.
- Productivity, in its broader sense, measures the ratio of planned effort to produce a unit quantity of work divided by the actual effort employed to achieve this unit of work.
- Completion time depends upon the speed with which the project is to be executed.
- Cost is the expenditure which the client has agreed to commit for creating the desired construction facility.

The above six parameters are interdependent and interactive, that is, each parameter is a function of the other. For example, consider the effect of repetition on completion time of a project containing 12 tasks of specified quality and cost, with each taking a unit time to execute. If there is no repetition of task, that is, if all the tasks are dissimilar, sequential and are taken one at a time, the earliest completion time for the project would be 12 units. But if four tasks can be repeated, each three times, as shown in Fig. 1.1, then the earliest completion time would be six units.

With an increase in the repetition of similar tasks, there is an improvement in resource productivity due to the experience gained, which consequently results in reduced overall costs.

The evaluation of interrelationship among the six project parameters is a complicated process. However, in a given project, the scope of work in terms of size, repetition and quality gets specified and these parameters thus can be treated as constants. Productivity standards for each item of resources needed to execute a work in a given time is estimated, and this forms the basis for determining the time and cost of the project. The achievement of the two parameters, that of time and cost, depends upon the effectiveness and efficiency with which the project resources are managed. Therefore, in a project with predetermined

**Figure 1.1**

**Completion Time of 12 Tasks
4 Tasks, Each of Unit Duration, Repeating 3 Times**

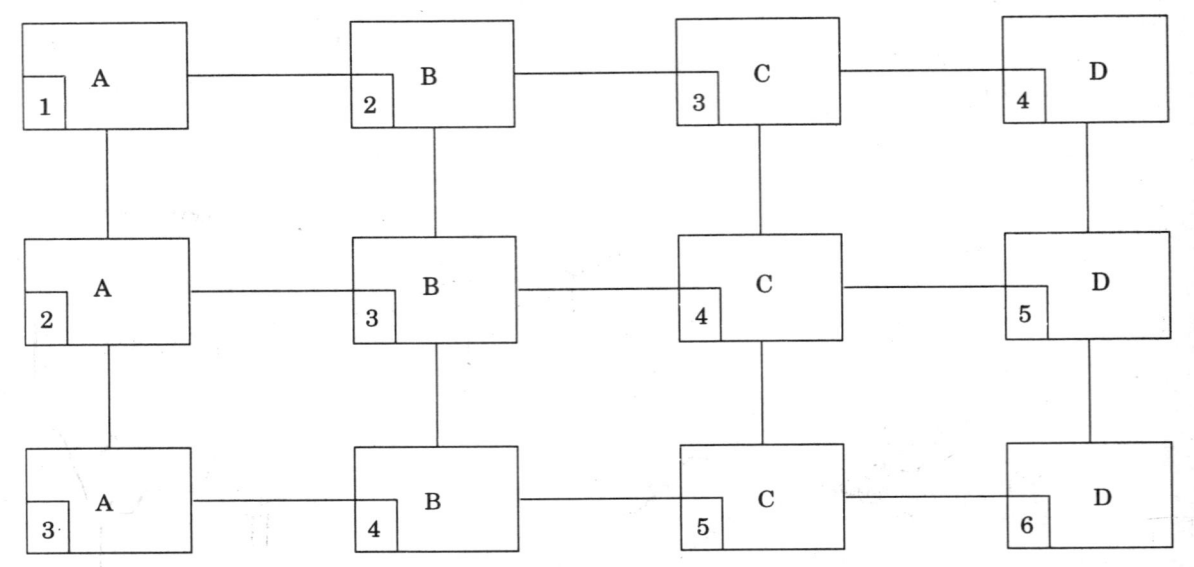

```
┌─────┐     ┌─────┐     ┌─────┐     ┌─────┐
│  A  │─────│  B  │─────│  C  │─────│  D  │
│1    │     │2    │     │3    │     │4    │
└──┬──┘     └─────┘     └──┬──┘     └──┬──┘
   │                       │           │
┌──┴──┐     ┌─────┐     ┌──┴──┐     ┌──┴──┐
│  A  │─────│  B  │─────│  C  │─────│  D  │
│2    │     │3    │     │4    │     │5    │
└──┬──┘     └─────┘     └──┬──┘     └──┬──┘
   │                       │           │
┌──┴──┐     ┌─────┐     ┌──┴──┐     ┌──┴──┐
│  A  │─────│  B  │─────│  C  │─────│  D  │
│3    │     │4    │     │5    │     │6    │
└─────┘     └─────┘     └─────┘     └─────┘
```

Data in box shows earliest completion time of the respective task.

productivity standards, specified completion time and construction cost become the project objectives, and the pattern of their relationship is shown in Figs 1.2 and 1.3.

The planning and controlling of the project objectives of time and cost, and setting up of the resources productivity standards to achieve these objectives, are the most important functions of the project management. The planning and controlling methodology employed for this purpose is loosely called the 'project management techniques' and these form the subject matter of this book.

### 1.2.5 Project Environment

Most construction projects have one or more of the following characteristics asociated with them:

- Details of work are not precisely defined.
- Scope of work gets modified during execution.
- Nature of work varies from job to job.
- Site of works are located in remote areas.
- Places of works are spread out.
- Resource requirements and organization of works differ with each task.
- Investments involved are large and the decisions entail risks.
- Performance is sensitive to the unexplored site geology, uncertain weather and unforeseen natural calamities. Engineering failures such as ill-defined scope of work,

### Figure 1.2

**Project Objectives Interrelation**

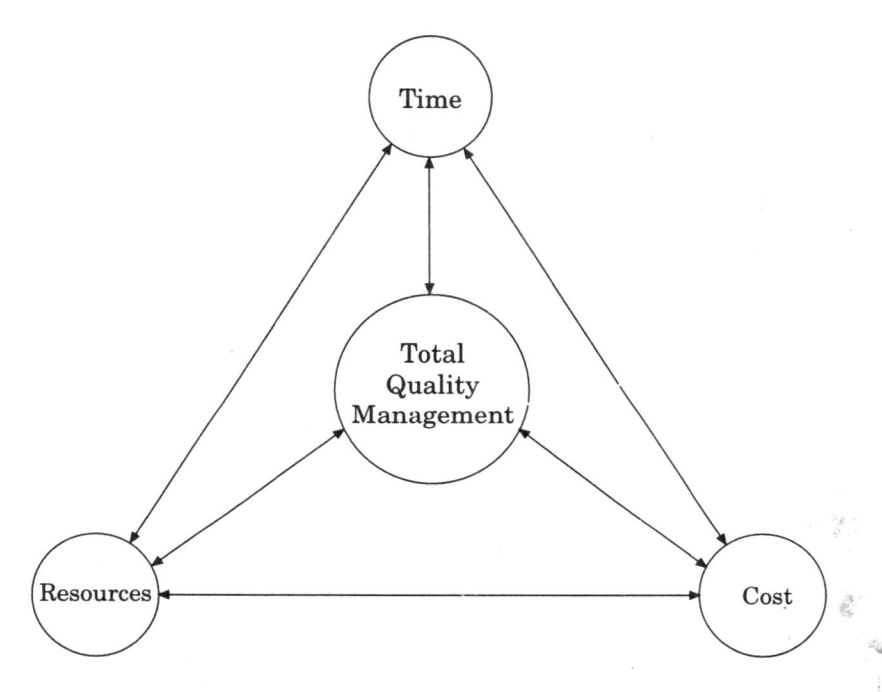

```
            Time
           /  |  \
          /   |   \
         / Total   \
        / Quality   \
       / Management  \
      /       |       \
  Resources ――――――― Cost
```

inadequate field investigations, faulty designs, absence of quality consciousness and lack of construction experience can delay completion and increase costs.
- Rapidly changing technology, fast moving economic conditions and susceptible environments and new dimensions to the complex nature of construction projects.

These difficulties, uncertainties and risks pose never-ending questions concerning the resources like: 'at what scale are the resources required?', where are they going to come from? when should they be inducted at site?', 'where should they be housed?', how to optimize their utilization?', and 'when to demobilize them?' Resources cost money. Generally, construction projects are capital intensive, requiring heavy investments. There is always a conflict between' how much it will cost?' and 'where to raise the finances from?'. The success of a project depends upon the efficiency with which the project management gets the work done by utilizing the planned resources of men, materials, machines, money and time.

Although management principles of forecasting, planning organizing, staffing, directing, motivating, monitoring, communicating, controlling and decision-making apply equally in traditional functional type management as well as project management, the risks, uncertainties and complexities make project management a relatively difficult process.

### Figure 1.3

**Project Time-cost Trade-off Pattern of a Small Size Project**
**(Costs in thousand dollars)**

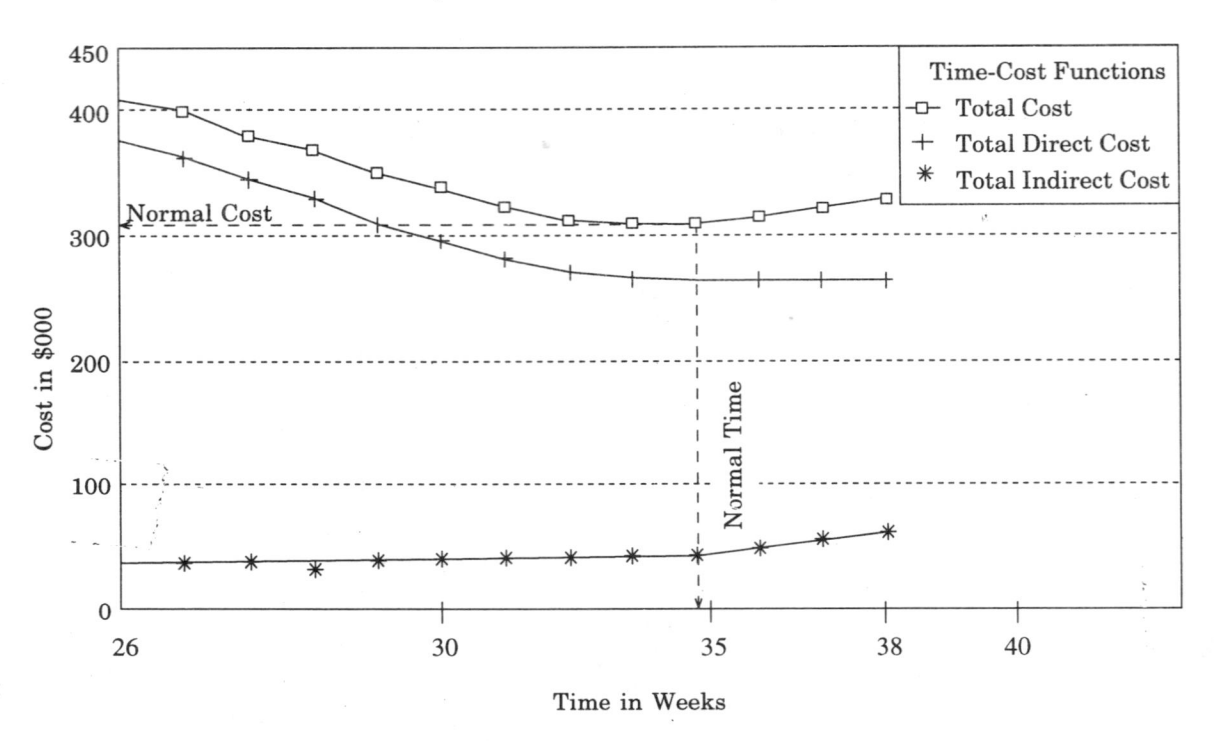

## 1.3 PROJECT DEVELOPMENT PROCESS

### 1.3.1 Project Life Cycle

Each project has a predetermined duration with a definite beginning and an identifiable end. Its starting point is the time when the idea is conceived by the client, and its end marks the time when the mission is accomplished. The time span between the start and completion of a project represents the project life cycle, which varies from few months to few years.

Although construction projects differ in many ways, the life span of a project follows a similar pattern. After conception there is a gradual build-up in the use of resources, it is followed by a long-duration plateau and towards the end, there is a rapid run-down till completion. See Fig. 1.4.

The life cycle of a typical construction project can be broadly divided into the following stages.

## Figure 1.4
## Typical Construction Project Life Cycle
## (Not to Scale)

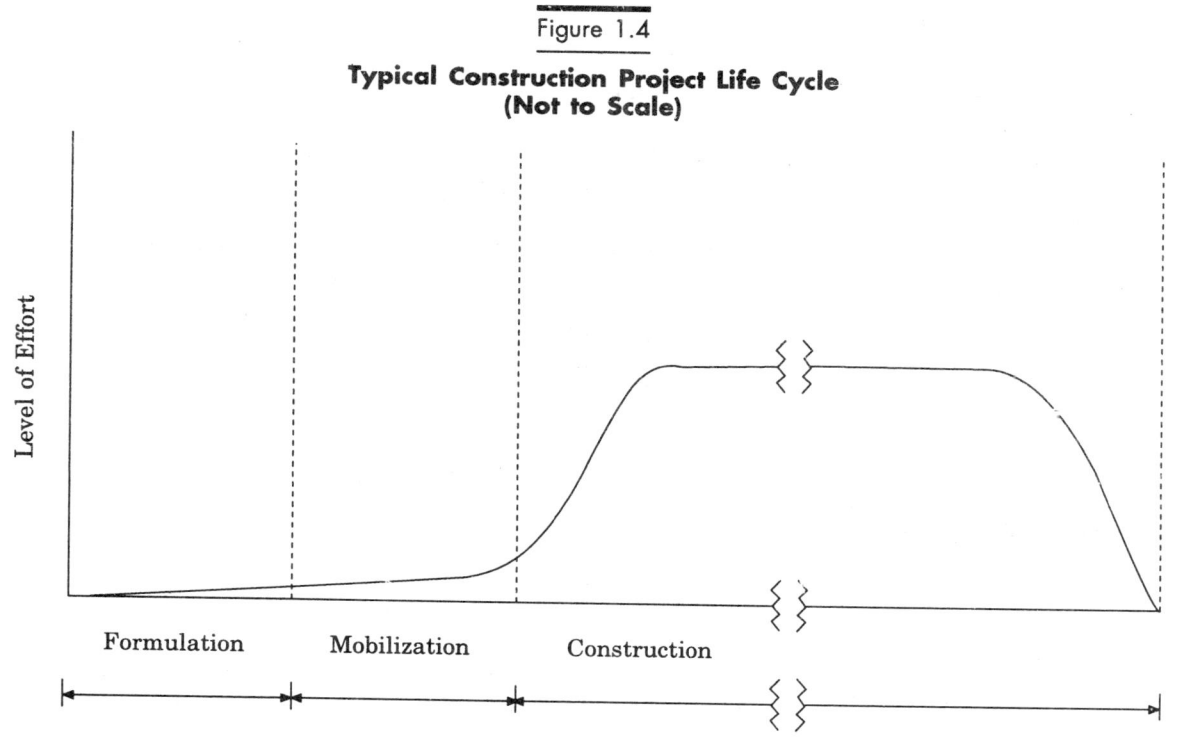

(a) **Formulation stage** This includes:

- Project idea conception
- Feasibility studies
- Investment appraisal
- Project definition

(b) **Mobilization stage** This covers preparation of:

- Project preliminary plan
- Designs and drawings
- Specifications and contract finalisation
- Resources mobilization and earmarking funds

(c) **Construction stage** This includes:

- Planning and controlling execution
- Inducting resources
- Construction and commissioning
- Final handling over to the client

Although some participants may separate out in one stage, the other move on the next one. The project manager is the key participant in all these stages and acts as a catalyst who motivates the participants for achieving the stage objectives.

## 1.3.2 Feasibility or Inception Stage

The major construction projects are undertaken to meet the particular needs of a client. Generally, a client is well-informed and clear about what he needs, but sometimes what he thinks he wants and what he really needs may actually be different.

The first step in the development of a project is to analyse the needs of the client. This requires a critical examination of the needs through feasibility studies.

The feasibility study evaluates project potential by examining technical feasibility, economic viability and financial implications.

The subject to be covered in the feasibility report of a construction project will depend upon the purpose of the report and the nature of the project. For example, the feasibility report of an industrial project may include the following aspects:

1. Proposed product features.
2. *Demand survey* It includes prospective customers, consumption pattern, existing market, government policy, demand forecast and sale potential.
3. *Technical studies* These cover production process selection, construction methodology, location study, power and local resources availability, means of transportation, scope of work, wastage disposal arrangement, construction cost estimates, preliminary time plan, resource forecasts, outline project organization, and statement of project time and cost objectives.
4. *Financial implications* It contains sales forecast, project budget, capital costs, profitability trend, payback period, net present worth, cash flow forecast, and sources of financing.
5. *Economic viability* It highlights social implications and cost benefit analysis.
6. Summary of recommendations.

The feasibility report, if found favourable, is followed up with investment appraisal. The purpose of appraisal is to conduct an objective asessment for invetment decision. It involves critical examination of the techno-economic analysis of feasibility findings, with particular reference to:

- Demand analysis
- Technical specifications feasibility
- Strength, weaknesses, opportunity and threat (SWOT) analysis
- Environments implications
- Financial analysis
- Economic analysis

Appraisal of feasibility stage enables a client to:

(a) Decide on the project concept, time and costs;
(b) Outline the approach needed to taking the project;
(c) Appoint key persons like construction project manager or project coordinator, to act as his representatives; and
(b) Nominate specialist associated agencies such as the architect, designer and consultants, as per the requirements.

Depending upon the nature and complexity of the project, the following may assist the client in making decisions.

(a) *Client representatives* These include the prospective project manager or his nominee, and the related officials.
(b) *Specialists* These include the architects, engineers, planners, and finance and management consultants.
(c) Concerned officials of administration and technical departments.

The process of formulation of needs, collection of information, critical examination of concepts and re-examination of needs, may have to be repeated several times over before a project inception finally takes shape.

Finally, the feasibility studies and its appraisal leads to the definition of the following aspects relating to the project:

- Broad scope of work involved.
- Project objectives.
- Outline execution methodology.
- Preliminary time plan.
- Resource forecasts.
- Cash flow pattern and sources of funding.
- Outline organization.
- Potential risks and problem areas.

## 1.3.3 Mobilization or Preparation Stage

The mobilization stage aims at processing the project preliminaries so as to enable the commencement of the construction stage. This is achieved by the following:

(a) Compiling detailed design and drawings, specifications, and bills of quantities, so as to complete all the documents necessary for contracting works.
(b) Planning project execution. This includes the work programme, manpower plan, materials plan, plant and machinery utilization plan, work-organization and mobilization plan, and project budget or cost plan. This process also continues during the construction stage.
(c) Tendering and appointing contracts, especially those needed for commencement of the work.

The composition of the team to prepare for commencement of the project depends upon many factors such as size and nature of the project, project characteristics, and the time and cost objectives. This team is lead by the project manager designate and, its works are coordinated by the project chief planner. The other participants of the team include the following:

(a) Architect and design engineers.
(b) Construction engineers from HVAC, civil, mechanical or electrical branches.

(c) Tendering staff, like the contracts managers and quantity surveyors.
(d) Specialists consultants, such as the town planners, geologists, and the environmentalists.
(e) Selected manager and the connected officials.

In this preparation stage, the project manager, assisted by the chief project planner, performs the key functions. These include, but are not limited to, the following:

(a) Participate in the finalization of design, drawings and specifications so as to formulate construction methodology.
(b) Prepare project execution preliminary plan and formulate the schedule for processing various contracts.
(c) Advise the client on an early purchase of the items of plant and equipment needing a long lead time for procurement.
(d) Evolve the pre-tender construction plan for each tender package.
(e) Scrutinize the tender packages, including drawings and specifications, so as to minimize the discrepancies.
(f) Conduct the pre-tender briefing to contractors to ensure that the bidders understand the tender documents and the work involved in each tender.
(g) Evaluate project costs and compile project budget including preliminary allocations for the various heads of expenditures.
(h) Compile a project directive covering the scope of work, work plan, organization, and the policies and procedures for implementing the project.

## 1.3.4 Execution Stage

Most of the construction projects are executed through the contract system. The contract documents define the contracted scope of the work of each contractor. They also provide the contractual relationship between the construction manager of the contractors and the project manager. The contract agreement is based on mutual trust between the contracting parties, both of whom have their share of responsibilities and obligations. In this process, disagreements sometimes arise. These may be on account of deviations in the scope of work and other factors like time delays, inflation and unforeseen circumstances. Contract provisions do provide a mechanism for the settlement of such disputes through arbitration.

Construction at the site of the contracted projects is supervised and carried out by two separate agencies. These are: the client team led by the project manager, and the contractor workforce managed by his construction manager. Both teams have the common goal of completing the project in time within specified costs and quality specification. However, their roles differ.

It is the *project manager* who plays the dominant role. He represents the client and acts as the boss at site. He ensures smooth functioning at site and makes decisions when the site faces problems. He manages the entire construction process so as to achieve the assigned project objectives. He manages the contractors employed at site, and the site activities, with the help of his supervisory team that reports to him for decisions. It is he who is accountable to the client for the construction of the project. The main functions of this constructions supervision team can be outlined as follows.

1. Scrutinize the contract documents to ensure that all amendments are incorporated into the drawings, specifications and bill of quantities held at site.
2. Scrutinize the contractor's plan of work, the mobilization plan, the construction procedures and the quality control measures to ensure that they are in order.
3. Scrutinize the pre-work preparation of work to ensure a smooth start of construction activities.
4. Scrutinize the work programmes to ensure that they are realistic, and monitor their progress regularly.
5. Scrutinize the quality of materials to ensure that they meet the contract specifications and also report any deviations.
6. Scrutinize the geotechnic investigations conducted by the contractor to ensure the adequacy of design parameters.
7. Scrutinize the field work regularly to ensure proper layouts, work conformity as per drawings and specifications, and good standards of workmanship.
8. Scrutinize the safety measures and working conditions to ensure healthy environments and prevention of accidents.
9. Hold review meetings to monitor progress, communicate observations, resolve problems and plan future works.
10. Scrutinize the payment of monthly bills of contractor to ensure correctness.
11. Exercise cost control and cost reduction measures.
12. Maintain project records, monitor the progress and submit management information reports at the predetermined frequency.
13. Report immediately to the project manager all cases amounting to breach of contract, non-adherence to specifications, slow progress and lack of co-operation.
14. Take over the project on completion, as per the contract stipulations.

At site, the contractor's *construction manager* manages the work execution as well as the resources, and the workforce. He operates to achieve the contractor's objectives, which include optimizing profit, maintaining a cooperative and harmonious relationship with the project manager and others engaged in the construction activity at site.

The completion of the construction phase of the project includes certain follow-up actions necessary to ensure that the facility constructed functions satisfactorily. These are as follows.

(a) The post-completion maintenance is usually entrusted to an agency familiar with the construction. In most cases, the contractor responsible for construction is given this responsibility one year after completion; and this aspect is included in the scope of work of the contractor.
(b) A proper record of the operating instructions and as-built drawings is maintained.
(c) The staff and workers necessary for operating and maintaining the facility are trained prior to its taking over.
(d) The site is cleared of the left-outs of the construction and unwanted materials.
(e) The client fully safeguards his interests prior to rendering the completion certificate to the contractor, and also before making the final payments.

After completion by the contractor, it is the project team of the client that hands over the project to him. The team also prepares a project completion report which includes the scope and schedule of work, the important events, the contract executed, the addresses of the suppliers of materials and equipment, the equipment maintenance manual, the as-built drawings, the costs involved, the problems encountered during execution, the lessons learned and the minor defects noticed at the time of handing over.

### 1.3.5 Fast-track Approach

Traditionally, the construction management process follows a sequential approach. It start with the owner's decision to procure a facility, and is followed by design finalisation by the architect engineering associates, and is delivered by the contractor under the supervision of the client consultant—each stage is completed prior to commencement of next stage. See Fig. 1.5.

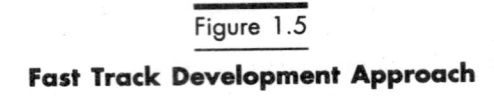

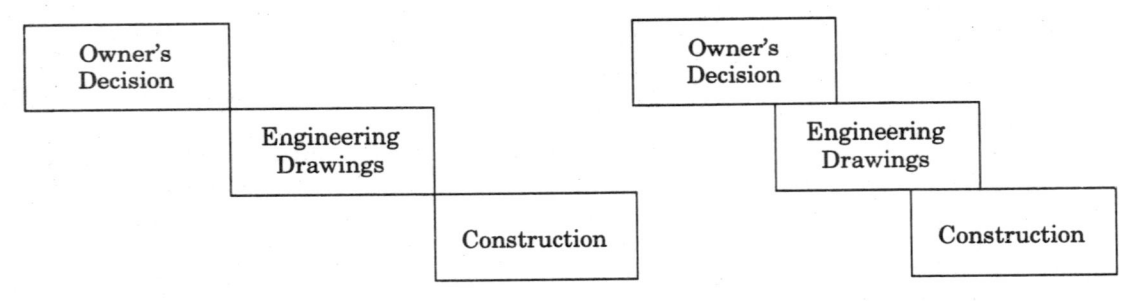

Figure 1.5

**Fast Track Development Approach**

*Sequential Traditional Approach*  *Fast Track Approach*

The above sequential traditional approach has the following disadvantages:

(a) The owner's decision regarding the budget for building the facility is generally based on the assessment of the feasibility report without tendering the work. Thus, it lacks the input from the contractor, which may not match the budgeted cost.
(b) It delays the project as the contract is finalized after the entire set of drawings and specification are completed by the designer for the tendering bids.
(c) Price to be paid by the client increases as the lowest quoted general contractor includes his mark up both on his department executed work, as well as the sub-contractor quotation received by him. Ultimately, it is the back-to-back specialist sub-contractor who remains responsible for the quality of work and whose performance guarantee remains with the client till completion of his contract.
(d) In order to secure the contract, the general contractor perceives the works to be of such quality that meets the minimum quality stipulation. Thus minimum quality and quantity attitudes result in conflict and claims between the client and the contractor.

In the end, it is the owner who pays for time delays and cost of inefficiency inherited in the sequential approach. Fast track development approach aims at reducing project construction time by overlapping project development phases. For example, in a building construction, foundation work can commence after its architectural and foundation drawing are ready and it need not wait till completion of all the building drawings.

The emerging trend for economically speeding up the construction process by a potential owner is to engage an experienced professional agent or agency to coordinate the entire construction process; including project feasibility, design guidance, contracting, planning and execution; with the objective of minimizing the construction time and cost, and maintaining the quality that meets the owner's requirement. This mode of processing construction is termed as 'professional construction management' (also referred to as 'CM'). It is designed to overview as well as assist working of the project manager, designers and specialize sub-contractors. The building of the World Trade Center consisting of twin 110 storey towers and some smaller buildings in Manhattan, New York, is a classic example of the application of the professional construction management approach.

Traditional build-only type of contracts, where designs and drawings are provided by the client to the contractor, is viewed by clients as time consuming, capital intensive and risky, specially for high cost infrastructure projects. Such infrastructure works include highways seaports, airports, railways, power plants, clear water supply and waste and sewerage disposal. The growing need for speedy implementation of infrastructural works, specially in developing countries facing a financial resource crunch, has given rise to new practices of procuring engineering high cost capital works. This emerging fast track approach uses the Build-Operate-Transfer (BOT) family of techniques. The BOT family includes a variety of techniques such a Build-Operate-Transfer (BOT), Build-Own-Operate (BOO) and Build-Own-Operate-Transfer (BOOT). Mostly, the upsurge in the Build-Operate-Transfer (BOT) family is driven by the government need to reduce public expenditure by involving private financial participation, while at the same time speeding up economic growth. (See Fig. 1.6.)

The basic concept behind BOT is that infrastructure works can be procured by the government or public sector, with private sector turnkey participation including designing, financing and building. The cost of these projects gets recovered by the builder from the consumer over a fixed period of time through a government-backed arrangement.

The outcome of this BOT fast track total-solution infrastructure construction results in a win situation for the participants. The government gets the work done at a marginal cost, in less time, and saves on specialist effort needed for high-tech projects. Builders promote their business and get a guaranteed surplus. The citizen gets the needed facilities by paying a nominal tool over a fixed period of time. Thus, all the participants gain in the bargain.

*Fast-track* approach requires a high degree of co-ordination and faster information processing to keep pace with the construction. It adds further complications to the already complex projects, but certainly makes them move faster.

## ❏ 1.4 PROJECT MANAGEMENT

### 1.4.1 Management and Organizational Implications

Project management is the art and science of mobilising and managing people, materials,

### Figure 1.6

## Models of Fast Track Approach in Capital Projects

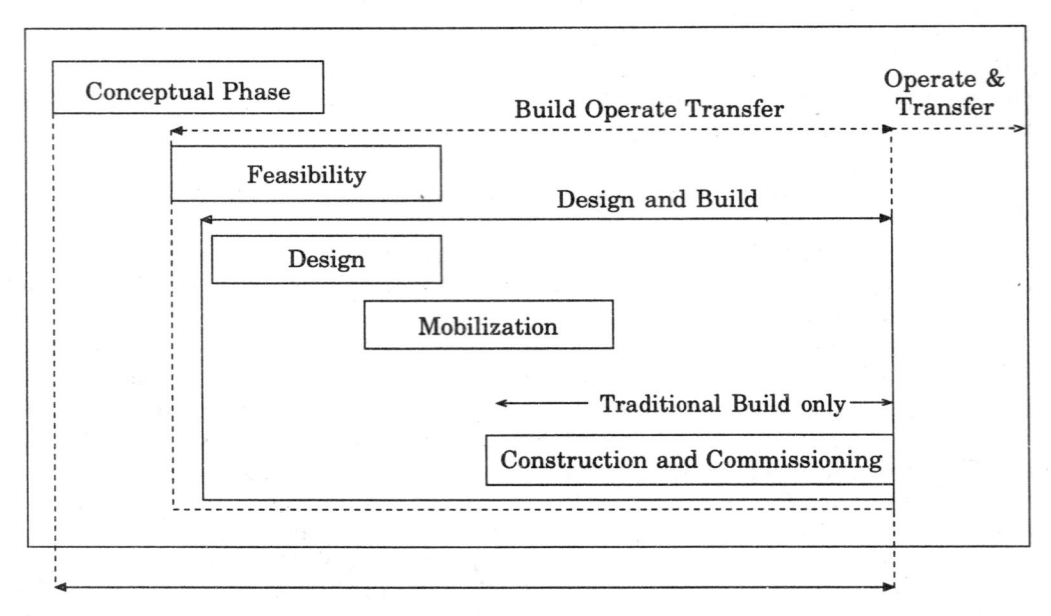

*Project Completion Period — Not to Scale*

- Conceptual Phase
- Build Operate Transfer → Operate & Transfer
- Feasibility
- Design and Build
- Design
- Mobilization
- Traditional Build only
- Construction and Commissioning

equipment and money to complete the assigned project work on time within budgeted costs and specified technical performance standards. It aims at achieving the specified objectives efficiently and effectively by managing human energies and optimising the non-human resources placed at their disposal.

Construction projects differ from other on-going steady state business enterprises like construction manufacturing and trading in many ways. The salient distinguishing features of project management and its organizational implications are as follows:

1. The project mission is unique. No two projects are alike. The type of work at each site differs, unlike in industry where a factory manufactures the same type of product repeatedly.
2. Projects are transient in nature. Unlike on-going steady state enterprises, a project comes to an end after its mission is fulfilled.
3. Projects consist of a variety of specialised works and need a wide range of tradesmen, who are casual employees. Since projects have a short life, workers move from job to job like nomads, whereas the stable industrial enterprises have more or less permanent employees.
4. Project sites are in open remote areas and are prone to weather changes, whereas industrial setups are housed in a permanent accommodation.
5. Project works are carried out at places that are far away from the corporate headoffices, unlike the industrial management, which is generally located at the place of work.

6. Project work, specially in high rise buildings, involves operations at heights making the accident rate higher than in industrial factories.
7. Construction projects operate under risk and uncertain conditions as compared to well-defined industrial processes.
8. The predetermined and specified start and completion dates of projects do not leave any time flexibility, specially when projects are to be executed speedily under relatively risk prone complex situations and resource constraints.
9. Project time and costs are correlated. Time delays in-between the project execution can alter the schedule of subsequent activities. Schedule slippages affect the project economy. Project delays attract heavy penalties. Cost on account of time delays, unless properly controlled, can increase exponentially instead of marginally as in case of other on-going enterprises.
10. Quality at each stage of project work is inspected. Construction quality judgement lies with the inspector of works, rather than the measurement of tolerances of an industrial product. Further acceptance of any work does not absolve the builder of defects appearing later on. In such situations generally the entire completed affected work gets rejected, whereas with the one product rejection in the manufacturing process.
11. Project tasks are generally non-routine. They are to be executed speedily. This hardly leaves any time for training or learning process. Accordingly projects employ experienced staff with proven skills. Comparatively, it is difficult to get state of the art experienced project operations and management personnel than the on-going enterprises.
12. Since projects are generally handled by various companies they result in social, organizational, technical and economic interactions. Unlike in on-going concerns, any adverse effects in one project can have its repercussions on other interdependent projects.
13. Most projects by nature contain several interrelated sub-systems. Integration of activities of several sub-systems requires coordination and needs information for making decisions. Information extraction for making decisions at various levels of management is relatively complex under dynamic complex project environments rather than in on-going stable enterprises.

Project organization is temporary, it ceases after completion of project. It is conceived during the project conception stage and it comes into existence at the start of planning stage. It grows gradually. It undergoes changes in various stages of the project life cycle to meet project needs. Towards the end, it runs down and ceases after completion of the project. Its special attributes include its innovation capacity to overcome problems as they arise. It is staffed with experienced person to respond speedily with changing situations and to speed up decision making.

The guidelines for designing of the project organization include the following

- Organizational groups are designed to generally conform with the project work breakdown structure.
- Each group is assigned responsibilities and allocated resources to meet the assigned tasks.
- The size and structure of the organization is changed due to alternation in requirements. However, the core project team continues till the end.

**24**  Construction Project Management

- Project groups are suitably structured with emphasis on team work and informal relationship.
- Organization structure is kept flat to avoid bureaucratic tendencies and reduce channels of communication with the project manager.
- Where possible, key staff is derived from their respective parent departments in corporate office and their interfaces and communication links and clearly defined.
- The heads of line and staff departments are generally grouped into project management team and planning chief is assigned responsibility of the coordination function.

Management of a construction project mission entails multidirectional interaction of dynamic forces represented by its time, resources constraints and the changing costs. There is always a dynamic link in how to manage time, how to manage resources and how to stay within budget. This dynamic linkage in the life span of a project, can be conceptualized by a typical project management model sketched Fig. 1.7.

Figure 1.7

**Project Management Model**

Project Environments

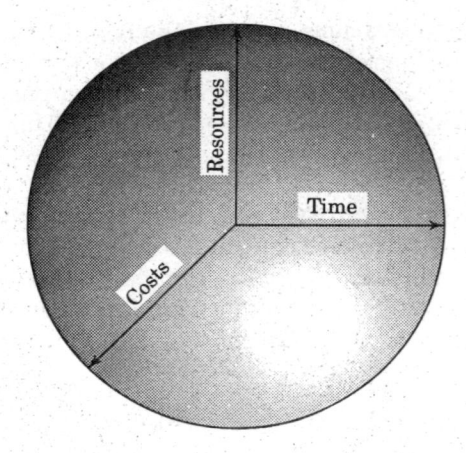

Despite diversities and multifarious activities, each project is an entity in itself. It is organized to achieve its mission, within pre-determined objectives. Its accomplishment is entrusted to a single responsibility centre, commanded by the project manager.

In such unpredictable fast-changing environments, the project manager aims at achieving the project mission

- Within the project time, cost, and quality;
- By planning, organizing, coordinating, monitoring and controlling the available resources;
- Managing the organizational behaviour with the assistance of the project team and the specialists.

### 1.4.2 Project Management Functions

The overall aim of the management in an enterprise is to create within the enterprise, an environment which will facilitate the accomplishment of its objectives. In doing this, management has to perform certain functions. Although the development of a theory and science of management suffers from disagreement among scholars and managers, a general pattern of functions which management has to perform, has emerged. Traditionally, management functions are grouped under six headings, namely planning, organizing, staffing, directing and controlling, and common to all these functions is the function of coordination. These functional areas, with some adjustments on account of the special characteristics of construction projects, are equally applicable in project management. The project management functions of planning, organizing, procuring, leading and controlling are outlined below:

**Planning** Planning involves deciding in advance what is to be done, how and in what order it is to be done in order to achieve the objectives. Planning aims at deciding upon the future course of action. A plan shows the committed course of action. Schedule depicts when the planned activities are to be carried, it puts the plan on calendar date scale. In brief, planning and scheduling involves the following:

(a) Crystallizing objectives.
(b) Collecting and synthesising information.
(c) Developing alternative courses of action within specified constraints
(d) Comparing alternatives in terms of objectives feasibility and consequences.
(e) Selecting and scheduling the optimum course of action.
(f) Establishing policies, procedures, methods, schedules, programmes, systems, standards and budgets for accomplishing project objectives.

**Organizing** Organizing is the process of establishing a structural relationship among functions of people, so as to formulate an effective machinery for streamlining the achievement of assigned objectives. Organizing involves the following main tasks:

(a) Dividing the work into component activities.
(b) Designing job structures.
(c) Defining performance targets and responsibilities.
(d) Allocating resources.
(e) Delegating authority commensurate with responsibility.
(f) Establishing structural relationship to secure coordination.

**Procuring** It implies managing and keeping manned, the positions created by organization structure and providing them the right quality resources at the right time. These resources include people, materials, machinery and money. The connected project management tasks include the following:

(a) Preparing resource procurement schedules.
(b) Developing specifications for required resources.
(c) Deciding appropriate sources of procurement.

(d) Budgeting resources and arranging approvals and purchases.
(e) Preventing wastage during resource holding at site.
(f) Supplying on time required quality and quantity of resources to project construction sites.

**Directing or Leading** It involves influencing people so as to enable them to contribute to organizational goals efficiently and effectively. Direction implies the following tasks:

(a) Providing effective leadership.
(b) Motivating participants behaviour.
(c) Communicating instructions and orders.
(d) Providing a suitable climate for subordinates' development.

**Controlling** Controlling involves monitoring of the performance and applying corrective measures in case of deviations from the plan. The process of control can be sub-divided into the following stages:

(a) Specifying the factors to be controlled.
(b) Stating the methods of measuring control factors.
(c) Evolving systems for generating performance data.
(d) Monitoring data received and formulating corrective options.
(e) Applying corrective measures to put a plan on the scheduled path.
(f) Replanning, when necessary.

### 1.4.3 Management Team

The project management team is led by a *project manager*, who is an agent of the client and acts on his behalf. He is either appointed by the client or is positioned at site by the construction management consultant (of the client). He coordinates and communicates with all the agencies engaged in project work. In particular, he is accountable for planning, mobilizing, motivation, directing, coordinating and controlling all the activities at the project site which are necessary for achieving the project objectives of time, cost and quality. Loosely, the site incharge of a major contractor is also referred as contractor's Project Manager or General Manager or Construction Manager.

The achievement of these project objectives is closely linked with the skill, effectiveness and efficiency of the project management team, and how it is organized for conducting its operations. This team consists of the functional heads or the body of managers in a project. To quote example, turnkey contractor's Project Management team comprising of heads of staff and line departments of a Typical Housing Units Building Construction Project, is shown in Exhibit 1.1.

The size of the project management team depends upon the nature and scope of the project work. In the medium and large-size projects, it may include specialists to manage: construction planning, architecture and engineering, tendering and contract administration, value analysis and quality assurance, materials and equipment handling, and finance and personnel administration.

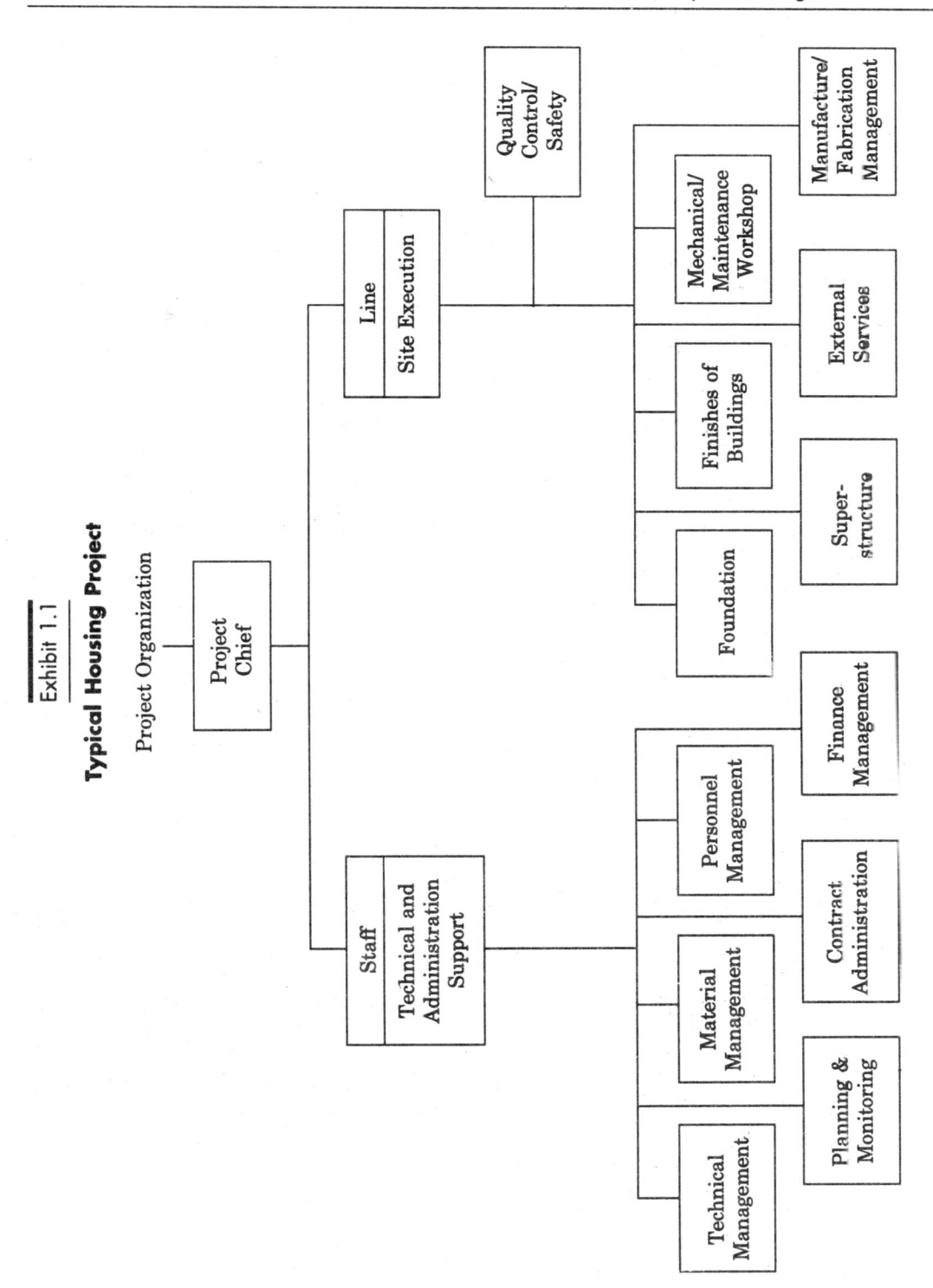

Construction Projects Management Framework **27**

Exhibit 1.1
## Typical Housing Project
Project Organization

- Project Chief
  - Staff — Technical and Administration Support
    - Technical Management
    - Material Management
    - Personnel Management
      - Planning & Monitoring
      - Contract Administration
      - Finance Management
  - Line — Site Execution
    - Quality Control/Safety
    - Foundation
    - Finishes of Buildings
    - Mechanical/Maintenance Workshop
      - Super-structure
      - External Services
      - Manufacture/Fabrication Management

Depending upon the size and nature of the project, the managers in the project team are entrusted with the responsibility to accomplish project tasks. A large complex project may have a manager incharge of each specialised task, whereas in smaller and less complex projects, only few managers can look into all the tasks. The various ways in which the duties of a manager can be combined with those of the project manager in a small project are:

(a) Project manager/construction superintendent/planning and controlling manager, can be a single individual.
(b) Project manager/resources procurement manager/construction superintendent, all can be centralised in one person.
(c) Project manager/planning and controlling manager/contract manager, can be the same person.

## 1.4.4 Project Management Organization and Staffing

Depending upon the nature of project and the corporate policy, the project management organization pattern can vary from highly centralised functional organization to a dedicated project team with fully decentralised authority. The matrix organization of project management lies in-between these two extreme organizational concepts. A typical matrix structure of project organization is shown in Fig. 1.8.

The matrix structure is viewed as a temporary organization having human and non-human resources with reduced vertical hierarchy so as to respond speedily in a changing complex situation for achieving the specified performance objectives.

The managers in a project team are its key personnel. They are drawn from their parent departments and are specialists in their field. They are charged with the responsibility of their respective areas of activity. In this way, communication and coordination between top management and project management is improved.

Following are the advantages of the matrix structure:

(a) It has a single project manager accountable for the whole project. The project management, working as a team, performs the basic management functions of planning, organizing, staffing, directing, controlling and coordinating the project work.
(b) All managers owe their allegiance to the project manager, and not to their parent departmental heads.
(c) Personal commitment to objectives is the key note of matrix organization. It provides a climate for motivation, effectiveness and personal development.
(d) The specialist staff is employed effectively. The matrix organization balances their conflicting objectives by reducing the communication gap.
(e) The top management is freed from making routine decisions, as the decision-making machinery forms an integral part of the matrix structure.
(f) It provides enough flexibility to meet uncertain and changing situations by establishing a project planning and control system at site to monitor the input flow of resources and the performance output.

However, if not properly conceived and directed, the matrix organization can result in increased conflicts, lack of coordination, low productivity, and enhanced costs.

**Figure 1.8**

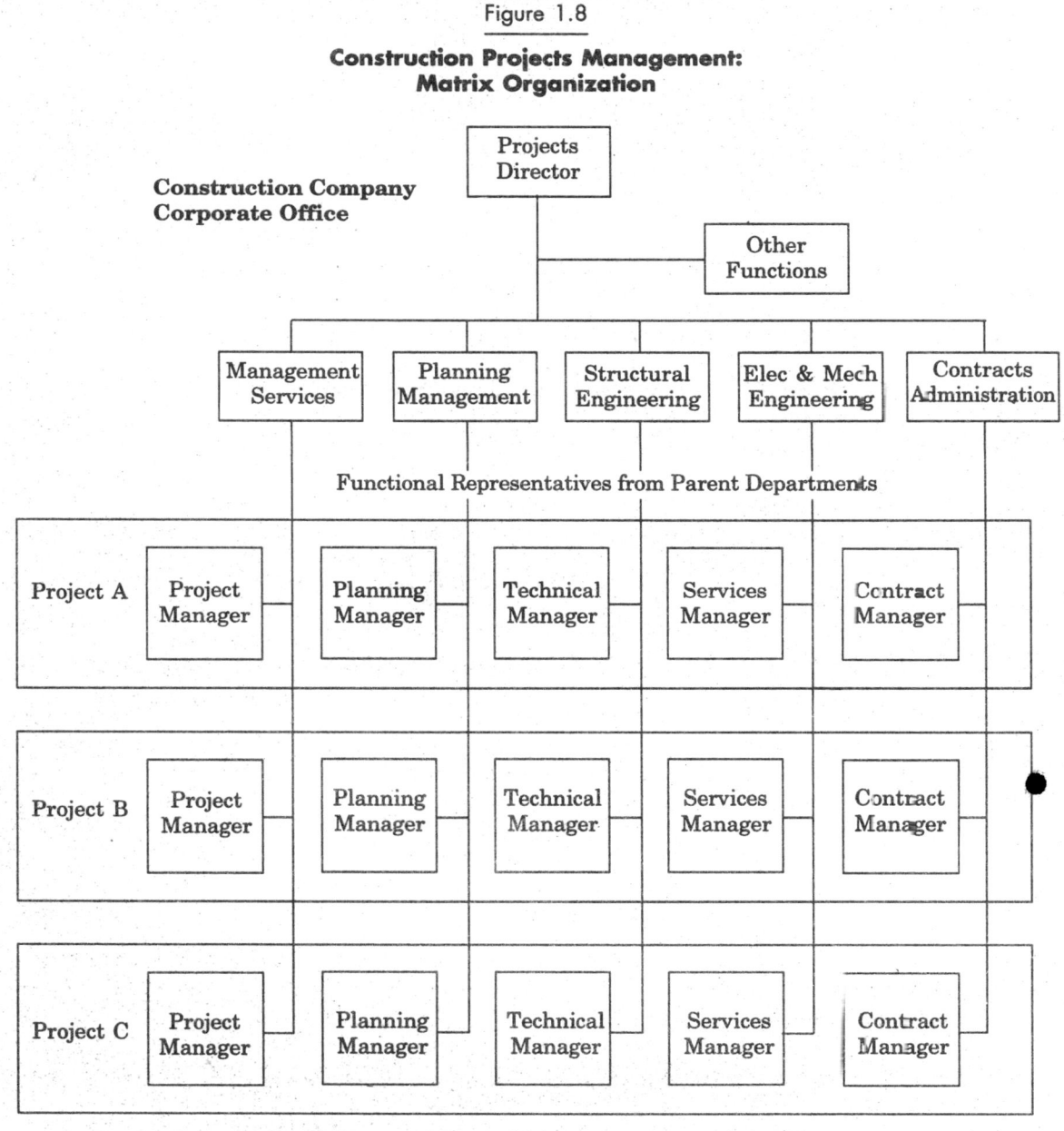

**Construction Projects Management: Matrix Organization**

```
Construction Company                    Projects
Corporate Office                        Director
                                           |
                                           |─────────── Other Functions
         ┌────────────┬──────────────┬──────────────┬──────────────┐
    Management      Planning      Structural    Elec & Mech    Contracts
    Services        Management    Engineering   Engineering    Administration
```

Functional Representatives from Parent Departments

| Project A | Project Manager | Planning Manager | Technical Manager | Services Manager | Contract Manager |
| Project B | Project Manager | Planning Manager | Technical Manager | Services Manager | Contract Manager |
| Project C | Project Manager | Planning Manager | Technical Manager | Services Manager | Contract Manager |

## 1.4.5 Role of a Project Manager

The project manager is the king pin around which the whole organization revolves. He is entrusted with the task of integrating the interdisciplinary and interorganizational efforts under changing environments for successful accomplishment of the specified objectives. He operates independently of the normal organisational chain of command, with the sole aim of achieving the specified goals within the available resources. He assumes total responsibility and accountability for the success or failure of the project. In particular his responsibilities include team building, financial control, contract management, technical management, resources management, interface management and quality management. His functions vary with the nature of the project and organizational setup, but his roles which refect the behaviour patterns identified with their specified position are similar in almost all types of projects.

Ten related roles of the project manager, generally, conforming to 'Managerial Role Constellation' advocated by Mintzberg are outlined below:

**(a) Figurehead role** The project manager, is the legal and social head of the project, is the single focal point for making decisions, ceremonial functions and symbolic duties.

**(b) Leadership role** As a leader, the project manager directs the interfunctional efforts through a complex web of relationships created in the project organization by building a performance-motivated organization a team of skilled and experienced people who collectively face the challenges posed by the people.

**(c) Liaisoning role** The project manager maintains contacts outside the organization, deals with those activities which may involve correspondence and contact with the concerned government officials contract vendors, professionals, and top persons of the construction industry.

**(d) Monitoring role** The project manager focuses a planned approach for performing tasks, and implements time, cost and quality planning and monitoring system for the project that highlights the commitment of the project team to provide assured results.

**(e) Disseminator's role** The project manager transmits the relevant information received from external sources and internal systems to the concerned people in the work place. This information may be written or verbal, formal or informal.

**(f) Spokesperson's role** The project manager acts as the sole representative through whom all communications with the client or other external parties are conducted outside the project site.

**(g) Entrepreneur's role** The project manager seeks and identifies opportunities to promote improvements and needed changes.

**(h) Disturbance handling role** The project manager maintains organizational harmony by resolving conflicts and diagnosing organizational behaviour an time. He applies corrective action when the organization faces important unexpected disturbances.

**(i) Resources allocator role** The project manager takes responsibility for allocating/ altering the project resources and makes any changes which are necessary to ensure the availability of adequate resources on time. This role also calls for developing and monitoring budgets and predicting future resource needs.

**(j) Negotiator's role** The project manager negotiates important conflicting issues and business related matters, both inside and outside of the project environment. He represents the organization on major negotiations.

In order to fulfil his assigned role effectively and efficiently a project manager has to have managerial skill, technical expertise, business acumen, leadership qualities and excellent communication and interpersonal skills. He should be a person with at least a degree or equivalent in engineering, architecture or quantity surveying. He should have relevant management qualifications and a wide construction experience, at least few years of which should be on senior positions in major projects.

## 1.5 MAIN CAUSES OF PROJECT FAILURE

It is not uncommon to see a project failing to achieve its mission of creating a facility within the specified cost and time. Hardly few projects get completed in time and within original costs. According to the annual year 1989–90 report of the Ministry of Programme Implementation of India, out of 351 projects each costing over Rs 20 crore are as follows:

- 56% had cost overruns (totalling 20% cost).
- 49% faced a time overrun from 1 to 157 months.

The factors contributing to these overruns are outlined below:

**Inadequate project formulation** Poor field investigation, inadequate project information, bad cost estimates, lack of experience, inadequate project analyses, poor investment decisions.

**Poor planning for implementation** Inadequate time plan, inadequate resource plan, inadequate equipment supply plan, inter-linking not anticipated, poor organization, poor cost planning.

**Lack of proper contract planning and management** Improper pre-contract actions, poor post award contract management.

**Lack of project management during execution** Inefficient and ineffective working, delays, changes in scope of work and location, law. There can be endless reasons for non-fulfillment of project objectives. Failures can be due to unforeseen natural calamities like earthquakes, floods and natural disasters. Failures can also result from deliberate attempts made by manipulators during the feasibility stage by incorporating inaccurate time and cost estimates with a view to secure business or start a project. These in-built intentional inaccuracies can lead to unrealistic objectives and thus create problems during the implementation stage. But, the main causes of such failures can be attributed to the cost estimation failure and management failure.

### 1.5.1 Cost Estimation Failure

Cost estimation is a continuous process. It calls for financial commitments at various levels and by various agencies involved in the project.

The client or the promoter, basing his judgement on the feasibility cost estimates, accepts engineering costs and signals the start of the engineering phase of the project. During this phase, his professional team or the consultants develop the design, the specifications, and the drawings which lead to the formulation of bill of quantities (BOQ). The BOQ contains work quantity estimates, and also indicates the approximate cost. At this stage, the client may review the cost commitments prior to giving the go-ahead for the tendering action.

On receipt of work tenders from the client's consultants, the contractor prepares his detailed estimates within the specified tendering period. He quotes his estimated price for the work itemized in the BOQ, and this tendered cost becomes his financial commitment for executing the works. Acceptance of the contractor's quoted tender by the client implies his commitment for the payment of the quoted costs.

Based on the quantities and costs reflected in the BOQ, the contractor's project planner draws up his plan of work. This plan forecasts the contractor's commitment for resources and input costs and, consequently, the revenue which he can expect.

This estimation process continues during the execution stage. The contractor's cost accountant, based on information from the site, undertakes the accounting commitment including accounting of actual costs, analyzing variances from estimated costs, and indicating the cost trends. The progress estimator (of the client) responsible for the interim payments estimates the contractors payments based on prices quoted in the BOQ, and thus implies a commitment for the correctness of part payment to the contractor. Finally, on completion, the final bill prepared by the contractor undergoes a scrutiny by the consultant, and this scrutinized bill gives the final estimate of project costs to be incurred by the client.

There are various methods employed for estimating the project costs. These include: unit cost estimation, parameter estimation, factor estimation, range estimation, and detailed contractor's estimation. The method used depends on the purpose for which the estimate is required, the degree of accuracy desired, and the estimating effort employed.

The following are the rough guidelines for selecting the appropriate method of estimation.

**(a) Inception stage** The estimation is initially based on the prevailing unit cost of the facility. Some examples of unit cost estimation are given below:

| *Nature of project* | *Method of estimation* |
| --- | --- |
| Building works | Cost per square meter of plinth area or floor area |
| School building | Cost per student |
| Hospital | Cost per bed |
| Motels | Cost per visitor or guest |
| Theater | Cost per seat |
| Water storage reservoirs | Cost per litre |
| Parking areas | Cost per space |
| Roads, highways, and airports | Cost per square meter of the surface area |

The prevailing cost depends upon many factors such as the location, specifications, resources availability, working conditions, and the political environment. This estimation method, called the unit cost method, needs little time and effort, sometimes just a few hours, to compute the cost, provided the prevailing rates are available.

The range of accuracy of this methods is roughly 40% and, therefore, it has to be further refined by using other estimating techniques when the architectural and structural drawings are prepared and other related information becomes available.

**(b) Preparatory stage**  The BOQ, prepared during the engineering stage, provides data for estimating the approximate cost by using any of the following two methods:

  (i) Computing direct costs for each item of work and adding fixed percentage for indirect costs, contractor's profit and consultancy charges.
  (ii) Computing costs using the factor estimate or parameter estimate methodology, provided sufficient past performance data is available.

The cost estimates thus derived are 10–20% on the accuracy range, and the time taken depends on the scope of the project, availability of the past performance data, and the method of execution.

**(c) Contractor's tendering and execution stage**  This estimate is based on the tendered BOQ and the contract stipulations. Tendering requires detailed estimation as inaccuracies both on plus and minus side can adversely affect the project feasibility and contractor's business respectively. Preparation of detailed estimation is a time consuming process and its accuracy (ranging from 2–10%) depends on the time and resources available for the preparation of estimation.

Despite the well-established methodology for project estimation, the glamour of hefty profits and the security of the everlasting market, financially, construction business still remains a risk proposition. Unlike other industries where the sale price of the product is determined after its manufacture, in construction, generally the works are priced before they are produced. This estimation of costs before the completion of the project adds to the business risk of the client as well as the contractors.

A construction contractor always gambles when he bids for a fixed price contract. A bid on the higher side (of what he considers reasonable) may mean an opportunity missed for new business, whereas a quotation on the lower side may imply less profits, or possibly a loss or, in some cases, even the contractor's bankruptcy. When the contractor wins a bid for quoting the lowest, his fellow bidders may question his judgement. Studies reveal that the failure rate of the construction contractors is one of the highest among the various types of businesses.

A construction project based on inaccurate cost estimates is bound to fail unless its performance objectives are revised and/or additional funds inducted.

### 1.5.2 Management Failure

A project environment comprises various interrelated constituents such as resources, tasks, and technology along with the people working against time under stress and strain: all of these combine together to achieve the common project objectives. The problems of management are so complex that they defy simple solutions. Some of these are beyond the management's control but some can be avoided. The following causes of project failure can be attributed to management failure.

**(a) Planning failure** It is due to unclear objectives and targets, unworkable plans, top management's failure to backup the plans, failure to identify critical items, lack of understanding of operating procedures and policy directions, reluctance to take timely decisions, and ignorance of appropriate planning tools and techniques.

**(b) Organizational failure** It is due to incorrect organizational structures resulting in conflicts, confusion of responsibility, inadequate delegation of authority at various levels, higher management interference, lack of stress on accountability, and a tendency of people to escape responsibility by passing on the buck.

**(c) Resource failure** It is due to an improper choice of the project manager, inexperienced staff, and failure to procure and position resources as per the planned schedules.

**(d) Directional failure** It can be attributed to a lack of team spirit, internal conflicts, poor human resource management, and labour strikes.

**(e) Controlling failure** It is due to unclear targets, inadequate information flow, incompetency in adopting appropriate monitoring techniques, and an absence of timely corrective measures.

**(f) Coordination failure** It can be attributed to a breakdown of communication at various levels, lack of day-to-day decisions to fill procedural gaps, and an absence of cooperation and *esprit de corps*.

**(g) Other failures** They may be due to faulty procurement of machinery and materials, bad workmanship, poor performance of sub-contractors, accidents, unforeseen bad weather, and a failure to adapt to the local conditions.

*Systematic planning, scheduling and controlling of projects can go a long way in preventing project collapse due to management failure. The scope and importance of planning, scheduling and controlling projects, covered in the book is outlined in Chapter 2.*

# CHAPTER 2

# Project Planning Scope

## ❑ 2.1 PLAN DEVELOPMENT PROCESS

### 2.1.1 Planning Process

Planning aims at formulation of a time-based plan of action for coordinating various activities and resources to achieve specified objectives. Planning is the process of developing the *project plan*. The plan outlines how the project is to be directed to achieve the assigned goals. It specifies a predetermined and committed future course of action, based on discussions and decisions made on the current knowledge and estimation of future trends.

Scheduling means putting the plan on a calendar time scale. During the execution stage, monitoring brings out the progress made against the scheduled base-line. Control deals with formulation and implementation of corrective actions necessary for achieving project objectives. In the construction phase of project development, planning and controlling are inseparable. During project implementation, the plan-do-monitor-communicate replan (when necessary) is a continuous process. In this context, the term planning broadly includes the plan-making, scheduling and controlling processes.

Planning, in its broader perspective, involves advance thinking as to *what* is to be done, what are the activities, *how* it is to be done, *when* it is to be done, where it is to be done, what is needed to do it, who is to do it and how to ensure that it is done; all of this is channelized to generate and evaluate options for evolving an action plan aimed at achieving the specified goals. The thought process involved in construction planning can broadly be divided into two following stages:

*Planning time*

- What is to be done?
- What are the activities involved?

- How it is to be done?
- When it is to be done?
- Where it is to be done?

*Planning resources*
- What is needed to do it?
- Who is to do it?

*Planning implementation*
- How to organize a control system?
- How to monitor what is done?
- How to analyze variances?
- How to forecast trends?
- How to communicate performance?

The construction planning process is stimulated through a study of project documents. These documents include—but are not limited to—the available technical and commercial studies and investigations, designs and drawings, estimate of quantities, construction method statements, project planning data, contract documents, site conditions, working regulations, market survey, local resources, project environment and the client's organization. The planning process takes into account the strengths and weaknesses of the organization as well as the anticipated opportunities and risks.

Planning follows a systematic approach. Various planning techniques are employed to systematize and transform the mental thought process into a concrete project plan. Generally, the following steps are involved in planning for a project:

(a) Define the scope of work to be performed.
(b) Identifying the activities involved, and assessing the approximate quantities of physical resources needed activity-wise.
(c) Preparing the logic or network diagram(s) to establish a relationship among activities, and integrating these diagram(s) to develop the project network or model.
(d) Analyzing the project network or model to determine project duration, and identifying critical and non-critical activities.
(e) Exploring trade-off between time and cost to arrive at the optimal time and costs for completing the project.
(f) Exploring work options within specified time and resource constraints, and deciding on the project-work schedule.
(g) Establishing standards for planning and controlling men, materials, equipment, costs and income of each work package.
(h) Forecasting input resources, production costs and the value of the work done.
(i) Assigning physical resources like men, materials and equipment activity-wise, and allocating these to the organizational units earmarked for execution.
(j) Forecasting the project budget and budget allocations for achieving targets assigned to each organizational unit.
(k) Designing a control system for the organization.

(l) Developing the resources, time, and cost control methodology.
(m) Evolving an information communication system.
(n) Computerizing the planning and control system.

The project planning process, techniques and methods employed to develop the project plan, are outlined in Tables 2.1 and 2.2.

Table 2.1

**Project Planning Process**

| | | |
|---|---|---|
| • Planning Data Collection | Where to look for data? | Studying relevant documents |
| • Planning Time | What is to be done? | Defining scope of work |
| | What are the activities involved? | Breaking down project work into activities |
| | How it can be done? | Developing network plans |
| | When it is to be done? | Scheduling work |
| | Where it is to be done? | Charting site layout |
| • Planning Resources | What is needed to do it? | Forecasting resources requirement |
| | | Planning manpower requirement |
| | | Planning materials procurement |
| | | Planning equipment procurement |
| | | Budgeting costs |
| | Who is to do it? | Designing organizational structure |
| | | Allocating tasks and resources |
| | | Establishing responsibility centres |
| • Planning Implementation | How to account performance? | Designing control system |
| | How to monitor performance? | Formulating monitoring methodology |
| | How to communicate information | Developing project Management Information system (PMIS) |

## 2.1.2 Type of Project Plans

Planning the entire project from its inception to completion requires a vast coverage, varied skills, and different types of plans. The nature of plans encountered in a typical construction project, are indicated below.

### Types of project plans

| *Development stage* | *Nature of plan* |
|---|---|
| Inception stage | Project feasibility plan |
| Engineering stage | Project preliminary plan |
| Implementation stage | Project construction plan |

**Project feasibility plan** Planning by the client begins as soon as he gets the idea about developing a facility to fulfil certain motives. His early thought process conceptualize the

## Table 2.2
### Project Planning Techniques

| Stages | Planning Process | Techniques/methods |
|---|---|---|
| Planning Time | Breaking down project work | Work breakdown |
| | Developing time network plans | Network analysis, Gantt chart |
| | | Line of Balance technique |
| | Scheduling work | Time limited scheduling |
| | | Resources limited scheduling |
| Planning Resources | Forecasting resource requirements | Forecasting |
| | Planning manpower requirements | Manpower scheduling |
| | Planning materials requirements | Materials scheduling |
| | Planning equipment procurement | Equipment selection and scheduling |
| | Budgeting costs | Cost planning and budgeting |
| | Designing organizational structure | Organisation design |
| | Allocating tasks and resources | Resource allocation |
| Planning Implementation | Formulating monitoring methodology | Resource productivity control |
| | | Time control |
| | | Contribution control |
| | | Budgetry control |

cost, time and benefit implications of the project. Only when he is convinced about the soundness of his idea does he decide to go ahead with the feasibility studies.

The feasibility study team examines the needs of the client and ways to fulfil them. It defines the overall scope of work and breaks it down into various task groups. It develops an outline plan of work, and assesses the time and costs of accomplishing the project. This outline plan, developed by the feasibility team during the inception stage, forms the basis for identifying project objectives and developing the project plan.

**Project preliminary plan** Acceptance of the feasibility studies marks the commencement of the preliminary plan-making process. Its main aim is to provide direction to the client managers and staff employed during the development phase of the project. The project preliminary plan forms the basis for developing the project construction plan. The preliminary plan may include the following:

(a) A project time schedule and the skeleton network to highlight the work dependencies, project milestones and the expected project completion time.
(b) The project designs and drawings preparation schedule.
(c) A breakdown of project work into contracts, along with a schedule of contracting activities, including the tender preparation period, tender finalization period, and the contracted works commencement and completion dates.
(d) A resources preliminary forecast indicating the phased requirement of men, important materials, plant and machinery.
(e) Resources procurement system.

(f) Project organization and staffing pattern.
(g) Preliminary forecast of funds requirement.

**Project construction plan** The client entrusts the construction of project facilities to the *project management team* headed by the project manager or the resident engineer. This team may be from the client's own construction agency or from a client-appointed construction management consulant firm or from a suitably organised combination of these. The planning chief, who is a member of the project management team, is entrusted with the task of developing the project construction plan. This plan includes the contracted works plans and the commissioning plan, as applicable. The work programmes are derived form the targets set out in the project plan.

The project construction plan as well as the contracted works plan further include the following plans:

(a) *Time plan* It depicts the schedule of project activities for completion of the project within the specified time.
(b) *Resources plan* It forecasts the required input resources of men, materials, machinery and money for achieving the project completion time target and cost objectives.
(c) *Plan for controlling project* It encompasses the design of control system, monitoring system, codification system and the computerized information system.

This book covers the methodology for developing the project construction plan, illustrated with real-life examples from projects handled by the author.

The construction projects plan development process is divided into three parts: time planning, resource planning and project control system planning. These parts are interdependent and not mutually exclusive.

The project plan-making approach outlined in this chapter is illustrated with a 2000 housing units turnkey construction project at Baghdad, Iraq, executed by the Makers Development Services of Bombay, India. The scope of the project included design and construction of 2000 residential apartments, educational buildings, public buildings, civic centre, connected external utility services and landscaping. The value of contracted works was to the tune of US $160 million and the project was contracted for completion in 36 months.

The residential accommodation was of precast concrete construction. The 2000 apartments were grouped into residential buildings consisting of 334 identical modules with each containing six flats. The precast production and erection was geared to achieve a peak of five flats per working day. The extent of construction work in this project is outlined in Exhibit 2.1.

## ❑ 2.2 TIME PLANNING PROCESS

In construction all projects are time bound. The project time objective specifies the project completion time. The project time and cost objective are correlated—it is the time factor which determines the project cost. Time is the essence of all construction contracts. Time delays attract penalties while early completion can earn rewards. However, inspite of one's best efforts to complete a project on time, changes from the original estimated project time plan do occur sometimes.

---

Exhibit 2.1

## 2000 Housing Units Project, Baghdad Scope of Work

**Residential buildings** 161 buildings, 3 storeyed high, modular construction having 334 modules each containing 6 flats, grouped into 52 dwelling clusters, distributed over 80 hectares.

- 3-bedroom flats : 1400
- 2-bedroom flats : 600
- Total built up area : 267,333 sq. m

### Educational buildings

- Nursery : 2
- Kindergarten : 4
- Primary school : 5
- High school : 4
- Total built up area : 32,804 sq. m

### Public buildings

Mosque, Baath Party office, super market, shopping centre, social centre, youth centre, health centre, police station, post office, *hammam*.

    Total built up area : 11,600 sq. m

### External utilities

- Filtered water supply/piping : 32 km
- Unfiltered water supply/piping : 36 km
- Sewage disposal/piping : 21 km
- Storm water drainage/piping : 12 km
- Pipe gas supply/piping : 27 km
- Electric power supply and distribution network/cabling : 111 km
- Telephones/cabling : 53 km
- Substations & pump houses : 3000 sq. m

### Roads, footpaths and pathways

### Sports facilities

Soccer fields, basketball courts, lawn tennis courts, Olympic-standard swimming pool etc.

**Gardens and landscaping** : 210,000 sq. m

---

There may be many reasons, both foreseen and unforeseen, for non-completion of a project on time. However, the absence of a project time plan almost makes certain that a project cannot be completed on schedule without incurring extra costs. A plan, prepared well before the commencement of construction in a project, can be instrumental in formulating directions, coordinating functions, setting targets, forecasting resources, budgeting costs, controlling performance and motivating people. It is for these reasons that the project planning starts with time planning as the first step. The time planning process involves the following three stages.

**(a) Project work breakdown** This means breaking down the scope of project work into its constituent sub-projects, tasks, work packages and activities.

**(b) Modelling and analyzing networks** This includes developing logic diagrams or sub-networks; integrating these to develop a time-planning model (usually a network) and; analyzing this model to determine the project completion time.

**(c) Scheduling work programmes** This involves putting the time plan on a calendar basis, and using the scheduled programme to forecast inputs and output.

## 2.2.1 Project Work Breakdown

The project work breakdown process involves splitting of the project works into its manageable constituents arranged in a hierarchical order till the desired level. The work-breakdown levels are categorised into sub-projects, tasks, work packages, activities and operations. These levels depend upon the plan type, the nature and complexity of the project and the expected degree of control.

The work-breakdown levels for various types of plans are given in Figure 2.1. It may be noted that the levels classification is a broad concept and, at times, overlapping of levels may become unavoidable.

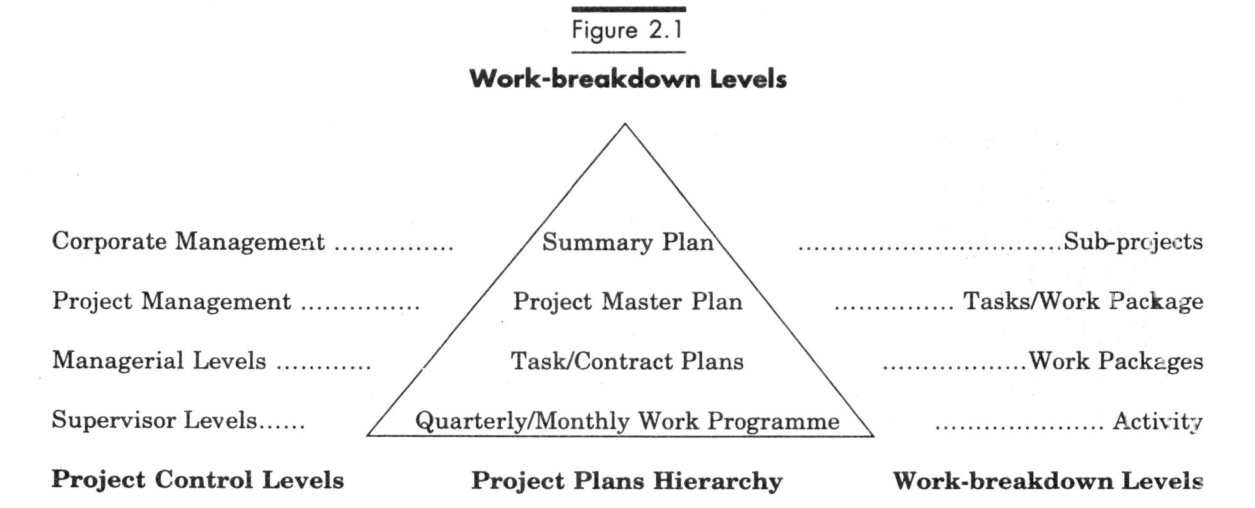

Figure 2.1

**Work-breakdown Levels**

| Project Control Levels | Project Plans Hierarchy | Work-breakdown Levels |
|---|---|---|
| Corporate Management ......... | Summary Plan | Sub-projects |
| Project Management ......... | Project Master Plan | Tasks/Work Package |
| Managerial Levels ......... | Task/Contract Plans | Work Packages |
| Supervisor Levels ...... | Quarterly/Monthly Work Programme | Activity |

The breaking down of a task/work package into its constituent activities requires a study of the methodology of execution of the work package. Generally, known by the term *method statement*, this methodology is evolved by the planning engineer on the basis of his construction experience and discussions with the respective project engineers.

Construction projects are best managed by work packages, which, in turn, are best planned and monitored by activities. A project planner, uses activity as the common data base for planning projects. Activity duration forms the basis for time planning and scheduling of project work. The inputs of labour, materials and machinery needed for execution of each activity enable preparation of resources forecasts. The activity sale price is used to determine income and cash-flow forecasts. The activity base is vital for monitoring progress of the project work.

The various methods of identifying tasks, work-packages and activities, and initial assessment of time duration and direct resources, activity-wise, are described in Chapter 3. It also includes work-breakdown illustrations from the 2000 Housing Units Project and other projects.

### 2.2.2 Modeling and Analyzing Networks

With the advancement of technology and the speed of construction, the traditional bar charts planning approach has become inadequate to tackle the modern complex construction projects. The bar charts provide very little information about the inter-relationship of the voluminous interdependent tasks. This traditional bar charts approach carry risk of schedule slippage's, time over-runs, improper decisions and contractual complications.

The network analysis techniques developed in sixties, is being effectively used as a management tool for planning and then scheduling of complex projects involving interlinking activities.

Project Networks analysis is a generic term that covers all network techniques used for planning scheduling and controlling of projects. The three commonly used techniques in this family are Critical Path Method (CPM), Program Evaluation and Review Technique (PERT) and the Precedence Network Analysis (PNA) Technique. The common features of these techniques are that they make use of network model for depicting time-plan of the project, apply critical path concept for determining project duration and identifying critical activities, and employ network analysis techniques for controlling project time objectives. But each technique has a distinct model and its field of application varies.

**Network analysis procedure** The modeling and analysis of a network involves the following steps:

- Defining scope of network
- Determining activities
- Developing network logic diagram
- Structuring model
- Incorporating activity durations
- Numbering events/activity
- Computing critical path
- Validating Network

**Illustrations** Some time analysed CPM, PERT and Precedence networks, given below are in Exhibits shown against each;

- CPM Network of Pumping Station Project—*Exhibit 4.1*
- PERT Network of Pumping Station Project—*Exhibit 4.3*

- Precedence Network of four rafts foundation construction—*Exhibit 5.2*
- Summary Precedence Network of Primary School—*Exhibit 5.4*
- Precedence Network of a group of similar Education Buildings—*Exhibit 5.5*
- Precedence Network of Raw Water Clarifier Tank—*Exhibit 5.7*

**Criteria for selection of network technique** Experience shows that:

- CPM is best suited for developing sub-project/task/work package sub-networks having activities with deterministic single-time duration.
- PERT is useful for work packages, tasks or sub-projects involving uncertainties. In such cases, probabilistic approach of three-times (or a mathematical time-related function) is used for assessing activity duration.
- Precedence Network is the most commonly used technique for time planning of construction sub-projects and projects.
- Networks containing 200 to 300 activities/work packages are manageable, and those having activities/work packages greater than 300 are difficult to comprehend.

A project schedule can be depicted by a bar chart, time-scale network or other pictorial displays. The 2000 Housing Units summary schedule of work as a bar chart is shown in Exhibit 2.2.

It is not necessary to draw networks for all projects/sub-projects, as some projects like repetitive type buildings can be better planned using Line-of-Balance technique.

## ❏ 2.3 WORK SCHEDULING PROCESS

### 2.3.1 Object of Scheduling

Scheduling means putting the plan on calendar basis. A project network shows the sequence and interdependencies of activities, their time durations and their earliest and latest completion time, but this needs to be scheduled to determine commencement and termination dates of each activity, using optimum resources or working within resource constraints. A time schedule outlines the project work programme, it is a time table of work.

### 2.3.2 Scheduling Procedure

Scheduling methodology varies with the planning technique and the nature of task. Tool kit containing commonly used techniques for planning, scheduling and monitoring is displayed in Table 2.3. Simple projects can be scheduled using bar chart methodology. Line-of-Balance (LOB) technique is widely accepted for scheduling repetitive works projects. Network scheduling methodology is suitable for all types of projects. There are many other scheduling techniques. Method of presentation of a schedule depends upon the technique used for scheduling. Generally, all scheduling techniques use time scale along horizontal axis. This time scale for most of the schedules, uses 'week' as the unit of time and the weeks are then

Exhibit 2.2

# 2000 Housing Units Project: Summary Schedule of Construction Tasks

| No. | Work Description | May | Jun | Jul | Aug | Sep | Oct | Nov | Dec | Jan | Feb | Mar | Apr | May | Jun | Jul | Aug | Sep | Oct | Nov | Dec | Jan |
|---|---|---|---|---|---|---|---|---|---|---|---|---|---|---|---|---|---|---|---|---|---|---|
|  | **Residential Buildings** | | | | | | | | | | | | | | | | | | | | | |
| 1. | Foundation | | | | | | | | | | | | | | | | | | | | | |
| 2. | Precast Reaction | | | | | | | | | | | | | | | | | | | | | |
| 3. | Finishes | | | | | | | | | | | | | | | | | | | | | |
|  | **Education & Public Buildings** | | | | | | | | | | | | | | | | | | | | | |
| 4. | Foundation | | | | | | | | | | | | | | | | | | | | | |
| 5. | Superstructure | | | | | | | | | | | | | | | | | | | | | |
| 6. | Finishes | | | | | | | | | | | | | | | | | | | | | |
|  | **External Utility Services** | | | | | | | | | | | | | | | | | | | | | |
| 7. | Sewage & Storm Water Pump Houses | | | | | | | | | | | | | | | | | | | | | |
| 8. | Receiving & Substations | | | | | | | | | | | | | | | | | | | | | |
| 9. | Sewage & Storm Water Drains | | | | | | | | | | | | | | | | | | | | | |
| 10. | Gas Supply | | | | | | | | | | | | | | | | | | | | | |
| 11. | Electric Supply | | | | | | | | | | | | | | | | | | | | | |
| 12. | Road & Parking Areas | | | | | | | | | | | | | | | | | | | | | |
| 13. | Landscaping & Sports Field | | | | | | | | | | | | | | | | | | | | | |

| Months | May | Jun | Jul | Aug | Sep | Oct | Nov | Dec | Jan | Feb | Mar | Apr | May | Jun | Jul | Aug | Sep | Oct | Nov | Dec | Jan |
|---|---|---|---|---|---|---|---|---|---|---|---|---|---|---|---|---|---|---|---|---|---|
| Working Days in a Month | 25 | 24 | 25 | 25 | 24 | 25 | 24 | 24 | 22 | 20 | 23 | 24 | 25 | 24 | 25 | 25 | 24 | 25 | 24 | 24 | 22 |
| Working Days Cumulative | 25 | 49 | 74 | 99 | 123 | 148 | 172 | 196 | 218 | 238 | 261 | 285 | 310 | 334 | 359 | 384 | 408 | 433 | 457 | 481 | 503 | 523 | 546 | 569 | 594 | 618 | 643 | 668 | 692 | 717 | 741 | 765 | 787 |

Note: Breakdown of Residential Building Monthly Physical Targets are detailed in Chapter 6.

related to calendar dates. Each techniques has its merits and demerits. But ultimately schedules are best presented in the bar chart form for case of comprehension and communication. These bar charts are supplemented with appropriate planning technique for monitoring time progress. It is mentioned that scheduling is not an automatic mechanical process, but it needs work experience to schedule the work.

The scheduling procedures, depending upon type of project can be broadly divided into two categories:

- Scheduling non-repetitive network based projects.
- Scheduling repetitive project using line of balance techniques.

### 2.3.3 Procedure for Scheduling Network-based Plan

- Outline scheduling constraints
- Design scheduling calendar
- List activities in order of sensitivity
- Draw earliest start time schedule
- Determine resource optimisation criteria
- Schedule critical activities
- Schedule non-critical activities
- Validate time objectives
- Schedule other resources
- Scheduling within resources constraints
- Scheduling repetitive works projects

Some illustrations of scheduling network based projects/tasks are given below:

- Time limited Site Development Project—*Exhibit 6.4*
- Resource limited Site Development Project—*Exhibit 6.5*
- Manpower optimised education building projects—*Exhibit 6.6*

### 2.3.4 Procedure for Scheduling Repetitive Projects Using Line-of-Balance Technique

- Outline scheduling constraints
- Tabulate scheduling data of a unit work cycle
- Prepare a logic diagram of a unit work cycle
- Chart scheduling calendar
- Prepare Earliest Start Time schedule
- Analyse Earliest Start Time schedule
- Prepare optimum schedule leaving adequate buffers
- Draw Line-of-Balance work schedule

Some illustration of scheduling repetitive projects using line of balance techniques are given below:

- Line-of-Balance Residential Building foundation—*Exhibit 6.7*
- Line-of-Balance Residential Building Finishes schedule—*Exhibit 6.9*
- Residential Buildings Monthly Work Targets—*Exhibit 6.10*

The schedule of work serves many purposes: it simplifies the project time plan by putting it on a calendar basis; it verifies fulfillment of time objectives; it aids in optimising resources; it evaluates implications of resources constraints, and; it enables forecasting of input resources, expenditure and income. These resource forecasts cover manpower, materials, machinery, sales-income and cash-flow. The scheduling work plan methodology is described in Chapter 6.

### 2.3.5 Time Planning Techniques

A project time plan depicts the sequence of accomplishment of the planning components plotted against project time scale. These components include activities and events. Time planning techniques are used to put these components on the time scale. The symbolic representation of these plan components varies with each planning technique.

There is a large variety of time planning techniques. The commonly known techniques are bar charts, network analysis, line of balance technique and linear programme charts.

Selection of planning technique from the techniques tool-kit, depends upon the nature of the project or sub-project. Time plan of simple projects, where activities and their logic can be visualized mentally, can be plotted directly on bar charts. The complex projects are best planned using network analysis techniques. These can then be scheduled to develop the time scale network schedule.

In case of projects having repetitive works, the line of balance techniques is used to depict graphical schedule of activities. Roads, airfields and similar linear-type construction projects can be planned in the form of linear programming charts to represent activity location, rate of work and time schedule.

There are many other time planning techniques which can serve the specific needs of construction projects. The commonly used planning techniques with their field of applications are shown in Table 2.3. These are covered in Chapters 4, 5 and 6.

## 2.4 RESOURCE PLANNING PROCESS

### 2.4.1 Forecasting Input and Output

A *forecast* is a prediction of what is anticipated in future. It represents current thinking about the future outcome. It is based on various assumptions and judgements. The assumptions made at the time of forecasting are based on the currently available information which may or may not hold good in future.

## Table 2.3
## Commonly Used Time Planning Techniques in Construction Project Management

| Sl. No. | Nature of Project | Planning | Scheduling | Monitoring | Displaying |
|---|---|---|---|---|---|
| 1. | Simple projects/sub-projects | | | | |
| | (a) Non-repetative work | Bar chart | Bar chart | Bar chart | Bar chart |
| | (b) Repetative works | LOB | LOB | LOB | LOB/Bar chart |
| 2. | Complex sub-projects | | | | |
| | (a) Deterministic | CPM | Time scale network | CPM | Bar chart |
| | (b) Probabilistics | PERT | ,, | PERT | Bar chart |
| 3. | Complex projects | | | | |
| | (a) Non-repetative works | PNA | Bar chart | PNA | Bar chart |
| | (b) Repetative works | PNA | LOB | LOB | Bar charts/LOB |
| | (c) Probabilistics | PERT | Time scale network | PERT | Bar chart |
| 4. | Linear projects | LPC | LPC | LPC | Bar chart/LPC |

*Abbreviations*     *Planning Technique*
- CPM — Critical Path Method.
- PERT — Programme Evaluation and Review Technique.
- PNA — Precedence Network Analysis.
- LOB — Line of Balance Technique.
- LPC — Linear Programme Chart.
- BC — Bar Chart.
- TSN — Time Scale Network or Logic Bar Chart.

The inputs and output forecast includes the data-wise requirement of project manpower, major materials, costly equipment, production costs, sales or earned value of work done and the expected income. The basis of forecasting is the schedule of work.

Resource forecasts are generally depicted graphically with time represented along abscissa and the resources along the ordinate axis to determine the data-wise and cumulative requirement pattern. The resulting graphical pattern for most of the cumulative forecasts is that of 'S' shaped curve. Exhibit 2.3 shows the cumulative forecast of value of work done and manpower requirements of the housing units project. The methodology for forecasting input resources and output is dealt with in Chapter 6.

Inputs and output forecast aids in conceptualization of the project. It indicates the quantum of resources required for executing is project and the output expected. The pattern of input resources form the base for evaluating such needs as workers' accommodation, materials storage, equipment work-load and project-funding pattern.

However, resource forecasts are, at best, educated guesses for predicting the future needs pattern. These forecasts, initially, for a short period, may be considered for mobilization of resources. To convert these *forecasts* into resource *plans,* the established principles of resources management has to be applied. For example a daily consumption of tiling material cannot be taken as the delivery schedule, as the plan for procurement of tiles will have to take into consideration the lot size, rate of consumption, procurement lead time, load transportation economy, shelf life and the predetermined inventory level.

## Exhibit 2.3

### 2000 Housing Units Project
### Man-month Requirement and Earned Value Forecasts

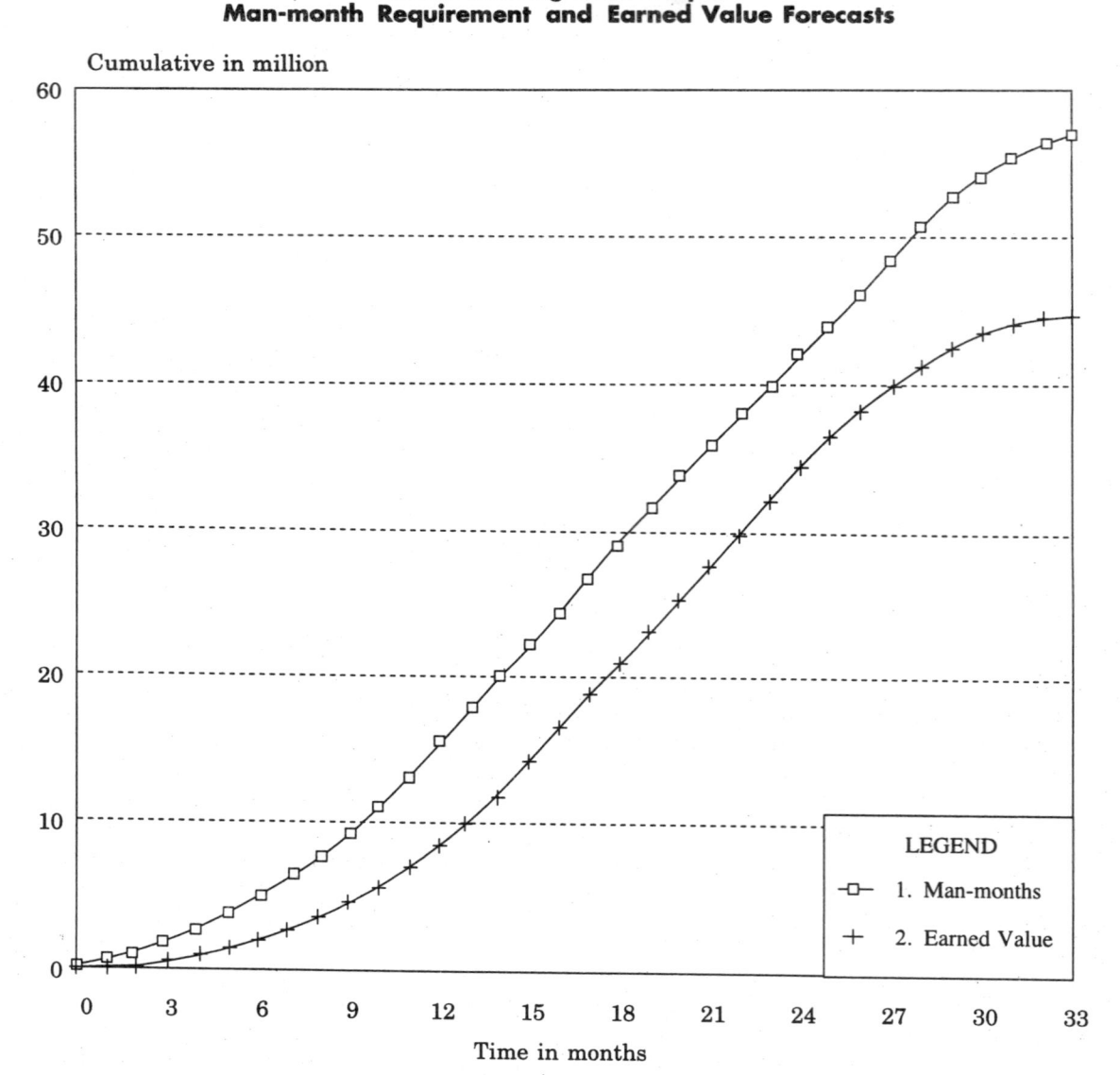

LEGEND
- —□— 1. Man-months
- + 2. Earned Value

1. Represents forecast in thousand man-months
2. Shows value of work done in million dinars

---

A resources plan shows when and in what quantity the resources are to be inducted at the project site. It specifies as to what the project management would like accomplished to achieve the project targets. The scope of construction resource planning spans manpower planning, materials planning, equipment planning, standard cost planning and budget planning.

### 2.4.2 Planning Construction Work Force

The project manpower planning primarily focuses on determining the size of the project work force, its structuring into functional groups and workers' teams, and scheduling the manpower recruitment/induction to match the task requirements.

This process chiefly involves identifying the trades or the skills required, establishing productivity standards to determine the number of workers needed to perform a given job in the specified time, data-wise forecasting of the workers' requirements for accomplishing the project work, and, finally, organizing the planned work force into operating work-teams having assigned programmed tasks. These aspects of manpower planning are covered in Chapter 7. The construction workers estimated date-wise for the housing units project are shown in Exhibit 2.4.

### 2.4.3 Planning Construction Materials

Efficient materials management in project environments calls for an integrated approach covering numerous functions such as materials planning and programming, materials purchasing, inventory control, store-keeping and ware housing, materials transportation and handling at site, materials codification and standardization, and the disposal of surpluses. The materials planning and programming, which is the key function of materials management is closely linked with the project planning and control set-up. Both these work together to develop a plan for procurement and stocking of construction materials so as to provide at site, materials of right quality, in right quantity, at right prices, from right source and at the right time.

The construction materials planning involves identifying the materials required, estimating quantities, defining specifications, forecasting requirements, locating sources for procurement, getting material samples approved, designing materials inventory, and developing the procurement plan to ensure a smooth flow of materials till the connected construction works are completed at the project site. These aspects of materials planning are covered in Chapter 8. The various materials needed for one module of residential building are listed in Exhibit 2.5.

### 2.4.4 Planning Construction Equipment

Production tasks needing equipment include excavating, handling, transporting, filling, compacting, grading, hoisting, concreting, pre-casting, plastering, finishing, trenching, and laying of pipes and cables. The supporting equipment at project site consists of generators, transmission lines, pumping sets, treatment plants and other utility services equipment.

Construction equipment is indispensable in the execution of modern high-cost, time-bound massive construction projects. It produces output with an accelerated speed in a

## Exhibit 2.4

### 2000 Housing Units Project
### Extract from Workers' Requirement for Crash Program

| No. | Work description | MAY | JUN | JUL | AUG | SEP | OCT | ~ | SEP |
|---|---|---|---|---|---|---|---|---|---|
| 1. | **Construction Works** | | | | | | | | |
| | *Carpentry Work* | | | | | | | | |
| | Furniture carpenter | | | | | | | | 56 |
| | Wood polisher | | | | | | | | 3 |
| | Shuttering carpenter | 41 | 77 | 122 | 124 | 124 | 124 | | 76 |
| | Carpenter helper | 10 | 38 | 60 | 60 | 60 | 60 | | 90 |
| | *Masonry Work* | | | | | | | | |
| | Concrete mason | 10 | 46 | 46 | 46 | 48 | 58 | | 112 |
| | Blockwork & plaster mason | 14 | 14 | 14 | 15 | 47 | 78 | | 41 |
| | Tiling mason | | | | | | 12 | | 104 |
| | Mason helper | 30 | 40 | 40 | 40 | 40 | 40 | | 272 |
| | *RCC Steel Work* | | | | | | | | |
| | Rebar fabricator | 22 | 45 | 74 | 91 | 99 | 104 | | 109 |
| | Rebar helper | 20 | 22 | 36 | 40 | 40 | 44 | | 67 |
| | *Painting work* | | | | | | | | |
| | Painter | 1 | 2 | 2 | 2 | 2 | 2 | | 20 |
| | Painter helper | | 2 | 2 | 2 | 2 | 2 | | 20 |
| | *Electrical works* | | | | | | | | |
| | Electrician | 10 | 16 | 16 | 16 | 18 | 27 | | 77 |
| | Electrical helper | | 1 | 5 | 5 | 15 | 24 | | 90 |
| | *Plumbing & Sanitary works* | | | | | | | | |
| | Plumber/Pipe fitter | 3 | 10 | 10 | 34 | 56 | 68 | | 47 |
| | Plumber helper | 1 | 10 | 10 | 34 | 50 | 59 | | 53 |
| | *Unskilled Work* | | | | | | | | |
| | General helpers | 70 | 70 | 124 | 142 | 164 | 204 | | 211 |
| 2. | **Mechanical Trades** | | | | | | | | |
| | Light vehicle drivers | 7 | 15 | 15 | 15 | 15 | 15 | | 23 |
| | Heavy vehicle drivers | 9 | 20 | 20 | 20 | 20 | 20 | | 38 |
| | Equipment operators | 1 | 18 | 38 | 55 | 57 | 59 | | 94 |
| | Blacksmith | 1 | 12 | 12 | 12 | 12 | 12 | | 43 |
| | Welder | 5 | 12 | 12 | 12 | 12 | 12 | | 15 |
| | Sheet fabricator | | | | | | 18 | | 26 |
| | Auto electrician | 1 | 2 | 2 | 2 | 2 | 2 | | 5 |
| | Mechanic diesel/petrol | 6 | 8 | 10 | 10 | 10 | 10 | | 16 |
| | Mechanic/operator helper | 1 | 8 | 30 | 41 | 46 | 48 | | 13 |
| | Riggers | 27 | 36 | 36 | 36 | 36 | 36 | | 97 |
| | Other categories | 3 | 3 | 3 | 28 | 28 | 28 | | 36 |
| | **Administration Staff** | | | | | | | | |
| | Cook | 4 | 10 | 10 | 10 | 10 | 10 | | 24 |
| | Mess helper | 1 | 26 | 26 | 26 | 26 | 26 | | 10 |
| | Security staff | | 6 | 6 | 6 | 6 | 6 | | 10 |
| 3. | **Administration helper** | 5 | 11 | 11 | 11 | 11 | 11 | | 44 |
| | Total | 303 | 580 | 792 | 896 | 953 | 1118 | ~ | 1942 |

Exhibit 2.5

## Residential Buildings with Precast Concrete Superstructure Main Materials Required

| Sl No. | Item & Description | % building materials Total Amount |
|---|---|---|
| **I** | **Bulk Materials** | |
| 1. | Cement | 19.43 |
| 2. | Sand | 6.39 |
| 3. | Aggregate | 5.75 |
| 4. | Admixtures | 4.80 |
| 5. | Steel | 15.22 |
| 6. | Weld mesh | 0.48 |
| 7. | Binding wire | 0.26 |
| 8. | Bitumen | 0.12 |
| 9. | Anti-termite chemicals | 0.50 |
| 10. | Polythene sheets | 0.36 |
| 11. | Imported soil | 0.93 |
| 12. | Softwood | 0.42 |
| **II** | **Wiring** | |
| 13. | PVC Conduits & accessories | 0.33 |
| 14. | Socket outlets | 0.32 |
| 15. | Armored cable | 0.39 |
| **III** | **Screed** | |
|  | Cement | Included in Sl No. 1 |
|  | Sand | Included in Sl. No. 2 |
| **IV** | **GRC Panels** | |
| 16. | GRC Panels | 6.25 |
| **V** | **PVC Plumbing** | |
| 17. | PVC Pipes & accessories | 2.64 |
| **VI** | **GI Plumbing** | |
| 18. | GI pipes & fittings | 0.56 |
| 19. | 15 mm valves | 0.26 |
| 20. | Hot water pipe | 0.29 |
| **VII** | **A/C Ducting** | |
| 21. | GI Sheet 24 g | 0.43 |
| 22. | GI Sheet 22 g | 0.39 |
| **VII** | **Staircase Metal Works** | |
| 23. | 40 mm GI pipe | 0.32 |
| **IX** | **False Ceiling** | |
|  | Softwood | Included in above |
| 24. | Asbestos sheet | 0.36 |

*(Contd.)*

| Sl No. | Item & Description | % building materials Total Amount |
|---|---|---|
| **X** | **Ceramic/Glazed tiles** | |
| 25. | Tiles Type A | 0.52 |
| 26. | Tiles Type B | 0.42 |
| 27. | Tiles Type C | 0.63 |
| 28. | Tiles Type D | 2.50 |
| **XI** | **Doors/Windows including shouttering/Glazing** | |
| | Softwood | Included in Sl No. 14 |
| 29. | Door/windows profiles | 1.99 |
| **XII** | **Sanitary fittings** | |
| 30. | European water closet | 0.22 |
| 31. | Bidet | 0.20 |
| **XIII** | **Painting** | |
| 32. | Spray plaster | 1.31 |
| 33. | Plastic emulsion paint | 0.71 |
| 34. | Paint primer | 0.46 |
| 35. | Paint putty | 1.09 |
| **XIV** | **Electrical Fittings** | |
| 36. | Electrical holders & fittings | 1.56 |
| **XV** | **Kitchen cabinets/Wardrobe** | |
| 37. | Kitchen cabinets | 2.92 |
| 38. | Wardrobe | 3.21 |
| **XVII** | **PVC Tiles** | |
| 39. | PVC tiles | 1.28 |
| 40. | PVC skirting | 1.16 |
| **XVIII** | **PVC Handrail** | |
| 41. | PVC handrail | 0.02 |
| **XIX** | **Roof Treatment** | |
| 42. | Roofing felt | 2.50 |
| 43. | Bitumen primer | 0.46 |
| **XX** | **External Finishes & Miscellaneous items** | |
| 44. | Waterproofing compound | 0.72 |

*Note:* Material needed for Residential Buildings are listed in Exhibit 8.1.

limited time. It saves manpower, which is becoming ever more costly and demanding. It improves productivity, quality and safety and also adds a sense of urgency. Acquisition of equipment mass involve initial heavy investment but, on the whole, its adds to profitability by reducing the overall costs, provided it is properly planned, economically procured and effectively managed.

Equipment planning for a project aims at identifying the construction tasks to be undertaken by mechanical equipment, assessing the equipment required, exploring the equipment

### Exhibit 2.6

## 2000 Housing Units Project: Major Plant and Equipment Planned

| Category | Quantity | Category | Quantity |
|---|---|---|---|
| **I. Earthmoving and road making maching machinery** | | **V. Power generation and water supply machinery** | |
| (1) Dozers | 2 Nos | (1) Generators—500 KVA | 1 Nos |
| (2) Loaders shovels | 7 ,, | (2) Generators—175 KVA | 10 ,, |
| (3) Excavators | 3 ,, | (3) Generators—25 to 55 KVA | 6 ,, |
| (4) Compressors | 8 ,, | (4) Pumps | 7 ,, |
| (5) Road rollers—Vibratory & pneumatic | 2 ,, | **VI. Precast factory machinery** | |
| (6) Motor grader | 1 ,, | (1) Batching plant 100 cu m/hr | 1 Nos |
| (7) Asphalt hot-mix plant | 1 ,, | (2) Gantry cranes | 10 ,, |
| (8) Asphalt paver | 1 ,, | (3) Steam boilers | 2 ,, |
| (9) Tarboiler | 1 ,, | (4) Moulds—vibratory | 75 ,, |
| (10) Bitumen sprayer | 1 ,, | (5) Electric cars | 4 ,, |
| (11) Soil compactors | 30 ,, | (6) Prime movers for trailors | 5 ,, |
| | | (7) 'A' frame trailors | 10 ,, |
| **II. Concreting machinery** | | (8) Flat head trailors | 5 ,, |
| (1) Batching plants 35 cu m | 2 Nos | | |
| (2) Transit mixers 6 cm | 4 ,, | **VII. Manufacturing and fabrication workshop** | |
| (3) Concrete pump | 1 ,, | | |
| (4) Concrete mixers 21/4 | 3 ,, | (1) Duct making machines | 10 Nos |
| (5) Screed pumps | 4 ,, | (2) Inserts manufacturing machines | 20 ,, |
| (6) Mobile conveyors | 4 ,, | (3) Metal work fabrication machines | 7 ,, |
| | | (4) GRC manufacturing machines | 9 ,, |
| **III. Erection and Handling machinery** | | (5) Plastic moulding machines | 2 ,, |
| (1) Crane—55 tons | 4 Nos | (6) Wood-work and carpentary machines | 15 ,, |
| (2) Cranes—20 to 35 tons | 4 ,, | (7) Steel doors and windows manufacturing machines | 13 ,, |
| (3) Cranes—6 to 10 tons | 3 ,, | (8) Rebar fabrication machines | 8 ,, |
| (4) Forklifts | 12 ,, | (9) Block making machine 2000 blocks/hr | 1 ,, |
| **IV. Transport fleet** | | (10) Spraying and plastering machines | 6 ,, |
| (1) Heavy duty tractors/tippers/ dumpers/tankers | 35 Nos | | |
| (2) Dumpers—2 ton capacity | 16 ,, | | |
| (3) Form tractors with trailors 81 HP | 5 ,, | | |

procurement options and, finally, participating in the decision-making for selecting the equipment. These aspects of equipment planning are covered in Chapters 9 and 10. The equipment planned for the housing units project is listed in Exhibit 2.6.

## 2.4.5 Planning Construction Standard Costs

The construction cost planning has as its aim the integration of planning judgement, costing techniques and accounting discipline for developing standard costs, financial forecasts, project budget and cost control measures with the ultimate goal of achieving project profit or cost objectives.

The construction cost plan uses standard cost concept for costing work-packages, work items or activities. The standard cost technique finds wide application in estimating, forecasting, budgeting, accounting and controlling of costs.

### Exhibit 2.7

**Foundation Construction Sub-project: Activity-wise Workers' Requirement Estimate for One Foundation Module Construction**

| No. | Activity | Unit | Quantity | Duration Hours | Direct labour crew Skilled | Direct labour crew Unskilled | B.O.Q. Code | Work centre Responsible |
|---|---|---|---|---|---|---|---|---|
| 1. | Layout for excavation | — | — | 4 | — | 2 | A1–1 | Earthwork |
| 2. | Excavation with machine | CM | 400 | 8 | — | 1 | ,, | ,, |
| 3. | Base preparation | SM | 360 | 16 | 4 | 10 | ,, | ,, |
| 4. | Anti-termite at base | SM | 362 | 4 | — | 2 | A1–4 | ,, |
| 5. | Polythene sheeting | SM | 362 | 6 | — | 3 | A1–6 | ,, |
| 6. | Shuttering for blinding | RM | 90 | 8 | 2 | 2 | A1–7 | ,, |
| 7. | Placing concrete M-100 | CM | 18 | 18 | 4 | 5 | A1–6 | Concreting |
| 8. | Layout for raft | — | — | 4 | 1 | 2 | A1–8 | Rebar |
| 9. | Shuttering for raft | SM | 22.5 | 8 | 2 | 2 | ,, | ,, |
| 10. | Reinforcement for raft | MT | 6.066 | 32 | 10 | 5 | A1–11 | ,, |
| 11. | Raft concreting M-250 | CM | 88.14 | 5 | 5 | 6 | A1–8 | Concreting |
| 12. | Curing raft | — | — | 4 | — | 1 | ,, | Back filling |
| 13. | Bitumen coating raft sides | SM | 362 | 3 | 2 | 3 | A1–5 | ,, |
| 14. | Layout for plinth wall | — | — | 4 | — | 2 | A1–8 | Shuttering |
| 15. | Wall shuttering | SM | 485 | 48 | 10 | 8 | ,, | ,, |
| 16. | Wall concreting M-250 | CM | 43.78 | 3 | 5 | 6 | ,, | Concreting |
| 17. | Deshuttering | — | — | 16 | 8 | 8 | ,, | Shuttering |
| 18. | Curing wall | — | — | 8 | — | 1 | ,, | Back filling |
| 19. | Bitumen coating wall & raft | SM | 319 | 3 | 2 | 3 | A1–5 | ,, |
| 20. | Back filling | CM | 120 | 8 | — | 4 | A1–2 | ,, |
| 21. | Plinth filling | CM | 305 | 16 | — | 8 | A1–3 | ,, |
| 22. | Anti-termite under GF slab | SM | 172 | 2 | — | 2 | A1–4 | ,, |
| 23. | Polythene sheeting | SM | 225 | 3 | — | 2 | | A1–6,, |
| 24. | Shuttering for GF slab | SM | 11 | 8 | 1 | 1 | A1–9 | Rebar |
| 25. | Weld mesh fixing | MT | 0.651 | 8 | 4 | 2 | A1–10 | ,, |
| 26. | GF concreting M-250 | CM | 28.34 | 2 | 5 | 6 | A1–9 | Concreting |
| 27. | Curing GF slab | — | — | 8 | — | 1 | ,, | Back filling |
| | Total manhours | | | | 1202 | 1304 | | |
| | All-in rate per manhour | | | | $ 1.50 | $ 1.25 | | |
| | Direct Labour Cost | | | | $ 1803 | $ 1630 | | |

Chapter 11 describes the cost classification and nature of production costs. It explains the methodology for establishing resource costing standards and apportioning indirect costs. It also highlights the salient features of the standard cost concept.

To quote an example, the direct standards labour cost and direct standard material cost for one module of foundation of the residential building is tabulated in Exhibits 2.7 and 2.8 respectively.

### 2.4.6 Planning Construction Budget

A project budget reflects the financial plan of operations with specified goals and the costs expected to be incurred for achieving these.

The primary purpose of having a budget is to assign financial targets and resources to each functional group so as to establish some basis for controlling their performance and to make participants plan with cost-consciousness instead of purpose-less routine-working.

The basis of budget is the project plan and its schedule of work. The budget preparation involves: structuring of project functional organization into production, services and administration responsibility centres; assigning each responsibility centre its goals in the form of sales budget and production targets; allocating resources with budgeted costs necessary to achieve the assigned goals, and; finally, compiling the project financial plan in the form of the project master budget. These aspects and the methodology for preparing the project construction budget are covered in Chapter 12. Tasks responsibility centres of the housing project are structured in Exhibit 2.9

## ❏ 2.5 PROJECT CONTROL PROCESS

The project plan indicates the path charted to achieve the objectives of the project. During the implementation stage, the project control system aims at ensuring the execution of work as per the planned schedule and the application of necessary corrective measures, including re-planning, to achieve the project objectives.

Even with the best of efforts, the probability of execution of a project exactly as per the original plan is negligible because the project implementation may undergo unpredictable resource problems and unforeseen time delays. These unforeseen factors demand constant vigilance and, from time to time, decisions have to be made for the smooth progressing of the project work. Like the guidance system of a missile, an effective control system corrects all deviations from the planned path. Planning and controlling, therefore, are inseparable.

Control involves organizing the control responsibility centres, designing accounting and monitoring methodology, codifying data and developing the information systems so as to make-decisions speedily. It also includes identifying the problem areas, making risk-taking decisions to tackle the problem, organizing and directing resources needed to carry out these decisions, and measuring the results of these decisions against targeted expectations through organized and systematic feedback.

An efficient control system improves productivity of men and materials, economizes employment of resources, enables understanding of time and cost behaviours, provides

**56** Construction Project Management

### Exhibit 2.8
### Foundation Construction Sub-project: Major Materials Requirement Estimate for One Foundation Module

| S. No. | Activity | Unit | Quantity | Concrete M100 CM | Concrete M250 CM | Rebar steel Tor MT | Rebar steel Mesh MT | Rebar steel Wire KG | Bitm KG | Trmt LTR | PVC Sht SM | Soil Import CM |
|---|---|---|---|---|---|---|---|---|---|---|---|---|
| 1. | Layout for excavation | — | — | | | | | | | | | |
| 2. | Excavation with machine | CM | 400 | | | | | | | | | |
| 3. | Base preparation | SM | 360 | | | | | | | | | |
| 4. | Anti-termite at base | SM | 362 | | | | | | | 75 | | |
| 5. | Polythene sheeting | SM | 362 | | | | | | | | 400 | |
| 6. | Shuttering for blinding | RM | 90 | | | | | | | | | |
| 7. | Placing concrete M-100 | CM | 18 | 18 | | | | | | | | |
| 8. | Layout for raft | — | — | | | | | | | | | |
| 9. | Shuttering for raft | SM | 22.5 | | | | | | | | | |
| 10. | Reinforcement for raft | MT | 6.066 | | | 6.066 | | 60.66 | | | | |
| 11. | Raft concreting M-250 | CM | 88.14 | | 88.14 | | | | | | | |
| 12. | Curing raft | — | — | | | | | | | | | |
| 13. | Bitumen coating raft sides | SM | 362 | | | | | | 91.2 | | | |
| 14. | Layout for plinth wall | — | — | | | | | | | | | |
| 15. | Wall shuttering | SM | 485 | | | | | | | | | |
| 16. | Wall concreting M-250 | CM | 43.78 | | 43.78 | | | | | | | |
| 17. | Deshuttering | — | — | | | | | | | | | |
| 18. | Curing wall | — | — | | | | | | | | | |
| 19. | Bitumen coating wall & raft | SM | 319 | | | | | | 103.4 | | | |
| 20. | Back filling | CM | 120 | | | | | | | | | |
| 21. | Plinth filling | CM | 305 | | | | | | | | | 80 |
| 22. | Anti-termite under GF slab | SM | 172 | | | | | | | 75 | | |
| 23. | Polythene sheeting | SM | 225 | | | | | | | | 250 | |
| 24. | Shuttering for GF Slab | SM | 11 | | | | | | | | | |
| 25. | Weld mesh fixing | MT | 0.651 | | | | 0.651 | | | | | |
| 26. | GF Concreting M-250 | CM | 28.34 | | 28.34 | | | | | | | |
| 27. | Curing GF Slab | — | — | | | | | | | | | |
| | Total | | | 18 | 160.26 | 6.066 | 0.651 | 60.66 | 194.6 | 75 | 650 | 80 |
| | Assessed wastage | | | 10% | 3% | 3% | 10% | 3% | — | — | 10% | 15% |
| | Materials required | | | 19.8 | 165.07 | 6.248 | 0.716 | 62.48 | 194.6 | 75 | 715 | 92 |
| | Unit Rate in $ | | | 77.8 | 111.7 | 557.1 | 640.0 | 0.96 | 0.56 | 6.4 | 0.36 | 9.6 |
| | Direct materials cost in $ | | | 1540 | 18438 | 3481 | 458 | 60 | 109 | 480 | 257 | 883 |

## Exhibit 2.9

### 2000 Housing Unit Project: Responsibility Centres

**Project Management**

- **Construction Responsibility Centre**
  - Building Foundation Centre.
  - Building Finishes Centre.
  - Precast Erection Centre.
  - Public Building Centre.
  - Pavement Construction Centre.
  - Landscaping Centre.

- **Service Responsibility Centre**
  - Precast Concrete Production Factory.
  - Readymix Concrete Production Plant.
  - Steel Fabrication Shop.
  - Quaring Establishment.
  - Plant & Machinery Maintenance Unit.

- **Functional Responsibility Centre**
  - Administration & Personnel Management.
  - Materials Management.
  - Plant & Machinery Management.
  - Finance Management.
  - Cost Management.
  - Engineering Services Management.
  - Contract Management.
  - Planning and Monitoring Cell.

yard-sticks for measuring performances, generates information for updating resource planning and costing norms, prevents pilferage and frauds and assists in formulating bonus or incentives schemes for motivating the people.

The project control system covered in this book deals with the project control methodology; controlling the productivity, cost and time; developing the codification system, and; finally, computerizing the project management information system.

### 2.5.1 Project Control Methodology

The project control follows the system concept. Each organizational unit in a project, usually referred to as the responsibility centre, can be viewed as a sub-system. These sub-systems are highly interdependent and interactive.

The performance objectives of a sub-system are stated in terms of the parameters to the controlled. These parameters include the time progress targets, resources productivity standards and the work-package standard costs and sales targets. Each sub-system accounts for its performance and reports its actual performance along with the deviation between the planned and the actual performance to the monitor. And it is these reports that serve as early warning signals of the ensuing dangers.

The project control centre, manned by the monitor, is at the heart of the system. It receives performance data from the responsibility centres and using scientific tools and techniques, transforms it into information which suggests remedial measures for achieving the objectives. This information, when fed at appropriate levels, results in steering of the organizational effort towards attainment of project objectives.

Project control methodology acts as a common language of understanding among all the participants. This methodology is covered in Chapter 13. It defines the performance parameters to be controlled and outlines the performance accounting and monitoring processes. It highlights the information feedback communication system, projects the control benefits and, finally, stresses the prerequisites for making the control system effective.

### 2.5.2 Controlling Resource Productivity

The success of a project depends upon the performance of the input resources. *Productivity* is a measure of performance of these resources.

Productivity control aims at ensuring efficient utilization of the inputs of men, materials and equipment by identifying causes of their wastage as well as affecting improvements to minimize it. The causes of wastage are located by analyzing variances and efficiency of planned and on-site actual productivity, as follows:

Productivity performance variance = Planned productivity − Actual productivity

Productivity performance index = Planned productivity/Actual productivity

The productivity parameters which need to be controlled in construction projects are: labour productivity, equipment productivity and materials productivity. The methodology used for controlling these is identical and can be divided into four stages, namely, defining the control purpose, measuring the actual performance, computing the productivity performance variances and identifying their causes for affecting improvements. The methodology for labour, equipment and materials productivity control and the role of management in improving productivity performance are covered in Chapter 14.

### 2.5.3 Controlling Costs

Cost control is the restraining of expenditure within the predetermined limits. It involves the processing of reports received from various responsibility centres or operating divisions, relating the cost incurred with the set standards, analyzing the reason for any variances and presenting the results to the project management for decision-making and initiating remedial measures.

The cost control process follows an active and forward-looking approach. It does not confuse itself to the historical data contained in cost reports and accounting documents, but goes further to indicate corrective measures so as to minimize inefficiencies and reduce costs. It fact, no project management can be effective without first installing and operating an effective cost control system.

Project costs without a control system can go astray and prove financially fatal not only for the project itself but also for the client and the connected contractors. Chapter 15 describes the methodology for exercising project cost control by the project monitoring team and for controlling the direct costs, contribution and the budgeted costs. It also outlines the responsibility for controlling costs and the approach needed to minimize them.

### 2.5.4 Controlling Time

Time is of essence in a project and all project activities are directed towards the achievement of project time objectives. The project time control aims at timely execution of work as per the work programme and application of corrective measures in case of deviations.

The time control process involves the monitoring of time status by updating the project networks and time schedules, reviewing duration of balance activities, computing deviations and evaluating the implications of deviations on project time objectives by time-analyzing the project network. It includes formulating remedial measures including what-if analysis, time crashing, re-planning, re-forecasting and re-mobilizing resources under changed situations with a view to accomplish the time objectives.

The time control methodology is described in Chapter 16. Time delays have serious repercussions on planned resources and produce inefficiency in their use. They alter the planned level of input resources and result in a revision of the materials inventories and accommodation for men and materials.

Delays necessitate re-mobilization of resources. Time over-runs increase costs exponentially and result in increased overheads and reduced planned sale receipts, thus causing liquidity problems. They also cause confusion and conflicts. All this has serious implications on the project resource needs and cost objectives. It is for this reason that the project controlling process starts with the resources productivity control. Next comes the cost control, followed by time control.

### 2.5.5 Codifying Data

A major turnkey construction project has architects, designers, estimators, planners, accountants and construction engineers with interrelated functions for managing it. In addition, the contractors' organization, which manages the execution of project work, also has a manager in charge of materials, plant and equipment, personnel and finances. These functional heads have their own requirement of information and some of them may process common data. Left to themselves, they will have to develop their own codes to identify, sort out and process data. In such a case a given information may have multiple codes resulting in confusion and duplication of effort. In fact, the organized control of a major project is not feasible without the proper codification of project data.

A well-designed codification system serves a threefold purpose: it aids in integration of the project data, it facilitates sorting out of information, and it enables easy computerization.

Chapter 17 describes the methodology for developing project codes. It includes the codification of project work components, construction work-packages and the related activities, architectural drawings and specifications, construction and materials types along with manpower categorization, plant and equipment grouping, bills of quantities, and interfacing of cost and finance heads of accounts.

### 2.5.6 Project Management Information System

Computers with their characteristic speed, accuracy, memory and interactive capabilities have revolutionized the data processing systems. They are an invaluable tool for managing the construction projects. Their application in project management spans planning and controlling projects, computer-aided designing and drafting, estimating and job costing, resource management, finance and cost accounting and office operations management.

Development of a computerized management system for a large-size firm involves conducting feasibility studies, formulating specifications, designing system, selecting system components, installing system and implementing system. All this is a specialized job. However, at the site project office, a microcomputer network with suitably designed programs can serve the needs of the project management.

Chapter 18 details the basics for developing the computerized project management information system. This chapter covers the scope for computerizing planning and control functions and the guidelines for selecting programme, matching software, choosing hardware, costing system, deciding supplier, installing system, and implementing system.

The coverage in Chapter 18 is aimed at familiarizing project planners with the methodology of setting up a computerized project management information system so as to enable them to appreciate their role as effective members of the project management system development team.

## ❏ 2.6 IMPORTANCE OF PLANNING, SCHEDULING AND CONTROLLING PROJECTS

### 2.6.1 Planning Benefits

The object of planning construction project is to per determine how the project objectives will be achieved. Planning precedes all managerial activities and the process combines systematic creative thinking with planning techniques to develop a project plan. The project plan comprises time plan, resources plan and plan for controlling project. It also includes schedules of design and drawing preparation, work quantities, progress of work planned resources allocations, budgeted costs and cash flow estimates.

- Project plan clearly defines project's scope of work. It breaks down project objectives into clear, identifiable, quantifiable, attainable and verifiable goals which are assigned to individuals and responsibility centres for accomplishment.
- Project Plan aids the management in performing its functions efficiently and effectively. It is the spine of the system and at the core of all management activities. It stream

lines the project management process and supports the management organizational structure and functioning.
- Project plan forms the basis of project operations and directions and shows how the project is to be run. It also specifies the committed future course of actions on the basis of current decision made with available knowledge of the future.
- Project plan identifies critical activities, thus enabling the managing of project by exceptions.
- Project plan provides the yard-stick for measuring progress and evaluating resources performance—it aids in developing information system and decision making during the implementation stage. It further simplifies and smoothens communication to enable coordination among all those involved in project management.
- Project plans provide the basis for coordinating the efforts of clients, consultants, architects, designers, quantity surveyors, specialists, suppliers, contractors and the project staff.
- A project plan maintains continuity of work, specially when project organisations is temporary and its staffing is transient in nature.
- Project plan has build in flexibility in the form of floats, to navigate changes in the planned path for meeting fast changing environments.
- Project plan creates healthy environment. It promotes unity of purpose among functional diversities to make people time and cost conscious. It commits individuals to tasks and motivates them to achieve challenging targets.

Therefore, a well-conceived project plan, developed before the commencement of project execution stage, can go a long way to prevent project collapse on account of management failures. But a Construction Project Plan, how-so-ever skillfully devised, cannot make up for bad management.

## 2.6.2 Scheduling Benefits

Work Scheduling serves a five-fold purpose:

(a) Schedule simplifying a project plan. The bar chart type work schedule provides a simplified version of the work plan which can be easily understood by all concerned with planning, coordination, execution and control of projects.
(b) Schedule validates time objectives. Work schedule shows the planned sequence of activities, data-wise. It takes into considerations, the reduction in efficiency resulting from climatic effects on resources while putting the plan of work on calendar basis. A schedule verifies the accomplishment of tasks on dates imposed for completion of the project and the achievement of milestones.
(c) Schedule aids in the optimization of resources employed. Work schedule is based on economical employment of the resources of men, materials, and machinery. It avoids abrupt changes from time to time.
(d) Schedule enables forecasting of input resources and earned value to indicate the pattern of requirement and the financial state of the project in terms of investment, expenditure, output and income.
(e) Schedule brings out implications of time and resources constraints.

## 2.6.3 Control Benefits

The control system aids the management at various levels to perform its functions efficiently and effectively for achieving the overall project objectives. The illustration given below shows the typical pyramidal management structure with the nature of control exercised at each level.

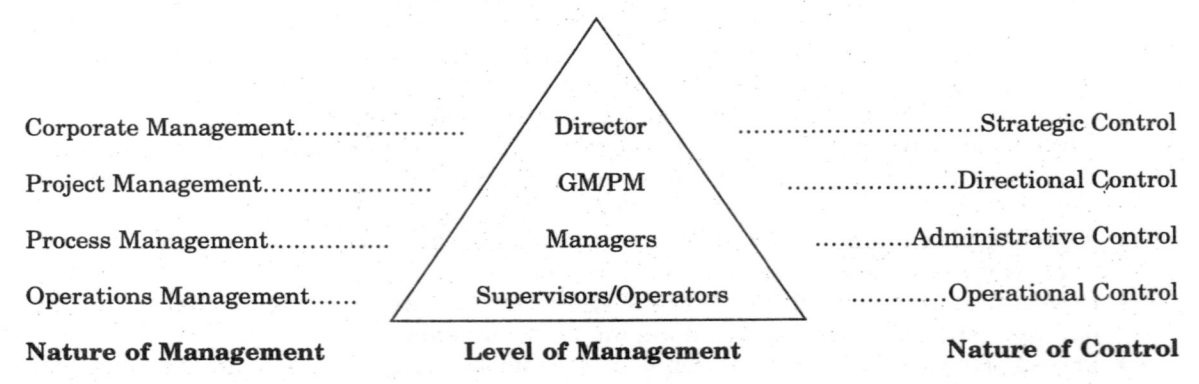

| Nature of Management | Level of Management | Nature of Control |
|---|---|---|
| Corporate Management | Director | Strategic Control |
| Project Management | GM/PM | Directional Control |
| Process Management | Managers | Administrative Control |
| Operations Management | Supervisors/Operators | Operational Control |

The benefits which can be derived at each level of management through an effective control system are outlined below:

**(a) Operational Control at Supervisory Level** It improves productivity by:

- Minimizing unproductive man hours
- Preventing wastage of materials
- Economizing plant and machinery utilization
- Reducing activity execution time

**(b) Administrative control at managerial level** It assists in ensuring project organizational efficiency and effectiveness by:

- Updating the work quantities status and determining the balance scope of work.
- Analyzing project time status and its implications on project time objectives.
- Evaluating production cost status and forecasting future trends.
- Calculating income status and forecasting cash inflows.
- Computing budget status and forecasting cash inflows.
- Computing budget status and analyzing the implications of variances of future expenditure.

**(c) Directional control at general manager's/project manager's level** It helps in formulating and directing policies for achievement of project objectives by:

- Analyzing project time cost behaviour and making decisions on time saving when required.
- Reviewing project costs and profitability, and making profitability improvement decisions

concerning wastage reduction through rigorous cost control, value engineering techniques, cost benefit analysis, workers incentive schemes and alternate methods of construction which cost less.
- Auditing management's performance.

**(d) Strategic control at corporate level** It provides information concerning corporate goals and assistance in formulating corporate strategies by:

- Determining overall profitability.
- Budgeting and allocating funds and resources.
- Updating the company's planning norms and unit rates for securing future works.

## ❑ 2.7 FUNCTIONS AND ROLE OF CHIEF PLANNER

### 2.7.1 Functions

The primary role of the project planning cell is to assist the project manager and the management team in planning, coordinating and controlling the project so as to achieve defined time goals with minimum costs. Within the framework of this role, the planning cell plans the project and provides planning information continuously to the management team on the planned targets, actual performance and the likely trends along with the remedial measures.

The functions to be performed by the project planning cell and its composition varies with the size and complexity of the project. For example, a large-size building construction project may have a planning cell consisting of a planning manager, a civil engineer, an electrical or mechanical engineer, a systems engineers and a draftsman. On the other hand, in a similar small-size project, all the functions may be entrusted to one planning engineer only. Further planning, estimation and cost accounting functions can be best performed if they are placed under one head and the participants work as a team sharing data and evaluating information.

Generally, the chief planner performs the following functions.

1. Formulating the planning and control policies and the data processing system.
2. Making the project time and resources plans, and replanning when necessary.
3. Formulating the work organization plan.
4. Establishing the planning and performance measuring standards.
5. Mobilizing and allocating resources for various construction sites.
6. Collecting and collating site data about the activities in progress; employment of manpower, equipment and materials, etc. and also evaluating the resources productivity.
7. Monitoring the progress of specified performance objectives.
8. Tracking variances of labour output and machinery utilization form productivity standards and providing feedback-based productivity information to the site executives.
9. Updating resource productivity norms, and planning the data and unit rates of work.
10. Maintaining the technical records, publications and the project library.
11. Participating in technical meetings and preparing their minutes.

12. Coordinating all technical activities.
13. Rendering assistance to the site executives on construction planning, formulating monthly targets and managing the project information system including submission of reports at pre-determined frequency to all concerned.
14. Setting up a project control room displaying vital up-to-date information.

The above list is indicative and not exhaustive. It may be noted that the pre-requisites for effective functioning of the planning personnel are: the management-backed drive for making site executive plan-conscious, the involvement of project engineers in planning and controlling activities, the existence of a well-coordinated and harmonious environment and, on top of all this, the role played by the project planning chief.

### 2.7.2 Role

The project environment often tends to create a conflict among the project executives. At times there may be a lack of mutual trust between them, especially when they dislike following a certain plan or when someone monitors their performance. Non-cooperation is also not uncommon. Occasionally, people may render incorrect data to mislead the planners or to cover up their unsatisfactory performance.

Instances are also not lacking where a conflict developed due to some inappropriate behavior pattern of the project planning cell itself, a situation which must be avoided at all cost by the chief planner. The smoothening of planning functions can be achieved to a large extent if the chief planner plays effectively the following key roles.

**Service role** The planning chief primarily performs a service function: he exists to render assistance to the executives and staff in performance of their planning and control function. He maintains close liaison with the heads of various departments including site supervisors, project engineers, designers, estimators, quantity surveyors, materials purchasers, accountants, personnel administrators, plant and machinery controllers and all the other managers in the project. He participates in almost all the meetings, discussions and decision-making exercises so as to assist the project manager in performing his planning functions.

**Information record-keeper role** The planning chief is the manager of the project data bank. He maintains the project information bureau. He runs the project information service, both for internal and external needs. He should be able to process data, produce and advertize information and provide it to the information seekers. In this information marketing role, the planning cell is expected to maintain up-to-date displays and records of the following.

(a) Contract documents including contract conditions, drawings, specifications, bill of quantities, and activity-wise cost breakdown.
(b) Project models, pictures, charts and tabulated data to illustrate the layout, scope and progress of the work.
(c) Project plans and planning assumptions including the planning data and output norms.
(d) Statistics of all reports and returns handled in the project and their pictorial displays.
(e) Records of minutes of all meetings and conferences, policies and important correspondence.

(f) Control charts showing progress of work, resource availability, cost status and anticipated trends.
(g) Revised unit rates and resources planning data for each item of work, for reference is future projects.

**Coordination role** Coordination is one of the most sensitive function of the management. It aims at an effective harmonization of the planned efforts for accomplishing the goals. If the situation variables are measurable, the policies and the procedures well defined, and communication flows smoothly in all directions, then *esprit de corps* prevails, every one is interested in his task, and all work collectively to achieve the ultimate project objectives in a fast changing project environment. Coordination is such a case is not required. However, such an ideal environment is rarely met in construction projects.

Coordination is essential both within and among the various departments to fill up the voids created by changing situations in the systems, procedures and policies.

The planning chief can play an important role in smoothening up the project coordination function by the following.

(a) Communicating promptly the monitored information to all concerned for taking corrective measures to prevent adverse situations.
(b) Creating a climate of cooperation by avoiding interdepartmental conflicts and resolving all issues affecting the progress of work.
(c) Providing a proper flow and record of the monitored information through monthly information reports, minutes of meetings, project bulletins and liaison letters.
(d) Pursuing all the planning and monitoring issues raised by the departments to their logical completion.

**Professional role** The effective implementation and smooth functioning of the planning system primarily depends upon the professional competency of the planning chief. He should be able to plan the project, organize the control system, employ monitoring tools and techniques, design the codification system, develop the management information system and create a conflict-free and harmonious working environment. All this requires a high degree of professional skills; some of these are acquired while others come with experience.

To make the planning system effective, the professional qualifications of the planning chief should be at least a degree in engineering, a post-graduation in construction management or business administration (MBA), and adequate construction experience in various fields including site-work, estimating and costing, and planning. He should have worked as the planner on a major project.

Additionally, a chief planner should have an analytical mind, a creative approach, highly developed conceptual skills, a past record of team-working, devotion to duty and a strong sense of purpose.

**Roles when 'planning starts' and when 'specialised planning function ceases'**
In the initial stages of preparation of a project plan, the chief planner needs to win over the confidence of the project team as well as the persons holding vital connected work documents like feasibility studies and quantity and cost estimates. No plan can be prepared

without studying these documents. For various reasons, the persons holding these may hesitate to part with them. While some may fear a criticism of their work others may consider planning a fault-finding exercise.

It may be mentioned here that the project plan preparation is not a one-man show. Although the project chief planner is chiefly accountable for developing the plan, others also share responsibility along with him. A typical responsibility matrix for evolving a construction plan in shown in Table 2.4. As can be seen from this table the plan development

Table 2.4

**Plan Preparation of Medium-size Turnkey Housing Project Responsibility Matrix**

| Sl. No. | Planning Actions | PM/CM | Plg | Dan | QS | Mtl | Eqt | Adm | Fin |
|---|---|---|---|---|---|---|---|---|---|
| 1. | Formulating planning assumptions | A | P | | | | | | |
| 2. | Developing construction methods. | A | C | P | | | | | |
| 3. | Listing work packages | A | P | P | P | | | | |
| 4. | Identifying activities | | P | | | | | | |
| 5. | Estimating quantity of work | | C | | P | | | | |
| 6. | Drawing sub-networks | | P | | | | | | |
| 7. | Formulating preliminary time plan. | A | P | | | | | | |
| 8. | Scheduling designs and drawings requirements | A | C | P | | | | | |
| 9. | Estimating materials | | C | | P | C | C | | C |
| 10. | Scheduling works to be sub-contracted | A | C | | P | | | | |
| 11. | Forecasting month-wise: | | | | | | | | |
| | (a) Workers requirements | A | P | | | | | C | |
| | (b) Shuttering movement and requirement | A | C | P | | | | | |
| | (c) Concrete requirement | | P | | | | | | |
| | (d) Imported materials requirements | A | C | | | P | | | |
| | (e) Equipment and vehicle needs | A | P | | | | C | | |
| | (f) Site staff requirement | A | P | C | C | C | C | C | C |
| | (g) Work done inflow | A | P | | C | | | | |
| | (h) Production costs | A | P | | C | C | C | C | C |
| 12. | Designing site organization and allocating responsibilities | A | P | | | | | | |
| 13. | Scheduling materials samples approval programme | A | P | | | P | | | |
| 14. | Finalising project master plan and resources induction plan | A | P | | | | | | |
| 15. | Preparing project preliminary budge | A | C | | | | | | P |
| 16. | Organising control system | A | P | | | | | | |
| 17. | Developing codification system | A | P | | | | | | |
| 18. | Designing Management Information System | A | P | | | | | | |

*Indicative Responsibility Legend:*
A = Approval authority, P = Preparation responsibility, C = Coordination responsibility.

proceeds stage-by-stage. It involves participation and acceptance of commitment by the various functional heads, especially the executive director, the project manager and the construction managers. Initially, only the project outline plan is made, which is subsequently supplemented when the project work unfolds and the execution methodology is finalized. Obviously, all this needs a highly skillful, matured and experienced chief planner who can win over the cooperation and controlling of the project team during the planning and controlling of the project.

The plan-do-monitor-replan continues during the construction phase of the project till a saturation point is reached when specialized planning is no longer needed. If the project implementation is based on a sound plan and the planning system functions effectively, this planning saturation stage arrives when the major portion of the project work (say 60–70%) has been executed. By then, all the members of the project team have become familiar with the plan for execution of the balance works and generally, the project plan does not need further replanning.

It is ironical that at the saturation stage, which marks the effectiveness of the planning system, the need for specialized planning and monitoring ceases and the planning team becomes almost redundant. Unless needed elsewhere, some short-sighted management may attempt to ease out the planning staff to save overhead costs.

No two projects are alike. Each enhances the planning skills of the planners. In every project, the planners have to conceptualize the development of the project right from scratch to near completion. They have to plan and monitor against inevitable and unforeseen situations and go through numerous stresses and strains of the projects activities. They have to compile the planning data from their experiences. It is not easy to find planners who are experienced in the development of project time and resource plans and can design and implement the project control system. It is thus advisable to well utilize their services, within the project or elsewhere, rather than easing them out halfway through.

# PART II

# Time Planning

- Project Work Breakdown
- Project CPM/PERT Network Analysis
- Precedence Network Analysis
- Project Work Scheduling

# CHAPTER 3

# Project Work Breakdown

Project work-breakdown methodology enables splitting of the project work into hierarchical work-breakdown levels of sub-projects, tasks, work packages and activities. Each activity represents an identifiable lower-level job which consumes time, and possibly resources.

Construction projects are best organized by tasks into task responsibility centres. They are best managed by work packages and best planned and monitored by activities.

This chapter defines the work-breakdown levels. It defines the project work-breakdown levels, outlines the methodology for determining the activities involved, method of assessing the activity duration, and correlating the activity and work items with budgeted earned value.

## ❑ 3.1 PROJECT WORK-BREAKDOWN LEVELS

The project work-breakdown process involves breaking down of the project work into manageable parts arranged in a hierarchical order till the desired level is reached. The work-breakdown levels are broadly categorized into five levels. These levels, arranged in a descending hierarchical order are given here

Sub-project level
Task level
Work-package level
Activity level
Operations level

Each level has certain features associated with it (Table 3.1). However, it may be noted that level categorization is a broad concept and at times their overlapping may become unavoidable.

Work breakdown of the 2000 Housing Units Project is outlined in Exhibit 3.1 through 3.3. The project work included construction of 2000 residential apartments, educational

## Table 3.1

**Typical Housing Project Work-breakdown Levels
Salient Features Generally Associated with Levels**

| Sl. No. | Features | Sub-project | Task | Work Package | Activity | Operations |
|---|---|---|---|---|---|---|
| 1. | Level designation | Level 1 | Level 2 | Level 3 | Level 4 | Level 5 |
| 2. | Work-breakdown hierarchy | Project to sub-project | Sub-project to tasks, project to tasks (directly) | Tasks to work packages | Work packages to activities | Activities to operations |
| 3. | Management responsibility | Project team | Task-responsibility unit | Work centres | Work centres | Site foreman |
| 4. | Planning level | Corporate plan | Project-summary plan, Design preparation plan, Contract-finalisation plan | Project master plan, Constructed works milestone plan, Project budget | Project detailed plan, Contracted works-control plan, Task/work package plan, Short-term work programmes, Resources mobilisation plan | Foreman-work programmes |
| 5. | Plan duration unit | Months | Months/weeks | Weeks | Weeks/days | Days/hours |
| 6. | Project control basis | Corporate control | Management control | Cost control | Time control, Productivity control, Sales control | Productivity control |
| 7. | Work inter-dependency with other jobs | Independent, can proceed without interference | Generally independent | Mostly inter-dependence | Interdepedent | Interdependent |

buildings, public buildings, a civic centre, connected external utility services and landscaping. The total value of contracted works was approximately US $160 million and the project was contracted for completion in 36 months. This project scope of work is described in Exhibit 2.1.

The work-breakdown structure of a cantonment-construction project up to sub-project levels is covered towards the end of this chapter.

The work breakdown structure of a project forms the basis for listing of activities, modification of systems, sorting data by hierarchy levels, structuring of work organisation and managing similar-scope multi-projects.

### 3.1.1 Sub-projects Level

Sub-projects are derived by dividing the project work into independent large-volume mini projects or task groups. For instance, in a housing project, each group of major works which can progress in a systematic manner, without interference from other works can be termed as a sub-project.

The number of sub-projects in a project varies with the nature of the project. Each sub-project comprises one or more substantial work tasks. The sub-project level aids in identifying tasks. In the 2000 Housing Units Project, each type of residential, educational and public building can be taken as a sub-project (See Exhibit 3.1).

### 3.1.2 Tasks Level

The project or sub-project work can be split up into various tasks. *A task is an identifiable and deliverable major work.* It is an entity in itself and can be performed without much interference from other tasks. A task is supported by its design package. Each task is assigned time and cost objectives and is provided with planned resources for accomplishing the task objectives. The task execution is entrusted to a task responsibility unit, headed by a manager or a senior engineer.

Task level is used in the project-summary plan, the design-preparation plan and the contract tendering plan. In the 2000 Housing Units Project, the construction works in each residential building can be grouped under three main tasks, i.e. foundation, superstructure and finishes (See Exhibit 3.1).

### 3.1.3 Work-packages Level

A project task can be further subdivided into one or more work packages. *Each work package contains a sizeable, identifiable, measurable, costable and controllable package of work.* Exhibit 3.2 shows the work packages for the construction of a residential building of the Housing Units Project.

In the project master plan or the contracted works-control plan, each work package is assigned its performance objectives. These are generally stated in terms of its completion period, standard cost, resource-productivity standards and the standard sale price. The measure of performance thus, gets closely linked with the execution of its work packages.

Work packages form a common base for linking the key functions in project management. The work-package concept leads to the simple-management theory of managing, designing, estimating, planning, organizing, directing, communicating and controlling, using these work packages as the base lines. In the 2000 Housing Units Project, foundation work of a residential building can be broken down into four work packages—base, raft, plinth wall, ground floor slab (See Exhibits 3.2 and 3.3).

**74** Construction Project Management

Exhibit 3.1

## 2000 Housing Units Project
## Sub-project and Task Level Work Breakdown

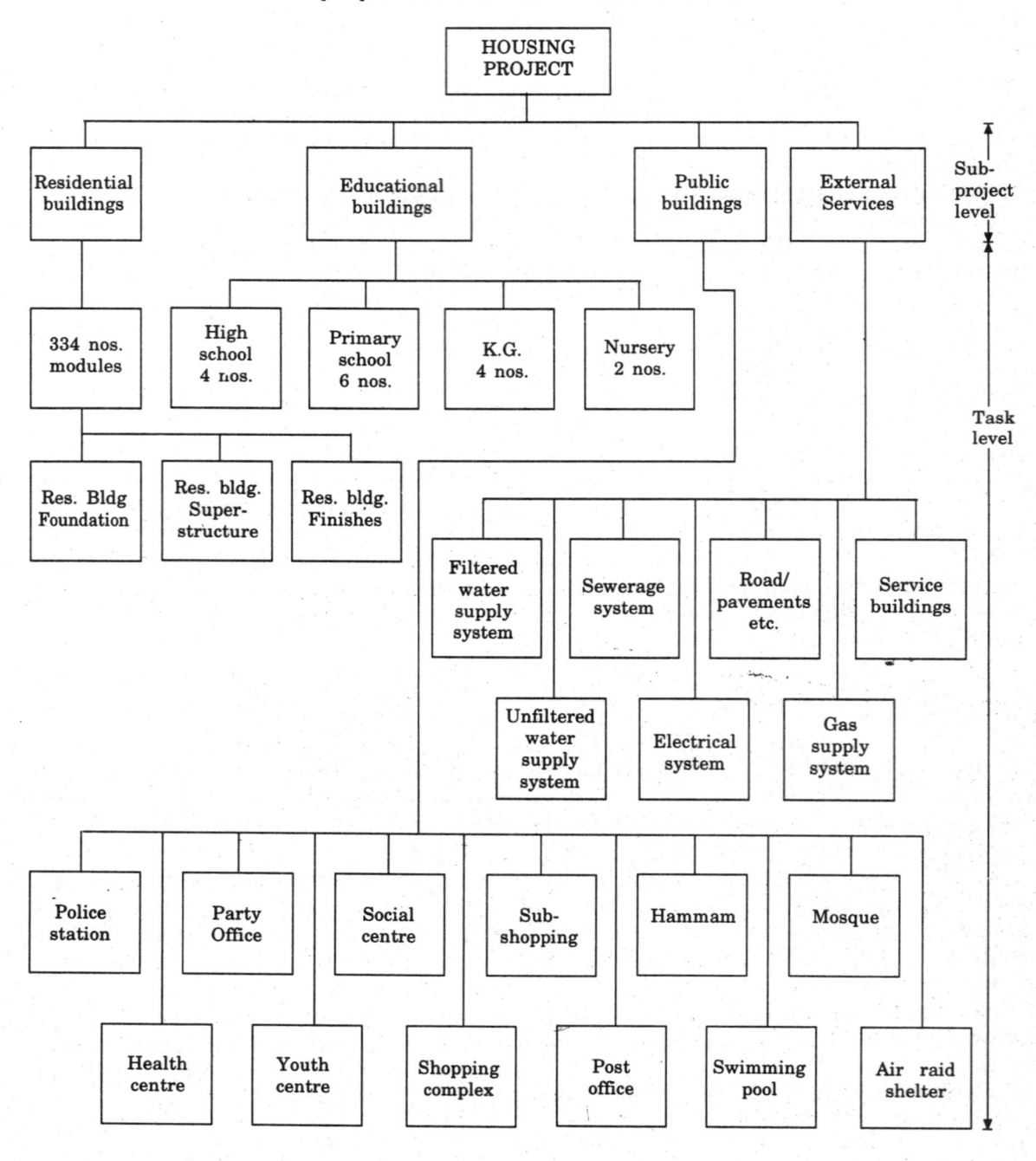

- HOUSING PROJECT
  - Residential buildings
    - 334 nos. modules
      - Res. Bldg Foundation
      - Res. bldg. Super-structure
      - Res. bldg. Finishes
  - Educational buildings
    - High school 4 nos.
    - Primary school 6 nos.
    - K.G. 4 nos.
    - Nursery 2 nos.
  - Public buildings
    - Police station
    - Party Office
    - Social centre
    - Sub-shopping
    - Hammam
    - Mosque
    - Health centre
    - Youth centre
    - Shopping complex
    - Post office
    - Swimming pool
    - Air raid shelter
  - External Services
    - Filtered water supply system
    - Sewerage system
    - Road/pavements etc.
    - Service buildings
    - Unfiltered water supply system
    - Electrical system
    - Gas supply system

Sub-project level

Task level

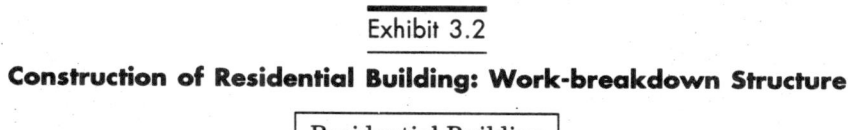

## Exhibit 3.2

**Construction of Residential Building: Work-breakdown Structure**

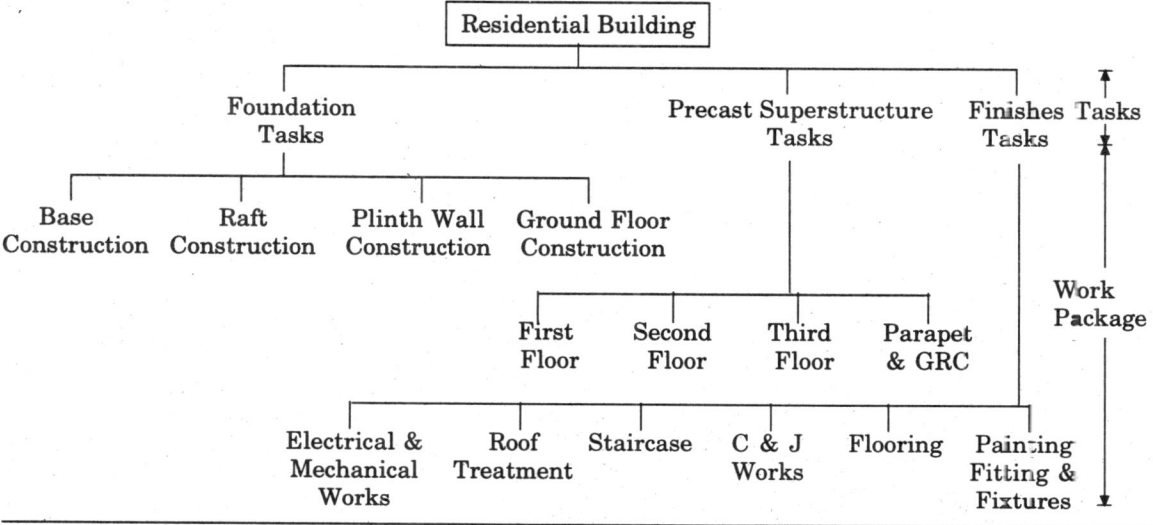

```
                        Residential Building
         ┌──────────────────────┼──────────────────────┐
    Foundation          Precast Superstructure      Finishes
      Tasks                    Tasks                  Tasks
┌──────┬──────┬──────┐   ┌──────┬──────┬──────┐
Base  Raft  Plinth  Ground  First Second Third Parapet
Const Const Wall    Floor   Floor Floor  Floor & GRC
      Const Const
                                                    Work
                                                   Package
   Electrical &  Roof    Staircase  C & J   Flooring  Painting
   Mechanical  Treatment            Works             Fitting &
   Works                                              Fixtures
```

## 3.1.4 Activity Level

A work package can further be broken down into various identifiable jobs, operations and processes, which consume time and possibly, other resources and are necessary for its completion. Each one of this is called an activity. As an example, the various activities involved in the construction of foundation of a residential building are listed in Exhibit 2.7 and Exhibit 3.3.

The breaking down of a work package into its constituent activities requires a study of the methodology of execution of the work package. This methodology, generally known by the term *method statement*, is evolved by the concerned planning engineer using his construction experience and through his discussions with the respective project engineers.

## 3.1.5 Operations Level

An activity comprises one or more operations. Each operation contains a part of the work content of the activity. It generally has a particular type or a fixed group of resources associated with it. It is performed during the scheduled time duration of the activity. Some operations may start with the commencement of the activity, while others may take place during its time duration. In some situations, performance periods of operations may overlap.

Operations are not considered during the network modelling and analysis stage except

**76** Construction Project Management

## Exhibit 3.3

## Construction of Residential Buildings: Work-breakdown Structure

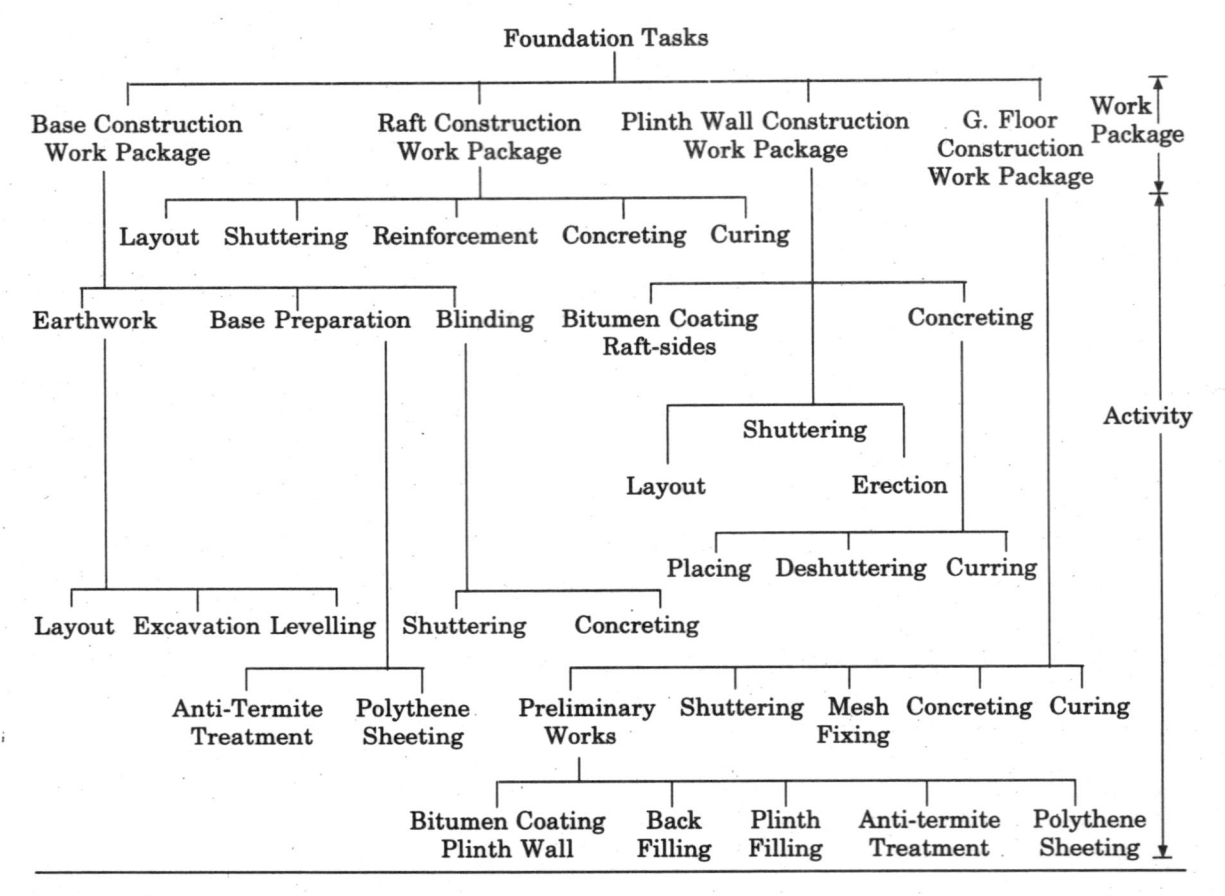

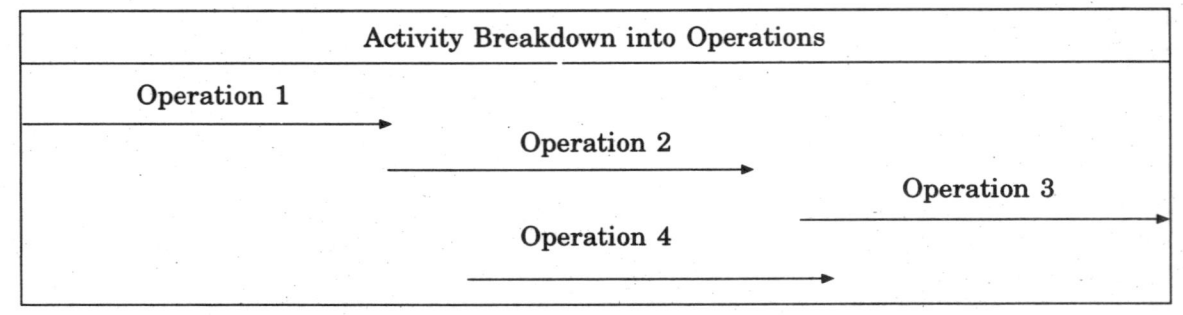

```
                              Foundation Tasks
         ┌──────────────┬──────────────────┬──────────────┐
Base Construction   Raft Construction   Plinth Wall Construction   G. Floor
Work Package        Work Package        Work Package               Construction
                                                                   Work Package
```

Work Package

Raft Construction Work Package: Layout, Shuttering, Reinforcement, Concreting, Curing

Base Construction Work Package: Earthwork, Base Preparation, Blinding

Plinth Wall Construction Work Package: Bitumen Coating Raft-sides, Concreting

Activity

Earthwork: Layout, Excavation, Levelling

Base Preparation: Anti-Termite Treatment, Polythene Sheeting

Blinding: Shuttering, Concreting

Concreting (Plinth Wall): Shuttering (Layout, Erection; Placing, Deshuttering, Curring)

G. Floor Construction Work Package: Preliminary Works, Shuttering, Mesh Fixing, Concreting, Curing

Preliminary Works: Bitumen Coating Plinth Wall, Back Filling, Plinth Filling, Anti-termite Treatment, Polythene Sheeting

---

| Activity Breakdown into Operations |
|---|
| Operation 1 ──────────────▶ |
|                 Operation 2 ──────────────▶ |
|                                   Operation 3 ──────▶ |
|                 Operation 4 ──────────▶ |

that the sum of the costs of operations equals the activity cost. They form the basis for allocation and scheduling of resources of each activity. In the 2000 Housing Units Project operation involved in activity 'concreting raft' of foundation work include

- Cleaning and preparing inner side of the raft for concreting
- Pumping concrete
- Spreading and vibrating concrete
- Finishing of top concrete surface

The construction projects are best controlled by the work packages, and best programmed for day work by using operational level best planned and monitored by the activities. A project planner uses activity as the common data base for project planning. The activity duration forms the basis for time planning and scheduling of project work. Detailed information about resources such as men, materials and machinery needed for execution of each activity enables the preparation of resource forecasts. The activity sale price is used to determine the income and cash-flow forecasts. The activity base is vital for monitoring the progress of the project work. In the 2000 Housing Units Project foundation construction task can be broken down into 27 activities (See Exhibit 3.3).

## 3.2 DETERMINING ACTIVITIES INVOLVED

In simple projects, an experienced engineer-in-change can visualize and list out the activities necessary for execution of the project. But in case of complex projects, the identification of activities can be systematized by using certain methods. The commonly used methods, depending upon the nature of activities, can be categorized as follows:

| Nature of Activity | Method Used |
| --- | --- |
| Construction activities | Work-breakdown structure |
| Functional activities | Task matrix |
| Repetitive activities | Structure and matrix combine |
| Building construction activities | CI/SfB Table 1 and similar indexing methods, specification standards etc. |

### 3.2.1 Work-breakdown Structure

The various construction activities can be identified by systematically developing a work-breakdown structure. This is done by dividing the project work into areas, sectors or task groups or a combination of these. These are further subdivided into work packages, workpackages into activities and, finally, activities into operations or processes. This work-breakdown process is continued till the desired level of activities is reached.

**Pumping station sub-project** In a cantonment construction project, the construction of a pump house of size 40,000 mm length × 8840 mm breadth, was tendered as one contract (Fig. 3.1). The scope of work included the construction of the pumping station building, the procurement and installation of six pumps and one gantry crane, the provision of connected internal services and, finally, the commissioning of the pump house.

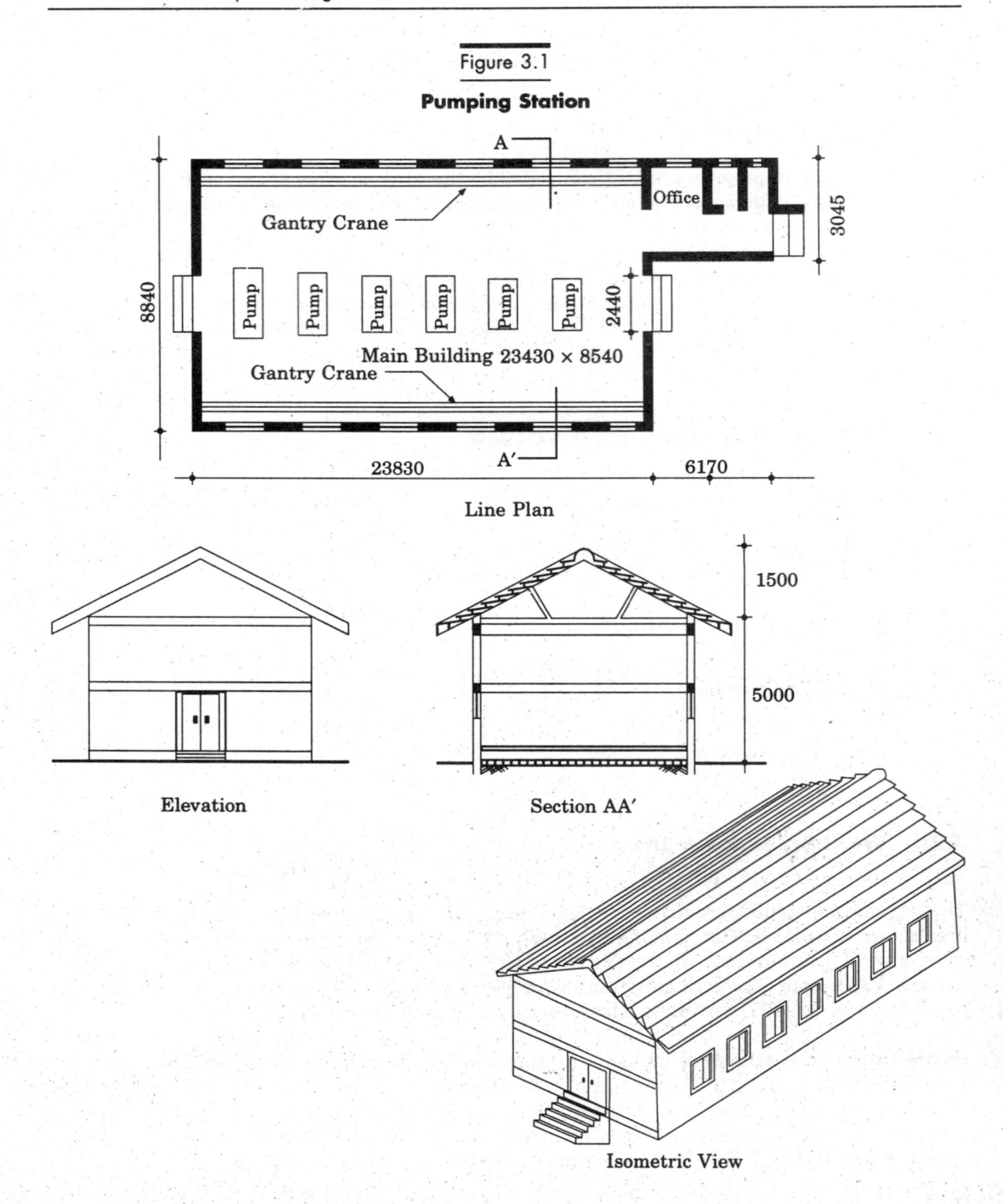

**78** Construction Project Management

Figure 3.1
**Pumping Station**

Line Plan

Elevation

Section AA'

Isometric View

The work-breakdown structure of the pumping station sub-project can be developed by splitting the work into divisions or levels till the desired activity level for controlling the progress of the work is achieved.

*(a) First division: Showing tasks* The works in the pumping station sub-project can broadly be divided into two task groups—building construction works; and electrical and mechanical works.

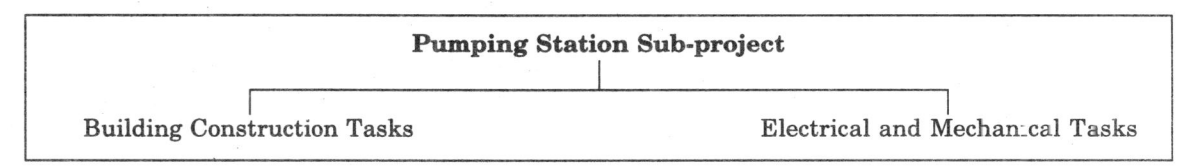

```
                    Pumping Station Sub-project
                    ┌──────────────┴──────────────┐
          Building Construction Tasks    Electrical and Mechanical Tasks
```

*(b) Second division: Depicting work packages* Each of the task group derived in the first division can further be subdivided into work packages as follows:

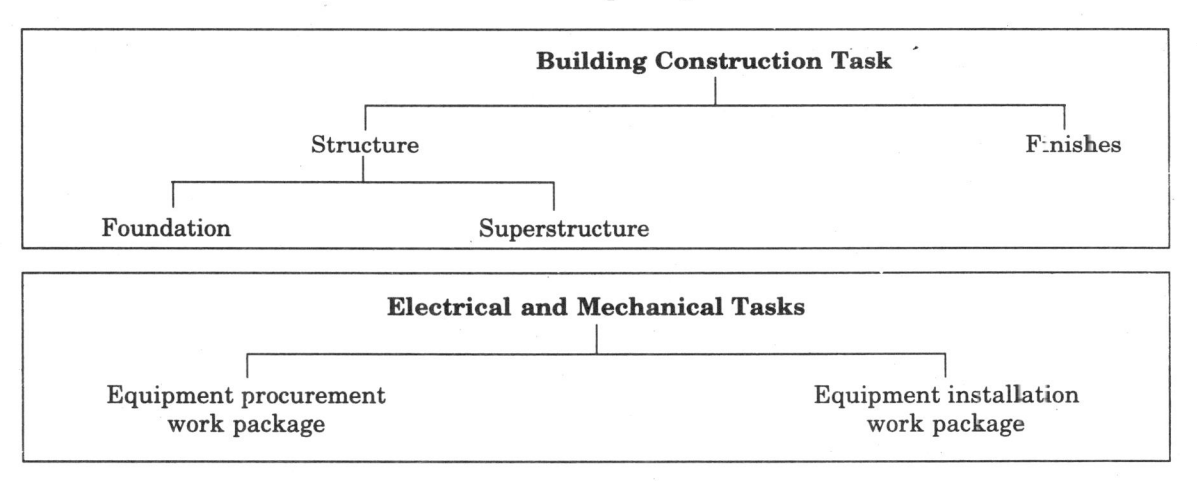

```
                    Building Construction Task
                    ┌──────────────┴──────────────┐
                 Structure                      Finishes
          ┌─────────┴─────────┐
      Foundation          Superstructure
```

```
                    Electrical and Mechanical Tasks
                    ┌──────────────┴──────────────┐
          Equipment procurement           Equipment installation
              work package                     work package
```

*(c) Third division: Representing activities* Each of the work packages can further be split into activities. For instance, activities constituting the work-package structure consist of the following:

| | |
|---|---|
| A | Excavation |
| B | Foundation walls |
| C | Walls up to sill |
| D | Walls up to lintel |
| E | Walls up to tie-band |
| F | Tie-band |
| G | Gable end |
| H | Roofing |

Similarly, the activities of the other work packages can also be derived.

The work-breakdown structure showing the activities involved is shown in Exhibit 3.4, while the activities derived are listed in Exhibit 4.2. It may be noted that the work-

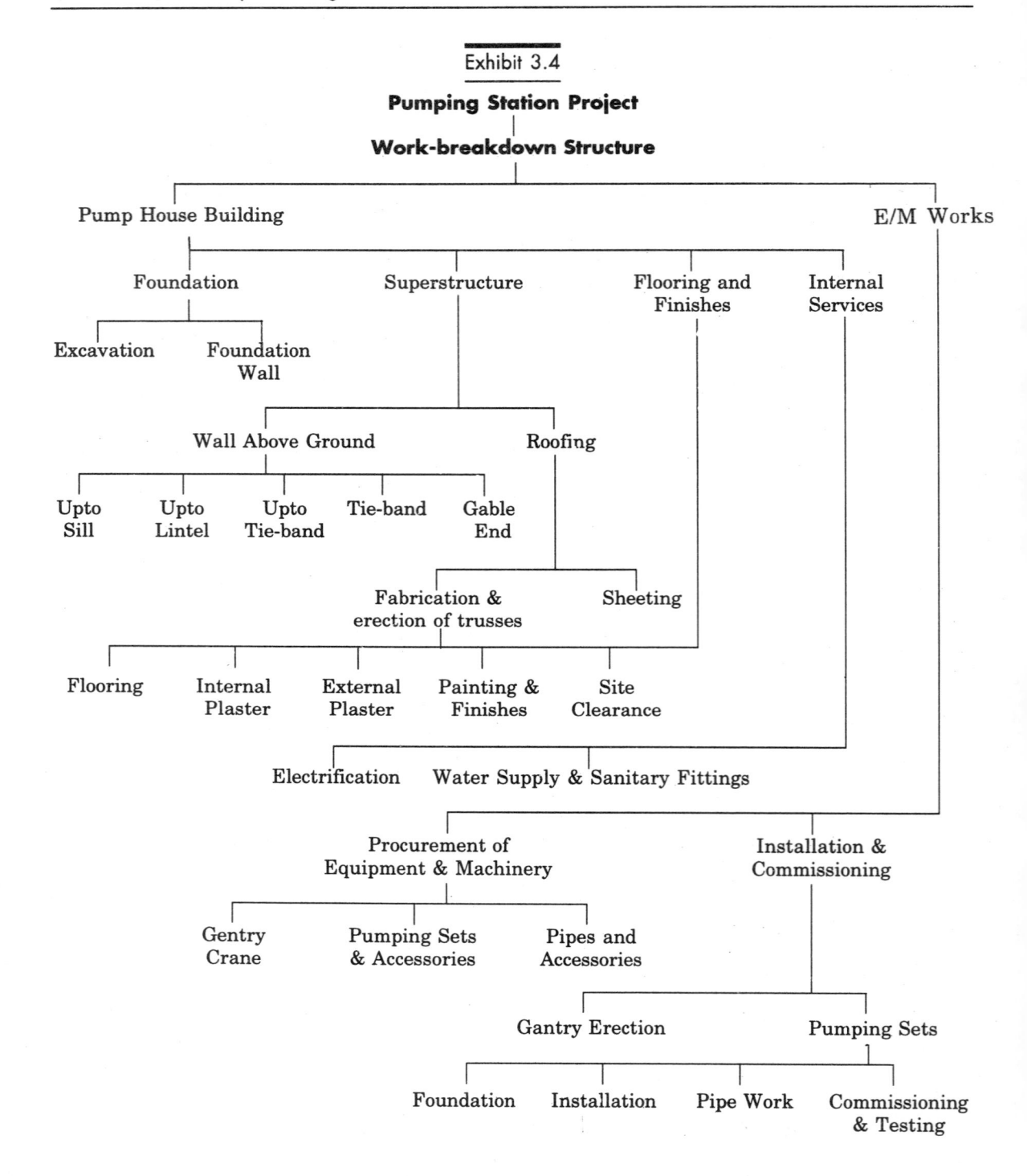

**Exhibit 3.4**

**Pumping Station Project**
**Work-breakdown Structure**

- Pump House Building
  - Foundation
    - Excavation
    - Foundation Wall
  - Superstructure
    - Wall Above Ground
      - Upto Sill
      - Upto Lintel
      - Upto Tie-band
      - Tie-band
      - Gable End
    - Roofing
      - Fabrication & erection of trusses
      - Sheeting
  - Flooring and Finishes
    - Flooring
    - Internal Plaster
    - External Plaster
    - Painting & Finishes
    - Site Clearance
  - Internal Services
    - Electrification
    - Water Supply & Sanitary Fittings
- E/M Works
  - Procurement of Equipment & Machinery
    - Gentry Crane
    - Pumping Sets & Accessories
    - Pipes and Accessories
  - Installation & Commissioning
    - Gantry Erection
    - Pumping Sets
      - Foundation
      - Installation
      - Pipe Work
      - Commissioning & Testing

breakdown here is restricted to the planning activity level only, and each activity can further be divided into one or more operations. For example, the activity 'surface preparation' can be split up into the following operations:

Layout
Excavation with machine
Dressing, levelling and compaction
Anti-termite treatment

### 3.2.2 Task Matrix

The task matrix method is generally used for determining functional activities at the feasibility stage or in the turnkey projects. In this, the tasks or work-packages in a project are listed vertically, while the various functions or connected aspects are drawn horizontally. The interconnection between the tasks and the functions, where applicable, suggests the activities.

**Factory construction project** Consider the case of a medium size factory which was accorded top priority for construction. Since the project was to be completed with foreign collaboration, it was decided to drastically cut down the usual departmental procedures to speed it up.

The project consisted of the construction of factory buildings, office and living accommodation, temporary accommodation for construction staff and the essential services. The siting board took a month to finalize the layout and other connected preliminaries. The go-ahead signal for the survey of land and project preliminaries was accorded immediately on the finalization of location studies. The final approval for the project was expected to take another month or so. All work connected with the procurement, installation and commissioning of the factory equipment was to be undertaken by the foreign consultant.

The project was planned for completion in two phases, which were:

**Phase I:** To commission the factory within 18 months after the project go-ahead signal is issued. This phase also included essential office and living accommodation.

**Phase II:** To complete the remaining accommodation within six months after the completion of phase I.

In order to plan and monitor the execution of the project, a project planning cell was established, and the planning chief was made a member of the project construction team.

The task matrix prepared by the planning chief to derive activities for developing the project preliminary plan is given in Exhibit 3.5.

### 3.2.3 Work Breakdown and Task Matrix for Repetitive Works

In projects involving repetitive or similar activities, the work-breakdown structure method can be used to identify activities in one building while the task-matrix method can assist in determining activities in the other buildings.

## Exhibit 3.5

**Planning of a Factory Project During Feasibility Stage**
**Task Matrix**

| Task code | Task description | Accomplishing | Designing | Contracting | Execution |
|---|---|---|---|---|---|
| A | Preliminaries | 1 | — | — | — |
| B | Project Sanction | 1 | — | — | — |
| C | Land Procurement and Survey | 2 | — | — | — |
| D | Factory Building | — | 1 | 2 | 12 |
| E | Office & Living Accomodation Phase-I | — | 1 | 2 | 9 |
| F | Office & Living Accomodation Phase-II | — | 1 | 2 | 6 |
| G | Temporary Storage Accomodation | — | — | 1 | 3 |
| H | Installation of Tube-wells | — | — | — | 2 |
| J | External Water Supply and Sanitation Phase-I & II | — | 1 | 2 | 3 |
| K | External Electrification | — | 1 | 2 | 3 |
| L | Air Conditioning—Factory & Office Building | — | 1 | 2 | 2 |
| M | Furniture for Phase I & II | — | 1 | 1 | 4 |

Activities with Durations in Months

**Schools construction sub-project** Consider the construction of schools in the housing units project described in Chapter 2. The project included two nursery, four kindergarten, five primary and four high schools. These schools had similar construction but varied in size. The work breakdown structure of the primary school, reflecting work packages and the connected activities, is shown in Exhibit 3.6. Its work packages and activities are as follows.

| Work Packages | Connected Activities |
|---|---|
| 1. Footing Wing-I and II | Excavation and footing, stub column and plinth beam, and ground floor slab. |
| 2. Superstructure Wings I & II | Wing I Ground floor column, first floor beam and slab, and roof structure.<br>Wing II First floor structure. |
| 3. Structure of gymnasium | Foundation, portals and slab. |
| 4. Building frame | Block work, concealed pipes or conduits, internal plaster, AC ducting and piping, roof treatment, wiring, and external plaster. |
| 5. Finishes | Tiling, preliminary paint, equipment installation, carpentry, joinery and metal work, fitting and fixtures, final paint and balance completion. |

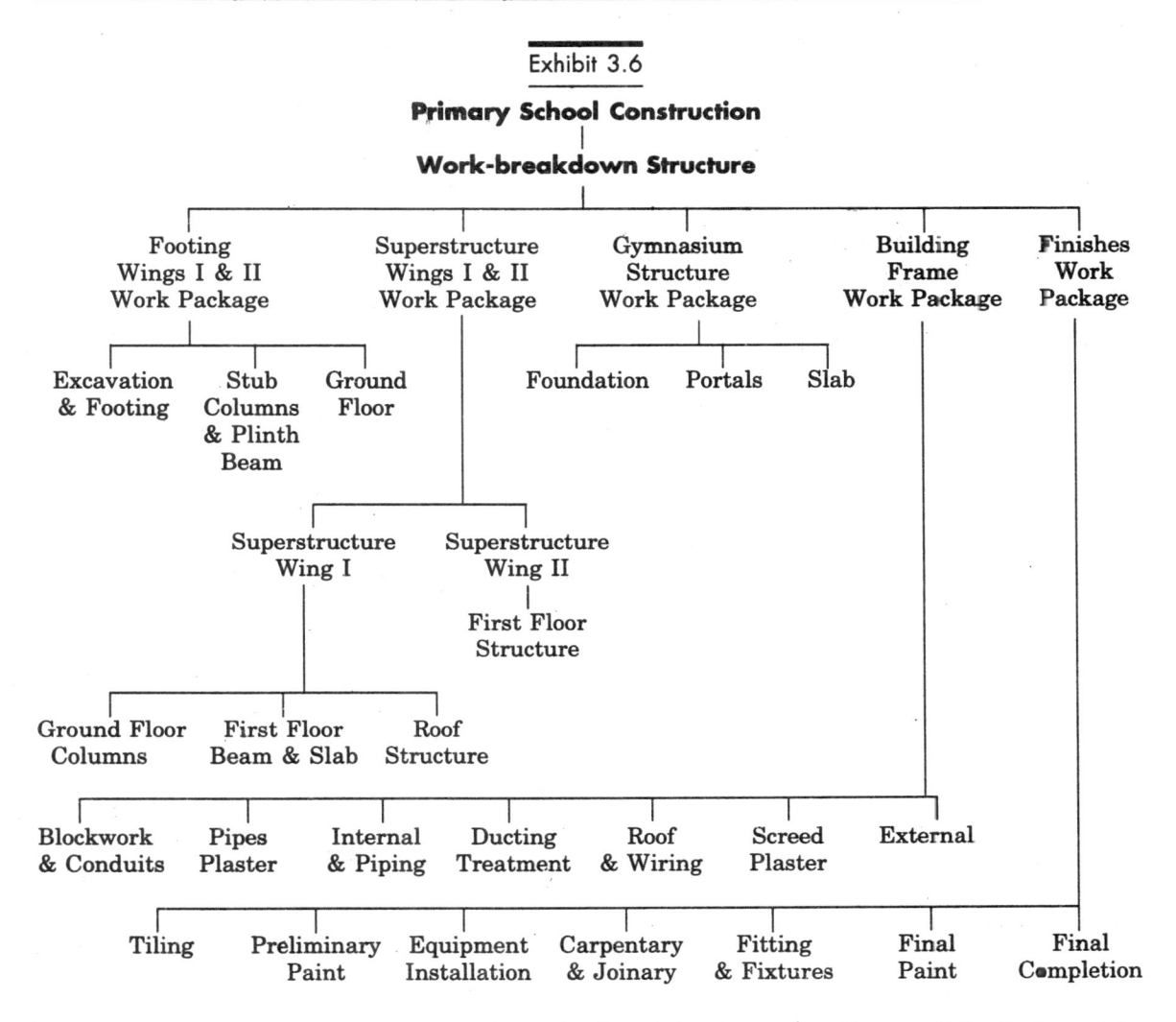

## Exhibit 3.6
## Primary School Construction
## Work-breakdown Structure

- Footing Wings I & II Work Package
  - Excavation & Footing
  - Stub Columns & Plinth Beam
  - Ground Floor
- Superstructure Wings I & II Work Package
  - Superstructure Wing I
  - Superstructure Wing II
    - First Floor Structure
  - Ground Floor Columns
  - First Floor Beam & Slab
  - Roof Structure
- Gymnasium Structure Work Package
  - Foundation
  - Portals
  - Slab
- Building Frame Work Package
- Finishes Work Package
  - Blockwork & Conduits
  - Pipes Plaster
  - Internal & Piping
  - Ducting Treatment
  - Roof & Wiring
  - Screed Plaster
  - External
  - Tiling
  - Preliminary Paint
  - Equipment Installation
  - Carpentary & Joinary
  - Fitting & Fixtures
  - Final Paint
  - Final Completion

The activities of the primary school can be listed in the main column of the task matrix as shown in Exhibit 3.7. The other school activities, being similar to that of the primary school, can be easily identified and tabulated in the task matrix. In particular, the duration of the activities can be incorporated as shown in Exhibit 3.7.

### 3.2.4 Deriving Building Construction Activities using CI/SfB Manual

**CI/SfB background** The CI/SfB Construction Index Manual, originally published in 1976 by the RIBA Publication Ltd, London, is primarily designed for use in project information and related applications such as preparation of bills of quantities and establishing the performance accounting linkages.

Exhibit 3.7

**Construction of Education Buildings: Activities Matrix with Duration**

| Sl. No. | Activity | Code | Primary School | High School | K.G. School | Nursery School |
|---|---|---|---|---|---|---|
| 1. | Excavation & footing | EF | 3 | 3 | 2 | 2 |
| 2. | Stub column & plinth beam | PB | 3 | 3 | 2 | 2 |
| 3. | Plinth filling | PF | 2 | 2 | 2 | 2 |
| 4. | Ground floor slab | GS | 3 | 3 | 2 | 2 |
| 5. | Ground floor column | GC | 2 | 2 | 2 | 2 |
| 6. | F.f. Slab & beam Wing I | FS | 3 | 4 | 3 | 3 |
| 7. | Roof struct URF Wing I | RS | 4 | 4 | 0 | 0 |
| 8. | First floor Wing II | FS | 3 | 4 | 0 | 0 |
| 9. | Foundation portals Wing II | FP | 3 | 3 | 0 | 0 |
| 10. | Construction Portals II | CP | 4 | 4 | 0 | 0 |
| 11. | Gymnasium slab Wing II | SC | 4 | 3 | 0 | 0 |
| 12. | Blockwork | BW | 4 | 4 | 1 | 1 |
| 13. | Pipes/conduit & frames | DW | 3 | 3 | 1 | 1 |
| 14. | Internal Plaster | IP | 4 | 4 | 2 | 2 |
| 15. | AC ducting & piping | AC | 2 | 2 | 6 | 6 |
| 16. | Roof treatment | RT | 2 | 2 | 2 | 2 |
| 17. | Screed & wiring | SC/EW | 2 | 2 | 2 | 2 |
| 18. | External plaster | EP | 2 | 2 | 2 | 2 |
| 19. | Tiling | TL | 3 | 3 | 2 | 2 |
| 20. | Preliminary paint | PT | 3 | 3 | 2 | 2 |
| 21. | A.C. equipment installation & testing | AE | 2 | 2 | 2 | 2 |
| 22. | C & J metal work | CJ | 4 | 3 | 2 | 2 |
| 23. | Fitting & fixtures | FF | 4 | 3 | 2 | 2 |
| 24. | Final paint & completion | CM | 4 | 4 | 2 | 2 |

The CI/SfB system is internationally recognized. It originated in Sweden in 1974 and was initially developed for coordinating the building processes. In 1952, it was adopted by the International Congress for Building Documentations (CIB) for standardizing the classification and filing system of documents.

**Work package** The construction elements in CI/SfB (extract in Table 3.2) represent the overall process of project construction, beginning with site development and proceeding vertically down to the external utility services.

The Table 3.2 matrix depicts primary divisions in the first column. Their corresponding subdivisions are reflected horizontally against each of them in CI/SfB.

Generally, each primary division can represent the work package of small projects, whereas for large projects, each subdivision or its further breakdown may have to be used to denote a work package. These subdivisions are shown in Table 3.2.

Project Work Breakdown  **85**

Table 3.2

**Construction Elements and Systems: CI/SfB Table I (Modified) Showing Process of Project Construction**

| Primary Division (—) | Sub-division (–0) | | | | | | | | |
|---|---|---|---|---|---|---|---|---|---|
| *General* (1–) Substructure | (10) Site | (01) Site Development | (02) Site Structures | (03) Site Enclosures | (04) Roads, Path & Pavings | (05) | (06) | (07) Sports Play Area | (08) Landscaping |
| | (10) Site | (11) Earthwork/ Excavation | (12) Backfilling | (13) Floor beds/ (slabs on grade) | (14) Tunnels/ ducts | (15) | (16) Foundations/ Retaining walls | (17) File Foundations | (18) Others |
| *(2–) Superstructures/Primary Elements* | (20) Site | (21) Exterior Wall Bearings | (22) Interior Wall Bearings | (23) Interior Floors | (24) Stairs/Ramps | (25) | (26) | (27) Roofs | (28) Structural Franc/ Chimneys |
| *(3–) Superstructure/Secondary Elements* | (30) Site Wall | (31) Exterior Wall Openings | (32) Interior Openings | (33) Interior Floor | (34) Railings Ceilings | (35) Suspended Bearings | (36) Walls Openings | (37) Roof | (38) Others |
| *(4–) Finishes* | (40) Site | (41) Exterior Wall Finishes | (42) Interior Wall Finishes | (43) Floor Finishes | (44) Stair Finishes | (45) Ceiling Finishes | (46) Roof finishes | (47) Other Finishes | (48) |
| *(5–) Mechanical Services* | (50) Site | (51) Refuse Disposal | (52) Drainage/ Waste Disposal | (53) Supply | (54) Gas supply | (55) Refrigeration/Space | (56) Space/ Systems | (57) NVAC/ Systems | (58) Other Services |
| *(6–) Electrical Services* | (60) Site | (61) Electrical Power | (62) Power Distribution | (63) Lighting | (64) Communication Audio/Visual | (65) | (66) Elevations/ Escalators | (67) | (68) Security Fire |
| *(7–) Fixed Equipment* | (70) Site | (71) Sign Display | (72) Furniture | (73) Cooking/ Eating | (74) Plumbing Fixtures | (75) Cleaning/ Maintenance | (76) Storage Activity | (77) Special | (78) Others |
| *(8–) Moveable Equipment* | (80) Site | (81) Circulation Furniture | (82) Furniture | (83) Cooking Eating | (84) Sanitary | (85) Cleaning Maintenance | (86) Storage | (87) Special Fire | (88) Other |
| *(9–) Site External Utility Services* | (90) Site Development | (91) Substructure | (92) Primary/ Elements | (93) Secondary/ Elements | (94) Finishes | (95) Mechanical Services | (96) Electrical Services | (97) Security Services | (98) Moveable Landscaping |

The Table-1 shown above is arranged to show the major headings of each primary division and sub-division. It is organised to reflect the overall process of project construction beginning with Division(1–) sub structure (foundations) and proceeding downward to Division (9–) site work.

| Code no. | Primary Division | Basis of Grouping Within Division |
|---|---|---|
| (00) | Site development | Information relating to external site development works. |
| (10) | Sub-structures | Foundation work below grade |
| (20) | Super-structure primary elements | Load bearing structural Elements above grades. |
| (30) | Super-structure Secondary elements | Non-load bearing elements |
| (40) | Finishes | Exposed surface treatment. |
| (50) | Mechanical services | All piping and ducting systems including materials and equipment. |
| (60) | Electrical services | All wired system, materials and equipment. |
| (70) | Fixed equipment | All fixed equipment, components & fixtures in a building. |
| (80) | Moveable equipment | All moveable equipment compoents and furnishes in a building. |
| (90) | External services | All services not within the enclosed limits of the buildings. |

**Activities** In CI/SfB, the primary divisions are further split up horizontally into subdivisions or activities. For example, subdivision 21 represents the external wall (load bearing) while subdivision 43 stands for the floor finishes. Further subdivision breakdown leads to connected activities. For instance, roof (27) is broken up into flat roof (27.1), pitched roof (27.2), folded plate roof (27.4), etc.

## 3.3 ASSESSING ACTIVITY DURATION

### 3.3.1 Concept

*Duration* of an activity is defined as the expected economical transaction time. The estimation of this time is based upon the current practices carried out in an organized manner under the normal prevailing conditions, and its assessment is done preferably, by the person responsible for its performance.

This definition of activity duration implies the following:

**Duration is transaction time** The transaction time of an activity is the time taken to change from one state to the next within the system. In other words, duration is the time delay incurred in moving from one event to its succeeding event.

**Duration is assessed** Generally, the smaller the level of details of an activity, the better the assessment of its duration. In the long run, during the progress of a project, the minor plus and minus variations in activity duration tend to get adjusted. It may be noted that duration is only an assessment. It may differ with the actual time which an activity may take for its transaction. If necessary, the activity could be work studied to determine the standard time of execution. The methods used for assessment of the duration are one-time and three-time estimates. These methods are explained in para 3.3.2.

**Duration is economical transaction time** The assessment of expected time should be based on the *most economical* method of execution of activity under the prevailing working conditions by using the available or earmarked resources.

Consider a job involving 50 cubic metre of manual excavation over an area of 15 × 6 m. It is possible to organise work by employing 18 men for one day in two shifts, or three men for five days; or four men for four days to complete this task. If each man is paid $5.00 per day, and assuming that tools required for digging are brought by the workers, the time for completion of excavation and the corresponding labour costs for this activity can be tabulated as follows:—

| Completion Time Days | Manpower Employed | Cost ($) |
|---|---|---|
| 1 | 18 | 90 |
| 2 | 8 | 80 |
| 3 | 5 | 75 |
| 4 | 4 | 80 |

The duration for this activity corresponding to the least cost of execution ($75.00) should be taken as three days. It may be noted that the duration of an activity is correlated with time and its cost. The time and cost at the least cost point in termed as normal time and normal cost of the activity.

**Duration is estimated in terms of predetermined units of time** The unit of time can be a month, a week, a day or even an hour. The unit considered depends upon the plan type. The guidelines given below may be adapted for selecting the unit of time for assessment of duration of activities in the following:

   (i) Project Summary Schedule    Months or weeks
   (ii) Project Master Schedule     Weeks
   (iii) Detailed Work Programme    Days or hours

The following conversion factors may be used for converting from one unit to another.

   (i) Working hours in a day     8 hours
   (ii) Working days in a week     5 or 6 days
   (iii) Weeks in a year       52 weeks

**All activities in the network or schedule use same unit of time** The duration assessed in weeks includes weekly holidays but excludes other holidays and non-productive period. Further, the seasonal and weather uncertainties are not considered; these are taken care of during scheduling stage. Overtime is not considered unless it is a standard practice.

The assessed duration estimate is expressed in terms of unit of time, in the nearest whole number.

**Duration estimation is based on current practices** This implies that the estimation is based on the present knowledge of the method of transaction in an economical way; it may undergo a change with the passage of time or with improved techniques.

**Duration estimation is based on work being carried out under normal prevailing site conditions** This implies that estimation is based on the method of work under normal working conditions at the site using economical resources. Adjustments for time delaying factors like rainy season and bad weather are considered at the time of scheduling of work and resource (refer Chapter 6).

**Duration estimation methods presuppose that activity is performed in an organized manner** Working in an organised manner implies breaking down the activity into elements, matching optimum resources for each element, laying down a systematic method of execution, and specifying objectives and responsibilities so that the task is performed efficiently and enthusiastically.

**Duration is assessed preferably by the person responsible for its performance** This makes the duration estimate realistic and meaningful.

### 3.3.2 Duration Estimation Basis

The construction activity accomplishment process combines resources like men, materials, and machinery. The first step in duration estimation is the *methodology* to be used for transforming these input resources into the desired activity.

The method of choosing and combining these resources may vary. For example, the activity of placing concrete in the foundation of a large building can be done in any of the following ways—manually, using crane and bucket arrangement, pumping by concrete pumps or transporting by a conveyor system. The time and cost for each of these methods will differ considerably, may be the same in all cases. Similarly, the time and manpower required for wall shuttering will depend upon the type of shuttering used from the available choices of custom-built steel wall forms and the conventional timber-plywood steel props support system.

The choice of the method of execution of an activity, depends upon the past experience, the market availability of appropriate resources, the resources available with the contractor, and the cost-benefit analysis of the various methods of reduction. In short, it is the method of production that dictates the resources required for accomplishment of an activity.

In the initial stages of time planning, it is necessary to make a preliminary assessment of the resources of men, machinery and materials required for the execution of each activity. This assessment is used to determine the duration of an activity, to develop a time schedule based on the optimum level of resources or on resource constraints and to evaluate the connected costs.

The preliminary estimate of resources needed to accomplish an activity can be made by using the planning norms developed from the past experience of companies or the published literature, suitably modified to conform to project environment.

The resource planning norms include the following:

(a) Workers output norms
(b) Plant and machinery output norms
(c) Materials quantity estimation and wastage norms

The typical resource planning norms that can be used for preliminary estimation of major item of resources are dealt with in Chapters 7, 8 and 9.

The methodology for costing of resources and activities is covered in Chapter 11.

### 3.3.3 Duration Estimation Methods

Generally any of the three methods are employed for assessing the duration of construction activities. These are termed as one-time estimate three-times estimate and non-linear distribution (e.g. trapezoidal) estimate.

**One-time estimate**

**Basis of estimation** The estimation of duration is based on one or more of the following.

1. Planning data.
2. Past experience on execution of a similar project.
3. Average time assessed by a group of executives.

*Example* In excavation of 3,000 cft of common earth, if output of a man is taken as 100 cft per day and six men can be effectively employed on the job, the duration of the activity would be five days.

**Application in construction projects** In most of the construction works, it is generally possible to assess the duration of an activity with reasonable certainty by using experience or the departmental planning data. The one-time estimate for activity durations is used in these projects. Further, the one-time estimate is task-oriented and the activity duration can be correlated to the cost and the resources employed. The method of the one-time estimate is simple and can easily be followed by all concerned with the planning or execution of construction works.

**Three-times estimate**

**Basis of estimation** When the exact duration of an activity, like research and development, is not certain, the three-times estimate is used to compute its expected duration. The following relation is used to calculate the expected duration of such an activity.

$$T_e = \frac{T_0 + 4T_m + T_p}{6}$$

Where, $T_e$ = expected completion time
$T_o$ = optimistic time, assuming that everything goes extremely well with no delays
$T_p$ = pessimistic time, assuming that everything goes wrong
$T_m$ = most likely time, assuming normal conditions

*Example* Let us take the activity of sanctioning of a government project. It has to pass through many channels and depends upon many factors. Let us assume that the sanction is most likely to take 8 weeks, and if all goes well, the earliest it can happen is 6 weeks, but in any case, it will certainly come through in 16 weeks. The expected duration of the activity can then be calculated as follows:

$$T_o = \frac{6 + (4 \times 8) + 16}{6} = 9 \text{ weeks}$$

**Application in construction projects** The three-time estimate can effectively be used in certain areas of construction projects where time is the main criterion and the resources employed are of secondary consideration. Some of these are as follows.

(i) The planning of projects especially, at the feasibility stage.
(ii) The skeleton networks enclosed with the tender documents.
(iii) The contracted works, where time is the main consideration for the management.
(iv) The complex structures, where the exact duration estimate is difficult to assess.

The analysis of networks using the three-times estimation is based on statistical methods. These are covered in Chapter 4.

**Trapezoidal distribution estimate** The one-time activity duration estimation methodology, given above, assumes average daily uniform manpower (or effort) of work throughout the execution of activity. But execution of some activities may need effort in a non-linear pattern. Such non-linear distributions may follow triangular, trapezoidal, binomial, beta, gama, normal or other pattern. In such cases, the activity duration estimation needs to be modified accordingly.

In practice, the profile of most activities takes the shape of trapezoidal distribution. A trapezoidal distribution has a build-up phase, peak period and rundown phase. The build-up and rundown phase can be expressed in terms of total activity duration. Assuming build-up and rundown time as 20% and 10% respectively of total duration, the activity duration can be assessed as under:

$$\text{Total man days} = \frac{0.2d}{2} \times p + 0.7d \times p + \frac{0.1d}{2} \times p = 0.85dp$$

$$\text{Duration } d = \frac{\text{Total man-days}}{0.85p}, \text{ in days}$$

*Example Brickwork of a building*
(a) Assessed scope of work using standard productivity standard = 1000 man-days
(b) Allow 20% for indirect labour and unforeseen reasons including absenteeism, bad weather, etc. = 200 man-days

Total effort required in standard man-days = 1200 man-days

*Trapezoidal Manpower Distribution Pattern*

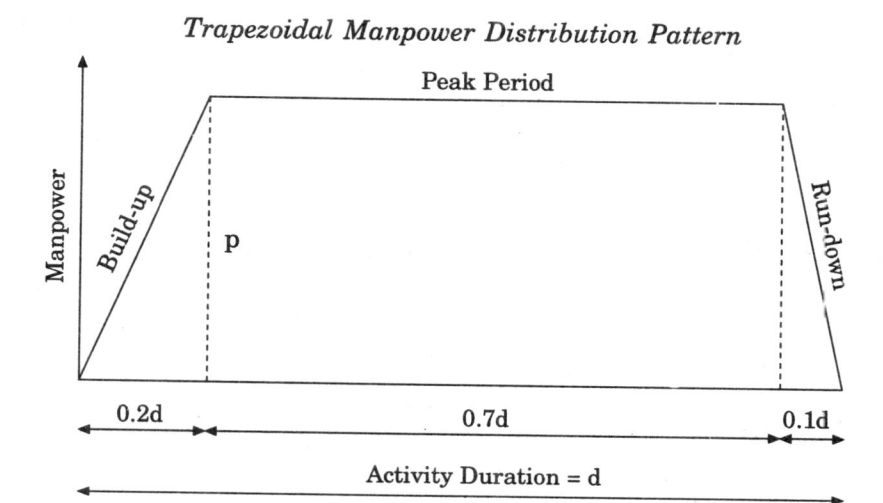

Assume:

(a) Work is to be done by a sub-contractor employing labour with 25% overtime, and working 5 days a week.
(b) Sub-contractor peak manpower per day is 40.
(c) Build-up period and rundown period is 20% and 10% respectively.

*Solution*

$$\text{Effort in man-days} = \text{peak manpower} \left\{ \frac{\text{(build up period)}}{2} + \text{peak level period} + \frac{\text{rundown period}}{2} \right\}$$

$$1200 = 40 \left( \frac{0.2d}{2} + 0.7d + \frac{0.1d}{2} \right)$$

$$= 40 \times 0.85d$$

$$\text{Duration} = d = \frac{1200}{40 \times 0.85} = 35.3 \text{ days}$$

$$= \frac{35.3}{5 \times 1.25} \approx 5.5 \text{ weeks}$$

weeks (taking 5 working days per week) and 25% overtime perday.

## 3.3.4 Duration Estimation Procedure

The various stages in duration estimation of a construction activity can be identified as follows:

**(a) Estimating the quantity of work** These estimates are worked out from the engineering drawings of the project. It is a common practice in all engineering projects to estimate the quantity of work prior to tendering.

**(b) Deciding the labour and material constants** The knowledge of these constants is essential to assess the activity duration. As is well known, these constants vary with place, environment and projects.

**(c) Assessing the effective activity-wise employment of resources** For each activity, assess the resources that can be employed effectively.

**(d) Estimating the activity completion period**

$$\text{Completion period} = \frac{\text{Quantity of work}}{\text{Output per unit of resource} \times \text{Resource earmarked}}$$

**(e) Rounding off the completion period to nearest value**

**(f) Using the three-times estimate or a non-linear estimate where it is not possible to predict reasonable activity duration by one-time method** The duration estimate of an activity assumes that the work will progress smoothly, but this is rarely true in construction tasks. It is general practice to make allowance for such contingencies while estimating the duration of individual activities, and the duration of each activity is evaluated independent of the others.

## 3.4 ACTIVITY COSTS AND EARNED VALUE

### 3.4.1 Costs Classification

In general, the term *cost* implies expenditure incurred in monetary terms by a person or an agency to acquire a product or a service, or to accomplish an objective. For a given product, the expenditure incurred or the money spent by the customer to acquire it, the manufacturer to produce it and the retailer to sell it, is not the same. The cost of an item is related to the purpose for which it is incurred; it varies when it passes through various agencies.

For example, suppose a customer purchases an apartment from a Realtor for one-million U.S. dollars. The total money paid by the Realtor to acquire it from the builder is $950,000, while the production cost incurred by the builder for the land and construction is U.S. $850,000. In each case, the cost is related to the specific purpose or activity for which it is incurred, and the cost associated for accomplishment of each activity becomes its cost objective.

In other words, the cost objective represents the cost which a person or agency has decided to pay for fulfilment of a specific purpose. In particular, the term *cost*, when singly used in this book, stands, for the production cost. The cost classification varies with the purpose. In general, the activity costs can be classified as follows:

| Cost Purpose | Cost Classification |
|---|---|
| 1. Estimating costs | Direct and indirect costs |
| 2. Accounting costs | Production cost and earned (sales) value. |

The above cost terms are outlined in the following paragraphs. These are further elaborated in Chapter 11.

**Activity direct cost**  This is the cost that can be traced in full with the execution of a specific activity. It consists of costs of direct materials, direct labour, direct equipment and other direct costs.

For example, in the activity of roof concreting, the following direct costs would be involved.

| Type of Costs | Items of Costs |
|---|---|
| Direct materials | Cost of concrete and steel |
| Direct labour | Cost of labour employed |
| Direct equipment | Cost of equipment hired for placing readymix concrete |
| Direct other expenses | Formwork hiring and repair charges |

**Activity indirect cost**  This is the cost that is incurred while performing an activity, but cannot be traced directly to its execution. In other words, all costs other than the direct ones fall in this category. These represent the apportioned share of supervision, general and administration costs, and are commonly referred to as *overheads*. Generally, the overheads charged to an activity are expressed as a percentage of its direct costs.

**Activity production cost**  This cost is the sum of direct cost and its apportioned indirect cost. It is built up as follows.

| Cost Elements | Amount |
|---|---|
| 1. Direct material costs | A |
| 2. Direct labour costs | B |
| 3. Direct equipment and other expenses | C |
| 4. Direct costs (A + B + C) | D |
| 5. Indirect costs | E |
| 6. Production cost (D + E) | F |

**Activity contract value**  It is the contract value of the work done. It is the amount which the client has agreed to pay for the satisfactorily completed works.

### 3.4.2 Activity and Work-item Sale Value

In contracted projects, the sales prices for various items of work are fixed and these are listed in the Bill of Quantities (BOQ). As an example, Table 3.3 shows an extract from the bill of quantities (BOQ), for the foundation work of a residential building complex (with actual data modified). In the (BOQ), the sale price is generally expressed in units of the work item. But for forecasting and monitoring the earned value, it is necessary to compute

## Table 3.3

### Bill of Quantities: Foundation of a Residential Building
### (Original Modified)

| Item No. | Description | Qty | Unit | Rate ($) | Amount ($) |
|---|---|---|---|---|---|
| A. 1 | Excavation in foundation include disposal of earth to a place within the work site, leveling and dressage and compaction of final source. | 44,400 | M3 | 5.00 | 222,000 |
| A. 2 | Backfilling and compaction around foundation in layers not exceeding 30 cm with excavated earth | 13,320 | M3 | 5.00 | 222,000 |
| A. 3 | Earthfilling and compaction in plinth with approved soil in layers not exceeding 30 cm level | 33,855 | M3 | 20.00 | 677,100 |
| A. 4 | Anti-termite treatment for bottom & sides of foundation plinth wall as per approved manufacturer's specifications | 59,274 | M2 | 7.50 | 444,555 |
| A. 5 | Painting with 2 coats of bitumen paint to foundation sides and plinth wall surface | 75,591 | M2 | 2.45 | 185,198 |
| A. 6 | Laying of polythene sheet 1000 G as separator between earth and concrete, and earth ad ground floor slabs | 65,157 | M2 | 1.00 | 65,157 |
| A. 7 | 75 thick blinding concrete Grade M-100 in foundation with sulphate resisting cement | 1,998 | M3 | 95.05 | 189,910 |
| A. 8 | Reinforced concrete Grade M-250 in foundation & plinth walls with sulphate resisting cement including. inserts, formwork and including expansion joints as necssary, but excluding reinforcement | 14,643 | M3 | 163.50 | 2,394,150 |
| A. 9 | Same as Item 1.8, but for ground floor slab | 3,146 | M3 | 144.95 | 455,975 |
| A. 10 | Mild steel weld mesh reinforcement as per BS 1221 for ground floor slab | 72.26 | T | 1,518.10 | 109,691 |
| A. 11 | High strength deformed bars reinforcement as per ASTM 1–615 Grade 60 or equivalent | 673.33 | T | 1,095.00 | 737,292 |

the sales price, preferably activity-wise. This computation is carried out by developing a correlation between each work item and activity by breaking down an item of work into activities, or subdividing an activity into items of works, as the case may be.

*Example 1* This example illustrates the splitting up of sales price of the BOQ work-item No. 8 into work package sales price.

Consider the BOQ item No. A8 in Table 3.3 relating to plinth wall concreting. It represents the concrete M 250 in the plinth wall of a building module of the repetitive-type residential building construction complex. This work item can be broken down into the sales price of connected activities of the work-package as shown in Table 3.4.

Standard unit sales price of work package 'plinth wall' expressed in work-unit of $m^3$ concrete placed works out as: $8031.85/43.70 = $183.80/m^3$

Table 3.4

**Sale Price Breakdown of Concreting Work Package**

| BOQ | Activity | Qty | Unit | Rate ($) | Amount ($) |
|---|---|---|---|---|---|
| A-5 | Bitumen painting | 362 | m² | 2.45 | 886.90 |
| A-8 | Layout | – | – | – | – |
| A-11 | Reinforcement fixing | | Included in raft work package | | |
| A-8 | Shuttering | 485 | m² | – | – |
| A-8 | Concreting | 43.7 | m³ | 163.50 | 7144.95 |
| A-8 | Deshuttering | – | – | – | – |
| A-8 | Curing | – | – | – | – |
| | Concrete placed | 43.7 | m³ | | $8031.85 |

*Example 2* This example shows the determination of sales price of work-package representing ground floor slab of one module from the given BOQ work item.

The sales price of the work package 'ground floor slab' in work units of m³ concrete placed works out to $515.82/m³, that is, $14618.42 divided by 28.34. See Table 3.5 for details.

Table 3.5

**Determination of Sales Price of Work Package**

| BOQ | Work Item | Qty. | Unit | Rate ($) | Amount ($) |
|---|---|---|---|---|---|
| A-5 | Bitumen painting | 319 | m² | 2.45 | 781.55 |
| A-2 | Back filling | 120 | m³ | 5.00 | 600.00 |
| A-5 | Plinth filling | 305 | m³ | 20.00 | 6100.00 |
| A4 | Anti-termite treatment | 172 | m² | 7.50 | 1290.00 |
| A6 | Polythene sheeting | 225 | m² | 1.00 | 225.00 |
| A-9 | Shuttering | 11 | m² | – | – |
| A-10 | Weld mesh laying | 0.651 | Ton | 1518.10 | 988.28 |
| A-9 | Concreting M 250 | 28.34 | m³ | 163.5 | 4633.59 |
| A-9 | Curing | – | – | – | – |
| | Concrete placed | 28.34 | m³ | | $14618.42 |

## 3.5 WORK BREAKDOWN OF A NEW CANTONMENT PROJECT

### 3.5.1 Introduction

This case history illustrates the application of the work-breakdown structure technique in developing the tasks involved for planning a military cantonment construction project costing over $22.5 million. This case can be used as a guide for breaking down work into new townships and housing complexes:

The team assigned for preparation of the project plan studied the information (then available) from the following sources:

(a) The sitting board report.
(b) The layout plan.
(c) The project administrative approval.
(d) The existing outline of ten-year plan for the construction of the project.
(e) The progress reports of the works under execution.
(f) The policy letters covering the brief history of the project, the scope of the work and the limitations or constraints imposed by the higher management from time to time.

On review of the above, it was found that the available data was not adequate to prepare a project work-breakdown structure for developing the project plan. The main drawbacks were as follows:

(a) The cantonment-layout plan was unrealistic. It did not give the correct development of zones and had no user bias.
(b) The external-services plan needed revision.

Keeping these aspects in view, a drive was launched by the higher management to prepare a user-oriented zonal development plan. Based on this, the external services schemes were prepared for the further planning of the project.

Further details required for making the time plan were obtained by discussing the relevant aspects with the heads of sections and applying the famous questioning technique of 'How? Why? What? When? and Where?', as applicable.

### 3.5.2 Cantonment Project Work-breakdown Approach

The sketch showing the layout (not to scale) of the cantonment is given in Fig. 3.2. The cantonment area is divided into 15 Zones, serially numbered from 1 to 16, excluding the number 13. Based on the work lead, source of water supply, plan of sewage disposal and the common road network, these zones are further grouped into four sectors, as follows.

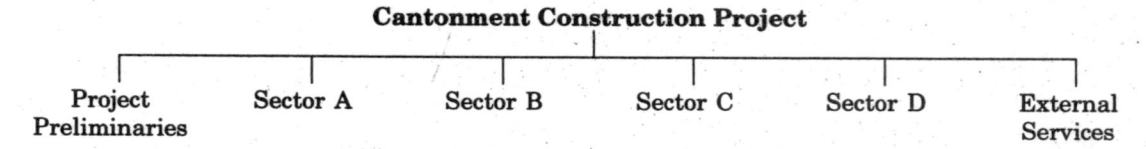

**Cantonment Construction Project**
- Project Preliminaries
- Sector A
- Sector B
- Sector C
- Sector D
- External Services

**Zonal accommodation including internal service** The accommodation, planned zone-wise, is as follows:

(i) *Unit accommodation other than married (OTM)*: Zones 1, 2, 3, 4, 8, 9, 10, 11, 12, 14, 15, and 16. Each zone has a major unit or its equivalent number of smaller units located in it.

Figure 3.2
**Zonal Layout of Cantonment Project**

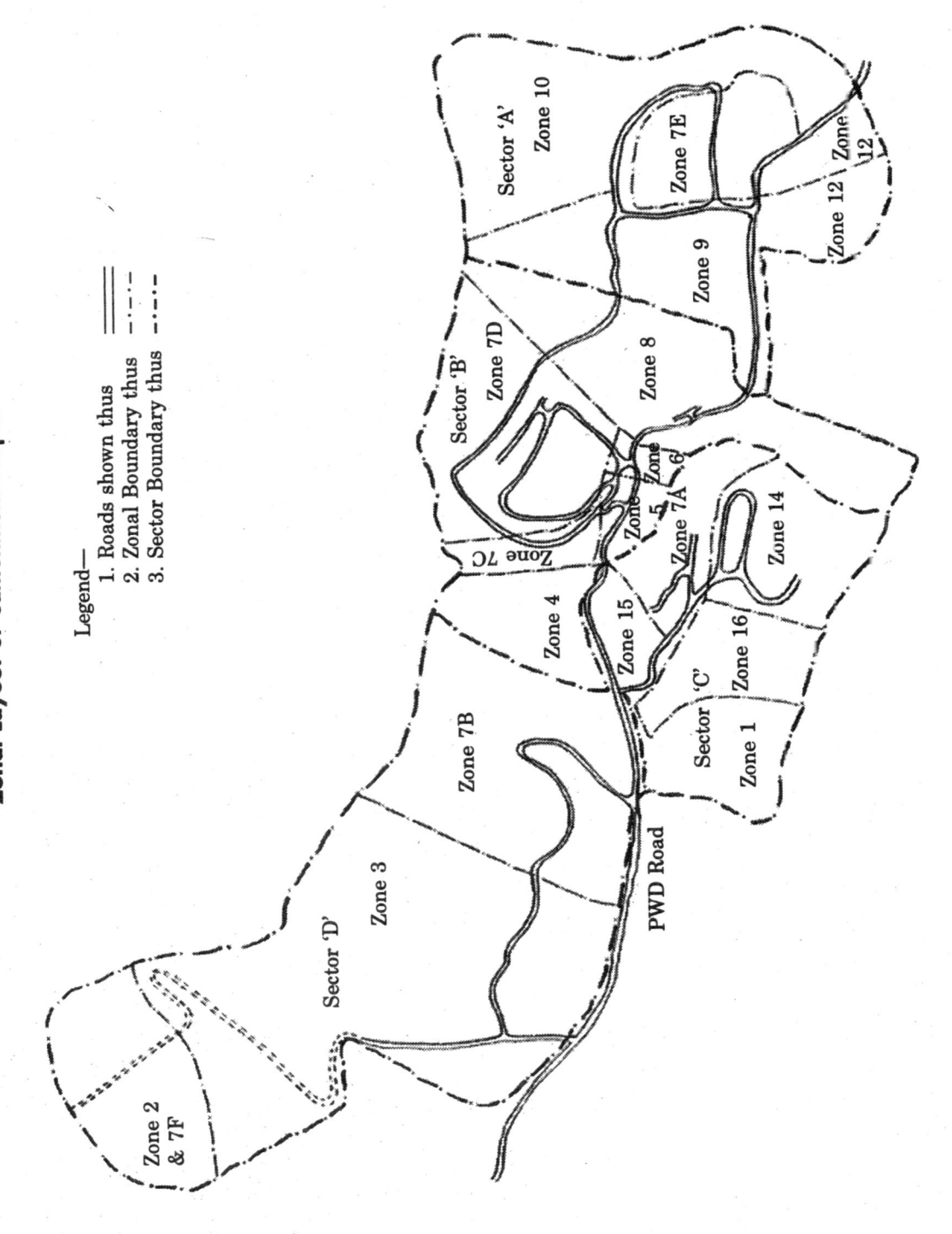

Legend—
1. Roads shown thus ═══
2. Zonal Boundary thus —·—·—
3. Sector Boundary thus —··—··—

(ii) *Married accommodation (Md)*: Zones 7A, 7B, 7C, 7D, 7E, and 7F.
(iii) *Accommodation for construction staff*: Zone 5.
(iv) *Cantonment hospital*: Zone 4.
(v) *Cantonment market*: Zone 6.

The sector-wise location of the zones is shown in the following Exhibit 3.8.

Proceeding similarly, each zone is further subdivided into sets of adjoining buildings. To give an example, the various subdivisions of Zone 16 are shown below:

**Inter-sector external services** These services include roads, power supply, water supply, sewage disposal, area drainage and arboriculture. These can be further subdivided into inter-sector works, inter-zonal works and the zonal works. The work breakdown of the inter-sector service tasks is shown in Exhibit 3.9. The tasks involved are outlined below.

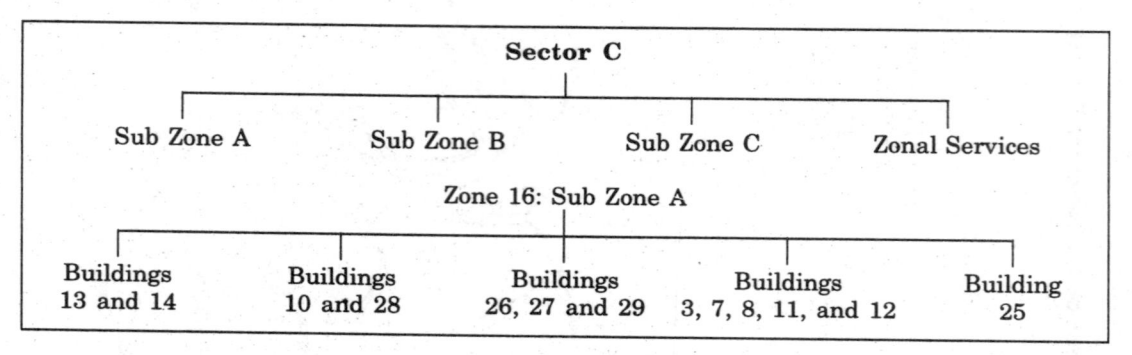

```
                           Sector C
       ┌──────────────┬──────────────┬──────────────┐
   Sub Zone A     Sub Zone B     Sub Zone C     Zonal Services

                     Zone 16: Sub Zone A
   ┌───────────┬──────────────┬──────────────┬──────────────┐
  Buildings   Buildings      Buildings       Buildings      Building
  13 and 14   10 and 28      26, 27 and 29   3, 7, 8, 11,   25
                                             and 12
```

**(a) Roads** The main road runs through the centre of the cantonment. There are a number of other roads which connect the zones.

**(b) Electrification** The main source of electric supply is from the hydel department. The hydel power is received at the receiving station in Zone 1. It is then transmitted to the various zones by HT transmission line. There are 17 sub stations which step down the high voltage to 440 volts and distribute it to the various zones by the LT lines. The power house, housing three generating sets, caters to important installations in an emergency.

**(c) Water supply** The main source of water supply is a stream. An irrigation channel connects this stream to the water treatment plant. The treated water is pumped to six water reservoirs which are distributed to the various Zones as follows.

  (i) *Three water reservoirs*: for Zones 9, 10, 11, 12 and 7E.
  (ii) *One water reservoirs*: for Zones 5, 6, 8, 7C and 7D.
  (iii) *One water reservoir*: for Zones 14, 15, 16 and 7A.
  (iv) *Two water reservoirs*: for Zones 1, 2, 3, 4, 7B and 7F.

**(d) Sewage disposal** It is based on the oxidation-pond method and is organized as follows:

  (i) The trunk sewer from Zones 9, 10, 11, 12 and 7E are connected to the oxidation pond in Zone 12.

## Exhibit 3.8
### Sector-wise Location of Zones in a Cantonment Construction Project

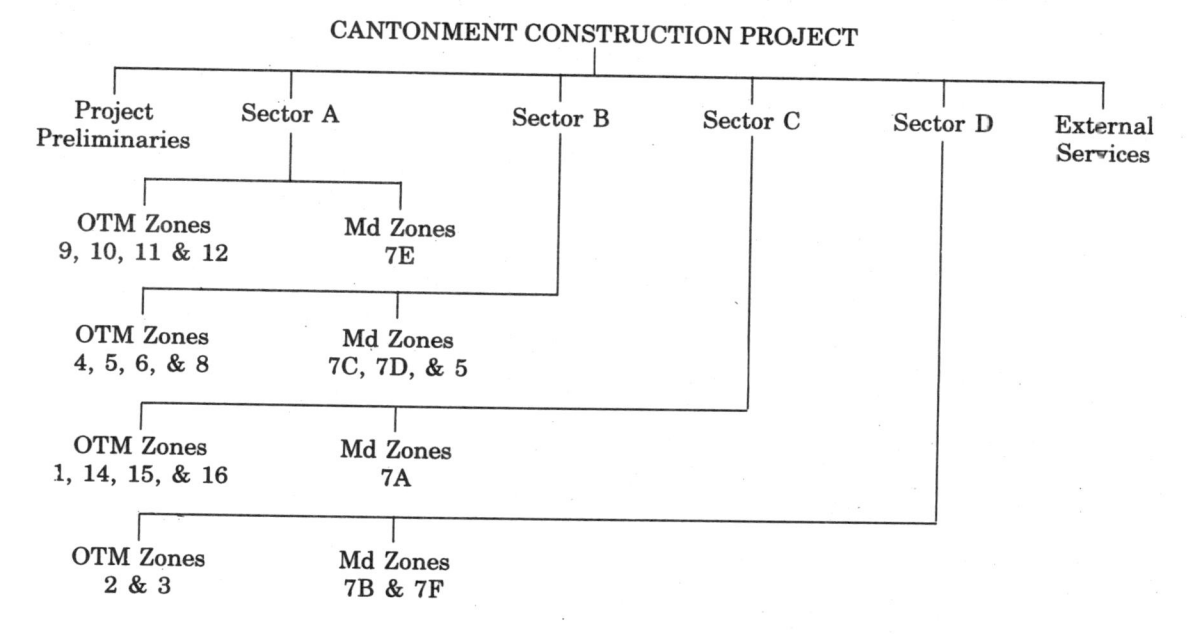

```
                        CANTONMENT CONSTRUCTION PROJECT
    ┌──────────┬──────────┬──────────┬──────────┬──────────┐
  Project    Sector A   Sector B   Sector C   Sector D  External
Preliminaries                                            Services

  OTM Zones    Md Zones
  9, 10, 11 & 12  7E

  OTM Zones    Md Zones
  4, 5, 6, & 8  7C, 7D, & 5

  OTM Zones    Md Zones
  1, 14, 15, & 16  7A

  OTM Zones    Md Zones
  2 & 3       7B & 7F
```

(ii) The trunk sewer from Zones 4, 5, 6, 7D and 8 terminates in the oxidation pond in Zone B.

(iii) The trunk sewer from Zones 7A, 14 and 15 is also connected to another set of oxidation ponds in Zone 8.

(iv) The trunk sewer from Zones 1, 3 and 7B are connected to oxidation ponds in Zone 1.

(v) All other Zones are connected with separate septic tanks.

**(e) Area drainage and arboriculture** These are planned on area basis.

### 3.5.3 Cantonment Project Work-breakdown Structure

The work-breakdown structure down to the task level developed for this project by integrating the various sub-project structures is shown in Exhibit 3.10. It also includes the additional tasks derived subsequently.

### 3.5.4 Project CPM Skeleton Network

The work-breakdown structure (Exhibit 3.10) was used to derive the list of sub-projects and the main tasks of the cantonmen- construction project. These sub-projects and tasks formed

**Exhibit 3.9**
**Inter-sector External Services**

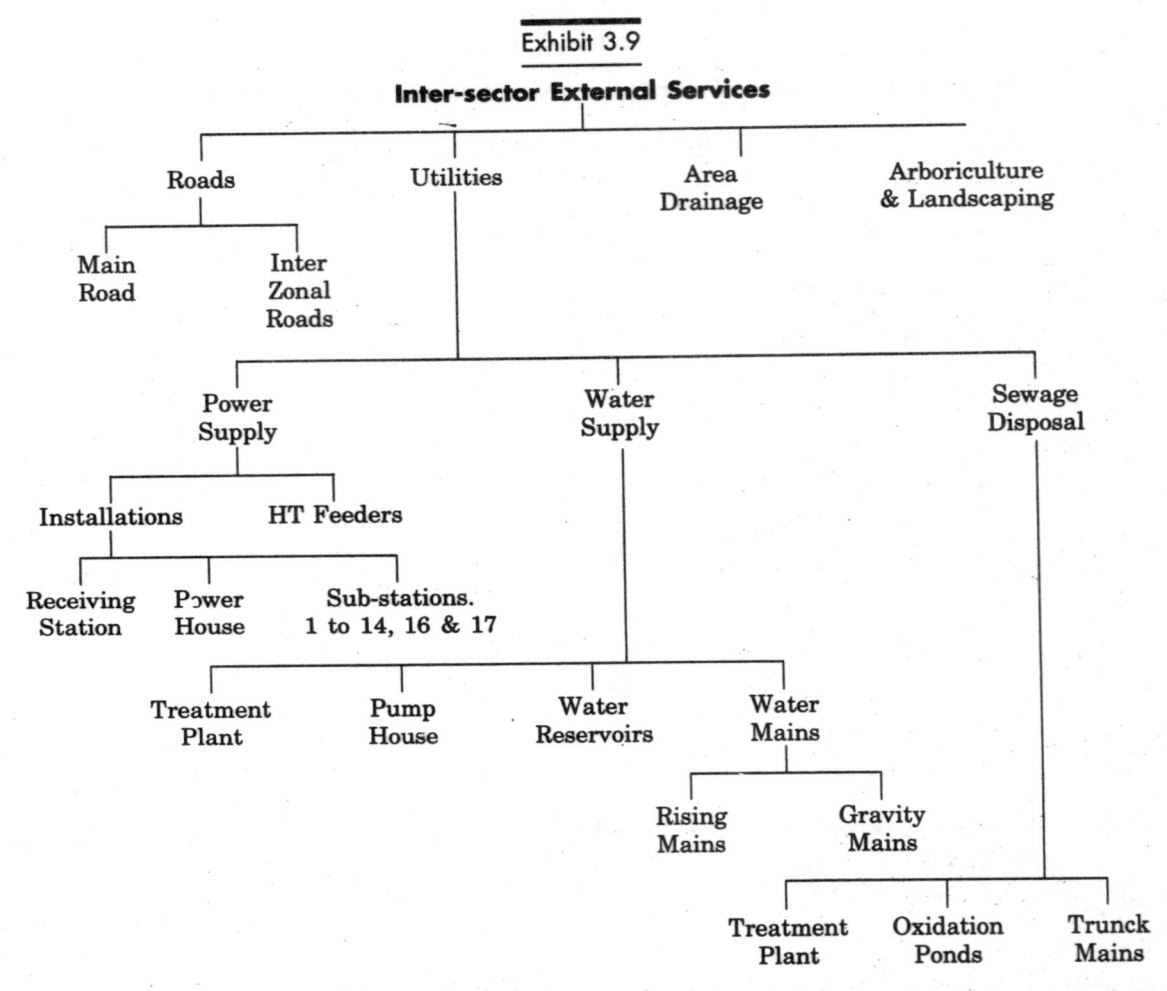

```
                    Inter-sector External Services
    ┌──────────────┬──────────────┬──────────────┐
   Roads        Utilities         Area       Arboriculture
                                Drainage     & Landscaping
   ┌────┴────┐
  Main     Inter
  Road     Zonal
           Roads

   Utilities
   ┌──────────────┬──────────────┐
  Power          Water          Sewage
  Supply         Supply         Disposal

  Power Supply
   ┌──────┴──────┐
 Installations  HT Feeders
  ┌──────┬──────────┐
Receiving Power   Sub-stations.
Station   House   1 to 14, 16 & 17

  Water Supply
   ┌──────┬──────────┬──────────┐
 Treatment  Pump    Water      Water
 Plant      House   Reservoirs Mains
                              ┌────┴────┐
                            Rising   Gravity
                            Mains    Mains

  Sewage Disposal
   ┌──────────┬──────────┐
 Treatment  Oxidation  Trunck
 Plant      Ponds      Mains
```

the basis for preparing the skeleton CPM network to conceptualize the long-term construction plan of the project within specified constraints. The project constraints were as follows:

**Priority of construction** This included the following.

  (a) The accommodation under construction.
  (b) The construction staff accommodation and, as per user requirements, the unit accommodation of Zone 8, Zone 9 (part), Zone 10 and Zone 16, in that order.
  (c) The remaining accommodation, in conformity with the command and control set-up.

**Phasing of unit accommodation** The unit accommodation within a zone was broadly grouped into the following:

  (a) The existing accommodation constructed prior to the formulation of network plan.
  (b) The minimum essential accommodations, as per the units requirements.
  (c) The remaining unit accommodation, where applicable.

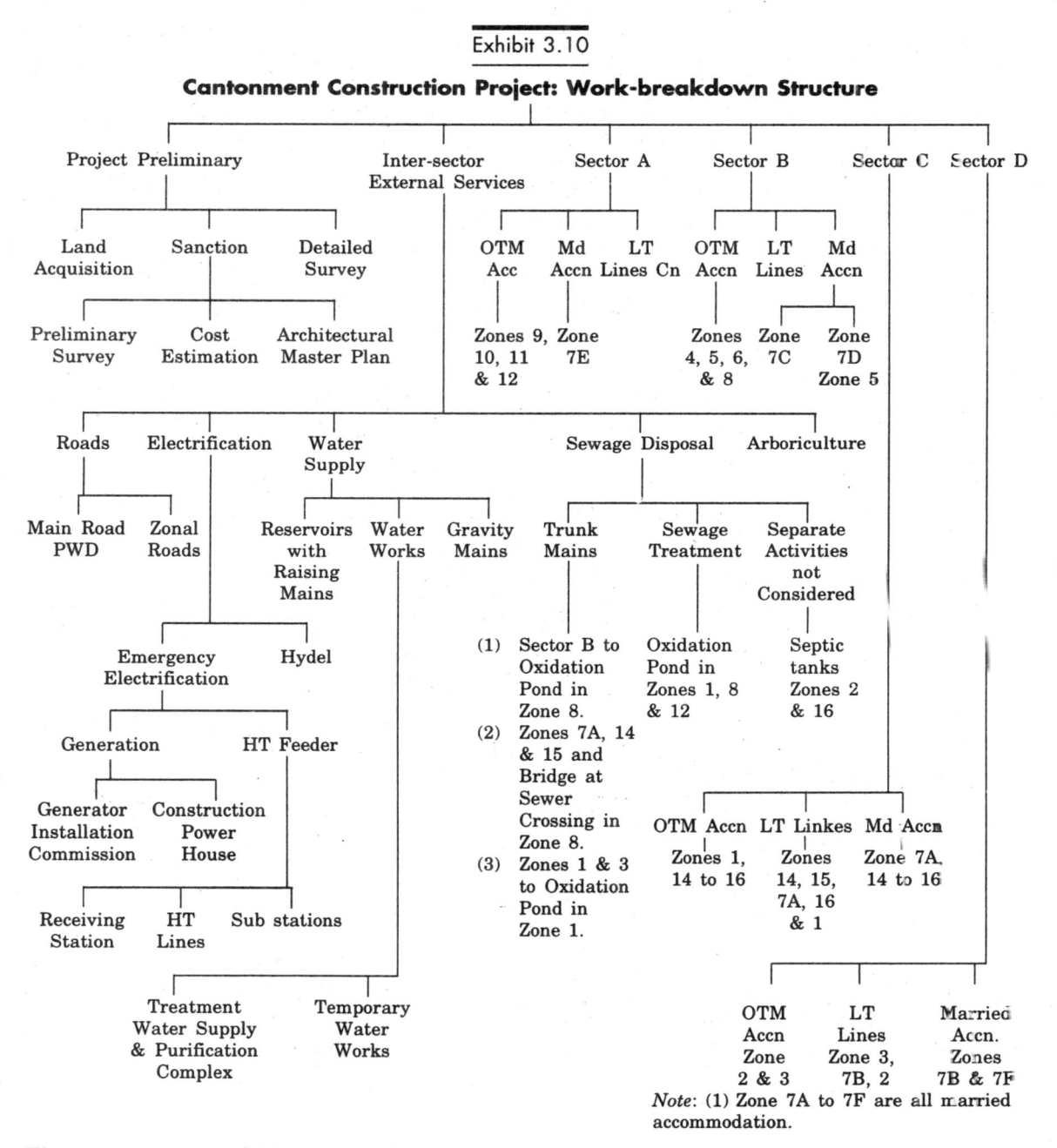

### Exhibit 3.10
## Cantonment Construction Project: Work-breakdown Structure

```
                        Cantonment Construction Project: Work-breakdown Structure
    ┌───────────────┬──────────────────┬──────────────┬──────────────┬────────────┬──────────┐
 Project         Inter-sector       Sector A       Sector B       Sector C    Sector D
 Preliminary     External Services
```

**Project Preliminary:** Land Acquisition; Sanction; Detailed Survey
- Preliminary Survey
- Cost Estimation
- Architectural Master Plan

**Sector A:** OTM Acc; Md Accn Lines; LT Lines Cn
- Zones 9, 10, 11 & 12
- Zone 7E

**Sector B:** OTM Accn; LT Lines; Md Accn
- Zones 4, 5, 6, & 8
- Zone 7C
- Zone 7D
- Zone 5

**Inter-sector External Services:**
- Roads
  - Main Road PWD
  - Zonal Roads
- Electrification
  - Emergency Electrification
    - Generation
      - Generator Installation Commission
      - Construction Power House
    - HT Feeder
  - Hydel
    - Receiving Station
    - HT Lines
    - Sub stations
- Water Supply
  - Reservoirs with Raising Mains
  - Water Works
    - Treatment Water Supply & Purification Complex
    - Temporary Water Works
  - Gravity Mains
- Sewage Disposal
  - Trunk Mains
    - (1) Sector B to Oxidation Pond in Zone 8.
    - (2) Zones 7A, 14 & 15 and Bridge at Sewer Crossing in Zone 8.
    - (3) Zones 1 & 3 to Oxidation Pond in Zone 1.
  - Sewage Treatment
    - Oxidation Pond in Zones 1, 8 & 12
  - Separate Activities not Considered
    - Septic tanks Zones 2 & 16
- Arboriculture

**Sector C:**
- OTM Accn — Zones 1, 14 to 16
- LT Linkes — Zones 14, 15, 7A, 16 & 1
- Md Accn — Zone 7A, 14 to 16

**Sector D:**
- OTM Accn Zone 2 & 3
- LT Lines Zone 3, 7B, 2
- Married Accn. Zones 7B & 7F

*Note:* (1) Zone 7A to 7F are all married accommodation.

The zone accommodation was split up into one or more part(s), broadly conforming to the above grouping.

**Married accommodation** To be ready with the completion of minimum essential unit or sub-unit accommodation, as applicable.

**Work under progress and connected external services** All works under progress to be completed as per the running contracts. The corresponding external services to be synchronized with the completion of the building.

**Assumptions** The main assumptions, made for making the network were as follows:

**Network logic** The tasks completed prior to preparation of network were also shown in the network to maintain its logic, though not necessarily in the order of their occurrence. The duration of the activities of the completed tasks were not considered.

**Employment of contractor** It was assumed that not more than one building contractor could work in a Zone at a given time.

**Duration estimate** The unit of time for duration estimation was taken as one month. The activities less than one unit duration were either merged with the neighbouring activities or were omitted. Duration of all works under execution was estimated in months from the date of making of network.

**Project sub-networks integration** Since the main purpose of drawing the network was to evolve a long term preliminary plan for the construction of the project, the level of details considered in the network was restricted to the sub-projects and major tasks, and sub-networks were prepared for most of them. Some of these sub-networks included the following.

(a) Skeleton network for planning the construction of accommodation in Zone 16.
(b) Skeleton network for planning the construction of married accommodation in Zone 7E.
(c) Skeleton network for planning the advanced landing ground.
(d) Skeleton network for planning the works in the military hospital.
(e) Master network for construction of the offices, mess.
(f) Master network of the multi-project contract.
(g) Master network for accommodation in Zone 10.
(h) Master network for sewage disposal of Sector B and C.
(i) Master network of the water purification plant.
(j) Summary network for the construction of married accommodation.
(k) Summary network of the multi-contracts complex.

These sub-networks were prepared by the graduate engineer trainees belonging to the military works services. Thereafter, the project skeleton network was developed by integrating the sub-networks of sub-projects and major tasks. Due to space constraints, the skeleton network of the Cantonment Project has not been included in the book.

The methodology for preparation of CPM network was used as a training device to teach network planning techniques to selected engineers of the Military Engineering Service in India. Most of the sub-networks mentioned above were drawn by the trainees.

It would be ideal to illustrate this case history step-by-step to give it the right combination of established theory and practical application, but that will need another volume. Keeping in mind the limited space available, the method of preparing the CPM/PERT sub-networks is described in Chapter 4, the precedence networks are covered in chapter 5 and the scheduling of networks is outlined in Chapter 6.

# CHAPTER 4

# Project CPM/PERT Network Analysis

The advancements in technology and the speed of execution of modern projects, have made the traditional bar chart planning approach outdated and inadequate to cope with the complexities of modern construction. Bar charts provide little information about the interrelationship of the voluminous interdependent tasks. These charts carry the risk of schedule slippages, time overruns, improper decisions and contractual complications. The network analysis techniques, developed in the sixties, have now come to be used as an effective management tool for planning and scheduling complex projects involving interlinking activities.

The term *project networks analysis* is a generic term covering all the network techniques used for planning, scheduling and controlling of projects. The three such commonly used techniques are: Critical Path Method (CPM), Program Evaluation and Review Technique (PERT) and Precedence Network Analysis (PNA). Their common features are that they make use of the network model for depicting the time plan of the project; apply the critical path concept for determining project duration and identifying critical activities, and; employ network analysis techniques for controlling the project-time objectives. But each of these techniques have a distinct model with a varying field of application.

Experience has shown the following:

(a) CPM is best suited for developing the sub-networks of sub-groups and task having activities with deterministic single-time duration.
(b) PERT is useful for project feasibility reports and sub-projects or tasks involving uncertainties. In such cases, probabalistic approach of three-times (or mathematical time-related functions) is used for assessing the activity duration.
(c) Precedence Network technique is commonly used technique for time planning of construction projects.

This chapter describes the CPM and PERT network analysis techniques. The topics covered can be used for planning short-duration projects or for developing sub-networks for the sub-projects, tasks or the work packages of major projects. The major project subnetworks can then be systematically integrated into a project network using the PNA technique.

## 4.1 CPM NETWORK ANALYSIS FUNDAMENTALS

A *network* shows the sequence and interdependence of the activities in a project in a diagrammatic form using standard symbols. For example, CPM network of a Pumping Station construction project is drawn in Exhibit 4.1

### 4.1.1 Network Elements

The two basic elements used in a network are *activity* and *event*. In addition, where necessary, dummy activities are introduced to maintain logic.

**Activity** A project can be broken down into various operations and processes necessary for its completion. Each of these operations or processes, which consume time and possibly, resources is called an activity. Acquiring land, fixing steel, collecting materials, building a wall, constructing a roof and curing the concrete are examples of some of the common activities in a building construction project.

The activities are represented by arrows pointing in the forward direction. The tail of the arrow depicts the commencement of an activity and the arrow head, its termination. The various ways by which the arrow of an activity 'A' can be drawn are:

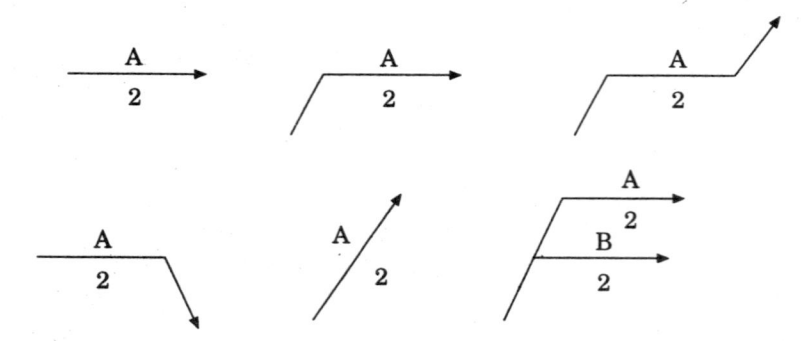

*Notes:* 1. The description of an activity is written above the arrow and its duration in the middle underneath. An activity involving excavation, and needing two units of time for its completion, would be shown as:

$$\text{Excavation} \atop 2$$

2. The length of the arrow is not drawn to scale. As far as possible, the arrow should be sufficiently long so that the description of the activity could be written over it.
3. Arrows are neither curved nor are they drawn in reverse direction.

Exhibit 4.1

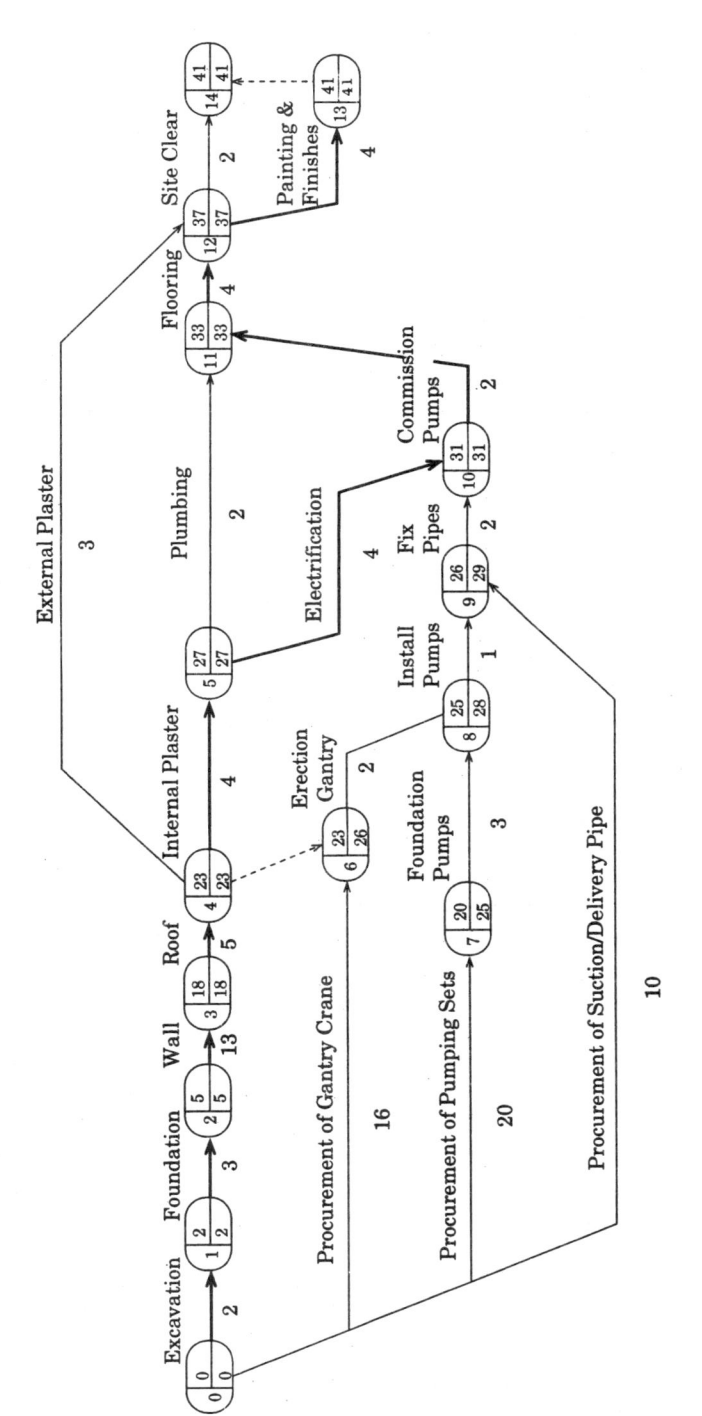

**Pumping Station Project
Time Analysed CPM Network**

**Event** It is the state between the completion of a preceding activity and the beginning of the succeeding one. It has no duration; it represents only a point in time. Symbolically, an event is shown by a circle or an ellipse, as:

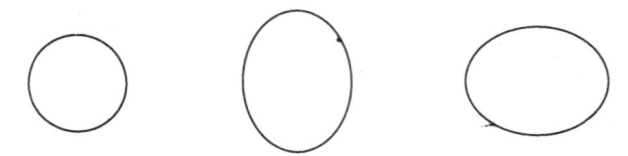

An event thus refers to a state in the progressing of a project. This state can be named in two ways: either it can describe the completion of the preceding activity, such as 'design approved' for the designing activity; or, it can depict the start of the succeeding activity, such as 'foundation commences'. The states are ordinarily described in terms of the completion of the preceding activity.

The events are labelled numerically to identify them and describe the connecting activities. The procedure for labelling events is covered in the subsequent paragraphs. An activity (i-j) would be shown as:

*Notes:* 1. The first event of a project is called the *start event* and the last, the *end event*.
2. An event at which an activity starts is termed as the *preceding event*. The event by which it terminates is called the *succeeding event*.
3. An event of significance, such as 'electrification complete', 'buildings ready for occupation' etc., is called a *key event*. The occurrence of a key event is termed as the *milestone*.

4. A key event common to two or more sub networks is called the *interface event*.

**Dummy activity** It is a superimposed activity, which does not represent any specific operation or process. It has zero duration and consumes no resources. Its purpose is twofold:

(a) To provide a logical link to maintain the correct relationship of activities.
(b) To simplify the description of concurrent activities in terms of event numbers.

The dummy activity is drawn like any other activity, but with dotted lines, as:

*Example* Consider a simple network consisting of six activities: A, B, C, D, E, and F. The durations of these activities are 2, 3, 2, 1, 3, and 2 days, respectively. The network is shown in Fig. 4.1.

## Figure 4.1

**Network of Activities and their Respective Durations**

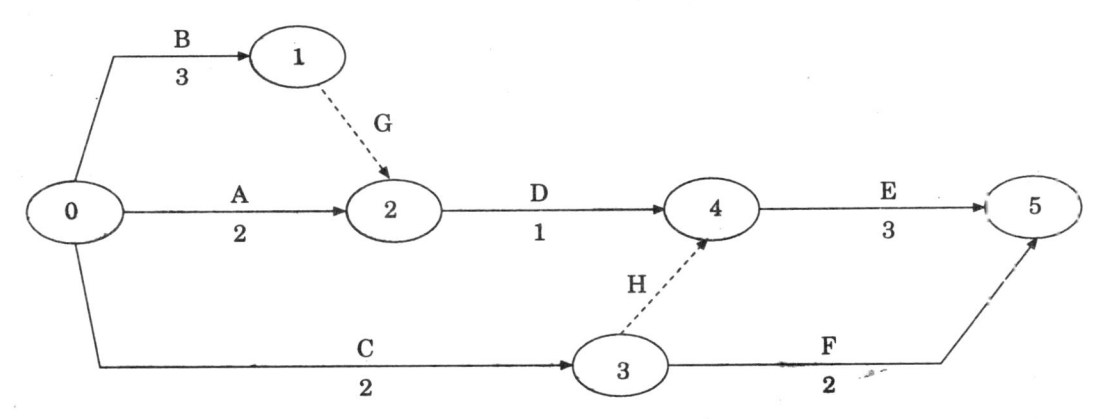

The network logic shows that: activities A, B and C start at the same time; D follows the completion of A and B: E starts after C and D are completed; and, F follows C. The project is over when E and F are completed. The points to note are:

(a) The activities A and B are concurrent (see Figs 4.2 and 4.3). To enable their description by event numbers, the dummy activity 'G' has been used.

## Figure 4.2

**Correct Representation of Concurrent Activities**

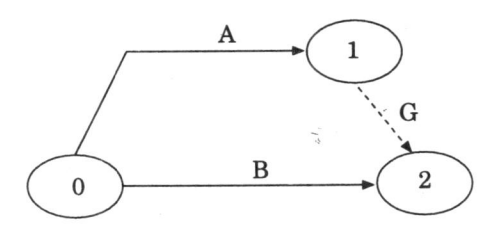

## Figure 4.3

**Incorrect Representation of Concurrent Activities**

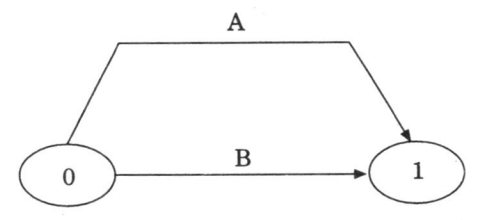

(b) To depict relationship among C, D, E, and F, the dummy activity 'H' is introduced (see Fig. 4.4)

Figure 4.4

**Part of Network Showing that F Follows C, and E Starts after Completion of C and D. The Dummy Activity H Provides The Logic Link.**

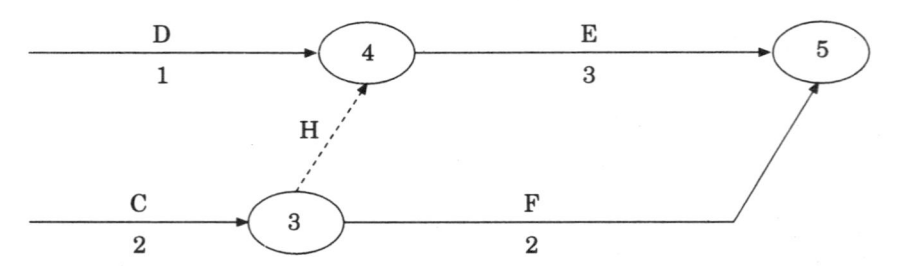

### 4.1.2 Network Preparation

The development of a network can be done by first tabulating the network logic and then drawing the arrow diagram step-by-step. This is illustrated below with a simple example. Consider a work package consisting of nine activities: A, B, C, D, E, F, G, H and J. Their durations are 4, 3, 2, 5, 2, 1, 3, 3 and 2 units, respectively.

The activities A, C and D can start at the same time; B follows the completion of A; G starts after B and D are completed; E starts after the completion of D, and is succeeded by F, H follows the completion of A and C; and J succeeds B and H. The tasks are over when F, G and J are completed.

The logic of activities can be tabulated as in Table 4.1 by questioning each activity as follows:

(a) Which activity/ies precede this activity?

Table 4.1

**Logic Table of Work Package**

| Activity | Preceding | Succeeding | Remarks |
|---|---|---|---|
| A | Nil | B, H | |
| B | A | G, J | |
| C | Nil | H | |
| D | Nil | E, G | |
| E | D | F | |
| F | E | Nil | Last Activity |
| G | B, D | Nil | Last Activity |
| H | A, C | J | |
| J | B, H | Nil | Last Activity |

(b) Which activity/ies succeed or follow this activity?
(c) Are there any logic constraints imposed on this activity?
(d) Is it the final activity?

The step-by-step development of the logic arrow diagram can proceed as follows:

* A, C and D can start concurrently in the beginning of the project. Therefore, their logic can be represented as:

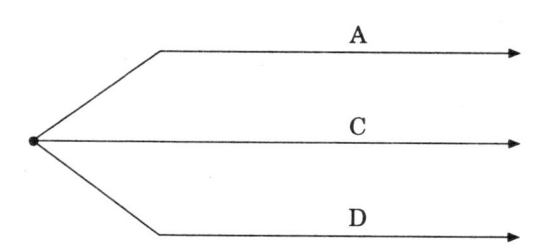

* B follow the completion of A.

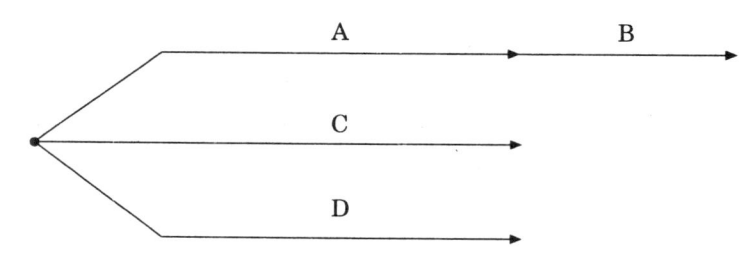

* E starts after the completion of D, and is succeeded by F.

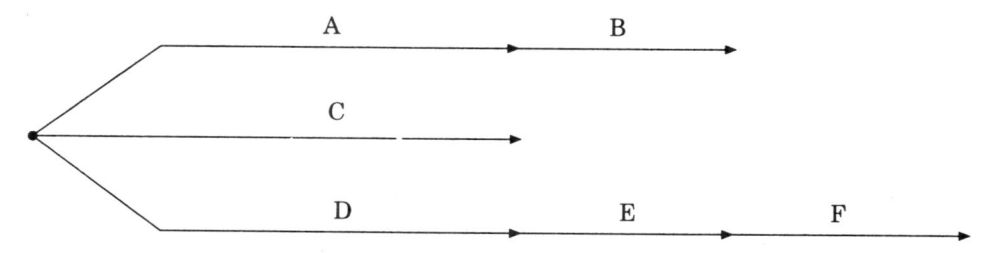

* G starts after B and D are complete.

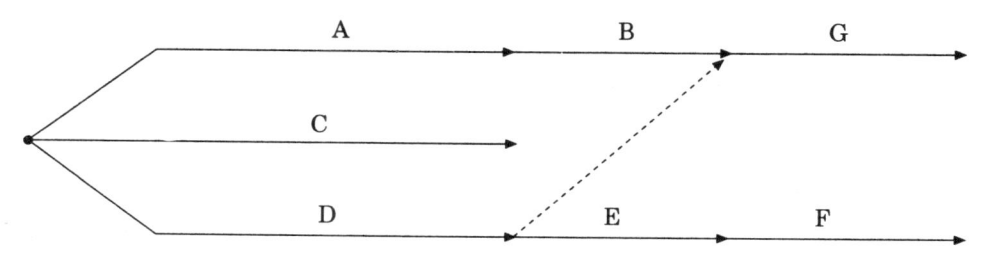

**110** Construction Project Management

* H follows the completion of A and C.

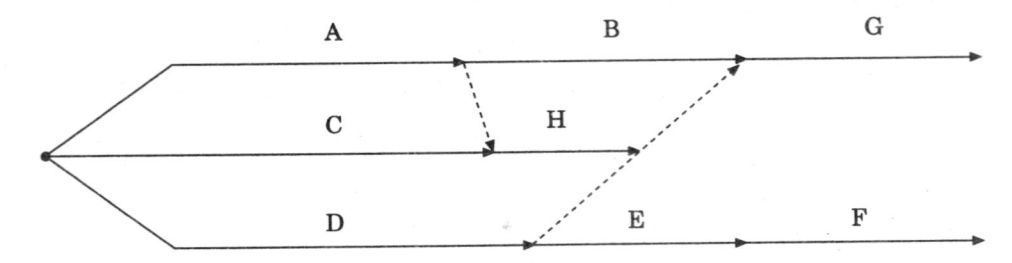

* J succeeds B and H.

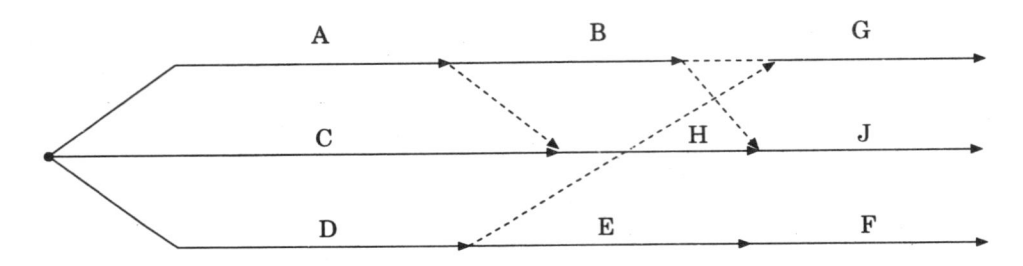

In order to maintain logic and provide the logical link, two dummy activities are introduced. The logic evolved shows that 'G' follows B and D, and 'J' starts after the completion of B and H.

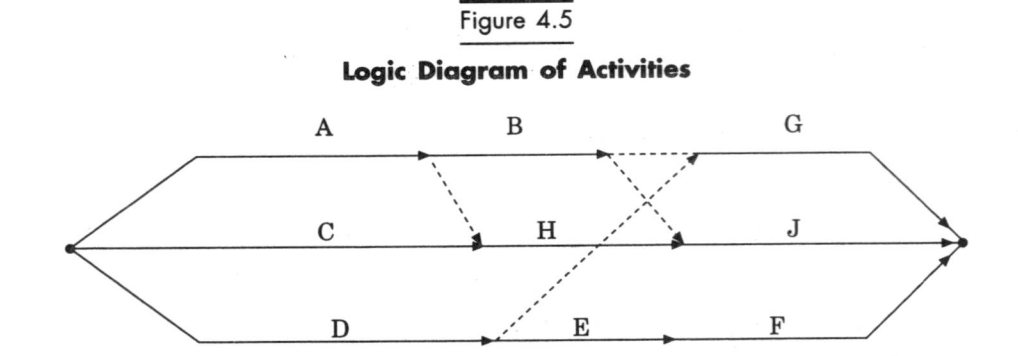

### Figure 4.5
**Logic Diagram of Activities**

- The tasks are over when F, G and J are completed (Fig. 4.5).
- The above logic diagram can be converted into the nine-activity networks by repositioning activities so as to avoid the crossing of arrows, inserting events to mark the start and completion of activities, and writing the duration of each activity. This work package network is shown in Fig. 4.6.

## Figure 4.6

### Logic Diagram of Nine Activities

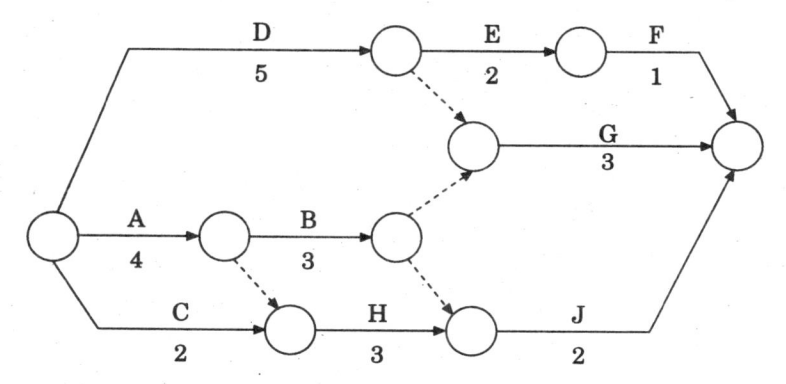

| | |
|---|---|
| D 5 | E 2 | F 1 |
| A 4 | B 3 | G 3 |
| C 2 | H 3 | J 2 |

## 4.1.3 Numbering Events

**Purpose** The numbering of the network serves a threefold purpose, as follows:

(a) It simplifies the identification and description of an activity in terms of event numbers. The activities are coded as '*i-j*', where i and j are the event numbers at the commencement and termination of an activity.
(b) It helps in developing identification code for computer application.
(c) It systematizes the computation of critical path. This point is illustrated under the network critical path.

**Rule** To codify the activities, their numbering can be done in an ad hoc manner, provided that different digits are used for numbering the events. For programming, however, the following rules of numbering help in detecting errors.

(a) For each activity, as far as possible, the number of the preceding event (i) should be less than that of the succeeding event (j).
(b) If the effort required in renumbering is considerable (as when the insertion of an event after the finalization of the network would require a renumbering of all the subsequent events), then the next (higher) number can be given to the new event without altering the other existing numbers. Alternately, events can be labelled in even digit sequence e.g. 0, 2, 4, to cater for insertion of subsequent events at a later time.

**Procedure** Various methods can be used for numbering events which are in conformity with the rule for numbering. The method given below has an added advantage—the numerical sequence indicates the order in which events are considered during time analysis. This procedure for numbering events is standardized as follows:

(a) The start event of the network is numbered as zero.
(b) Starting with the top chain, the subsequent events in the chain are numbered serially

till more than one activity emerges out of an event, or where the tail event of an activity converging into it is not numbered.
(c) Where more than one activity emerge out of an event, the events in the topmost activity or chain are serially numbered first, till an event is reached where the tail event of the activity converging into it is not numbered.
(d) Where the tail event of the converging activity is not labelled, one proceeds with the next activity chain from the top and in that order, following similar procedure, till all events are numbered.

The networks in this book generally follow the above procedure for numbering events. This procedure is illustrated with simple examples given below.

**Numbering Events:** *Example* 1. Figure 4.7(a)

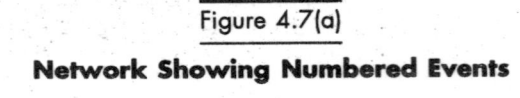

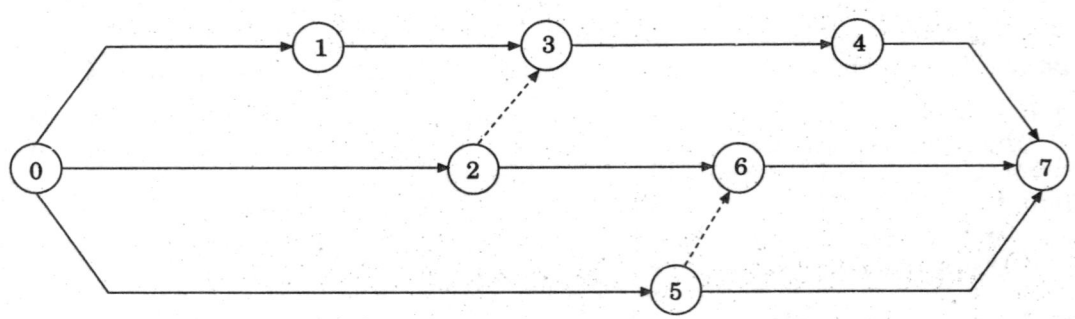

Figure 4.7(a)

**Network Showing Numbered Events**

(a) Consider the network given in Figure 4.7(a). The start event is numbered as zero.
(b) Proceeding with the top chain first, the next event is numbered as 1.
(c) The event subsequent to event 1 cannot be numbered as the tail event of the dummy activity converging into it is not numbered.
(d) Starting with the second chain from top, event 2 is numbered.
(e) There are two activities emerging out of event 2; proceeding first with the top chain, events 3 and 4 are numbered.
(f) Proceeding similarly, other events can be numbered as shown in the above network.

**Numbering Events:** *Example* 2. Figure 4.7(b)

(a) The start event is numbered as zero.
(b) In the top chain first event is numbered as 1, and the event subsequent to it is labelled as 2.
(c) The event subsequent to event 2 cannot be numbered as the tail events of the activities G and J converging into it are not numbered.
(d) Starting with the second chain from top, the events 3, 4, and 5 are numbered serially. Note that the succeeding event of activity G still cannot be numbered as the tail of activity J is not numbered.

### Figure 4.7(b)
**Network Showing Procedure for Numbered Events**

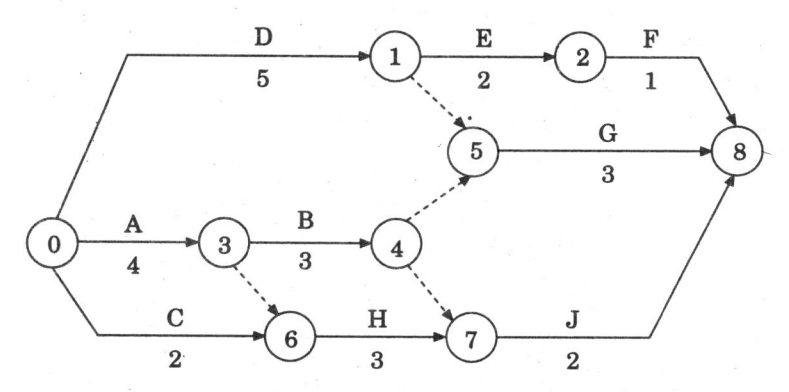

(e) Proceeding similarly with the bottom chain, the other events can be numbered as 6, 7 and 8, as shown in Fig. 4.7(b).

## 4.1.4 Event Timings and Associated Terms

Each event has two timings associated with it. These are the Earliest Event Time (EET) and the Latest Event Time (LET). The other connected terms are *slack* and *critical* events.

**Earliest event time (EET)** It is the earliest time an event can take place, assuming that all the events prior to it also occur at their earliest time.

The value of EET is inserted into the circle or ellipse representing the event by suitably dividing them into parts, as shown below:

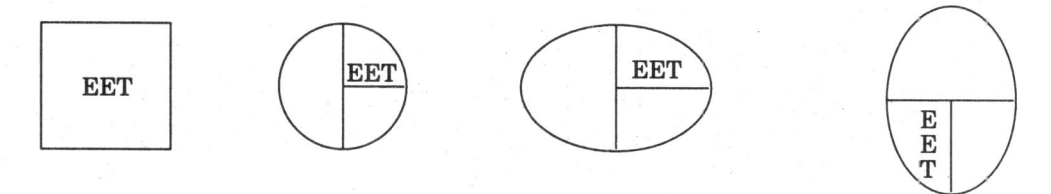

The EET of the first event is taken as zero, while the EET of subsequent event is calculated by adding the activity duration to it. If there are more than one activities terminating into an event, the EET of that event is the highest value obtained by adding activity duration to the EETs of the preceding events. This process of determining EET is called *forward pass*.

Take, for example the network given in Fig. 4.8. The EET of event zero (EET 0) is taken as zero. The subsequent activities are B, A and C. The earliest timing of the event marking the completion of activity B, designated as EET 1, is 0 + 3 = 3.

EET 2 has the highest value (3) of the duration along paths 0 – 1 and 0 – 2. EET 3 is 0 + 2 = 2. Similarly, EET 4 and EET 5 are 4 and 7, respectively.

### Figure 4.8
### Network Illustrating Calculation of Earliest Event Time (EET)

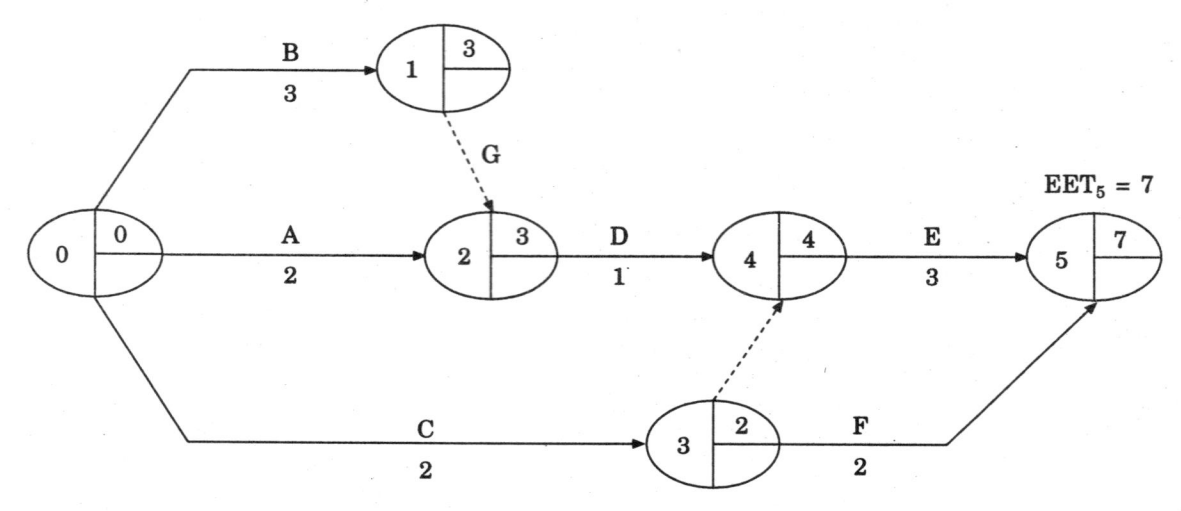

**Latest event time (LET).** It is the latest time by which an event can occur, if the project is to be completed within the specified time. The LETs are written as:

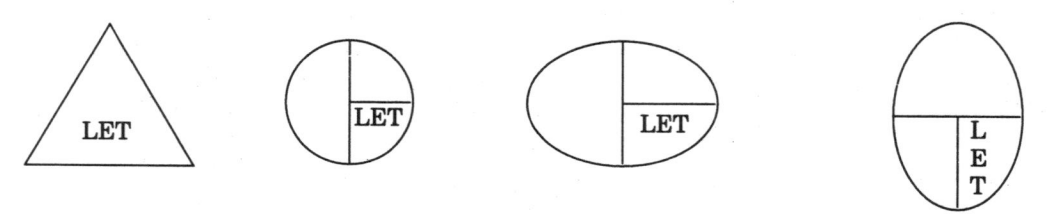

Unless otherwise specified, the LET of the end event is taken equal to its EET. The LETs of the remaining events are calculated by moving in a reverse path and subtracting the activity duration from the LET at the head of the activity.

If more than one activity diverges from an event, then its LET would be the lowest value obtained by subtracting the duration of each activity from the LET of the respective succeeding event. This process of determining LET is called *back pass or backward pass*.

The LETs of the sample network discussed earlier are shown in Fig. 4.9. Note that the LET of event 3 (LET 3) is the lowest value (4) of paths connecting events 3–4–5 and events 3–5.

**Slack**  The difference between the LET and EET of an event is called *slack* or *event slack*. It gives the range of time available within which the event must take place if the project is to be completed on schedule.

For example, the slack of the event 3 would be:

$$= \text{LET 3} - \text{EET 3} = 4 - 2 = 2$$

## Figure 4.9
### Network Illustrating Calculation of Latest Event Time (LET)

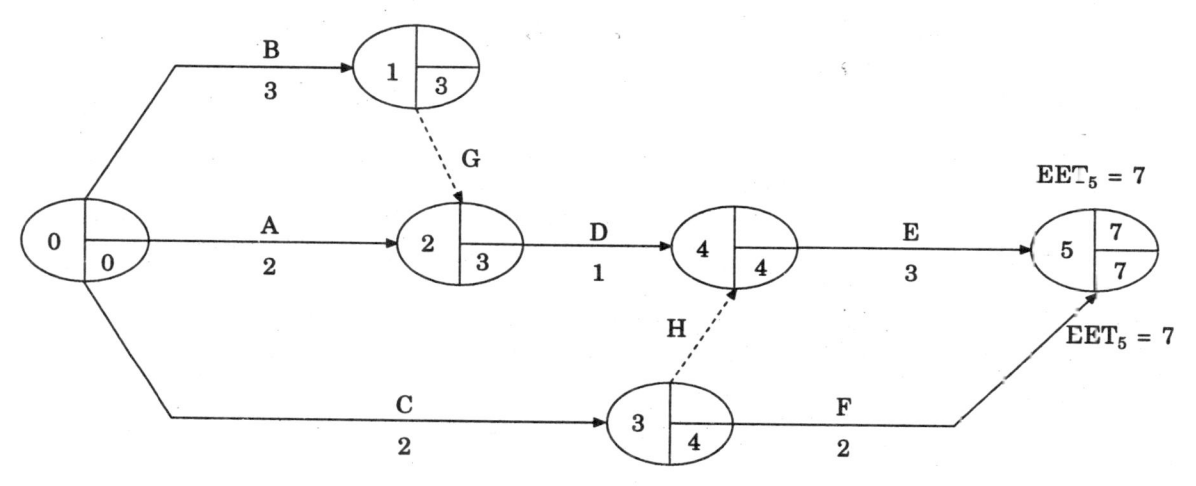

**Critical events** The events having a zero slack are called critical events. They must take place at a stipulated time without fail. There is no flexibility in their schedule. Any change in their occurrence would affect the project completion time. For example, the events 0, 1, 2, 4, and 5, of the network given in Fig. 4.10, have LETs equal to EETs. These are its critical events.

## Figure 4.10
### Network Showing Critical Events

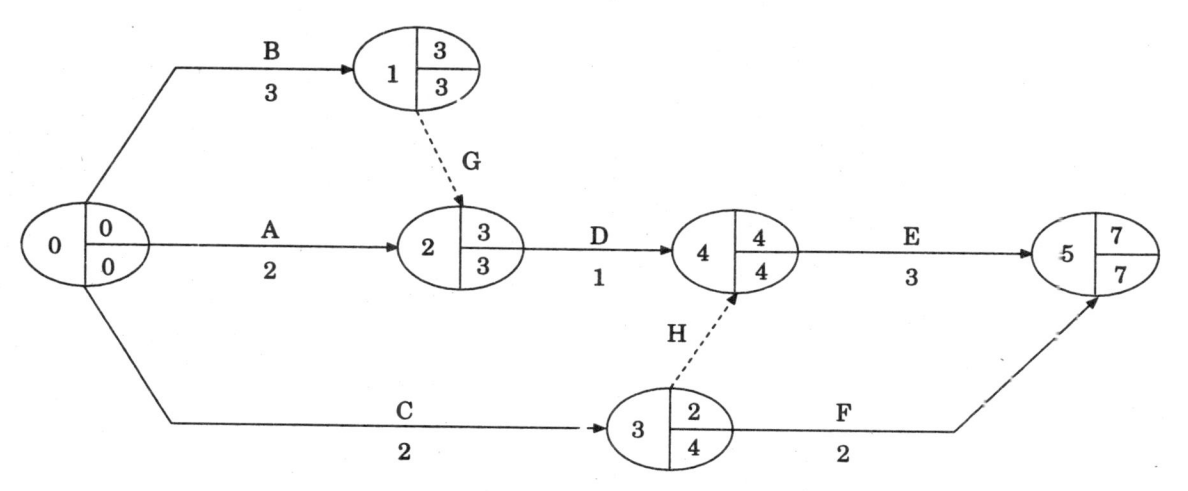

## 4.1.5 Activity Timings and Connected Terms

Corresponding to the event timings at its beginning and termination, each activity has four timings associated with it. These are the Earliest Start Time (EST), the Latest Start Time (LST), the Earliest Finish Time (EFT) and the Latest Finish Time (LFT). The other connected terms are *float* and *critical activities*.

**Earliest start time (EST)** This is the earliest time an activity can be started, assuming that all the activities prior to it have taken place as early as possible.

The EST of an activity is equal to the EET of the preceding event, that is,

$$EST = EET_i$$

**Latest start time (LST)** This is the latest time an activity can start consistent, with the completion of the project in the stipulated time. The LST of an activity is determined by subtracting the activity duration from the LET of the succeeding event, that is,

$$LST = LET_j - d$$

For example, the LST of activity 'F' in the network shown in Exhibit 4.10.

$$= LET_5 - d = 7 - 2 = 5$$

*Note:* That the LST of activity 'F' is not the same as the LET of its preceding event.

**Earliest finish time (EFT)** It is the earliest time by which an activity can be completed, assuming that all the activities prior to it begin at their ESTs. The earliest finish time (EFT) is calculated by adding the activity duration to EST.

For example, the EFT of activity F

$$EFT = EET_3 + d = 2 + 2 = 4$$

**Latest finish time (LFT)** It is the latest time by which an activity must be completed to ensure the completion of project within the stipulated time, that is,

$$LFT = LET_j$$

**Float** The difference between the latest start time (LST and the earliest start time (EST) of an activity is called variously as *float, total float* or *activity slack*. Float is a measure of the amount of time by which the start of an activity can be delayed consistent with the completion of the project on time. Mathematically, the float is represented as:

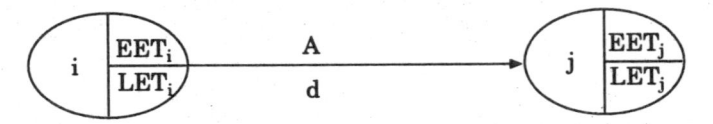

$$\text{Float} = LST - EST = LET_j - d - EET_i$$

For example, for an activity 'C', the float would be:

Float = LST − EST
     = LET 3 − d − EETo
     = 4 − 2 − 0 = 2

Chapter 6 deals with the various types of floats and their applications.

**Critical activities** The activities (including dummy ones) having a zero float are called *critical activities*. For example, in Network drawn in Fig. 4.11 the activities B, C, D and E are critical activities as their float is zero. The activity A connects two critical events, 0 and 2, but it is not a critical activity as its float is 1. All critical activities must join two critical events, but all activities joining two critical events are not necessarily critical themselves.

For easy identification, the critical activities are shown by any or a combination of the following:

(i) Two small vertical lines in the middle of an arrow
(ii) A thick line;

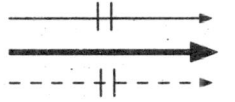

In the network shown in Fig. 4.11, B, G, D, and E are critical activities and the sum of duration along the critical path is 7 time units. (i.e $3 + 0 + 1 + 3 = 7$)

Figure 4.11

**Network Showing Critical Activities**

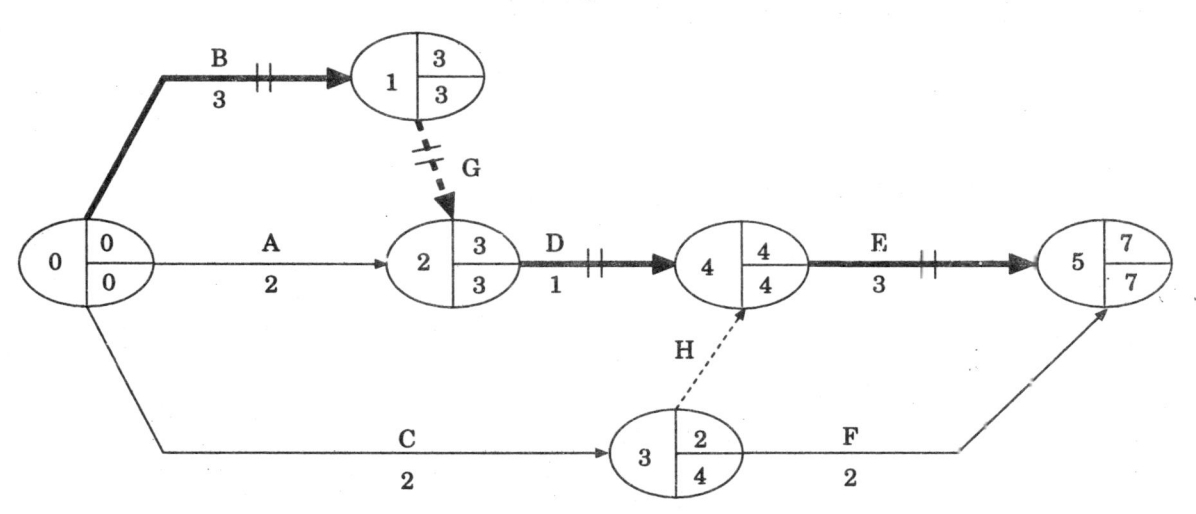

The term *zero float* implies that the activity must commence and terminate at the specified time. Any delay in the start and completion time of a critical activity will increase the duration of the project by that much time.

## 4.1.6 Network Critical Path

The path of critical activities (including dummy activities) which links the start and end events is called *critical path*. In other words, it is the path of activities having zero float and events having zero slack. The sum of the duration of the critical activities along a critical path gives the duration of the project.

The various stages involved in the computation of critical path are discussed below. These are illustrated with the network given in Fig. 4.7(b).

**Determining earliest event times (EET)** The EET of the start event is set as zero time. Then, moving in the forward direction, the succeeding events are selected one by one in the ascending order of their event number code. The EETs are processed systematically. If there is more than one path converging into an event, its EET is the value obtained along the longest path. Further, during analysis, the earliest event timings can be mentally worked out and written directly on the network, as shown in Fig. 4.12.

### Figure 4.12
**Network Showing Earliest Event Times (EET)**

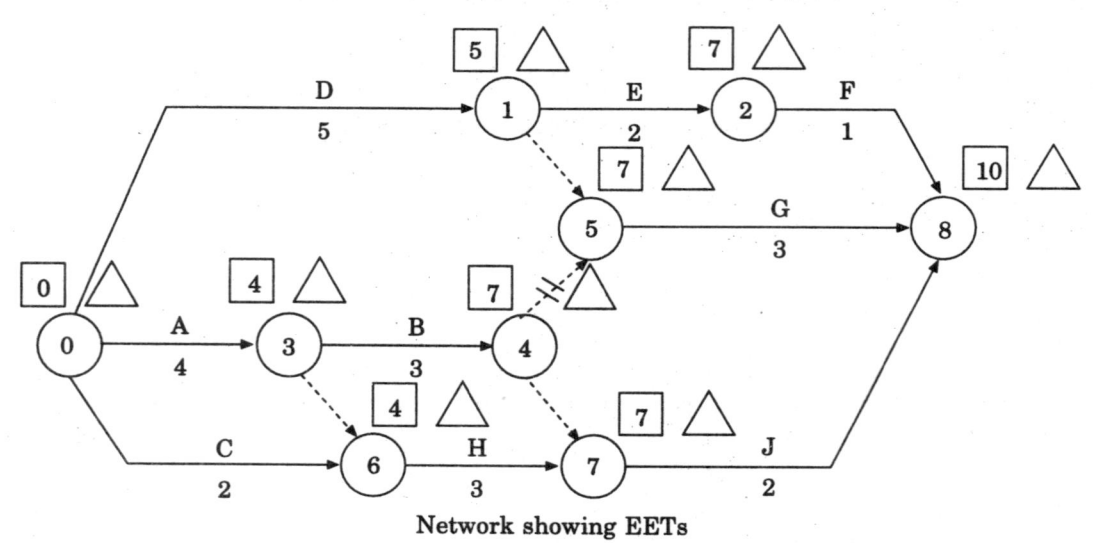

Network showing EETs

*Note*: The minimum project duration is equal to the EET of the end event.

**Calculating latest event times (LET)** If the project is to be completed on schedule, the LET of the end event must be taken equal to the laid down completion time. Generally, in the initial stages the project completion time constraints are not considered and the LET of the end event is taken equal to the minimum project duration indicated by the EET of the end event. The LET of the remaining events are calculated by reversing the method followed for determination of the EET. In practice, the LETs are directly worked out on the network, as shown in Fig. 4.13.

Figure 4.13

**Network Depicting Latest Event Times (LET)**

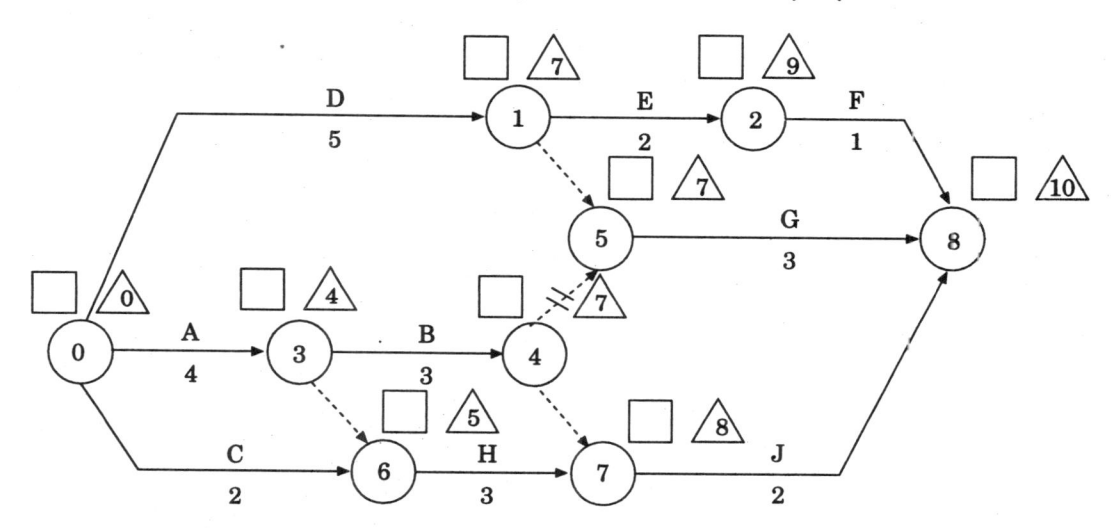

**Isolating critical events** The slack of an event is equal to the difference between its LET and EET. The events having zero slack are termed *critical events*. After the LETs and EETs of all the events on the network have been worked out, the critical events having zero slack can be spotted visually. In the network shown in Fig. 4.14, the critical events are 0, 3, 4, 5 and 8.

**Identifying critical activities** The critical activities are always joined by critical events, but an activity joining two critical events may not necessarily be a critical activity. It is therefore essential that floats of all activities (including dummies) linking critical events be worked out and activities having zero floats identified.

$$\text{Float} = \text{LET}_j - d - \text{LET}_i$$

After identification, the critical activities should be marked on the network using the conventional symbol. (Fig. 4.14).

## 4.1.7 Significance of Critical Path

(a) It is the longest path in the network. However, it is possible for a network to have more than one critical path. The sum of the durations of critical activities along the critical path determines the duration of the project.

**Figure 4.14**

**Network Showing Critical Path**

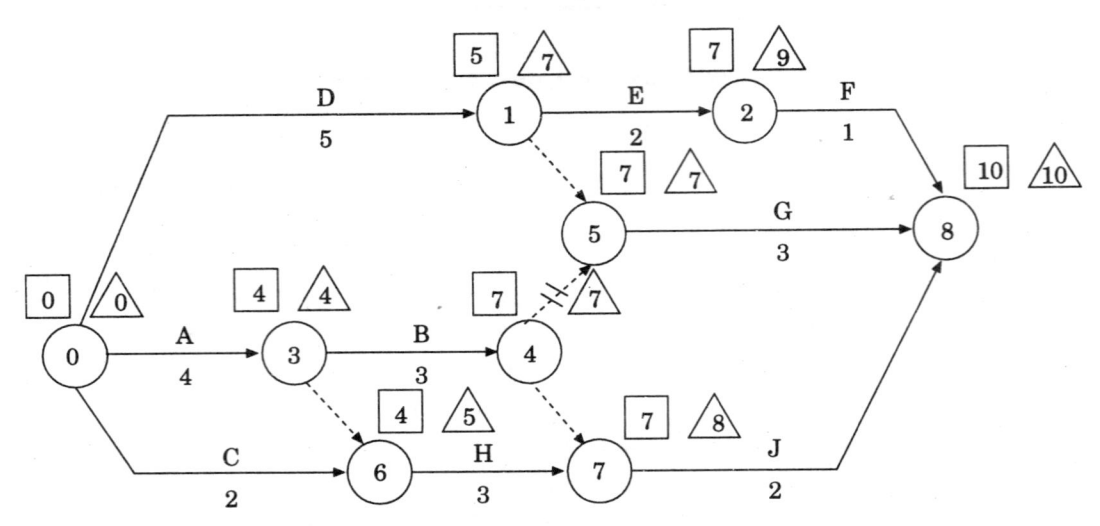

(b) It is the most sensitive path; any change in duration critical activities along the critical path is bound to affect the duration of the entire project.

(c) By isolating critical path, the project management can exercise 'management by exception', thereby focusing its attention on the critical activities.

## 4.2 CPM NETWORK MODELLING AND ANALYSIS PROCEDURE

An experienced planner can develop the CPM sub network of a sub-project or a task, working straight from its work-breakdown structure or task matrix. However, for a beginner, a step-wise approach can systematize modelling and time analysis of network. This step-by-step procedure involves defining the scope of network, listing activities, developing logic diagram, structuring network, incorporating activity durations, numbering events and computing the critical path.

The network analysis procedure is illustrated with the help of a simple pumping station sub-project, discussed in Chapter 3. The scope of work of this sub-project included construction of a pumping-station building, procurement and installation of the pumping sets, erection of gantry crane and commissioning of the installation. The contract for the sub-project has been finalized and the network is to be drawn for controlling the execution of the contracted works.

It is emphasized that the network should be drawn after the construction methodology is finalized. Accordingly, one should focus on the procedure of modelling and analysis of network illustrated in the following paragraphs, rather than debate the method of construction.

## 4.2.1 Defining the Scope of Network

From its conception to its evolution and completion, a project has innumerable activities associated with it, but it is not necessary to include all of them in the network.

For example, a network drawn for systematic execution of contracted work need not include the pre-contract planning and designing activities. The first step in network modelling, therefore, is to define the scope of the network by fixing start and end events, stating suitable assumptions and laying own constraints.

**(a) Start and end events** These define the extent of the network. The contract period of a contracted work commences from the time of handing over of site to the contractor; this can be taken as the start event. The clearance of site after completion of work is generally the last activity of a contract; its completion becomes the end event. For the major multi-project networks, there may be more than one start and end event.

**(b) Assumptions** These aim at reducing the size of the network by omitting unnecessary details. Suitable assumptions can also be made about the 'unpredictables'.

**(c) Constraints** These are the restrictions and limitations imposed by the management on the method of execution, such as priorities of the work and availability of resources.

Consider the example of pumping station sub-project. The scope of the network can be defined as follows:

1. *Extent of network*

    (i) *Start event*   Handing over the site to the contractor.
    (ii) *End event*   Clearance of site, after completion of the works.

2. *Main assumptions*   The contractor has ascertained the availability and delivery period of the specified pumps, gantry crane and fittings prior to tendering. But, he shall be placing the supply order for these after the award of the contract.

3. *Constraints*

    (i) The work on concreting of foundation for pumping sets must not commence before the procurement of the equipment. This is to ensure that foundation bolts and other inserts are correctly embedded.
    (ii) The gantry crane must be erected prior to the installation of pumping sets, and roofing of the building.
    (iii) The flooring work must not commence prior to the installation of the pumping sets.

## 4.2.2 Determining Activities

The various stages in the execution of a project can easily be visualised by breaking down the work into major tasks or work packages. Each one of these can further be split into sub tasks, and these sub-tasks can be further sub-divided; this process continues till the desired level of activities is reached. The technique of breaking down the project into its component activities has already been described in Chapter 3. The activities derived for the pumping station sub-project are given in Exhibit 4.2

### Exhibit 4.2

### Activities of Pumping Station Project

| | | |
|---|---|---|
| **Work Package No. 1** | | **– Building Structure** |
| | A | – Excavation |
| | B | – Foundation walls |
| | C | – Wall upto sill |
| | D | – Wall upto lintel |
| | E | – Wall upto tie-band |
| | F | – Tie-band |
| | G | – Gable end |
| | H | – Roofing |
| **Work Package No. 2** | | **– Procurement of Equipment** |
| | J | – Procurement of crane gantry |
| | K | – Procurement of pumping sets |
| | L | – Procurement of suction/delivery pipes |
| **Work Package No. 3** | | **– Installation and Commissioning of Pumping Sets** |
| | M | – Erection of gantry |
| | N | – Foundation of pumps |
| | O | – Installation of pumping set |
| | P | – Fixing of suction and delivery pipes |
| | Q | – Commissioning of pumping sets |
| **Work Package No. 4** | | **– Finishes and Essential Services** |
| | R | – Laying floor |
| | S | – Internal plaster |
| | T | – External plaster |
| | U | – Painting and finishes |
| | V | – Electrification |
| | W | – Plumbing and sanitary fittings |
| | X | – Site clearance |

## 4.2.3 Establishing Work-package Logic

The logic of activities within the work package can easily be established by the following questions relating to each activity.
  (a) Which activity/ies precede this activity?
  (b) Which activity/ies succeed or follow the completion of this activity?
  (c) Are there any constraints imposed on starting of this activity?

(d) Is it the final activity within the work package? If so, are there any other activity/ies from other work package(s) that precede or succeed this activity.

The above questioning technique enables determination of the logic showing preceding and succeeding activities of each activity. The activity logic thus obtained can be compiled in the form of an activity-dependence table.

To quote an example, activity-dependence table of Pumping Station Project is given in Table 4.2.

### Table 4.2

**Pumping Station Project Activity Dependence Table**

| Activity Code | Activity Description | Activity Duration | Preceding Activity(s) | Succeeding Activity(s) |
|---|---|---|---|---|
| **Work-package No. 1 – Building Structure** | | | | |
| A | – Excavation | 2 | – | B |
| B | – Foundation walls | 3 | A | C |
| C | – Wall upto sill | 2 | B | D |
| D | – Wall upto lintel | 4 | C | E |
| E | – Wall upto tie-band/roof | 2 | D | F |
| F | – Tie-band | 4 | E | G |
| G | – Gable end | 1 | F | H |
| H | – Roofing | 5 | G | M.S.T |
| **Work-package No. 2 – Procurement of Equipment** | | | | |
| J | – Procurement of crane gantry | 16 | – | M |
| K | – Procurement of pumping sets | 20 | – | N |
| L | – Procurement of suction/delivery pipes | 10 | – | P |
| **Work-package No. 3 – Installation and Commissioning of pumping sets** | | | | |
| M | – Erection of gantry | 2 | H, J | O |
| N | – Foundation of pumps | 3 | K | O |
| O | – Installation of pumping set | 1 | M, N | P |
| P | – Fixing of suction and delivery pipes | 2 | O, L | Q |
| Q | – Commissioning of pumping sets | 2 | P, V | R |
| **Work-package No. 4 – Finishes and Essential Services** | | | | |
| R | – Laying floor | 4 | Q, W | U, X |
| S | – Internal plaster | 4 | H | V, W |
| T | – External plaster | 2 | H | U, X |
| U | – Painting and finishes | 4 | T, R | – |
| V | – Electrification | 4 | S | Q |
| W | – Plumbing and sanitary fitting | 2 | S | R |
| X | – Site clearance | 2 | R, T | – |

At times, in the initial stages, the preceding and succeeding activities connecting the work packages are difficult to determine, but they become apparent during integration.

## 4.2.4 Developing Network Logic Diagram

The preparation of logic diagram can be divided into three stages: (i) developing logic diagram for each work package, (ii) integrating work packages, and (iii) transforming integrated work package logic diagrams into a project logic diagram. In practice, work-packages are considered in the sequence they occur. Further the drawing of work-package logic diagrams and the process of integration can be carried out simultaneously.

**Developing work-package logic diagram** The activity-dependence table provides the necessary data for developing the work-package logic arrow diagram.

Logic diagrams can be developed for each work-package. These diagrams based on the logic, given in the activity-dependence table for each work package of the pumping station sub-project are shown in Fig. 4.15

**Integration of work-package logic diagrams** The term *integration* implies the connecting of logic diagrams of the work packages into a single-project logic diagram.

Prior to the commencement of integration, it is essential that, as far as possible, the paper on which the project logic diagram is to be drawn is divided into various strata. The term *stratification* means a division of the diagram in such a way that activities pertaining to the same department, contract, site, location or method of construction can be suitably grouped by drawing horizontal and/or vertical imaginary lines. Generally, the integration link can be visualized from the work-breakdown structure.

The process of integration of work-package logic diagram is commenced from the beginning of the project, and work packages falling in the same strata are connected in the sequence of their occurrence. While integrating, the sequence of activities terminating into and emerging out and the connecting key events must be verified by questioning each about its preceding and succeeding activity.

Broadly, the integration of the work packages of the pumping station sub-project can be divided into two strata, namely, civil works and mechanical works. The key events can be positioned as shown in Fig. 4.16.

While integrating the work-package diagrams, the logic of all the activities should be re-examined to find their interdependence. This interdependence can initially be correlated with dummy activities. In some cases, the activities may have to be re-drawn to conform to a given logic.

The sub-project logic diagram, derived after integrating the work-package logic diagrams of civil and mechanical works of the pumping station sub-project, is shown in Fig. 4.17. The main points to be noted are as follows:

(a) The start event is common to both civil and mechanical works logic diagram.
(b) The erection of gantry is to start with completion of roofing. A dummy activity has been interposed to maintain this logic.
(c) The commissioning of pumping set can commence after the electric lines have been laid inside the building. This is shown by a dummy activity.
(d) It is desirable to complete the plumbing and sanitary works and commission the pumping set prior to the laying of floor, so as to avoid breaking floor surface in case of defects. A dummy, connecting circle 3 and 4, has been used to show this logic.

## Figure 4.15
## Pumping Station Project
## Work Package Sub-Network

1. *Building structure sub network.*

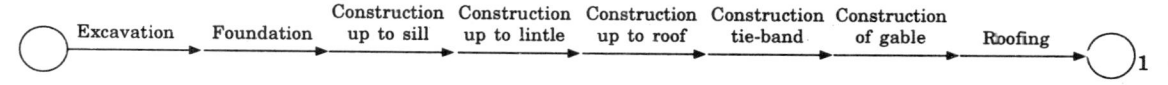

○ →Excavation→ Foundation→ Construction up to sill→ Construction up to lintle→ Construction up to roof→ Construction tie-band→ Construction of gable→ Roofing→ ○1

*Note*: Start event is circled and numbered zero; last circle is labelled 1.

2. *Equipment procurement sub network.*

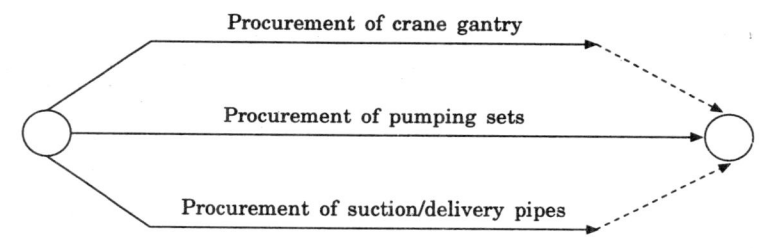

○ → Procurement of crane gantry → ○
○ → Procurement of pumping sets → ○
○ → Procurement of suction/delivery pipes → ○

3. *Building finishes sub network.*

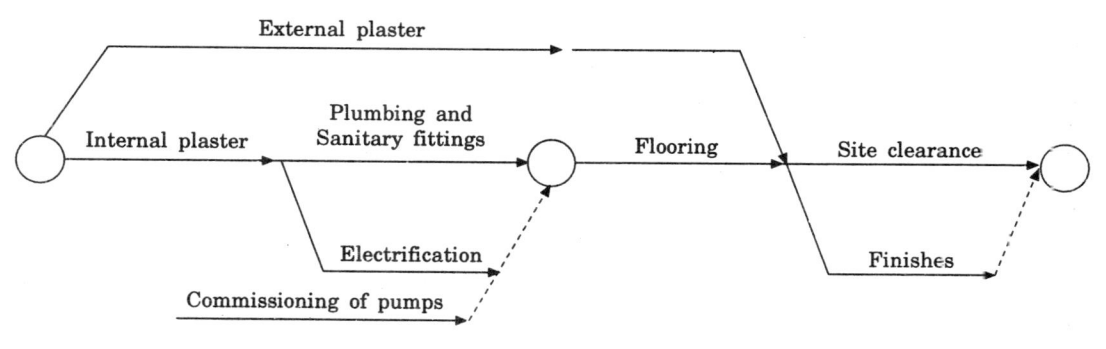

- External plaster
- Internal plaster
- Plumbing and Sanitary fittings
- Flooring
- Site clearance
- Electrification
- Commissioning of pumps
- Finishes

*Note*: All the above activities can be commenced from the start event and they can run concurrently.

4. *Equipment installation and commissioning sub network.*

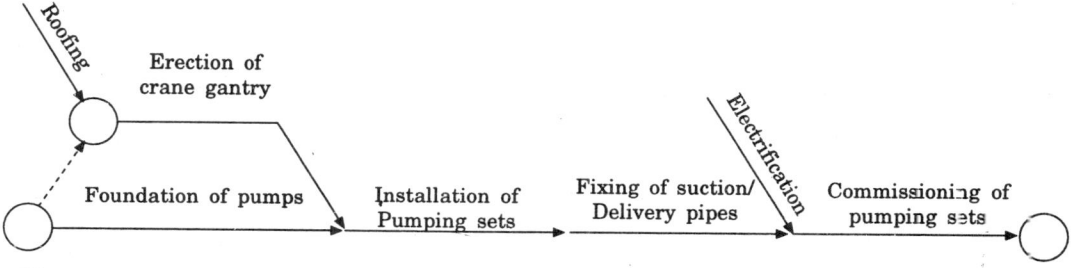

Roofing ↓ → Erection of crane gantry → Foundation of pumps → Installation of Pumping sets → Fixing of suction/Delivery pipes → (Electrification ↘) Commissioning of pumping sets → ○

*Note* The activities linking other work packages.

**126** Construction Project Management

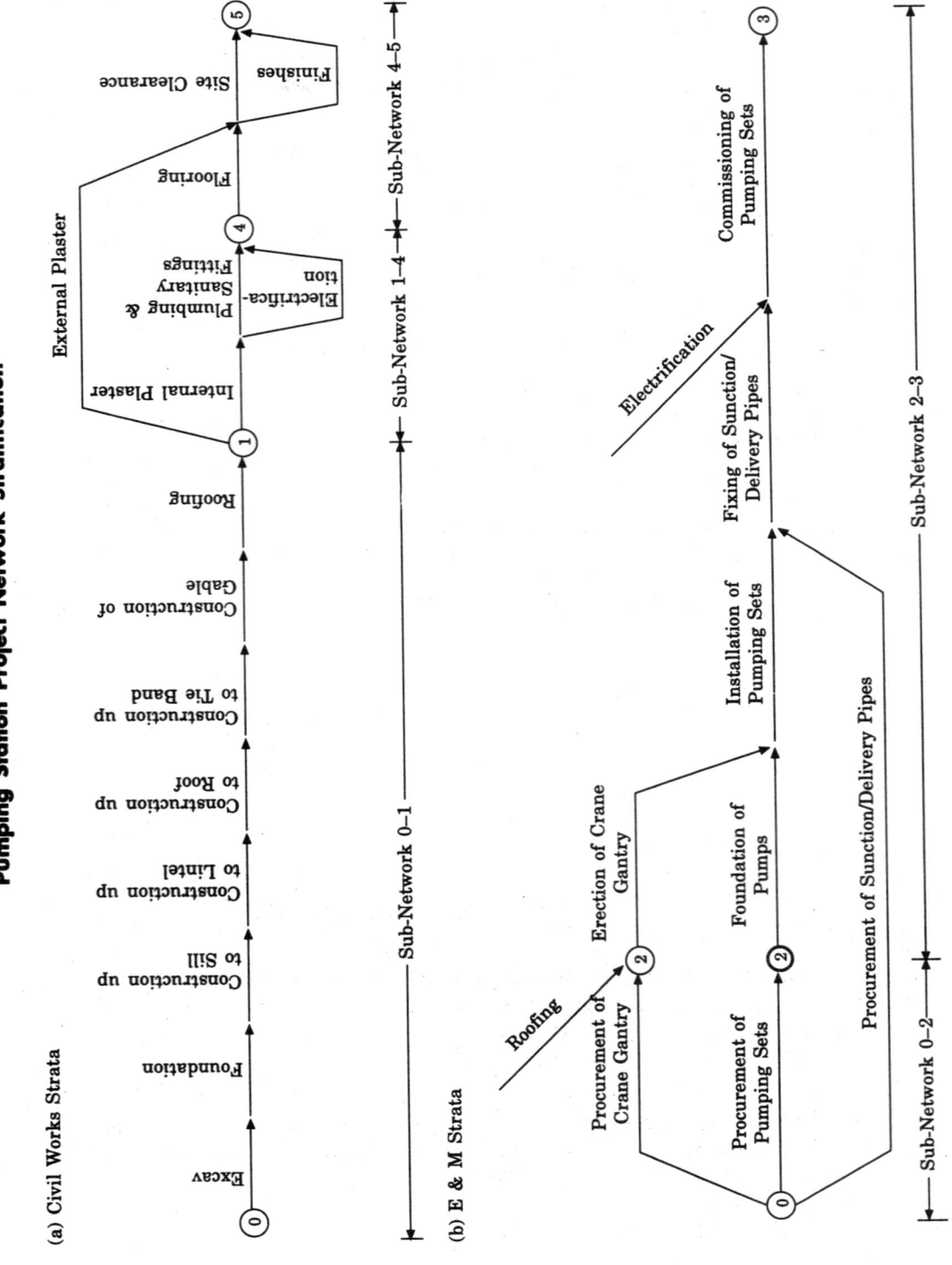

### Figure 4.16
### Pumping Station Project Network Stratification

(a) Civil Works Strata

(b) E & M Strata

Project CPM/PERT Network Analysis **127**

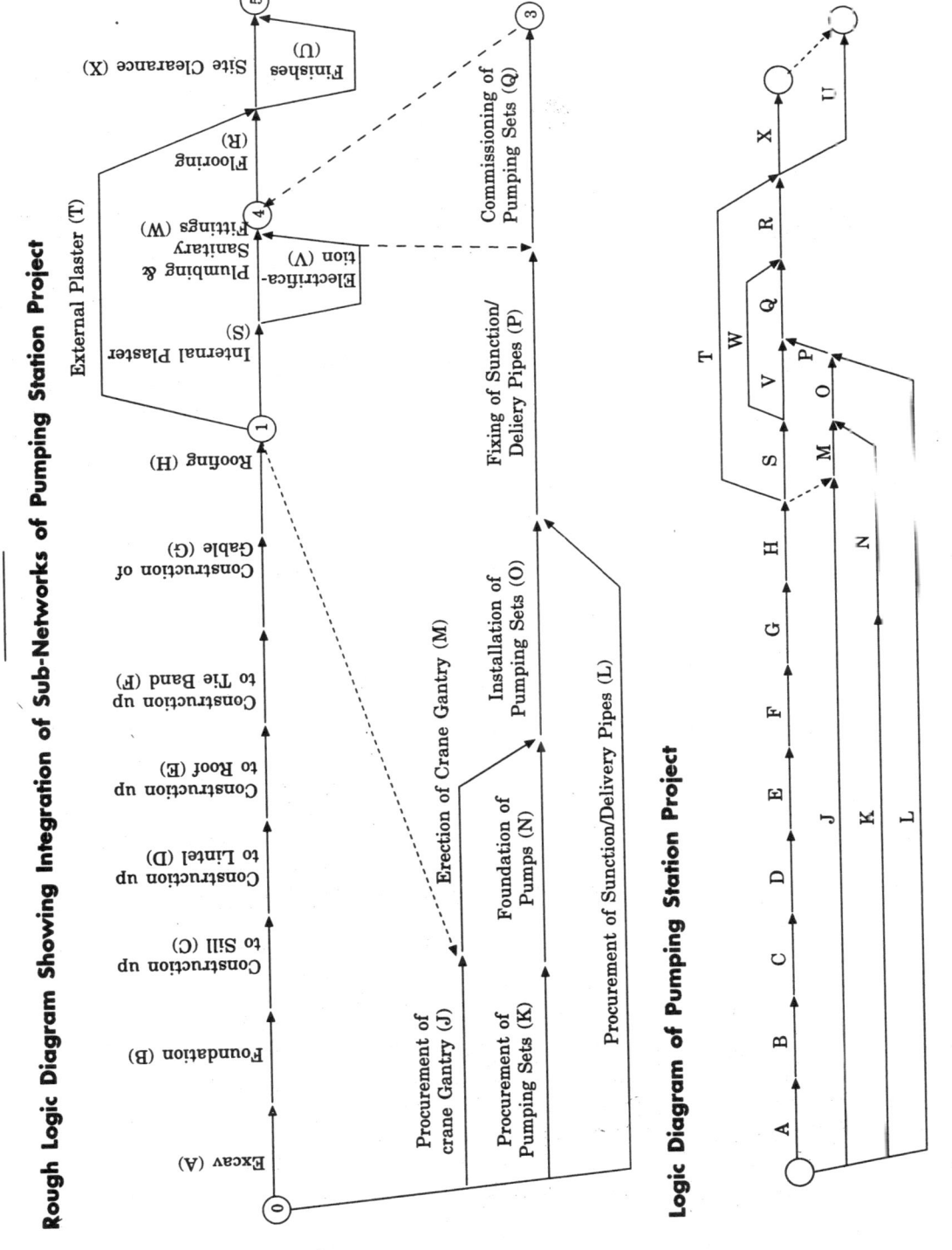

#### Figure 4.17

**Rough Logic Diagram Showing Integration of Sub-Networks of Pumping Station Project**

**Logic Diagram of Pumping Station Project**

## 4.2.5 Preparation of Logic Diagram and Draft Network

The main purpose of the flow diagram is to facilitate a systematic drawing of the draft of network. The guidelines for converting the logic diagrams into draft network are:

(a) The dummies should be reduced to minimum.
(b) The crossing of arrows should be avoided by a suitable re-positioning of the activities.
(c) The new activities should be incorporated, if visualized during the preparation of logic diagrams.
(d) Logic of all the activities should be verified for its correctness.

The Fig. 4.18 also shows the draft network diagram of the pumping station sub-project.

## 4.2.6 Structuring Model Using Network Drawing Rules

The project networks are constantly read, referred to and reviewed. Therefore, it is essential that they should be suitably titled and numbered, neatly drawn by readable lettering printed horizontally, and divided into strata for easy reference.

The various conventions and rules for drawing CPM network are given below. The master network of pumping station project is shown in Exhibit 4.1, while the cantonment construction project is given in Exhibit 3.11.

(a) All arrows must run from left to right. Turning arrows in the reverse direction is not correct.
(b) The arrows should have sufficient horizontal length so that a description could be written over it.
(c) The crossing of arrows should be avoided by suitably re-positioning them.
(d) Arrows running close to each other should be avoided. The intervening space should be sufficient to permit writing of activity description.
(e) The concurrent activities (commencing and terminating into common events) should be separated by inserting additional events followed by dummy activities.
(f) The activities emerging from an event should takeoff from a line rather than a point. Similarly, activities terminating into an event should finish into a common line.
(g) Wherever possible, the network should be drawn in such a way that activities belonging to the same strata can be demarcated by drawing vertical and/or horizontal lines.
(h) Use of large sheets should be avoided. If required, a large network can be split into two or more sheets having common interface events. For easy recognition, the interface events can be represented by double circle or ellipse.
(i) The network should be re-drawn, if necessary, to give a neat appearance.
(j) Prints of important networks should be taken and circulated to all concerned for comments. Amendments should be carried out, if necessary.

Figure 4.18

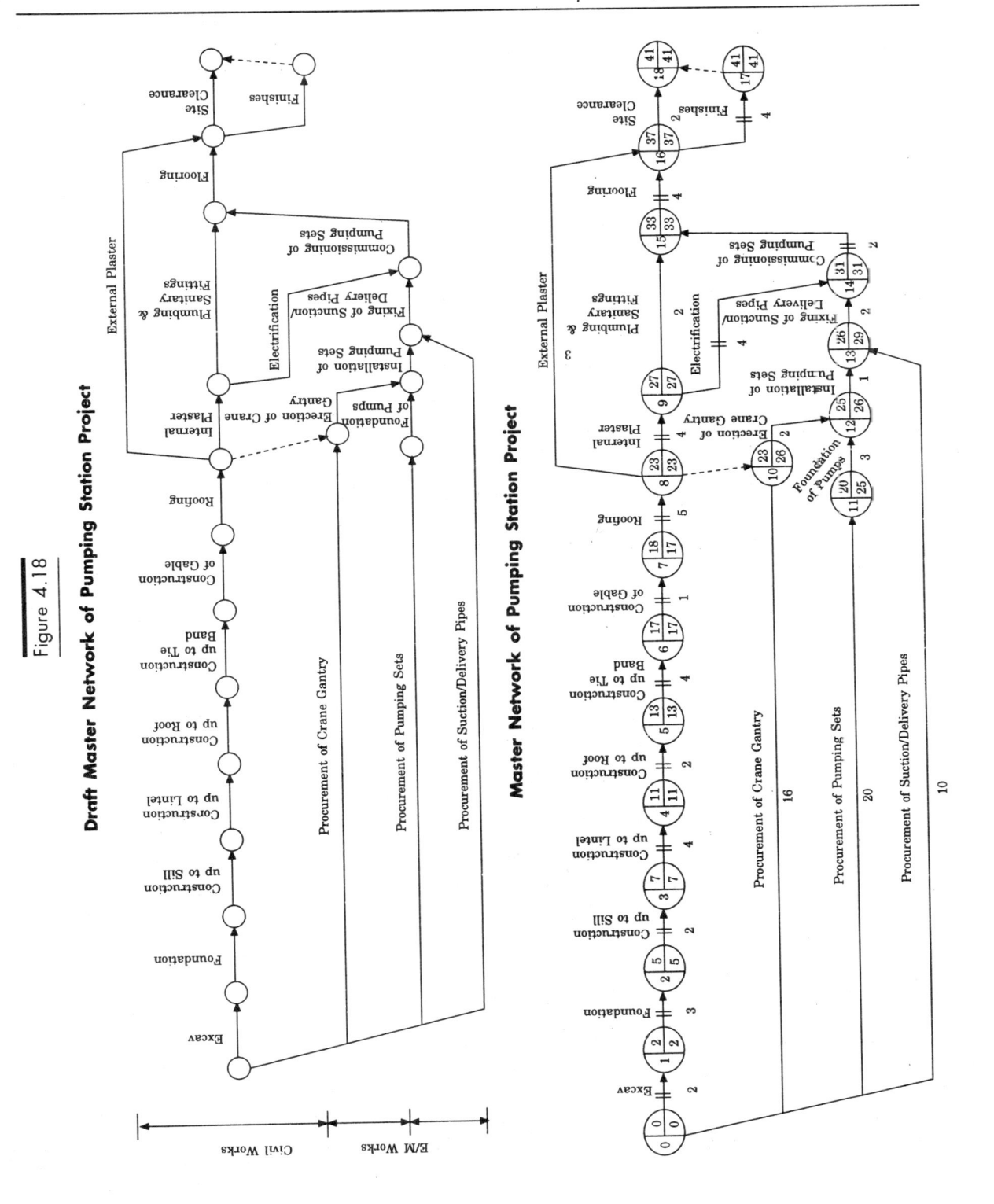

**Draft Master Network of Pumping Station Project**

**Master Network of Pumping Station Project**

### 4.2.7 Incorporating Activity Duration

The duration of activities are estimated while breaking down the project into activities. Further, some new activities may also get added during the preparation of network. Therefore, after drawing the network, the duration of all the activities should be re-checked and necessary corrections made.

### 4.2.8 Numbering of Events

It is the last operation in the modelling of the network. Using the procedure for numbering events described earlier, the events for the pumping station sub-project can be numbered as shown in Fig. 4.19.

### 4.2.9 Time Analysing Network

The focus of time analysis of a CPM network is to calculate float for each activity by conducting forward pass and backward pass with a view to determine critical path. The critical-path computation procedure involves determination of the Earliest Event Times (foreward pass), calculation of the Latest Event Times, identification of the critical events and critical activities, (having zero float) and, finally, evaluation of the project duration by summing up the duration of critical activities along the critical path connecting the start and the end events. This computation process can be carried out directly on the network, as illustrated for the pumping station sub-project in Fig. 4.19.

## ❏ 4.3 PERT NETWORK ANALYSIS

The Programme Evaluation and Review Technique (PERT) is employed for planning and controlling the projects involving uncertainties.

PERT is an event-oriented technique. Its basis is a network of events in which the activities are derived by connecting the events. It lays stress on measuring the uncertainty in activity times by using the three-times duration estimation method. For computation of critical path, the PERT three-times probabilistic network is converted into a single-time deterministic CPM Model. PERT studies the implications of uncertainties on project time scheduling and slack of events by employing statistical tools.

### 4.3.1 Modelling PERT Network

Two special features of PERT distinguish it from the other network analysis techniques. These are—emphasis upon events rather than activities; and the use of three-times estimate for activity duration. Exhibit 4.3 illustrates the PERT network of pumping station sub-project.

The PERT network-making approach is to identify the milestones necessary for successful completion of the project. These milestones are then depicted in the from of a key-events

Project CPM/PERT Network Analysis **131**

## Figure 4.19 (a)
## Pumping Station Project Network Critical Path Calculation

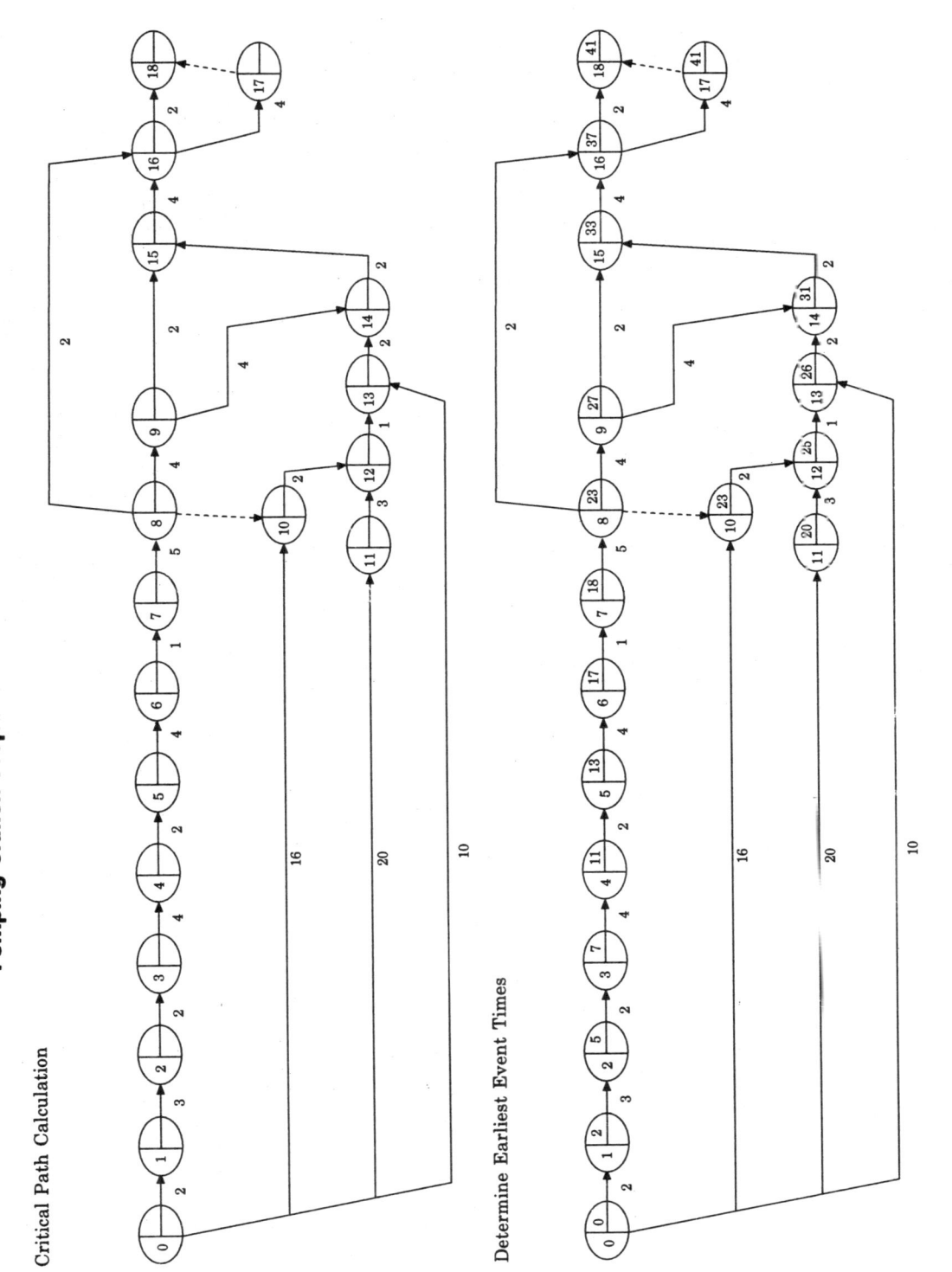

Critical Path Calculation

Determine Earliest Event Times

**132** Construction Project Management

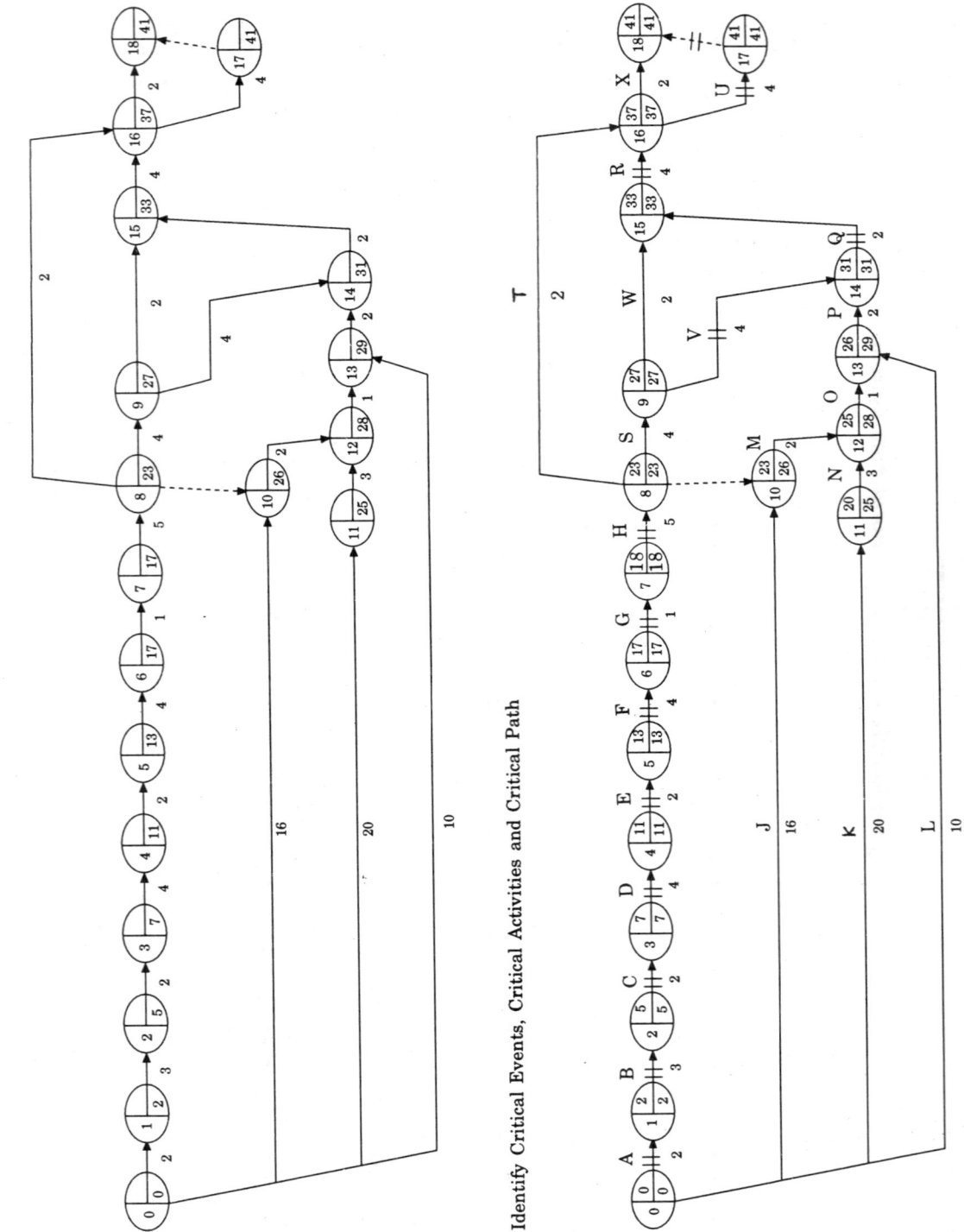

Calculate Latest Event Times

Identify Critical Events, Critical Activities and Critical Path

Project CPM/PERT Network Analysis 133

Exhibit 4.3
## PERT Network of Pumping Station Project

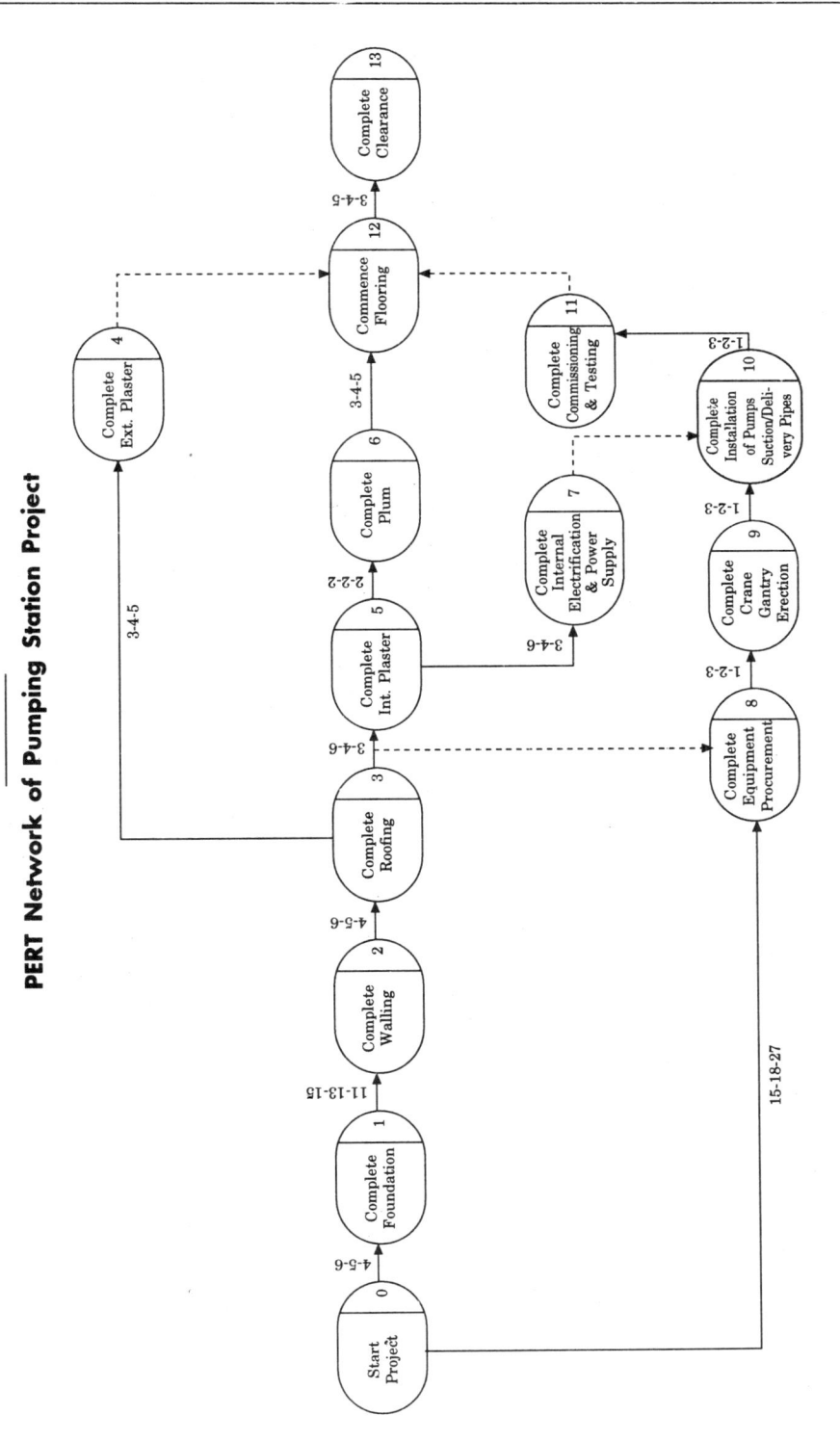

network showing their sequence and interdependence. After this, the events visualized between the milestones are added and their interelationship established. These event nodes represent points in time which are generaly terminal in nature. The activities are derived by interconnecting the events. The event diagram thus obtained is converted into event-oriented PERT network using the network drawing rules.

The steps involved in this technique are:—

(a) Identification of key events or milestones which must occur during the project execution.
(b) Determination of the sequence and interdependence of the key events.
(c) Incorporation of events (or activities) between the milestones, generally conforming to their sequence of occurrence.
(d) Connection of events, maintaining their interdependence.

This gives the project flow diagram from which the network can be drawn directly using the network drawing rules.

It may be noted that while determining the three-time estimate, the optimistic and pessimistic times should be assessed first. These two extremes bracket the most likely time, thus helping the planners to concentrate within this range. There is also a tendency of planners to either use the same figure for all the three times (say, 9, 9 and 9), or arrive at the most likely time first and then arrive at the optimistic and pessimistic time by subtracting and adding an equal amount (say, 6, 9 and 12). These trends should be avoided because such estimates are likely to be conservative.

### 4.3.2 Computing Critical Path

The first step in computing the critical path in PERT network is to reduce the three-time activity durations estimate into single expected time estimate. The rest of the procedure for computing critical path of PERT network is exactly the same as of the CPM network. The steps involved in computing critical path are as follows:

**(a) Estimate the expected activity duration**   It is given by the following formula:

$$T_e = \frac{T_0 + 4T_m + T_p}{6}$$

where, $T_e$ = Expected activity duration
$T_o$ = Optimistic time, assuming that everything goes extremely well with no delays
$T_p$ = Pessimistic time, assuming that everything occurs at its worst, with the exception being delays due to acts which cannot be foreseen.
$T_m$ = Most likely time, assuming the normal prevailing conditions.

As an example, consider PERT network outlined in Fig. 4.20.

Using the three-time activity duration estimation formula, the expected activity timings can be calculated as in Table 4.3.

**(b) Convert PERT network into deterministic model**   It is done by changing the three-time activity durations in PERT to the one-time expected estimates as shown in Fig. 4.21.

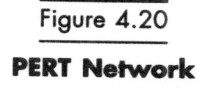

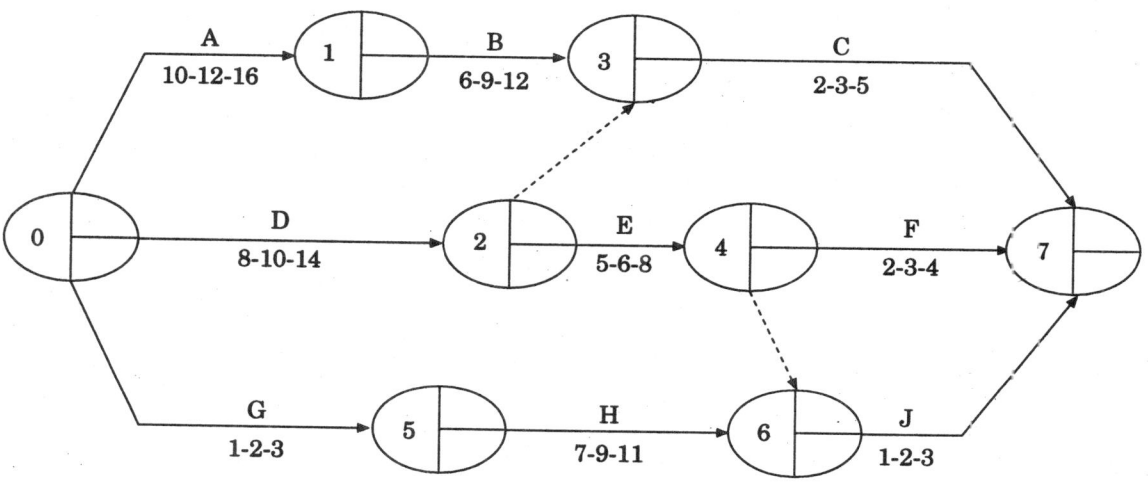

## Figure 4.20
### PERT Network

```
         A            B              C
     ──────→ ( 1 ) ──────→ ( 3 ) ──────→
    10-12-16      6-9-12         2-3-5   ╲
                          ↑               ╲
                          ┊                ╲
         D            E              F      
( 0 ) ──────→ ( 2 ) ──────→ ( 4 ) ──────→ ( 7 )
     8-10-14       5-6-8          2-3-4   ╱
                                  ┊      ╱
                                  ↓     ╱
         G            H              J
     ──────→ ( 5 ) ──────→ ( 6 ) ──────→
     1-2-3         7-9-11         1-2-3
```

### Table 4.3
### Table Showing Expected Activity Timings

| S. No. | Activity | $T_o$ | $T_m$ | $T_p$ | $T_e$ |
|---|---|---|---|---|---|
| 1. | A | 10 | 12 | 16 | 12.3 |
| 2. | B | 6 | 9 | 12 | 9.0 |
| 3. | C | 2 | 3 | 5 | 3.2 |
| 4. | D | 8 | 10 | 14 | 10.3 |
| 5. | E | 5 | 6 | 8 | 6.2 |
| 6. | F | 2 | 3 | 4 | 3.0 |
| 7. | G | 1 | 2 | 3 | 2.0 |
| 8. | H | 7 | 9 | 11 | 9.0 |
| 9. | J | 1 | 2 | 3 | 2.0 |

**(c) Determine critical path** It is obtained by analyzing the one-time deterministic model, as worked out in Fig. 4.22.

**(d) Transfer deterministic model into PERT network** This is achieved by replacing the one-time estimate with the three-time activity estimates, and marking the critical path, as shown in Fig. 4.23.

*Note*: If more than one critical path is discovered during the analysis, then the path having the maximum level of uncertainty is termed as the critical path. The method of measuring uncertainty is covered in the next section.

### Figure 4.21
**Converting PERT Network into Deterministic Model**

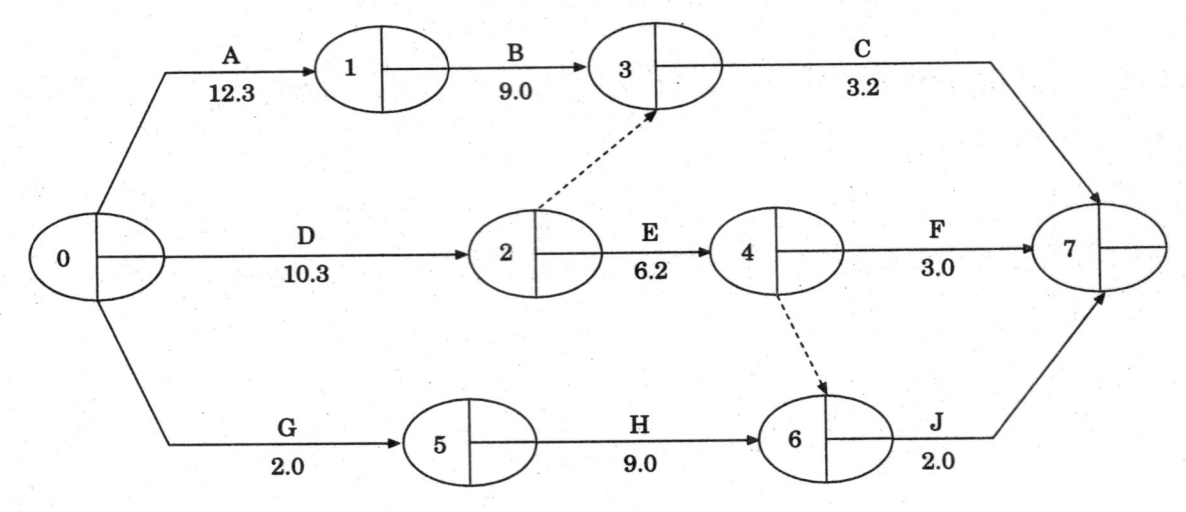

### Figure 4.22
**Determining Critical Path**

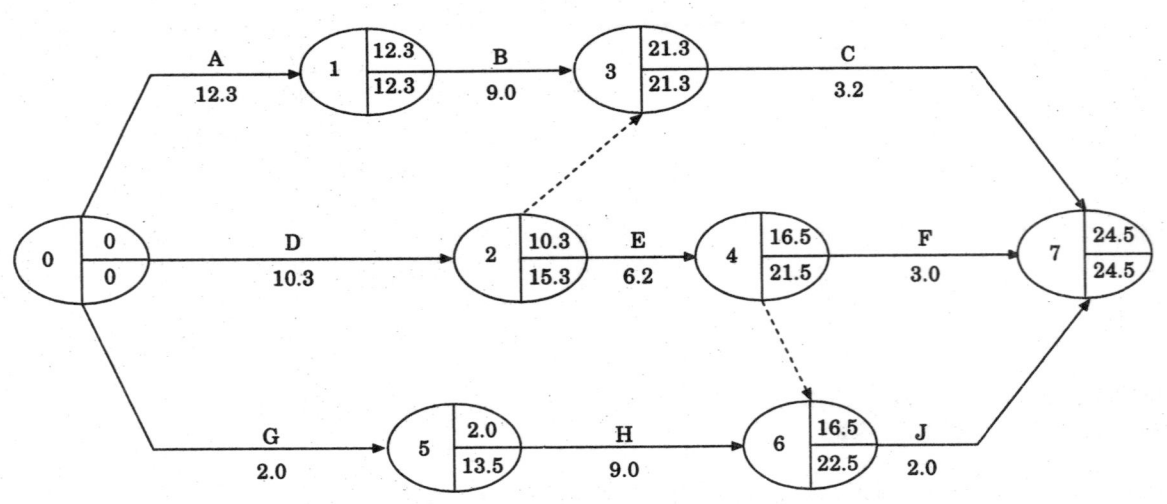

### 4.3.3 Uncertainty in Project Duration Estimation

The duration of an activity is defined as the expected economical transaction time. Its estimation is based on the current practices carried out in an organized manner under the normal prevailing conditions at the place of execution. Its assessment is done preferably, by the person responsible for its performance.

## Figure 4.23
### Transferring a Deterministic Model into PERT Network

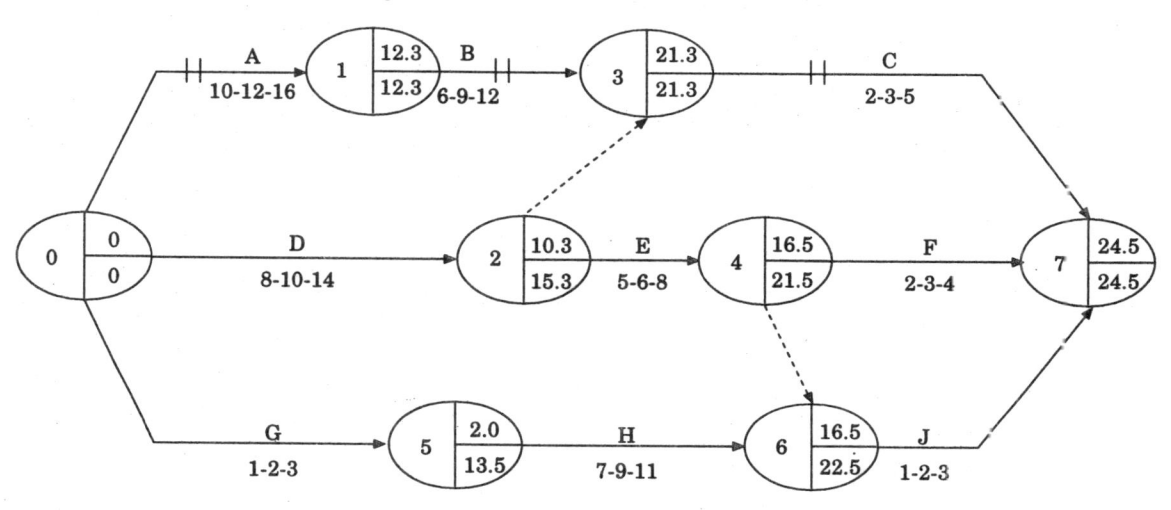

The duration estimation of an activity, however, cannot be taken as exact. It has fringes: it may be a bit this side or the other. These slight variations add to the uncertainty in the network. When they are considerably less, the one-time estimate is used for activity-duration estimation and determination of resources. To cater to the uncertainty prevalent in activity estimation, the PERT statisticians developed the three-time estimate, assuming that activity estimation trend follows the beta probability distribution. (See Fig. 4.24.)

To reduce the number of parameters in the beta distribution and to simplify calculations, it is assumed that:

(a) The expected activity duration corresponds to the 50% probability of performance. Its value is estimated from:

$$\text{Mean value} = \frac{a + 4m + b}{6} = T_e$$

(b) 'm' is taken as the most likely time, assessed by the planners.
(c) 'a' and 'b' are defined as the optimistic and pessimistic times which an activity takes for its performance.
(d) It is assumed that 'a' and 'b' are non-negative and:

$$a < m < b$$

(e) The beta curve is taken as unimodel and continuous.

(f) Standard deviation, which is a measure of uncertainity, is taken as $\left(\frac{b-a}{6}\right)$. The greater the spread $(b - a)$, the higher will be the value of standard deviation, and more will be the uncertainity.

**138** Construction Project Management

#### Figure 4.24
### Activity Distribution

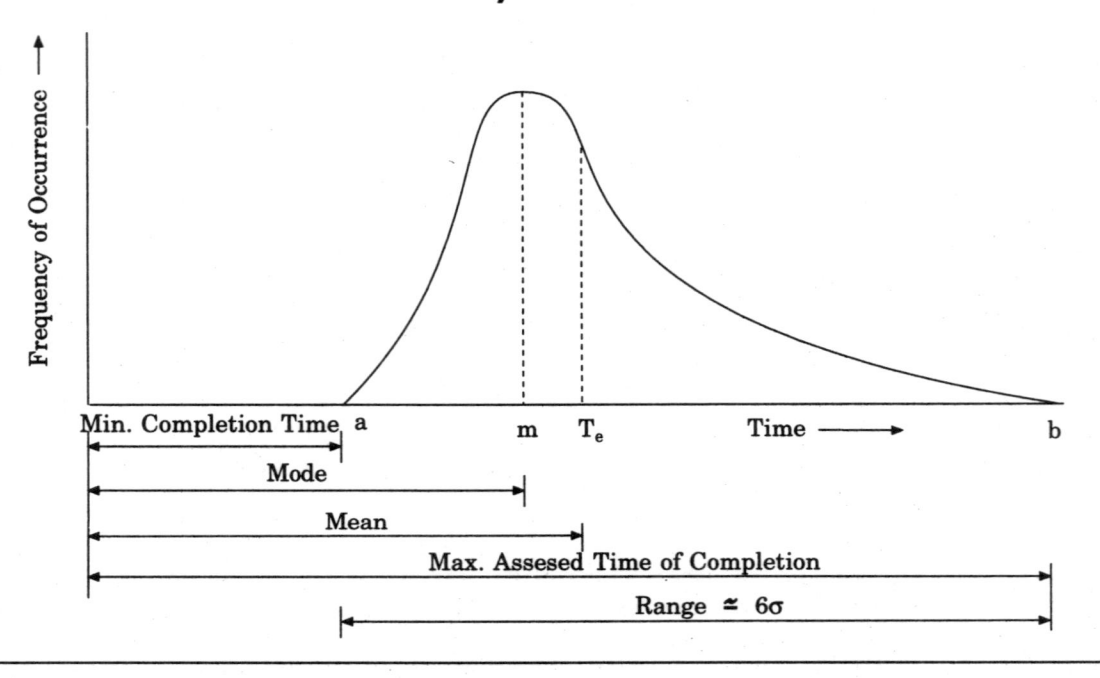

*[Graph showing frequency of occurrence vs time, with labels: Min. Completion Time a, Mode, Mean, m, $T_e$, Max. Assesed Time of Completion, b, Range ≈ 6σ]*

Consider $A$ and $B$ as two activities of a project.

| A | B |
|---|---|
| $T_o = 4$ | $T_o = 1$ |
| $T_m = 7$ | $T_m = 6$ |
| $T_p = 16$ | $T_p = 23$ |

For activity $A$:

$$T_e = \frac{T_0 + 4T_m + T_p}{6}$$

$$T_e(A) = \frac{4 + 4 \times 7 + 16}{6} = 8$$

For activity $B$:

$$T_e(B) = \frac{1 + 4 \times 6 + 23}{6} = 8$$

Standard deviation of Activity $A = \dfrac{16 - 4}{6} = 2$

Standard deviation of Activity $B = \dfrac{23 - 1}{6} = 3.67$

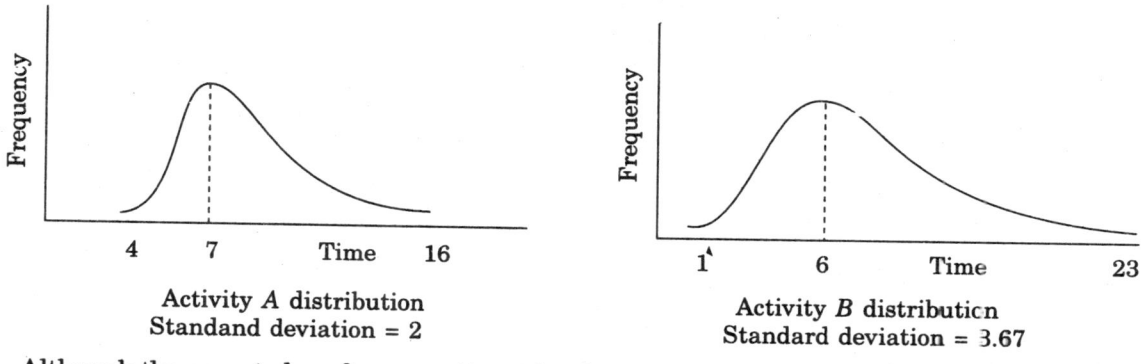

**Activity A distribution**
Standard deviation = 2

**Activity B distribution**
Standard deviation = 3.67

Although the expected performance time of activities A and B is eight, their range (difference between the highest an the lowest value, that is, $T_p - T_o$) differs. The greater the range, the higher is the value of standard deviation and higher is the uncertainty.

The duration of a project is computed by adding the duration of activities along a critical path. In order to evaluate uncertainty in project time, the originators of PERT assumed that the means of distribution of critical activities, lying on a critical path, follow the normal distribution, and thus the pattern of variation of project time approximates the normal distribution with the characteristics shown in Fig. 4.25.

## Figure 4.25
### Pattern of Variation of Project Time

Normal Distribution Curve

$$y^2 = \frac{1}{\sigma\sqrt{2\pi}} e^{-(x-x)^2/2\sigma^2}$$

where $x$ = Mean Time (expect time $t_2$
$\sigma$ = Standard deviation

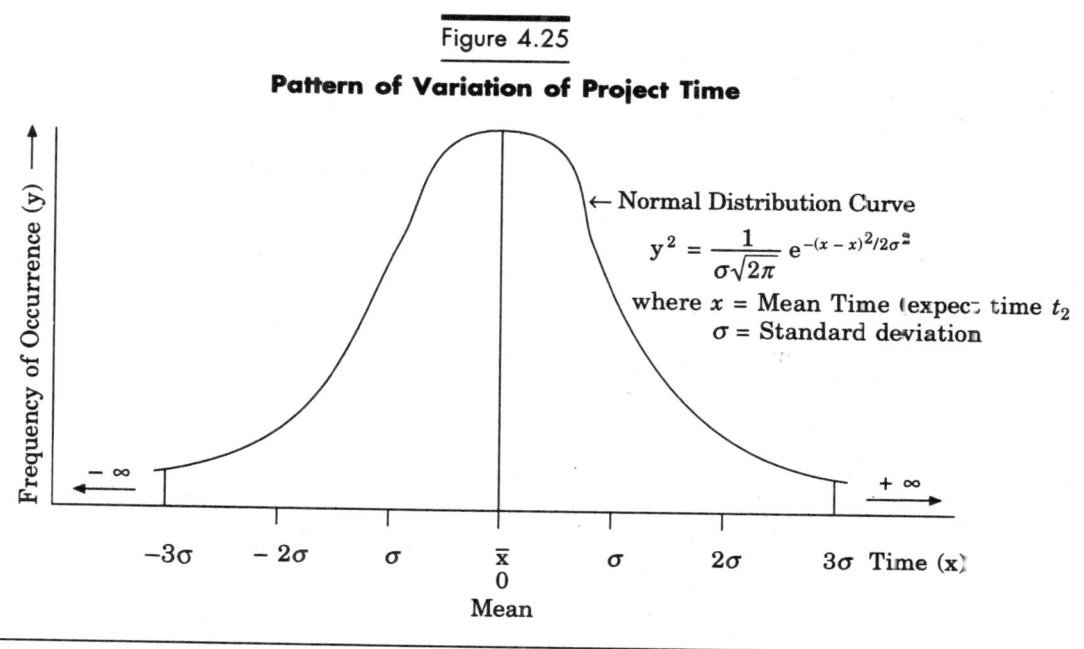

(a) Mean = Sum of the means of critical activities:

$\bar{x} = x_1 + x_2 + \ldots + x_n$

= Expected project duration corresponding to 50% probability.

= Mean of Normal Distribution

(b) Variance = Sum of variance of critical activities:
$$\bar{V} = V_1 + V_2 + \ldots + V_n$$
= Variance of Normal Distribution

(c) Standard deviation = $\sqrt{\text{variance}}$
$$\sigma = \sqrt{\bar{V}}$$
= Standard deviation of Normal Distribution

It may be noted that a normal distribution curve is fully defined and can be plotted when its mean and standard deviation are known.

To simplify calculations, the effect of variance of non-critical activities is not considered. Further, if there are more than one critical path, the path having the maximum variance is used for determining uncertainty.

Consider the case of the PERT network discussed in Fig. 4.26.

**Figure 4.26**

**Time Analysed PERT Network**

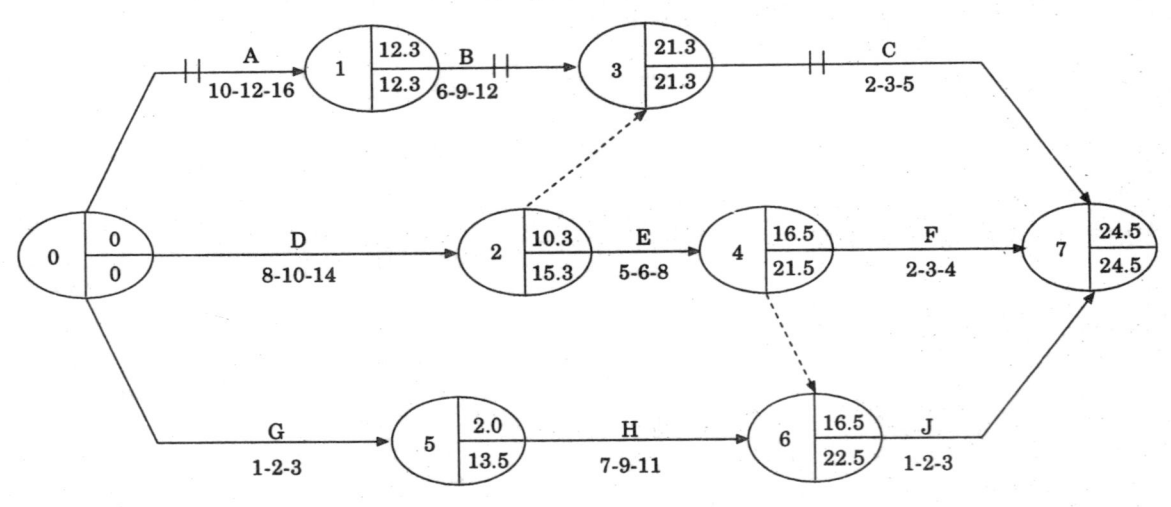

(a) *Expected project duration* It is given by adding the expected duration of critical activities.
Expected project duration:
$$= A + B + C = 12.3 + 9.0 + 3.2 = 24.5$$

(b) *Standard deviation* Variance is equal to the sum of variances of critical activities.
$$V = Va + Vb + Vc$$
$$= \left\{\frac{16-10}{6}\right\}^2 + \left\{\frac{12-6}{6}\right\}^2 + \left\{\frac{5-2}{6}\right\}^2$$
$$= 1.00 + 1.00 + 0.25 = 2.25$$

Therefore, project standard deviation is given by:

$$\sigma = \sqrt{V}$$
$$\sigma = \sqrt{2.25}$$
$$\sigma = 1.5$$

Hence, the normal probability distribution of this project has the following characteristics:

Means = Project duration corresponding to 50% probability
= 24.5

Standard deviation = 1.5

The graph of the distribution is shown in Fig. 4.27.

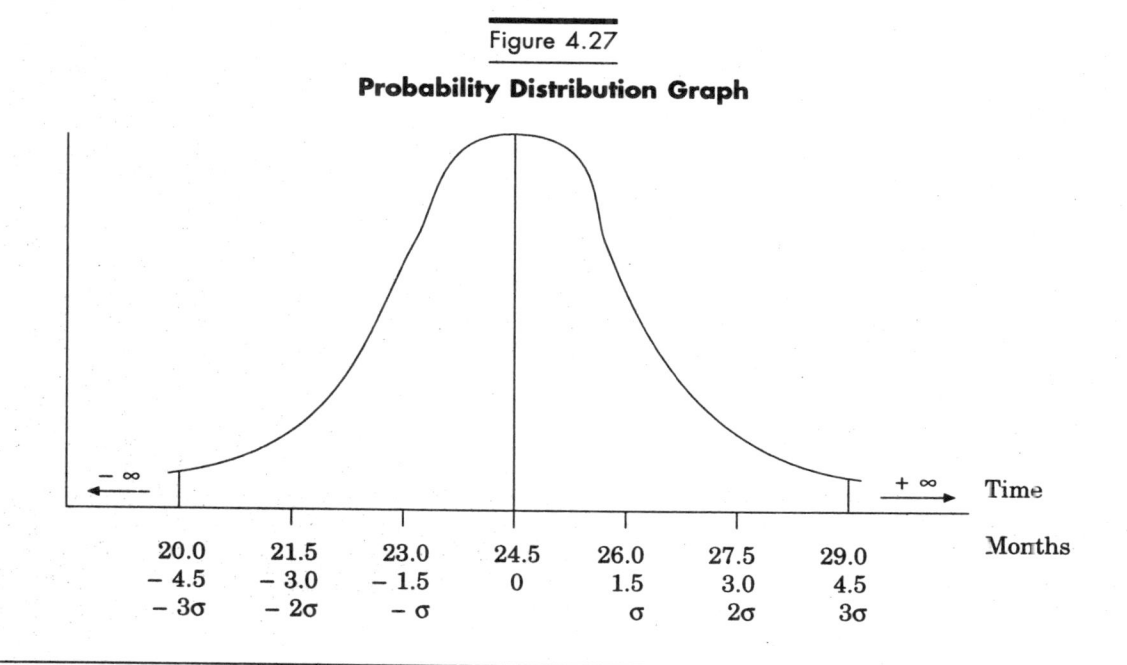

Figure 4.27

**Probability Distribution Graph**

| 20.0 | 21.5 | 23.0 | 24.5 | 26.0 | 27.5 | 29.0 | Months |
| – 4.5 | – 3.0 | – 1.5 | 0 | 1.5 | 3.0 | 4.5 | |
| – 3σ | – 2σ | – σ | | σ | 2σ | 3σ | |

**Network time scheduling** Unlike the network using the single-time estimate where the emphasis is on activities and their related cost (or resources), the network using the three-times estimate contains information that enables calculation of the probability of meeting a given schedule.

The chances of meeting a given project time schedule (say $x$) are equal to the area of the project probability distribution Fig. 4.28.

$$\text{Probability} = \text{Shaded area under the curve} \times 100.$$

### Figure 4.28
**Probability of Project Completion Time at x = Shaded Area of Curve**

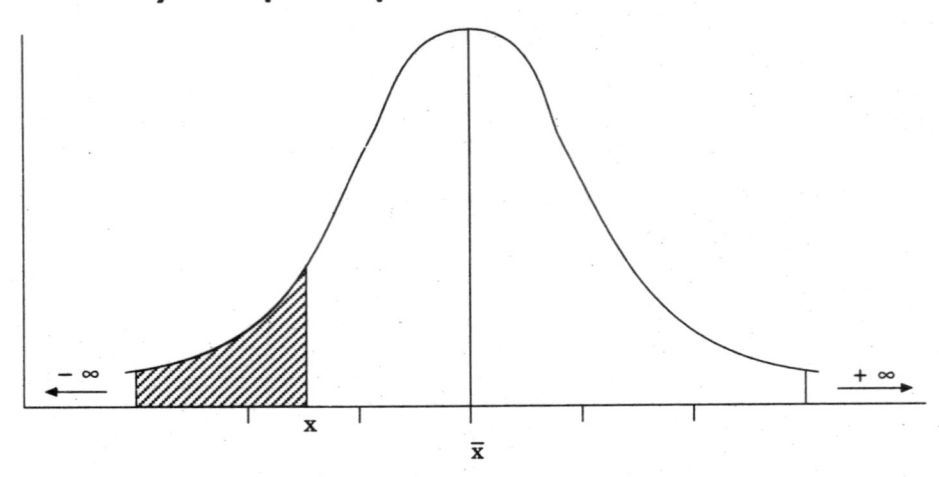

The shaded area of the normal distribution corresponding to the value 'x' (expressed in standard deviation units) can be directly read from the standard normal distribution table given in Table 4.4. The value of 'x' in standard deviation units can be worked out as:

$$x = \frac{\text{Scheduled date} - \text{Expected date}}{\text{Standard deviation}}$$

Q.1. Calculate the probability of completion in 23 months.

$$x = \frac{\text{Scheduled date} - \text{Expected date}}{\text{Standard deviation}} = \frac{23 - 24.5}{1.5} = -1$$

The normal distribution for the project is shown in Fig. 4.29, with the value of x marked on it.

The probability of project completion in 23 months is given by the area under the curve corresponding to $x = -1$. Referring to the table 4.4 the area under the curve at $x = -1$ gives this probability as 15.87%.

Q.2. Estimate project duration corresponding to 98.00% probability of completion.

$$x = \frac{\text{Scheduled date} - \text{Expected date}}{\text{Standard deviation}}$$

Scheduled date = Expected date + x . Standard deviation

Value of x corresponding to 98% probability as read from the table in Table 4.4 is 2.0 Hence, the probable completion date is:

$$= 24.5 + 2.0 \times 1.5 = 27.5 \text{ months (Fig. 4.30)}$$

## Table 4.4

## Area Under the Normal Curve

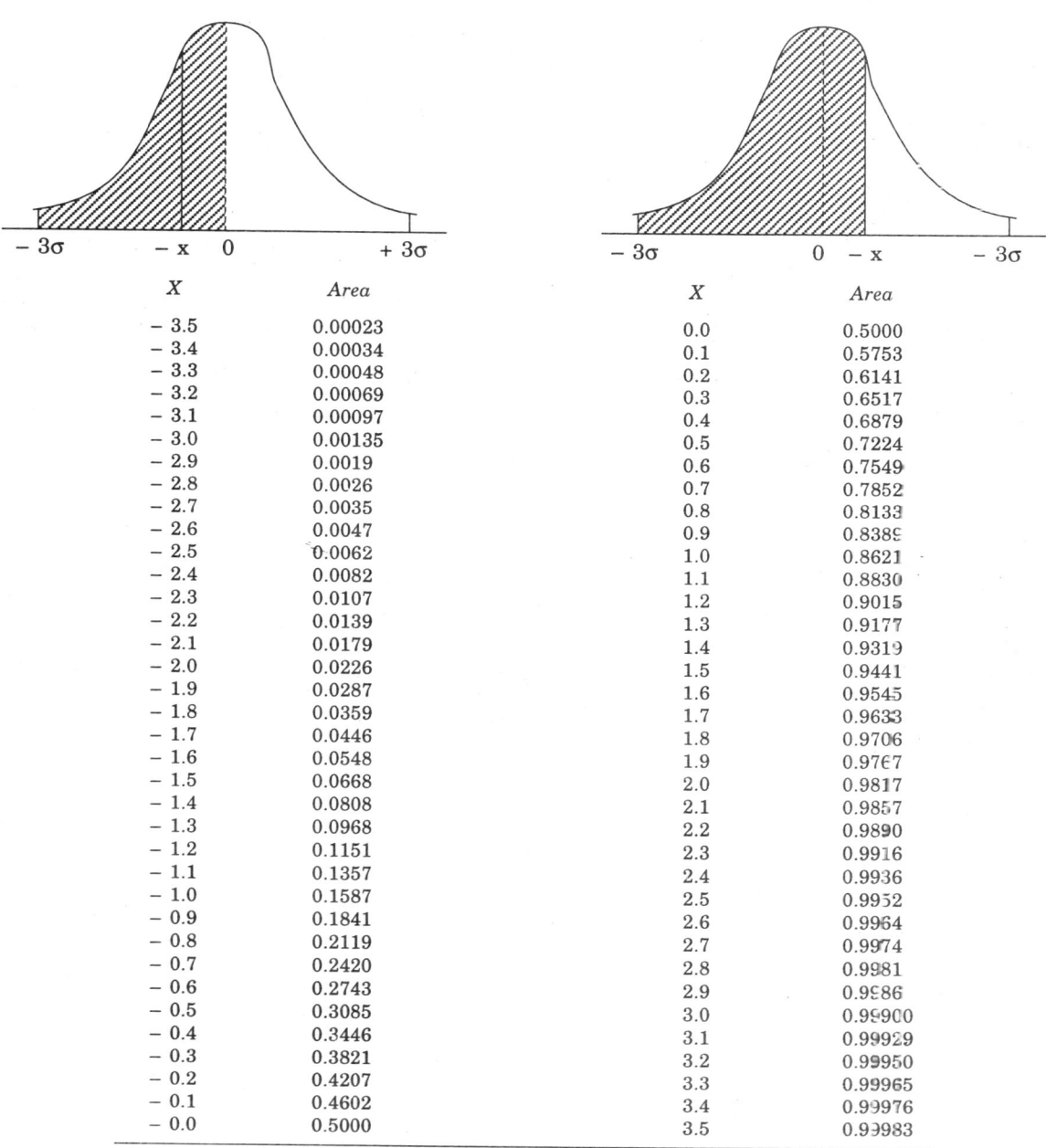

| X | Area | X | Area |
|---|---|---|---|
| −3.5 | 0.00023 | 0.0 | 0.5000 |
| −3.4 | 0.00034 | 0.1 | 0.5753 |
| −3.3 | 0.00048 | 0.2 | 0.6141 |
| −3.2 | 0.00069 | 0.3 | 0.6517 |
| −3.1 | 0.00097 | 0.4 | 0.6879 |
| −3.0 | 0.00135 | 0.5 | 0.7224 |
| −2.9 | 0.0019 | 0.6 | 0.7549 |
| −2.8 | 0.0026 | 0.7 | 0.7852 |
| −2.7 | 0.0035 | 0.8 | 0.8133 |
| −2.6 | 0.0047 | 0.9 | 0.8389 |
| −2.5 | 0.0062 | 1.0 | 0.8621 |
| −2.4 | 0.0082 | 1.1 | 0.8830 |
| −2.3 | 0.0107 | 1.2 | 0.9015 |
| −2.2 | 0.0139 | 1.3 | 0.9177 |
| −2.1 | 0.0179 | 1.4 | 0.9319 |
| −2.0 | 0.0226 | 1.5 | 0.9441 |
| −1.9 | 0.0287 | 1.6 | 0.9545 |
| −1.8 | 0.0359 | 1.7 | 0.9633 |
| −1.7 | 0.0446 | 1.8 | 0.9706 |
| −1.6 | 0.0548 | 1.9 | 0.9767 |
| −1.5 | 0.0668 | 2.0 | 0.9817 |
| −1.4 | 0.0808 | 2.1 | 0.9857 |
| −1.3 | 0.0968 | 2.2 | 0.9890 |
| −1.2 | 0.1151 | 2.3 | 0.9916 |
| −1.1 | 0.1357 | 2.4 | 0.9936 |
| −1.0 | 0.1587 | 2.5 | 0.9952 |
| −0.9 | 0.1841 | 2.6 | 0.9964 |
| −0.8 | 0.2119 | 2.7 | 0.9974 |
| −0.7 | 0.2420 | 2.8 | 0.9981 |
| −0.6 | 0.2743 | 2.9 | 0.9986 |
| −0.5 | 0.3085 | 3.0 | 0.99900 |
| −0.4 | 0.3446 | 3.1 | 0.99929 |
| −0.3 | 0.3821 | 3.2 | 0.99950 |
| −0.2 | 0.4207 | 3.3 | 0.99965 |
| −0.1 | 0.4602 | 3.4 | 0.99976 |
| −0.0 | 0.5000 | 3.5 | 0.99983 |

$$\bar{x} = \frac{\text{Scheduled date} - \text{Expected date}}{\text{Standard deviation}}$$

#### Figure 4.29
### Normal Distribution For The Project

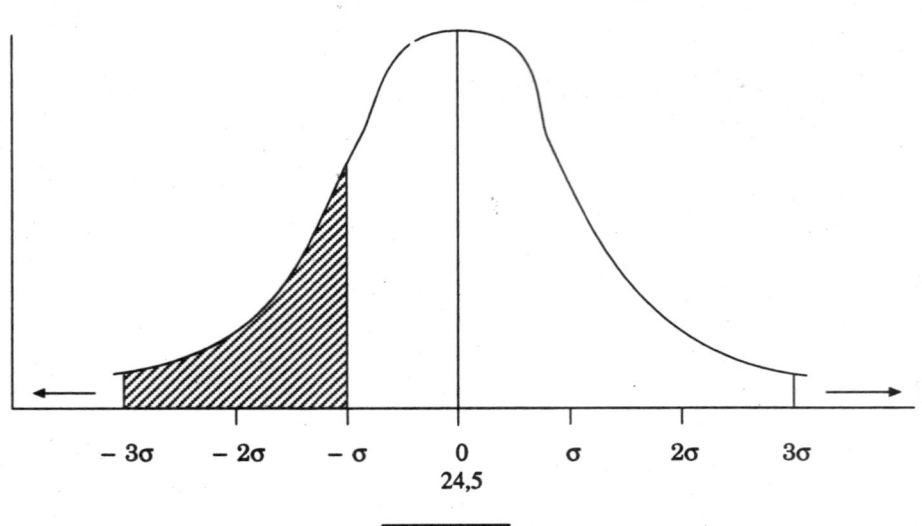

#### Figure 4.30
### Probability of Project Completion

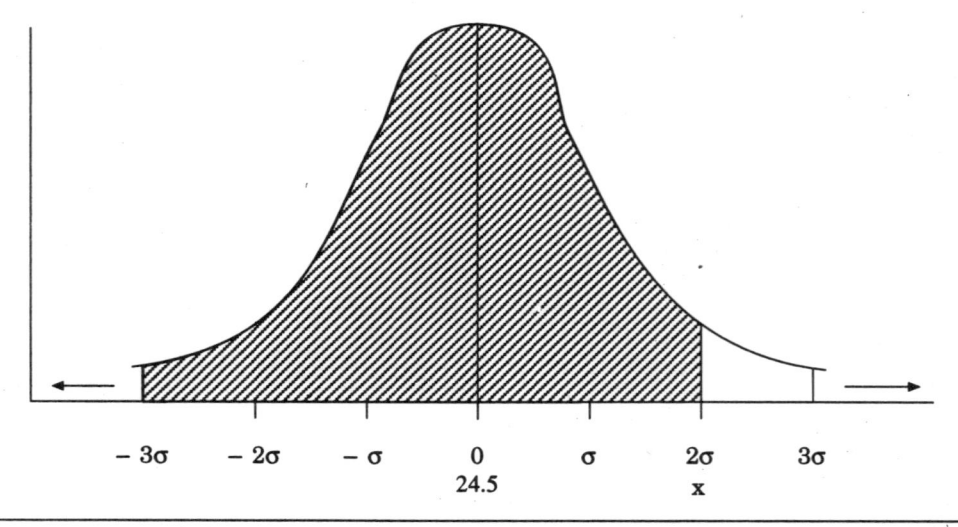

Q.3. Assess expected duration corresponding to 25% probability. Proceeding as above, see Fig. 4.31.

From Table 4.4 the value of $x$ corresponding to 25% probability = $-0.675$.

Hence, expected date = $24.50 - 0.675 \times 1.5 = 24.50 - 1.01$
= 23.49 months

The procedure used to calculate the probability of meeting a given schedule can be summarized as follows.

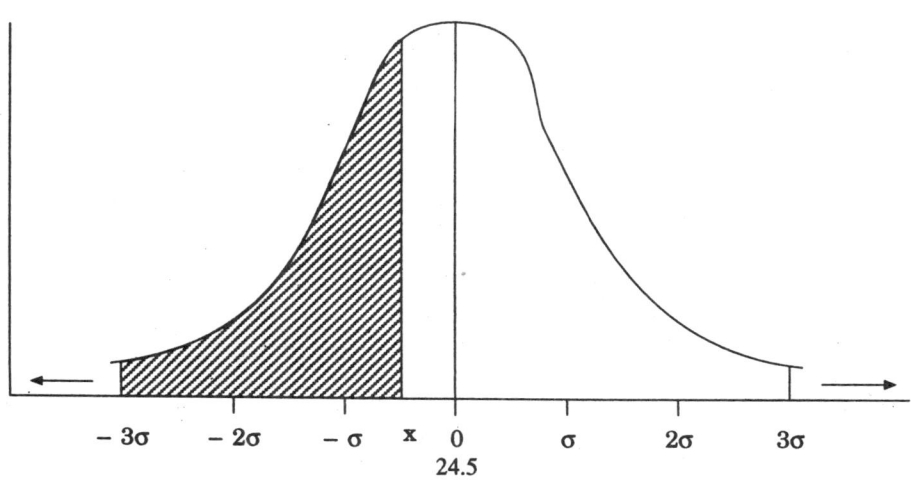

### Figure 4.31
**Assessment of Expected Project Duration**

*Step 1:* Determine the expected durations ($T_e$) of all the activities of the network.

*Step 2:* Compute critical path, considering the expected duration of all activities.

*Step 3:* Assess the expected completion time of the project by adding the expected durations of critical activities along a path.

*Step 4:* Calculate the variance of the project probability distribution by adding variances of critical activities along each critical path. If there is more than one path, take the maximum value.

$$\text{Standard deviation} = \sqrt{\text{Variance}}$$

The standard deviation is a measure of dispersion. The larger the variance. The bigger the spread and more uncertain is the achievement of the scheduled time.

*Step 5:* Determine the value of abscissa of normal curve in standard deviation units as:

$$x = \frac{\text{Scheduled date} - \text{Expected duration}}{\text{Standard deviation}}$$

*Step 6:* The probability of completing the project in $x$ units of time is equal to the area under the normal curve from $-\infty$ to $x$. The area under the curve is read from the table given in Table 4.4.

The important values of area under the curve for different values of $x$ are:

$$
\begin{array}{lll}
x = -3\sigma, & \text{area} = & 0.135\% \\
x = -2\sigma, & \text{area} = & 2.28\% \\
x = -\sigma, & \text{area} = & 15.87\% \\
x = 0, & \text{area} = & 50.00\% \\
x = \sigma, & \text{area} = & 84.13\% \\
x = 2\sigma, & \text{area} = & 97.73\% \\
x = 3\sigma, & \text{area} = & 99.865\% \\
\end{array}
$$

Probabilities less than 50% signify the need for using additional resources or effort.

## 4.4 PERT VS CPM

A controversy has developed over the years between the proponents of PERT and CPM. The commonly debated questions are: Which of these methods originated first? Which is the better one? Are both of them practically the same? To understand the various distinguishing features of the two and their spheres of application, let us first discuss their original differences and then the subsequent developments. All controversial issues, which are only of an academic interest with no practical significance have been avoided.

### 4.4.1 Original Differences

CPM was developed for planning, scheduling and control of *civil works*, while PERT originated in response to the complexities of the uncertainity in *research and development projects* for controlling their multifarious time schedules. Originally, thus, their fields of application were quite different.

In network modelling, CPM laid emphasis on breaking the projects into various works or activities. In PERT, the project breakdown was in terms of milestones which were planned to occur during its execution. Therefore, CPM was *activity-oriented* whereas PERT was *event-oriented*.

Originally, the application of CPM was confined to construction works where the activities were familiar and their duration could be easily estimated from the *one-time estimate*. Since PERT was designed to cope with uncertainties, it used the *three-time estimate*.

In CPM, activity durations were related to costs. This provided a means of assessment of different activity durations with varying costs and made crashing of activities possible. PERT dealt with events and their probable time of occurrence. This enabled adoption of probabilistic approach in time scheduling.

The CPM schedule enabled optimization of resources as the activity durations were defined in terms of resources employed. This was not possible with PERT.

CPM, which used the one-time estimate, was simpler to follow, while PERT required a statistician to interpret the results.

**Later developments** As the various drawbacks of PERT gradually became apparent, further studies were initiated by the US Defence Department. Notable among these were the PERT/TIME and PERT/COST. In the later, the concept of single-time estimate of activities could be equally employed.

In the CPM field, the concept of three-time estimate was introduced into networks which were primarily designed for controlling the time factor rather than the resources. In recent years, further developments in PERT and CPM have made CPM appear more like PERT, and the subject of network analysis has come to be known as PERT/CPM. To distinguish these two main network techniques, the event-oriented networks using three-time estimate for activity durations having uncertainties can be termed as a PERT network, while the other which is activities-oriented and uses one-time estimate may be referred to as the CPM.

# CHAPTER 5

# Precedence Network Analysis

Each activity in a precedence network (PN) is represented by a rectangular or square box. The boxes portray activities-on-nodes, unlike the CPM/PERT networks which show activities-on-arrows. The time duration of the activity is incorporated inside the nodal box. The logic relationship in a PN is shown by connecting activity nodes with lines drawn from the preceding activity(ies). Precedence Network Analysis (PNA) technique is also known as Precedence Diagramming Method (PDM) or Activity-on-node Network.

In CPM/PERT networks, activities are connected according to the finish-to-start logic, i.e. an activity starts only after its preceding activity is accomplished. But in reality, a certain overlapping of time between the adjoining activities is inevitable. For example, in a multi-housing construction project, the CPM network may show the activity of wall-plastering as starting after the completion of masonry work of a particular building. In practice, however, plastering can start as soon as the first room is complete; it need not wait for completion of masonry work of all the rooms. Such inaccuracies in a CPM network may misrepresent the actual situation unless a detailed one is drawn to include each minor operation and process.

A detailed CPM network, on the other hand, may become unmanageable and defeat the very purpose of project planning. A PN incorporates the concept of delays (lags) while depicting the relationship of various start and finish activities. They represent a real time-realistic plan which shows the dependency and interrelationship of various activities in a much better way than the other project-network analysis techniques. The PN is thus best suited for planning complex construction projects.

## ❑ 5.1 PRECEDENCE NETWORK ANALYSIS (PNA) FUNDAMENTALS

### 5.1.1 Modelling Procedure

The procedure for drawing PN is similar to CPM. For beginners, the step-by-step network modelling procedure involves defining the scope of the network, listing activities, developing logic diagrams, structuring networks, incorporating activity duration, super-imposing construction constraints and, finally, numbering the various activities. Though the procedure of drawing PN is similar to CPM, its model presents a different look (Exhibit 5.1). The salient features of PN technique are explained below using a simple task involving the construction of raft foundation of a typical building.

Exhibit 5.1

**Precedence Network of Raft Foundation Construction**

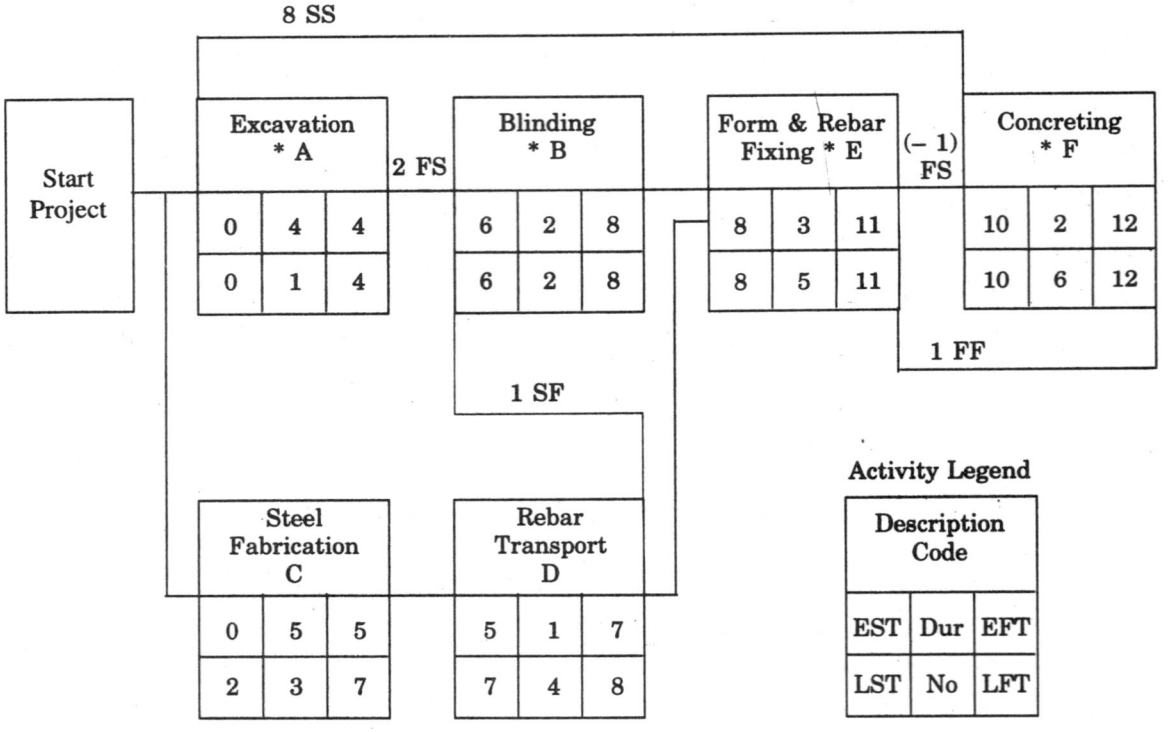

*[Precedence network diagram showing Start Project → Excavation *A (0,4,4 / 0,1,4) → 2 FS → Blinding *B (6,2,8 / 6,2,8) → Form & Rebar Fixing *E (8,3,11 / 8,5,11) → (−1) FS → Concreting *F (10,2,12 / 10,6,12); with 8 SS link from Start to Excavation; Steel Fabrication C (0,5,5 / 2,3,7) and Rebar Transport D (5,1,7 / 7,4,8) branching below; 1 SF link from Rebar Transport to Blinding; 1 FF link to Concreting]*

Activity Legend

| Description Code | | |
|---|---|---|
| EST | Dur | EFT |
| LST | No | LFT |

*Critical Activities for time analysis refer to page 153.

**PN of raft foundation** The various activities involved in the raft construction are as follows:

| Code | Description | Duration (days) |
|---|---|---|
| A | Excavation | 4 |
| B | Blinding base | 2 |
| C | Steel fabrication | 5 |
| D | Transportation of rebar steel to site | 1 |
| E | Formwork setting and rebar fixing | 3 |
| F | Raft concreting | 2 |

Excavation starts at the commencement of the building construction and takes four days to complete. After excavation, it takes two days to clear the area, conduct compaction tests and mark the layout prior to the commencement of blinding.

Excavation is followed by placing of blinding concrete on the base. This is completed in two days. The raft formwork and reinforcement steel bar fixing is commenced after the blinding of base. Transportation to site of rebar steel takes one day. Formwork and steel fixing is finished in three days, after the completion of blinding.

Procurement and fabrication of steel required for the raft can start at the fabrication shop at the commencement of the building. This is expected to take five days. But fabricated steel can be transported from workshop to site only after a part of the blinding area is cleared of the excavated material. This area clearance is expected to take one day from the start of blinding.

The formwork setting and fixing of reinforcement proceed concurrently, and are completed in three days. Expansion joint in the middle of the raft divides this work into two parts with the first taking two days for completion and the second, one more day. This is followed by raft concreting.

Raft concreting is also subject to approval of concrete mix compressive strength testing, which is scheduled on the eighth day from the commencement of excavation for the building. Concrete placing is completed in two days. Concreting can start after the first part of preceding activity is completed.

PN for this simple task is shown in Exhibit 5.1. The main points to note are:

**Network start and end**  Generally, a PN starts with a single 'start activity' and terminates on a single 'final activity'.

**Activity listing and activity dependence table**  It can be prepared in a manner similar to CPM network, as follows:

| Activity | Code | Preceding | Succeeding | Construction Constraints Type | Extent | Preceding |
|---|---|---|---|---|---|---|
| Start | S | — | A, C | — | — | — |
| Excavation | A | S | B | — | — | — |
| Blinding base | B | A | E | FS | 2 | A |
| Steel fabrication | C | S | D | — | — | — |
| Rebar transportation | D | C | E | SF | 1 | B |
| Formwork and rebar | E | B, D | F | — | — | — |
| Raft concreting | F | E | — | FS | (−1) | E |
|  |  |  |  | FF | 1 | E |
|  |  |  |  | SS | 8 | A |

**Activity representation**  PN depicts activities on square or rectangular nodes. The activity data is incorporated inside these nodes. Activities can be represented in different ways (Fig. 5.1). A typical activity box is given below:

| EST | Dur | EFT |
|---|---|---|
| \multicolumn{3}{c}{ACTIVITY DESCRIPTION} |
| LST | No. | LFT |

## Figure 5.1

**Alternate Methods of Activity Representation in Precedence Network**

| EST | Dur | EFT |
|---|---|---|
| \multicolumn{3}{c}{DESCRIPTION RESOURCE} |
| LST | No. | LFT |

| EST | Dur | EFT |
|---|---|---|
| \multicolumn{3}{c}{NO. & DESCRIPTION RESOURCE} |
| LST | TF | LFT |

| \multicolumn{3}{c}{DESCRIPTION RESOURCE} |
|---|---|---|
| EST | Dur | EFT |
| LST | No. | LFT |

| EST | | EFT |
|---|---|---|
| \multicolumn{3}{c}{DESCRIPTION RESOURCE} |
| Dur | | TF |

EST = Earliest Start Time
LST = Latest Start Time
EFT = Earliest Finish Time
LFT = Latest Finish Time
Dur = Duration
No. = Activity number or identification label
TF = Total Float
Resource = Gang size or mandays or cost or earned value etc. can be written below description, if considered necessary.

The activity description is written in the middle portion of the node box. The duration is written in the rectangular space above it on top while the activity number is written below it at the bottom of the box. The activity data in the box also includes activity timings. The box shape and the writing inside the activity box can be modified, as would be seen in illustrations covered in this chapter.

**Network logic** Generally, the extreme left vertical side of the activity box marks the start of the activity and the extreme right, its completion. The connecting lines show the relationship among the various activities. A logic diagram showing the start of activity B after completion of activity A is shown below:

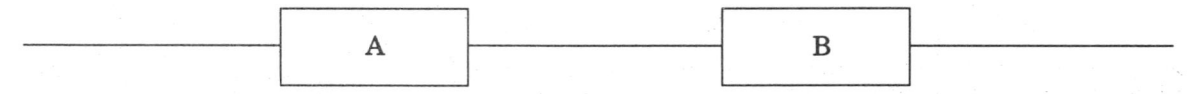

───[ A ]───────[ B ]───

The logic between the activities is indicated by connecting them with lines. The length of these lines has no significance. Generally, they move from left to right. Arrow heads are not normally shown unless considered essential for clarity of logic. Crossing of lines should be minimized. Where unavoidable, line crossings may be depicted with symbols used in electrical circuits.

In PN, the precedence logic between activities is of two types, namely, job dependency logic and construction constraints logic:

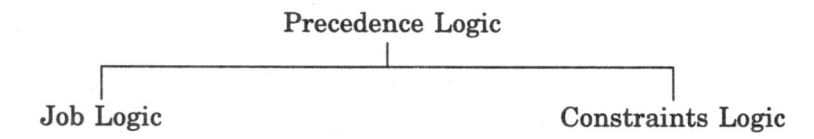

```
                    Precedence Logic
                    |
          ┌─────────┴─────────┐
       Job Logic         Constraints Logic
```

The *job dependency logic* shows the sequence in which the jobs or activities progress, e.g. blinding activity starts after the completion of excavation. It generally follows the rule that except the start activity, each activity starts after its preceding activity(ies) is completed.

The *construction constraints logic* arises from the restrain on start and completion of dependent activities imposed due to construction process at site. For example, the start of blinding activity may get delayed by two days after completion of excavation for grading and soil testing of the excavated surface. The construction constraints, can be of the following types (Fig. 5.2):

(a) *Finish-to-start,* i.e. delay from the finish of preceding activity to the start of the succeeding one.
(b) *Start-to-start,* i.e. delay from the start of preceding activity to the start of the succeeding one.
(c) *Finish-to-finish,* i.e. delay from the finish of preceding activity to the finish of the succeeding one.
(d) *Start-to-finish,* i.e. delay from the start of preceding activity to the finish of the succeeding one.

The precedence relationships of the raft construction task, showing job logic and construction constraints, are shown in Exhibit 5.1.

Representation of construction constraints on starting and finishing of activities, generally stated in terms of time delays, is a unique feature of PN. Unlike CPM/PERT networks, PN depict the overlap in activities to provide a realistic sequence of engineering tasks as they occur in the actual execution of works.

**Precedence logic diagram**  The first step while drawing the network is to establish network logic, either by making activity-dependence table or with experience, by directly sketching the network outline. In PN, a flow diagram can be easily plotted on pre-printed box pattern drawing sheets, tracing papers or box-type stickers similar to the box pattern sheet (Fig. 5.3). Each box can be taken to represent an activity, and the flow diagram can be developed by connecting these boxes logically with lines.

The formal PN can then be drawn by using the standard symbols and network drawing conventions outlined in Section 5.4.

**Duration estimation**  The duration of activity in PN is assessed by the one-time estimate method. Generally, delays are expressed in terms of time unit, though they can also be

## Figure 5.2
## Types of Precedence Relationships

*Finish-to-Start*

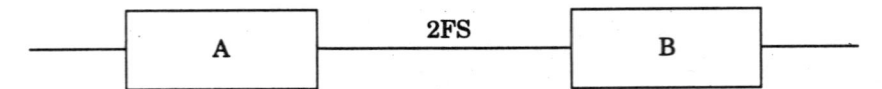

Activity B starts after 2 time-units delay constraints from completion of activity A.

*Start-to-Start*

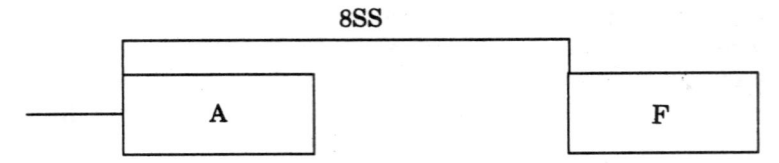

Activity F starts after 8 time-unit delay constraints from commencement of activity A

*Finish-to-Finish*

Completion of activity F will take atleast one time-unit after completion of activity E.

*Start-to-Finish*

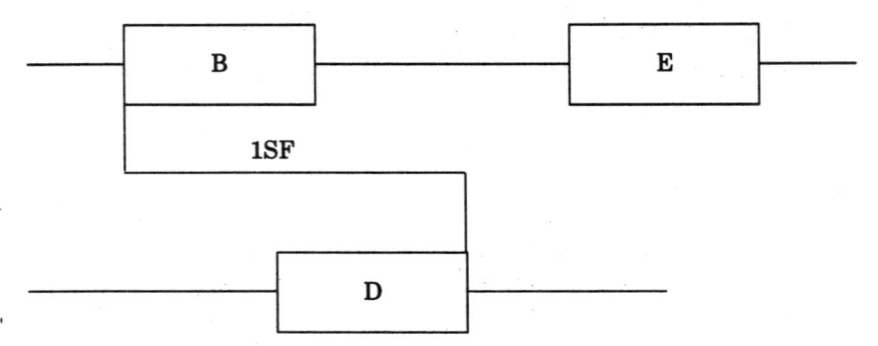

Activity D is finished after atleast 1 time unit delay from start of activity B.

*Notes:*
1. Relationships are always defined from preceding activity to its successor activity.
2. Lag means the delay time from start or finish of an activity to its successor. It can be specified in positive or negative time units. Lead implies a negative Lag.

## Figure 5.3
**Raft Foundation Construction: Precedence Logic Diagram**

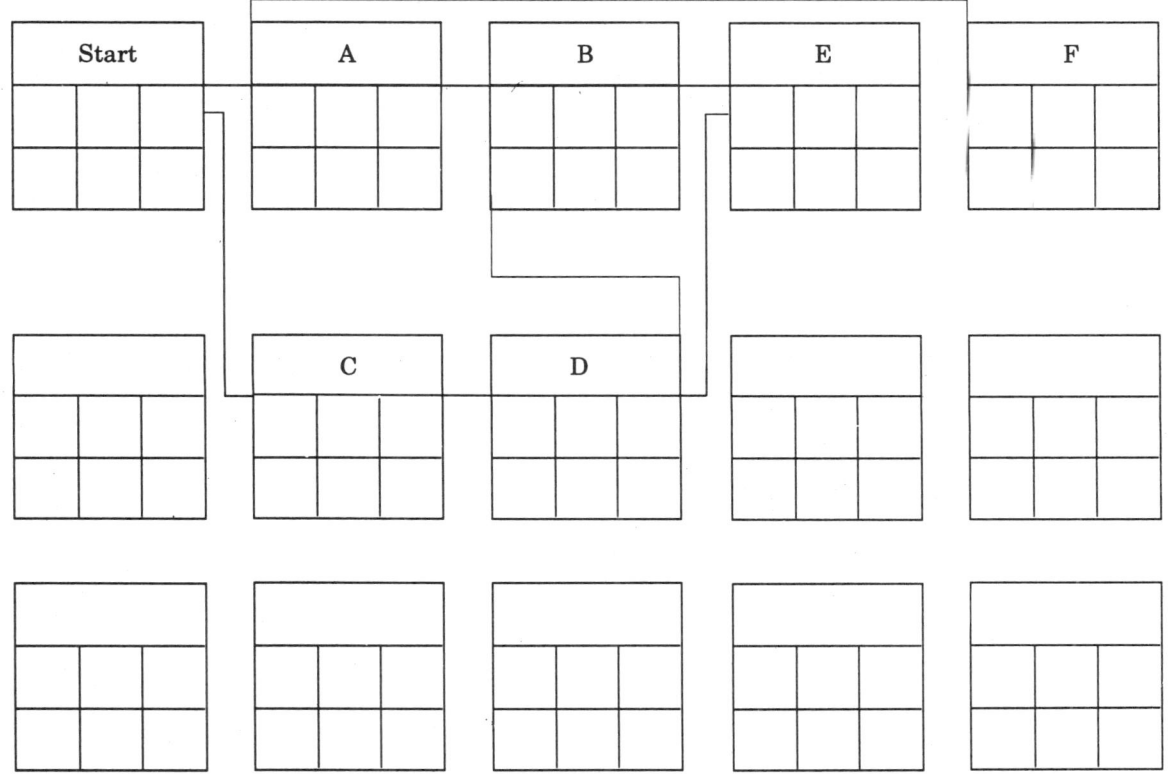

reflected as percentage of the preceding activity duration. In the later case, the percentages have to be converted to time units for the purpose of time analysis.

The three-time estimate of activities can also be used in PN. In such cases, analysis of network is carried out by reducing three-times to a single expected time and then proceeding in a manner similar to PERT.

**Activity numbering** The activity numbering methodology is similar to CPM. Numbering commences from the start activity and finishes with the last one. It is a standard practice to number activities after the network model is finalized.

## 5.1.2 Time Analysis

In PN, it is activity times and not the event times that are shown on the network. Like CPM network, the time analysis process can be divided into two stages, namely, forward-pass computation and back-pass computation. These timings facilitate determination of

**154** Construction Project Management

critical path and various types of floats. The method of time analysis of raft concreting network drawn in Exhibit 5.1, is as follows.

**Forward-pass computation** Set the Earliest Start Time (EST) of nodes depicting the start of the project as zero and write it in the space provided. Nodes shall follow in the ascending numerical order.

(a) *Activity A node No. 1*

$EST_1 = 0$
$EFT_1 = EST_1 + d_1 = 0 + 4 = 4$

(b) *Activity B Node No. 2*

$EST_2 = EFT_1 + \text{delay} = 4 + 2 = 6$
$EFT_2 = EST_2 + d_2 = 6 + 2 = 8$

(c) *Activity Node No. 3*

$EST_3 = 0$
$EFT_3 = EST_3 + d_3 = 0 + 5 = 5$

(d) *Activity D Node No. 4*

$EST_4 = 5$
$EFT_4 = (EST_4 + d_4)$ or $(EST_2 + 1SF)$, greater of these
  $= $ Greater of $(5 + 1)$ and $(6 + 1) = 7$

(e) *Activity E Node No. 5*

$EST_5 = $ Greater of $EFT_4$ and $EFT_2$
  $= $ Greater of 7 and 8
  $= 8$
$EFT_5 = EST_5 + d_5 = 8 + 3 = 11$

(f) *Activity F Node 6*

$EST_6 = $ Greater of $EFT_5 - 1$, and $EST_0 + 8$

  $= 11 - 1$, and 8

  $= 10$
$EFT_6 = EST_6 + d_6$ or $EFT_5 + 1$, which ever is greater
  $= 10 + 2$ or $11 + 1 = 12$ ( in both cases)

**Back-pass computation** Proceeding systematically with nodes in descending order, the latest timings of the activities can be worked out, as shown in Table 5.1.

**Critical path** Activities A, B, E and F have zero float (Float = LST − EST). These are critical activities. The parth from start to end connecting these critical activities is the critical path. The length of this longest path in the network is 12 time units.

## Table 5.1

| Node No. | Activity | Duration | LFT | LST |
|---|---|---|---|---|
| 6 | F | 2 | 12 | 10 |
| 5 | E | 3 | 11 | 8 |
| 4 | D | 1 | 8 | 7 |
| 3 | C | 5 | 7 | 2 |
| 2 | B | 2 | 8 | 6 |
| 1 | A | 4 | 4 | 0 |

### 5.1.3 Repetitive Works Network

The PNA technique can be usefully applied to prepare the network plan of projects involving repetitive works. Such networks also facilitate scheduling of manpower as well as other resources.

As an example, take a building complex involving construction of four similar raft foundations. The scope of work and the network for completion of the first raft is given in Exhibit 5.1. This network indicates that the first raft takes two working week for completion. Assuming that rebar steel fabrication would be carried out in the central rebar fabrication yard, the network for construction of subsequent rafts can be easily developed as follows:

(a) Decide the order of priorities of construction of rafts.
(b) Plan each construction activity into a work-team with the assigned manpower, equipment and other resources required for its completion.

The raft-construction network plan can then be developed by vertically linking the work-teams (Exhibit 5.2). In particular, the backward-pass time calculations should be thoroughly scrutinized.

Note that one work-team for each activity continues working on similar activities of subsequent rafts till completion.

The above example highlights the usefulness of using PNA network technique for planning repetitive works project.

As another example, an extract from the repetitive works summary network prepared for constructing the first four education buildings of the western sector in 2000 Housing Units Project is given in Exhibit 5.5.

### 5.1.4 Project Network

The network of a project is developed by logically integrating its sub networks. It covers the entire scope of the project and depicts its execution plan. It highlights the milestones and contracts or sub-contracts planned during the project life. It provides the yardstick for measuring and analyzing progress. It is supported by the various sub-networks of the project.

Integration of sub-network logic commences from the beginning of the project. Work packages falling in the same strata are connected in order of their occurrence.

**156** Construction Project Management

---

Exhibit 5.2

**Repetitive Works Project**
**Precedence Network of Four Rafts Foundation Construction**

8 SS

RAFT No. 1

| Excavation | | | | Blinding | | | Formwork & Rebar | | | Concreting | | |
|---|---|---|---|---|---|---|---|---|---|---|---|---|
| 0 | 4 | 4 | 2 FS | 6 | 2 | 8 | 8 | 3 | 11 | 10 | 2 | 12 |
| 0 | 1 | 4 | | 9 | 2 | 11 | 11 | 3 | 14 | 16 | 4 | 18 |

−1 FS (between Formwork & Rebar and Concreting)

RAFT No. 2

| Excavation | | | | Blinding | | | Formwork & Rebar | | | Concreting | | |
|---|---|---|---|---|---|---|---|---|---|---|---|---|
| 4 | 4 | 8 | 2 FS | 10 | 2 | 12 | 12 | 3 | 15 | 14 | 2 | 16 |
| 4 | 5 | 8 | | 12 | 6 | 14 | 14 | 7 | 17 | 18 | 8 | 20 |

−1 FS

RAFT No. 3

| Excavation | | | | Blinding | | | Formwork & Rebar | | | Concreting | | |
|---|---|---|---|---|---|---|---|---|---|---|---|---|
| 8 | 4 | 12 | 2 FS | 14 | 2 | 16 | 16 | 3 | 19 | 18 | 2 | 20 |
| 8 | 9 | 12 | | 15 | 10 | 17 | 17 | 11 | 20 | 20 | 12 | 22 |

−1 FS

RAFT No. 4

| Excavation | | | | Blinding | | | Formwork & Rebar | | | Concreting | | |
|---|---|---|---|---|---|---|---|---|---|---|---|---|
| 12 | 4 | 16 | 2 FS | 18 | 2 | 20 | 20 | 3 | 23 | 22 | 2 | 24 |
| 12 | 13 | 16 | | 18 | 14 | 20 | 20 | 15 | 23 | 22 | 16 | 24 |

−1 FS

Precedence Network Analysis **157**

While integrating, the sequence of activities is verified by its preceding and succeeding activities, the procedure and rules for drawing project network are outlined in Section 5.4.

### 5.1.5 Validating Project Time Objectives

Normally, a project should be planned for the completion period determined from the network. Increasing the duration of the project beyond its optimum completion time is out of question since, it would only add to the project cost. On the other hand, in some exceptional circumstances, the project completion time may have to be set less than the time-analyzed optimum completion time. This may be done to:

(a) Meet the management's need for an early completion of the project when the cost incurred for gaining time is acceptable.
(b) Avoid delays which may attract heavy penalty or a loss of goodwill.
(c) Venture on another project in the offing.
(d) Earn bonus for early completion, if found feasible and advantageous.
(e) Transfer elsewhere the resources needed.
(f) Conform to a given resource-availability schedule.

If the analyzed completion time is greater than the specified time objective, the time reduction of the project is achieved by modifying the network or activity durations. This modification process is divided into divided into two stages:

(a) Time compression of critical path, and
(b) Time crashing of critical path.

Time compression is the reduction of project completion time without any appreciable increase in the cost of activities. It involves splitting (where feasible) the critical activities into smaller ones, either by using different methods of execution without any appreciable change in resources, or by switching over to a lower level of activity details. Some of these smaller activities may form a chain of activities while others may be in parallel. Generally, it is the parallel component of the critical activities that enables a compression of the project completion time.

The method of time crashing in network analysis aims at keeping the increase in cost of speeding up the project from its optimum completion period to its minimum. In other words, it means buying time with the least price. Unlike the traditional method, where crashing implies speeding up all the works, in network analysis it is carried out only for selected activities.

The time compresion and time-crashing methodology is explained in Chapter 16.

### ❏ 5.2 CASE ILLUSTRATIONS

### 5.2.1 Primary School Construction PN

This illustrates the methodology of developing the network for construction of a primary school by integrating its sub networks, summarising this network by introducing hammock activities, and preparing the network of a group of similar educational buildings.

The primary school building is broadly divided into three parts: Wing 1, Wing 2 and gymnasium. Wings 1 and 2 have a common foundation, and both are two-storeyed. The roof of the gymnasium is supported on portals. The Wing 2 and gymnasium share a common beam, with the gymnasium roof starting a week later than Wing 2 roof. The construction of school involves the following stages:

(a) Foundation of Wing 1 and Wing 2 up to the ground floor slab.
(b) Foundation of gymnasium portal to start eight weeks after the commencement of the foundation of wings. It is due to site constraints.
(c) Frame structure of Wing 1, Wing 2 and gymnasium.
(d) Block work and finishes.

The primary school work-breakdown structure is shown in Exhibit 3.6. The activities thus derived are shown in Exhibit 3.7. After examining the construction methodology and the sequence and logic of activities, the PN of the primary school can be developed by integrating the following logic sub network diagrams:

## Foundation Wing 1 and Wing 2 and gymnasium activities

1. Excavation and footing      EF
2. Stub column and plinth beam      PB
3. Plinth filing      PF
4. Ground floor slab      GS
5. Foundation portals gymnasium      FP

The logic diagram of foundation is:

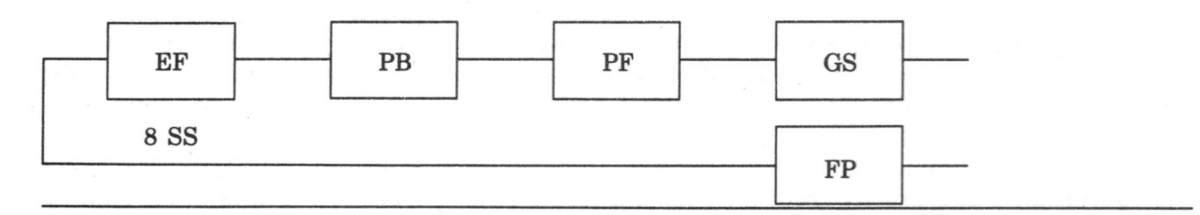

```
┌─────┐     ┌─────┐     ┌─────┐     ┌─────┐
│ EF  │────▶│ PB  │────▶│ PF  │────▶│ GS  │
└─────┘     └─────┘     └─────┘     └─────┘
  8 SS                                ┌─────┐
  └──────────────────────────────────▶│ FP  │
                                      └─────┘
```

## Frame structure of Wing 1, Wing 2 and gymnasium activities

6. First floor column Wing 1      FC
7. FF slab and beam Wing 1      FS
8. Roof structure Wing 1      RS
9. First floor Wing 2      FF
10. Construction portals      CP
11. Slab of gymnasium and Wing 2      SG

The logic diagram of frame structures is:

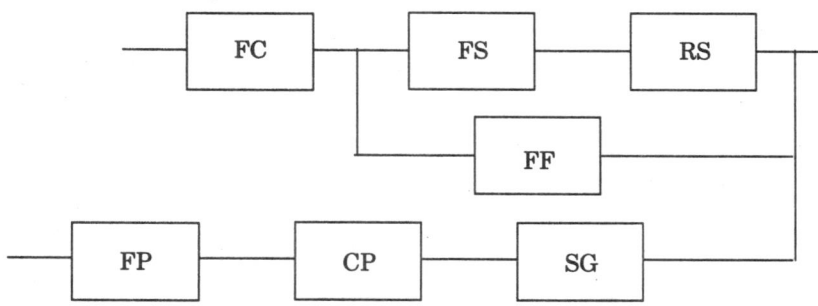

```
─── FC ───┬─── FS ─── RS ───
          │                  
          └─── FF ───┐       
                     │       
─── FP ─── CP ─── SG ────────
```

## Block work and finishes

12. Block work — BW
13. Pipes and conduit, and frames — PC
14. Internal plaster — IP
15. Ducting and wiring — DW
16. External plaster — EP
17. Roof treatment — RT
18. Screed — SC
19. Tiling — TL
20. Preliminary paint treatment — PT
21. Air-conditioning equipment installation & testing — AC
22. Carpentry and Joinery — CJ
23. Fittings, fixtures and metal works — FM
24. Final paint and completion — CM

The logic diagram of block work and finishes is:

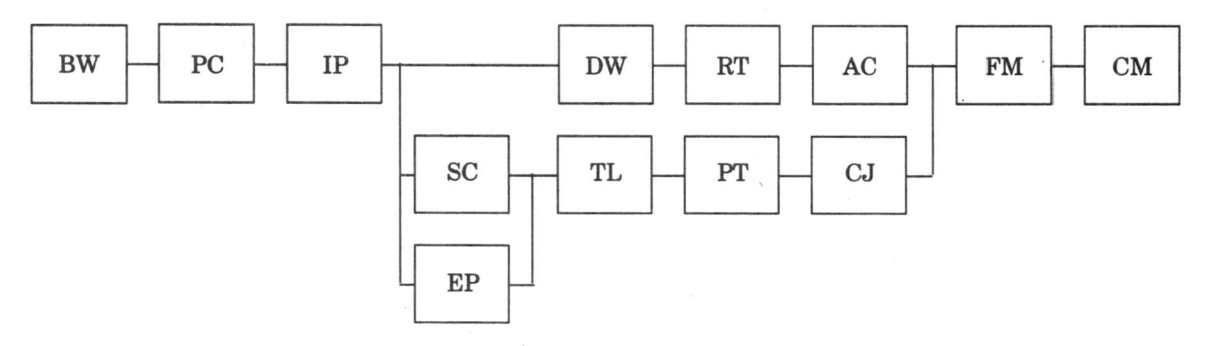

```
BW ── PC ── IP ──┬── DW ── RT ── AC ──┬── FM ── CM
                 │                     │
                 └── SC ── TL ── PT ── CJ
                      │
                      └── EP
```

The integration of work-package logic diagrams in construction sequence produces the project logic diagram. The flow diagram of the primary school construction showing box-type activities and the logic build-up is shown in Fig. 5.4.

The project flow diagram can be converted to PN using the network drawing rules similar to CPM. The primary school structure construction precedence sub-network, duly time analyzed, is shown in Exhibit 5.3. Similarly, the 'finishes', sub-network can be added

**160** Construction Project Management

## Figure 5.4
## Primary School Construction: Flow Diagram

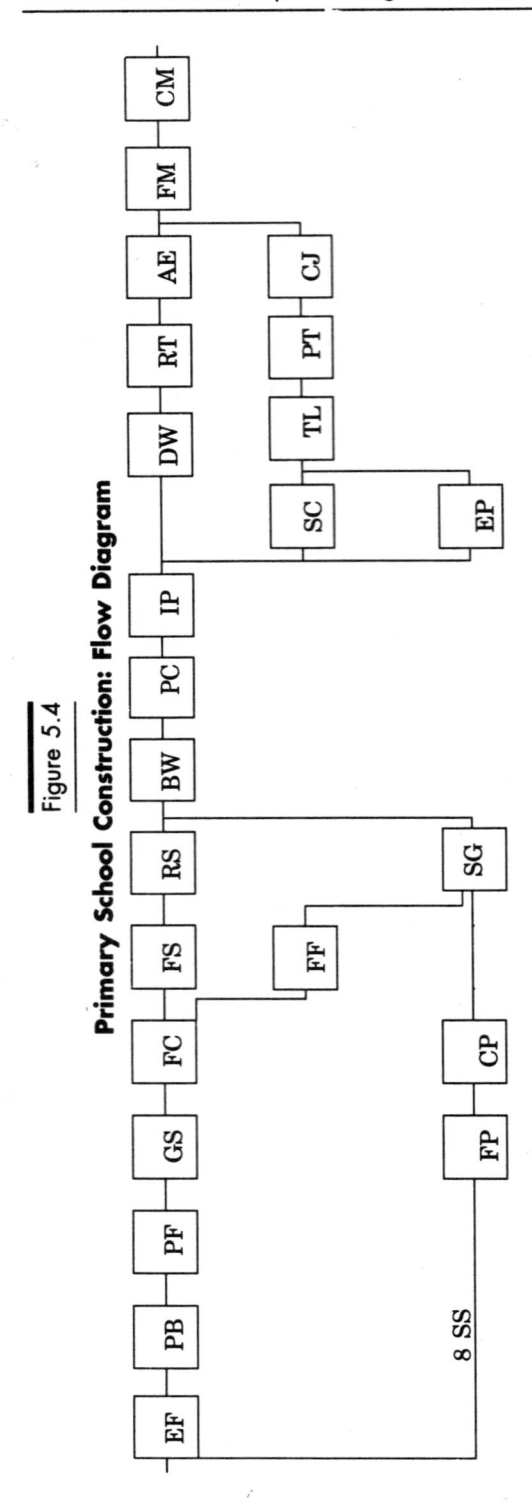

Logic Diagram of Foundation    Logic Diagram of Frame Structure    Logic Diagram of Block Work and Finishes

to the structure construction sub network to develop the primary school construction network.

A network can be summarized by creating hammock activities to cover a sub network or agroup of activities. Exhibit 5.3 shows the hammock activity 'Foundation Wings 1 and 2' spanning over the foundation sub-network of primary school project.

The main purpose of introducing hammock activities is to facilitate preparation of higher level network and summarize the schedule of work. These activities are numbered and they have a description, but their duration is derived after time analysis. It has start-to-start (SS) relation with the start activity of the sub-network being summarized, and finish-to-finish (FF) relationship with the last activity of the sub-network. The hammock activity EST and LST are set equal to the start activity of the sub-network, while its EFT and LFT are made equal to the last activity of the sub-network. Thus, the duration of hammock activity gets determined only after the time analysis.

In computerized networks, whenever a change occurs in the sub-network, the connected hammock activities automatically get time analyzed to fit between the preceding and succeeding activity of the sub network.

The hammock activity concept can also be used to represent activities like supervision, whose duration is related to the period covered by two or more activities.

The summarized network of the primary school project is shown in Exhibit 5.4. This network, in addition to controlling the progress of work, was also used to prepare the network plan for a group of educational buildings in the 2000 Housing Units Project. This project involved construction of a nursery, a kindergarten, a primary and a high school on the western sector of the project area. These schools were of similar design and construction but varied in construction areas. The activities and their durations, school-wise, are reflected in Exhibit 3.7.

Taking into consideration the development plan, the priorities for completion of the construction of schools were determined. Thereafter, the repetitive works education buildings project network was developed by logically interconnecting the networks of each school listed in the order of construction priorities. The network containing these four typical school buildings is summarized in Exhibit 5.5.

## 5.2.2 Raw Water Clarifier Construction Project

The civil works in a raw-water treatment plant of a refinery project included construction of a clarifier, mixer chamber, sludge transfer basin and foundations to support pipes and pump. Since the commissioning of the refinery depended upon the clarified water supply from the raw-water treatment plant, this work was accorded highest priority and a time limit of seven months commencing from February 1, 1986 was fixed for the completion of all civil works (Exhibit 5.6).

The clarifier RCC tank had an outer diameter of 22.0 m. It had both an underground chamber and an above-ground level 4.5 m high structure. The underground chamber had conical and trapezoidal RCC sumps. The heavily reinforced floor slab of the main tank acted as the roof for the underground chamber.

The main clarifier tank had an inner chamber of 7 m diameter constructed over the RCC columns. The inner chamber was encircled by twin circular RCC baffle walls. These circular twin narrow-spaced baffle walls had a semicircular raised spillway at the bottom.

## Exhibit 5.3

### Primary School Structure Construction Precedence Network

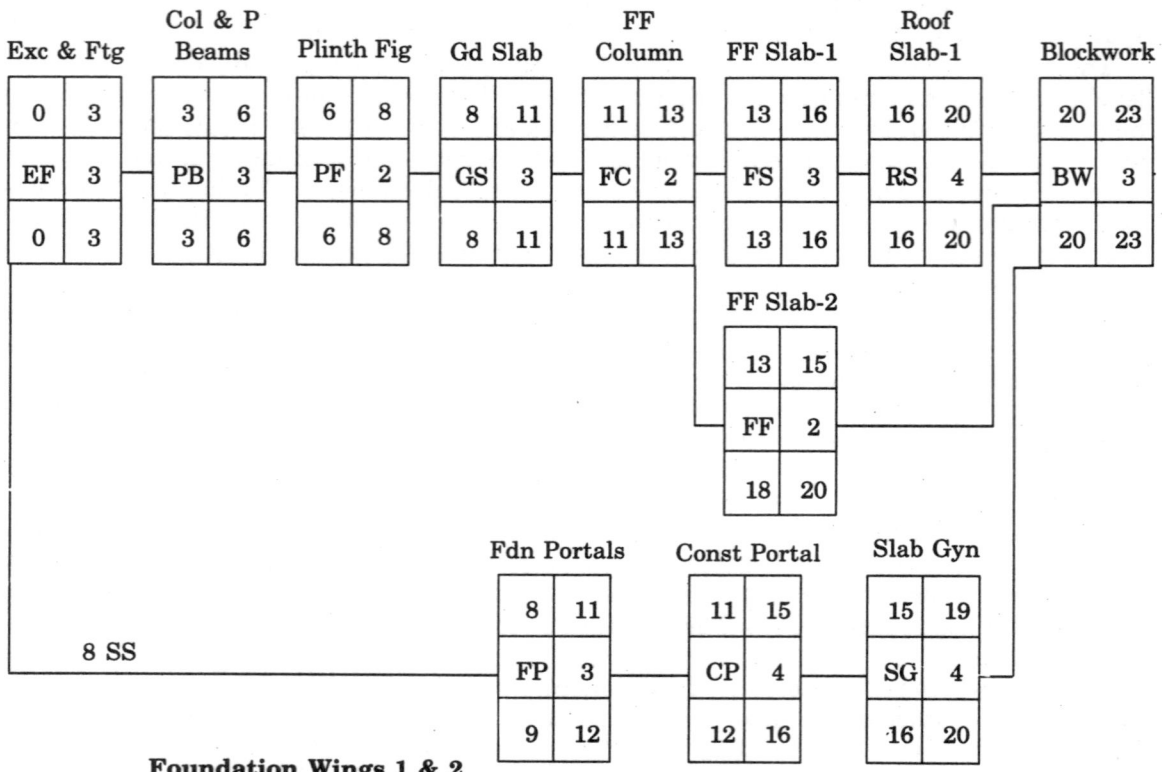

| Exc & Ftg | Col & P Beams | Plinth Fig | Gd Slab | FF Column | FF Slab-1 | Roof Slab-1 | Blockwork |
|---|---|---|---|---|---|---|---|
| 0 / 3 | 3 / 6 | 6 / 8 | 8 / 11 | 11 / 13 | 13 / 16 | 16 / 20 | 20 / 23 |
| EF / 3 | PB / 3 | PF / 2 | GS / 3 | FC / 2 | FS / 3 | RS / 4 | BW / 3 |
| 0 / 3 | 3 / 6 | 6 / 8 | 8 / 11 | 11 / 13 | 13 / 16 | 16 / 20 | 20 / 23 |

FF Slab-2:
| 13 | 15 |
| FF | 2 |
| 18 | 20 |

8 SS

Fdn Portals:
| 8 | 11 |
| FP | 3 |
| 9 | 12 |

Const Portal:
| 11 | 15 |
| CP | 4 |
| 12 | 16 |

Slab Gyn:
| 15 | 19 |
| SG | 4 |
| 16 | 20 |

### Foundation Wings 1 & 2 Hammock activity

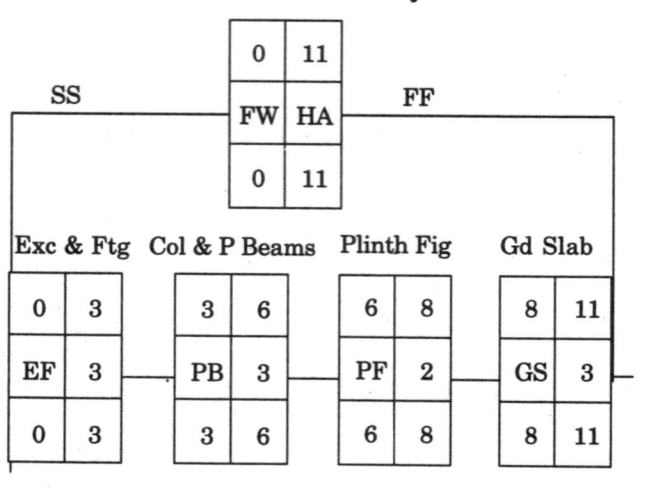

SS — FW HA — FF
| 0 | 11 |
| FW | HA |
| 0 | 11 |

| Exc & Ftg | Col & P Beams | Plinth Fig | Gd Slab |
|---|---|---|---|
| 0 / 3 | 3 / 6 | 6 / 8 | 8 / 11 |
| EF / 3 | PB / 3 | PF / 2 | GS / 3 |
| 0 / 3 | 3 / 6 | 6 / 8 | 8 / 11 |

*Note*: A hammock activity is used to summarise a group of activities. Hammock activities have description, but no duration. Its start timing is equal to the start time of its preceding activity and finish time is made equal to finish time of its succeeding activity.

Precedence Network Analysis  **163**

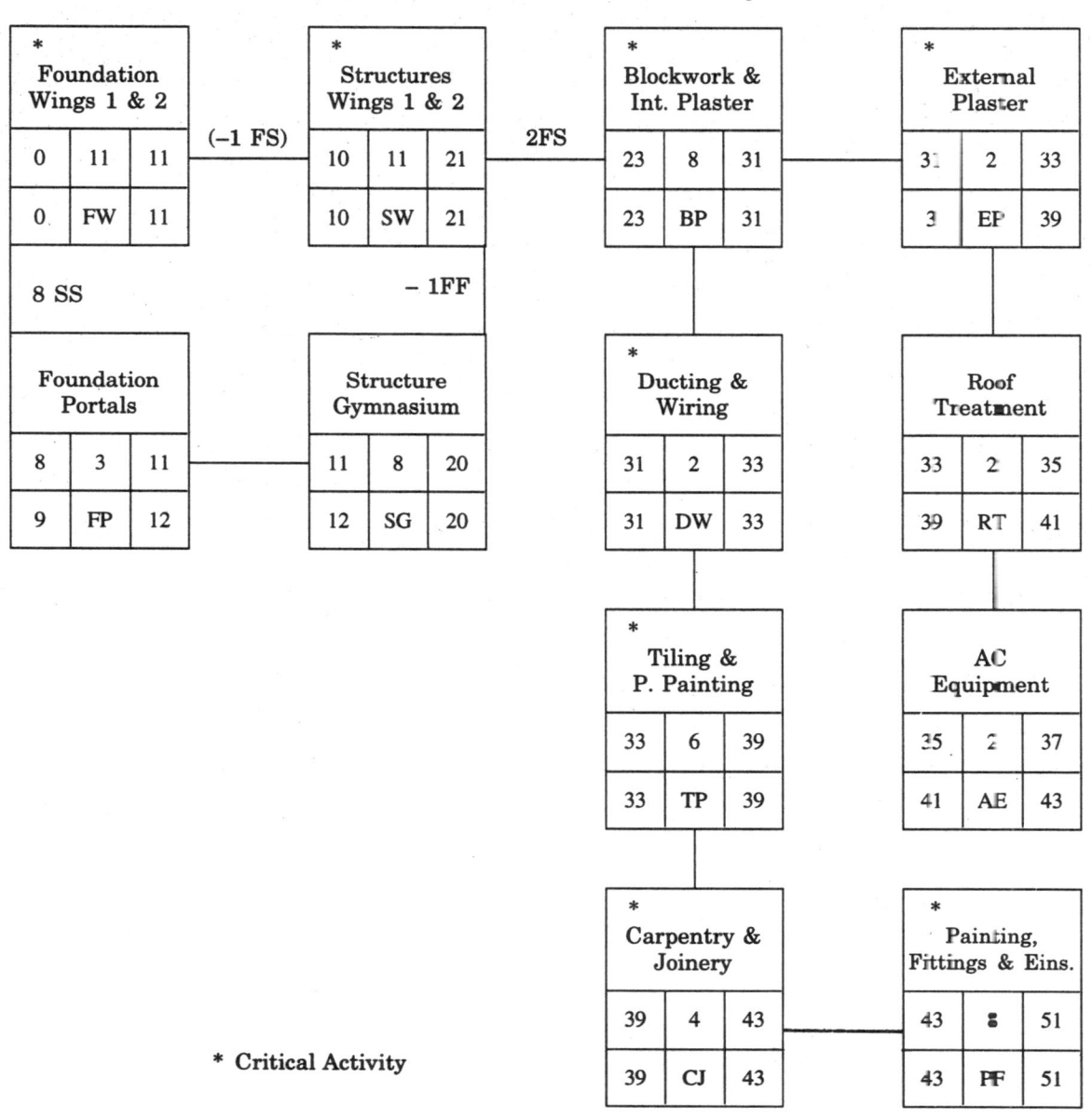

Exhibit 5.4

## Summary Precedence Network of Primary School

```
┌─────────────────┐         ┌─────────────────┐        ┌─────────────────┐        ┌─────────────────┐
│   *             │         │   *             │        │   *             │        │   *             │
│  Foundation     │         │   Structures    │        │  Blockwork &    │        │   External      │
│  Wings 1 & 2    │         │  Wings 1 & 2    │        │  Int. Plaster   │        │   Plaster       │
├────┬─────┬──────┤ (−1 FS) ├────┬─────┬──────┤  2FS   ├────┬─────┬──────┤        ├────┬─────┬──────┤
│ 0  │ 11  │ 11   │─────────│ 10 │ 11  │ 21   │────────│ 23 │  8  │ 31   │────────│ 31 │  2  │ 33   │
├────┼─────┼──────┤         ├────┼─────┼──────┤        ├────┼─────┼──────┤        ├────┼─────┼──────┤
│ 0  │ FW  │ 11   │         │ 10 │ SW  │ 21   │        │ 23 │ BP  │ 31   │        │ 3  │ EP  │ 39   │
└────┴─────┴──────┘         └────┴─────┴──────┘        └────┴─────┴──────┘        └────┴─────┴──────┘
   8 SS                         − 1FF
┌─────────────────┐         ┌─────────────────┐        ┌─────────────────┐        ┌─────────────────┐
│  Foundation     │         │   Structure     │        │   *             │        │     Roof        │
│   Portals       │         │   Gymnasium     │        │  Ducting &      │        │   Treatment     │
├────┬─────┬──────┤         ├────┬─────┬──────┤        │   Wiring        │        ├────┬─────┬──────┤
│ 8  │  3  │ 11   │─────────│ 11 │  8  │ 20   │        ├────┬─────┬──────┤        │ 33 │  2  │ 35   │
├────┼─────┼──────┤         ├────┼─────┼──────┤        │ 31 │  2  │ 33   │        ├────┼─────┼──────┤
│ 9  │ FP  │ 12   │         │ 12 │ SG  │ 20   │        ├────┼─────┼──────┤        │ 39 │ RT  │ 41   │
└────┴─────┴──────┘         └────┴─────┴──────┘        │ 31 │ DW  │ 33   │        └────┴─────┴──────┘
                                                       └────┴─────┴──────┘
                                                       ┌─────────────────┐        ┌─────────────────┐
                                                       │   *             │        │      AC         │
                                                       │  Tiling &       │        │   Equipment     │
                                                       │  P. Painting    │        ├────┬─────┬──────┤
                                                       ├────┬─────┬──────┤        │ 35 │  2  │ 37   │
                                                       │ 33 │  6  │ 39   │        ├────┼─────┼──────┤
                                                       ├────┼─────┼──────┤        │ 41 │ AE  │ 43   │
                                                       │ 33 │ TP  │ 39   │        └────┴─────┴──────┘
                                                       └────┴─────┴──────┘
                                                       ┌─────────────────┐        ┌─────────────────┐
                                                       │   *             │        │   *             │
                                                       │  Carpentry &    │        │   Painting,     │
                                                       │   Joinery       │        │ Fittings & Eins.│
                                                       ├────┬─────┬──────┤        ├────┬─────┬──────┤
                                                       │ 39 │  4  │ 43   │────────│ 43 │  8  │ 51   │
                                                       ├────┼─────┼──────┤        ├────┼─────┼──────┤
                                                       │ 39 │ CJ  │ 43   │        │ 43 │ PF  │ 51   │
                                                       └────┴─────┴──────┘        └────┴─────┴──────┘
```

\* Critical Activity

## Exhibit 5.5
## Summary Precedence Network of Educational Buildings

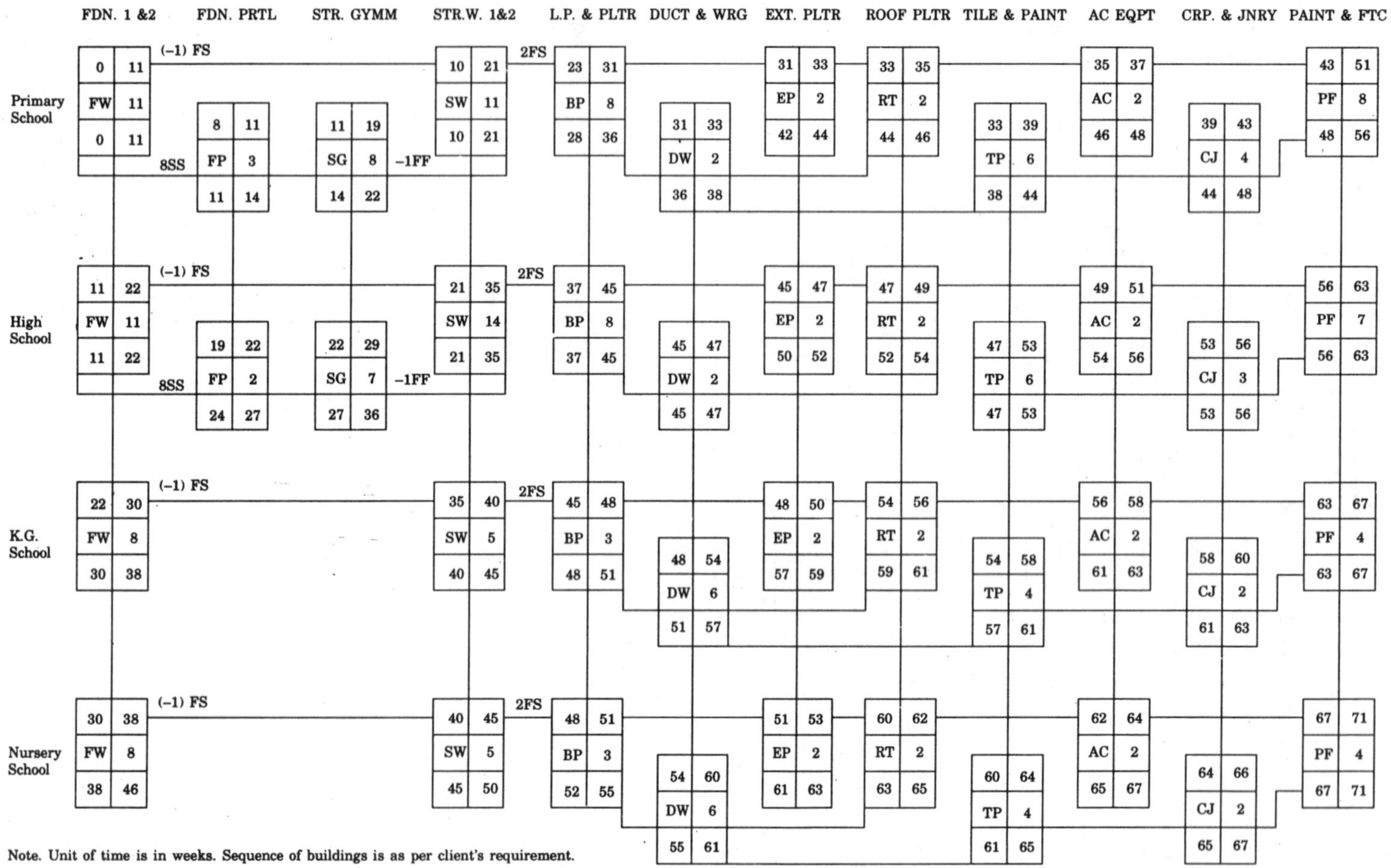

Note. Unit of time is in weeks. Sequence of buildings is as per client's requirement.

## Precedence Network Analysis 165

Exhibit 5.6

**Raw Water Treatment Clarifier**

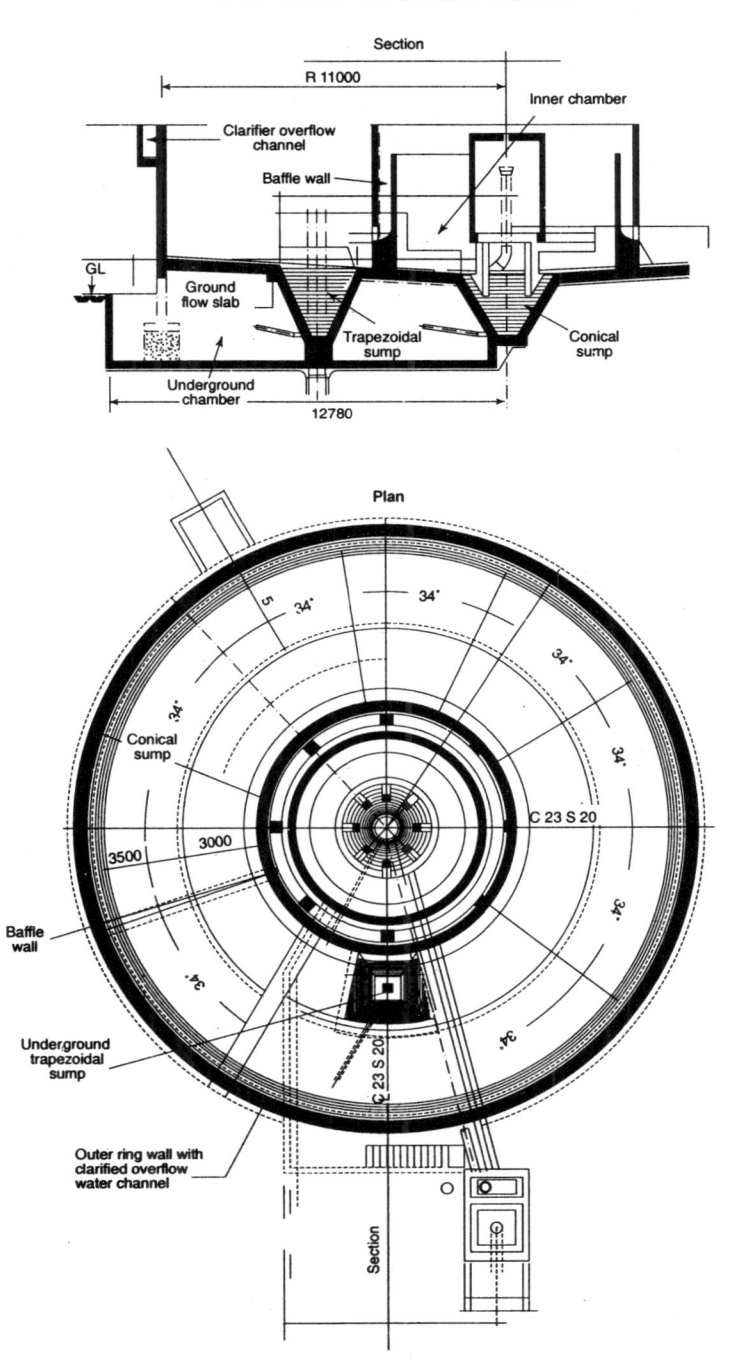

The outer ring wall was 4.5 m high above the RCC circular floor and the floor was supported on a circular base-wall of 1.8 m height. The outer ring wall (dia. 22 m) had an overflow channel, which was to be cast along with the outer ring wall.

**Construction sequence**  The various stages in the construction of clarifier tank are:
1. Construction raft of underground chamber.
2. Building the perimeter wall of underground chamber up to conical sump.
3. Elevating central circular areas of inner conical chamber up to the bottom level ground slab.
4. Building baffle wall in three stages, namely, base, spillway inner wall and outer wall columns, and the outer wall.
5. Raising the outer ring wall up to the bottom level of ground floor slab, followed by filling with lean concrete, except for two sectors on the opposite face to the entrance of underground chamber. This gap is left to provide approach for concreting of the remaining structure using 22 m boom-length concrete pump.
6. Filling the below ground area, enclosed by ring wall, with lean concrete for laying the central ground floor slab except the two approach sectors.
7. Concreting the ground floor slab over the central circular area including slab of the underground chamber, baffle wall (dia. 7 m ), both the sumps.
8. Laying the remaining ground floor slab, sector-wise, with 10 cm kickers of outer ring wall (internal dia. 22 m). except the two approach sectors.
9. Building the inner chamber in two stages, namely, column and ring beam, followed by cylindrical wall with slab.
10. Raising the ring wall (internal dia. 22 m) , sector by sector, above the central ground floor slab, except for the two approach sectors.
11. Constructing the remaining two sectors of outer ring wall.
12. Screeding after installation of mechanical equipment.

**Work breakdown**  The construction of the water clarifier tank involves the following work packages, the activities involved are shown against each:

| *Work packages* | *Activities* |
|---|---|
| 1. Field location | Survey and layout. |
| 2. Underground chamber | Excavation, blinding, raft concreting, wall concreting, and central ground floor slab. |
| 3. Inner conical sump | Excavation, blinding, columns and beams, central ground floor slab, above-ground level wall and slab. |
| 4. Baffle wall | Excavation, blinding, base, wall, and central roof slab. |
| 5. Outer ring wall | Excavation, blinding, below-ground level wall (in three lifts), central ground floor slab, and level above-ground and outer ring wall (10 sectors). |

**Time analyzed PN**  The network of a raw water clarifier is shown in Exhibit 5.7. The completion time of civil works was fixed as 140 working days corresponding to the scheduled start date of February 1, 1986 and the completion date of July 12, 1986.

# Precedence Network Analysis

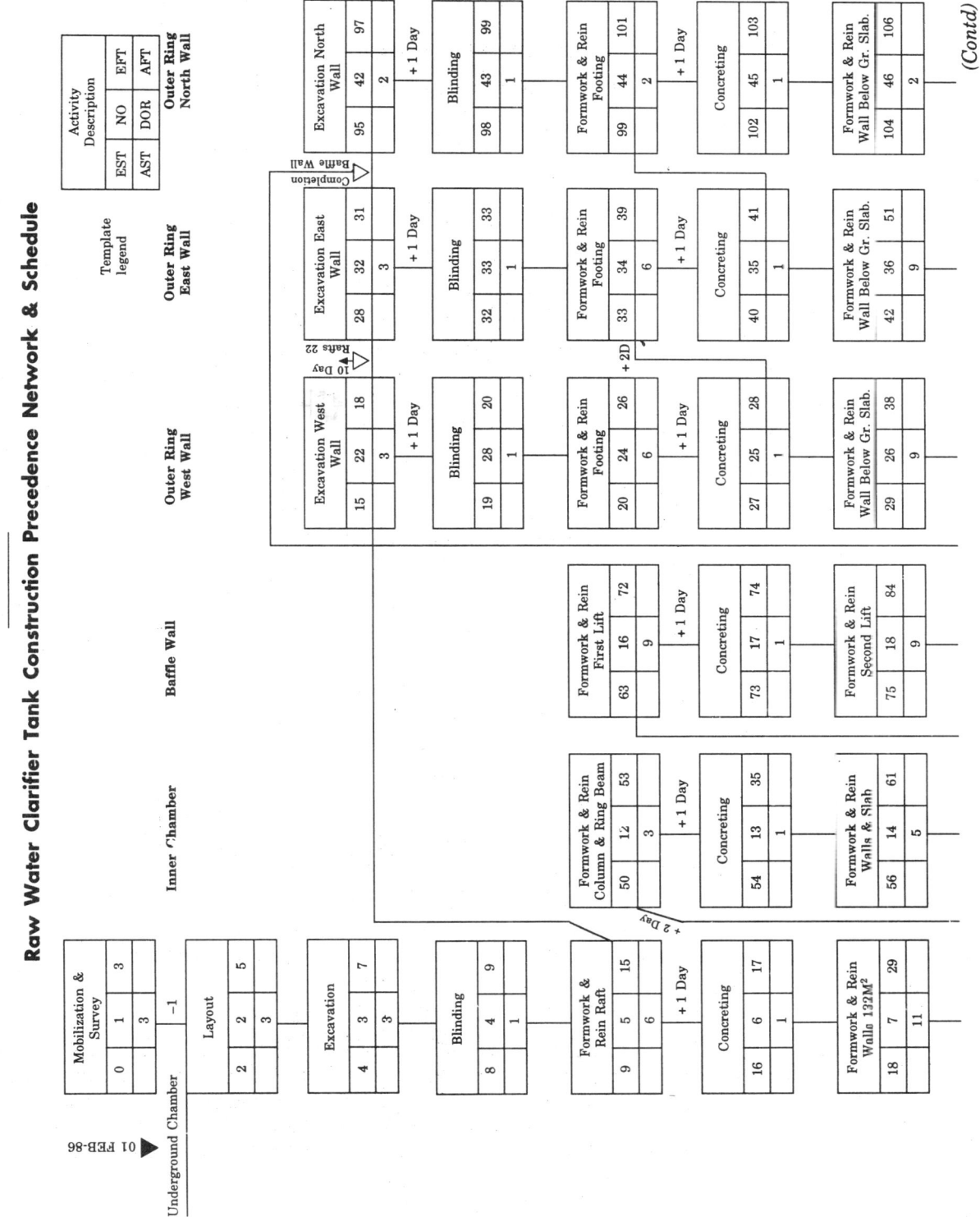

## Exhibit 5.7
## Raw Water Clarifier Tank Construction Precedence Network & Schedule

*(Contd)*

# 168 Construction Project Management

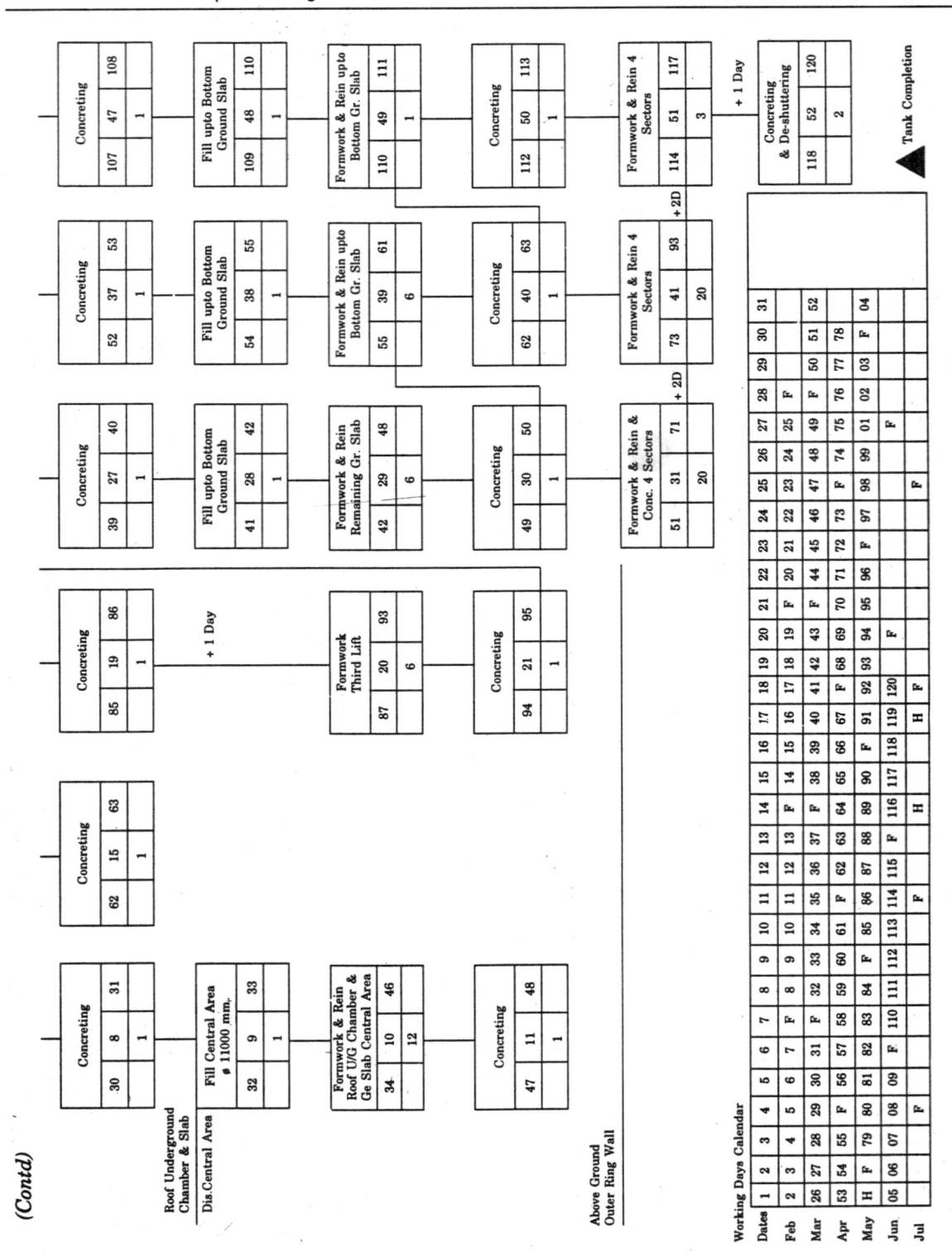

*(Contd)*

The contractor planned for completion of work in 120 fair-weather working days, earmarking the remaining 20 days as his reserve for rains and bad weather. The contractor's work programme, based on the earliest start time, is also given in Exhibit 5.7.

## 5.3 CLASSIFICATION OF NETWORKS

From the functional angle, the networks in a project, are classified into four categories: skeleton network, master network, detailed network and summary network.

The purpose of these networks, the level of activity used, the unit adopted for estimation of duration and the rough cost of each activity are given below.

### 5.3.1 Skeleton Network

The project skeleton network depicts the preliminary or outline plan of the project using (sub-projects and tasks) level of activities. The duration of each activity is estimated in months or weeks.

The rough cost of each activity varies from 0.5–5% of the project cost. Skeleton networks are prepared during the feasibility or engineering stage with a view to provide direction to the project management team.

### 5.3.2 Master Network

This network is designed for controlling the systematic execution of a project or contract. It generally uses work packages as database. Its unit of time for duration estimation is taken in weeks. The rough cost of each activity is 0.1–2.5% of the project cost.

### 5.3.3 Detailed Network

This network is prepared for the execution of day-to-day work, conforming to the sequence of activities given in the master network. It contains lower-level activities, whose duration is assessed in days. These are prepared for controlling the extremely important sub-projects, tasks or contracts where the progress of work is to be watched and controlled on a day-to-day basis. Detailed networks are also prepared for determining the duration of a work package.

### 5.3.4 Summary Network

This network depicts the summary of a master network. In the summary network, sub-projector task level is used and their duration is assessed in weeks. The project summary network and its schedule are used in project information reporting to the top management.

One of the methods of summarizing a master network is to introduce the hammock activities to link a sub-network or a group of activities, as explained earlier.

## 5.4 GUIDELINES FOR DRAWING PROJECT PN

The networks drawn using standard conventions are easily readable and acceptable. These rules for drawing networks depend upon the network technique employed.

The rules for drawing the CPM/PERT sub-networks are covered in Chapter 4. The PN drawing conventions are described herewith to standardize details presentation.

### 5.4.1 Network Purpose

A project needs different types of networks like master network, summary network and contract control network, at various levels of control. The first step in drawing a network is to decide upon the type of network required and then draw separate networks incorporating relevant information for each level of control.

Initially, the draft of the network should be prepared in pencil, discussion at various levels. As far as possible, the level of activities within a network should be kept consistent.

### 5.4.2 Network Drawing Sheet Size

Each type of network should be drawn on convenient size sheet not exceeding A0 size (1189 mm × 841 mm). An A0 size drawing sheet is sufficient for as many as 200 activities. Networks should be split into various sub-networks linked by the interfacing activities or events (shown in boxes or circles) and should be drawn on smaller size (A3 or A4) paper.

### 5.4.3 Project Network Layout Stratification

Prior to the commencement of integration, the paper on which the project network diagram is to be drawn should be divided into various strata. *Stratification* means division of the network diagram in such a way that activities pertaining to the same department, contract, location or method of construction, can be grouped by drawing horizontal and/or vertical lines. Generally, the strata can be visualized from a prior knowledge of the scope of work in a project. These can also be easily deduced from the work-breakdown structure. The method of stratification is covered in Chapter 4.

### 5.4.4 Network Layout

The non-repetitive networks should be developed horizontally, starting from left to right. The path containing the maximum activities should be positioned in the middle portion of the network, and the remaining activities should be suitably positioned on its upper and lower sides (as far as possible). For repetitive work networks, the linking of activities should be horizontal or vertical, as convenient.

Check that all activities are included in the network. The standard network symbols and method of linking symbols should be used. The non-standard symbols if used, should be clarified.

### 5.4.5 Network Logic

The following guidelines may reduce complications arising from the multiple nature of dependency logic:

(a) Outgoing dependency lines can be drawn on the activity box, either from left top or bottom, or from the right edge of the activity box. For repetitive works projects, the middle of bottom side may be used to link up repetitive activities vertically.
(b) Activities heading to an activity box, depending upon logic, are mostly linked with the left edge of the activity box. In rare cases, the right edge or top side of the box is used to represent the start-to-finish and finish-to-finish logic.
(c) Crossing and/or reversing of dependency lines should be minimized by suitably positioning the activities.
(d) Arrowheads should be drawn wherever necessary to clarify the direction of flow.

It may be noted that in case of logic constraints:

(a) There can be more than one different types of relationships between any two given activities.
(b) The relationship time can be positive or negative to show overlapping or separation, respectively, of activities. For example, a succeeding activity completion constraint imposed on the completion of preceding activity, can have a negative delay effect.
(c) Too many relationships can complicate a network. It can also result in conservative estimates as there is a tendency to use extensive overlapping while attempting to meet a predetermined objective.
(d) Unless absolutely essential, it is a general practice to restrict the precedence relationships to a minimum. It can be done by restructuring logic in such a way that the succeeding activity starts only after the preceding activity(ies) has been completed, even if this amounts to a further splitting of related activities.

### 5.4.6 Events and Dummy Activities

Generally, PNs do not have events and dummy activities. However, there are few exceptions. Where a PN starts (or ends) with more than one activity, its start (or end) can be shown by a start event (or an end event).

In large networks, connectors are used to separate part of a network or to provide logical links. Further interface in the form of dummy event can be introduced to mark overlapping of sub networks. The connectors and dummy events of are shown in Fig. 5.5.

## Figure 5.5
## Dummy Events and Connectors to Link Precedence Activities/Sub-networks

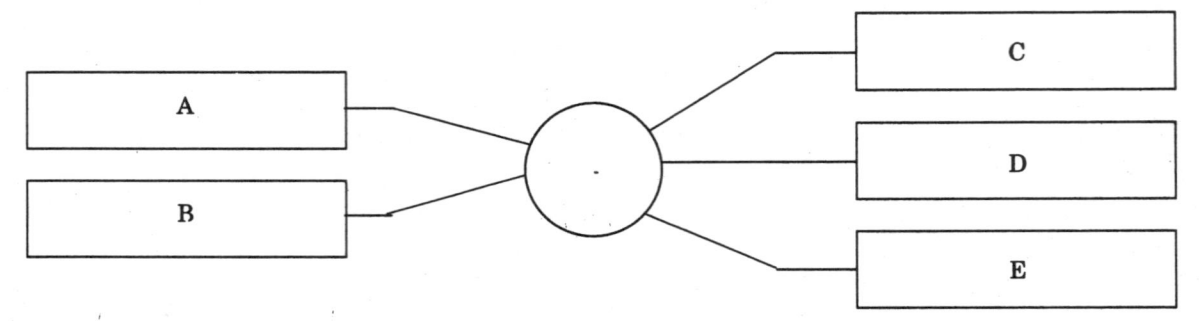

(a) Use of dummy event to link multiple activities, where logic permits so as to avoid congestion. Dummy events can be drawn as boxes or circles.

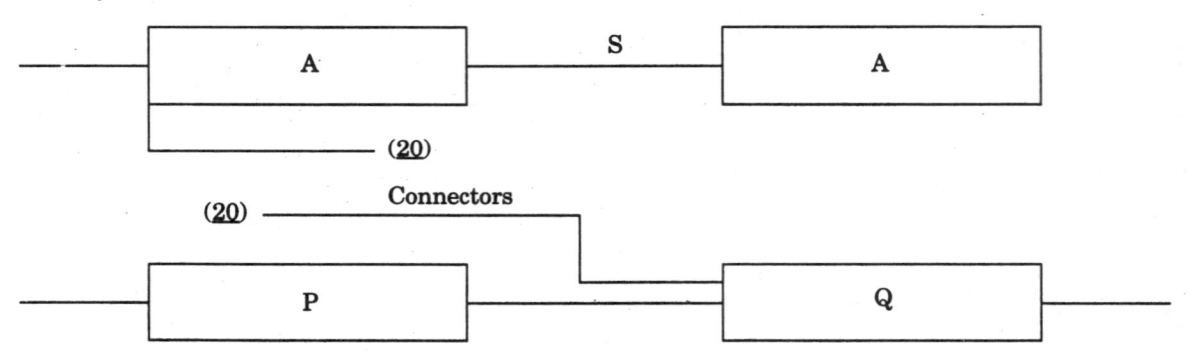

(b) Use of connectors to separate parts of networks.

### 5.4.7 Network Presentation

Some more points for improving the presentations for making them more readable and acceptable:

(a) Make the text of activity description brief but significant. Avoid describing activities by using non-standard abbreviations or alphabetic or numerical codes like A, B, C, 0-2, 5-9, etc. as they need frequent reference to a list of legends. (In this chapter, however, the description of activities in network illustrations has been abbreviated or coded due to limited printing space.)

(b) Draw information index by stratifying the network into broad horizontal and/or vertical bands for demarcating departments and grouping similar type of works.

(c) Use the drawing method specified for writing titles of network, drawing number, sheet number, revision data, names of persons drawing and approving the network, date of issue, and the signature. Notes on network drawing should highlight the unit of time, the non-standard symbols used and other important drawing features including distribution. Generally, all this information is written on the right hand side of the drawing sheet.

## 5.5 PNA VERSUS CPM

### 5.5.1 Same Family

Both Critical Path Method (CPM) and Precedence Network Analysis (PNA) belong to family of network analysis techniques. The common features, as already mentioned in Chapter 4, are that they:

(a) make use of the network-type graphic model to depict the time plan for execution of the project;
(b) apply the critical path analysis concept for determining project duration and identifying critical activities; and
(c) employ these network analysis techniques for scheduling and controlling of projects.

Although CPM and PNA network models may appear different, logically they are similar. For a given project, both CPM and PNA network contain same job activities and durations. In case of networks using finish-to-start logic, even activity times and extent of floats are equal. This can easily be seen from the CPM and PNA networks of the Site Development Project shown in Exhibit 5.8.

Generally, a CPM network can be converted into a PNA network by the following steps:

(a) Delete dummy activities and isolated start and end events.
(b) Identify preceding events of all the non-dummy activities.
(c) Draw boxes around the non-dummy activities to enclose the preceding event, activity description and its duration.
(d) Develop PN by linking activity boxes with dependency lines using the finish-to-start relationship.

To quote another example, the PN of the factory project thus developed, along with its CPM network for comparison, is shown in Exhibit 5.9. Note that PNs having multiple logic constraints cannot be converted into CPM networks without further splitting the affected activities.

Both PNA and CPM are used extensively for planning construction projects. They have some common features as well as significant differences.

### 5.5.2 Common Features

(a) Both separate planning and scheduling. In network-based project, network planning precedes scheduling of work and budgeting of resources.
(b) Both enable systematic and logical development of time programme of complex projects with resource constraints. In these programmes, the scope of work and interconnection between activities get clearly defined.

## Exhibit 5.8

## Site Development Project CPM and PNA Networks

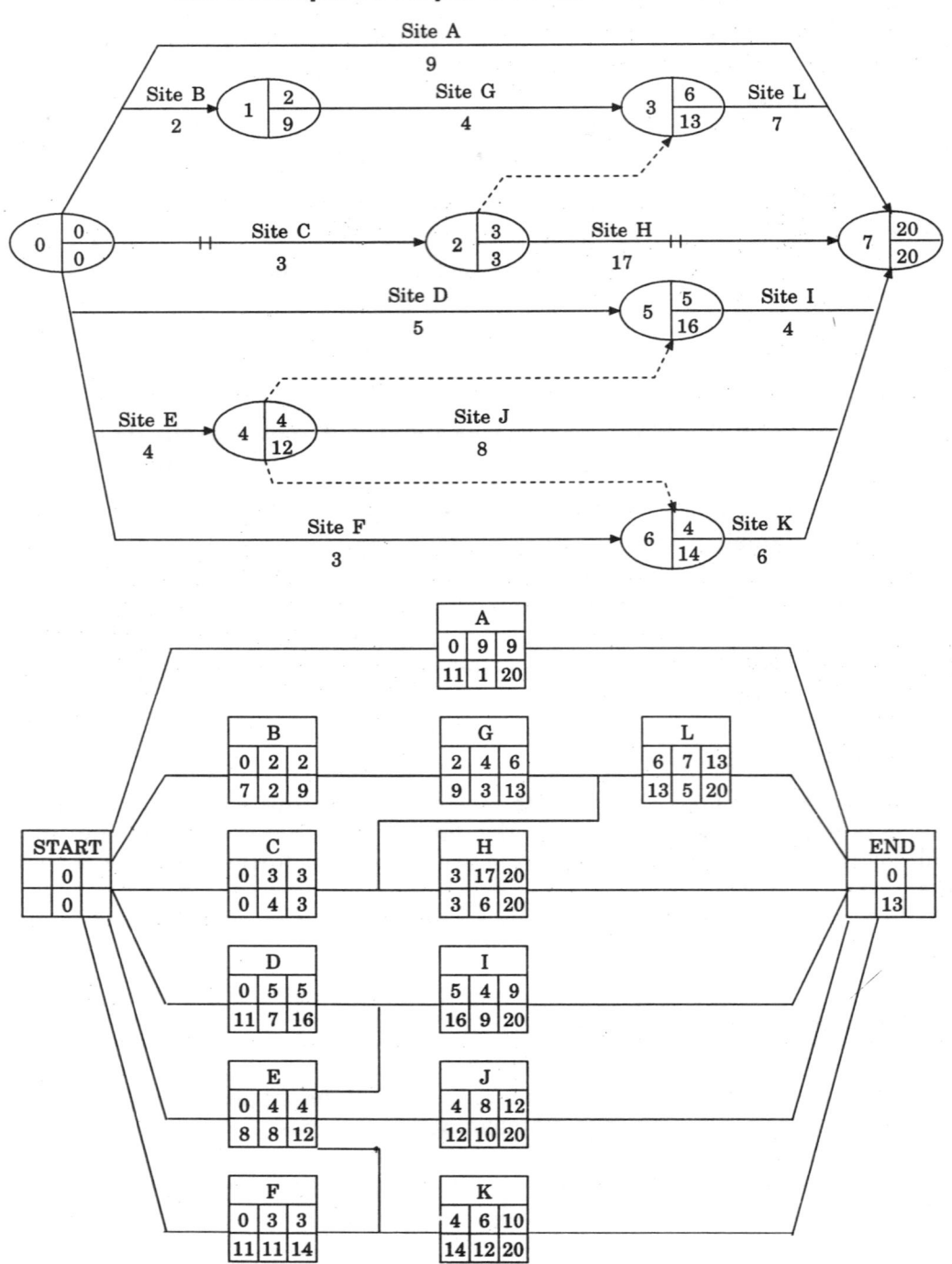

Precedence Network Analysis 175

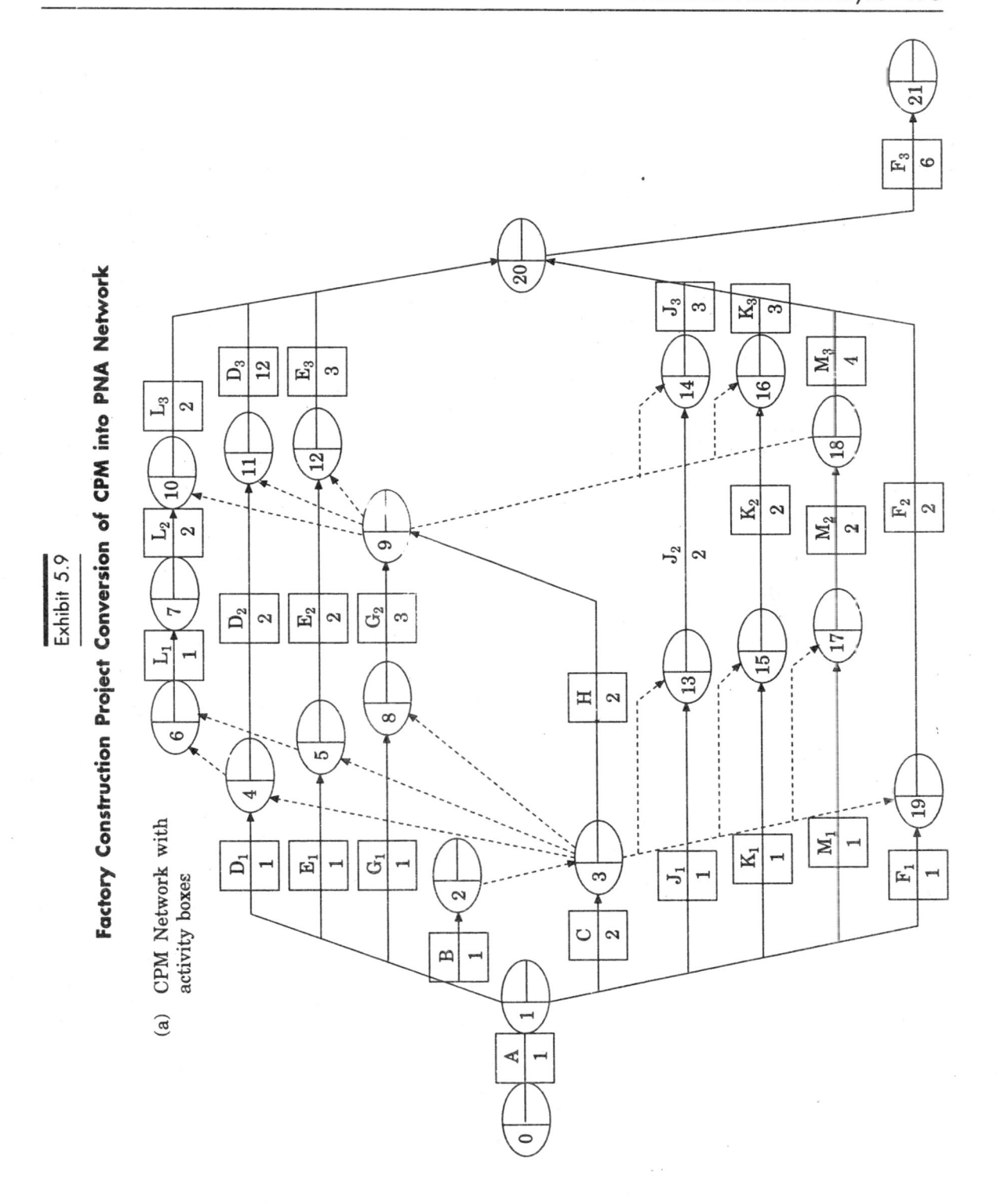

Exhibit 5.9
**Factory Construction Project Conversion of CPM into PNA Network**

(a) CPM Network with activity boxes

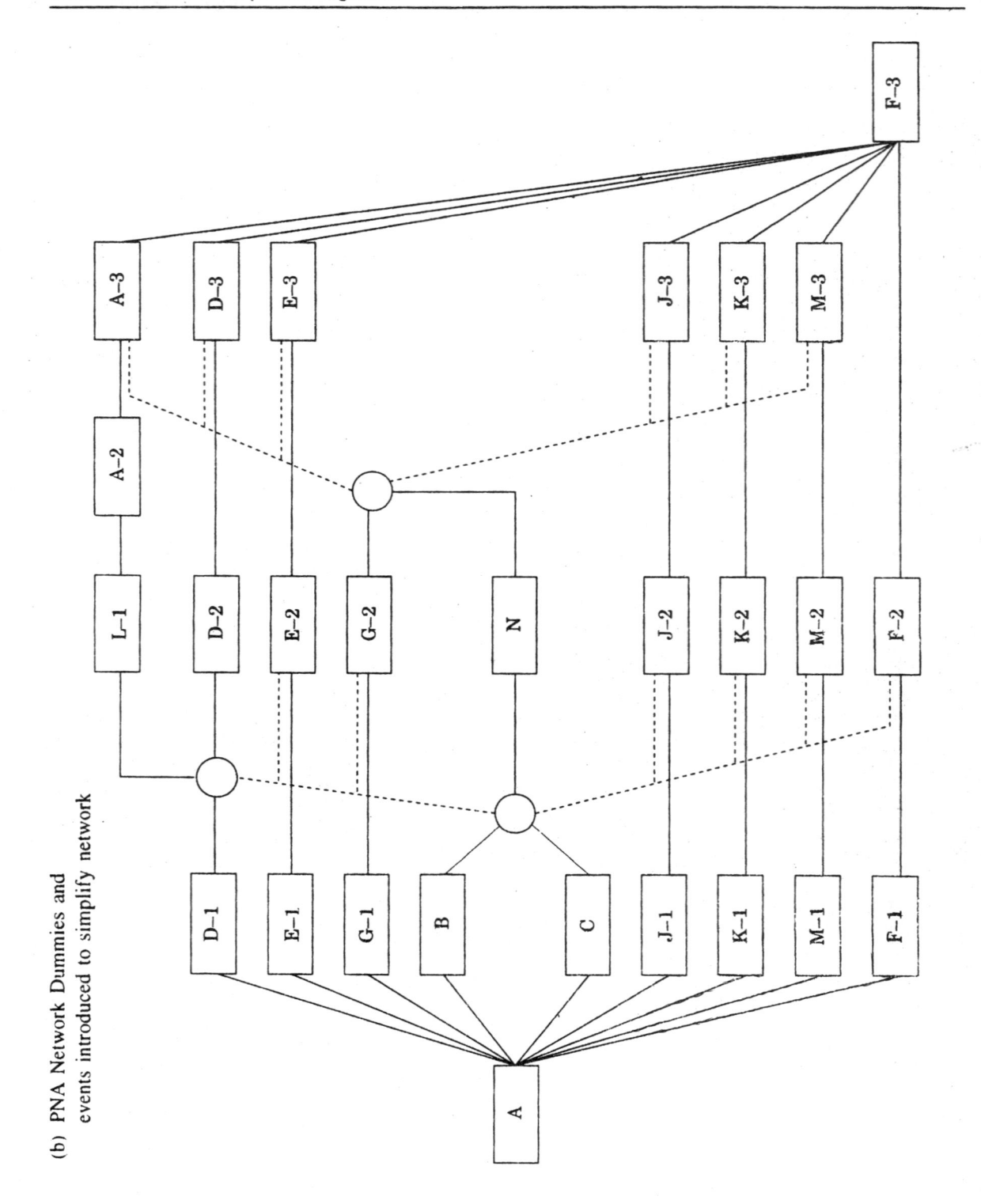

**176** Construction Project Management

(b) PNA Network Dummies and events introduced to simplify network

(c) Both depict interdependence diagrammatically. This makes for easy comprehension of the tasks involved, anticipation of potential problem areas and judging the implication of changes.
(d) Both help in establishing a relationship between time and cost, thus enabling optimization of resources.
(e) Both are independent of time axis and, therefore, do not become outdated with the passage of time.
(f) Both aid in establishing key events, scheduling of work, budgeting of resources and measuring of risks on a scientific basis.
(g) Both provide basis for monitoring progress and analysing effect of deviations.
(h) Both help in exercising management-by-exception, by focusing thought of the management on critical activities.
(i) Both provide the common language for communication among all those connected with management of projects thus reducing communication gaps, coordination effort and contractual disputes.

## 5.5.3 Major Differences

**Comprehensive appearance** The PNA presents a better appearance than CPM. In PNA, activities are generally arranged in rows of symmetrically placed horizontal boxes connected with dependency lines, whereas CPM contains arrows, dummy arrows and events drawn in forward direction at various angles.

PNA is simpler. It does not contain dummies, events or unnecessary low order activities. This reduces chances of error, size of network and the data processing effort.

Colour code, if used for activity boxes in PNA enables easy identification of critical and non-critical activities. Different colour codes on these boxes can also represent responsibilities and resources.

In PNA each activity box includes relevant data for time and, possibly, resources needed for analysis, but in CPM it is distributed on arrows and connecting events.

**Ease of drawing** The logic-arrow diagram of CPM is easy to draw whereas PNA takes more time to develop its logic sketch. After finalization of logic diagram, PNA is quicker to draw than CPM.

**Realistic logic representation** PNA takes into consideration overlapping of activities. These overlapped activities present a realistic sequence of engineering tasks as they occur in actual execution. PNA can represent four types of logic, namely, finish-to-start, start-to-start, start-to-finish and finish-to-finish. These cover real life situations better than the CPM's single finish-to-start relationship approach.

**Ease of logic alteration** PNA enables easy alteration as it involves connecting dependency lines instead of shifting of arrows and events as in the CPM network.

**Ease of understanding and communication** The CPM network with its distinct events and simple logic relationship can be easily understood by those not familiar with network analysis. This is difficult in the case of PNA with its multiple logic relationship.

**Computerization of network** CPM having single logic relationship of finish-to-start generally, needs less input data than PNA with its multi-logic approach. However, for a network of the same project, PNA has less activity input as there are no dummies.

PNA networks can be zoomed in various sizes and levels on computer screen according to the information needs of various levels of management. The detailed activity networks can be easily transformed to the summarized versions.

**Manual analysis of network** CPM is comparatively easier to analyze than PNA. In case of PNA, all the time data has to be transferred from one activity to its adjoining activity before the adjoining activity can be analyzed.

**Activity label** In PNA, each activity is given a unique label number. This label can also be used to indicate the activity resources, whereas in CPM, the label of activity changes with alteration of logic or addition of new activities.

**Time scale network schedule** The schedule derived from CPM can be drawn both in bar charts as well as the 'time scale network' format in which each activity is drawn to time scale. The 'time scale network' schedule is difficult (but possible) in PNA as distortion of activity boxes can result in confusion.

### 5.5.4 Application

Networks are the tools employed by planners for planning and controlling the project time objectives. These are instruments representing the mutually agreed plan of action between client and the project executing agencies. Although their preparation, monitoring and revision is generally confined within the planning department, they form the basis for discussion and communication of information among the project management team and with the client.

Network-analysis is the most useful technique developed to help the project management perform its functions efficiently. Experience shows that in complex construction projects:

(a) The CPM is best suited for developing sub project, task or work-package sub networks having activities with deterministic single-time duration.
(b) The PN is better suited for time planning of construction projects.
(c) Network containing up to 300 activities or work-packages are manageable while those above this are difficult to comprehend. Generally, the large-sized projects employing PNA technique use the following levels of details:

| Network Classification | Level of Details |
|---|---|
| Project summary networks | Sub projects or tasks |
| Project master networks | Work packages |
| Sub-project networks | Activities |

### 5.5.5 Limitations of Network Techniques

(a) Though simple and straightforward, the introduction of network analysis requires specialized training.
(b) Network analysis is not very useful for planning repetitive type of work. The planning of such projects needs scheduling rather than preparation of a ladder-type network. However, an integrated use of project network and line-of-balance technique (see Chapter 6) can be usefully adopted for repetitive projects.
(c) Network analysis provides the means for taking decisions, but the actual decisions have to be made by the management itself. It is not a substitute for bad management.
(d) Network analysis indicates practical courses of action to accomplish specified time objectives. A project network shows the sequence and interdependence of activities. A network is scheduled to determine the commencement and termination date of each activity for accomplishing the task within stipulated time by using the optimum level of resources. It is the schedule which outlines plan for execution of work and not the network itself.

# CHAPTER 6

# Project Work Scheduling

A *schedule* is a work programme, set date-wise in a logical sequence; it is a time table for action. Time scheduling is the process of developing a work programme. It implies programming of the chosen work plan on a calender basis and provides the base against which all progress is measured.

The scheduling methodology varies with the planning technique and the nature of task to be performed. A tool kit containing the commonly used techniques for planning, scheduling and monitoring is shown in Table 2.3 of Chapter 2. Simple projects can be scheduled using the 'bar chart methodology'. The Line-of-Balance (LOB) technique is widely accepted for scheduling the repetitive work projects, while network scheduling is suitable for all types of projects. There are many other scheduling techniques.

The method of presentation of a schedule depends upon the scheduling technique used. Generally, all of them use time scale along the horizontal axis. This time scale mostly uses a 'week' as the unit of time; these weeks are then related to the calendar dates and months. Each scheduling technique has its own merits and demerits. But ultimately schedules are best presented in the bar chart form for ease of comprehension and communication. These bar charts are supplemented with the appropriate planning technique for monitoring the progress of the projects.

This Chapter describes the scheduling methodology under the following heads.

(a) Purpose of Scheduling Work
(b) Scheduling using Bar Chart
(c) Scheduling the Network Plan
(d) Line-of-Balance (LOB) Method of Scheduling Repetitive Projects
(e) Factors affecting work scheduling
(f) Forecasting Inputs and Outputs
(g) Schedule Hierarchy

## ◻ 6.1 PURPOSE OF WORK SCHEDULING

Work scheduling serves the following purposes:

**(a) It simplifies the project plan**  The bar-chart type work schedule provides a simplified version of the work plan, which can easily be understood by all concerned with planning, coordination, execution and control of the project.

**(b) It validates the time objectives**  A work schedule shows the planned sequence of activities, date-wise. While putting the work plan on a calendar basis, it takes into account reduced efficiency of resources to adverse climatic conditions and other factors. It verifies the deadlines imposed for completion of the project and achievement of the milestones.

**(c) It optimizes the resources employed**  A work schedule is based on the most economical employment of the resources of men, materials and machinery. It smoothens abrupt changes which may occur from time to time.

Resource optimization is achieved by a systematic utilization of the floats of non-critical activities. Unless otherwise constrained, a project is scheduled using either the optimum or the available pattern of resources.

**(d) It forecasts the input resources, and predicts the output**  A work schedule enables the forecasting of resources and also indicates the pattern of resource consumption. The time schedule of work forms the basis for predicting the resource requirement as well as the financial state of the project in terms of investment, expenditure, output and income.

**(e) It evaluates the implications of scheduling constraints**  A work schedule brings out the implications of constraints, and enables preparation of a plan of work within the framework of these constraints.

## ◻ 6.2 BAR CHART METHOD OF WORK SCHEDULING

In the bar chart method, works are first split into activities. These activities are then listed in the order of construction priorities, generally on the lefthand side column, while the time scale is plotted horizontally on the top and/or bottom of the chart (Exhibit 2 2). The bar against each activity represents its schedule of work. The start of the bar marks the commencement of the activity and the end of the bar, its completion. The length of the bar on the calendar scale represents the duration of the activity. Horizontally, each row depicts the activity description, activity data and the rectangular shape bar represents the activity schedule.

The time base of bar charts—and, for that matter, all scheduling techniques is the project calendar. Generally, this calendar covers a bar or tabulated format, a project's life span from the date it started to the date of its final completion. It specifies the dates when the activities can be scheduled for execution. It shows all calendar months, weeks, working days, weekend non-working days and holidays. The calendar weeks may have the standard five or six working days. The detailed calendar also highlights the various non-working days such as the weekends and national and other holidays. The project calendar and its parts are invariably, represented in a bar format as shown in various exhibits of this chapter.

The chart can be vertically divided into three divisions. The left division group activities are listed in the sequence of their execution. The central portion contains the data of activities. The right division depicts the calendar and the schedule of activities. Graphically, the three vertical segments of a bar chart can be arranged in the following ways:

(a) Activity description, data and calendar. This is a commonly adopted sequence.
(b) Activity description and calendar. This is used where data is omitted.
(c) Calendar with activity (or work package or task) only with description written inside or at the end of the bar. It is particularly useful for making a schedule for a large project.
(d) Data followed by calendar with description inside or at the end of the bar. This facilitates scheduling of long duration projects.

Schedules are prepared in the form of bar charts as shown in Exhibit 6.1. Bar chart schedule of 2000 Housing Units Project is shown in Exhibit 2.2.

Bar charts are easy to plot, comprehend and communicate, and are most appropriate for presentation of schedules. However, as a planning technique, the bar chart is not suitable for complex projects due to the following reasons:

(a) It does not reflect the relationship between various activities which are a common feature of all complex projects.
(b) It cannot identify and highlight the emerging critical tasks needing special attention for preventing schedule slippages, time overruns, and other bottlenecks.
(c) In complex projects, time durations are often educated guesses. Any change in schedule or time duration would require a redrawing of the multi-task bar chart schedule.

Thus, it can be said that the bar chart format is most useful for presentation of schedules, but as a planning technique, it is not suitable for scheduling of complex projects. The method of conversion of a Network Plan into a bar chart schedule is described in subsequent paragraphs.

## ❑ 6.3 SCHEDULING THE NETWORK PLAN

A schedule aims at optimizing resources for completion of the project within stipulated time objectives. Resource optimization implies scheduling of resources according to the given pattern of their employment. Optimization is achieved by suitably adjusting the schedule of non-critical activities using available floats in such a manner that fluctuations from the desired pattern of resource utilization are minimized.

Mathematically, there are a large number of ways for adjusting the floats of activities. For example, if an activity 'A' has a float of three days, and the parallel activity 'B' has a float of two days, then 12 schedules of these activities can be obtained by adjusting the floats between them. This means that activity A may consume 0, 1, 2, or 3 days float, and

Project Work Scheduling **183**

Exhibit 6.1

## Site Development Project: Work Programme

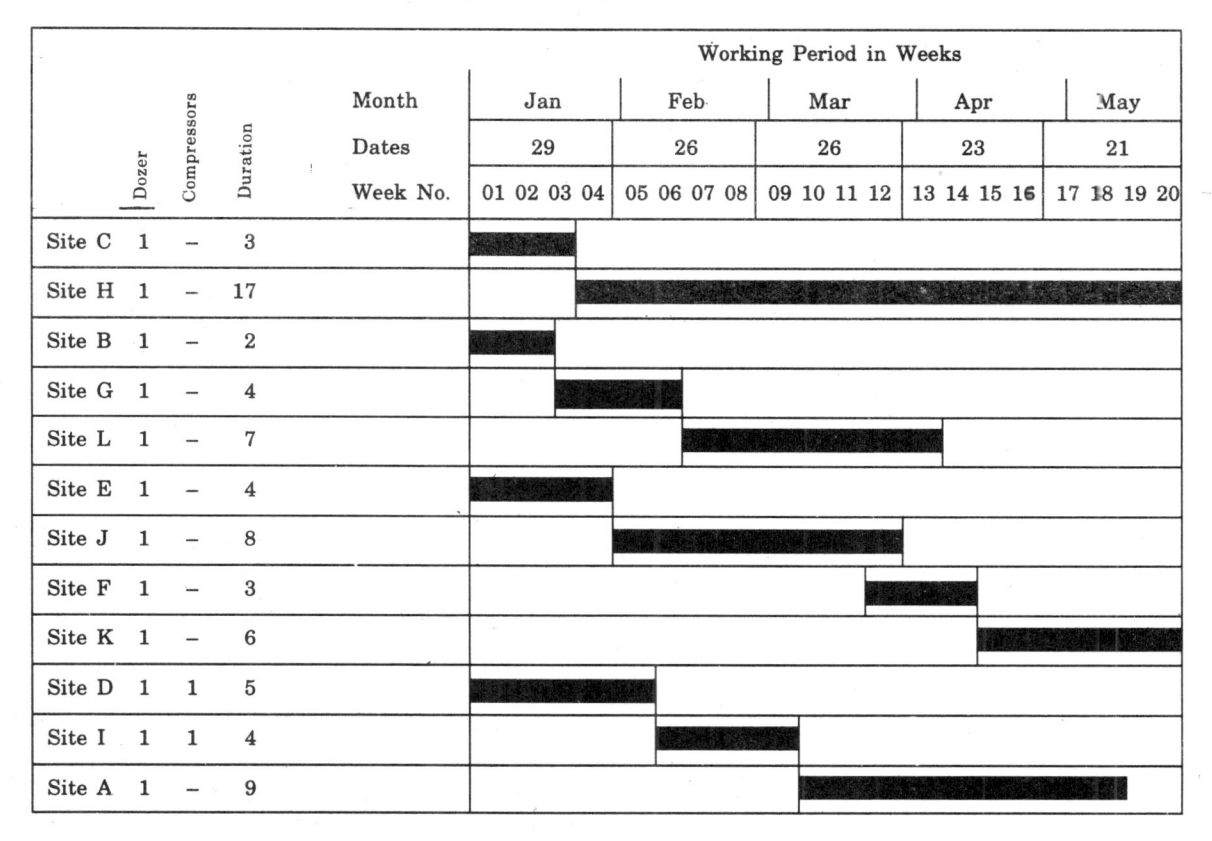

| | Dozer | Compressors | Duration | Month | Jan | Feb | Mar | Apr | May |
|---|---|---|---|---|---|---|---|---|---|
| | | | | Dates | 29 | 26 | 26 | 23 | 21 |
| | | | | Week No. | 01 02 03 04 | 05 06 07 08 | 09 10 11 12 | 13 14 15 16 | 17 18 19 20 |
| Site C | 1 | – | 3 | | ▇▇▇ | | | | |
| Site H | 1 | – | 17 | | | ▇▇▇▇ | ▇▇▇▇ | ▇▇▇▇ | ▇▇▇▇ |
| Site B | 1 | – | 2 | | ▇▇ | | | | |
| Site G | 1 | – | 4 | | | ▇▇▇▇ | | | |
| Site L | 1 | – | 7 | | | | ▇▇▇▇▇▇▇ | | |
| Site E | 1 | – | 4 | | ▇▇▇▇ | | | | |
| Site J | 1 | – | 8 | | | ▇▇▇▇ | ▇▇▇▇ | | |
| Site F | 1 | – | 3 | | | | | ▇▇▇ | |
| Site K | 1 | – | 6 | | | | | | ▇▇▇▇▇▇ |
| Site D | 1 | 1 | 5 | | ▇▇▇▇▇ | | | | |
| Site I | 1 | 1 | 4 | | | ▇▇▇▇ | | | |
| Site A | 1 | – | 9 | | | | ▇▇▇▇ | ▇▇▇▇▇ | |

## Site Development Project: Time Scale Network Logic Chart

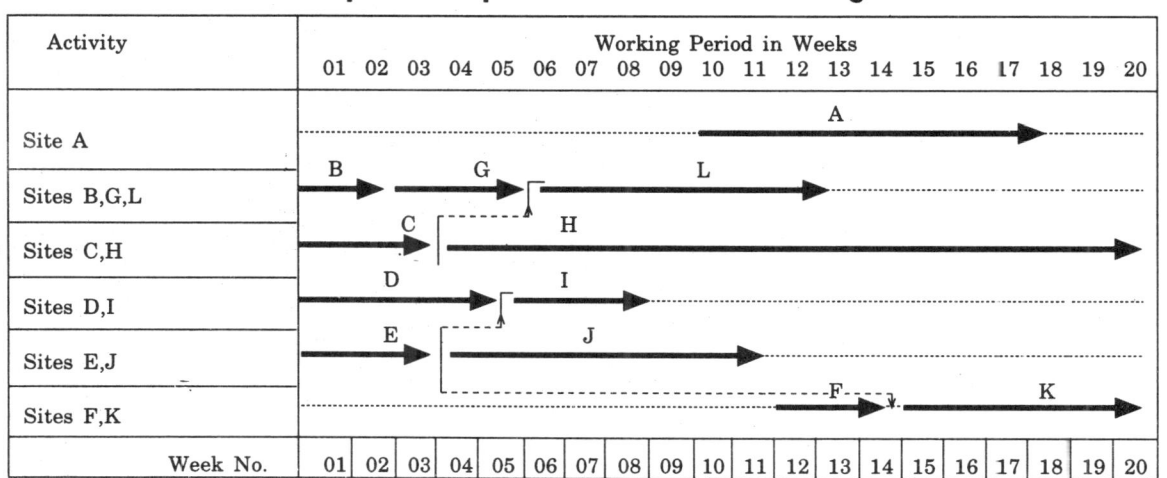

| Activity | Working Period in Weeks |
|---|---|
| | 01 02 03 04 05 06 07 08 09 10 11 12 13 14 15 16 17 18 19 20 |
| Site A | A (weeks 10–18) |
| Sites B,G,L | B (1–2), G (4–7), L (8–14) |
| Sites C,H | C (1–3), H (4–20) |
| Sites D,I | D (1–5), I (6–9) |
| Sites E,J | E (1–4), J (5–12) |
| Sites F,K | F (12–14), K (15–20) |
| Week No. | 01 02 03 04 05 06 07 08 09 10 11 12 13 14 15 16 17 18 19 20 |

**184** Construction Project Management

that for each schedule of A, three schedules of B are possible. The procedure explained below can be adopted to systematically reduce the number of possible solutions for optimizing resources.

The process of network scheduling is described step by step with the help of the CPM network of a simple site development project as shown in Exhibit 5.8. This network is reproduce in Exhibit 6.2. The scheduling of PN-based projects also follows a similar procedure and is comparatively simpler as there are no dummies or event timings. The scheduling of network plan involves the following steps:

- (a) Outlining scheduling constraints.
- (b) Identifying the floats of each activity and tabulate activities to order of (ascending order of floats) sensitivity.
- (c) Preparing the earliest start time (EST) schedule.
- (d) Determining resource scheduling criteria.
- (e) Scheduling critical activities at their EST.
- (f) Scheduling non-critical activities.
- (g) Optimizing other resources.
- (h) Validating time objectives.

Exhibit 6.2

### Site Development Project CPM Network

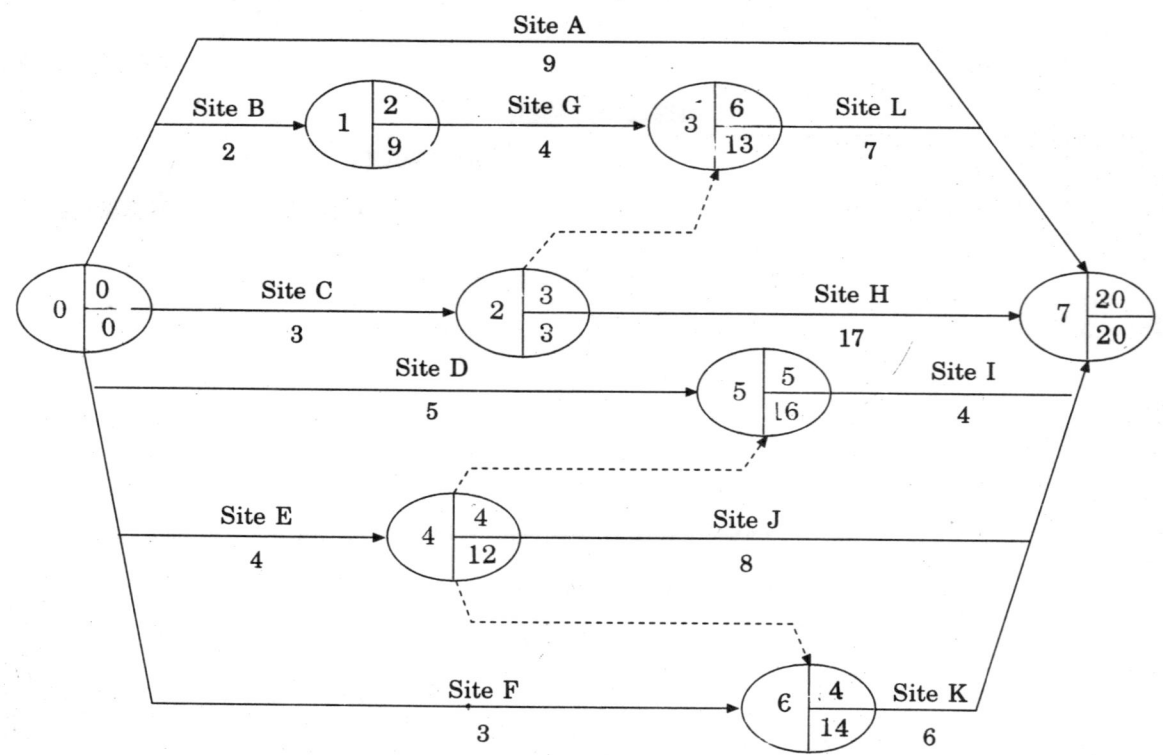

(i) Scheduling within resource constraints.
(j) Scheduling networks of repetitive projects

It would have been ideal to illustrate the optimisation procedure with a major project in the text, but due to space limitations, the process of network scheduling is described step-by-step with the help of a simple Site Clearance Project CPM network Exhibit 6.2. This has been followed by more examples on scheduling of work.

### 6.3.1 Outlining the Scheduling Constraints

These constraints may include the following:

(a) Time objectives of the project and the milestones specified in terms of imposed dates.
(b) The working period and the dates of holidays.
(c) Availability of men, material and machinery, and restrictions on their use
(d) Terms of the labour employed.
(e) Degree of uncertainty, where applicable.

The following assumptions and constraints are considered while scheduling the CPM network of the site development project:

(a) The date of commencement of work is January 1, 1990.
(b) Four bulldozers in excellent working condition are available for the work. However, due to restricted space, not more than one dozer team can work at any site at a given time. Further, in case of a breakdown of dozers, their replacement can be provided by hiring dozers locally.
(c) Compressors are available on demand.
(d) Five working days have been considered in a calendar week, leaving the rest of the days as spare, reserve, holidays or bad weather days.

### 6.3.2 Identifying the Floats of Activities

Floats provide the time margins which can be utilized during scheduling of activities without affecting the time objectives. The amount of float available is a measure of the sensitivity of the activity, with less float meaning a higher sensitivity to delays.

Floats can be divided into three categories namely, total float, free float and interference float.

**Total Float (TF)** It is the maximum period by which the start of an activity can be delayed from its earliest start time (EST) without affecting the project duration. For an activity (i – j) having duration 'd'.

$$TF = LST - EST$$
But
$$LST = LET_j - d$$
$$EST = EET_i$$
Therefore,
$$TF = LET_j - d - EET_i$$

**Free Float (FF)** It is the maximum period by which the start of an activity can be delayed from its EST without effecting the EST of the subsequent activity/ies.

|  | FF | = | $EST_j - d - EST_i$ |
|---|---|---|---|
| But | $EST_j$ | = | $EET_j$ |
|  | $EST_i$ | = | $EET_i$ |
| Therefore | FF | = | $EET_j - d - EET_i$. |

**Interference Float (IF)** It is the overlapping time between LFT of an activity and EST of the succeeding activity.

$$IF = LFT_j - EST_j$$
$$= LET_j - EET_j$$

For example, in the site development project given below:

| TF of site F | = | LET 6 − d − EET 0 |
|---|---|---|
|  | = | 14 − 3 − 0 |
|  | = | 11 |
| FF of site F | = | EET 6 − d − EET 0 |
|  | = | 4 − 3 − 0 |
|  | = | 1 |
| IF of site F | = | LET 6 − EET 6 |
|  | = | 14 − 4 |
|  | = | 10 |

**Tabulation of float** The tabulation of float has a twofold purpose:

(a) To serve as a ready reckoner to determine the time margin available for each non-critical activity.
(b) To calculate the order of sensitivity of the activities for charting during scheduling. Critical activities have zero floats, they are the most sensitive activities.

The float table for the site clearance project and the order of sensitivity is shown in Table 6.1. The following points may be noted:

(a) The order of sensitivity shows the availability of float in descending order. Thus, a higher sensitivity means lesser float.
(b) For activities having the same amount of total float, interference float is considered to determine the order of sensitivity.
(c) For activities having the same amount of interference float, the path of activities is taken as a guide.

The dummy activities must also be listed and given appropriate numbers.

With experience, the preparation of float table can be dispensed with, and the order of listing based on the degree of sensitivity can be directly determined from the network. This data can then be reflected into the EST schedule (Table 6.2).

Listing the activities in the order of sensitivity in the float table or directly in the scheduling chart can proceed as follows:

## Table 6.1

### Site Development Project
### Float Table

| Sl. No. | Activity | Duration | EET$_i$ | EET$_j$ | LET$_j$ | Total Float | Inter. Float | Free Float | Sensitivity Rank |
|---|---|---|---|---|---|---|---|---|---|
| 1 | 0-2 | 3 | 0 | 3 | 3 | 0 | 0 | 0 | 1 |
| 2 | 2-7 | 17 | 3 | 20 | 20 | 0 | 0 | 0 | 2 |
| 3 | 0-1 | 2 | 0 | 2 | 9 | 7 | 7 | 0 | 3 |
| 4 | 1-3 | 4 | 2 | 6 | 13 | 7 | 7 | 0 | 4 |
| 5 | 3-7 | 7 | 6 | 20 | 20 | 7 | 0 | 7 | 5 |
| 6 | 2-3 | 0 | 3 | 6 | 13 | 10 | 7 | 3 | *6 |
| 7 | 0-5 | 5 | 0 | 5 | 16 | 11 | 11 | 0 | 12 |
| 8 | 5-7 | 4 | 5 | 20 | 20 | 11 | 0 | 11 | 13 |
| 9 | 0-7 | 9 | 0 | 20 | 20 | 11 | 0 | 11 | 14 |
| 10 | 0-4 | 4 | 0 | 4 | 12 | 8 | 8 | 0 | 7 |
| 11 | 4-7 | 8 | 4 | 20 | 20 | 8 | 0 | 8 | 8 |
| 12 | 4-5 | 0 | 4 | 5 | 16 | 12 | 11 | 1 | 15 |
| 13 | 0-6 | 3 | 0 | 4 | 14 | 11 | 10 | 1 | *10 |
| 14 | 6-7 | 6 | 4 | 20 | 20 | 10 | 0 | 10 | 11 |
| 15 | 4-6 | 0 | 4 | 4 | 14 | 10 | 10 | 0 | 9 |

*Note*: For activities marked with asterisk (*), continuity of chain of activities is given preference over extent of availability of float, while labelling rank of sensitivity.

(a) First, serially list all critical activities commencing from the start event to the end event.
(b) Next, list all activities of the sub-critical path, preferably following the numerical order of the activity code, even if slight adjustment may have to be made in the order or sensitivity.
(c) Finally, list remaining chains of activities in the ascending order of availability of float in each activity. Some minor inaccuracy in the order of listing of activities does not materially affect the scheduling process.

### 6.3.3 Preparing the EST Schedule

The earliest start time (EST) schedule of the site development project is shown in Table 6.2. This format may vary with the nature of the project and the types of resources to be forecast. The following steps are involved:

(a) List all activities with connected durations and event times, in the order of their sensitivity.
(b) For each activity draw vertical lines, joining EET$_i$, EET$_j$ and LET$_j$ of each activity.
(c) Against each activity starting from EET$_i$ mark the activity duration. Note first division of calendar starts with 1 and not zero. Accordingly add 'one' to all start timings to

## Table 6.2

**Site Development Project
Earliest Start Time Schedule**

| Activity | Dura-tion | $EET_i$ | $EET_j$ | $LET_j$ | Working Period in Weeks<br>01 02 03 04 05 06 07 08 09 10 11 12 13 14 15 16 17 18 19 20 |
|---|---|---|---|---|---|
| 1  0–2 | 3 | 0 | 3 | 3 | 1 1 1 |
| 2  2–7 | 17 | 3 | 20 | 20 |     1 1 1 1 1 1 1 1 1 1 1 1 1 1 1 1 1 |
| 3  0–1 | 2 | 0 | 2 | 9 | 1 1      IF |
| 4  1–3 | 4 | 2 | 6 | 13 |    1 1 1 1    IF |
| 5  3–7 | 7 | 6 | 20 | 20 |       1 1 1 1 1 1 1   FF |
| 6  2–3 | 0 | 3 | 6 | 13 |     - FF -  - - - - IF - - - |
| 7  0–4 | 4 | 0 | 4 | 12 | 1 1 1 1      IF |
| 8  4–7 | 8 | 4 | 20 | 20 |     1 1 1 1 1 1 1 1   FF |
| 9  4–6 | 0 | 4 | 4 | 14 |     - - - - IF - - - - - |
| 10  0–6 | 3 | 0 | 4 | 14 | 1 1 1 FF    IF |
| 11  6–7 | 6 | 4 | 20 | 20 |     1 1 1 1 1 1   FF |
| 12  0–5 | 5 | 0 | 5 | 16 | 1 1 1 1 1     IF |
| 13  5–7 | 4 | 5 | 20 | 20 |      1 1 1 1   FF |
| 14  0–7 | 9 | 0 | 20 | 20 | 1 1 1 1 1 1 1 1 1  FF |
| 15  4–5 | 0 | 4 | 5 | 16 |      FF - - - - - IF - - - - - |
| Total Dozers Required per Week | | | | | 6 6 6 5 6 6 6 6 6 4 3 3 2 1 1 1 1 1 1 1 |

DOZER REQUIREMENT PROFILE

OPTIMUM REQUIREMENT = 4

Week No.  01 02 03 04 05 06 07 08 09 10 11 12 13 14 15 16 17 18 19 20

obtain calendar schedule date. For example, $EET_2$ marking start of activity 2–7 (H) is 3, but while scheduling its start, the bar commences at the end of 3 and beginning of 4.

(d) Draw free floats and interference floats against each activity. They can be easily identified as following:

   (i) Free float (FF) $\quad = EET_j - d - EET_i$
                                    $= $ Portion between $EET_j$ and end of the bar representing activity earliest start time schedule.

   (ii) Interference float (IF) $\quad = $ Total float – free float
                                      $= (LET_j - d - EET_i) - (EET_j - d - EET_i)$
                                      $= LET_j - EET_j$
                                      $= $ Portion between two vertical lines representing $LET_j - EET_j$.

$EET_i = EST_i$                                                              $EET_j$       $LET_j = LFT$

| d | FF | IF |
|---|----|----|

                                                            ←———Total float———→

EST schedule of a non-critical activity

Graphically the floats of a non-critical activity i-j scheduled at $EST_i$ can be represented as under:

(e) Select the most critical item of resources required for performance of each activity (dozers in case of the site development project).

(g) Aggregate the critical resource date-wise.

**Latest Start Time (LST) Schedule** The procedure for drawing LST schedule is similar to EST schedule, and it can be drawn on the same chart as shown in Exhibit 6.3.

### 6.3.4 Determining the Scheduling Criteria

Resource analysis of the site clearance project reveals that the cumulative requirement of dozers and compressors for 20 weeks duration of the project comes to 72 dozer-weeks. Therefore, the average requirement of these machines can be worked out as follows:

**Dozer requirement** The dozer requirement can be calculated as:

$$\text{Dozer required} = \frac{\text{Cumulative requirement}}{\text{Duration of project}}$$

$$= \frac{72}{20}$$

$$= 4 \text{ approximately.}$$

Exhibit 6.3

**Site Development Project**

| | Activity | Duration | $EET_i$ | $EET_j$ | $LET_j$ | Earliest Start Time Schedule Working Period in Weeks 01 | 02 | 03 | 04 | 05 | 06 | 07 | 08 | 09 | 10 | 11 | 12 | 13 | 14 | 15 | 16 | 17 | 18 | 19 | 20 |
|---|---|---|---|---|---|---|---|---|---|---|---|---|---|---|---|---|---|---|---|---|---|---|---|---|---|
| 1 | 0–2 | 3 | 0 | 3 | 3 | 1 | 1 | 1 | | | | | | | | | | | | | | | | | |
| 2 | 2–7 | 17 | 3 | 20 | 20 | | | | 1 | 1 | 1 | 1 | 1 | 1 | 1 | 1 | 1 | 1 | 1 | 1 | 1 | 1 | 1 | 1 | 1 |
| 3 | 0–1 | 2 | 0 | 2 | 9 | 1 | 1 | | | | IF | | | | | | | | | | | | | | |
| 4 | 1–3 | 4 | 2 | 6 | 13 | | | 1 | 1 | 1 | 1 | | | | IF | | | | | | | | | | |
| 5 | 3–7 | 7 | 6 | 20 | 20 | | | | | | | 1 | 1 | 1 | 1 | 1 | 1 | 1 | | | | FF | | | |
| 6 | 2–3 | 0 | 3 | 6 | 13 | | | | - | FF | - | - | - | - | IF | - | - | - | | | | | | | |
| 7 | 0–4 | 4 | 0 | 4 | 12 | 1 | 1 | 1 | 1 | | | | IF | | | | | | | | | | | | |
| 8 | 4–7 | 8 | 4 | 20 | 20 | | | | | 1 | 1 | 1 | 1 | 1 | 1 | 1 | 1 | | | | | FF | | | |
| 9 | 4–6 | 0 | 4 | 4 | 14 | | | | | - | - | - | - | IF | - | - | - | - | - | | | | | | |
| 10 | 0–6 | 3 | 0 | 4 | 14 | 1 | 1 | 1 | F | | | | | IF | | | | | | | | | | | |
| 11 | 6–7 | 6 | 4 | 20 | 20 | | | | | 1 | 1 | 1 | 1 | 1 | 1 | | | | | IF | | | | | |
| 12 | 0–5 | 5 | 0 | 5 | 15 | 1 | 1 | 1 | 1 | 1 | | | | | | IF | | | | | | | | | |
| 13 | 5–7 | 4 | 5 | 20 | 20 | | | | | | 1 | 1 | 1 | 1 | | | | IF | | | | | | | |
| 14 | 0–7 | 5 | 0 | 20 | 20 | 1 | 1 | 1 | 1 | 1 | 1 | 1 | 1 | 1 | | | | | | FF | | | | | |
| 15 | 4–5 | 6 | 4 | 5 | 16 | | | | | 1 | - | - | - | - | - | IF | - | - | - | - | - | | | | |
| Total Dozers Required per Week | | | | | | 6 | 6 | 6 | 5 | 6 | 5 | 6 | 6 | 6 | 4 | 3 | 3 | 2 | 1 | 1 | 1 | 1 | 1 | 1 | 1 |
| Week No. | | | | | | 01 | 02 | 03 | 04 | 05 | 06 | 07 | 08 | 09 | 10 | 11 | 12 | 13 | 14 | 15 | 16 | 17 | 18 | 19 | 20 |

| | Activity | Duration | $EET_i$ | $EET_j$ | $LET_j$ | Latest Start Time Schedule Working Period in Weeks 01 | 02 | 03 | 04 | 05 | 06 | 07 | 08 | 09 | 10 | 11 | 12 | 13 | 14 | 15 | 16 | 17 | 18 | 19 | 20 |
|---|---|---|---|---|---|---|---|---|---|---|---|---|---|---|---|---|---|---|---|---|---|---|---|---|---|
| 1 | 0–2 | 3 | 0 | 3 | 3 | 1 | 1 | 1 | | | | | | | | | | | | | | | | | |
| 2 | 2–7 | 17 | 3 | 20 | 20 | | | | 1 | 1 | 1 | 1 | 1 | 1 | 1 | 1 | 1 | 1 | 1 | 1 | 1 | 1 | 1 | 1 | 1 |
| 3 | 0–1 | 2 | 0 | 2 | 9 | | | | | | | | 1 | 1 | | | | | | | | | | | |
| 4 | 1–3 | 4 | 2 | 6 | 13 | | | | | | | | | | 1 | 1 | 1 | 1 | | | | | | | |
| 5 | 3–7 | 7 | 6 | 20 | 20 | | | | | | | | | | | | | | 1 | 1 | 1 | 1 | 1 | 1 | 1 |
| 6 | 2–3 | 0 | 3 | 6 | 13 | | | | | | | | | | | | | | | | | | | | |
| 7 | 0–4 | 4 | 0 | 4 | 12 | | | | | | | | 1 | 1 | 1 | 1 | | | | | | | | | |
| 8 | 4–7 | 8 | 4 | 20 | 20 | | | | | | | | | | | | | 1 | 1 | 1 | 1 | 1 | 1 | 1 | 1 |
| 9 | 4–6 | 0 | 4 | 4 | 14 | | | | | | | | | | | | | | | | | | | | |
| 10 | 0–6 | 3 | 0 | 4 | 14 | | | | | | | | | | | | 1 | 1 | 1 | | | | | | |
| 11 | 6–7 | 6 | 4 | 20 | 20 | | | | | | | | | | | | | | | 1 | 1 | 1 | 1 | 1 | 1 |
| 12 | 0–5 | 5 | 0 | 5 | 15 | | | | | | | | | | | | | 1 | 1 | 1 | 1 | 1 | | | |
| 13 | 5–7 | 4 | 5 | 20 | 20 | | | | | | | | | | | | | | | | | 1 | 1 | 1 | 1 |
| 14 | 0–7 | 5 | 0 | 20 | 20 | | | | | | | | | | | | 1 | 1 | 1 | 1 | 1 | 1 | 1 | 1 | 1 |
| 15 | 4–5 | 6 | 4 | 5 | 16 | | | | | | | | | | | | | | | | | | | | |
| Total Dozers Required per Week | | | | | | 4 | 4 | 4 | 3 | 4 | 4 | 4 | 4 | 4 | 4 | 3 | 3 | 2 | 1 | 6 | 6 | 6 | 6 | 6 | 6 |
| Week No. | | | | | | 01 | 02 | 03 | 04 | 05 | 06 | 07 | 08 | 09 | 10 | 11 | 12 | 13 | 14 | 15 | 16 | 17 | 18 | 19 | 20 |

Since, the site has four new dozers and in case of any breakdown, the replacement can be easily provided by hiring, the desired level of dozer requirement for site development project can be taken as four.

The important resources required date-wise and their estimated desired level can be plotted graphically, to depict the loading pattern of resources. The area above and below the desired resource line give the typical peaks and valleys look. Both sides of the desired resource level line indicate the possible area needing adjustment.

The first draft of the optimum schedule is based on the most vital resources. For the site development project, the dozers for excavation of the site form the most critical resource, and as far as feasible, their daily requirement should not exceed four.

### 6.3.5 Scheduling Critical Activities at their EST

For the project to be completed on time, all critical activities have to commence at their ESTs, and the resources required have to be earmarked, accordingly. The extent of remaining resources needing leveling can then be easily assessed by subtracting date-wise the resources required for critical activities from the desired level of resources.

### 6.3.6 Scheduling the Non-critical Activities

The procedure for scheduling non-critical activities can be divided into the following two stages:

(a) Schedule non-critical activities in order of sensitivity at EST till loading does not exceed the desired level of optimum resource (Table 6.3).
(b) Thereafter, take the next non-critical activity in the order of sensitivity, and suitably schedule it within the desired level of vital resource by:

- Consuming free float (if available) to smoothen resources. Note that the EST of the subsequent activity/ies in the chain is not affected.
- If free float is not available, then utilize interference float and adjust the EST of subsequent affected activity/ies.
- If available floats are not sufficient to smoothen resources, then adjust floats existing in the already scheduled activities.

(c) Proceed similarly, with the next non-critical activity and continue till all the activities are scheduled.

Let us again consider the case of the site clearance project. The time-limited optimum resources schedule of this project is shown in Exhibit 6.4. As can be seen from this exhibit, the schedule of work up to activity 6–7 does not cause overload from the desired level of resource (dozers). The scheduling of remaining non-critical activities can be carried out as follows:

**Activity 0–5** The starting activity at EST causes overload. However, there are many ways of scheduling this activity without causing overload. Assuming that the continuity of work in a chain is to be maintained, the two options are:

## Table 6.3

### Site Development Project
### Earliest Start Time Schedule Till Resources Reach Optimum Level

| Activity | Dura-tion | $EET_i$ i | $EET_j$ j | $LET_j$ j | 01 | 02 | 03 | 04 | 05 | 06 | 07 | 08 | 09 | 10 | 11 | 12 | 13 | 14 | 15 | 16 | 17 | 18 | 19 | 20 |
|---|---|---|---|---|---|---|---|---|---|---|---|---|---|---|---|---|---|---|---|---|---|---|---|---|
| 1 0–2 | 3 | 0 | 3 | 3 | 1 | 1 | 1 | | | | | | | | | | | | | | | | | |
| 2 2–7 | 17 | 3 | 20 | 20 | | | | 1 | 1 | 1 | 1 | 1 | 1 | 1 | 1 | 1 | 1 | 1 | 1 | 1 | 1 | 1 | 1 | 1 |
| 3 0–1 | 2 | 0 | 2 | 9 | 1 | 1 | | | IF | | | | | | | | | | | | | | | |
| 4 1–3 | 4 | 2 | 6 | 13 | | | 1 | 1 | 1 | 1 | | | IF | | | | | | | | | | | |
| 5 3–7 | 7 | 6 | 20 | 20 | | | | | | | 1 | 1 | 1 | 1 | 1 | 1 | 1 | | | FF | | | | |
| 6 2–3 | 0 | 3 | 6 | 13 | | | | | -FF | - | - | - | - IF | - | - | - | | | | | | | | |
| 7 0–4 | 4 | 0 | 4 | 12 | 1 | 1 | 1 | 1 | | | | IF | | | | | | | | | | | | |
| 8 4–7 | 8 | 4 | 20 | 20 | | | | | 1 | 1 | 1 | 1 | 1 | 1 | 1 | 1 | | | | FF | | | | |
| 9 4–6 | 0 | 4 | 4 | 14 | | | | | - | - | - | - IF | - | - | - | - | | | | | | | | |
| 10 0–6 | 3 | 0 | 4 | 14 | 1 | 1 | 1 | FF | | | | IF | | | | | | | | | | | | |
| 11 6–7 | 6 | 4 | 20 | 20 | | | | | 1 | 1 | 1 | 1 | 1 | 1 | | | | | | FF | | | | |
| Total Dozers Required per Week | | | | | 4 | 4 | 4 | 3 | 4 | 4 | 4 | 4 | 4 | 4 | 3 | 3 | 2 | 1 | 1 | 1 | 1 | 1 | 1 | 1 |
| Week No. | | | | | 01 | 02 | 03 | 04 | 05 | 06 | 07 | 08 | 09 | 10 | 11 | 12 | 13 | 14 | 15 | 16 | 17 | 18 | 19 | 20 |

**(a) Option 1** Schedule activity 0–5 starting from the eleventh week (after completion of activity 6–7). Its implication is that one dozer will remain idle in the fourth week.

**(b) Option 2** Reschedule the non-critical activities 0–6 and 6–7, with activity 0–6 starting in the tenth week (after completion of activity 6–7).

Implications of the above are also to be examined from the construction priority and slippage of completion date angles. Considering these factors, the activity 0–6 and activity 6–7 are rescheduled as per Option 2 above, and activities 0–5 and 5–7 are scheduled at their earliest start.

**Remaining Activities** Proceeding similarly, activity 0–7 and dummy activity 4–5 can be scheduled as shown in Exhibit 6.4.

**Charting Schedule** Generally, schedules are plotted graphically on bar charts. These bars may also show the extent of total float and free float available against each activity. A bar chart is easy to read, understand and communicate.

## Exhibit 6.4
## Site Development Project
## Time Limited Optimum Resources Schedule

| Activity No | Code | Resources DZ | CP | Dura-tion | EET$_i$ | LET$_i$ | LET$_j$ | 01 | 02 | 03 | 04 | 05 | 06 | 07 | 08 | 09 | 10 | 11 | 12 | 13 | 14 | 15 | 16 | 17 | 18 | 19 | 20 |
|---|---|---|---|---|---|---|---|---|---|---|---|---|---|---|---|---|---|---|---|---|---|---|---|---|---|---|---|
| 1 | 0–2 | 1 | – | 3 | 0 | 3 | 3 | 1 | 1 | 1 | | | | | | | | | | | | | | | | | |
| 2 | 2–7 | 1 | – | 17 | 3 | 20 | 20 | | | | 1 | 1 | 1 | 1 | 1 | 1 | 1 | 1 | 1 | 1 | 1 | 1 | 1 | 1 | 1 | 1 | 1 |
| 3 | 0–1 | 1 | – | 2 | 0 | 2 | 9 | 1 | 1 | | | | IF | | | | | | | | | | | | | | |
| 4 | 1–3 | 1 | – | 4 | 2 | 6 | 13 | | | 1 | 1 | 1 | 1 | | | | IF | | | | | | | | | | |
| 5 | 3–7 | 1 | 1 | 7 | 6 | 20 | 20 | | | | | | | 1 | 1 | 1 | 1 | 1 | 1 | 1 | | | | FF | | | |
| 6 | 2–3 | 1 | – | 0 | 3 | 6 | 13 | | | | | FF | | | | | IF | | | · | | | | | | | |
| 7 | 0–4 | 1 | – | 4 | 0 | 4 | 12 | 1 | 1 | 1 | 1 | | | | IF | | | | | | | | | | | | |
| 8 | 4–7 | 1 | – | 8 | 4 | 20 | 20 | | | | | 1 | 1 | 1 | 1 | 1 | 1 | 1 | 1 | | | | | FF | | | |
| 9 | 4–6 | 1 | – | 0 | 4 | 4 | 14 | | | | | · | · | · | IF | · | · | · | · | · | | | | | | | |
| 10 | 0–6 | 1 | – | 3 | 0 | 4 | 14 | | | | | | | | | | | | 1 | 1 | 1 | | | | | | | |
| 11 | 6–7 | 1 | – | 6 | 4 | 20 | 20 | | | | | | | | | | | | | | 1 | 1 | 1 | 1 | 1 | 1 | | |
| 12 | 0–5 | 1 | 1 | 5 | 0 | 5 | 16 | 1 | 1 | 1 | 1 | 1 | | | | | | | | | | | | | | | |
| 13 | 5–7 | 1 | 1 | 4 | 5 | 20 | 20 | | | | | | 1 | 1 | 1 | 1 | | | | | FF | | | | | | | |
| 14 | 0–7 | 1 | – | 9 | 0 | 20 | 20 | | | | | | | | | | 1 | 1 | 1 | 1 | 1 | 1 | 1 | 1 | 1 | | |
| 15 | 4–5 | – | – | 0 | 4 | 5 | 16 | | | | | F | · | · | · | · | · | IF | · | · | · | | | | | | | |
| Total Dozers Required Per Week | | | | | | | | 4 | 4 | 4 | 4 | 4 | 4 | 4 | 4 | 4 | 4 | 4 | 4 | 4 | 3 | 3 | 3 | 3 | 3 | 2 | 2 |
| Week No. | | | | | | | | 01 | 02 | 03 | 04 | 05 | 06 | 07 | 08 | 09 | 10 | 11 | 12 | 13 | 14 | 15 | 16 | 17 | 18 | 19 | 20 |

Each row of the bar chart depicts activity description, data and its time schedule. The scheduled bar length is made equal to the time duration of the activity. The start of the bar marks the commencement of the activity, the bar end represents its completion.

Vertically, the bar chart is stratified into three-column segments demarcating work breakdown, scheduling data and the project time calendar. Generally but not necessarily, the work breakdown is listed in the left column, calendar is drawn on top and/or bottom of the right column and scheduling data is entered in the middle segment.

The work-breakdown column lists activities, one in each row, in the order of priorities of their execution. Each activity is given a serial number (or identification code) and is described horizontally in the space earmarked in the row.

The activity data segment contains a number of columns, each column containing basic data relating to activity schedule and connected resources. Such data includes, work quantity activity duration, earliest start date, latest start date, earliest finish date, latest finish date, schedule time constraints. Schedule data may also include resources, cost and earned value. These are needed to draw bar charts and resources profile. The activity data reflected in the bar chart should be restricted to the barest minimum, depending upon the purpose of the bar chart.

*A word of caution:* Scheduling is not a mere mechanical process—it needs construction experience. The methodology for scheduling of non-critical activities described above should be viewed only as guidelines. In particular the following should be kept in mind while developing a schedule:

(a) Schedule activities in a realistic manner by maintaining the continuity of work. Avoid splitting up of activities, uneconomical shifting of resources and frequent changes in the organization of work gangs.
(b) Consume less float of activities carrying higher risk of time slippages, and vice versa.
(c) Consume free float in preference to interference floats as free floats do not affect start of subsequent activities.
(d) Do not omit dummies, as floats in dummies get altered after the floats of their preceding activities are consumed, and these changes in float of dummies may affect start of the subsequent activities.

### 6.3.7 Optimizing Other Resources

The first estimate of resource optimization is derived by using the vital items of resources (dozers). Based on this schedule other important resources are date-wise aggregated and compared with the desired level. The loading profile is then plotted and the desired resource line drawn to get a pictorial representation of the comparison. These resources are smoothened or rounded off as far as possible within the framework of resource constraints till a suitable schedule of all the resources is achieved.

During rescheduling, free floats should be consumed first, even overlooking the order of sensitivity, as they do not alter the EST of subsequent activities. Whenever interference float is utilized, the first step should be to change the ESTs of affected activities.

### 6.3.8 Validating the Project Time Objectives

Validation means verification of the achievement of project objectives. Before the work programme based on network time schedule is finalized, it should be validated to ensure that it meets the purpose for which it is drawn. In particular, the achievement of project objectives of time and resource constraints should be studied carefully and the project management apprised of any limitation or implications in the critical stages of the project.

### 6.3.9 Scheduling within the Resource Constraints

Normally, the resources should be allotted as per the optimum resource schedule, but this may not always be possible. There can be many slippages: a particular machine may not be available in the market or the resources earmarked earlier may have to be shifted to another project. The network schedule provides the measure of resources required datewise and also gives the implications in case of any change in allocation. For the site development project, the schedule based on availability of three dozers is shown in Exhibit 6.5. It may be noted that the project duration has increased to 24 weeks.

### 6.3.10 Scheduling Networks of Repetitive Projects

The repetitive projects contain a large number of similar activities, each of which is organized into work-units or work-centres with assigned manpower, equipment and other resources necessary for its accomplishment. In case of similar activities, these organized work-units continue working till the completion of the same type of job. The schedule of work of these work-units can be easily derived from the project networks.

For example, consider the four-raft construction network depicted in Exhibit 5.2. It can be easily scheduled by first scheduling the critical activities, and then suitably adjusting the non-critical activities by maintaining continuity in employment of each activity resource.

Take the case of education buildings construction network (Exhibit 5.5) involving the construction of one primary school, one high school, one KG school and one nursery school. This network was developed by logically interconnecting the activities of each school listed in the order of construction priorities.

The schedule of work of the education buildings, is given in Exhibit 6.6.

It may be noted that the repetitive-type network is drawn for projects having only a limited similar activities. When the number of repetitive activities become very large (say, more than ten of each type, then it is preferable to use the 'line of balance' technique for scheduling them.

## ❑ 6.4 LOB METHOD OF SCHEDULING REPETITIVE PROJECTS

The 'line-of-balance' (LOB) technique originated in the manufacturing industry during the second world war. It is primarily used for planning, scheduling and controlling of projects

**196** Construction Project Management

Exhibit 6.5

## Site Development Project
## Resources Limited Schedule

| Activity Code No | Resources DZ | CP | Duration weeks | EET i | LET j | LET j | Working Period in Weeks |
|---|---|---|---|---|---|---|---|
| | | | | | | | 01 02 03 04 05 06 07 08 09 10 11 12 13 14 15 16 17 18 19 20 21 22 23 24 |
| C 0-2 | 1 | – | 3 | 0 | 3 | 7 | 1 1 1 · · IF · · · · · · · · · · · · · · · · · · |
| H 2-7 | 1 | – | 17 | 3 | 20 | 24 | · · · 1 1 1 1 1 1 1 1 1 1 1 1 1 1 1 1 1 IF · · · |
| B 0-1 | 1 | – | 2 | 0 | 2 | 13 | 1 1 · · · · · · · · · IF · · · · · · · · · · · · |
| G 1-3 | 1 | – | 4 | 2 | 6 | 17 | · · 1 1 1 1 · · · · · · · IF · · · · · · · · · · |
| L 3-7 | 1 | 1 | 7 | 6 | 20 | 24 | · · · · · · 1 1 1 1 1 1 1 FF · · · · · · · · · · |
| 2-3 | – | 1 | – | 0 | 3 | 17 | · · · · · FF · · · · · IF · · · · · · · · · · · · |
| E 0-4 | 1 | 1 | 4 | 0 | 4 | 16 | 1 1 1 1 · · · · · · · · · · · IF · · · · · · · · |
| J 4-7 | 1 | – | 8 | 4 | 20 | 24 | · · · · · · · · · · · · 1 1 1 1 1 1 1 1 IF · · · |
| 4-6 | – | 1 | 0 | 4 | 4 | 18 | · · · · · · · · IF · · · · · · · · · · · · · · · |
| F 0-6 | 1 | – | 3 | 0 | 3 | 18 | · · · · 1 1 1 · · · · · · · · · IF · · · · · · · |
| K 6-7 | 1 | – | 6 | 4 | 20 | 24 | · · · · · · · · 1 1 1 1 1 1 · · · · 1 1 1 1 1 1 |
| D 0-5 | 1 | 1 | 5 | 0 | 5 | 20 | · · · · · · · 1 1 1 1 1 · · · · · · · · IF · · · |
| I 5-7 | 1 | 1 | 4 | 5 | 20 | 24 | · · · · · · · · · · · 1 1 1 1 1 1 1 1 1 · · · · |
| A 0-7 | 1 | – | 9 | 0 | 20 | 24 | · · · · · · · · · · · · IF · · · 1 1 1 1 1 1 1 1 |
| 4-5 | – | 1 | 0 | 4 | 5 | 20 | · · · · FF · · · · · · · · · · · · · · · IF · · · |
| Total Dozers Required Per Week | | | | | | | 3 3 3 3 3 3 3 3 3 3 3 3 3 3 3 3 3 3 3 3 3 3 3 3 |
| Week No. | | | | | | | 01 02 03 04 05 06 07 08 09 10 11 12 13 14 15 16 17 18 19 20 21 22 23 24 |
| Dozer 1 | | | | | | | C | B | G | F | D | H | A | I |
| Dozer 2 | | | | | | | B | G | F | D | H | A | I | L | K |
| Dozer 3 | | | | | | | E | | | L | | J | | | |

Exhibit 6.6
## 2000 Housing Units Project
## Summary Schedule of Educational Buildings

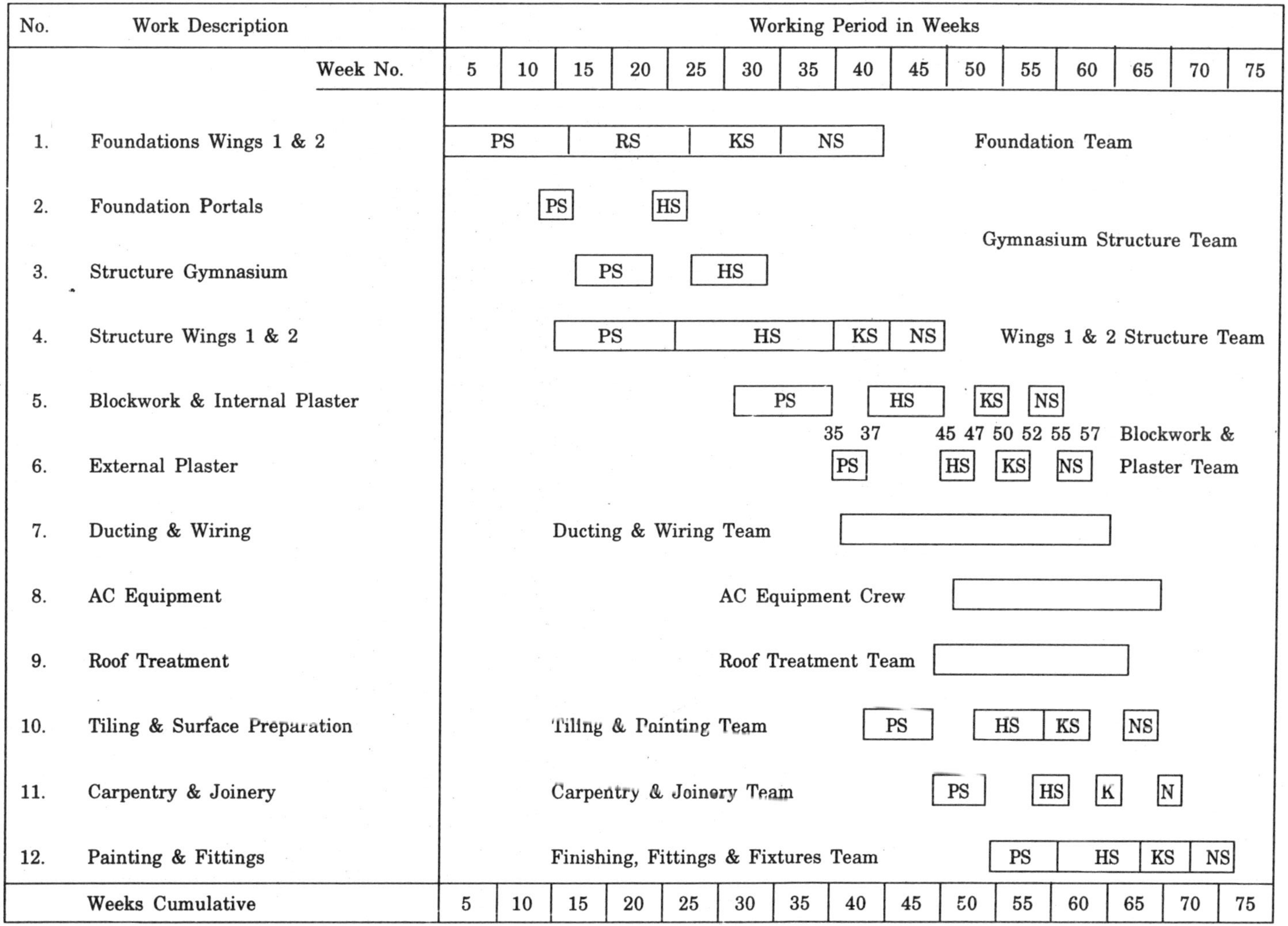

| No. | Work Description | Working Period in Weeks |
|---|---|---|
| 1. | Foundations Wings 1 & 2 | Weeks 5–30: PS, RS, KS, NS — Foundation Team |
| 2. | Foundation Portals | Week 10: PS; Week 20: HS |
| 3. | Structure Gymnasium | Week 25: PS; Week 35: HS — Gymnasium Structure Team |
| 4. | Structure Wings 1 & 2 | Weeks 25–45: PS, HS, KS, NS — Wings 1 & 2 Structure Team |
| 5. | Blockwork & Internal Plaster | Weeks 35, 37, 45, 47, 50, 52, 55, 57: PS, HS, KS, NS — Blockwork & Plaster Team |
| 6. | External Plaster | |
| 7. | Ducting & Wiring | Ducting & Wiring Team |
| 8. | AC Equipment | AC Equipment Crew |
| 9. | Roof Treatment | Roof Treatment Team |
| 10. | Tiling & Surface Preparation | Week 50: PS; Week 55: HS; Week 60: KS; Week 65: NS — Tiling & Painting Team |
| 11. | Carpentry & Joinery | Week 55: HS; Week 60: K; Week 65: N — Carpentry & Joinery Team |
| 12. | Painting & Fittings | Week 55: PS; Week 60: HS; Week 65: KS; Week 70: NS — Finishing, Fittings & Fixtures Team |

Weeks Cumulative: 5, 10, 15, 20, 25, 30, 35, 40, 45, 50, 55, 60, 65, 70, 75

involving construction of a large number of *repetitive works* such as similar buildings and multi-storeyed skyscrapers, and the *linear-type segmented works* like roads, airfields, tunnels and pipelines. It enables the optimum utilization of resources, improvement in work efficiency and interference-free scheduling of a wide range of activities.

The LOB scheduling technique entails preparation of two types of charts, termed as the setback chart, and the activities schedule chart. The preparation of these charts is illustrated here with the construction of *10 base construction of foundations of buildings*. It is followed by examples from the 334-module residential building construction project with a view to demonstrate the LOB technique application in repetitive works projects.

## 6.4.1 Setback Chart

This chart shows the logic of construction of unit-work cycle of the repetitive works project. The network logic diagram is drawn in the form of bar chart for simple works, and time scale network for complex projects, but its time scale is reversed, that is, completion of end event of unit work is taken as zero. (See Fig. 6.1.)

Figure 6.1

**Setback Chart of Base Construction (Not to Scale)**

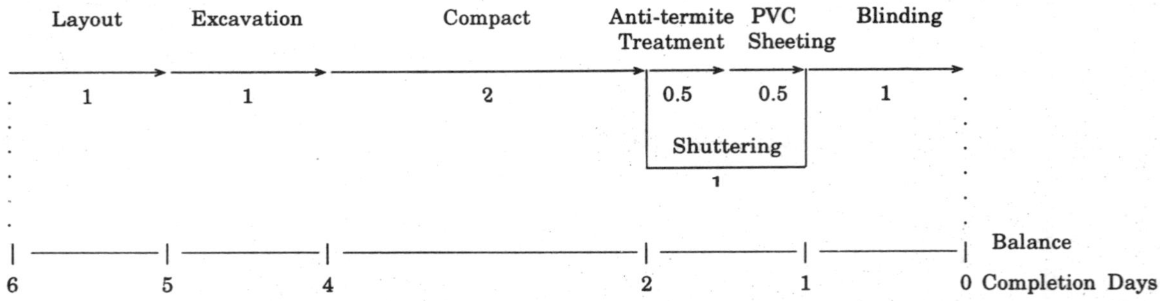

| Layout | Excavation | Compact | Anti-termite Treatment | PVC Sheeting | Blinding |
|--------|------------|---------|------------------------|--------------|----------|
| 1      | 1          | 2       | 0.5                    | 0.5          | 1        |

Shuttering
1

| 6 | 5 | 4 | 2 | 1 | 0 | Balance Completion Days |

The preparation of a typical setback chart involves the following steps; number of steps can be omitted after some practice:

(a) Break the unit-work cycle into activities.
(b) Estimate the duration and manpower required for each activity.
(c) Group these activities in a logical order, having well-defined stages of work.
(d) Draw the activities logic diagram.
(e) Time analyze the logic diagram.
(f) Draw the project bar chart schedule or time-scale network.
(g) Determine the activity setback completion time of the unit work cycle.
(h) Calculate the rate of work per unit of time, say per day or week (Table 6.4).

Further, in case of major repetitive projects, it is preferable to consider work-packages or even tasks instead of activities as illustrated in this example.

Table 6.4

**Base Construction Activities**

| Code | Activity | Duration (Day) | Output Rate (Unit/day) |
|------|----------|----------------|------------------------|
| A | Layout | 1 | 1 |
| B | Excavation | 1 | 1 |
| C | Compaction | 2 | 0.5 |
| D | Anti-termite treatment | 0.5 | 2 |
| E | PVC sheeting | 0.5 | 2 |
| F | Shuttering | 1 | 1 |
| G | Blinding | 1 | 1 |

## 6.4.2 Activities Schedule Chart

The LOB activity schedule chart shows the graphical plan of work execution. These graphs representing the cycles of work are referred to as *cyclographs* or *cyclograms*. The time unit (day or week) in cyclographs are represented along the horizontal axis, while the vertical axis shows the number of similar work-units of the project. The time unit reflected on the horizontal axis can further be divided into calendar months (or weeks) after assessing the working days available in each month.

Development of the scheduling chart depends upon three main factors i.e the activity start time, the activity rate of build up, the activity latest completion data (as read from setback chart) and the buffer (or float) available for starting the subsequent activity. The scheduling chart showing number of work-units (cumulative) planned for completion takes linear or 'S' curve shape.

For example, the earliest start time schedule of activities of base construction tasks of the 10 foundations can be prepared by plotting time along the horizontal axis and 10 foundations along the vertical axis. The rate of execution of each activity is then plotted graphically as shown in Fig. 6.2. The steps involved in preparation of this graph are given below:

(a) Select the EST point of activity 'layout' on the graph, and draw a line sloping equal to its rate of execution, that is, one unit/day.
(b) Proceed similarly with the subsequent activities, (providing buffers in-between for unforeseen delays, and keeping margins, to avoid interferences) till the activity having the least rate of execution (slope) is reached. In this case 'compaction' with execution at 0.5 unit/day is the lowest rate.
(c) Plot the lowest rate sloping line and mark its intersection with the top 10-foundation horizontal line.
(d) Starting from this (top) point of intersection, move forward horizontally on top line and identify the latest completion point of subsequent activity as indicated by the setback chart.
(e) From this activity latest completion points, draw reverse line with slopes equal to the

## Figure 6.2

### 10 Foundations Base Constructions Cyclograph: Using One Team Per Activity Earliest Start Time Schedule.

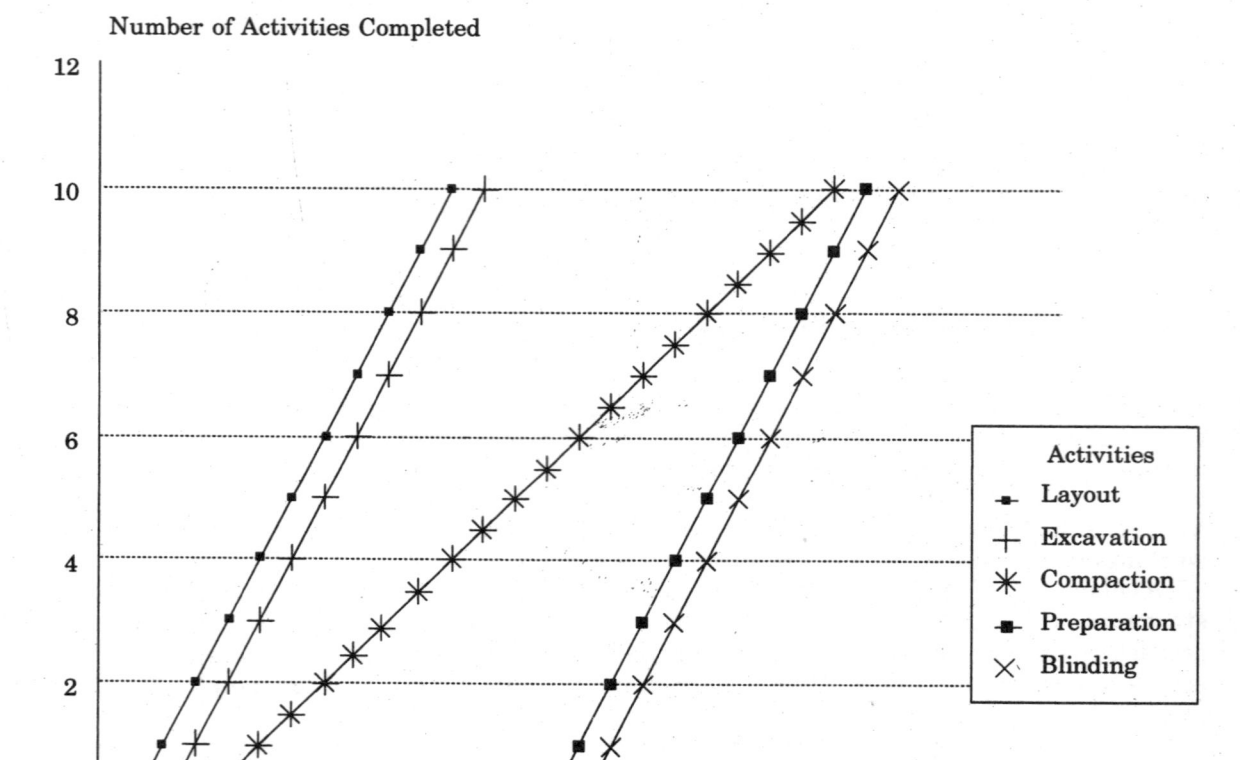

Activities:
- ■ Layout
- + Excavation
- ✱ Compaction
- ■ Preparation
- × Blinding

rate of execution of the activity. The graph thus drawn (Fig. 6.2) would show a typical earliest start time schedule, depicting the number of activities planned (cumulative) for completion at a given point of time.

Generally, the construction targets are specified in terms of the number of activities to be completed on a given date, and the rate of progress depends upon the resource teams employed. For example, in the base construction task, the target for completion of one base per day can be achieved by increasing the resources as given in Table 6.5.

The activities with increase resources for completion at the uniform rate of one unit per day can be scheduled as shown in Fig. 6.3. It includes buffer of one day between 'compaction' and preparation.

### Table 6.5

**Target: One Base Unit Per Day**

| Code | Activity | Duration (Day) | Completed work-unit by one team/day | Resources teams unit-work per day |
|------|----------|----------------|-------------------------------------|------------------------------------|
| A | Layout | 1 | 1 | 1 |
| B | Excavation | 1 | 1 | 1 |
| C | Compaction | 2 | 0.5 | 2 |
| D | Anti-termite treatment | 0.5 | 2 | 0.5 |
| E | PVC sheeting | 0.5 | 2 | 0.5 |
| F | Shuttering | 1 | 1 | 1 |
| G | Blinding | 1 | 1 | 1 |

### Figure 6.3

**10 Base Constructions Cyclograph: Activity Progress at the Rate of Unit Activity Per Day (Optimum resources schedule)**

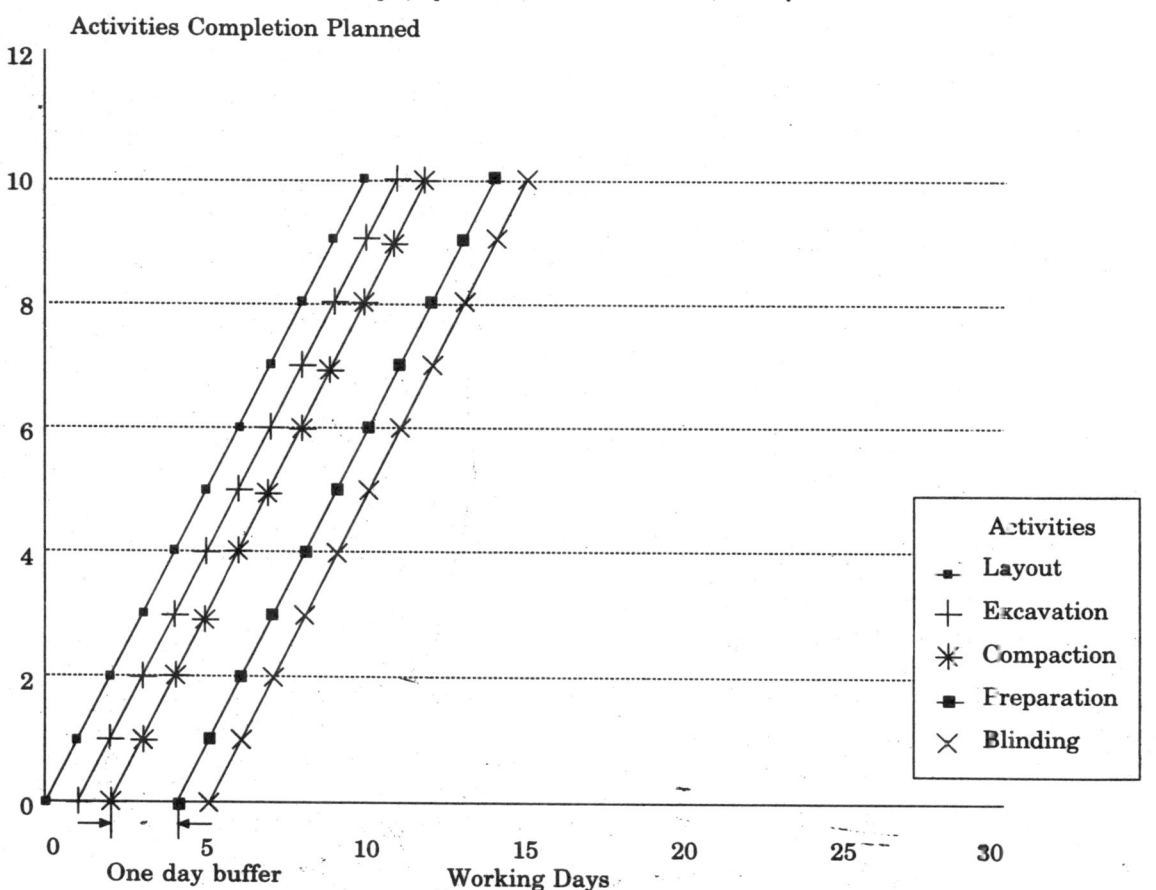

## 6.4.3 Residential Appartments Construction Schedule

**Scope and constraints** A residential housing project involves the construction of 2000 apartments of 334 similar modules, with six apartments per module. The construction is to be completed in 785 working days. The construction task is entrusted to the following three task forces:

(a) Foundation construction task force.
(b) Precast superstructure production and erection task force.
(c) Finishing task force.

The foundation construction task force is assigned the task of producing one foundation per working day at peak level, subject to the following constraints:

(a) Work to commence on the first (M01) month and to progress gradually to one raft per day within two months.
(b) Two sets of timber conventional formwork for plinth walls to be manufactured locally in the first month. The balance imported custom-made steel shuttering are expected to reach the project site by the end of the third (M03) month.
(c) The ground floor design is expected to be finalized by the end of the fourth (M04) month.
(d) The manpower required for the plinth walls and ground floor can be inducted earlier provided, it can be effectively utilized to increase the rate of progress of other foundation activities.

The rate of production starting in the beginning of the sixth (M06) month, as indicated by the pre-cast consultant is given in Table 6.6.

Table 6.6

**Rate of Precast Production in Modules/Month**

| Period | Modules Total |
|---|---|
| M06 to M11 | 56 |
| M12 to M17 | 104 |
| M18 to M23 | 114 |
| M24 onwards | 60 |
| Total | 334 |

The erection of superstructure is linked with the production of pre-cast concrete components in the factory. The total peak erection capability of the five erection teams at project site is 5/6 modules per working day.

The finishes in the erected buildings are to be progressed so as to complete the entire project at the earliest.

## 6.4.4 Project Planning Approach Using LOB Technique

To prepare an outline time plan of work using LOB technique, the planning process can be carried out as follows:

**Foundation task force work schedule** The work-breakdown structure of one module of foundation is shown in Exhibit 3.3 and its activities with duration and manpower needed for execution are reflected in Exhibit 2.7.

Each work cycle for construction of the foundation module can be grouped into work-packages, as follows:

| Work Package | Detailed Activities |
| --- | --- |
| Base Construction | Layout, excavation, compaction, anti-termite treatment, PVC sheeting, shuttering and blinding concrete. |
| Raft Construction | Layout, shuttering, reinforcement, raft concreting. |
| Plinth wall Construction | Raft curing, Bitumen coating, reinforcement fixing, shuttering, wall concreting. |
| Ground floor Construction | Preliminaries, backfilling, shuttering, mesh fixing, floor concreting. |

The foundation construction setback diagram can be deduced as given in Fig. 6.4.

Figure 6.4

**Setback Chart for Foundation Module**

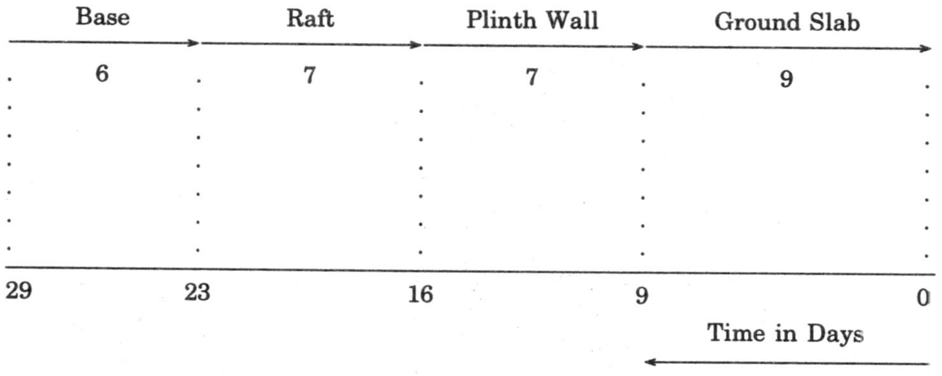

```
       Base          Raft        Plinth Wall      Ground Slab
        6             7              7                9

  29           23              16            9              0
                                              Time in Days
```

The rate of execution of the workpackages and desired buffer, is shown in Table 6.7.
The LOB work schedule cyclograph for foundation work packages is shown in Exhibit 6.7.

*Note*: A buffer is provided to cater for unforeseen delays in completion of the preceding work package.

## Table 6.7
### Rate of Execution of the Work Packages and Desired Buffer

| Work Package Description | Duration (Days) | Execution Rate (Unit/Day) Commencement | (Unit/day) Peak | Buffer [from start of preceding activity(Days)] |
|---|---|---|---|---|
| Base | 6 | 0.5 /day | 1.2/day | – |
| Raft | 7 | 0.25/day | 1.2/day | 12 days |
| Plinth Wall | 7 | 0.2 /day | 1/day | 12 days |
| Ground Floor | 9 | 0.2 /day | 1/day | 75 days |

## Exhibit 6.7
### Residential Buildings Foundations Work Packages Construction Cyclograph

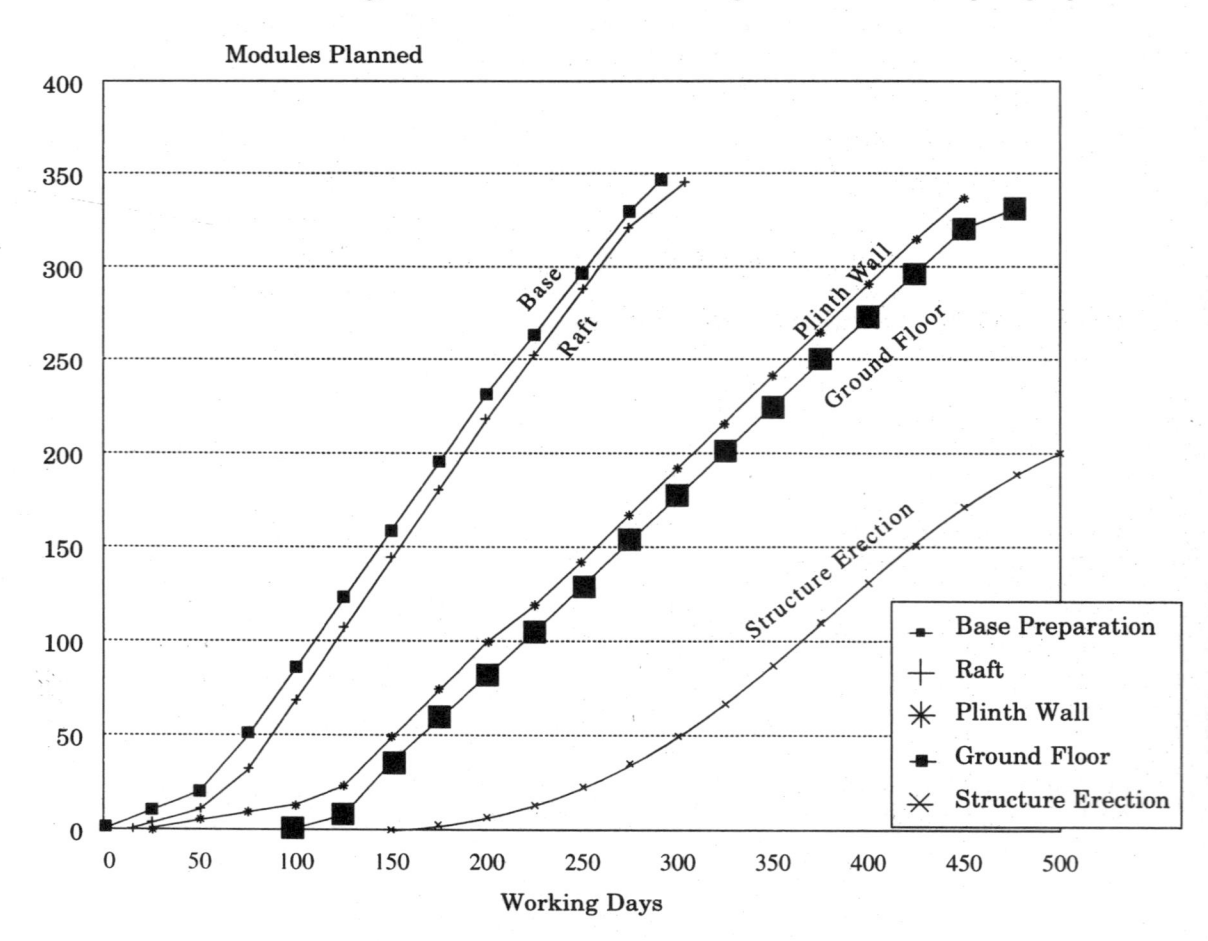

**Erection task force** The erection of superstructure is linked with the production of precast concrete components in the factory. The rate of erection can be considered as follows:

| Period | First Month | Second Month | Third Month | Fourth Month | Fifth Month | Sixth Month | Total |
|---|---|---|---|---|---|---|---|
| M06 to M11 | 4 | 6 | 8 | 10 | 12 | 14 | 54 |
| M12 to M17 | 15 | 16 | 17 | 18 | 19 | 19 | 104 |
| M18 to M23 | 19 | 19 | 19 | 19 | 19 | 19 | 114 |
| M24 onwards | 19 | 19 | 19 | 5 | – | – | 62 |
| Total | | | | | | | 334 |

The schedule of erection is shown in Exhibit 6.8.

Exhibit 6.8

**Residential Building Finishes Plan Derived Using Line-of-Balance Technique (in Units of Modules)**

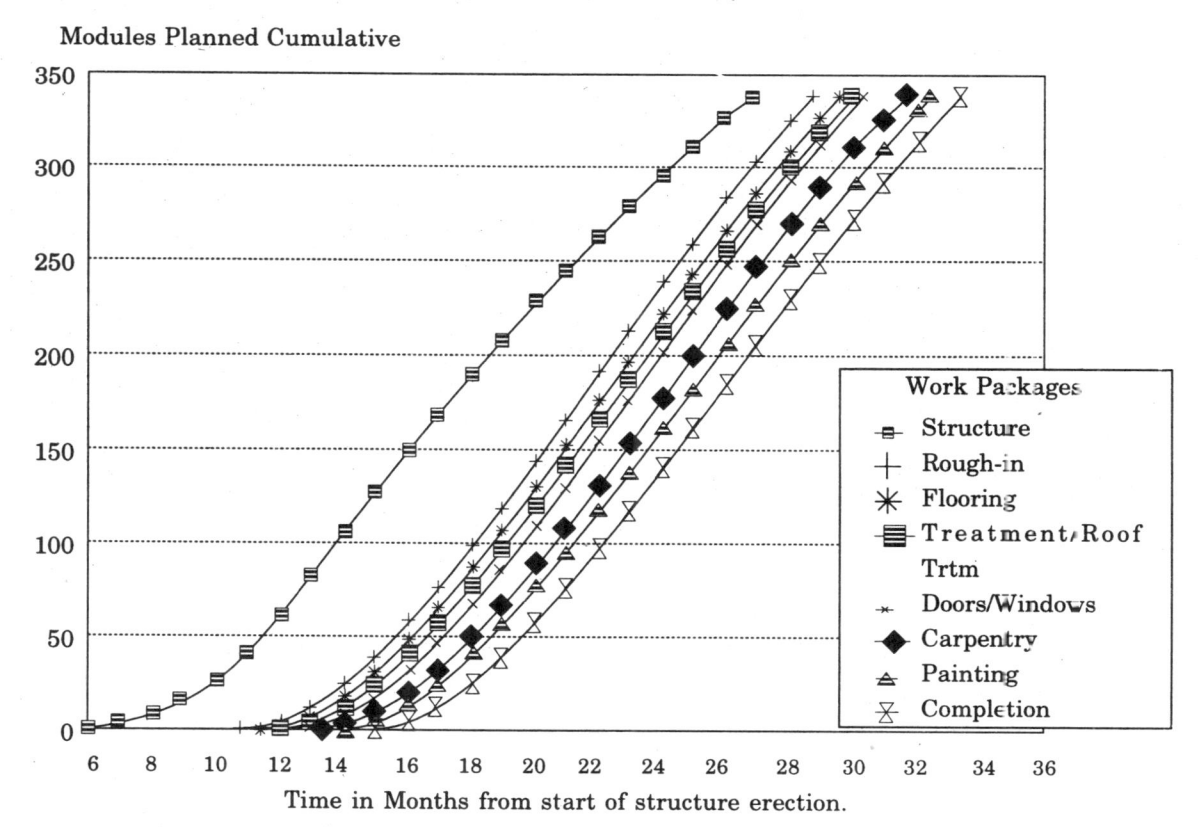

Modules Planned Cumulative

Work Packages
- Structure
- Rough-in
- Flooring
- Treatment/Roof Trtm
- Doors/Windows
- Carpentry
- Painting
- Completion

Time in Months from start of structure erection.

**Finishes task force** The finishes in the erected buildings are to be progressed at the rate of one module/day so as to complete the entire project at the earliest. These finishes can be broadly divided into the work packages indicated in Table 6.8.

### Table 6.8
### Residential Building Finishing Works

| Work package | Activities Included |
| --- | --- |
| Rough-in | Wire pulling and circuit checking. GRC panel fixing and sealing of edges. |
| | PVC and GI plumbing. A/C ducting, and staircase metal work, balustrade. |
| Flooring | Screed, ceramic tiles. |
| Roof treatment | Insulation, polythene sheet separation layer, screed, primer and tarfelt. |
| Doors & Windows | Dooirs and windows and joinery including shutters. |
| Carpentry | False ceiling, glazing, kitchen cabinet fixing and built-in wardrobe. |
| Painting, fittings and fixture. | Surface preparation, and preliminary painting. Sanitary fittings, electrical fittings and fixtures, staircase and PVC handrail. |
| Completion | Final painting, masonry decoration work, PVC tiling. |

The earliest the finishing works can start is after a buffer of at least 4 month from the erection of the first module. Initially, the rate of finishes can be slow and then increase gradually, till erection reaches its peak rate. The workers, gang sizes can be suitably mobilized. The rate of finishing key activities for earliest completion thus derived from start of erection of structure is shown in Exhibit 6.8.

## LOB Control Chart

The LOB control chart is used to monitor the progress of works. In this, the vertical axis scale is same as that of the activity schedule chart, and each activity is represented by a column along the horizontal axis as shown in Exhibit 6.9, drawn for controlling important finishing targets.

At a given point of time usually, the last date of each month, the number and types of activities planned for completion are read from the activity schedule chart and tabulated in the LOB control chart inside each activity column. The line joining the horizontal segments of the number of various activities, planned for completion on a given date, represents the line of balance for achieving the planned targets. The actual progress at the end of the month is reflected in the LOB control chart to determine variances from the planned targets.

The activity progress beyond the LOB line shows progress ahead of schedule while that below it shows progress behind the schedule. The activities falling behind schedule are

## Exhibit 6.9

**Residential Building Finishes Control: Derived Using Line-of-Balance Technique (in Units of Module)**

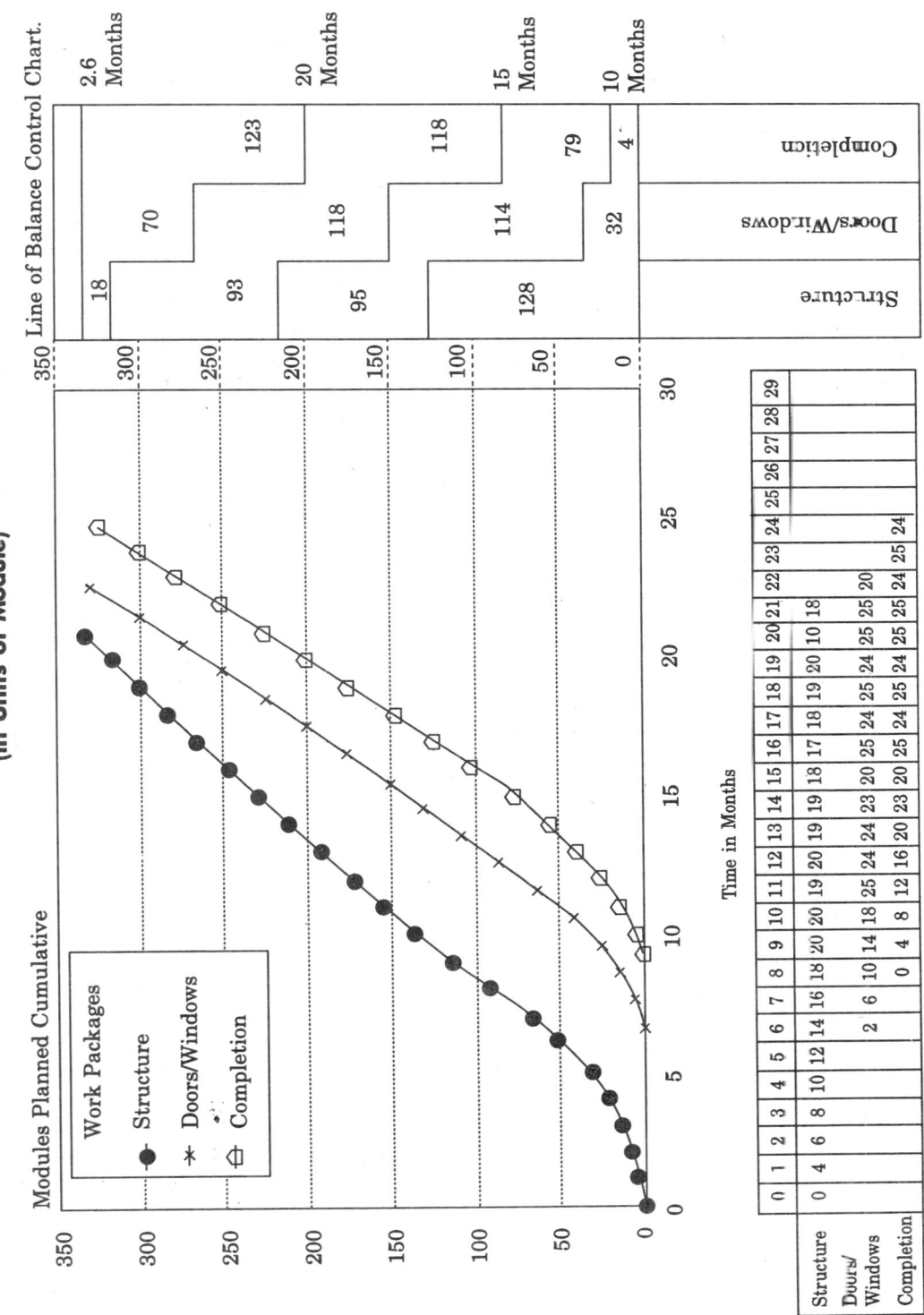

| | 0 | 1 | 2 | 3 | 4 | 5 | 6 | 7 | 8 | 9 | 10 | 11 | 12 | 13 | 14 | 15 | 16 | 17 | 18 | 19 | 20 | 21 | 22 | 23 | 24 | 25 | 26 | 27 | 28 | 29 |
|---|---|---|---|---|---|---|---|---|---|---|---|---|---|---|---|---|---|---|---|---|---|---|---|---|---|---|---|---|---|---|
| Structure | 0 | 4 | 6 | 8 | 10 | 12 | 14 | 16 | 18 | 20 | 20 | 19 | 19 | 19 | 19 | 18 | 17 | 18 | 19 | 19 | 20 | 18 | | | | | | | | |
| Doors/Windows | | | | | | 2 | 6 | 10 | 14 | 18 | 25 | 24 | 24 | 23 | 20 | 25 | 25 | 25 | 25 | 24 | 25 | 25 | 20 | | | | | | | |
| Completion | | | | | | | | | 0 | 4 | 8 | 12 | 16 | 20 | 23 | 20 | 25 | 24 | 24 | 24 | 24 | 25 | 24 | 25 | 24 | | | | | |

Time in Months

Line of Balance Control Chart:
- Structure: 18 / 93 / 95 / 128 — 2.6 Months
- Doors/Windows: 70 / 118 / 114 / 32 — 20 Months
- Completion: 123 / 118 / 79 / 4 — 15 Months / 10 Months

analyzed to determine the degree of criticality. (The method of time control of repetitive projects based on LOB technique is covered in Chapter 16.)

Generally, where space permits, the LOB control chart and the activity schedule chart are plotted on the same sheet (Exhibit 6.9) and targets are tabulated as shown in Exhibit 6.10.

## ❑ 6.5 FACTORS AFFECTING WORK SCHEDULING

The scheduling of a project plan has to take into consideration many variables like time, resources, and financial constraints. It is difficult to enumerate principles governing all such factorss which may vary from project to project. However, the guidelines given in the following can be considered for developing the schedule of a project work.

**Time** The availability of time is a crucial limiting factor in a project. More time normally, implies less investment. Time and cost are correlated factors (refer Chapter 16). There are three aspects of time which have to be considered during scheduling:

(a) Most of the projects carry time constraints in the form of imposed dates. These dates may include constraints on start and completion of activities. A schedule must meet the project time constraints, in such a way that project duration is not exceeded, such a Schedule is called *time limited schedule*.
(b) The schedule must account for holidays, bad weather days and the non-working periods. Further, affect of the working season on production efficiency must also be considered while scheduling activities, and the schedule and connecting resources adjusted suitably. Such a schedule details the work programme for execution.
(c) Scheduling must make use of the reserve of time available in floats of non-critical activities to reduce fluctuations in resource requirements or conform to a given predetermined pattern of resources. For minor fluctuations, working overtime may also be resorted to. The schedule prepared under resource constraints is termed as *resource limited schedule*.

**Manpower** Manpower is one of the main factors in the successful execution of projects. No amount of automation or machinery can replace the manpower needed for completion of a project. It cannot be treated like a commodity and cannot be dismissed or re-employed at will. Technical hands once employed are normally continued till their requirement ceases. The idle labour time is paid for and the strikes and breakdown of work are kept in view by the management. The task efficiency of labour, weather conditions, nature of work and the supervisors, leadership—all of these affect labour productivity.

The non-availability of suitable labour is generally, a limiting factor. The labour turnover, sickness and absenteeism further aggravate the problem. The working hours, overtime and other incentives have to be considered while deciding the manpower schedule. The management-labour agreements and the governing labour laws considerably, affect labour employment. A schedule cannot take care of all the variables but these can be reduced considerably, by working out a uniform trade category-wise manpower requirement

Exhibit 6.10

## 2000 Housing Units Project
### Residential Building Monthly Target Tracking Chart

| No. | Work Description | May | Jun | Jul | Aug | Sep | Oct | Nov | Dec | Jan | Feb | Mar | Apr | May | Jun | Jul | Aug | Sep | Oct | Nov | Dec | Jan |
|---|---|---|---|---|---|---|---|---|---|---|---|---|---|---|---|---|---|---|---|---|---|---|
| 1 | Base Construction | 12 | 16 | 25 | 37 | 36 | 37 | 36 | 36 | 33 | 30 | 34 | 2 | | | | | | | | | |
| 2 | Foundation Rafts | 6 | 12 | 25 | 37 | 36 | 37 | 36 | 36 | 33 | 30 | 34 | 12 | | | | | | | | | |
| 3 | Plinth Walls | 5 | 5 | 5 | 12 | 25 | 24 | 24 | 22 | 20 | 23 | 24 | 25 | 24 | 25 | 25 | 24 | 22 | 25 | 12 | 19 | 19 |
| 4 | Ground Slabs | | | | | 12 | 25 | 24 | 24 | 22 | 20 | 23 | 24 | 25 | 24 | 25 | 25 | 24 | 19 | 20 | 24 | 23 |
| 5 | Super Structure | | | | | | | | 4 | 6 | 8 | 10 | 12 | 14 | 16 | 18 | 20 | 20 | 25 | 24 | 24 | 23 |
| 6. Wiring | | | | | | | | | | | | | 4 | 8 | 12 | 16 | 20 | 24 | 23 | 20 | 25 | 24 |
| 7 | Plumbing | | | | | | | | | 4 | | | 4 | 8 | 12 | 16 | 20 | 24 | 24 | 24 | 23 | 20 |
| 8 | Air Cooling Ducts | | | | | | | | | | 8 | 12 | 16 | 20 | 24 | 25 | 24 | 25 | 24 | 24 | 23 | 20 |
| 9 | Door Frames | | | | | | | | | | | 4 | 8 | 12 | 16 | 20 | 24 | 25 | 24 | 24 | 24 | 24 |
| 10 | Screeding | | | | | | | | | | | 2 | 6 | 10 | 14 | 18 | 24 | 16 | 20 | 25 | | |
| 11 | Roof Treatment | | | | | | | | | | | | | | 4 | 8 | 12 | | | | | |
| 12 | Terrazzo-Ceramic Tiles | | | | | | | | | | | | | 4 | 8 | 12 | 16 | 20 | 25 | 24 | 24 | 23 |
| 13 | Doors/Windows Shutters | | | | | | | | | | | | | 2 | 6 | 10 | 14 | 18 | 25 | 24 | 24 | 23 |
| 14 | Preliminary Paint | | | | | | | | | | | | | 4 | 8 | 12 | 16 | 20 | 24 | 24 | 23 | 20 |
| 15 | Carpentry/Joinery, Glazing | | | | | | | | | | | | | 2 | 6 | 10 | 14 | 18 | 24 | 24 | 23 | 20 |
| 16 | P.V.C. Tiles | | | | | | | | | | | | | | | 4 | 8 | 12 | 16 | 20 | 24 | 23 |
| 17 | Fittings/Fixtures | | | | | | | | | | | | | | | 2 | 6 | 10 | 14 | 18 | 24 | 23 |
| 18 | Final Completion | | | | | | | | | | | | | | | | 4 | 8 | 12 | 16 | 20 | 23 |

| Months | May | Jun | Jul | Aug | Sep | Oct | Nov | Dec | Jan | Feb | Mar | Apr | May | Jun | Jul | Aug | Sep | Oct | Nov | Dec | Jan |
|---|---|---|---|---|---|---|---|---|---|---|---|---|---|---|---|---|---|---|---|---|---|
| Working Days in a Month | 25 | 24 | 25 | 25 | 24 | 25 | 24 | 24 | 22 | 20 | 23 | 24 | 25 | 24 | 25 | 25 | 24 | 25 | 24 | 24 | 22 |
| Working Days Cumulative | 25 | 43 | 74 | 99 | 123 | 148 | 172 | 196 | 218 | 238 | 261 | 285 | 310 | 334 | 359 | 384 | 408 | 433 | 457 | 481 | 503 |

(Contd.)

*(Contd.)*

| No. | Work Description | Feb | Mar | Apr | May | Jun | Jul | Aug | Sep | Oct | Nov | Dec | Jan |
|---|---|---|---|---|---|---|---|---|---|---|---|---|---|
| 1 | Base Construction | 18 | 17 | | | | | | | | | | |
| 2 | Foundation Rafts | 20 | 25 | 18 | 19 | 20 | 19 | 18 | | | | | |
| 3 | Plinth Walls | 20 | 25 | 24 | 25 | 24 | 25 | 11 | | | | | |
| 4 | Ground Slabs | 25 | 24 | 25 | 25 | 24 | 25 | 11 | | | | | |
| 5 | Super Structure | 25 | 24 | 25 | 11 | 25 | 11 | | | | | | |
| 6. | Wiring | 25 | 24 | 25 | 24 | 25 | 21 | | | | | | |
| 7 | Plumbing | 23 | 20 | 25 | 24 | 25 | 24 | 25 | 25 | 10 | | | |
| 8 | Air Cooling Ducts | | | | | | | | | | | | |
| 9 | Door Frames | 20 | 25 | 24 | 25 | 24 | 25 | 25 | 10 | | | | |
| 10 | Screeding | | | | | | | | | | | | |
| 11 | Roof Treatment | 20 | 25 | 24 | 25 | 24 | 25 | 25 | 20 | | | | |
| 12 | Terrazzo-Ceramic Tiles | 25 | 24 | 25 | 24 | 25 | 25 | 24 | 11 | | | | |
| 13 | Doors/Windows Shutters | 25 | 24 | 25 | 24 | 25 | 25 | 24 | 21 | 10 | | | |
| 14 | Preliminary Paint | 20 | 25 | 24 | 25 | 24 | 25 | 2524 | 25 | 25 | 20 | | |
| 15 | Carpentary/Joinery, Glazing | 20 | 25 | 24 | 25 | 24 | 25 | 25 | 24 | 25 | 24 | | |
| 16 | P.V.C. Tiles | 20 | 25 | 24 | 25 | 24 | 25 | 25 | 24 | 25 | 24 | 10 | |
| 17 | Fittings/Fixtures | | | | | | | | | | | | |
| 18 | Final Completion | | | | | | | | | | | | |

| Months | Feb | Mar | Apr | May | Jun | Jul | Aug | Sep | Oct | Nov | Dec | Jan |
|---|---|---|---|---|---|---|---|---|---|---|---|---|
| Working Days in a Month | 20 | 23 | 23 | 25 | 24 | 25 | 25 | 24 | 25 | 24 | 24 | 22 |
| Working Days Cumulative | 523 | 546 | 569 | 594 | 618 | 643 | 668 | 692 | 717 | 741 | 765 | 787 |

schedule, or by fixing a pattern depending upon the manpower availability and working conditions.

**Materials** No project can ever be started without materials. Construction materials are increasingly becoming scarce, and their procurement is a time consuming process. The schedule aids in forecasting of materials, and their timely supply determines the economics and progress of work.

One method could be, to stock materials well before they are required so as to ensure timely supply, but the stock inventory costs money. Generally, the inventory should be zero before the commencement and after the completion of the project. To go a step forward, this rule should be made applicable to each activity. But for certain materials, the procurement action can be based on the guiding principle that materials inventory must be kept to the minimum. In case of materials in short supply, the schedule may have to be based on availability constraints.

**Machinery** The availability of machinery is normally, a limiting factor. For example, in an activity involving excavation, the schedule may specify a requirement of two dozers, but one may actually be available or allotted. This would entail a recasting of the whole schedule. In such circumstances, various alternatives like delay-penalty costs, cost of time crashing and the cost of procurement or hiring of additional machinery have to be weighed before making the final decision. The aim of machinery-and-equipment scheduling should be to find out the minimum duration schedule in which the employment of equipment and machinery is systematically and uniformly distributed based on its availability or allotment.

**Capital** Capital is the core of all project activities. The project management aims at economies and the contractor works for earning profits. The proper management of money results in savings while its improper use proves ruinous. For example, consider the investment implications of starting works at their EST and LST, as can be seen from the graph shown in Fig. 6.5.

In EST schedule, the large production costs get staggered over a longer period of time, thus reducing investments. But this schedule may not prove attractive to a builder as the saving on investments in the earliest stages can be best utilized either on another project or even in earning interest. Therefore, a builder's schedule, would generally aim to execute those jobs earlier which are more profitable, involve least investment and benefit his cash flow. On the other hand, the client would aim at phasing of construction for early completion. The network schedule must balance these conflicting requirements.

## ❏ 6.6 FORECASTING INPUTS AND OUTPUTS

The work schedule can form the basis for making forecasts. The forecasts predict, datewise, the future projections, in respect of input resources and production outputs. They are educated guesses based on assumptions and judgement. The assumptions made at the time of forecasting are based on the then available information which may or may not hold good in the future. Unforeseen situations may arise which affect the decisions made at the time of preparation of forecasts.

## Figure 6.5

**Graph Showing Investment Implications of Starting Works at their EST and LST**

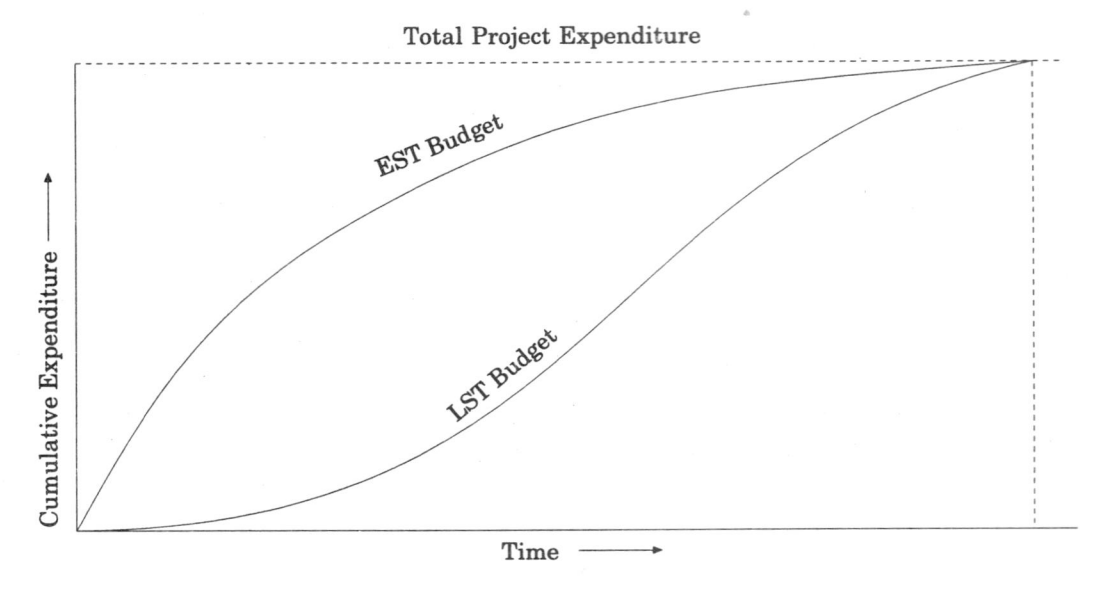

The economies of projects depend upon the accuracy of the forecasts. This accuracy, in turn, depends upon the experience and ability of the person making the forecasts. Inspite of the risk of proving wrong, forecasts for inputs and outputs should be made and regularly reviewed, as they assist in taking crucial decisions.

The work schedule can form the basis for making forecasts. Take the example of the site development project. The contractor has estimated his quoted prices for each work site as follows:

| | | |
|---|---|---|
| Activity direct cost | = | A |
| Activity variable indirect costs | = | B = 1.1A |
| Site fixed indirect cost | = | $ 2000 per week |
| Activity contract price | = | 2A |

The direct costs, activity-wise, estimated by the contractor are as follows:

| Code | Direct Cost ($) |
|---|---|
| 0–2 | 27000 |
| 0–1 | 18000 |
| 1–3 | 36000 |
| 0–4 | 72000 |
| 4–7 | 54000 |
| 6–7 | 45000 |

| Code | Direct Cost ($) |
|---|---|
| 0–5 | 45000 |
| 0–6 | 27000 |
| 2–7 | 153000 |
| 3–7 | 63000 |
| 0–7 | 81000 |
| 5–7 | 36000 |
| Total | 657000 |

The contractor's forecast for the value of work done and production cost based on the optimum resource employment schedule (Exhibit 6.4) can be worked out by week-wise aggregating the activity direct costs, and then evaluating the other costs (Exhibit 6.11). Similarly, forecasts can be prepared for the daily rate of work, input resources and outputs, and cash-in-flow and cash-out-flow.

## 6.6.1 Forecasting Daily Rate of Works

The schedule of work can be used to forecast date-wise the major items of works to be performed, that is, their rate of execution. These works include earthwork, reinforcement, shuttering, concreting, masonry, plastering, carpentry and joinery, metal work tiling, painting, and other finishing items. It may be noted that the 'rate of work' forecast gives both the extent of work to be done date-wise, as well as the time period in which the work is to be executed. This forecast forms the basis for determining the input resource forecast, as is evident from the following typical cases:

| Daily rate of work forecast | Typical items of input resource requirement |
|---|---|
| Excavation in m$^3$ | Excavators and dumpers teams. |
| Reinforcement fixing (in tonnes) | Steel, fabrication machinery and steel-fixing gang. |
| Suttering in m$^2$ | Shuttering materials, equipment and shuttering gangs. |
| Concreting | Concreting materials, equipment and manpower. |
| Pre-cast concrete erection (in nos.) | Precast elements, cranes and erection gangs. |
| Masonry in m$^2$ | Hollow block and masonry gang. |
| Plastering in m$^2$ | Materials, mortar-mixer and masonry gang. |

## 6.6.2 Forecasting Inputs

Inputs, in the form of resources, comprise men, materials, machines and money. These are inducted into the project from time-to-time as the work progresses. The schedule of work provides the framework for forecasting these inputs which can be directly identified with the activities. The direct resource input forecasts, which can be developed from the schedule of work, include the following:

## Exhibit 6.11

### Site Development
### Project Input-Output Costs Forecast Based on Optimum Resources Time Schedule
(In thousands of dollars)

| Activity Code | No. | Duration Weeks | Earned Value | Output Per Week | 01 | 02 | 03 | 04 | 05 | 06 | 07 | 08 | 09 | 10 | 11 | 12 | 13 | 14 | 15 | 16 | 17 | 18 | 19 | 20 |
|---|---|---|---|---|---|---|---|---|---|---|---|---|---|---|---|---|---|---|---|---|---|---|---|---|
| C | 0-2 | 3 | 6 | 2 | 2 | 2 | 2 | | | | | | | | | | | | | | | | | |
| H | 2-7 | 17 | 34 | 2 | | | | 2 | 2 | 2 | 2 | 2 | 2 | 2 | 2 | 2 | 2 | 2 | 2 | 2 | 2 | 2 | 2 | 2 |
| B | 0-1 | 2 | 4 | 2 | 2 | 2 | | | | | | | | | | | | | | | | | | |
| G | 1-3 | 4 | 8 | 2 | | | 2 | 2 | 2 | 2 | | | | | | | | | | | | | | |
| L | 3-7 | 7 | 21 | 3 | | | | | | | 3 | 3 | 3 | 3 | 3 | 3 | 3 | | | | | | | |
| E | 0-4 | 4 | 8 | 2 | 2 | 2 | 2 | 2 | | | | | | | | | | | | | | | | |
| J | 4-7 | 8 | 16 | 2 | | | | | 2 | 2 | 2 | 2 | 2 | 2 | 2 | 2 | | | | | | | | |
| F | 0-6 | 3 | 6 | 2 | | | | | | | | | | | | 2 | 2 | 2 | | | | | | |
| K | 6-7 | 6 | 12 | 2 | | | | | | | | | | | | | | | 2 | 2 | 2 | 2 | 2 | 2 |
| D | 0-5 | 5 | 15 | 3 | 3 | 3 | 3 | 3 | 3 | | | | | | | | | | | | | | | |
| I | 5-7 | 4 | 12 | 3 | | | | | | 3 | 3 | 3 | 3 | | | | | | | | | | | |
| A | 0-7 | 9 | 18 | 2 | | | | | | | | | | 2 | 2 | 2 | 2 | 2 | 2 | 2 | 2 | 2 | | |
| Output/Week | | | | | 9 | 9 | 9 | 9 | 9 | 9 | 10 | 10 | 10 | 9 | 11 | 9 | 6 | 6 | 6 | 6 | 6 | 6 | 4 | 4 |
| Variable Costs @ 70% of Output | | | | | 6.3 | 6.3 | 6.3 | 6.3 | 6.3 | 6.3 | 7.0 | 7.0 | 7.0 | 6.3 | 7.7 | 6.3 | 4.2 | 4.2 | 4.2 | 4.2 | 4.2 | 4.2 | 2.8 | 2.8 |
| Fixed Costs (Estimated) | | | | | 3.0 | 2.5 | 2.0 | 1.5 | 1.5 | 1.5 | 1.5 | 1.5 | 1.5 | 1.5 | 1.5 | 1.5 | 1.5 | 1.0 | 1.0 | 1.0 | 1.0 | 1.0 | 1.0 | 1.0 |
| Input Costs | | | | | 9.3 | 8.8 | 8.3 | 7.8 | 7.8 | 7.8 | 8.5 | 8.5 | 8.5 | 7.8 | 9.2 | 7.8 | 5.2 | 5.2 | 5.2 | 5.2 | 5.2 | 5.2 | 3.0 | 3.0 |
| Input Costs Cumulative | | | | | 9.3 | | | 34 | | | 67 | | | 100 | | | 124 | | | 142 | | | | |
| Output Cumulative | | | | | | | | 36 | | | 74 | | | 113 | | | 140 | | | 160 | | | | |
| Week No. | | | | | 01 | 02 | 03 | 04 | 05 | 06 | 07 | 08 | 09 | 10 | 11 | 12 | 13 | 14 | 15 | 16 | 17 | 18 | 19 | 20 |

**(a) Direct labour forecast** It shows date-wise the number and trade categories of workers required. It forms the basis for manpower planning and mobilization.

**(b) Direct materials forecast** These indicate, date-wise the quantity of various items of major materials required. This enables formulation of the materials procuement plan and the stock-inventory.

**(c) Special-purpose plant and machinery forecast** This is used to plan the procurement of special-purpose plant and machinery such as earthwork machinery, concrete production, transportation and placing machinery, shuttering equipment, reinforcement fabrication machinery, and lifting and erection machinery.

**(d) Direct production costs forecast** This shows the trend and the extent of direct product costs of input resources.

The procedure for forecasting each item of resources is similar. It involves the following steps:

(a) Assess item-wise the resources required for each activity by making appropriate assumptions and using standard engineering constants. Write important items of resources in the scheduling chart under appropriate column, or inside the bar representing the schedule of activity.
(b) Calculate activity-wise, the daily rate of expenditure of each item of resources. The rate of consumption would depend upon the nature of the activity. Mostly the rate of consumption can be assumed to be constant, and can be determined by dividing the resources required by the activity duration; sometimes, it may be expressed in terms of units of time, say, expenditure per four weeks.
(c) Prepare the resources aggregate by adding date-wise the requirement of each item, as per the scheduled dates of activities. This is normally worked out on the schedule chart.
(d) Determine date-wise the cumulative requirement of resources. This data gives the forecast of resources.
(e) Plot the forecast of resources graphically. Generally the cumulative forecasts are in the form of S-shaped curve, (Exhibit 6.12).

*Note*: It is not necessary to prepare the forecast of each item of resources down to the last nails, nuts and bolts. Forecasting, as discussed above, is a laborious process and should be restricted only to the important items.

Further forecasting predicts the date on which the resources are required, but this must not be mixed up with the provisioning action. For example, the materials forecasts provide the planning programme, whereas the indenting, purchasing and inventories of the materials must be based on the well-established principles of materials management.

## 6.6.3 Forecasting Output

Output is what is produced with the given input resources. It is measured in monetary terms. In other words, output represents the earned value of workdone. It is the sum total

## Exhibit 6.12

**Site Development Project: Forecasts of Input Costs and Workdone Value**
**(In thousands dollars)**

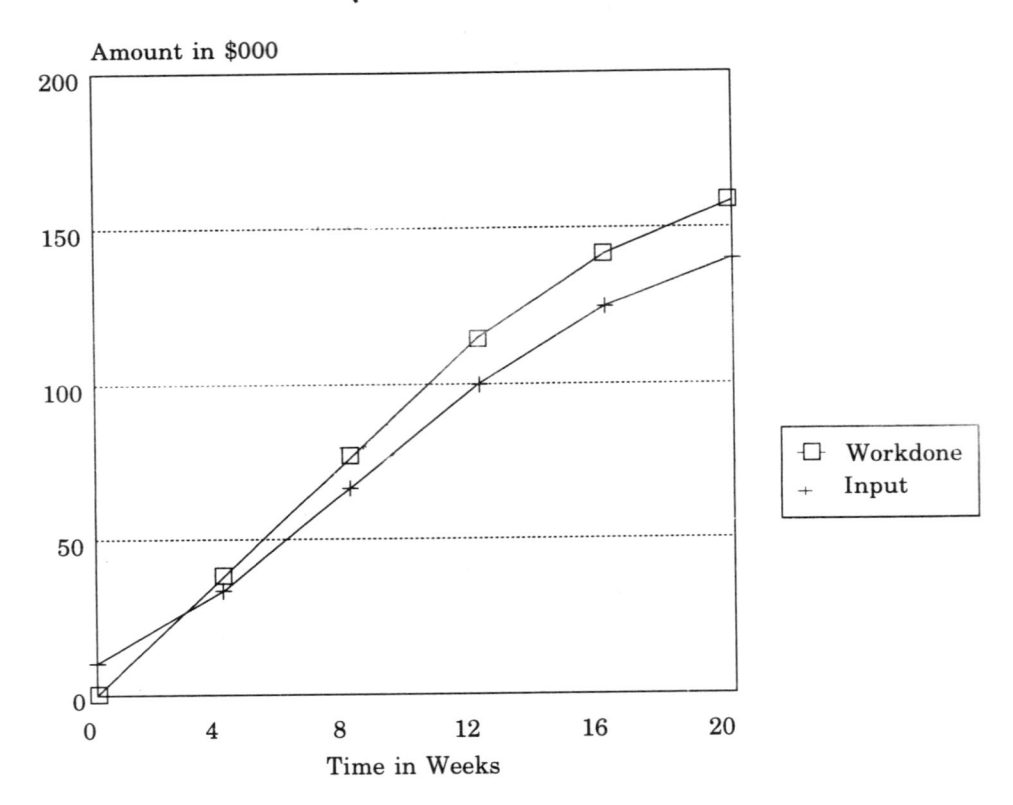

of direct costs, indirect costs and profits. In the work schedule, each activity output is costed at its sale price. The schedule provides the framework for evaluating output date-wise. The procedure of determining the output is similar to the forecasting of inputs. It involves the following steps:

(a) Assess the cost of activity at sale price.
(b) Calculate, activity-wise, the output per unit of time by dividing the activity cost with activity duration.
(c) Aggregate, date-wise, the activity outputs from the schedule of the work.
(d) Determine, date-wise, the cumulative effect of output and plot it against the time scale. The cumulative effect of output generally follows the S-curve pattern.

## ❏ 6.7 SCHEDULE HIERARCHY

The schedule hierarchy depicts the levels of various schedules in relation to each other.

Each level of schedules is meant to serve the information needs of the corresponding management level.

A typical pyramidal structure of schedule hierarchy having five levels is shown in Fig. 6.6. This schedule consists of the following:

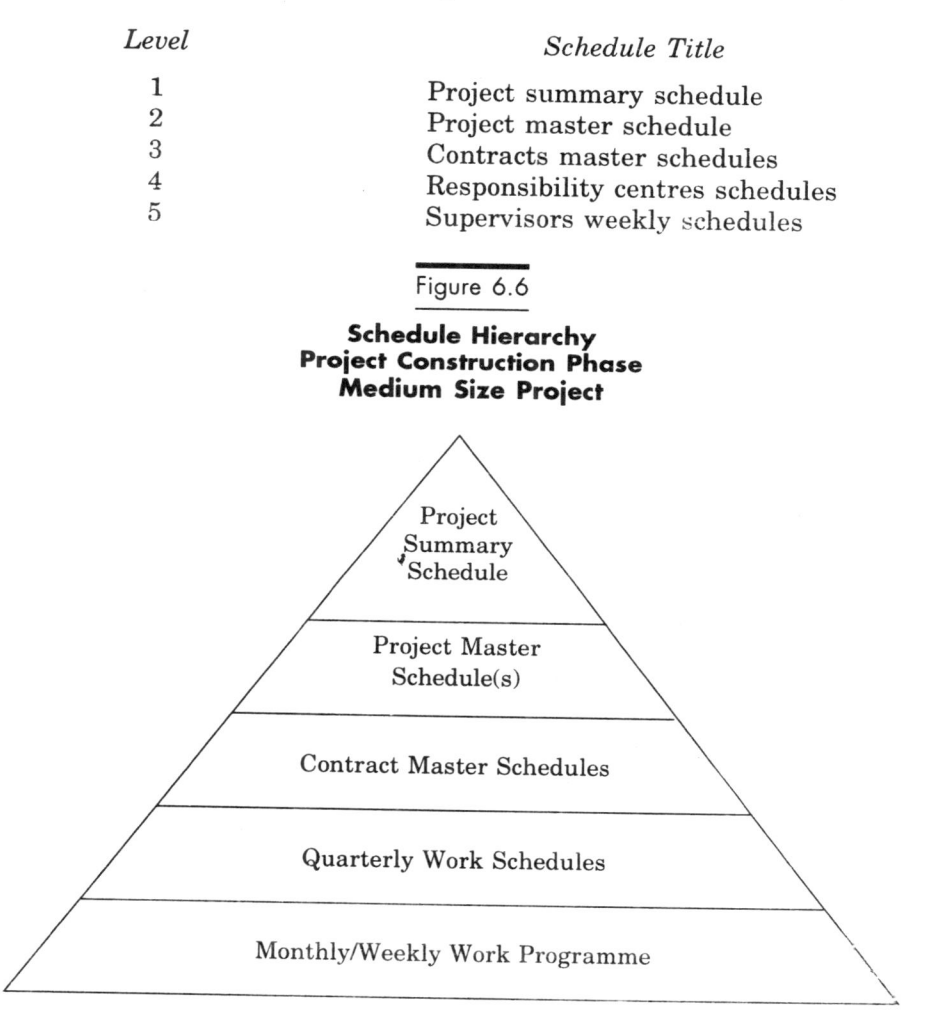

| Level | Schedule Title |
|---|---|
| 1 | Project summary schedule |
| 2 | Project master schedule |
| 3 | Contracts master schedules |
| 4 | Responsibility centres schedules |
| 5 | Supervisors weekly schedules |

Figure 6.6

**Schedule Hierarchy
Project Construction Phase
Medium Size Project**

Project Summary Schedule

Project Master Schedule(s)

Contract Master Schedules

Quarterly Work Schedules

Monthly/Weekly Work Programme

The characteristics associated with the various levels of schedules are given in Table 3.1. The purpose of each schedule is outlined in the following:

**1. Project summary schedule** It shows the outline of the time plan for executing the project. It contains the schedule of sub-projects and tasks. The time scale unit is taken as a month or a week. These schedules are used at the top management level to highlight the plan and progress of various project milestones.

**2. Project master schedule** It shows the project plan for execution of work packages and other important activities. It is the project management's plan for commencing, progressing, monitoring and controlling of works. It is prepared by integrating the schedules of sub-projects and tasks, or by scheduling the project network.

**3. Contracts master schedule** A contract schedule depicts the plan of execution of activities involved in the execution of contracted works. The contract master schedule is used to:

- systematically control the contracted works, and
- determine the time effect of work deviation and unforeseen circumstances.

The contract master schedule is linked up with the project master schedule and is supplemented by the respective contract master network.

**4. Responsibility centre work schedule** It reflects the work programme of the responsibility centre and its scope ranges from a quarter or a month to the entire life span of the centre. It is prepared in sufficient details to enable the supervisors to plan their weekly work programme.

**5. Supervisors' work programme** This shows the day-to-day work execution schedule of the supervisors or foremen incharge of work. These programmes are prepared on a fortnightly or weekly basis, and are detailed enough to include the operations or processes of each construction activity.

The number of levels in a schedule hierarchy is not fixed, but depends upon the nature, type and complexity of the project. A simple project being executed by a contractor may hardly need two or three schedule levels, where as a large size complex project may require even more than five levels.

In the schedule hierarchy structure, the schedule levels are related to the management and work breakdown sructure levels. The consistency in this correlation can go a long way in building up an integrated schedule for planning and monitoring the project work and providing appropriate information at the various management levels.

# PART III

# Resource Planning

- Planning Construction Manpower
- Planning Construction Materials
- Project Construction Equipment
- Selecting Construction Equipment
- Planning Construction Costs
- Planning Construction Budget

# CHAPTER 7

# Planning Construction Manpower

The corporate personnel management broadly covers a wide spectrum of functions including forecasting needs, formulation of pay scales and service conditions, recruitment and induction, training and development, morale and motivation, health and welfare, safety and security, and maintenance of harmonious industrial relations. It thus entails an interdisciplinary approach employing the combined skills of system planners, behavioural scientists, management practitioners, economists, statisticians and industrial relation experts. Being a critical resource, manpower is of paramount concern to those planning and managing construction projects.

The project construction manpower planning is primarily concerned with estimating the workers' productivity, scheduling manpower employment, and structuring it into workers' teams and work-groups, with a view to economically match manpower supply with the task requirements. The various functions performed by the project planning team with respect to manpower planning are listed in Table 7.1.

The scope of construction manpower planning, covered in this chapter is restricted to:

(a) Establishing workers' productivity standards
(b) Scheduling construction site workers
(c) Grouping project manpower
(d) Designing workers' financial incentive schemes.

This chapter excludes indirect manpower planning needed for local personnel administration and other departments in the project office as it varies from site to site. The worker productivity control methodology is described in Chapter 14.

## Table 7.1

**Project Planning Team: Typical Manpower Planning Functions**

1. Determining expected labour productivity.
2. Estimating workers requirement for each work package.
3. Scheduling date-wise, category-wise, project direct labour.
4. Establishing a construction teams.
5. Organising task forces.
6. Allocating labour during execution stage.
7. Monitoring workers productivity at site.
8. Recording productivity data.
9. Costing and controlling manpower costs.
10. Controlling manpower mobilisation, distribution and demobilisation.
11. Defining job requirement for key executive and staff appointments.
12. Assist in recruitment of personnel.
13. Assist in designing incentive system.
14. Assist in controlling manpower costs.
15. Assist in training and induction of manpower.

## ❑ 7.1 ESTABLISHING WORKERS' PRODUCTIVITY STANDARDS

### 7.1.1 The Challenging Task

The basic equation for determining the workers required for accomplishing a specific activity is given by:

(a) Workers required

$$= \frac{\text{Work quantity} \times \text{Workers' productivity standard}}{\text{Completion period}}$$

(b) Workers' productivity standard

$$= \text{Worker output norms} \times \text{production efficiency factor}$$

Where

- Workers' productivity standard is defined as the effort in man-days or man-hours needed for accomplishing a unit quantity of work, while working efficiently but allowing for normal delays and wastage.
- Work quantity of the activity involved is expressed in standard work units.
- Completion period is taken as working days or hours planned or earmarked to accomplish the task.
- Workers' production norms are expressed in man-days or man-hours, category-wise, required for accomplishing the unit work.
- Production efficiency factor is the multiplier used to convert production norms into productivity standards expected under job conditions at the site.

In this basic equation for determining manpower, the quantity of work to be performed can be accurately estimated from the construction drawings and specifications. If the work is to be completed within the stipulated period, the variable in assessment of workers' requirement is the productivity standard.

The method of computation of workers' requirement as illustrated above may appear simple, but in actual practice assessment of production efficiency and thereby workers' productivity standards are the most challenging tasks faced by the project planners.

### 7.1.2 Identifying Requisite Skills

Construction involves multi-skill technology for its wide range of related activities. These skills vary with the nature of job, type of project and corporate policy of the contractor. The first step towards determining productivity standard is to identify the trade workers needed for execution of the project.

A typical trade categorisation of construction workers encountered in a building project is shown in Table 7.2.

*I.S 10302: 1982,* Indian Standards on "Unified nomenclature of workmen for civil engineering", published by its Construction Management Section Committee includes around 95 categories of labours. The trade categories and crew sizes used for determining construction output also varies with various agencies publishing output planning norms. On the whole, for a given project, nomenclature of the trade categories needed for workers planning, mobilising and monitoring productivity, should be identified and standardised.

### 7.1.3 Workers' Production Planning Norms

The workers' production planning norms (or planning data) indicate the extent of effort required in terms of man-hours (MH) to accomplish a unit quantity of specified work or activity. These norms are sometimes loosely referred to as 'workers' productivity norms'.

They express the effort, in direct man-hours, of workers which can be identified with the execution of some work or activity. They do not include the indirect supporting or administrative personnel, who are estimated separately. To illustrate the, workers productivity norms used by a construction company in the United Arab Emirates for estimating and planning their building construction activities are shown in Table 7.3.

Consider a task involving 160 m² of fixing timber formwork for the roof slab of a single-storey building. The time earmarked for completion is four days, working eight hours per day. If a workers' team consisting of two skilled workers and an unskilled worker can install the formwork at the rate of 1.25 m²/hour, then:

$$\text{Effort required} = \frac{\text{Formwork quantity}}{\text{Output per team}}$$

$$= \frac{160 \text{ m}^2}{125 \text{ m}^2 \text{ per team-hours}}$$

$$= 128 \text{ team-hours}$$

## Table 7.2
## Building Construction Workers Trade Classification

**Building Trades**

*Carpentry Work*
Shuttering carpenter
Furniture carpenter
Wood polisher
Carpenter helper

*Masonry Work*
Concrete mason
Blockwork & plaster mason
Tiling mason
Marble mason
Mason helper

*RCC Steel Work*
Rebar fabricator
Rebar helper

*Painting Work*
Painter
Painter helper

*Electrical Works*
Electrician
Cable jointer
Cable layer
Electrical helper

*Plumbing & Sanitary Works*
Plumber
Pipe fitter
Plumber helper

*Unskilled Work*
General helpers

**Mechanical Trades**
Fitter
Machinist
Welder
AC mechanic
Sheet fabricator
Auto electrician
Diesel mechanic
Petrol mechanic
Mechanic helper
Riggers

**Drivers & Operators**
Light vehicle drivers
Heavy vehicle drivers
Equipment operators

**Administration Staff**
Office helper
Medical helper
Security staff
Store keeper
Cook
Mess helper
Janitor
Tailor
Laundry man
General helpers

$$\begin{aligned}
\text{Teams required} &= \frac{\text{Team-hours}}{\text{Completion period}} \\
&= \frac{128}{4 \times 8} \\
&= 4 \\
\text{Workers required} &= 4 \ (2 \text{ skilled} + 1 \text{ unskilled}) \\
&= 8 \text{ skilled} + 4 \text{ unskilled}.
\end{aligned}$$

## Table 7.3

**Typical Building Construction Project Workers' Production Planning Data for Building Works**

| Sl. No. | Activities | Units | Gang Size Skilled | Gang Size Unskilled | Output per day (8 Hours) |
|---|---|---|---|---|---|
| 1. | Excavation in ordinary soil (manually) | CM | – | 2 | 7.00 |
| 2. | Backfilling with excavate earth (manually) | CM | – | 3 | 15.00 |
| 3. | Concrete mixing and pouring in place | CM | 2 | 10 | 17.50 |
| 4. | Making, fixing & removing of fairface formwork | SM | 2 | 1 | 10.00 |
| 5. | Making, fixing & removing of ordinary formwork | SM | 2 | 1 | 11.50 |
| 6. | Reinforcement making & fixing | MT | 2 | 1 | 0.30 |
| 7. | B.R.C fabric cutting & fixing | SM | 2 | 1 | 165.00 |
| 8. | Bitumen paints (2 Coats) | SM | – | 2 | 40.00 |
| 9. | Blockwork & plaster (including scaffolding upto 4) | | | | |
| | (i) Solid blockwork | SM | 2 | 2 | 15.00 |
| | (ii) Hollow blockwork | SM | 2 | 2 | 17.00 |
| | (iii) Fairface blockwork | SM | 2 | 2 | 12.00 |
| | (iv) Internal plaster (single coat) | SM | 2 | 2 | 30.00 |
| | (v) Internal plaster (double coat) | SM | 2 | 2 | 20.00 |
| | (vi) External plaster (single coat) | SM | 2 | 2 | 20.00 |
| | (vii) External plaster | SM | 2 | 2 | 15.00 |
| | (viii) Screed in flooring (upto 75 mm thick) | SM | 2 | 2 | 20.00 |
| | (ix) Erection of scaffolding (above 4 m upto 15 m nt) | SM | – | 2 | 35.00 |
| | (x) Dismantling of scaffolding | SM | – | 2 | 100.00 |
| 10. | Tiling work | | | | |
| | (A) Ceramic wall tiles | SM | 1 | 1 | 6.00 |
| | (B) Ceramic floor tiles with cement back | SM | 1 | 1 | 7.50 |
| | (C) Ceramic tiles with adhesive backing | SM | 1 | 1 | 7.50 |
| | (D) Mosaic tile work | SM | 1 | 1 | 9.00 |
| | (E) Mosaic skirting | RM | 1 | 1 | 27.00 |
| | (F) P.V.C tiles work with adhesive | SM | 1 | 1 | 45.00 |
| | (G) P.V.C skirting with adhesive | SM | 1 | 1 | 60.00 |
| | (H) P.V.C steps | No. | 1 | 1 | 5.00 |
| | (I) Mosaic steps making | No. | 1 | 1 | 5.00 |
| | (J) Mosaic steps fixing | No. | 1 | 1 | 6.00 |
| 11. | Situ flooring | SM | 1 | 1 | 2.50 |
| | Situ skirting | RM | 1 | 1 | 8.75 |
| | Situ steps | RM | 1 | 1 | 1.50 |
| 12. | Threshold fixing | No. | 1 | 1 | 12.00 |
| 13. | Sanitary accessory fixing (including cutting of fixed tile if necessary) | No. | 1 | 1 | 10.00 |
| 14. | Marble work—Floor | SM | 1 | 1 | 10.00 |
| 15. | Painting: | | | | |
| | (i) 2 Coats of Snowcem | SM | 1 | – | 24.00 |
| | (ii) 3 Coats of emulsion | SM | 1 | – | 12.00 |
| | (iii) 4 Coats of enamel paint | SM | 1 | – | 10.00 |

Experienced estimators and planners compile the workers' production planning norms for estimating the manpower requirements. In the absence of such planning data, appropriate norms can be evolved using one or a combination of the following methods:

(a) Analyzing the past performance data.
(b) Abstracting data from published norms.
(c) Work-studying the actual work process.

**Analyzing past performance data** The long-standing construction firms compile their basic production norms by analyzing the past performance data of similar works, using statistical techniques. This analysis for each item of work is carried out by statistically averaging the historical data of output achieved. For example, consider the performance data of steel fixer work of a project shown in Fig. 7.1

Figure 7.1

**Raft Foundation of Residential Buildings: Output Pattern in Initial Stages (Fixing Steel Reinforcement Bars)**

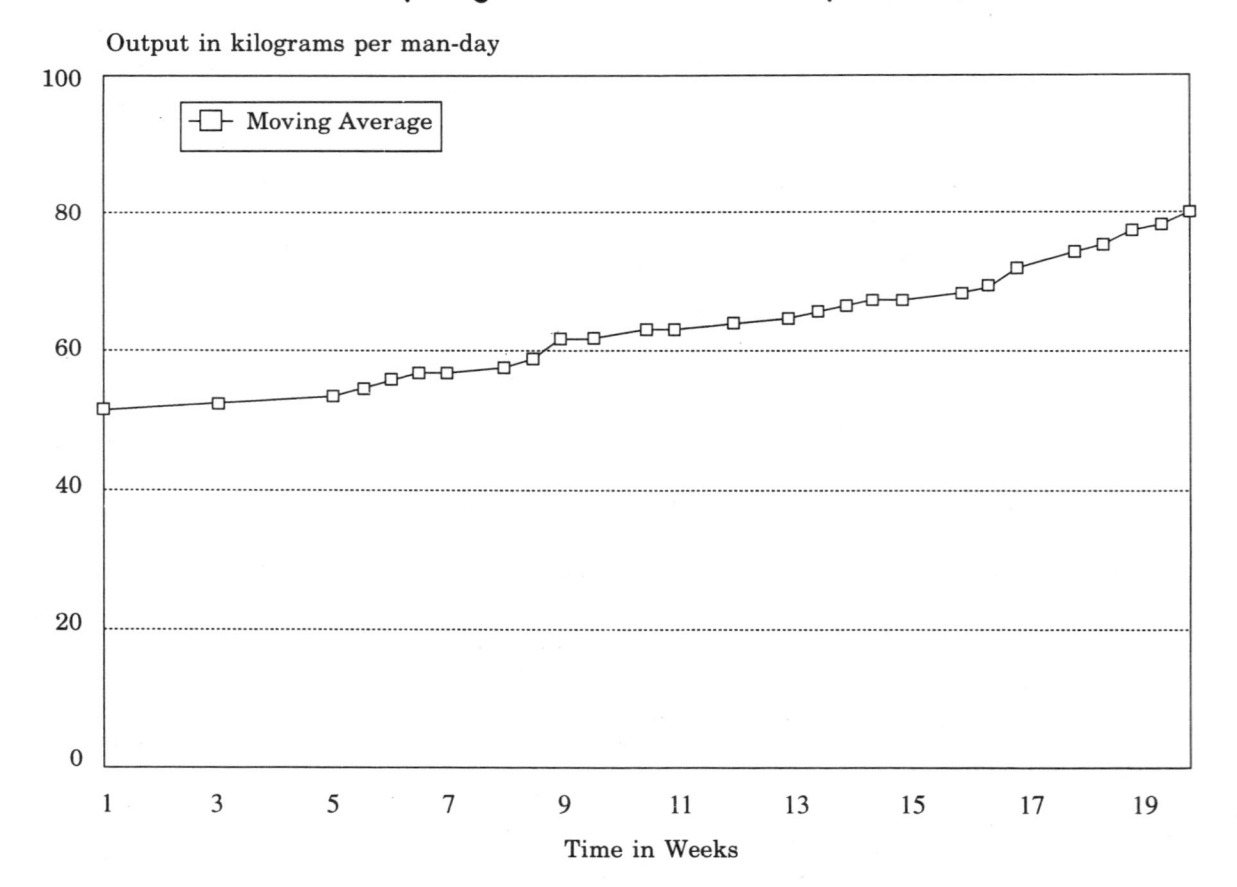

The moving average of this data after 19 weeks works out as 81 kg/man-day. The steel fixer output for planning purposes after 20 weeks can be taken as 80 kg/man-day.

Another statistical approach for analyzing the past performance is to develop a productivity model for each major work-item. In this method, the productivity function of a work-item is generalized as:

$$Q = CX^a \cdot Y^b$$

Where $Q$ = Output quantity
  $X$ = Skilled workers man-hours
  $Y$ = Unskilled workers man-hours
  $C$, $a$ and $b$ are constants.

This model is evaluated by substituting various values of output quantity achieved and their corresponding inputs.

It enables the determination of man-hours as well as crew composition for performing a unit quantity of work.

However, the statistical analysis techniques of evaluating workers production norms have certain drawbacks as well. These drawbacks, outlined in the following, should be studied carefully, prior to data processing.

(a) No two projects are exactly alike, and therefore the past performance data of various projects have to be critically examined for their suitability while determining the norms for a given project.
(b) The construction production output is constantly improving over time because of induction of better techniques and latest equipment. The statistical analysis of past performance therefore may not conform to the state-of-the-art.
(c) Analysis of past data is useful only if the data available is reliable. The degree of reliability of such data needs to the ascertained prior to analysis.
(d) Statistical analysis must not blindly compound the inefficiencies or problems of the past. The actual context in which the past performance data was recorded should be studied, and the data of inefficient or problematic working periods should be discarded prior to processing.

**Selecting published production norms** A planner can derive production norms for a project by relating them with the published production norms of professional institutions like the Institute of Quantity Surveyors, the Builders' Associations and other corporate and practicing bodies. For example, the Bureau of Indian Standards has published *I.S. 7272 (Part 1): 1974*, containing 'recommendations for labour output constants for building work: Part 1, North zone'.

The workers productivity norms vary from area to area. Workers coming from different areas, even when employed on a similar job, have different productivity. This difference is due to a blend of many ethnic and environmental factors. Considering the production norms of one of these areas (or a project) as the base, the production norms for other areas can be assessed using a relative published index or experiences, as illustrated.

| Area Location | Relative Productivity Index |
|---|---|
| Zone A | 0.95 |
| Zone B | 1.00 |
| Zone C | 0.93 |
| Zone D | 0.91 |
| Zone E | 0.95 |
| Zone F | 1.10 |

**Workstudying construction process** Workstudy, using the method study and time study techniques, aims at finding the optimum method of production with specified resources and the time required to perform the production tasks, so as to establish production norms of workers and production capacity of a machine. It is a specialized field, and workstudy is carried out by professionals.

The *method study* aims to find an optimum method of execution of work by minimizing all waste. In this, the purpose of the study is defined, the method of execution is recorded, the sequence of work and resources employed are critically examined, and areas of inefficiency are identified with the aim of reducing wastage. The various studies of construction activity show that a workman devotes only 40–60% of his time in the actual execution of work, with the rest spent on wasteful and unproductive activities like waiting, travelling, and personal breaks.

Consider a typical work process where the recorded productivity and non-productivity time is in the proportion of 40 : 60. If by using method study, a better method emerges in which the non-productive time of a worker crew is reduced by (say) 15%, and the time thus saved is utilized for productive work then the productivity increase would be to the time of 22.5%. This shows that the proportionate increase in productivity is higher than the percentage reduction in non-productive time (Table 7.4).

Table 7.4

**Table Showing Analysis of Improved Productivity**

| Work Effort | Hourly Productivity ||||| Increase in Productivity |
|---|---|---|---|---|---|
| | Existing Method || Improved Method (15% Reduction of non-productive time) || |
| | Time | Output | Time | Output | |
| Productive | 24 min | Z | 29.4* min | $\frac{29.4 \times Z}{24}$ | 22.5% |
| Non-productive | 36 min | – | 30.6 min | – | – |
| Total | 60 min | Z | 60 min | 1.225Z | 22.5% |

*Productive time + 15% non-productive time = 24 + 15% of 36 = 29.4 min

Consider a project with the production cost of $100 million, having 20,000 man-months as direct labour, of which 60% is non-productive time. If 15% of the wastage resulting from non-productive time is eliminated by using improved methods then the resulting saving in labour cost would be:

$$\text{Labour costed} = 20\% \text{ of project cost (estimated while tendering)}$$
$$= 0.20 \times 100 \text{ million}$$
$$= 20 \text{ million}$$

Non-productive labour time at 60% of labour cost, $0.6 \times 20 = 12$ million

Saving in cost by reduction of 15% of non-productive time $= 0.15 \times 12$ million
$$= \$1.8 \text{ million}$$

$$\text{Saving as percentage of productive work value} = \frac{\$1.8 \text{ million} \times 100}{40\% \text{ of } 20 \text{ million}}$$
$$= 22.5\%$$

After the method study has established the methodology for accomplishing the work, *time study* establishes the time needed by a qualified worker to carry out the specified work at a defined level of performance.

The concept of workstudy has found wide acceptance in manufacturing industries, but in the construction field it is not so effective as each project has unique tasks which are affected by varying situations. The workstudy-trained planners and supervisors, during the execution stage are able to achieve better productivity at site, but at the planning stage, off-the-job workstudy has only a limited value.

## 7.1.4 Factors Affecting Production Efficiency

The computation of production efficiency factors depends upon numerous variable which affect workers' productivity in actual job conditions at the project site. These variables vary from project to project, and over place and time. Some of the typical factors affecting the works' production efficiency are given in the following. The values, for changes in the productivity rate or human effort are indicated for conceptual purposes; these should be considered as guidelines and not mathematical rules.

**Work complexity** A simple, familiar work, is easier to execute than an unfamiliar, complex one. The extra effort needed for the latter type of work, specially in the initial stages, may range from 10–100% of the normal expected productivity.

**Repetition of work** While the first-time execution of an unfamiliar work needs extra effort and results in low output, the skill acquired in the process, when utilized over a period of time to execute similar works, improves productivity rate, especially when crew of workers is the same. This improvement in productivity rate continues till a certain limit is reached.

This limit corresponds to the stage when the crew acquires the necessary skill and becomes throughly conversant with the process, and the work is performed at its peak productivity rate. This impact of repetitive work on the productivity rate varies with time, nature of task and the characteristics of the crew. As thumb rule, the improvement in productivity rate can be taken from 5–15% for each repetition, from its initially assessed rate of about 60–80% of the average output rate till it reaches about 120% of the average rate.

**Quality control** Stringent quality control is sensitive projects, like in the construction of a nuclear reactor calls for frequent inspections, which involve elaborate documentation and is a time consuming task. They increase the non-productive time of workers and, in turn, reduces productivity by 10–25%.

**Equipment-intensive tasks** The construction tasks which can be performed wholly or partly with equipments include excavating, handling, transporting, filling, compaction, grading, hoisting, fabricating, precasting, erecting, plastering, finishing, paving, trenching, cable-laying, pipe-laying, and so on. Generally, special-purpose equipments are required for performing these tasks.

The construction equipment executes works speedily, but it needs operators. The productivity of this man-machine combination depends upon many factors, which are covered in chapter 10. However, the equipment-intensive tasks are less susceptible to productivity changes than the labour-intensive ones.

**Supervision** A supervisor manages his assigned technical work as well as the workers under him. The accomplishment of tasks economically and on schedule mostly depends upon the competence of the supervisor, which in turn affects the workers' productivity. An efficient and effective supervisor can get a higher productivity from workers.

**Climatic and weather conditions** Generally, under average weather conditions with temperature varying from 40–70°F and relative humidity of 60%, the workers continue working at the same productivity level. But extreme weather situations and seasonal changes like extreme hot or cold climate, high humidity, and strong winds and rains affect both productivity as well as the work performance.

Since construction projects are spread over several months or even years, it is necessary to adjust the effect of weather changes month-by-month on workers productivity as well as work execution. This adjustment in productivity can best the assessed by experience or it can be derived from available area productivity index.

The effect of weather on performance of equipment is explained in Chapter 10.

**Labour availability** The labour productivity also depends upon the employment opportunities available in the market. If jobs are plenty and labour is scarce, the labour productivity tends to become less. During a slump in the construction market, labour is easily available while there is a dearth of jobs. In such situations, employers can afford to be selective as hiring and firing of workers become easy. In scarce job situation, the overall productivity improves since the employers can then sort out labour with a light produvtivity.

There is also a tendency among labour to move to high-value, large-sized projects since they offer them longer service, better job opportunities and more stability.

**Role of management** The project management has a key role to play in planning and controlling productivity. It is responsible for specifying the weekly target of work to be accomplished by the workers as well as how the works are to be executed and using which resources.

During the execution stage, the management provides the necessary resource support and closely monitors the performance. Each week, it compares the planned target with the work accomplished, evaluates variances, analyzes causes for variances, and takes corrective measures.

It provides feedback to the workers on their past performance, and communicates performance improvement measures. It suitably rewards the workers who have done exceptionally well, and keeps the morale of the work force high. The productivity is bound to suffer if the management fails to fulfil its role and obligations effectively.

**Determining production efficiency factor** There is no single or exact method to determine production efficiency factor as there are too many factors involved, and, it is neither feasible nor desirable to evaluate the effect of all such factors affecting production efficiency. At the planning stage, a project planner or estimator cannot take care of all the controllable and enforceable factors. It is possible that some of these may have been considered while establishing the basic productivity norms.

Further, it is not necessary to consider the effect of all the factors while modifying basic norms as some of these may overlap, while a few may have only a marginal effect on overall productivity. It is better to limit the computation of adjustment in productivity to four to six prominent factors which contribute significantly to overall productivity, and omit other factors. By using his experience and skill, the planner identifies the main factors that affect productivity, evaluates their implications, and finally transforms the basic productivity norms into workers productivity standards conforming to the characteristics of the project under consideration.

Another approach to evaluate the main factors that influence workers production efficiency is to divide the production efficiency range into three basic ranges corresponding to 'low', 'average', and 'high' productivity conditions. The low condition ranges from 40–60% efficiency, average from 60–80% and high from 80–100%.

Each major factor affecting efficiency is the evaluated considering the site conditions. This evaluation, for a typical project, is given below:

| Production Elements | Efficiency (in %) |
|---|---|
| Nature of work | 75 |
| Supervision | 90 |
| Labour market | 80 |
| Climate and working conditions | 60 |
| Equipment orientation | 50 |
| Total | 355 |

The average production efficiency (355/5) is 71.0% of the basic productivity norms. The standard productivity for each item of work is then obtained by multiplying the basic norms with the evaluated average production efficiency factor of the work process. However, this structured approach only provides guidelines and its outcome can best be taken as an approximate to be further scrutinized by the planners and construction engineers.

The workers' productivity data used in the initial stages of the planning process may not necessarily be the workers' productivity standards used for controlling workers' performance. During the execution stage, the initially assessed productivity is subjected to further reviews, if necessary.

## ❏ 7.2 SCHEDULING CONSTRUCTION SITE WORKERS

### 7.2.1 Direct and Indirect Workers

The workers at the project site are inducted to perform a specified function and its connected tasks. These workers include supervisors, construction workers, operators and drivers and administrative personnel. For ease of estimating, planning, accounting and controlling, the project workers are broadly divided into two categories, namely—direct workers or construction site workers and indirect workers or support manpower.

**Direct manpower** These are the construction site workers who can be identified with execution of the client's permanent works such as those listed in the bill of quantities. The direct manpower constitutes 75–90% of the total manpower employed at the project site.

The direct construction workers include foremen and tradesmen, skilled in various engineering trades, in addition to the semi-skilled and unskilled manpower. The tradesmen include shuttering carpenters, fabricators, steel fixers or iron workers, masons, plumbers, electricians, furniture carpenters, metal workers, painters and decorators.

Generally the wages of construction site workers are accounted on a daily or hourly basis, and their activity-wise requirement is computed using the workers' productivity standards.

**Indirect manpower** The indirect manpower covers all supervisors, staff and workers other than those in the direct manpower. It is required to support the direct manpower, both technically and administratively. It generally consists of the project management and administration group.

The indirect manpower is generally accounted on monthly basis with some exceptions like plant and machinery operators who can be accounted on daily wages like direct manpower. Most of the indirect manpower can be assessed while formulating organisation of work and can also be estimated using thumb-rules based on experience.

*Examples* The following are some examples of direct and indirect construction site workers.
  (a) A shuttering carpenter employed in the preparation of formwork during construction of the roof slab of a building, which forms a part of the contract, is categorized as a direct worker, while another carpenter engaged in the construction of a workers'

camp (temporary accommodation) for housing labour is an indirect worker. Similarly a welder employed in the manufacture of metallic inserts for fixing in the ground slab of a permanent building is a direct worker, while a welder in the vehicle and plant maintenance and repair workshop is considered an indirect worker.

(b) A vehicle driver of a concrete truck mixer used for transporting ready-mix concrete from site batching plant and the concreting site is classified as direct worker of the ready-mix concrete supply work-centre, whereas a driver of a personnel-carrying vehicle is taken as an indirect worker.

(c) Generally all persons in a project engaged in the administrative duties such as office functioning, supervision, repair and maintenance workshop, and operation and maintenance of utility services are grouped as indirect workers.

The workers' scheduling methodology involves the following two steps:

(a) Scheduling direct construction site workers.
(b) Adding indirect construction site workers.

## 7.2.2. Scheduling Direct Workers

The project direct manpower constitutes a major portion of the labour strength. It comprises of production workers who can be identified with the execution of an activity of permanent works.

The direct manpower schedule indicates, data-wise as well as category-wise, the worker strength required to accomplish the scheduled work. The past performance data is invaluable for conceptualising manpower forecasts. For example, the actual workers utilized for a project shown in Table 7.5 can roughly indicate the effort in man-months and the peak manpower required for similar projects. This illustration shows that for similar works peak worker strength may be around 1.5 times the average manpower. But, then, no two projects are alike, and the manpower schedule for each project has to be compiled separately.

The bar chart of construction work schedule with its date of commencement and completion of each activity of work-item forms the basis for developing direct worker's schedule. Since activity has a specified duration, work content, and manpower required for its accomplishment, the daily average manpower required for each scheduled activity can be assessed as:

= Quantity of work × labour productivity standard in man-days ÷ duration in days.

The ratio of skilled and unskilled workers in a construction team depends upon their characteristics and the nature of work. A typical skilled and helper ratio used for building construction activity by a company in the Middle East, employing workers, is shown in Table 7.3.

The date-wise aggregation of manpower required for the scheduled activities (or work-items) indicates the daily strength of manpower, category-wise, required to accomplish the scheduled work as per the project plan.

Daily manpower required for scheduled work:

= Sum of manpower of construction of scheduled activity on date.

The methodology of aggregating for forecasting manpower requirement is covered in Chapter 6.

**234** Construction Project Management

## Table 7.5
### Workers' Employment Pattern on Building Projects

Table showing actual strength of workers category wise for civil works

| Month | Shuttering Carpenter | Mason Conc | Mason Finishes | Steel Fixer | Plumber | Electrician | Operators | Trade Helpers | Gen. Helpers | Total | % | Cum % |
|---|---|---|---|---|---|---|---|---|---|---|---|---|
| 1 | 18 | 2 | 0 | 10 | 4 | 2 | 2 | 17 | 7 | 62 | 0.51% | 0.51% |
| 2 | 33 | 15 | 0 | 17 | 6 | 5 | 4 | 25 | 32 | 137 | 1.14% | 1.65% |
| 3 | 47 | 13 | 0 | 27 | 6 | 7 | 11 | 37 | 59 | 207 | 1.72% | 3.37% |
| 4 | 48 | 21 | 0 | 32 | 6 | 8 | 12 | 39 | 82 | 248 | 2.06% | 5.42% |
| 5 | 63 | 26 | 8 | 32 | 6 | 8 | 14 | 58 | 105 | 320 | 2.65% | 8.07% |
| 6 | 63 | 26 | 21 | 24 | 6 | 9 | 21 | 95 | 120 | 385 | 3.19% | 11.27% |
| 7 | 98 | 26 | 27 | 35 | 9 | 9 | 24 | 84 | 195 | 507 | 4.20% | 15.47% |
| 8 | 115 | 28 | 30 | 40 | 9 | 9 | 35 | 156 | 162 | 584 | 4.84% | 20.31% |
| 9 | 121 | 31 | 48 | 41 | 12 | 10 | 39 | 173 | 192 | 667 | 5.53% | 25.84% |
| 10 | 156 | 24 | 55 | 50 | 13 | 10 | 39 | 196 | 199 | 742 | 6.15% | 31.99% |
| 11 | 193 | 30 | 62 | 54 | 14 | 13 | 43 | 247 | 170 | 826 | 6.85% | 38.84% |
| 12 | 199 | 33 | 68 | 55 | 14 | 18 | 47 | 278 | 283 | 995 | 8.25% | 47.09% |
| 13 | 202 | 23 | 83 | 61 | 16 | 19 | 50 | 277 | 288 | 1019 | 8.45% | 55.53% |
| 14 | 202 | 23 | 83 | 61 | 16 | 19 | 50 | 300 | 265 | 1019 | 8.45% | 63.98% |
| 15 | 197 | 23 | 83 | 60 | 19 | 22 | 46 | 302 | 263 | 1015 | 8.41% | 72.39% |
| 16 | 186 | 0 | 83 | 60 | 20 | 22 | 47 | 280 | 268 | 966 | 8.01% | 80.40% |
| 17 | 153 | 0 | 83 | 60 | 20 | 22 | 46 | 280 | 286 | 950 | 7.88% | 88.28% |
| 18 | 104 | 0 | 83 | 47 | 20 | 22 | 38 | 212 | 258 | 784 | 6.50% | 94.78% |
| 19 | 72 | 0 | 70 | 27 | 20 | 22 | 29 | 143 | 247 | 630 | 5.22% | 100.00% |
| Total | 2270 | 244 | 887 | 793 | 236 | 256 | 597 | 3199 | 3481 | 12063 | 100.00% | |

Planning Construction Manpower  **235**

To cite an example, the number of workers required, category and date-wise, for the 2000 Housing Units Project, worked out by aggregating the daily requirement of manpower for each scheduled activity, is shown in Exhibit 7.1.

### Exhibit 7.1

### 2000 Housing Units Project
### Extract from Workers' Requirement Forecast

| No. | Work description | MAY | JUN | JUL | AUG | SEP | OCT | NOV | DEC | JAN | FEB | MAR | APR |
|---|---|---|---|---|---|---|---|---|---|---|---|---|---|
| 1. | **Construction Works** | | | | | | | | | | | | |
| | Carpentry Work | | | | | | | | | | | | |
| | Furniture carpenter | | | | | | | 20 | 39 | 50 | 50 | 50 | |
| | Wood polisher | | | | | | | | 7 | 16 | 16 | 16 | |
| | Shuttering carpenter | 41 | 77 | 122 | 124 | 124 | 124 | 124 | 124 | 124 | 124 | 124 | |
| | Carpenter helper | 10 | 38 | 60 | 60 | 60 | 60 | 67 | 81 | 91 | 91 | 91 | |
| | Masonry Work | | | | | | | | | | | | |
| | Concrete mason | 10 | 46 | 46 | 46 | 48 | 58 | 58 | 58 | 58 | 58 | 58 | |
| | Blockwork & plaster mason | 14 | 14 | 14 | 15 | 47 | 78 | 78 | 78 | 78 | 78 | 78 | |
| | Tiling mason | | | | | | 12 | 34 | 50 | 50 | 54 | 54 | |
| | Mason helper | 30 | 40 | 40 | 40 | 40 | 40 | 92 | 108 | 108 | 112 | 112 | |
| | RCC Steel Work | | | | | | | | | | | | |
| | Rebar fabricator | 22 | 45 | 74 | 91 | 99 | 104 | 104 | 104 | 104 | 104 | 104 | |
| | Rebar helper | 20 | 22 | 36 | 40 | 40 | 44 | 44 | 44 | 44 | 44 | 44 | |
| | Painting work | | | | | | | | | | | | |
| | Painter | 1 | 2 | 2 | 2 | 2 | 2 | 48 | 100 | 144 | 144 | 144 | |
| | Painter helper | | 2 | 2 | 2 | 2 | 2 | 13 | 13 | 15 | 15 | 15 | |
| | Electrical works | | | | | | | | | | | | |
| | Electrician | 10 | 16 | 16 | 16 | 18 | 27 | 38 | 44 | 44 | 77 | 77 | |
| | Electrical helper | | 1 | 5 | 5 | 15 | 24 | 34 | 39 | 39 | 82 | 82 | |
| | Plumbing & Sanitary works | | | | | | | | | | | | |
| | Plumber/Pipe fitter | 3 | 10 | 10 | 34 | 56 | 68 | 85 | 99 | 104 | 116 | 116 | |
| | Plumber helper | 1 | 10 | 10 | 34 | 50 | 59 | 59 | 87 | 93 | 109 | 109 | |
| | Unskilled Work | | | | | | | | | | | | |
| | General helpers | 70 | 70 | 124 | 142 | 164 | 204 | 235 | 251 | 274 | 274 | 274 | |
| 2. | **Mechanical Trades** | | | | | | | | | | | | |
| | Light vehicle drivers | 7 | 15 | 15 | 15 | 15 | 15 | 15 | 15 | 15 | 15 | 15 | |
| | Heavy vehicle drivers | 9 | 20 | 20 | 20 | 20 | 20 | 20 | 20 | 20 | 20 | 20 | |
| | Equipment operators | 1 | 18 | 38 | 55 | 57 | 59 | 59 | 59 | 59 | 59 | 59 | |
| | Blacksmith | 1 | 12 | 12 | 12 | 12 | 12 | 12 | 12 | 12 | 12 | 12 | |
| | Welder | 5 | 12 | 12 | 12 | 12 | 12 | 12 | 12 | 12 | 12 | 12 | |
| | Sheet fabricator | | | | | | | 18 | 24 | 24 | 24 | 24 | |
| | Auto electrician | 1 | 2 | 2 | 2 | 2 | 2 | 2 | 2 | 2 | 2 | 2 | |
| | Mechanic diesel/petrol | 6 | 8 | 10 | 10 | 10 | 10 | 10 | 10 | 10 | 10 | 10 | |
| | Mechanic/operator helper | 1 | 8 | 30 | 41 | 46 | 48 | 48 | 48 | 48 | 48 | 48 | |
| | Riggers | 27 | 36 | 36 | 36 | 36 | 36 | 36 | 36 | 32 | 32 | 32 | |
| | Other categories | 3 | 3 | 3 | 28 | 28 | 28 | 28 | 28 | 28 | 28 | 28 | |
| 3. | **Administration Staff** | | | | | | | | | | | | |
| | Cook | 4 | 10 | 10 | 10 | 10 | 10 | 10 | 10 | 10 | 10 | 10 | |
| | Mess helper | 1 | 26 | 26 | 26 | 26 | 26 | 26 | 26 | 26 | 26 | 26 | |
| | Security staff | | 6 | 6 | 6 | 6 | 6 | 6 | 6 | 6 | 6 | 6 | |
| | Administration helper | 5 | 11 | 11 | 11 | 11 | 11 | 11 | 11 | 11 | 11 | 11 | |
| | Total | 303 | 580 | 792 | 896 | 953 | 1118 | 1392 | 1566 | 1661 | 1702 | 1713 | |
| | Months | MAY | JUN | JUL | AUG | SEP | OCT | NOV | DEC | JAN | FEB | MAR | APR |
| | Working days in a month | 25 | 24 | 25 | 25 | 24 | 25 | 24 | 24 | 22 | 20 | 23 | 24 |
| | Working days cumulative | 25 | 49 | 74 | 99 | 123 | 148 | 172 | 196 | 218 | 238 | 261 | 285 |

### 7.2.3 Adding Indirect Construction Site Workers

Requirement of indirect workers varies with the nature and size of the project. There are some yardsticks for assessing administrative persons, but on the whole the number of indirect workers required for each project has to be estimated and scheduled separately, on case-by-case basis.

### 7.2.4 Adjustments for Daily Manpower Requirement

The daily forecast of manpower can best be considered an approximate estimate of the work force required under the normal operating conditions. The factors such as learning process, weather conditions, labour turnover, strikes, absenteeism, sickness and the overtime working policy affect the day-to-day aggregated manpower requirement. Though it is difficult to quantify such variables, for planning proposes the aggregated manpower in each category may be increased by 5% or so to cater to these factors.

On the other hand, it is also possible to decrease manpower. Though it is difficult to replace skilled workers by machines, the overall strength of the work force can be reduced by increasing productivity as follows:

(a) Replacing unskilled labour by machines, wherever feasible, in jobs like loading, unloading, shifting, bar-cutting, etc.
(b) Using appropriate and efficient tools as equipment.
(c) Constantly improving the methods of production.
(d) Increasing productivity through improved working conditions and incentives.
(e) Implementing the job-oriented financial incentive schemes.
(f) Training workers to overcome the initial learning period.

In particular, overtime working based on job-oriented financial incentive schemes, if properly implemented, can cut down the daily manpower requirement by a substantial amount, say 10–15%.

## ❏ 7.3 PROJECT MANPOWER GROUPING

### 7.3.1 Nature of groups

The project manpower organization depicts the hierarchy of organizational groups of people. Each group is headed by a leader. Each leader is assigned specific tasks, resources, responsibilities and authority that enables him to manage the group efficiently and effectively for accomplishing the assigned objectives.

The number of organizational groups depend upon the magnitude and complexity of a project—a simple project may have only a few while a large, complex one may have many.

In a major project, each organizational group is usually headed by a manager. To illustrate, the outline organizational structure of a typical Housing Project as shown in Exhibit 7.2. The project manpower groups can be broadly divided into the following function units.

## Planning Construction Manpower 237

Exhibit 7.2
**Typical Housing Project**

Project Organization

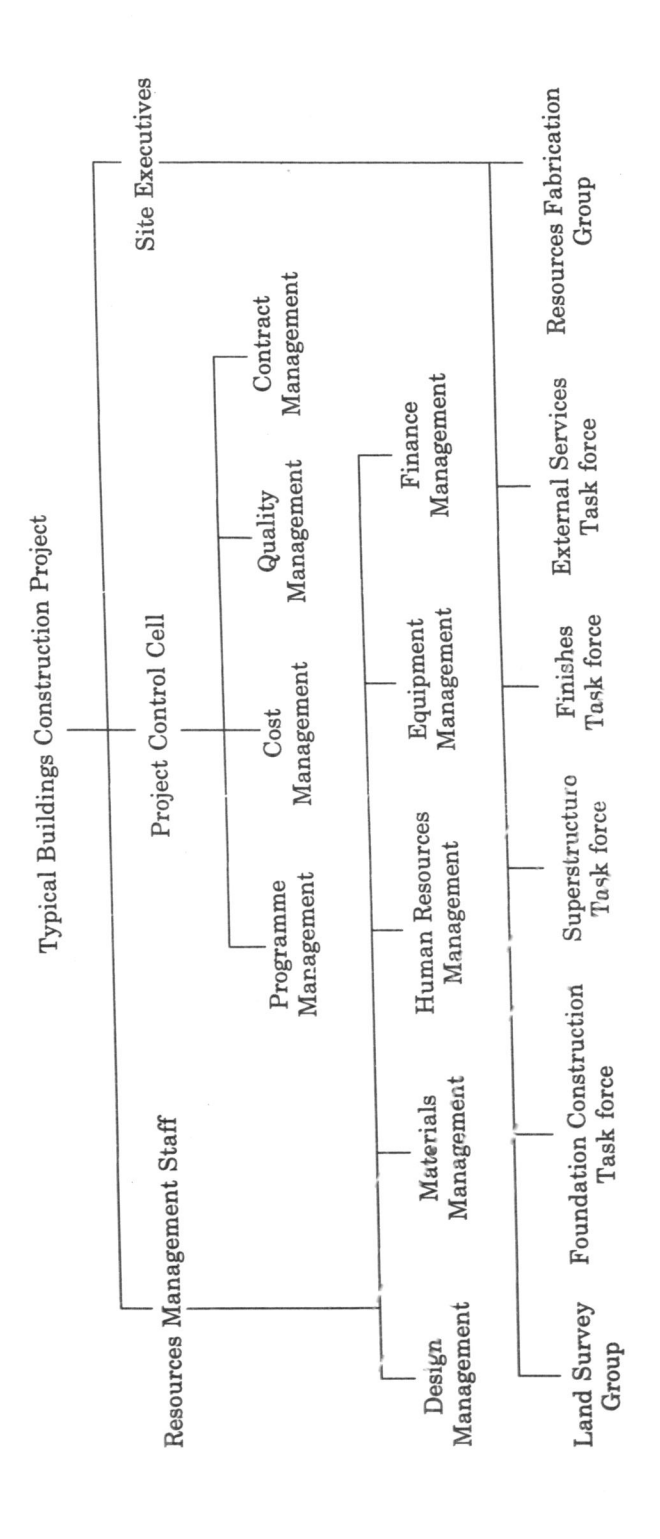

Typical Buildings Construction Project

- Resources Management Staff
  - Site Executives
- Project Control Cell
  - Programme Management
  - Cost Management
  - Quality Management
  - Contract Management
- Human Resources Management
  - Equipment Management
  - Finance Management
- Materials Management
- Resources Fabrication Group
- Design Management
- Foundation Construction Task force
- Superstructure Task force
- Finishes Task force
- External Services Task force
- Land Survey Group

(a) *Command and control group:* to manage the project and to provide necessary logistic support.
(b) *Construction task forces:* to execute the construction works.
(c) *Resource/Support centres:* to provide men, materials, and machinery support to the construction task forces.

**Command and control group** This group includes the project manager and his key staff. The Command and Control key staff of a medium-sized project would include the following:

(a) Planning and monitoring staff.
(b) Costing and contract administration staff.
(c) Technical staff, including the manpower of design and drawing office, site laboratory and technical library.
(d) Administration and personnel staff and workers connected with temporary housing, catering, camp utility services, medicine and welfare, safety and security, and other facilities, for the entire project.
(e) Material handling staff and workers.
(f) Plant and machinery workshop engineers, staff, operators, mechanics, drivers, electricians, fabricators, welders, riggers, and so on.
(g) Finance management and cost accounting staff.

Command and control staff falls in the category of indirect manpower.

**Construction task forces** These are responsible for transforming inputs into outputs. The construction task forces of the typical Housing Project, as is evident from its organizational chart, include the following:

(a) Building structure construction task force.
(b) Precast building production and erection task force.
(c) Building finishes construction task force.
(d) External services construction task force.

A construction task force consists of one or more work centres. A work centre is entrusted with the execution of a group of activities constituting one or more work packages.

A task force generally operates without much interference from the other executing agencies. It is an independent and significant unit of project organization. It is fully supported with design and drawing packages, construction plan and allocated resources. It has a specified scope of work and assigned performance objectives Fig. 7.2.

The project direct manpower is divided into several construction teams, with each having a clearly defined task assigned to it. These teams possess the skill to perform their respective tasks. They are formal groups with informal bondage, where each person understands the needs of the other. The strength of a construction team depends upon the nature of the task: it may range from 2 to 30.

Each team consists of a predetermined category of tradesmen, skilled and unskilled. It is headed by a team leader, who may be an engineer, a foreman, a change-hand, a labour subcontractor or even an experienced skilled worker.

## Figure 7.2
## Construction Task Force Heirarchy and Relationship

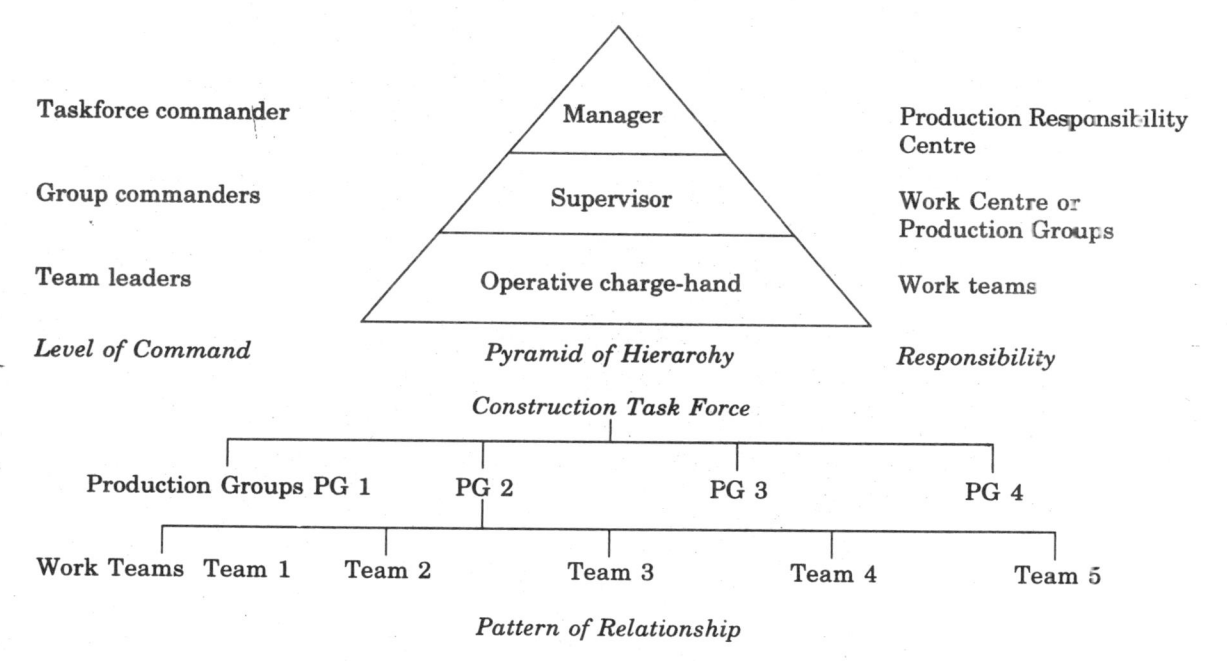

| Level of Command | Pyramid of Hierarchy | Responsibility |
|---|---|---|
| Taskforce commander | Manager | Production Responsibility Centre |
| Group commanders | Supervisor | Work Centre or Production Groups |
| Team leaders | Operative charge-hand | Work teams |

Construction Task Force
- Production Groups PG 1, PG 2, PG 3, PG 4
- Work Teams: Team 1, Team 2, Team 3, Team 4, Team 5

*Pattern of Relationship*

Some example of these teams, also called crew or gangs, are brick-layers team, steel-fixers team, concretor team, plasters team, tilers team, painters team, plumbers team, electricians team, and so on.

The construction teams are combined together to form various work-groups. Each work-group is entrusted with the task of executing one or more work packages. Depending upon the volume of work, each work group consists of one or more construction teams. Each team is headed by a supervisor who may be a charge-hand, foreman or a labour subcontractor.

**Support centres** These centres provide construction centres with technical support, materials, manpower, equipment and general services like accommodation and temporary utility services. Some of these centres contain capital-intensive machinery, and are self-supporting divisions. Examples of such investment-oriented centres are; ready-mix concrete production plant, steel reinforcement fabrication workshop, GRC elements manufacturing factory, metallic doors and windows fabrication unit, and plant and machinery operation and maintenance establishment.

Support centres manpower is a mix of direct and indirect supportcentres.

## 7.3.2 Forecasting Indirect Manpower

As stated earlier, the indirect manpower requirement is related to the management functions. In construction projects, these functions can broadly be grouped as.

(a) Project office management
(b) Design and drawing management
(c) Estimation and contracts management
(d) Planning and monitoring management
(e) Project administration and personnel management
(f) Cost and finance management
(g) Materials management
(h) Plant and equipment management
(i) Quality management
(j) Construction supervision management
(k) Support services management

In general, the extent of indirect manpower needed to perform the project functions depends upon the type and size of the project. A small project may need few indirect personnel to supervise and manage whereas a large-sized project may require far more indirect manpower of various categories including managers, engineers, staff, and skilled technical and administration assistants and workers. Further, the period of employment of the indirect manpower varies with the project needs.

To cite an example the indirect manpower of a small road construction project (contract value: $5 million; contract period: 12 months) employing special-purpose road-making plant and equipment is listed below:

| Category | Employment Period (in weeks) |
|---|---|
| Project manager | 72 |
| Senior engineer | 66 |
| Supervisors (3) | 54 |
| Senior officer clerk | 72 |
| Junior office clerk | 56 |
| Draftsman | 56 |
| Stores officer | 56 |
| Stores assistant | 40 |
| Time keeper | 56 |
| Cost accountant | 56 |
| Field surveyor | 56 |
| Personnel carrier driver | 56 |
| Load carrier driver | 56 |
| Plant workshop foreman | 56 |
| Equipment mechanics (2) | 40 |
| (2) | 40 |
| General helpers (3) | 40 |
| (2) | 56 |

*Note*: Above figures exclude special-purpose equipment operators and drivers, as these are covered under the direct workers.

The format given in Table 7.6 can be used to assess the indirect manpower of a project. The period of employment for each category can then be determined, and its forecast plotted graphically on the project calendar.

### Table 7.6
### Project Management and Administration Group Indirect Manpower Data Sheet

| Sl.No. | Departments | Manager | | Senior Engineer | | Junior Engineer | | Supervisor | | Staff | | | Workers | | |
|---|---|---|---|---|---|---|---|---|---|---|---|---|---|---|---|
| | | No. | Period | No. | Period | No. | Period | No. | Period | Category | No. | Period | Category | No. | Period |
| 1. | Office management | | | | | | | | | | | | | | |
| 2. | Planning management | | | | | | | | | | | | | | |
| 3. | Technical management | | | | | | | | | | | | | | |
| 4. | Contract management | | | | | | | | | | | | | | |
| 5. | Personnel management | | | | | | | | | | | | | | |
| 6. | Materials management | | | | | | | | | | | | | | |
| 7. | Equipment management | | | | | | | | | | | | | | |
| 8. | Cost management | | | | | | | | | | | | | | |
| 9. | Finance management | | | | | | | | | | | | | | |
| 10. | Quality management | | | | | | | | | | | | | | |
| 11. | Miscellaneous | | | | | | | | | | | | | | |

### 7.3.3 Structuring Site Organization

The project organization is temporary—it ceases to be on completion of the project. It is conceived during the project conception stage and comes into existence at the start of planning stage. Gradually, it grows and undergoes changes with the various stages of the project life cycle to meet project needs. Towards the end, it runs down and ceases on completion of the project. It's special attributes include the innovation capacity to overcome problems as they arise. Usually it is staffed with experienced people to respond speedily to changing situations and to speed up decision making.

Thus the guidelines for designing the project organization will include.

- Organizational groups are designed to generally conform with the project work-breakdown structure.
- Each group is assigned responsibilities and allocated resources to meet the assigned tasks.
- The size and structure of the organization changes with the alternation in requirements. However, the core project team continues till the end.
- Project groups are suitably structured with emphasis on team work and informal relationship.
- Organization structure is kept flat to avoid bureaucratic tendencies and to reduce channels of communication with the project manager.
- Where possible, key staff is derived from their respective parent departments in the corporate office and their interfaces and communication links are clearly defined.
- The heads of line and staff departments are generally grouped into a project management team and the planning chief is assigned responsibility of the coordination function.

The structuring of work-groups into construction task forces and direct support service centres is accomplished by a applying the three classic principles of designing formal organizations. These principles are outlined below.

**(a) Unity of command** According to this no man can serve two bosses simultaneously that is, a person should receive orders from and be responsible to only one superior.

**(b) Scalar principle** This implies that within an organization, the chain of command or hierarchy showing the superior-subordinate relationship should be well defined, that is, it should clearly lay down the channel of authority, decision-making and communication. A construction task force hierarchy generally follows the pattern given in Fig. 7.2.

**(c) Span of control** This principle puts a limit to the number of subordinates (span of control) reporting to a superior. In other words, an executive should be made accountable for the actions of only a limited number of subordinates. The span of control depends upon many factors such as:

(i) Nature of work.
(ii) Project characteristics, including execution times.
(iii) Moral and competence of the people.

(iv) Capability of the leaders at various levels.
(v) Management policy regarding decentralization, information system and the degree of control.

A limited span leads to strict control but it has adverse implications: the senior leaders tend to interfere with the work of their subordinates, thus restricting their initiative.

Further, project organization undergoes changes in various phases of the project life cycle. Unlike on-going enterprises, there are on standard methods of organizing the project management. Generally, efficient management of project resources is effected by organizing the project management structure similar to the army's special purpose task-force concept. The leader of this organization is the project manager. Although management principles of forecasting, planning, organizing, staffing, directing, motivating, monitoring, communicating, controlling and decision making, are equally applicable in the traditional functional type management as well as project management, but the risks, uncertainty and complexity make project management a relatively difficult process.

## ❑ 7.4 DESIGNING WORKERS FINANCIAL INCENTIVE SCHEME

The project management aims at achieving objectives economically. It employs motivational tools to increase production and productivity. The art of motivating lies in creating environment, developing systems, and directing efforts in such a way that they meet the organizational goals as well as the needs of those participating in the process, with everyone working enthusiastically as one team under the leadership of the project manager.

The motivational approach, in general, can be divided into behavioural approach and financial incentive schemes. In a construction project the behaviour motivational approach is essential to create a healthy work environment, while the financial incentive scheme benefits the participants in the following ways:

(a) It assists the project management in increasing production and productivity, without any appreciable increase in estimated costs, by curtailing supervision time, obtaining reliable feedback in progress of work and productivity, and exercising effective control on the employment of workers. The feedback also generates output information for planning and costing future works and improving incentive schemes.

(b) It helps workers in increasing their earnings and gaining job satisfaction without affecting the estimated costs of work. It also encourages workers to develop better methods of working.

In the construction industry, many financial incentives schemes have been developed to motivate workers. These vary with the type of project, nature of task and employment teams of workers. Broadly, the financial incentive schemes can be divided in the following categories:

| | |
|---|---|
| (i) Time-related schemes | Employee is paid according to the overtime worked in proportion to the basic hourly wages. |
| (ii) Job-related schemes | Employee is paid according to the measurable job completed. |

(iii) Lump-sum work payment    Employee is paid according to: scheme
- Time saved from standard time fixed for completing the job.
- A lump-sum amount paid for completing the fixed quantity of a specified job.

(iv) Profit sharing bonus    These can be paid as bonus after a predetermined time, say, quarterly, half-yearly or yearly.

The basis of financial incentive schemes is the setting of attainable output target rates for time or task. Generally, for direct workers, these output targets are derived from the productivity standards. For indirect manpower, the time employed and profit-sharing may be the only method of offering financial incentives.

Finalizing a financial incentive scheme for a given work is a difficult process. A scheme once agreed upon cannot be altered without concurrence of the parties concerned. The following guidelines can help in designing a financial incentive scheme for the direct workers. The scheme should be:

(a) *Attainable enough,* so that the workers find prospects of higher earning than their guaranteed minimum wages.
(b) *Simple enough,* so that the workers can easily comprehend it.
(c) *Specific enough,* so that the output can be measured without any controversy.
(d) *Concise enough,* so that the unforeseen and unavoidable holdups in progressing works can be easily determined and workers compensated for the time wasted during execution.
(e) *Supervised enough,* so that work progresses smoothly as per standard engineering practices and quality specifications.
(f) *Comprehensive enough,* so that all the statutory requirements are fulfilled.

An incentive scheme needs to be designed carefully. It is difficult to sell to workers. It faces teething problems during implementation. Once implemented, it cannot be altered without concurrence of the affected workers. With all its drawbacks, however, an incentive scheme is still necessary to induce the workers to give their best. In conclusion, it can said that workers work harder if there is a financial reward linked to their performance, and the management saves upon time and costs if it is properly implemented.

# CHAPTER 8

# Planning Construction Materials

Broadly, the term 'materials' denotes all purchased items utilized at the project site including construction materials, supporting plant and equipment, and administrative facilities and stores. Supporting plant and equipment consists of all machinery, vehicles, custom–build form work, construction equipment and their operational repair and maintenance materials.

Construction materials cover all types of materials used in construction including electrical and mechanical fittings fixtures, devices and instruments that are incorporated during the construction of permanent works and temporary supporting works at site.

In construction projects, materials account for more than 40% of the project cost. A small saving in materials cost, say even 5%, through efficient management of materials, can result in a large contribution specially, when competitive bidding is for small profit margins varying from 3.5% to 10% of the project cost.

Efficient materials management in project environments calls for an integrated approach covering numerous functions such as materials planning, purchasing, inventory control, store-keeping and warehousing, handling and transportation, codification and standardization, and the disposal of surpluses. Materials planning, which is the key function of materials management, is closely linked with project planning and control set-up. Both these work together to develop a plan for procurement and stocking of construction materials so as to provide at the site materials of the right quality in right quantity at the right prices from the right sources at the right time.

Construction materials planning involves identifying materials, estimating quantities, defining specifications, forecasting requirements, locating sources for procurement, getting samples of materials approved, designing materials inventory, developing procurement plans, and monitoring flow of materials till the connected construction works are completed.

In contracted construction projects, materials management is the responsibility of the contractor executing the works. Accordingly, in this chapter, construction materials planning is viewed from the contractor's angle. Further, construction materials planning in building construction projects involves a variety of materials. The planning process described in the chapter is illustrated with examples from such projects. The costing and monitoring of construction materials is covered in Chapters 11 and 14, respectively.

## 8.1 ABC CLASSIFICATION OF CONSTRUCTION MATERIALS

### 8.1.1 Concept

In the manufacturing industry, where manufactured end-products are usually similar, the materials used are broadly divided into: *repetitive items* and *non-repetitive* items. The repetitive items include the raw materials and other stores consumed regularly for production, maintenance and administration. All other items, such as capital purchases of plant and machinery including its major repairs, capital goods, and special one-time requirements for various jobs, are categorized as non-repetitive items. In the manufacturing industry, repetitive items are included in the regular stock list and their procurement and inventory is generally, guided by the ABC analysis technique explained in subsequent paragraphs. On the other hand, non-repetitive items are inducted when required. Each item is considered for purchase on its own merit and it is subject to selective inventory control.

However, in construction no two projects are similar. The type and quality of construction materials differ from project to project. Although some basic materials like cement, aggregate, steel, water, and timber are common items, others vary with the type of the project. For example, most of the finishing materials used in housing projects are not required in industrial projects.

The primary purpose of classifying materials is to control quality, cost and timely supply. There are many factors that need consideration while classifying materials. These include storage space, shelf life, supply reliability, inventory costs, ease of identification, construction sequence, transportation requirement, price, procurement time, procurement source and project life. In general, the construction materials can be grouped into any one or a combination of the following categories:

(a) Bulky, one-time purchases, repetitive use, and minor materials.
(b) Vital, essential and desirable materials.
(c) Indigenous and imported materials.
(d) High price, medium price and low-price materials.
(e) High usage value, medium usage value and low-usage value materials.

The most commonly used method for classifying construction materials is to group them into high-value, medium-value and low-value materials. This classification is achieved using the ABC analysis, (Fig. 8.1). The prerequisite for applying the ABC analysis technique is that the project should have a standardized bill of materials listing the physical quantities (including standard wastage), unit rate and total cost for each item. The following is the format of a bill-of-materials table.

| BILL OF MATERIALS |||||| 
|---|---|---|---|---|---|
| S. No. | Item of Materials | Unit | Quantity | Rate | Amount |
| 1. | | | | | |
| 2. | | | | | |

The materials management technique of ABC analysis is based on the principle of 'control by selection' which implies that it is not necessary to give the same degree of attention to procurement, storage, issue and control of all types of materials.

ABC analysis is generally used for control of regular stock items. Studies show that

Figure 8.1

**ABC Analysis Concept**

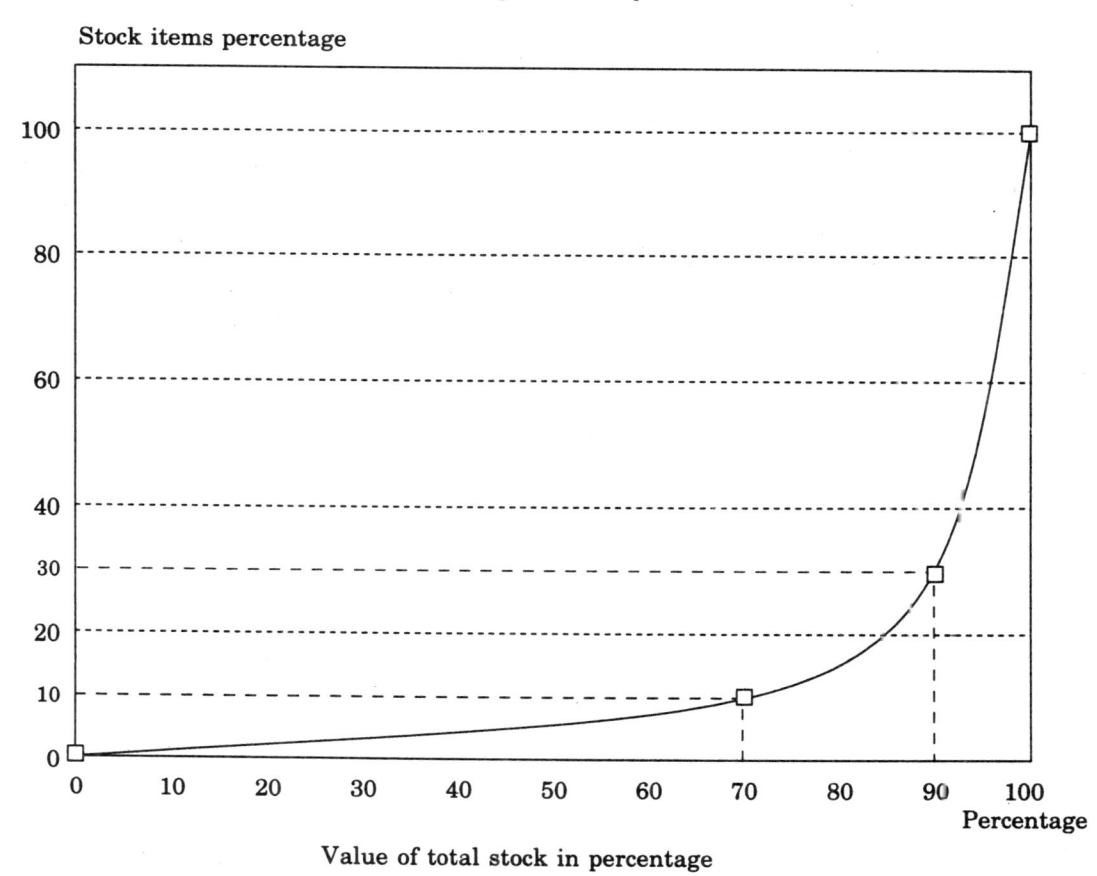

Stock items percentage

Value of total stock in percentage

10 % Items cost 70% of Stock Usage Value
20 % Items have 20% of Stock Usage Value
70 % Items account for 10% of Stock Usage Value

regular stock items, depending upon their periodic requirement and costs (say quarterly or yearly), can be grouped into three groups of materials, i.e. A, B and C, generally confirming to the following pattern:

| Group class | Total items | Inventory costs |
|---|---|---|
| A | 10% | 70% |
| B | 20% | 20% |
| C | 70% | 10% |

(a) *Group A Items*—These are high usage value items which account for 70% of the inventory cost. Number of a items is about 5% to 15 of all items.
(b) *Group B Items*—These are medium usage value items, which account for 20% of the inventory costs. Their number is also in the range of 15% to 25% of the total number of items.
(c) *Group C Items*—These are the remaining about 65% to 75% of the items which account for hardly 10% of the inventory cost.

The above concept of ABC analysis can be applied for the categorization of repetitive construction materials where the period of usage can be taken as the project completion period or on an yearly basis. The number of items can be considered as those required for the execution of the project. For further simplification, these can be restricted to the construction materials estimated for the works.

## 8.1.2 Methodology

The ABC group of construction materials can thus be grouped in the following manner: an example, from Residential Project is depicted in Exhibit 8.1.

(a) Identify materials required and estimate quantity and quality of each material.
(b) Obtain the approximate unit rate for each item.
(c) Assess the requirement during the period under consideration, i.e. yearly or project completion basis.
(d) Determine the usage value of each type by multiplying the quantity required with the corresponding unit rates.
(e) Calculate the percentage usage value of each material with respect to total project or yearly usage cost. Write this percentage against each item in the appropriate column.
(f) Arrange the items in the descending order of usage value.
(g) Consider materials in the descending order of usage value. Compute cumulative usage value against each item.
(h) Draw two horizontal lines demarcating the descending order of the cumulative purchase values at 70% level and 20% level.
(i) The three groups separated by the above two horizontal lines starting in descending order of usage value can then be classified as 'A' group, 'B' group and 'C' group.

### Exhibit 8.1
### Residential Buildings Sub-project
### ABC Classification of Direct Material

| Sl No. | Item & Description | Amount (in 000$) | % to Total Amount | Rank | Class |
|---|---|---|---|---|---|
| **I- Bulk Materials** | | | | | |
| 1. | Cement | 6235.88 | 19.43 | 1 | A |
| 2. | Sand | 2052.63 | 6.39 | 3 | A |
| 3. | Aggregate | 1844.21 | 5.75 | 5 | A |
| 4. | Admixtures | 1540.62 | 4.80 | 6 | A |
| 5. | Steel | 4884.37 | 15.22 | 2 | A |
| 6. | Weld mesh | 153.91 | 0.48 | 27 | B |
| 7. | Binding wire | 84.17 | 0.26 | | C |
| 8. | Bitumen | 36.40 | 0.12 | | C |
| 9. | Anti-termite chemicals | 160.32 | 0.50 | 26 | B |
| 10. | Polythene sheets | 114.77 | 0.36 | 35 | C |
| 11. | Imported soil | 294.99 | 0.93 | 19 | B |
| 12. | Inserts for precast | 1375.34 | 4.28 | 7 | A |
| 13. | Hardwood | 39.57 | 0.13 | | C |
| 14. | Softwood | 135.70 | 0.42 | 31 | C |
| 15. | Teakwood | 2.18 | 0.02 | | C |
| 16. | Commercial plywood | 12.85 | 0.05 | | C |
| 17. | Teakface plywood | 5.63 | 0.02 | | C |
| **II-Wiring** | | | | | |
| 18. | PVC Conduits & accessories | 105.21 | 0.33 | 37 | C |
| 19. | Switches | 54.46 | 0.17 | | C |
| 20. | Socket outlets | 102.39 | 0.32 | 38 | C |
| 21. | 6 mm$^2$ electric cable | 5.10 | 0.02 | | C |
| 22. | Electric buzzer | 28.11 | 0.09 | | C |
| 23. | Telephone cable | 2.21 | 0.01 | | C |
| 24. | Shaver unit | 28.11 | 0.09 | | C |
| 25. | Rawl plugs | 59.60 | 0.19 | | C |
| 26. | Screws | 59.60 | 0.19 | | C |
| 27. | Telephone socket | 1.97 | 0.01 | | C |
| 28. | Armored cable | 125.40 | 0.39 | 34 | C |
| 29. | 2.5 mm flexible wire | 89.25 | 0.28 | 41 | C |
| 30. | 4 mm$^2$ flexible wire | 36.63 | 0.12 | | C |
| **III-Screed** | | | | | |
| | Cement | Included in Sl No. 1 | | | |
| | Sand | Included in Sl No. 2 | | | |
| **IV-GRC Panels** | | | | | |
| 31. | GRC Panels | 2006.76 | 6.25 | 4 | A |
| **V-PVC Plumbing** | | | | | |
| 32. | PVC Pipes & accessories | 843.40 | 2.64 | 10 | A |

*(Contd)*

*(Contd)*

| Sl No. | Item & Description | Amount (in 000$) | % to Total Amount | Rank | Class |
|---|---|---|---|---|---|
| **VI-GI Plumbing** | | | | | |
| 33. | GI pipes & fittings | 179.68 | 0.56 | 24 | B |
| 34. | 40 mm valves | 18.47 | 0.07 | | C |
| 35. | 25 mm valves | 56.91 | 0.18 | | C |
| 36. | 20 mm valves | 28.57 | 0.09 | | C |
| 37. | 15 mm valves | 85.66 | 0.26 | | C |
| 38. | Hot water pipe | 92.34 | 0.29 | 40 | C |
| 39. | Teflon tape | 10.00 | 0.04 | | C |
| 40. | Dense tape | 18.70 | 0.07 | | C |
| **VII-A/C Ducting** | | | | | |
| 41. | GI Sheet 24 g | 136.93 | 0.43 | 30 | C |
| 42. | GI Sheet 22 g | 126.43 | 0.39 | 33 | C |
| 43. | GI Sheet 18 g | 17.21 | 0.05 | | C |
| 44. | I-Glasswool | 17.73 | 0.05 | | C |
| **VII- Staircase Metal Works** | | | | | |
| 45. | M.S. flat/round | 14.04 | 0.05 | | C |
| 46. | 40 mm GI pipe | 98.48 | 0.32 | 39 | C |
| 47. | Inserts/bolts | 19.00 | 0.06 | | C |
| 48. | Sealant | 1.32 | 0.02 | | C |
| **IX- False Ceiling** | | | | | |
| | Softwood | Included in Sl No.14 | | | |
| 49. | Metal screws | 14.04 | 0.04 | | C |
| 50. | Wood screws | 1.41 | 0.02 | | C |
| 51. | Plastic rawl plugs | 2.04 | 0.02 | | C |
| 52. | Asbestos sheet | 112.68 | 0.36 | 36 | C |
| **X-Ceramic/Glazed tiles** | | | | | |
| 53. | Tiles Type A | 167.33 | 0.52 | 25 | B |
| 54. | Tiles Type B | 134.93 | 0.42 | 32 | C |
| 55. | Tiles Type C | 200.80 | 0.63 | 23 | B |
| 56. | Tiles Type D | 802.25 | 2.50 | 11 | B |
| 57. | Tiles adhesive | 67.27 | 0.22 | | C |
| 58. | Bonding agent | 14.34 | 0.05 | | C |
| 59. | Tile grout | 29.14 | 0.09 | | C |
| **XI-Doors/Windows including shuttering/Glazing** | | | | | |
| | Hardwood | Included in Sl No. 13 | | | |
| | Softwood | Included in Sl No. 14 | | | |
| | Commercial plywood | Included in Sl No. 16 | | | |
| | Teak faced plywood | Included in Sl No. 17 | | | |
| 60. | Hot pressing glue | 1.71 | 0.02 | | C |
| 61. | Nails/pins | | 0.02 | | C |
| 62. | Wood screws | | 0.02 | | C |
| 63. | Door/windows profiles | | 1.99 | 13 | B |

*(Contd)*

*(Contd)*

| Sl No. | Item & Description | Amount (in 000$) | % to Total Amount | Rank | Class |
|---|---|---|---|---|---|
| **XII-Sanitary fittings** | | | | | |
| 64. | Wash hand basin | 64.87 | 0.16 | | C |
| 65. | Shower tray | 29.95 | 0.09 | | C |
| 66. | European water closet | 68.64 | 0.22 | | C |
| 67. | Bidet | 63.68 | 0.20 | | C |
| **XIII-Painting** | | | | | |
| 68. | Spray plaster | 421.33 | 1.31 | 15 | B |
| 69. | Plaster spatula | 1.00 | 0.02 | | C |
| 70. | Plastic emulsion paint | 228.95 | 0.71 | 22 | B |
| 71. | Oil paint | 44.30 | 0.15 | | C |
| 72. | Paint primer | 147.29 | 0.46 | 28 | B |
| 73. | Paint putty | 350.70 | 1.09 | 18 | B |
| 74. | Fibre glass scrims | 6.01 | 0.03 | | C |
| 75. | Masking tape | 1.20 | 0.02 | | C |
| **XIV-Electrical Fittings** | | | | | |
| 76. | Electrical holders & fittings | 501.00 | 1.56 | 14 | B |
| **XV-Kitchen cabinets/Wardrobe** | | | | | |
| 77. | Kitchen cabinets | 938.69 | 2.92 | 9 | A |
| 78. | Wardrobe | 1030.88 | 3.21 | 8 | A |
| 79. | Kitchen sink | 70.66 | 0.23 | | C |
| **XVII-PVCTiles** | | | | | |
| 80. | PVC tiles | 411.41 | 1.28 | 16 | B |
| 81. | PVC skirting | 372.63 | 1.16 | 17 | B |
| 82. | MV cement glue | 40.03 | 0.13 | | C |
| 83. | SV cement | 10.30 | 0.03 | | B |
| 84. | Bar emulsion | 256.00 | 0.80 | 20 | B |
| 85. | Levelling compound | 1.90 | 0.02 | | C |
| 86. | Polishing stone | 22.50 | 0.07 | | C |
| **XVIII-PVC Handrail** | | | | | |
| 87. | PVC handrail | 7.70 | 0.02 | | C |
| **XIX-Roof Treatment** | | | | | |
| 88. | Roofing felt | 801.93 | 2.50 | 12 | B |
| 89. | Bitumen primer | 146.97 | 0.46 | 29 | C |
| 90. | Super penetration primer | 78.25 | 0.24 | | C |
| | Polythene sheets | Included in Sl. No. 10 | | | |
| **XX-External Finishes & Miscellaneous items** | | | | | |
| 91. | Waterproofing compound | 230.46 | 0.72 | 21 | B |
| 92. | Terrazo tiles | 19.95 | 0.06 | | C |
| | | | 100.00 | | |

Exhibit 8.1 shows the tabulated A, B and C grouping of construction materials with respective usage values of a typical residential buildings construction project. It may be noted that:

(a) A, B and C grouping is based on the estimated consumption costs of materials over a selected period.
(b) The classification based on 70%, 20% and 10% of the purchase costs is not rigid. This percentage can be varied to suit project procurement sources.
(c) 'A' items need tighter control while 'B' items need fairly tight control. For 'C' items, control can be moderate.
(d) The number of Economical Order Quantities (EOQ) for 'A' and 'B' items can be worked out by using the EOQ technique (described under materials inventory).

## 8.1.3 Applications

In materials management, ABC analysis is used in areas needing selective control such as policy development, procurement planning, inventory planning and control, quality inspection, and store-keeping. For example, ABC analysis can assist in developing policy guidelines for exercising selective control on material supplies as shown in Table 8.1.

Table 8.1

**Use of ABC Analysis for Developing Policy Guidelines**

| Policy consideration | 'A' items | 'B' items | 'C' items |
|---|---|---|---|
| Degree of control required | Strict | Moderate | Loose |
| Forecast accuracy | Accurate quantities | Approximate quantities | Rough quantities |
| Authority for ordering purchases | Senior level | Middle level | Junior level |
| Suppliers to be contacted for enquiries | Maximum suppliers | 3 to 5 reliable suppliers | 2 to 3 reliable suppliers |
| Safety stock | Low | Moderate | Adequate |
| Ordering frequency | When required | EOQ basis | Bulk ordering |
| Follow-up need | Maximum | Moderate | When necessary |
| Monitoring inflow and stock status | Weekly | Monthly | Quarterly |
| Control reports | Weekly | Monthly stock-taking | Quarterly accounting period |

It is worth noting that the ABC analysis depends upon the usage value of the item of the material consumed during the project life and not on the unit cost of the material. It does not rely on the importance of the material. It is not related to construction sequence. A, B and C items can be further split up into categories like locally available items and imported items. Further, bulky locally available materials can be taken out of the category of A, B and C items, and these can be classified as a separate item.

## 8.2 MATERIALS USAGE STANDARD

Generally, the materials and labour costs in a project are conceptualised during the inception stage by using past experience (see Table 8.2 for illustration). While contracting the quantities of work involved in a project are detailed in the contract bill of quantities. These are derived from the design and drawings. But there is inherent materials wastage associated with all types of materials.

For example, the actual requirement of concrete for the floor slab of a building may be 2% more than the theoretical quantities measured from the drawing, as certain wastage does occur while placing concrete specially, due to inaccuracies in the levelling of form work. Further, the quantities of aggregate, sand, cement and water though correctly weighed prior to mixing, also have a certain element of handling wastage. Similarly, some steel gets wasted when the standard bars are bent into designed lengths and shapes for reinforcement work. Some wastage is inevitable in actual work. This wastage in materials is generally expressed as a percentage of the materials calculated theoretically from the quantities of work involved, and are termed as 'Standard Wastage'. The total quantity of materials to be provisioned should cater for the standard wastage by increasing the theoretical quantity, proportionately.

Materials to be provisioned

$$= \text{Theoretical quantity of materials} \times \frac{\{100 + \text{standard wastage (\%)}\}}{100}$$

Standard wastage of the construction materials depends upon many variables such as the nature of work, type of materials, method of application, etc. The standard wastage can best be specified from experience. The typical standard wastage considered while estimating some of the materials in a housing project are shown in Table 8.3.

It may be noted that standard wastage caters for wastage during utilization only for causes considered beyond control at the site. In addition to the uncontrollable wastage, there is wastage/pilferage which falls in the category of controllable wastage. The main causes of controllable wastage at various stages can be due to the following:

(a) Wastage on account of designers specifying non-standard materials having unattainable specifications.
(b) Wastage due to incorrect purchasing resulting in over buying, wrong buying, unnecessary buying and untimely buying.
(c) Wastage in transportation and handling including breakage and pilferage.
(d) Wastage during storage resulting from deterioration, improper storage, breakage, obsolescence and theft.

Since, controllable wastage falls under the purview of the materials management staff the additional provisions to compensate for such wastage should be made by them so as to ensure that the right quantity and right quality of materials are available at the right time.

Table 8.2

**Building Construction Conceptualising Costs Breakdown**

| Sl No. | Description of the material/labour | Residential building upto 3 storeys with brick walls and RCC upper floors and roof | Residential multistoreyed building—more than 3 storeys with brick RCC structure |
|---|---|---|---|
| 1. | Bricks | 14.0% | 5.0% |
| 2. | Sand | 3.0% | 4.0% |
| 3. | Cement | 9.0% | 12.0% |
| 4. | Aggregate | 3.0% | 4.0% |
| 5. | Timber | 16.5% | 11.0% |
| 6. | Steel | 11.0% | 19.5% |
| 7. | Sheet glass 3 mm thick | 1.0% | 0.7% |
| 8. | Paints | 1.5% | 1.0% |
| 9. | CI pipes (water supply pipes) and fittings. | 3.0% | 3.0% |
| 10. | Electric wiring including conduit | 6.0% | 6.0% |
| 11. | CI soil, waste and vent pipes | 4.0% | 4.0% |
| 12. | Sanitary fittings | 2.5% | 2.5% |
| 13. | Mazdoors | 11.0% | 12.0% |
| 14. | Mason | 6.0% | 7.0% |
| 15. | Carpenter | 3.5% | 3.5% |
| 16. | Painter | 0.5% | 0.5% |
| 17. | Blacksmith | 2.0% | 2.2% |
| 18. | Plumber | 1.0% | 1.0% |
| 19. | Electrician | 1.0% | 1.0% |
| Total | | 100.0% | 100.0% |

*Note:*
(1) For steel windows, reduce timber percentage by 7% and correspondingly, increase percentage of steel by 7%.
(2) Minor materials are ignored in this table.

## 8.3 MATERIALS PROVISIONING PROCESS

Construction materials needed for a project work vary with the nature of the project. For example, in a road construction project, the type of materials required may be few in number whereas, in the building construction project, it may run into hundreds. The determination of the type, quantity and specifications of the construction materials needs a detailed study of the contract documents, including the bill of quantities, drawings, specifications, pre-tender estimates, and preliminary vendor enquiries. Such a study consumes considerable time, and is a systematic and gradual process.

Table 8.3

**Construction Materials Wastage Planning Norms**

| Sl No. | Type of Materials | Planned Wastage |
|---|---|---|
| 1. | Cement | 2% |
| 2. | Sand | 10% |
| 3. | Aggregate | 5% |
| 4. | Concrete structural | 2% |
| 5. | Concrete blinding (lean) | 10% |
| 6. | Reinforcement steel bars | 3% |
| 7. | Reinforcement steel mesh | 10% |
| 8. | PVC sheeting | 15% |
| 9. | Steel for windows | 7% |
| 9. | Timbering in trenches | 5% |
| 10. | Stone masonry | 5% |
| 11. | Marble lining | 20% |
| 12. | Wood for door frames | 5 to 7.5% |
| 13. | Wood for shutters | 10% |
| 14 | Wood for flooring/walling | 5 to 10% |
| 15. | Sheet sheet roofing | 2.1/2% |
| 16. | Tile roofing | 5% |
| 17. | Floor tiling | 2 to 5% |
| 18. | Wall tiling | 3% |
| 19. | Pigments (for colours other than natural grey) | 5% |
| 20. | Paints | 5% |

Materials planning considers materials in the order of requirement at the site. For example, in a building construction project, bulk materials and other items for site development, foundation work and superstructure frame, which are needed in the early stages of construction, are considered first. The others are taken up in the sequence of their requirement. The materials selection process for each item generally, follows the sequence outlined below and this sequence is also depicted in Table 8.4.

## 8.3.1 Identification of Materials Package

Materials breakdown specially, of bulk materials, can be determined from the bill of quantities which contain work-items with quantities of work involved generally, listed in the order of execution. Similarly, details regarding finishes can be read from the architectural drawings specially, the schedule of finishes. In case of electrical and mechanical items, a detailed scrutiny is required to identify the item and its components. In some cases these may have to be designed.

Materials package includes all types and qualities of materials needed to perform a given activity or a work-item. For example, the concreting of the foundation not only requires

## Table 8.4

### Materials Provisioning Process

1. Study contract documents to identify items for purchase.
2. Estimate quantities to be purchased.
3. Float inquiry indents to locate sources of supply.
4. Invite quotations from selected vendors.
5. Analyse quotations received and vendors' prequalifications.
6. Submit proposals for technical, financial and client's approval.
7. Negotiate with vendors and finalise supply orders.
8. Place purchase orders and monitor order execution.
9. Conduit pre-shipment inspections, where necessary.
10. Inspect goods received at site and initiate action where warranted for in-transit losses/theft/damages, short shipments and rejections of sub-standard supply item.
11. Close materials supply contract after confirming no-further demand from concerned site manager. Inform accounts, planning, costing and the project manager, accordingly.

cement, sand, aggregate and water, but it may also need polythene sheets to be laid under the concreting surface. Further, each one of these items should meet the contract specifications.

A typical combination of materials needed activity-wise for finishes are identified in Exhibit 8.1. This list also highlights that the materials should be identified activity-wise as one package.

### 8.3.2 Materials Quantity Estimation

Material quantities estimates are based on the abstract of quantities of work calculated by the quantity surveyors from the contract drawings. The work quantities when multiplied by the respective estimated materials required for a unit item of work, give the quantity of materials required for the activity. To quote example, Bureau of Indian Standard Code I.S. 10067: 1982 gives the materials constants in building works. In particular, materials estimates must include standard wastage in materials estimates which occur during execution of work. Table 8.3 shows typical wastage percentage which may be included in the materials estimates.

The final materials quantities specially, of the A and B items which constitute the major portion of the materials costs, are then compared with the preliminary materials estimates prepared at the time of tendering, so as to know the variations from the original estimates. In case of appreciable variations the approval of the appropriate authority is obtained prior to floating materials cost inquiries/quotations.

### 8.3.3 Scheduling Materials Requirements

After the quantity of materials required for the work are evaluated, a usage schedule at the site based on the project construction plan is prepared with a view to evolve their delivery schedules and the stocking policy. The method of forecasting is covered in Chapter 6.

### 8.3.4 Materials Procurement Enquiries

Preliminary investigations for developing sources for procurement of materials are made by floating enquiry indents. Materials enquiry indents containing quantities, specifications and delivery times are jointly prepared by the project planning cell and materials procurement department. These are processed by the materials procurement department for inviting quotations with samples of materials, where applicable.

On receipt of the quotations, a comparative study of the price, quality, delivery time, terms of delivery and payment terms is made jointly by both materials and project planning incharges. During the course of this study, vendors' proposals are compared with enquiry specifications and stipulated requirements, and the resulting deviations are examined for acceptability. Thereafter each acceptable quotation is analyzed for prices, delivery timings and payment terms.

Vendor's enlistment is based on its size, capability, past performance, market reputation and, if necessary, these may be confirmed by a visit to the vendor's works. The key criteria for evaluating the potential of the supplier to deliver the right quantity product at the right time should include the following:

(i) Quality of the material—its past records, recent test reports, performance reports, performance reports from old users, etc.
(ii) Company's financial status.
(iii) Company's management team and their professional competency and engineering skills.
(iv) Support services.

This study of various acceptable quotations is compiled in the form of a quotation comparison sheet for each of the major items of materials. In particular, all deviations from stipulated specifications and delivery timings should be discussed with the project manager/manager concerned and if required with the consultants also. Their views, are ascertained prior to preparing the quotation comparison sheet. These informal discussions with the consultant in the early stages prior to the finalization of the source for procurement can avoid costly delays at a later stage.

### 8.3.5 Finalization of Source of Materials Procurement

The quotation comparison sheet can be best termed as a summary of the alternate proposals for the procurement of given materials. These proposals undergo further processing before making a decision about placing of purchase order. The various stages encountered prior to the purchase decisions are as follows.

(a) *Approval in principle for processing proposals*—The quotation comparison sheet containing various proposals has financial implications. These implications include the effect on profitability is case of major deviations from original estimates and budgeted funds. The necessity to take up further changes or improvements in the offers needs to be approved in principle by the project management prior to commencing further negotiations with the suppliers. This approval in principle strengthens the company's representatives engaged in further negotiations and to avoid situations which may ultimately, affect the reputation and credibility of the company.

(b) *Client's approval of proposed materials*—As per the terms of agreement and standard construction practices, the contractor submits proposals to the client/consultant for approval of the materials. These proposals can be in the form of samples of materials, the manufacturer's write-up on the materials, the materials test results, its previous performance or a combination of these. The proposals for approval of materials can be submitted to the client at any time prior to procurement. Generally, a contractor will like to get those materials approved which are economical to him whereas the client's side will aim at approving materials which in their opinion meet the quality requirement and give best performance. No materials procurement plan can work unless, the materials are approved by the client prior to the placing of supply orders for procurement. In major projects, contractors also get more than one vendor approved for the same type of materials so as to ensure continuity of materials in case of breakdown of supplies from one vendor.

(c) *Negotiations of terms of supply*—Final negotiations with the vendor prior to the placing of order are carried out to evolve mutually agreed terms for supply particularly, with respect to the following:

   (i) To finalize prices through negotiations by securing a better price offer.
   (ii) To finalize mode of transportation of materials up to site.
   (iii) To finalize the payment terms including the opening of the letter of credit, if required.
   (iv) To finalize prior delivery and post delivery inspection/quality control procedures with particular reference to the contract stipulations and design specifications.
   (v) To finalize the materials delivery schedule.
   (vi) To finalize guarantees and penalties.

Before closing the final negotiations, a re-check is done to ensure that the necessary documents needed for manufacturing and making supplies as per contract have been provided to the vendor by the contractor.

## 8.3.6 Monitoring Materials Delivery Schedule

After the purchase order is placed with the vendor, a number of steps are necessary to ensure that the right quality and right quantity of materials arrive at the site at the right time. These steps include the following:

(a) Preparation and monitoring the materials movement schedule as shown in Table 8.5

(b) Conduct pre-transportation inspections where necessary.
(c) Obtain periodic information on shipment/transportation status.
(d) Keep ready the documents necessary for clearing customs and other formalities during transit.
(e) Plan in advance for receiving materials at the site. This includes unloading place; machinery for handling at site; persons for inspecting materials for correctness; storage arrangement and the construction site/persons who are to be intimated on arrival.
(f) Assisting the construction management in checking the materials when received at the site for correctness of quality and quantity as per requirement and bringing out discrepancies, if any, to the notice of the materials management for further action including timely replacement/reordering and claiming insurance/compensation if applicable.

## ❑ 8.4 PLANNING MATERIALS INVENTORY

### 8.4.1 Need for Planning Inventory

Generally, each project starts with zero material stock and after the left-outs are disposed off, it ends up with zero-stock. Ideally, each construction activity prior to commencement should have zero-stock; during execution there should be working stock sufficient for a very short period and should get replenished regularly as soon as it is about to finish; and finally, it should end up with zero-stock when the activity is completed. But such an ideal materials stocking policy is rarely feasible in construction projects, as materials need for each activity have to cater for lead time necessary to procure materials, build up sufficient working stock, hold safety stock, and at the same time, exercise economy in procuring materials. All this results in materials stock build-up at the project site.

Construction materials stock costs money, it locks up the capital invested for making purchases, and occupies built-in accommodation and open storage space. The magnitude of materials stock and inventory of each item will depend upon many factors, which are discussed in subsequent paragraphs. The variety of items and their value pattern can be conceptualized using ABC analysis, which indicates that around 10% of the materials stock items may account for 70% of the total value, whilst the 70% of the items may amount to 10% of the total value of the stock.

It may be noted that the total number of items of construction materials at any one time during peak stock period may run into hundreds and their corresponding value may be of the order of 5–15% of the material cost. It is therefore necessary to hold a planned stock of construction materials at the project site to ensure a timely supply of the expected quantity of materials at the appropriate time for smooth execution of planned construction activities with least investment on inventory.

The term 'inventory' implies the cost of materials in stock at a given time. This stock of materials is held to act as a cushion between supply and demand. The monetary value of inventory indicates the extent of investment required to maintain minimum stock of materials for the smooth running of the project. Higher inventory implies higher investment, and less inventory carries the risk of supplies falling behind demand. A balanced inventory acts as a cushion between supply and site requirement till supplies are received. It includes predetermined safety stock to cater for slippages in delivery schedules.

## 8.4.2 Inventory Cost

**Cost components** Inventory cost (C) of an item of materials is made up of inventory carrying costs and ordering costs and it is related as under:

$$\text{Inventory cost C} = \text{Ordering cost} + \text{Inventory carrying cost}$$

where,

$$\text{Ordering cost} = \text{Cost per Order} \times \text{Number of Orders}$$
$$= C_o \cdot N$$

and,

$$\text{Inventory Carrying Cost} = \text{Carrying Cost of an Item} \times \text{Average Stock}$$
$$= \frac{C_i \cdot P \cdot Q}{2}$$
$$= \frac{C_i \cdot P \cdot Q \cdot N}{2N}$$
$$= \frac{C_i \cdot A}{2N}$$

where,
$C_i$ = Carrying cost expressed as % of unit price of an Item.
P = Price per Item
Q = Quantity per Order
N = Number of Orders
A = Total Consumption Cost
 = Total Consumption Quantity × Unit Price
 = Q · N · P

Therefore,

$$\text{Inventory Cost (c)} = C_o \cdot N + \frac{C_i \cdot A}{2N}$$

For example, take the case of stocking of 'an imported store' at a project site:

- (a) Site requirement = 480 tons spread uniformly over 6 months.
- (b) Ordering cost ($C_o$) = $50/order.
- (c) Inventory carrying cost ($C_i$) = 25% of unit rate
- (d) Unit rate (P) = $80 per ton
- (e) Transporter capacity = 20 tons per trip

The inventory cost corresponding to various demand patterns can be worked out as shown in Table 8.6 and Figure 8.3.

Therefore, the least inventory cost is $980 for 12 orders distributed uniformly in 6 months, and it corresponds to 40 tons per order per fortnight (two trips of 20 tons each).

Table 8.5

## Materials Procurement and Monitoring Sheet (Specimen)

| Sl No. | Status | | Item of Material | RE SM | # | Samples Plan | | | Procurement Plan | | | | | | | | | Remarks |
|---|---|---|---|---|---|---|---|---|---|---|---|---|---|---|---|---|---|---|
| | | | | | | Re-ciept | Sub-mission | Apro-val | Prog. lead | Order confmn | | Order placed | | Vendor Details | L/C | Delivery | | Site requirement | |
| | Samp | Proc | | | | | | | Date | Date | No | Date | No | | Open-ing | Std essu-rence | ETA Bagh-dad | Date phases | |
| 1 | 2 | 3 | 4 | 5 | 6 | 7 | 8 | 9 | 10 | 11 | | 12 | 13 | 14 | 15 | 16 | 17 | 18  19 | 20 |
| 8.1.2 | | | Solid Core Flush Door | | S | | | | | | | | | Site Manufactured | | | | | |
| | | | | | A | | | | | | | | | | | | | | |
| 8.1.2 | | | Semi-Solid Core Door | | S | | | | | | | | | -do- | | | | | |
| | | | | | A | | | | | | | | | | | | | | |
| | | | | | S | | | | | | | | | | | | | | |
| | | | | | A | | | | | | | | | | | | | | |
| | | | | | S | | | | | | | | | | | | | | |
| | | | | | A | | | | | | | | | | | | | | |
| 8.2 | | | Window | | S | | | | | | | | | | | | | | |
| | | | | | A | | | | | | | | | | | | | | |
| 8.2.1 | ☒ | | Window sections | | S | | | | $22^3/_{82}$ | R377 | | | | | | | | At earliest | |
| | | | | | A | | | | | | | | | | | | | | |
| | | | | | S | | | | | | | | | | | | | | |
| | | | | | A | | | | | | | | | | | | | | |
| | | | | | S | | | | | | | | | | | | | | |
| | | | | | A | | | | | | | | | | | | | | |
| | | | | | S | | | | | | | | | | | | | | |
| | | | | | A | | | | | | | | | | | | | | |
| | | | | | S | | | | | | | | | | | | | | |
| | | | | | A | | | | | | | | | | | | | | |

| # | | | | | | | | | | | | | | | | |
|---|---|---|---|---|---|---|---|---|---|---|---|---|---|---|---|---|
| 9.1 | Steel Doors | S | | | | | | | | | | | | | | |
| | | A | | | | | | | | | | | | | | |
| | | S | | | | | | | | | | | | | | |
| | | A | | | | | | | | | | | | | | |
| | | S | | | | | | | | | | | | | | |
| | | A | | | | | | | | | | | | | | |
| | | S | | | | | | | | | | | | | | |
| | | A | | | | | | | | | | | | | | |
| 9.2 | Windows (Openable) | S | | | | | | | | | | | | | | |
| | | A | | | | | | | | | | | | | | |
| 9.2.1 | Windows (Fixed Shutters) | S | | | | | | | | | | | | | | |
| | | A | | | | | | | | | | | | | | |
| | Toilet Window | S | | | | | | | | | | | | | | |
| | | A | | | | | | | | | | | | | | |
| | | S | | | | | | | | | | | | | | |
| | | A | | | | | | | | | | | | | | |
| | | S | | | | | | | | | | | | | | |
| | | A | | | | | | | | | | | | | | |
| | | S | | | | | | | | | | | | | | |
| | | A | | | | | | | | | | | | | | |
| | | S | | | | | | | | | | | | | | |
| | | A | | | | | | | | | | | | | | |
| | | S | | | | | | | | | | | | | | |
| | | A | | | | | | | | | | | | | | |

\# S: Scheduled  
A: Actual

Sample   Procurement  
☒ Order   ☒ Placed   ☒ Material   ☒ Received

## Table 8.6

### Inventory Cost Corresponding to Various Demand Patterns

| Number of orders N | Quantity per order Q | (Tons) average Q/2 | Ordering cost ($) Co · N | Carrying cost ($) Ci. P. Q/2 | Inventory cost ($) C |
|---|---|---|---|---|---|
| 4  | 120 | 60 | 200  | 0.25 × 80 × 60 | 1400 |
| 6  | 80  | 40 | 300  | 0.25 × 80 × 40 | 1100 |
| 8  | 60  | 30 | 400  | 0.25 × 80 × 30 | 1000 |
| 10 | 48  | 24 | 500  | 0.25 × 80 × 24 | 980  |
| 12 | 40  | 20 | 600  | 0.25 × 80 × 20 | 1000 |
| 16 | 30  | 15 | 800  | 0.25 × 80 × 15 | 1100 |
| 20 | 24  | 12 | 1000 | 0.25 × 80 × 12 | 1240 |

where $C_o$ = $ 50 per order

**Factors affecting inventory costs** The construction materials inventory differs from project to project. Considering that in a project, the required quantities of each material are known, and assuming that the prices of frequently required items remain unchanged, the factors which affect the inventory cost are $C_o$, $C_i$, N and A.

(a) $C_o$ Ordering cost per order, includes costs connected with ordering such as clerical work for placing an order for delivery, follow-up using various communication channels, inspection on receipt, and the share of salaries of connected personnel.
$C_o$ varies with the source of item (local or imported) and the communication effectiveness between the purchasing department and the supplier's organisation. For all purposes, it can be assumed that the ordering cost per order is constant for a group of items having similar characteristics of the type or source of materials. For locally readily available items in particular, $C_o$ becomes negligible.

(b) $C_i$ Inventory carrying cost, is expressed as a percentage of the unit price of the material. It comprises of costs connected with interest on investments of inventory, insurance, storage rental value, bins and racks, wastage, obsolence, surplus disposal and warehouse staffing expenses. For on-demand readily available items, $C_i$ reduces with increase in number of orders.

(c) N stands for the number of orders and it determines the correspondening quantity (Q) for each order. N depends upon the type of materials, which can be broadly divided into non-repetitive and repetitive materials:

    (i) For one-time order, non-repetitive materials, N = I and $C_i$ becomes negligible if there is no stocking period.

    (ii) For repetitive materials, number of orders and economic order quantity can be determined mathematically (explained in subsequent paragraphs).

(d) A denotes the consumption or the usage cost. From the usage cost criteria, materials can be classified into A, B and C categories. Alternately, using Pareto's Rule, materials can be grouped into High Value; and Low Value, about 20% of high value items contribute to 80% of the usage cost and the remaining 80% low value items make up nearly 20% of the materials cost. Selective items inventory planning lays stress on planning of high value items.

### 8.4.3 Inventory Planning Approach

The construction materials inventory plan aims at evolving materials stock-holding levels to meet project execution plan, with minimum investment on inventory.

If all the items with similar characteristics are stored under similar conditions and are procured from a similar source, then $C_o$ and $C_i$ can generally, be considered as constant. However, in real life situations, $C_i$ (percentage) is not constant for all types of materials, but varies with consumption value, the volumetric size of material as well as with type of storage, while $C_o$ depends upon the location of the source. For these reasons, while planning inventory, materials with similar source and storage characteristics can be grouped together, and the $C_o$ and $C_i$ for each group can be determined separately.

In a typical Housing Project, from the inventory point of view, construction materials can be classified as under, and their subgrouping along with relevant factors affecting inventory cost is shown in Table 8.7.

Table 8.7

**Factors Affecting Inventory Cost**

| | Materials Demand Pattern | Order Cost Per Order ($C_o$) | Carrying Cost Per Item ($C_i$) | Purchase Orders (N) |
|---|---|---|---|---|
| 1. | *Frequently Required High-Value Items* | | | |
| | (a) Local | Negligible | Item Type & Price | N = Maximum feasible |
| | (b) Imported | Appreciable | ,, | $N = \sqrt{\dfrac{C_i \cdot A}{2 \cdot C_o}}$ |
| 2. | *One-Time Required High-Value Item* | | | |
| | (a) Local | Negligible | Negligible | N=1 |
| | (b) Imported | Fixed | ,, | N=1 |
| 3. | *Minor Low-Value Items* | | | |
| | (a) Local | Negligible | Low | N = Maximum feasible |
| | (b) Imported | Appreciable | ,, | N = Minimum feasible |

Construction materials, listed in the above categories based on location of the source of supply, can be further subdivided into locally available materials and imported materials. These materials, from storage considerations, can be further divided into bulky and non-bulky items. It is also appropriate to consider lead time for the supply of these materials. The approach for planning inventory for these groups of materials is outlined in subsequent paragraphs.

### 8.4.4 Planning Inventory of Repetitive Materials

The inventory planning for the repetitive construction materials involves determining of economic order quantity, fixing of maximum and minimum stock limits, lead time for stock replenishment and reordering point (ROP) for each item of 'A' and 'B' category construction materials i.e. high value materials.

The basic simplified model of inventory replenishment pattern as shown in Figure 8.2, depicts the economic order quantity, (working stock), the safety stock, the minimum stock level, the maximum stock level and the number of replenishment or re-order points (ROP) during the usage period, for each item of material.

Figure 8.2

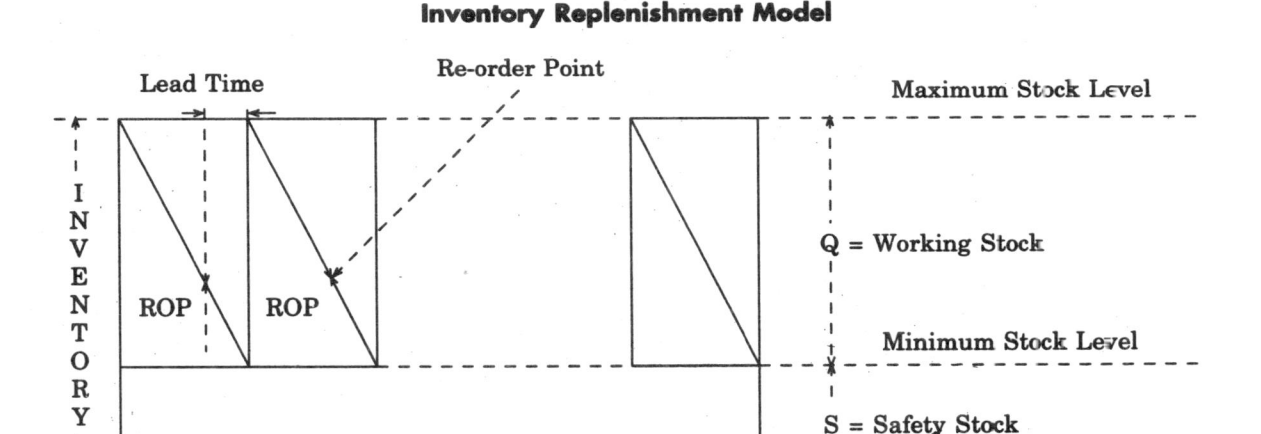

**Inventory Replenishment Model**

The inventory replenishment model shows the number of cycles of replenishment during the usage period. The initial inventory of materials at the start of the work, consists of working stock (Q) and safety stock (S).

**Economic order quantity (Q)** Two important decisions to be taken while planning repetitive materials inventory are how much to order at one time and when to order this quantity, or, in other words, to decide the reorder quantity level and the reorder time cycle so as to effect economy in cost of purchasing and holding inventory. This Economic Order Quantity (EOQ) and the Number of Orders are determined mathematically as under:

Inventory cost     C = Ordering cost + Inventory carrying cost

$$C = C_o \cdot N + \frac{C_i \cdot A}{2N} \quad \ldots(i)$$

For cost to be minimum:

$$\frac{dC}{dN} = C_o - \frac{C_i A}{2 \cdot N^2} = 0$$

$$N^2 = \frac{C_i A}{2 \cdot C_o}$$

and

$$C = C_0 N + \frac{C_i A}{2N} = \frac{1}{2N}(2C_0 N^2 + C_i A) = \frac{2C_i A}{2N} \qquad \text{...(ii)}$$

Therefore,

$$\text{Least Inventory Cost} = \sqrt{2C_0 C_i A}$$

Consider the imported item example covered above. The number of orders (N) and inventory cost (C) can be determined as follows:

$$N = \sqrt{\frac{\{C_i \cdot A\}}{2C_o}} = \sqrt{\frac{0.25 \times \$80 \times 480 \text{ tons}}{2 \times \$50}} = 10$$

$$C = \sqrt{\{2 \cdot C_0 \, C_i A\}} = \sqrt{2 \times \$50 \times 0.25 \times \$80 \times 480 \text{ tons}\}}$$
$$= \$980$$

**Working stock** It is equal to the normal consumption quantity during each cycle, and assuming the rate of consumption to be uniform in each cycle, it can be determined by dividing the total quantity required during the period with the number of cycles:

$$\text{Working stock} = Q = \frac{\text{Total quantity during the period}}{\text{Number of replenishment cycles}}$$

**Safety stock** It is the floating stock held to cater for changes in rate of consumption, delays in delivery of materials from the agreed dates, and other unforeseen causes, so as to prevent stock-outs resulting in production hold-ups.

The safety stock for a given situation can be determined using statistical techniques. Generally, a minimum safety stock can be taken as equal to consumption quantity in lead time period.

**Lead time** It is defined as the total time required for replenishment of an item of material from the time an indent is submitted to the purchase department, to the time that ready-for-use materials are received at the project stock-yard for storage or delivered at the site of work.

**Maximum stock level** It can ideally be determined by adding working stock and safety stock, and the minimum stock level is generally taken as equal to safety stock. The other factors considered for fixing maximum stock level include rate of consumption of materials, lead time to obtain new deliveries, risk of deterioration, storage space available, cost of storage, market fluctuations, seasonal considerations and the funds earmarked.

**Reorder level** It is the level at which the stock is ordered. This is determined by adding assessed consumption during the lead time period to the minimum stock level.

**Replenish level** It is the desired level of inventory. The quantity to be ordered is determined with reference to this level. At the time of placing of an order, the quantity to be ordered, the quantity already ordered but not received, and the quantity in hand, all sum up to this level.

For example, take the case of stocking of cement at a project site:

(a) Site requirement = 500 tons/month for 12 months.
(b) Ordering cost ($C_o$) = $40/order
(c) Inventory carrying cost ($C_i$) = 20% of unit rate
(d) Unit rate (P) = $100/ton
(e) Transport capacity = 20 tons
(f) Lead time = 5 days
(g) Safety stock = 100 tons
(h) Materials life = 2 months

Calculate N, EOQ, Minimum Stock level, Maximum Stock Level and ROL.

$$\text{Economic Order Quantity} = \frac{1}{P} \cdot \sqrt{\frac{2 \cdot C_0 \cdot A}{C_i}}$$

$$Q = \frac{1}{\$100} \sqrt{\frac{2 \times \$40 \times \$100 \times 6000 \text{ Tons}}{0.2}}$$

$$= 155 \text{ tons approximate}$$

$$= 160 \text{ tons, 8 trailor trips}$$

$$\text{Number of Orders } N = \frac{\text{Total Quantity}}{\text{Quantity per Order}}$$

$$= 6000/160$$

$$= 38$$

Minimum Stock Level = Safety Stock
= 100 tons

Maximum Stock Level = Safety Stock + EOQ
= 100 + 160
= 260, Say 300    tons

$$\text{Re-order Level} = \text{Minimum Stock Level} + \text{Lead Time} \times \text{Daily Usage}$$
$$= 100 + 5 \times 25$$
$$= 225, \text{ tons}$$
$$\text{Inventory Cost} = \sqrt{2 \, C_o \, C_i \, A}$$
$$= \$3098.39$$

Since, the daily consumption of cement is about 25 tons and cement is being replenished at the rate of 160 tons per week, the cement stock (maximum level 260 tons) gets rotated within two weeks, and hence its quality during storage is not affected.

*Practical applications of repetitive inventory model*  The simple model outlined above shows the relationship between Economic Order Quantity (Q) and the Number of Orders (N), involving least investment, for an item of material needed repeatedly during its usage. In its simplified version, it presupposes that materials are available freely, in any quantity and at predetermined fixed prices. It also assumes that the usage schedule depicting requirements of materials is fairly accurate. In its presented form, the inventory model is deterministic in character, i.e. there are no fluctuations in requirement and price of materials with passage of time. The probabilistic model, which includes fluctuation in parameters, is not covered in this chapter.

The graphical pattern of the relationship between 'Q' and 'N' of the Inventory Model is shown in Fig. 8.3. The Inventory Cost function, plotted in Fig. 8.3 (data Table 8.6) is made

Figure 8.3

**Repeitive Materials Inventory Cost Function Economic Order Quantity**

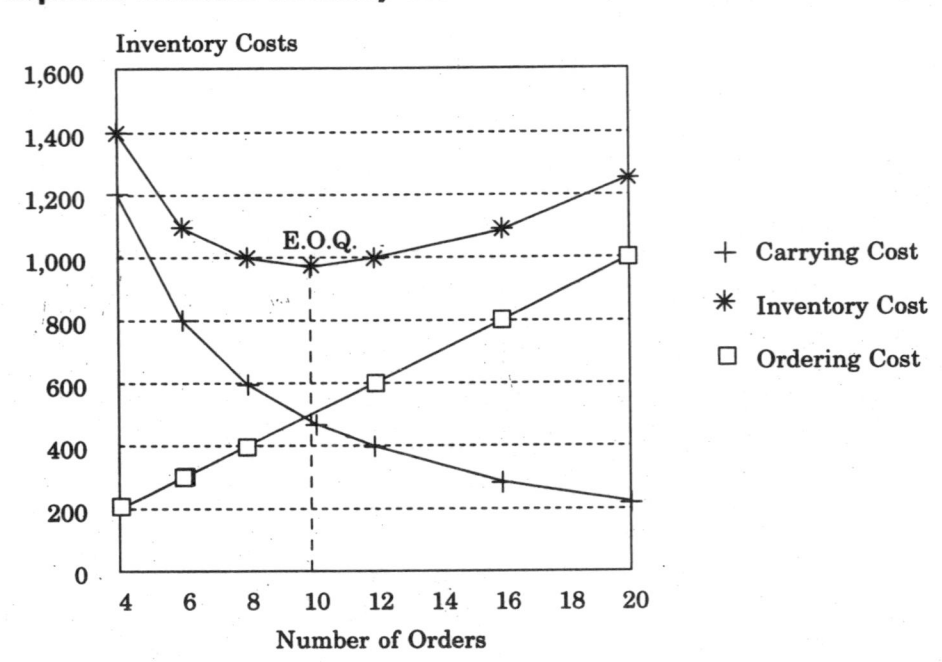

up of Inventory Carrying Cost function and Ordering cost function. The inventory carrying cost (Ci) and ordering cost (Co) vary with the order quantity (Q), but they move in opposite directions, i.e. when Q increases, Ci increases and Co decreases. The intersection point of these two functions indicate the Economic Order Quantity which result in least investment.

The Inventory Cost function at EOQ point is nearly flat for a short range. This shows that the marginal change in EOQ quantity within this range does not appreciably, affect the total inventory cost. This EOQ flat range characteristic is used in practical applications as under:

(1) Simplify the number of orders. For example, if N = 38, instead of ordering in an irregular manner, (i.e at a frequency of 52/38 weeks, the orders can be placed thrice a month or weekly, and the quantity of order adjusted suitably, as per the actual situation.
(2) Order in terms of standard lot supply. For example, if cement is being supplied in bulk bouzers of 20 ton capacity, then the order should be for multiples of 20 ton.
(3) Order perishable quantities keeping their shelf-life in view, so as to prevent wastage due to deterioration in quality.
(4) Adjust the order quantity in case of better discount offers, seasonal variation in prices, weather conditions and other similar causes.
(5) Reduce the number of orders for low value 'C' category items, as these do not affect the overall inventory cost appreciably, provided the storage space permits.

Bulk items include raw materials and semi-finished bulky stores such as soil, sand, aggregate, cement, lime, reinforcement steel, masonry blocks, timber, water and other similar items, The common features of bulky items is that they occupy a large space and need extensive transportation facilities for their movement. Most of the bulky materials are frequently required over a long period of time. In particular, locally available bulk items can be replenished on a day-to-day basis and their procurement planned in such a way that their stock position is kept within pre-determined minimum and maximum levels.

## 8.4.5 Planning Inventory of Non-repetitive One-Time Purchase Materials

These are non-regular and mostly one-time purchased items of construction materials. These materials are purchased for a specific purpose such as architectural fittings and fixtures, water supply and sanitation, HVAC and electrical and mechanical works, and moveable and fixed equipment.

It is important that non-repetitive materials must be interlinked with connected construction activities and specifications, and possibly, codified during the identification stage. The CI/SfB indexing system and other methods covered in Chapter 17, provide a means of correlating and coding work-activities and connected materials with their specifications.

In case of non-repetitive items, the aim should be to have a zero inventory prior to commencement of activity and after completion of the job, with low average during execution.

The requirement for non-repetitive items, which are mostly one-time use, can be derived date-wise from the project plan, and these can be procured when required and need not be stocked for a long time provided market permits. In such cases, based on lead time for procurement of materials, the delivery schedule can be easily worked out and supply orders can be placed accordingly. The important consideration is that the materials of right quality and quantity from a right source should be negotiated for purchase well in advance, and adhoc purchase should be discouraged as they generally, cost 10–15% more than the timely planned purchases.

Further, the procurement of non-repetitive materials should be properly scrutinised so that no surplus material is left-over after the activity is completed. However, it should be remembered that it is better to stock in advance if there is a chance of non-availability in the market when these non-repetitive items are actually required.

### 8.4.6 Minor Materials Items Inventory

Minor materials consist of low-cost, common use and frequently needed stores or items for various construction activities. These stores include tradesmen tools and frequently used minor, indirect, regularly consumed materials like screws, nails, cordage. The list of minor items held at site warehouse vaires with the size of the project and most of these stores needed time for mobilisation are listed in Exhibit 8.2.

Exhibit 8.2

**Minor Materials Mobilisation Stock**

| Sl. No. | Item | Unit | Project Small | Project Medium | Project Large |
|---|---|---|---|---|---|
| | **General Stores** | | | | |
| 1. | Buckets (plastic) | Nos | 2 | 4 | 6 |
| 2. | Petromax complete | Nos | 2 | 4 | 4 |
| 3. | Glass for Petromax | Nos | 2 | 4 | 4 |
| 4. | Mantle for Petromax | Nos | 2 | 4 | 4 |
| 5. | Lantern complete | Nos | 2 | 4 | 4 |
| 6. | Glass for lantern | Nos | 2 | 4 | 4 |
| 7. | Torch (Battery) with cells | Nos | 2 | 4 | 4 |
| 8. | Shuttering oil | Ltrs | 50 | 50 | 100 |
| 9. | Spades (Hand showels) | Nos | 10 | 12 | 16 |
| 10. | Iron pans (Tasla) | Nos | 10 | 12 | 16 |
| 11. | Pick axe | Nos | 10 | 12 | 16 |
| 12. | Handles for pickaxe/showels | Nos | 6 each | 6 each | 8 each |
| 13. | Coir strings | Nos | 6 | 10 | 12 |
| 14. | Tile cutter (Electrical) | Nos | 1 | 1 | 1 |
| 15. | Wire mesh cutter Hammer | Nos | 1 | 1 | 1 |
| 16. | ,, 1/2 Lb | Nos | — | — | 2 |
| 17. | ,, 1 Lb | Nos | 2 | 4 | 4 |
| 18. | ,, 1.1/2 Lb | Nos | 4 | 6 | 10 |

*(Contd)*

## Planning Construction Materials

| Sl. No. | Item | Unit | Project Small | Medium | Large |
|---|---|---|---|---|---|
| 19. | ,, 2 Lb | Nos | 4 | 8 | 12 |
| 20. | ,, 10 Lb | Nos | 2 | 2 | 4 |
| 21. | ,, 18 Lb | Nos | 2 | 2 | 4 |
| 22. | Screw driver (Assorted) | Nos | 6 | 16 | 20 |
| 23. | Spenner (sets) | sets | 4 | 6 | 8 |
| 24. | Turn buckle | Nos | 2 | 4 | 6 |
| 25. | Files assorted | Sets | 4 | 6 | 8 |
| 26. | 12" Hacksaw frame | Nos | 2 | 4 | 6 |
| 27. | Hacksaw blades | Nos | 4 | 8 | 8 |
| 28. | Adjustable spanner 8" & 12" | Nos | 2 Each | 4 Each | 6 Each |
| 29. | Concrete chisel 10" long flat & pointed | Set | — | 1 | 2 |
| 30. | Bolt threading die set | Set | 1 | 1 | 2 |
| 31. | Manila rope 1.1/2 " Dia | Bundle | 2 | 2 | 4 |
| 32. | Nylon rope 3/4" Dia | Bundle | 2 | 2 | 4 |
| 33. | Screw 1" ,1.1/2" & 3" (144 Nos) | Pkt | 20 Each | 20 Each | 20 Each |
| 34. | Wire nails 1" to 4" (144 Nos) | Pkt | 20 Each | 20 Each | 20 Each |
| 35. | Steel nails 1" to 4" | Pkt | 20 Each | 20 Each | 20 Each |
| 36. | Katoni (nail Beri) | Nos | 2 | 4 | 6 |
| 37. | GI washers | Nos | As Required | | |
| 38. | M.S washers | Nos | ,, | | |
| 39. | GI Pipes & fittings | Nos | | | |
| 40. | " 1/2" | Nos | ,, | | |
| 41. | " 3/4" | Nos | ,, | | |
| 42. | " 1" | Nos | ,, | | |
| 43. | Crow Bars 4" × 1" | Nos | 1 | 1 | 1 |
| 44. | Crow bars | Nos | 1 Each | 1 Each | 2 Each |
| 45. | Nuts of various diameters | Nos | As Required | | |
| 46. | Bolts of various dia/sizes | Nos | ,, | | |
| 47. | GI buckets 5 Ltrs | Nos | 4 | 6 | 8 |
| 48. | GI buckets 12 Ltrs | Nos | 4 | 6 | 8 |
| 49. | Wire brush | Nos | 6 | 12 | 20 |
| 50. | Ladders (aluminium) | Nos | 4 | 4 | 8 |
| 51. | Sand paper (fine to ruogh) | Dozen | 4 | 6 | 8 |
| 52. | Cotton waste | Kg | 8 | 10 | 16 |
| 53. | Water level pipe | Nos | 2 | 4 | 4 |
| 54. | Slump cone | Nos | 1 | 1 | 1 |
| 55. | Cube moulds | Nos | 6 | 6 | 18 |
| 56. | Jute cloth | Bundle | 1 | 1 | 2 |
| 57. | Plywood 4/6/12/18 mm | — | As Required | | |
| 58. | Asorted softwood/hard wood for shuttering | — | ,, | | |
| 59. | Wooden pegs | Nos | 50 | 100 | 200 |
| 60. | Steel rods for marking | Nos | 50 | 100 | 100 |
| 61. | Masking tape 2"/3"/4" | roll | 8 Each | 8 Each | 12 Each |
| 62. | Hard hat (safety Hat) | Nos | 10 | 20 | 40 |

*(Contd)*

| Sl. No. | Item | Unit | Small | Medium | Large |
|---|---|---|---|---|---|
| 63. | Measuring tape steel 3 M | Nos | 8 | 12 | 20 |
| 64. | Measuring tape steel 5 M | Nos | 2 | 4 | 6 |
| 65. | Measuring tape steel 30M | Nos | 1 | 2 | 2 |
| | **Masons Tools** | | | | |
| 1. | Gum boots | Pairs | 6 | 6 | 12 |
| 2. | Aluminium float 4'or 6' | Nos | 8 | 12 | 16 |
| 3. | 3'–4" Wide wooden float | Nos | 4 | 6 | 8 |
| 4. | 2'–3" Wide wooden float | Nos | 4 | 6 | 8 |
| 5. | 1'–2" Wide wooden float | Nos | 4 | 6 | 8 |
| 6. | Right angles | Nos | 6 | 10 | 12 |
| 7. | Plumb bob | Nos | 6 | 10 | 12 |
| 8. | Spirit level 2'/3'/4' | Nos | 2 Each | 3 Each | 4 Each |
| 9. | Mason trowel (big & small) | Nos | 3 Each | 4 Each | 6 Each |
| 10. | Sponge | Nos | 10 | 10 | 18 |
| 11. | Handgloves | Pairs | 20 | 20 | 30 |
| 12. | Steel Gurmala | Nos | 4 | 6 | 8 |
| | **Carpenters Tools** | | | | |
| 1. | Planner | Nos | 4 | 6 | 8 |
| 2. | Carpenters chisels 1/4" to 2" | Set | 4 | 6 | 8 |
| 3. | Sharpening stone for chisels | Nos | 1 | 2 | 2 |
| 4. | Glass cutter | Nos | 1 | 1 | 1 |
| 5. | Carpenters right angle | Nos | 6 | 10 | 18 |
| 6. | Carpenters pencil | Doz | 2 | 4 | 6 |
| 7. | Carpenters hammer | Nos | 6 | 10 | 18 |
| 8. | Carpenters woodsaw 12" | Ltrs | 4 | 4 | 4 |
| 9. | Carpenters woodsaw 18" | Nos | 4 | 8 | 8 |
| 10. | Carpenters woodsaw 24" | Nos | 4 | 4 | 4 |
| 11. | Carpenters vice | Nos | 1 | 2 | 4 |
| | **Steel Fitters Tools** | | | | |
| 1. | Bar bendering keys | Nos | 1Each | 1Each | 1Each |
| 2. | Cutting pliers | Nos | 6 | 12 | 30 |
| 3. | Binding wire | As Required | | | |
| 4. | Steel bending die | Nos | 2 | 4 | 4 |
| | **Painters stores** | | | | |
| 1. | Tyrolene M/C | Nos | 2 | 2 | 4 |
| 2. | Painting brush 2" & 4" | No3 | 12Each | 24Each | 24Each |
| 3. | Paint roller 9" | Nos | 6 | 12 | 12 |
| 4. | Paint tray | Nos | 6 | 12 | 12 |
| 5. | Paint thinner | Ltrs | 20 | 40 | 80 |
| | **Welders Tools** | | | | |
| 1. | Hand gloves for welding | Nos | 1 | 1 | 2 |
| 2. | Screen glass | Nos | 1 | 1 | 2 |
| 3. | Welding rods | Pkts | 2 | 2 | 4 |
| 4. | Welding set | Set | 1 | 1 | 1 |

*(Contd)*

|  |  |  | Project | | |
|---|---|---|---|---|---|
| Sl. No. | Item | Unit | Small | Medium | Large |
| 5. | Gas nozzels | Nos | 1 | 1 | 2 |
| 6. | Nozzle cleaner set | Nos | 1 | 1 | 2 |
|  | **Plumber Stores** | | | | |
| 1. | Die set 1/2″ to 1.1/2″ | Set | 1 | 1 | 1 |
| 2. | Pipe cutter | Nos | - | 1 | 2 |
| 3. | Chain spanner | Nos | - | 1 | 2 |
| 4. | Table vice | Nos | - | 1 | 2 |
| 5. | Pipe wrench 10″/14″/18″ | Nos | 1 | 1 | 2 |
| 6. | Blow lamp | Nos | 1Each | 1Each | 2Each |
| 7. | Jute for plumber | Nos | 1 | 1 | 2 |
| 8. | Tape | Rolls | 20 | 40 | 40 |
|  | **Electrician tools** | | | | |
| 1. | Screw driver (assorted) | Nos | 4 | 10 | 20 |
| 2. | Insulation tape | Rolls | 2Doz | 6 | 18Doz |
| 3. | Flexible wire | Rolls | 4 | 10 | 20 |
| 4. | Lamp holders | Nos | 10 | 20 | 40 |
| 5. | Bulbs | Nos | 20 | 40 | 80 |
| 6. | Tube light fittings | Nos | 4 | 12 | 36 |
| 7. | Fluorescent tube 4′ | Nos | 4 | 12 | 36 |
| 8. | Starters for tubes | Nos | 4 | 12 | 36 |
| 9. | Switches | Nos | 24 | 48 | 96 |
| 10. | Knife | Nos | 1 | 2 | 4 |
| 11. | Insulated Nose plier | Nos | 1 | 2 | 4 |
| 12. | Insulated cutting plier | Nos | 1 | 2 | 4 |
| 13. | Multimeter | Nos | - | 1 | 2 |
|  | **Admin. Materials** | | | | |
| 1. | Flying insets killer | Tins | 4 | 4 | 6 |
| 2. | First aid box | Set | 1 | 4 | 4 |
| 3. | Toilet cleaning chemical | Tins | 4 | 4 | 4 |
| 4. | Sweep brush long handle | Nos | 4 | 6 | 12 |
| 5. | Sweep brush small handle | Nos | 4 | 6 | 12 |
| 6. | Cotton caps | Nos | 40 | 80 | 150 |
| 7. | Trash bags | Nos | 40 | 80 | 150 |

## ❏ 8.5 USE OF OPERATIONS RESEARCH IN MATERIALS PLANNING

Operations research and statistical techniques can be usefully employed to plan procurement of materials. Some of the typical applications of these techniques in this field are as under:

(a) **Linear programming**—for minimizing transportation costs and time.
(b) **Allocation**—for quantities to be purchased from each of the various sources of supply.
(c) **Make or buy decisions**—for setting up materials manufacturing and fabrication units at the project site.

(d) **Materials inventory models**—for meeting the given production schedule.
(e) **Materials mix**—for various end products and site manufactured items.
(f) **Queuing problems**—for inventory stocking and transportation.
(g) **Statistical analysis**—for various types of distribution and risks.

It is desirable that the engineers involved in materials planning should jointly work on the problems requiring solutions by the applications of operation research and other analytical methods. If necessary, assistance of the operations research experts may be sought to make decisions.

CHAPTER 9

# Project Construction Equipment

Construction equipment plays a significant role in the execution of modern high-cost time-bound construction projects. An indispensable item of resources, it produces output at accelerated speed, and enables completion of tasks in a limited time. Equipment saves manpower which is becoming scarce, costly and more demanding day-by-day. Equipment improves productivity, quality and safety.

The nature of production tasks which can be performed with equipment include excavating, hauling, transporting, compacting, grading, hoisting, concreting, precasting, plastering, finishing, trenching, pipe-laying, cable-laying, and so on. In addition, the support equipment at the project site consists of generators, pumping sets, treatment plants and other utility services equipment.

Construction equipment planning aims at identifying the construction equipment for executing project tasks, assessing equipment performance capability, forecasting the date-wise requirement of numbers and types of equipment, and finally participating in the selection of the equipment to be acquired.

This Chapter outlines the commonly used construction equipment. It introduces the suitability of equipment for executing various tasks. It describes the approach generally followed for assessing the ideal output of the equipment. This ideal output is multiplied by the correction factors and the performance factor to derive the output planning data of the equipment considered during the project-planning stage, with a view to forecast equipment requirement.

The subject covered in this chapter is divided as under:

(a) Classification of major equipment.
(b) Earth factor in earthwork.
(c) Earth excavating equipment.
(d) Earth cutting and hauling equipment.
(e) Earth compaction equipment.
(f) Concreting plant and equipment.
(g) Cranes for materials handling.

The earthwork equipment output planning data used for illustrating is tabulated at the end of this chapter.

The criteria governing the selection of the equipment are outlined in Chapter 10. The equipment, described in this chapter, is generally confined to the major items required in building construction projects. The methodology for planning of equipment for heavy construction and utility services is similar, but requires specialized equipment know-how. Planning of equipment for such specialized projects is beyond the scope of this Chapter as there are limitations of space. Readers are advised to refer to the equipment manufacturers' manuals and standard books on construction equipment for a detailed study. The contents of this chapter be viewed as guidelines for planning purposes.

## ❑ 9.1 CLASSIFICATION OF MAJOR EQUIPMENT

Construction equipment classification facilitates identifying equipment, verifying stock, locating spares, recording repairs, accounting costs, indexing catalogues, logging performance, monitoring effectiveness, estimating outputs, and planning procurements.

There are many methods for classifying construction equipment. These include dividing the equipment into special purpose and general purpose machines; classifying equipment according to the alphanumeric code generally, conforming to the description of equipment; and categorizing equipment into its functional use. In particular, functional classification of major equipment is reflected in Exhibit 9.1.

Major equipment commonly employed for the execution of a medium sized building construction project, with its task suitability and ideal output capability, are outlined in subsequent paragraphs.

## ❑ 9.2 EARTH FACTOR IN EARTHWORK

The most important factor that determines the suitability of equipment for earthwork is the earth itself. The earthwork process is affected by the ground condition. The main ground characteristics which influence the performance of the equipment are the suitability of equipment, the digging effort, the resulting output, and the output measurement.

### 9.2.1 Equipment Suitability

The type of earthmoving equipment required varies with the nature of the soil and tasks to be performed. Typical job-related equipment used in building projects are given below:

(1) **Excavating and lifting in soft earth**

    (a) Deep pits excavation — Clamshell and dragline.
    (b) Shallow pit excavation — Backhoes.
    (c) Ground level excavation — Shovels.
    (d) Shallow trenching — Trenchers, excavators (backhoes).
    (e) Wet soil excavation — Excavators (dragline or grab).

## Exhibit 9.1

## Functional Classification of Construction Equipment

**Earthwork Equipment**
- Excavation and lifting equipment—backactor (or backhoes), face shovels, draglines, grabs or clamshell and trenchers.
- Earth cutting and moving equipment—bulldozers, scrapers, front-end loaders
- Transportation equipment—tippers dumps truck, scrapers rail wagons and conveyors.
- Compacting and finishing equipment—tamping foot rollers, smooth wheel rollers, pneumatic rollers, vibratory rollers, plate compactors, impact compactors and graders.

**Materials Hoisting Plant**
- Mobile cranes—crawler mounted, self-propelled rubber-tyred, truck-mounted.
- Tower cranes—stationary, travelling and climbing types.
- Hoists—mobile, fixed, fork-lifts.

**Concreting Plant & Equipment**
- Production equipment-batching plants, concrete mixers.
- Transportation equipment—truck mixers, concrete dumpers
- Placing equipment—concrete pumps, concrete buckets, elevators, conveyors, hoists, grouting equipment.
- Precasting special equipment—vibrating and tilting tables, battery moulds, surface finishes equipment, prestressing equipment, GRC equipment, steam curing equipment, shifting equipment, erection equipment.
- Concrete vibrating, repairing and curing equipment.
- Concrete laboratory testing equipment.

**Support and Utility Services Equipment**
- Pumping equipment.
- Sewage treatment equipment.
- Pipeline laying equipment.
- Power generation and transmission line erection equipment.
- Compressed air equipment.
- Heating, ventilation and air-conditioning (HVAC) equipment.
- Workshop including wood working equipment.

**Special Purpose Heavy Construction Plant**
- Aggregate production plant & rock blasting equipment.
- Hot mix plant and paving equipment.
- Marine equipment.
- Large-diameter pipe laying equipment.
- Piles and pile driving equipment.
- Coffer dams and caissons equipment.
- Bridge construction equipment.
- Railway construction equipment.

(2) **Cutting over areas**

    (a) Short–hauls    —   Dozers.
    (b) Long–hauls    —   Scrappers.

(3) **Loading and transporting excavated soil**

    (a) Loading soil    —   Loaders, shovels, excavators.
    (b) Transporting soil    —   Tippers, dumpers, scrapers. rail wagons, conveyors.

## 9.2.2 Digging Effort

The digging effort of an equipment depends upon the nature of the soil. For example, it is easy to dig in common earth than in stiff clayey soil. The typical soil factor which determines the comparative equipment effort required in various types of soils can be taken as under:

| Nature of soil | Digging effort | Soil factor |
|---|---|---|
| Loam, sand, gravel | Easy digging | 1.0 |
| Common earth | Medium digging | 0.85 |
| Stiff clay, soft rock | Hard digging | 0.67 |

## 9.2.3 Volume Conversion

The volume measure varies with the state of the soil. Three states of soil encountered in earthmoving operations are in-place natural soil, loose excavated bulk soil, and compacted soil. The volume of soil in its in-place natural state is usually, referred to as the bank volume. It swells when heaped in a loose state after excavation, and shrinks when mechanically compacted.

The typical relationship for volume conversion of soil into its three states can be taken as shown in Table 9.1.

Table 9.1

**Volume Conversion of Soil into its Three States**

| Nature of soil | Bank volume | Loose volume | Compacted volume |
|---|---|---|---|
| Common earth | 1.00 | 1.25 | 0.90 |
| Sand | 1.00 | 1.12 | 0.95 |
| Clay | 1.00 | 1.27 | 0.90 |
| Rock (blasted) | 1.00 | 1.50 | 1.30 |

For a given weight of soil, the swell factor and shrinkage factor are defined as under:

$$\text{Swell factor} = \text{Loose volume/bank volume.}$$

$$\text{Shrinkage factor} = \text{Compacted volume/bank volume.}$$

### 9.2.4 Equipment Output

The equipment capability to perform an assigned earthwork task can best be determined from the on-site actual trials or can be assessed from its past performance records of operation under similar site conditions.

The equipment's hourly output is determined by multiplying the earth quantity moved (load) per cycle by the number of cycles per hour.

$$\text{Equipment actual hourly output} = \text{Actual load/cycle} \times \text{cycles/hour.}$$

For example, a front-end loader on a given job moves a load of 1.5 m$^3$ of loose soil in one cycle consisting of loading-lifting-travelling-unloading-return trip-and ready for loading. If each cycle time is 1.2 minutes, then

$$\text{Actual output per working hour} = \text{Load per cycle} \times \text{cycles per hour}$$
$$= 1.5 \text{ m}^3 \times 60 \text{ minutes}/1.2 \text{ minutes}$$
$$= 75 \text{ m}^3 \text{ per hour.}$$

But at the planning stage the actual on-site trials may not be feasible, and the past performance data may not always be available, or it may not be adequate as the site conditions vary from place to place and project to project. In the absence of these reliable performance methods, the equipment output norms can be derived from the performance data given in the manuacturer's manuals. This off-the-job equipment hourly ideal output data is reflected in these manuals in the form of charts, graphs, performance curves, and tables. This 'ideal output' is multiplied by 'correction factor' to determine the 'optimum output'.

$$\text{Optimum output} = \text{Ideal output} \times \text{Correction factor.}$$

Correction factor depends upon the operating characteristics of the equipment and the site conditions like excavator swing factor, earth grade factor, soil factor, rolling resistance, traction factor, and so on. The ideal output and correction factor are covered in subsequent paragraphs under each equipment.

The equipment planned performance at site of work depends upon many situational factors that influence the output. These situational factors can be broadly grouped under two headings, i.e. controllable factors and uncontrollable factors. The output adopted for planning purposes can be determined as under:

$$\text{Planned output} = \text{Optimum output} \times \text{Performance factor.}$$

Table 9.2

**Estimation of Performance Factor**

| Assessed Equipment Effective Working Minutes/hour | Performance Efficiency Factor |
|---|---|
| 60 minutes/hour | 1.00 |
| 55 minutes/hour | 0.92 |
| 50 minutes/hour | 0.83 |
| 45 minutes/hour | 0.75 |
| 40 minutes/hour | 0.67 |

The method of estimation of performance factor is covered in Chapter 10. Broadly, it can be expressed as in Table 9.2.

Earthmoving equipment comes in various sizes, and its rate of output depends upon types, sizes and salient job suitability features. Output capabilities of commonly used earthmoving equipment are outlined in subsequent paragraphs under appropriate heads.

## ❑ 9.3 EARTH EXCAVATING EQUIPMENT

Primary earth excavating equipment is the tractor-mounted excavator. Excavators operate in a stationary mode. They dump excavated materials on the sides, or directly into waiting tippers/dump trucks and they gradually, shift their position as the work progresses. Various types of earth excavating equipment are listed in Exhibit 9.2.

The excavating equipment is divided into four categories, viz. face shovels, backhoes, draglines and grab or clamshell. Further, excavators can be rope-operated or hydraulically operated. The type and size of the equipment depends upon the nature of the task, the type of soil, digging depth and the desired level of production.

### 9.3.1 Face Shovel

It operates from a flat surface, producing upward digging action, excavating and filling the bucket as it climbs. After the bucket is filled, its upper part swings to the dumping position where the bucket is emptied in a waiting truck or on to a stockpile. Thereafter, it returns to its original position and starts the next cycle of excavation. It is capable of working in all types of dry soils. The struck-bucket capacity of the face shovel bucket varies from $1/2$ yd$^3$ (0.38 m$^3$) to $4/1/2$ yd$^3$ (3.25 m$^3$), and depending upon the size of the machine and bucket, its cutting length varies from 7 m to 10.5 m.

### 9.3.2 Backhoe

It is primarily used for excavating materials below its track level, i.e. excavation of small and large pits, basements and large trenches. Backhoe are generally track-mounted but small capacity equipment do have wheel-mounting to add to their mobility.

Project Construction Equipment  **281**

Exhibit 9.2

**Earth Excavating and Lifting Equipment**

| Types of Equipment | Features | | | Bucket Struck Capacity | | | | |
|---|---|---|---|---|---|---|---|---|
| | Bucket Size | YD$^3$ | 0.50 | 0.75 | 1.00 | 1.50 | 2.00 | 3.00 |
| | | M$^3$ | 0.38 | 0.57 | 0.76 | 1.14 | 1.53 | 2.30 |
| | Engine HP | | 50 | 75 | 100 | 130 | 160 | 200 |
| 1. Face Shovel 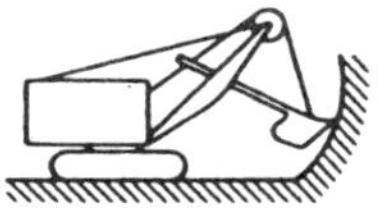 | Maximum Cutting Height | M | 7.0 | 7.0 | 7.0 | 7.5 | 8.5 | 10.0 |
| | Ideal Output/ Hour (Loose, easy dig) | LM$^3$ | 60 | 90 | 120 | 180 | 220 | 300 |
| 2. Backhoe or Excavator 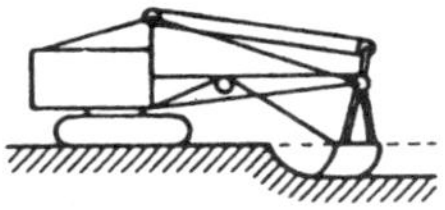 | Maximum Digging Depth | M | 5.0 | 6.5 | 7.5 | 8.0 | 9.0 | 9.0 |
| | Ideal Output/ Hour (Loose, easy dig) | LM$^3$ | 48 | 72 | 96 | 144 | 173 | 240 |
| 3. Dragline 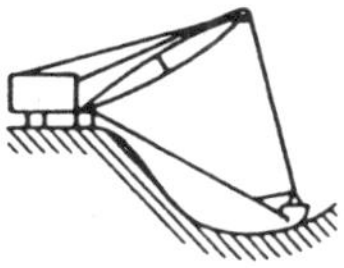 | Maximum Boom Length | M | 21 | 21 | 21-27 | 21-27 | 27-30 | 30-33 |
| | Ideal Output/ Hour (Loose, easy dig) | LM$^3$ | 45 | 67 | 78 | 135 | 135 | 225 |
| 4. Clamshell 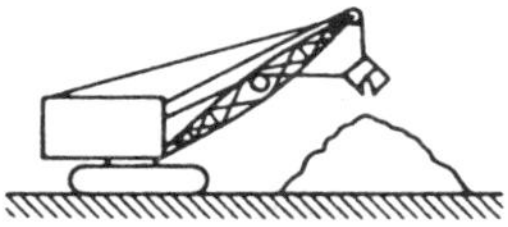 | Maximum Boom Length | M | 21 | 21-27 | 21-27 | 21-27 | 27-30 | 30-33 |
| | Ideal Output/ Hour (Loose, easy dig) | LM$^3$ | 24 | 36 | 48 | 72 | 89 | 120 |

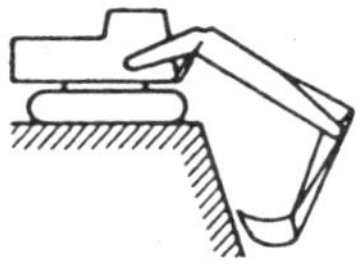

*Note*: Planning output norms = Ideal Output × Correction Factor × Performance Factor

The backhoers are fitted with buckets having struck capacity varying from 1/2 Yd$^3$ (0.38 m) to 4 1/4 Yd$^3$ (3.25 m$^3$) and their corresponding digging depth capability is from 5 m to a maximum of 9.5 m.

### 9.3.3 Dragline

It is a rope-operated boom-fitted crane type machine. The bucket is thrown into the excavation area, and the cable-controlled hook is rotated, so that, the bucket gets filled by scraping the surface to be excavated. It is used for digging below the ground level specially, in loose soils or marshy and underwater areas with soft beds.

The dragline can operate in a depth approximately up to 1/3 of its boom length for broad sweeping type excavated work. Its boom length varies from 21 m to 36 m and the struck bucket capacity extends from 1/2 Yd$^3$ (0.38 m$^3$) to 4 Yd$^3$ (3.06 m$^3$).

### 9.3.4 Grab or Clamshell

Like dragline, it is a rope-operated boom-fitted crane type machine having a grab or clamshell bucket. The grab bucket has interlocking teeth to penetrate loose soil whereas the clamshell bucket has no teeth. These buckets are dropped with their sides open like open jaws on the soil to be grabbed, and thereafter, these jaws are closed by rope machines prior to hauling. These machines are used primarily for deep confined excavations such as shafts, wells and spoil heaps removal. The depth of the excavation can be roughly taken as 1/3 of the boom length. The range of the size of the grab bucket and its length of boom are similar to those of the dragline.

### 9.3.5 Output Planning Data

$$\text{Planned output} = \text{Ideal output} \times \text{Correction factor} \times \text{Performance factor.}$$

Ideal output in Loose cubic meters (LCM):

$$\text{Ideal output} = \text{Bucket output/Cycle} \times \text{Cycles/hour}$$

These are explained as under:

(a) Bucket output/cycle—A cycle of a bucket starts from the point it strides the excavation place to its return to the next excavation point after unloading the excavated materials at the specified place in the transporter or on a heap of loose excavated materials. The maximum loose material in cubic meters (LCM) it can carry in its bucket per cycle is equal to its bucket struck capacity.

(b) Cycles/hour—The cycle time is the time taken by the cycle of bucket movements which includes load, swing, unload and return to start the cycle again.

Maximum number of cycles/hour = 60 minutes/cycle time in; minutes.

Considering that a face shovel can perform 100 cycles/hour of cutting loose soil and casting load after a 90 degrees swing in an open area, while operating under ideal conditions at optimum cutting levels, its maximium output can be 100 buckets per hour. The ideal output under ideal conditions, for the face shovels of different capacity and bucket sizes, is shown in Appendix 9.1.

### 9.3.6 Correction Factors

These include the following and their implications on the equipment output are shown in Exhibit 9.3.

**Exhibit 9.3**

**Excavator Output Adjustment Factors for Secondary Tasks**

| Equipment | Nature of Secondary Tasks | Task Efficiency |
|---|---|---|
| Shovel | Movement from excavating place to unloading place: | |
| | a. Within vicinity | 1.0 |
| | b. Little movement | 0.6 to 0.9 |
| | c. Appreciable; movement or delays | 0.4 to 0.6 |
| Backhoe | Trenching | |
| | a. Equal to bucket width | 1.0 |
| | b. More than bucket width | 0.7 to 0.9 |
| Dragline | a. Bulk excavation | 1.0 |
| | b. Wide open ditches | 0.7 to 0.9 |
| | c. Confined, restricted places | 0.5 to 0.7 |
| Clam shell | a. Dry soil Pits | 0.9 |
| | b. Wet soil pits | 0.5 to 0.9 |

(a) **Equipment conversion factor**: It relates to the type of equipment employed.

| Equipment | Factor multiplier |
|---|---|
| Face shovel | 1.00 |
| Backhoe | 0.80 |
| Dragline | 0.75 |
| Grab | 0.40 |

(b) **Soil digging factor**: It depends upon the digging effort.

| Digging effort | Factor multiplier |
|---|---|
| Easy digging | 1.00 |
| Medium digging | 0.85 |
| Hard digging | 0.67 |

(c) Swing factor: The output varies with the angle of the swing of the bucket carrying arm, in the horizontal plan, enclosed by the arc connecting loaded bucket swing starting point and bucket unloading point on heap or transporter.

*Typical swing factor*

| Angle of swing: | 45° | 60° | 75° | 90° | 120° | 150° | 180° |
|---|---|---|---|---|---|---|---|
| Factor value : | 1.20 | 1.16 | 1.07 | 1.0 | 0.88 | 0.79 | 0.71 |

(d) Load casting factor: Output varies with the method of casting of load.

| Method of casting | Factor multiplier | |
|---|---|---|
| | Open area | Restricted area |
| Side casting | 1.0 | 0.8 |
| Loading in vehicle | 0.8 | 0.6 |

(e) Task efficiency factor: Each equipment is designed for a primary task. There are occasions when equipment is employed on secondary tasks. For example, a backhoe excavating trenches using a bucket of width equal to the width of the trenches will yield more output than if the same bucket is used for excavating trenches of more than the bucket's width.

The efficiency of the equipment, when employed on the primary task, is taken as 100% and it can be suitably adjusted using the following guide lines for typical secondary tasks, given in Exhibit 9.3.

### 9.3.7 Procedure for Determining Output from Equipment Output

**Planning chart** The output of an excavating equipment, for planning purposes, can be easily determined from the equipment output planning table shown in Appendix 9.1. The procedure involved is explained with the following example:

*Example* Estimate the hourly production in bulk volume (LCM) of a backhoe with bucket capacity of 0.96 $M^3$ employed on excavation of a foundation four meters deep in hard digging soil. The excavated earth is to be loaded in waiting dump trucks, placed at a swing angle of 75 degrees. The expected performance efficiency is 83%.

(a) Ideal output of loose soil in cubic meter (LCM) for an equivalent face shovel of bucket capacity of 0.96 $m^3$ from Appendix 9.1. = 150 LCM (approximate)
(b) Backhoe output using equipment conversion factor of 0.8 operating at optimum depth = A × 0.80 = 120 LCM
(c) Correction factors applicable are
—Soil factor for hard digging = 0. 67
—Load factor for loading into vehicle = 0.80
—Swing factor for 75 degrees = 1.05

Therefore, correction factor
 = 0.67 × 0. 80 × 1.05 = 0.56
(d) Performance efficiency = 0.83

Hence expected output/h
 = Ideal output × correction factor × performance efficiency.
 = $B \times C \times D$
 = $0.8A \times C \times D$
 = 120 × 0.56 × 0 . 83
 Say = 56 LCM/h.

## 9.4 EARTH CUTTING AND HAULING EQUIPMENT

These machines are used to cut and shift earth from one place to another. These machines include bulldozers, scrapers, front-end loaders, and other hauling equipment. Typical cutting and hauling equipment is sketched in Exhibit 9.4.

### 9.4.1 Bulldozers

The bulldozer is a versatile machine. It can be used for moving earth over distances upto 100 m, clearing and grubbing sites, stripping top unwanted soil, excavating to a shallow depth say upto 200 mm at a time, pushing scrapers, spreading soil for leveling areas, ripping bare soft rock, and maintaining roads. Bulldozers normally are Track-mounted, however there are four-wheeled dozers with large-powered engine. The wheel dozers exert higher bearing pressure as compared to track-dozers.

Dozers excavate and push earth with the help of a stiff welded steel blade fitted in front and controlled by two hydraulic cylinders. Blades are of four types. The straight S-blade is used for forward pushing of earth. U-blades have large capacity, and are used for pushing loose materials. Angle A-blades are used for pushing soil to one side rather than hauling it forward as is required in hill road formation cutting. Push P-blades are used for push loading a scraper. A dozer can also be fitted with a bachhoe attachment for ripping hard soil and rock, and a winch for uprooting trees, skidding boulders and heavy materials.

Ideal output for dozing soft soil depend upon the engine power, straight-blade capacity and dozing distance. The ideal output of bulldozers is shown in Appendix 9.1.

This ideal output, measured in the bulk volume (loose soil), assumes forward dozing speed of 3 km/h, return speed of 6 km/h, manoeuvring time of 0.15 minutes, easy going on generally level ground and dozing of (bank) materials using a strainght S-blade. This ideal production is corrected to conform to varying conditions as under:

Dozer optimum output = Dozer ideal output × Correction factor

Output planning data = Dozer optimum output × performance factor

where, correction factor leads to the following effect.

**286** Construction Project Management

---

### Exhibit 9.4
### Earth Cutting and Hauling Equipment

---

1. Bull dozers

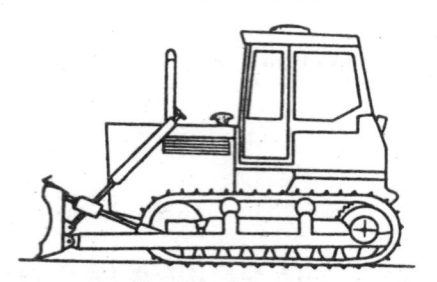

   Tracked dozer

2. Front-End Loaders

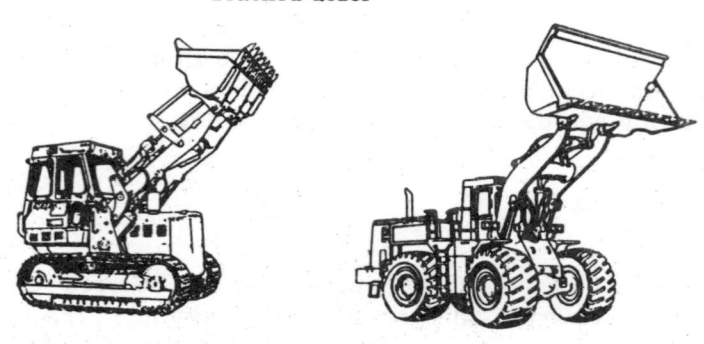

3. Towed Scrapers

   Towed

4. Motorised Scrapers

   Single engine conventional      Twin engine conventional

   Elevating

(a) *Blade factor*—Multiply ideal output by the blade factor value.

| Type of blade | Blade factor |
|---|---|
| S blade | 1.0 |
| A blade | 0.75 |
| U blade | 1.25 (used only for loose soil). |

(b) *Transmission system*—For direct drive, take 80% of the ideal output which is based on the power shift system. Direct drive system output = 0.8 power shift system output.

(c) *Grade factor*—The manufacturer's manual provides the data for a change of output with varying slope, but for planning purposes it can be taken as under:

| Nature of slope | Effect on output (%) |
|---|---|
| Downhill working | Increase 2.5 × grade (%) |
| Uphill working | Decrease 2 × grade (%). |

(d) *Soil factor*—The ideal output is based on easy–dig and loose soil. This ideal output should be multiplied by the follwing soil factors where the nature of soil differs:

| Digging effort | Nature of soil | Soil factor |
|---|---|---|
| Easy–dig | Loam, sand, gravel | 1.0 |
| Medium–dig | Common earth in natural state | 0.85 |
| Hard–dig | Hard stiff clay, soft rock | 0.67 |

(e) *Swing factor*—The ideal output is stated in terms of bulk (or loose) volume excavated. This output can be converted into in–place (or bank) volume by dividing the bulk materials with the swell factor.

$$\text{In-place (or bank) volume (BCM)} = \frac{\text{Bulk (or loose) volume}}{\text{Swell factor}}$$

*Example* Determine the output of a bulldozer having 215 HP engine, fitted with A-blade rated capacity $4.40 M^3$. The dozer is employed for excavating a hard clayey area with average haulage of 50 meters, on a ground with down slope of 10%. It has direct drive transmission, and its expected performance is 50 minutes per hour.

*Solution* Output/h = Ideal output/h × correction factor × performance factor.

(a) Ideal output/h for 50 meter haulage of 215 HP dozer with 'S' blade of capacity 4.40 m³ from Appendix 9.1.  = 160 LCM (approximate)

(b) Correction factors applicable are:
—Soil factor for hard digging = 0.67
—Blade factor for A blade = 0.65
—Grade factor for 10 % down grade = 1 + 2.5 × 10%
 (assistance) = 1.25

|  |  |
| --- | --- |
| —Transmission factor for direct drive | = 0.8 |
| —Swell factor of clayey soil | = 1.3 |

Therefore correction factor

$$= 0.67 \times 0.65 \times 1.25 \times 0.8 \times \frac{1}{1.3} \qquad = 0.42$$

(C) Performance factor for 50 min/hour working  = 0.83
(D) Therefore expected output in BCM
$= A \times B \times C$
$= 160 \times 0.42 \times 0.83 = 55.8.$      Say 56 BCM

### 9.4.2 Scraper

It is the equipment commonly used for scraping, loading, hauling and discharging including spreading large quantities of earth over long distances, say around three Km. It can scrape soils in layers of 15 cm to 30 cm in depth. Basically, a scraper has a soil container or bowl mounted on two wheels. It digs into the earth after the forward portion of the container is lowered, and it collects the earth as the scraper moves forward. Unloading and spreading takes place in controlled layers in the discharge area with the aid of a tractor plate while the unit keeps on moving. Scrapers come in many sizes varying from $8m^3$ to $50\ m^3$. There are two main categories of scrapers—(i) towed scrapers and (ii) motorized scrapers. They are shown in Exhibit 9.4.

**(i) Towed scrapers** These are pulled by a tractor or a bulldozer capable of 300 HP or more. Although the loading cycle may take hardly two to three minutes, its travelling speed is slow. Its main advantage over the motorized scraper is that it can operate in small areas and can scrape in heavy soil areas. Towed scrapers are best suited for medium distances up to 400 m. Towed scrapers range from $8\ m^3$ to $30\ m^3$.

**(ii) Motorized scrapers** Several types of motorized scrapers with heaped capacity ranging from $15\ m^3$ to $50\ m^3$ are available to suit varying job requirements. These include single engine scraper, double engine scraper and elevating scraper.

(a) Single engine scraper requires a pusher bulldozer to provide the necessary tractive force. Generally one medium–sized crawler tractor is sufficient to serve four to five scrapers.

$$\text{Scrapers per pusher} = \frac{\text{Cycle time of each scraper}}{\text{Cycle time of pusher}}$$

*Example* Cycle time of a scraper is 6 minutes and a pusher to fill a scraper is 1.5 minutes. Calculate the number of scrapers which a pusher can serve. Determine the number of pushers to serve 10 scrapers.

*Solution* Number of scrapers per pusher $= \frac{6.0}{1.5} = 4.$

$$\text{Number of pushers for 10 scrapers} = \frac{\text{No. of scrapers}}{\text{No. served by one pusher}}$$

$$= \frac{10}{4} = 3.$$

(b) Double-engine scrapers are fitted with two engines, one in the front and the other in the rear axle. For scrapers having capacity 35 m³ and above, two engines are preferred instead of one very large equivalent engine. Although the engine in the rear provides a four-wheel drive, double-engine scrapers do require a pusher specially in hard soil excavations. In the push-pull method, two double-engine scrapers are used to mutually load each other in turn, without the aid of a pusher.

(c) Elevating scrapers are fitted with an elevating mechanism for self-loading. Due to their heavy weight, they are at a disadvantage over long hauls.

**Scraper output planning data** The ideal indicative outputs of towed scraper and motorized scraper are reflected in Appendix 9.1. This ideal output is for good haulage by road, and this has to be modified by taking into consideration various corrections and efficiency factors discussed above.

$$\text{Output/h in Lm}^3 = \text{Ideal output} \times \text{correction factor} \times \text{performance factor}$$

*Example* A new motorised scraper, working under average conditions, employed in spreading of excavated materials along a road alignment 1.5 km long using the following data:

| | |
|---|---|
| Scraper capacity | = 16/23.7 (struck/heap in loose soil m³) |
| Gross vehicle weight (empty) | = 36 tons |
| Maximum pay load | = 34020 kg |
| Material density | = 1500 kg Lm³ |
| Job efficiency | = 50 min/h |
| Rated power of engine | = 450 HP |
| Correction factor | = 0.91 (estimated from equipment manual) |

Evaluate the output per hour after making adjustments for various factors affecting production.

*Solution*

Production per hour in Lm³ = Load per cycle (m³) × 60 min × Operation efficiency ÷ Cycle time in minutes

1. Load per cycle (Lm³)

    = Weight of heaped capacity

    = 23.7 m³ × 1500 kg / m³

    = 35.550 kg.

But this weight exceeds pay load of 34,020 kg.
Therefore maximum load carriage capacity

$$= 34020 \text{ kg}$$

$$= \frac{34020}{1500} \text{ Lm}^3$$

$$= 22.68 \text{ Lm}^3, \text{ and not } 23.7 \text{ Lm}^3.$$

2. Approximate output from Appendix 9.1 works out as under:
Ideal production per hour for 16m³ (struck capacity scraper) with 23.7 Lm³ heaped capacity

$$= 150 \text{ m}^3 \text{ (approximate)}$$

Correction factor = 0.91

Performance factor = 0.84

Load carriage capacity factor = $\dfrac{\text{Maximum load carrying capacity}}{\text{Scraper heaped capacity}} = \dfrac{22.68}{23.7}$

$$= 0.96$$

Therefore scraper output = 150 × 0.91 × 0.84 × 0.96

= 110 LCM/Hour.

3. *Note*: The Gross Vehicle Weight—(GVW), the effective grade (%), the maximum travel speed and the rimpull (or the drawbar pull) can be determined from the equipment performance charts which are provided by the manufacturer. This information aids in determining the cycle time, output data and usable rimpull (i.e. adjusted rimpull) necessary to overcome traction of the haulage road.

## 9.4.3 Loader Shovel

This machine, also called as the front–end loader, can be used as earth loader, earth transporter over short distances, and earth excavator in loose soil. It can operate like a face shovel and bulldozer. It is available with wheel mounting and track mounting.

The loader shovel can also be fitted with a backactor attachment. This backactor type loader can be used for light excavation like manholes, drain trenches, small pits, etc. and for loading of materials into tippers. The ideal output data for loader shovel is given in Appendix 9.1.

The quantity of materials that can be hauled by the loader depends upon its bucket capacity. Loader bucket capacities are specified by the manufacturer either in terms of heaped capacity or struck capacity. However, planning can be based on the loose soil struck capacity of the bucket, and the heaped capacity (loose soil) can be converted into struck capacity (loose soil) as under:

**Bucket struck capacity = Bucket heaped capacity × Fill-factor where fill-factor can be taken as:**

| Nature of soil | Bucket fill factor |
|---|---|
| Common earth | 0.95 |
| Sand and gravel | 0.95 |
| Hard clay | 0.80 |
| Blasted rock | 0.70 |

### 9.4.4 Hauling Equipment

The type of earth hauling equipment primarily depends upon the haulage distance. A rough guideline for selecting equipment based on haulage distance is given in Table 9.3

Table 9.3

**Guidelines for Selecting Equipment Based on Haulage Distance (in metres)**

| Type of Equipment | Range of Haulage Distance |
|---|---|
| 1. Front-end loader track | Up to 80 |
| 2. Front-end loader (wheeled) | Up to 200 |
| 3. Bulldozers | Up to 80 |
| 4. Towed scrapers | 100–300 |
| 5. Elevating self-loading scrapers | 100–1000 |
| 6. Single engine scrapers (dozer pusher arrangement) | 500–1500 |
| 7. Double engine motorised scrapers (push pull arrangement) | 2000 and above |
| 8. Tippers and dump trucks | 800 and above |

Mostly the excavated earth is hauled in heavy duty rubber-tyred tippers, lorries, and rear-opening dump trucks. Over long distances these vehicles vary in capacity from 5 m$^3$ to 30 m$^3$ dumpers. Tipping lorries are employed for transporting materials over level grounds where as dumpers are used for moving large quantities of materials across rough areas. Generally, front-end loaders and excavators are used to load tippers and dumpers.

The number of haulage vehicles required can be calculated as under:

$$\text{Haulage vehicle required} = 1 + \frac{\text{Cycle time per trip of vehicle}}{\text{Load filling time of vehicle}}$$

*Example* Construction of a military helipad at an altitude of 2400 m involves 80,000 m$^3$ (loose) of area excavation in soft soil. This task is to be completed in 200 working hours. The company entrusted with the execution of the task has two dozers each with an output of 220 m$^3$/h under job conditions. It also holds wheel loaders and 22 m$^3$ dump trucks. One loader can load in trucks about 120 m$^3$ of excavated soil per hour. The dump truck cycle time for disposal of excavated materials is 35 minutes. This includes 7 minutes of loading time by a loader team consisting of 2 loaders. Estimate the output of front-end loader for loading excavated soil heap into dump trucks and determine approximately the number of dozers, loaders and dumpers required to complete the task on time.

*Solution*

(a) Dozers required $= \dfrac{\text{Excavation quantity}}{\text{Output/h} \times \text{Working hour}}$

$= \dfrac{80{,}000}{220 \times 200} \simeq \text{(say)}$

(b) Loaders required $= \dfrac{\text{Excavation/h by dozers}}{\text{Loader output/h}}$

$= \dfrac{\text{No. of dozers} \times \text{dozer output/h}}{\text{Loader output/h}}$

$= \dfrac{2 \times 220}{120}$

$\simeq 4 = 2$ loader teams, each team consisting of 2 dozers.

(c) Dumpers required $= 1 + \dfrac{\text{Dumper cycle time}}{\text{loading time}}$

For each loading team of 2 front end loaders

$= 1 + \dfrac{35}{7}$

$= 1 + 5 = 6$

Total dumpers required $= 2 \times 6 = 12.$

## ❑ 9.5 EARTH COMPACTING AND GRADING EQUIPMENT

The compacting process increases the density of soil by reducing air void space. Consolidation, on the other hand, increases soil density by reducing water voids. Consolidation is a long-term process spread over years, whereas compaction can be achieved in a few hours. Compaction improves bearing strength, permeability and compressibility. Compacting equipment combine their static weigh with tamping, vibration, impact and kneading action to produce the desired compacting effort. Compaction equipment requirement varies with soil characteristics and compacting effort. Exhibit 9.5 shows the type of compacting effort and equipment required to compact different soils. The compacting equipment can be broadly classified into tamping foot rollers, pneumatic tyred rollers, vibratory rollers, impactors, plate vibrators, and smooth steel-wheel rollers.

### 9.5.1 Segmented Pads and Tamping Rollers

A tamping roller consists of one or more hollow steel cylindrical drums with rows of steel studs like sheep's feet mounted on it. As the roller is towed with a crawler tractor, these studs punch into the soil and compact it by tamping and kneading action. Generally, the

Exhibit 9.5

**Common Earth Compacting Equipment**

| Types of Rollers | Nature of Soil | | |
|---|---|---|---|
| | 100% Clay | 100% Sand | Rock |
| 1. Sheep Foot Rollers | Sheep Foot | | |
| Towed Sheeps Foot roller | | | |
| 2. Vibratory Rollers | | Vibratory | |
| Self-propelled vibrating roller | | | |
| 3. Steel Drum Rollers | | Steel Drum | |
| Smooth, steel wheel roller. | | | |
| 4. Multi-Tyred Pneumatic Rollers | | Pneumatic Tyred | |
| Small, mutli-tyred pneumatic roller. | | | |

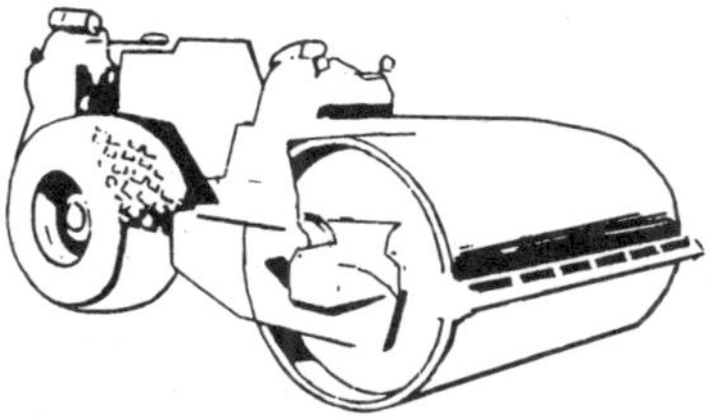

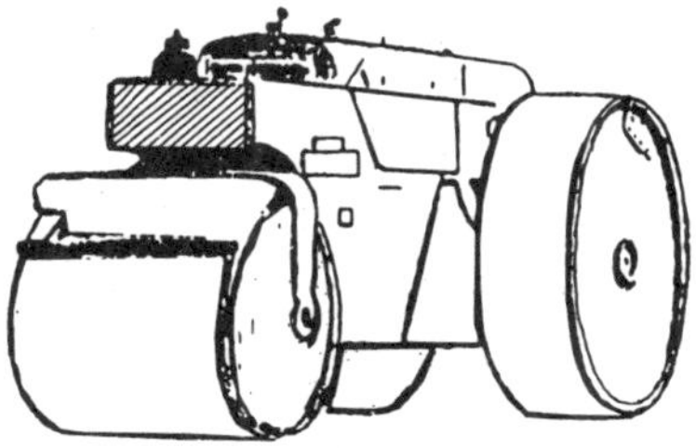

compaction gets carried out to a depth of 150 mm. The cylinder drum can also be filled with water or sand to add extra weight while compacting.

The compaction depends upon the nature of the soil and the roller passes are continued till the feet do not dig into the surface being compacted. There are many varieties of tamping foot rollers. These include sheep's foot rollers for compacting very cohesive soils, tamping foot rollers for compacting soil with low to medium cohesiveness, and grid or mesh segmented rollers for compacting granular soils, specially gravels. In general, the depth of compaction achieved in layers with the sheep's foot roller is nearly equal to the depth of the stud. Tamping foot rollers are rated in terms of static load or foot pressure (termed the ground contact pressure) on the soil surface unit area.

### 9.5.2 Smooth Wheeled Rollers

These rollers have one or more smooth steel wheels, and the latest variety rollers are self-propelled. The self-propelled tandem and 3-wheeled rollers are used for finishing compaction of layers up to 150 mm of sand, gravel and water bound macadam used in base courses. Smooth wheeled rollers are employed for compacting bituminous materials specially the top layers in road surfacing operation. Smooth wheeled rollers are classified either by type or weight or both. Various types of rollers include 3-wheel two axles, 2-wheel tandem and 3-wheel tandem The weight of the rollers can also be increased by ballasting with water, sand, or pig iron. Rollers are designated in terms of static weight and ballasted weight, i.e. 15/20 tons means that the static weight of the roller is 15 tons and the maximum weight when ballasted is 20 tons. In order to indicate the pressure exerted, these rollers are also designated by specifying the minimum weight per linear width of roller, i.e. 60 kg/cm width.

### 9.5.3 Pneumatic Rollers

Pneumatic rollers are available in light, medium and heavy weights. They compact soil by a kneading action. The weight of the equipment can be nearly doubled with ballasting using water, sand or pig iron, and the ground pressure can be maintained as desired by controlling the weight of the ballast, the number of the wheels, the width of the tyres and the tyre pressure. The pneumatic tyred rollers are rated in terms of tyre pressure (ground contact pressure) per unit area. It may be noted that the load on the tyres determines the depth to which compaction is possible, where as both the tyre pressure and the tyre load are important for achieving compaction near the surface. (See Table 9.4.)

### 9.5.4 Vibratory Rollers and Compactors

Vibration improve compaction and save time when compared with the static weight method of compaction. Vibrations set the rim roller in oscillation, and these in turn transmit vibrations to the soil. Vibrations are induced by installing a rotating eccentric weight inside the roller drum. Vibratory rollers combine the static weight with dynamic forces. Maximum

## Table 9.4
### Load Requirements for Compaction at Different Depths

| Passes | Job Characteristics | Maximum Depth of Layer (in mm) | Load Desired (in tons) |
|---|---|---|---|
| 4 to 8 | Compaction of loamy sand | 300 mm | 1.5 to 1.7 |
|  |  | 500 mm | 2.0 to 2.5 |
|  |  | 700 mm | 4.0 to 4.5 |
| 4 to 6 | Compacting bituminous material | 80 mm | 1.5 |
|  |  | 130 mm | 2.5 |
|  |  | 200 mm | 4.0 |

compacting effort is produced when the resonance frequency of the roller and soil coincide. Generally, the rating for the vibratory compactor is stated as total applied force' expressed in tons and it is the numerical sum of the dynamic forces plus static weight. The vibrating frequency is specified as cycles/minute. Vibration frequencies range from 1400 to 3000 cycles per minute. Further, a slow displacement speed of say 2.5 to 4 km/h produces a better effect than speedier movement.

Vibratory compactors are of various types and sizes. These include smooth drum vibratory rollers and tamping foot vibratory rollers. These are widely used for compacting non-cohesive soils.

### 9.5.5 Manually Operated Plate and Impact Compactors

These are used for compaction of small stretches like base and trenches in a building foundation work, and are operated manually. In plate compactors, vibrations are provided by installing two eccentric weights rotating in opposite directions around the centre of gravity of the plate. Plate compactors are more effective on granular materials, whereas impact compactors are preferred for cohesive materials. The compacting effort in the impact or tamping compactor is delivered by raising a heavy weight and then dropping it on the surface of the soil. These compactors are mostly hand operated. However, track-mounted cranes can also be improvised to provide a free fall hammer effect on the soil surface.

### 9.5.6 Production Output of Roller Compactors

The nature of soil dictates the type of compacting equipment required, and the dry density which can be achieved. After the compacting equipment is selected, its average output can be calculated as under:

$$\text{Compaction in m}^3/\text{hr} = \frac{WSTEC}{P}$$

where  W = Width compacted per pass (M)
       S = Compactor speed in M/h
       T = Thickness of compacted layer in m$^3$
       E = Job efficiency factor
       C = Compacting factor
       P = Number of passes required—varies from 4 to 6

and the approximate value of the compacting factor for the changing state of soil. In the absence of actual data, the compacting factor can be assumed as shown in Table 9.5.

Table 9.5

**Compacting Factor for Different Types of Soil**

|  | Compacted Volume | Loose Volume | In-place Volume | In-place Dry Density |
|---|---|---|---|---|
| Common earth | 1.0 | 1.41 | 1.18 | 1.8 |
| Sand | 1.0 | 1.21 | 1.18 | 1.7 |
| Clay | 1.0 | 1.48 | 1.11 | 1.9 |
| Gravel | 1.0 | 1.17 | 1.11 | 2.0 |
| Crushed stone | 1.0 | 1.30 | 0.75 | 2.2 |

*Notes*
(1) The above data can be used for initial planning purposes. However, field trials are necessary to determine the optimum moisture content, loose layer (lift) thickness, roller weight and the number of passes that yield a certain compacted thickness of the layer having a specified field dry density.
(2) It is necessary to assess the requirement of water for compaction so as to develop a water distribution system including requirement of water tenders.

Water requirement in litres per hour = weight of loose soil to be compacted per hour in kg × (optimum moisture content–natural moisture content).

For example, water required per hour for compacting loose soil being spread by a shovel and dozer at the rate of 230 m$^3$/h for a soil having density of 1.5 g/cm$^3$ and 8% moisture content, needing 12% optimum moisture content for compaction

$$= 230 \times 10^6 \times 1.5 \times \frac{12-8}{100} \times \frac{1}{1000} = 13800 \text{ litres water/hour}$$

## 9.5.7 Graders

These are used to grade earthen road formations and embankments to their finished shape within specified limits by trimming the surface. The graders can also be used for forming ditches, mixing and spreading soils, backfilling and scarifying ground.

The motor grader is the equipment mostly used for grading and finishing of large areas. Motor graders generally have engines up to 300 HP and the latest models are provided with hydraulically controlled attachments. These attachments include an excavation blade similar to the bulldozer, scarifier, ripper and backhoe. The blade of the motor grader has replaceable cutting edges. These blades come in flat, curved and serrated styles. Motor graders are fitted with articulated frames for increasing manoeuvrability. Motor graders are now available with automatic grade controls for achieving the desired grading. Grading distance of 500 meters and above give optimum output. For shorter distances, task efficiency gets reduced:

| Distance in meters | 50 | 100 | 200 | 500 |
|---|---|---|---|---|
| Task efficiency | 0.4 | 0.6 | 0.8 | 1.0 |

Graders' optimum output for finishing is measured in $M^2$/hour on an area basis or km/hour on an linear basis:

$$\text{Output in } m^2/\text{hour} = \frac{W.S.E.}{P}$$

where,
$W$ = Width graded per pass
$S$ = Average speed in m/h
$E$ = Job efficiency factor
$P$ = Number of passes (generally 4 to 6)

and the grader speed for various operations can be taken as under:

| Operation | Speed km/h |
|---|---|
| Rough grading | 4≃10 |
| Finishing (including grading) | 6≃15 |
| Mixing | 15≃30 |
| Spreading | 6≃15 |
| Self transporting | 10≃40 |

*Example* Calculate the time required to grade and finish 30 km of road formation with width equal to thrice the width of the motor grader, using six passes of the motor grader with speed for each of the successive two passes as 6 km/h, 8 km/h and 10 km/h respectively. Assume machine efficiency based on operator's skill, machine characteristics and working conditions as 75%

$$\text{Average speed} = \frac{2 \times 6 + 2 \times 8 \times 2 \times 10}{6}$$

$$= 8 \text{ km/h}$$

Area to be graded per hour

$$= \frac{\text{Width graded per pass} \times \text{Average speed} \times \text{Machine efficiency}}{\text{Number of passes}}$$

$$= \frac{W \times 8 \times 1000 \times 0.75}{6}$$

Number of hours required to grade and finish 30 km long and 3 W wide area

$$= \frac{\text{Total area}}{\text{Area/hr}}$$

$$= \frac{30 \times 1000 \times 3W}{[W \times 8 \times 1000 \times 0.75] \div 6}$$

= 90 hours.

### 9.5.8 Equipment Selection Criteria

Equipment selection criteria depends upon the following factors:

(a) Compacting equipment—nature of materials, depth of fill, daily work load, and working condition. Exhibits 9.5 and 9.6 provide guidelines for selecting the type of compacting equipment for the given soil conditions.
(b) Grading equipment—nature of materials, daily workload, finishing accuracy, and working conditions.

## 9.6 CONCRETING PLANT AND EQUIPMENT

Concrete is produced by combining basic materials like cement, aggregate and water into a homogeneous, suitably designed, plastic mix that solidifies into structural and non-structural building members. The process of production of concrete involves batching, mixing, transportation, placing, consolidating and curing. The major equipment used for production, transportation and pumping of concrete are outlined in the subsequent paragraphs and these are shown in Exhibit 9.7. The designing and erection of the formwork needed for shaping concrete is a subject in itself and is not covered in this chapter.

### 9.6.1 Concrete Batching and Mixing Equipment

Batching is the process of proportioning cement, aggregates, water and admixture (where added), by weight (commonly used method) or volume, prior to mixing. The equipment used for batching and mixing can be divided into three categories, viz. mobile concrete mixers, commonly called concrete mixers: centralized batching and mixing plant: and mobile truck-mixers which are covered under concrete transportation.

### 9.6.2 Mobile Concrete Mixers

These mixers have a conical or circular rotating drum with baffle fittings inside. These are mounted on pedestals with facilities for batching of various concreting materials. There are

Project Construction Equipment **299**

Exhibit 9.6

## Typical Major Compacting Equipment: Salient Features

| Type | Weight (Tons) Static | Weight (Tons) Other | Rated hose power | Working Speed K.M.P.H average | Rolling width m³ | Other features | Soil loose lift maximum cm |
|---|---|---|---|---|---|---|---|
| **Pneumatic Rollers** | | **Ballasted** | | | | **Maximum wheel loading tons** | |
| (a) Light 15 inch dia wheels 9 to13 wheels | 3 to 9 | 10 to 15 | 40–110 | 5–12 | 170–250 | 1.25–2.00 | 70 cm |
| (b) Medium 20 inch dia wheels 7 to 11 wheels | 6 to 10 | 21–30 | 80–130 | 6–15 | 185–240 | 2.25–3.00 | 70 cm |
| (c) Heavy 24 inch dia wheels, 7 wheels | 10 to 12 | 30–35 | 100–130 | 6–16 | 200–240 | 4.50–5.00 | 70 cm |
| **Segmented and Tamping Foot** | | | | | | **Production Capacity LPH** | |
| (a) Light self-propelled | 15 to 18 | — | 130–250 | 5–20 | 21–27 | 700–900 | Upto depth of foot |
| (b) Medium self-propelled | 20 to 28 | — | 250–350 | 5–20 | 24–30 | 900–1200 | Upto depth of foot |
| (c) Heavy, self-propelled | 30 to 50 | — | 400–600 | 5–20 | 36–42 | 1600–2500 | — |
| (d) Towed | — | — | — | 3–8 | 18–30 | 300–600 | Upto depth of foot |
| **Vibratory** | | **Dynamic Force** | | | | **Frequency Vibration/min** | |
| (a) Roller self-Propelled (with) pneumatic rear wheels) | 6 to 25 | 7.5–37.5 | 65–150 | — | 150–250 | 1400–1800 | 100 cm |
| (b) Towed | 3 12.5 | 7.5–30.0 | 25–75 | — | 150–210 | 1300–2200 | 100 cm |
| (c) Tandemself-propelled | 1.5–2.5 | 2.0–40.0 | 25–35 | — | 75–90 | 2500–3000 | 100 cm |
| (d) Plate self-propelled | 4–6.5 | 15.0–30.0 | 50–75 | — | 375 400 | 2100–420 | 100 cm |

# Construction Project Management

| Type | Weight (Tons) Static | Weight (Tons) Other | Rated horse power | Working Speed K.M.P.H average | Rolling width m³ | Other features | Soil loose lift maximum cm |
|---|---|---|---|---|---|---|---|
| **Smooth Steel Wheel** | | **Blasted** | | | | | |
| (a) 2-Axle Tandem | — | 5–14 | 40–150 | 6–12 | 100–135 | — | 30 cm |
| (b) 3-Axle Tandem | — | 16–20 | 75–120 | 8–12 | 100–135 | — | 30 cm |
| (c) 3-wheel | — | 6–14 | 75–120 | 6–12 | 175–210 | — | — |
| | | | | | | **Frequency Vibration/min** | |
| **Small Scale Work** | | | | | | | |
| (a) Vibratory roller | 0.2–6.0 | — | 5–40 | 3–10 | — | Upto 80 | 100 cm |
| (b) Vibratory plate Compactors | 0.1–1.0 | — | 2–10 | 1.0–1.5 | — | Upto 80 | 70 cm |
| (c) Stampers | Approx 0.1 | — | 2–4 | — | — | Upto 80 | 50 cm |

Project Construction Equipment **301**

Exhibit 9.7
## Major Concreting Equipment

- Mixing Equipment
  - Portable Concrete
  - Batching Plants
- Transportation Equipment
  - Transit Mixers
  - Concrete Dumpers
- Delivery Equipment
  - Concrete Pumps
  - Others
    - Hoist
    - Conveyors
    - Concrete Buckets
- Compacting Equipment
  - Needle vibrators
  - Surface vibrators

Batching Plant

Transit Mixer

Concrete Pump

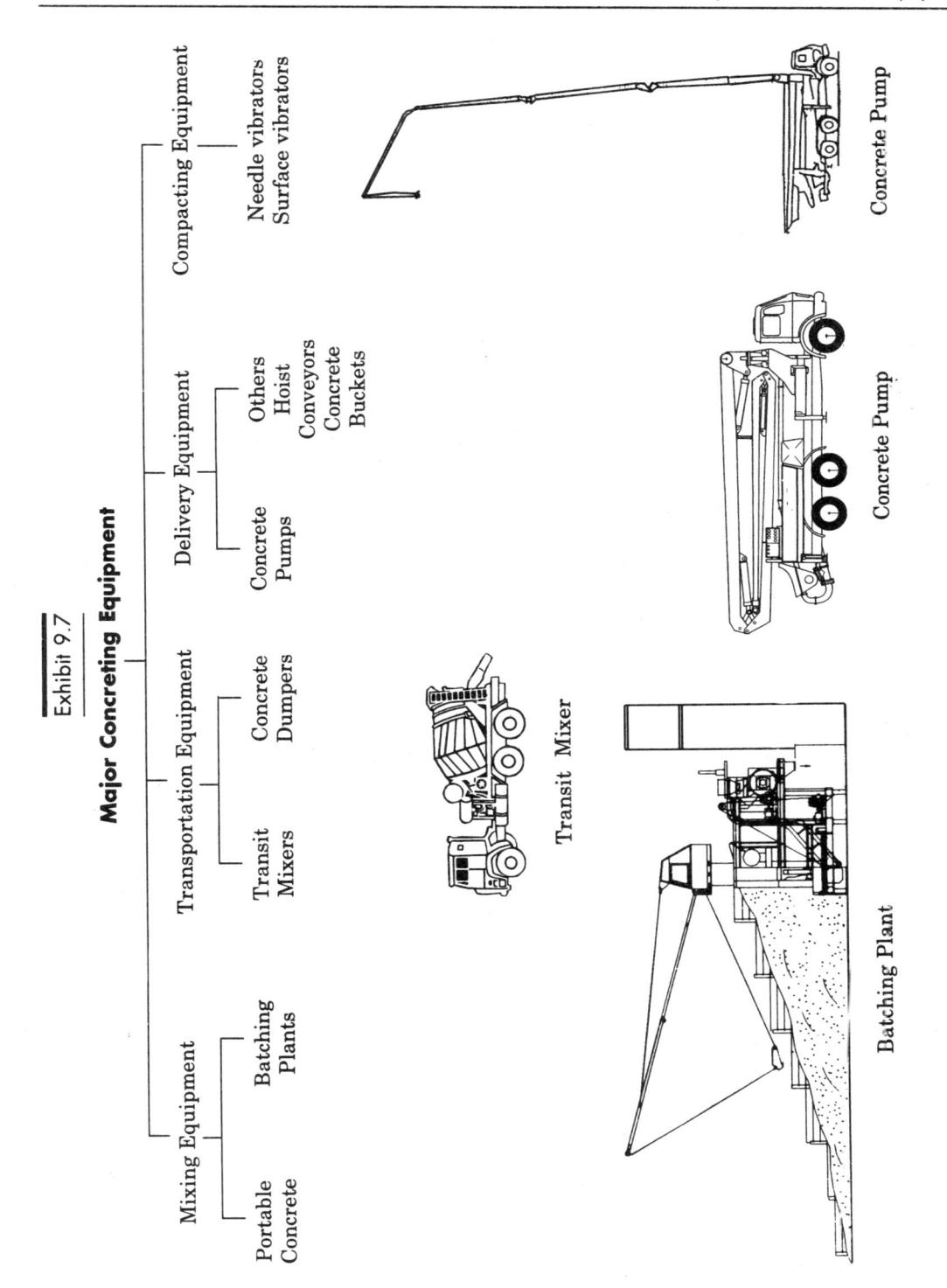

Concrete Pump

three types of concrete mixers, viz. tilting drum mixers, non-tilting drum mixers and reverse drum mixers. Tilting drum mixers discharge the concrete by tilting the drum. Tilting drum mixers are used for producing very small quantities of concrete or mortar mixes.

Non–tilting drums are suitable for requirements say up to 10 m³/h. These have a hopper-fitted outlet on the top for loading and another chute-fitted outlet on the bottom for discharge. The reverse-drum mixers mix in one direction and discharge in the opposite direction.

The mobile concrete mixers vary in size from as slow as 100 litres to 400 litres or more per cycle. The size of the concrete mixers denotes the volume of concrete that can be mixed in a single cycle, and usually it is expressed in cubic feet or cubic meters, or the ratio of the concreting materials volume to the wet concrete volume, for example 21/14 means a concrete mixer having maximum capacity to hold dry concreting materials up to 21 cubic feet capable of producing wet concrete of 14 cubic feet.

Concrete mixers are available as static units and trailer-mounted towed units.

The hourly output of a concrete mixer can be calculated by multiplying production in m³ per batch or cycle into the number of batches per hour. In the absence of actual data, for planning purposes, the hourly output for various sizes of concrete mixers can be taken as shown in Table 9.6.

Table 9.6

**Hourly Output for Various Sizes of Compact Mixers Output of Concrete Mixers**

| Mixer size | | Batches/hour | Output (M³/hour) |
|---|---|---|---|
| 7/3.5  | (100)         | 17 | 1.7 |
| 7/5    | (140 litres)  | 16 | 2.3 |
| 10/7   | (200 litres)  | 15 | 3.0 |
| 14/10  | (280 litres)  | 14 | 3.9 |
| 21/14  | (400l litres) | 12 | 4.8 |
| 32/21  | (600 litres)  | 10 | 6.0 |

### 9.6.3 Central Batching Plant

A central batching plant includes all types of equipment and materials necessary to provide input to the mixers and to deliver output to the concrete transporting system. Batching plants can be divide into two categories, viz. medium size or low profile batching plants, and large volume or high profile batching plants. Generally medium size batching plants have a rated capacity of 25 m³/h to 60 m³/h and are used for producing concrete for building construction projects where as batching plants having higher capacity, say 120 m³/h, are employed for heavy construction or are used in the ready-mix concrete supply business.

Experience dictates that for planning purposes, the average output of the central concrete batching plants be taken as 60% to 70% of the hourly rated capacity for each working hour so as to cater for various correction factors specially idle-time on account of non-utilization period and repairs.

## 9.6.4 Transportation Equipment

Equipment used for transportation of concrete, from mixer to placing site, depends upon the distance involved and the volume of concrete to be placed. Wheelbarrows, with limited capacity say 0.04 m$^3$, and small motorized dumpers, with capacity up to 1.0 m$^3$ are used for transporting and placing small quantities of concrete.

Concrete transit mixers are employed for transporting large quantities of concrete over long distances. These mixers have a rotating drum mixer mounted on a truck. These transit mixers transport wet concrete from the mixer to the placing site, and their rotating drums carrying capacity varies from 3 m$^3$ to 9 m$^3$ concrete. Concrete specifications restrict the time from loading to discharge of the concrete mixer as one hour without retarders, provided the drum is kept rotating to agitate the wet mix. For long distances, say exceeding two hour's travel time, the dry mix can be transported in specially designed truck-mixers, and the concrete is manufactured at the placing site by mixing these materials with water.

The number of truck-mixers required for transporting concrete can be worked out by evaluating the cycle-time. Consider a typical mixer cycle-time data of 6 m$^3$ truck-mixer, given below:

| | |
|---|---|
| Loading time for 6 m$^3$ truck-mixer | = 14 minutes |
| Travel time of loaded truck-mixer to site | = 7.5 " |
| Average waiting time at site | = 7.5 " |
| Discharge time at site using concrete pump | = 15 " |
| Travel time for return trip | = 5 " |
| Total cycle time | = 49 minutes |

Therefore truck-mixers required for continuous supply

$$= \frac{\text{Cycle time}}{\text{Discharge time}} + 1 \text{ (spare)}$$

$$= \frac{49}{15} + 1$$

$$= 5 \text{ Nos.}$$

*Notes*

(1) Cycle time should be divided by discharge time (as illustrated above) or loading time, whichever is higher.
(2) Concrete placing rate at delivery site (m$^3$/h) should be kept marginally less than the loading (or production) rate due to the following reasons:

   (a) Concrete placing should proceed continuously as waiting in between can result in improper jointing, specially if the time interval between the initial deposit of concrete and subsequent deposit exceeds concrete initial-set period.
   (b) Concrete loading at the batching plant can be suitably controlled as and when the queue of loaded truck-mixers starts building-up at the placing site.

## 9.6.5 Hauling and Placing Concrete

At the delivery site the concrete transported by truck-mixers is hauled horizontally and/or vertically for final placing into the forms.

A small quantity of concrete can be hauled at the site by using wheelbarrows, chutes, portable belt-conveyors or hoisting units. But haulage of a large quantity of concrete needs a crane-and-bucket arrangement. Or the latest trend is to use concrete pumps.

Concrete buckets come in varying sizes. These are attached to hooks of suitable cranes for lifting concrete at desired heights. These buckets have a bottom gate which can be released manually for discharging concrete at the desired location. Concrete buckets can also be tied up with fork-lifts for moving concrete over short horizontal distances. The use of cranes, fork-lifts and hoists for handling materials is covered separately in this chapter.

Concrete pumps provide the most acceptable, easy, and quick method of placing concreting. These are commonly used in the industrialized countries. Concrete pumps can be broadly divided into two categories, viz. truck-mounted mobile pumps and trailer-mounted stationery pumps.

Truck-mounted mobile pumps have the ability to deliver concrete up to 120 $m^3/h$ at a height above 40 metres. But it creates handling and logistic difficulties. Usually mobile concrete pumps operate in the range of 35-45 $m^3/h$ or even less. The pumping distance and the price of the pump depends upon the boom length of the pump. For planning purposes, the vertical distance at which a concrete pump can deliver concrete with its boom can be taken as 2/3 of the boom length with remaining boom length being used for placing concrete horizontally. The mobile concrete pumps are frequently moved from place to place. They can also be used in the stationery mode of delivering concrete, horizontally or vertically up to designed distances, by fixing and suitably anchoring extension pipes.

The stationery concrete pumps are mounted on trailers and are moved occasionally. These are positioned in th vicinity of the place where concrete is to be delivered by pumping concrete vertically or horizontally. The pump is connected to the delivery site by a pipeline through which the concrete is pumped. Pumping distance depends upon the capacity of the pump, horizontal and vertical pumping distance. and the nature of bends in the pipeline. These details can be found in the manual of the concrete pump.

The truck-mounted mobile concrete pumps are preferred to trailer-mounted stationery pumps due to their mobility, flexibility, ease of maintenance and higher pumping capacity. Gradually the stationery pumps, though cheaper for certain work situations, are being replaced by the truck-mounted mobile concrete pumps.

## 9.6.6 Consolidating and Finishing

Consolidation aims at removing air voids in the concrete at the time of placing. Consolidation is achieved with the help of concrete vibrators, which come in many sizes depending upon the nature of their vibrating application such as in narrow slits, columns, slabs, mass concreting, etc. Finishing operations make use of screed vibrators, manual/power troveels, and tools necessary for undertaking various types of finishes such as exposed aggregate, broom, and textured pattern-shape finishes.

## 9.7 CRANES FOR MATERIAL HOISTING

Cranes are predominantly used for handling including lifting, lowering and swing shifting of small to heavy loads. Cranes come in many types such as crawler-mounted mobile cranes, self-propelled rubber-tyred wheels, telescopic jib cranes, truck-mounted strut-jib cranes and tower cranes. The commonly used cranes are shown in Exhibit 9.8.

### 9.7.1 Mobile Cranes

In wide spread project sites, mobile cranes provide the best means for lifting and shifting of small to heavy loads. These cranes can move over level firm surfaces as well as on rough terrains. Mobile cranes are of the following types:

(a) **Crawler-mounted cranes** These cranes spread their dead load over larger area through their long tracks, and as such are useful while working in unprepared surfaces. The boom of these cranes comes in sections which are joined by pin connections. The straight boom thus formed can lift loads over a radius of 30 to 40 metres. In order to overcome the ground obstruction to the inclined boom, a fly-jib (say, 18 meters in length) is attached to the top of the end boom, as shown in Exhibit 9 8. The fly-jib is generally inclined at 30 degrees offset from the main boom and it acts as its extension. The crawler jib crane can also be converted into a grabbing crane or dragline crane by fitting appropriate attachments.

(b) **Self-propelled rubber-tyred wheels cranes** These cranes have greater mobility over hard surfaces and are in great demand for shifting and transporting light loads over short distances, and for off-loading of medium to heavy loads. Self-propelled cranes can be broadly divided into three categories:

   (a) Strut-jib cranes for shifting small loads at a distance, where ground obstruction restricts the utility of the crane.
   (b) Cantilever-jib crane provides greater clearance under the jib for heavy and bulky loads.
   (c) Telescopic-jib crane provides flexibility in adjusting distances and heights of lifts. It has greater mobility on roads than other self-propelled cranes.

(c) **Truck-mounted cranes** These cranes are used for lifting medium to heavy loads over high and wide reaches, such as placing precast concrete slab panels in a high rise building, or installation of heavy mechanical equipment such as vessels in production industries. These cranes have a capacity ranging from 10 tons to 100 tons. Cranes of capacity greater than 100 tons are custom-made. Their main advantage is that they can move on roads, and they take hardly a few minutes to prepare for the lifting operation.

Truck-mounted cranes are available with telescopic-jib and strut-jib. These cranes have hydraulically operated outriggers, which get stretched out and are made to rest on firm ground so as to provide a stable base.

**Exhibit 9.8**

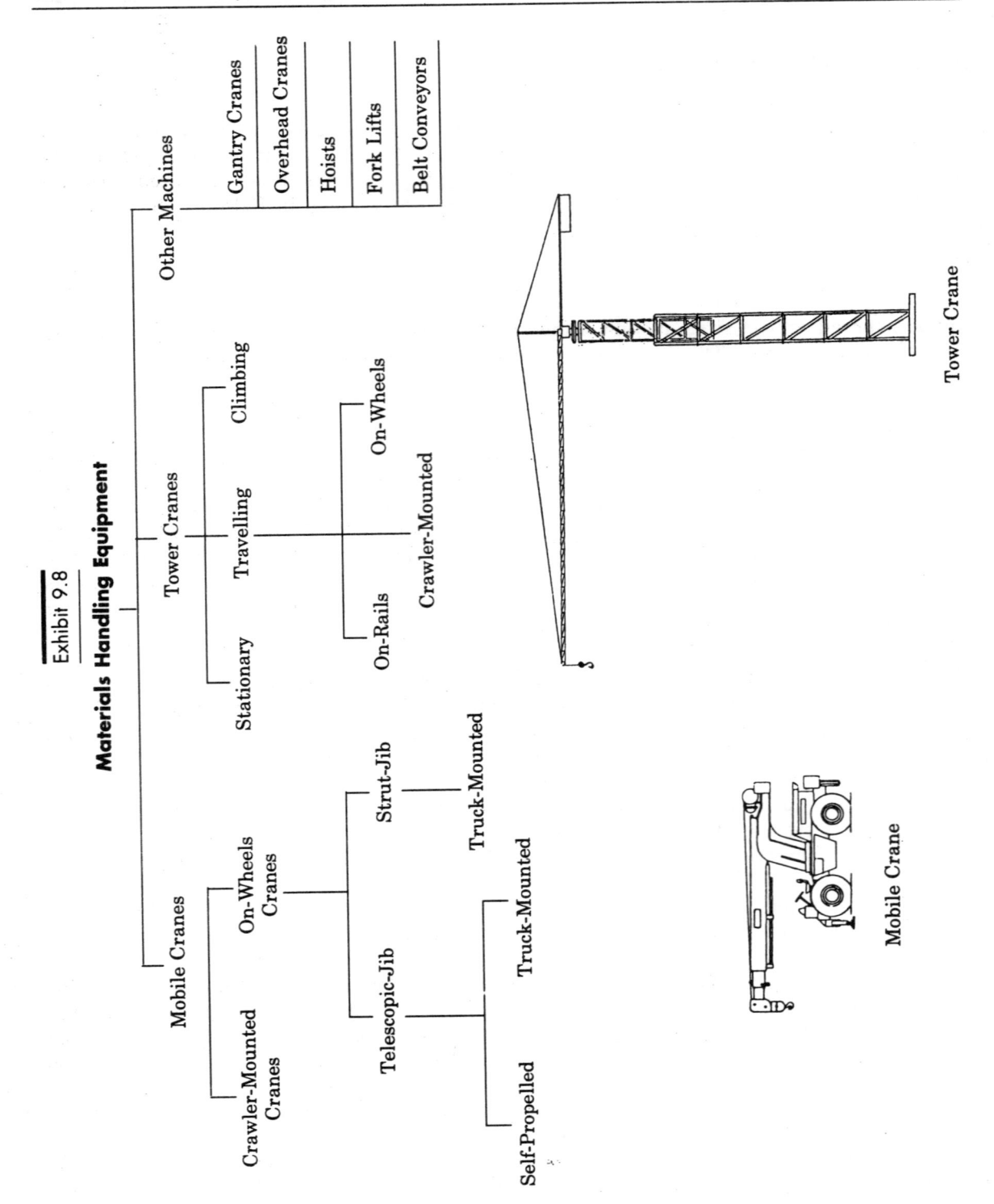

## Materials Handling Equipment

- Mobile Cranes
  - Crawler-Mounted Cranes
  - On-Wheels Cranes
    - Strut-Jib
      - Truck-Mounted
    - Telescopic-Jib
      - Truck-Mounted
      - Self-Propelled
- Tower Cranes
  - Stationary
  - Travelling
    - On-Rails
    - On-Wheels
    - Crawler-Mounted
  - Climbing
- Other Machines
  - Gantry Cranes
  - Overhead Cranes
  - Hoists
  - Fork Lifts
  - Belt Conveyors

Tower Crane

Mobile Crane

## 9.7.2 Tower cranes

Tower cranes are extensively used in building projects, specially in high rise construction sites where work concentration is in a limited area. The tower crane configuration enables the crane to be erected close to the building, and its height enables its jib to swing clear of obstructions. These cranes have 360 degree slewing capability, and are electrically powered.

Depending upon the nature of the primary task, the tower cranes (both horizontal-jib and luffing cranes) can be grouped into following types:

(a) **Stationery cranes** These are supported on foundations. Their mast is bolted to a fixed-position steel base placed on top of the foundations and their ballast counterweight rests on the base. These cranes can go up to 100 meters in height and are mostly used for high rise buildings. The height of these cranes can be increased further by suitably bracing the mast with the structure of the building.

(b) **Travelling cranes** The steel base of these cranes is mounted on travel-gear, resting on rail-tracks embedded in the foundation. This enables the crane to travel along the track. The load travelling cranes can be used for constructing long buildings, and shifting heavy materials like precast elements, and batched concrete from the production site to the adjoining places or transportation areas.

(c) **Climbing cranes** These cranes are positioned on solid cores like the lift shaft inside a multistorey building. Initially about two storeys of the building are constructed by placing the crane outside the core on a selected part of the building foundation. The crane is then positioned in the core by securing it with special collars, resting on the walls of the core. Thereafter, the crane erects the building around itself, and climbs up when the mast supported on the collars is raised by winches or hydraulic jacks. Climbing cranes are economical and are specially useful where the shortage of sufficient external space around the building does not permit the erection of other tower cranes.

It may be noted that the erection of the tower cranes needs careful planning, and is generally entrusted to experienced persons or agencies.

## 9.7.3 Estimating Crane Output

The crane's capacity to handle loads from one location to another is given by:

$$\text{Crane output/Hour} = \text{Load/cycle} \times \text{cycles/hour}.$$

Calculation of the output and cycle time depends upon many variables, and it can best be determined by referring to machinery manuals and site trials.

It is important that manufacturers' manuals must be referred to in order to determine the tipping load at a given radius and the safe working load of the crane. Generally the safe working load varies from 67 to 75% of the theoretical crane tipping load.

For initial planning purposes, the cycle time can be computed as outlined below. However, the data indicated is for illustration purposes only:

| S. No. | Activity | Time in minutes (medium-sized crane) |
|---|---|---|
| 1. | Hooking load at ground level | = 1.0 minute |
| 2. | Raising load from ground level to a height or 30 meters at 60 metres/minute | = 0.5 ,, |
| 3. | Slewing through 120 degrees at 60 degree/minutes | = 0.5 ,, |
| 4. | Travelling on rails for 45 meters at 30 metres per minute | = 1.5 ,, |
| 5. | Moving trolley at jib level for unloading and positioning by 15 metres at 15 metres per minute | = 1.0 ,, |
| 6. | Unhooking load | = 1.0 ,, |
| 7. | Lowering load by 5 metres at 60 to 100 meters/minute, and resting at the proper place | = 1.0 ,, |
| 8. | Raising hook by 5 meters (overlapping) | = 0.0 ,, |
| 9. | Slewing to original loading position | = 1.0 minute |
| 10. | Moving trolley at jib level to loading position | = 0.5 ,, |
| 11. | Travelling on rails to original loading position | = 1.5 ,, |
| 12. | Lowering hook | = 0.5 ,, |
| | Total cycle time after disregarding effect of small overlapping activities | = 11.0 ,, |

Therefore, the above crane, operating with job efficiency of 44 mins/h and shifting a 5 Tons load in each cycle, shall handle 5 ton load × cycles in one hour (of 44 minutes).

$$= 5 \times \frac{44 \text{ min}}{11 \text{ min}}$$

$$= 20 \text{ tons/h}$$

It may be noted that the rated crane capacity is equal to the maximum load lifting capacity at the minimum operating radius.

## APPENDIX 9.1

## EARTHMOVING EQUIPMENT
## APPROXIMATE PRODUCTION DATA FOR PRIMARY TASKS

(Planning Output Norms = Ideal Output × Performance Factor × Correction Factor)

### ❏ Tracked Bull Dozer Ideal Output Per Hour In Bulk Volume In Easy-To-Doze Loose Soil

**Job Conditions.** Assumed dozing speed 3 km/h, return speed 6 km/h and manoeuvering time as 0.15 min. Ideal output in one hour = St blade capacity × cycles in one hour

| HP range | Straight Yd³ | Blade capacity m³ | Dozing Distance in Metres (one way) ||||
|---|---|---|---|---|---|---|
| | | | Up to 25 | 50 | 75 | 100 |
| 250-300 | 8   | 6.11 | 400 | 220 | 150 | 110 |
| 180-250 | 6   | 4.58 | 300 | 160 | 110 | 80  |
| 120-180 | 4   | 3.06 | 200 | 110 | 70  | 60  |
| 100-120 | 3   | 2.23 | 150 | 80  | 50  | 40  |
| 75-100  | 2   | 1.53 | 100 | 50  | 40  | 30  |
| 50-75   | 1.5 | 1.14 | 70  | 40  | 30  | 20  |

### ❏ Front-End Loader Ideal Output Per Hour In Bulk Volume Easy-To Haul Loose Soil

*Ideal output of the wheeled loader shovel.*

**Job Conditions.** Assumed manoeuvring digging and dumping time 0.4 min and speed (loaded) as 4 km/h and return empty as 12 km/h

| Bucket Capacity | Output per hour in m³ ||||||||| Bucket Capacity |
|---|---|---|---|---|---|---|---|---|---|
| 6.12 m³ | 410 | 265 | 245 | 155 | 130 | 110 | 95 | 85 | 8 Yd³ |
| 4.6 m³  | 310 | 200 | 185 | 115 | 95  | 80  | 70 | 60 | 6 Yd³ |
| 3.06 m³ | 205 | 135 | 125 | 75  | 65  | 55  | 50 | 40 | 4 Yd³ |
| 2.3 m³  | 155 | 100 | 95  | 60  | 50  | 40  | 35 | 30 | 3 Yd³ |
| 1.5 m³  | 100 | 65  | 60  | 40  | 30  | 25  | 25 | 20 | 2 Yd³ |
| 0.76 m³ | 50  | 35  | 30  | 20  | 15  | 15  | 10 | 10 | 1 Yd³ |
| Distance m | 25 | 50 | 75 | 100 | 125 | 150 | 175 | 200 | One way |

Hauling Distance in Metres

## Ideal output of the tracked loader shovel

**Job Conditions.** Assumed digging manoeuvring and dumping time 0.4 min and speed (loaded) as 3 km/h and empty return as 6 km/h

| Bucket Capacity | Output Per Hour in m$^3$ | | | | | | | Bucket Capacity |
|---|---|---|---|---|---|---|---|---|
| 3.06 m$^3$ | 260 | 185 | 140 | 115 | 95 | 85 | 75 | 60 | 4 Yd$^3$ |
| 1.53 m$^3$ | 130 | 90 | 70 | 60 | 50 | 40 | 35 | 30 | 2 Yd$^3$ |
| 0.76 m$^3$ | 65 | 45 | 35 | 30 | 25 | 20 | 15 | 15 | 1 Yd$^3$ |
| Distance m | 10 | 20 | 30 | 40 | 50 | 60 | 70 | 80 | One way |

Hauling Distance in Metres

❑ **Excavating and Lifting Equipment Ideal Output Per Hour In Bulk Volume In Easy To Dig Soil Swing 90 Degree with 23 seconds cycle.**

| Types of Equipment | Features | | | Bucket Struck Capacity | | | | | |
|---|---|---|---|---|---|---|---|---|---|
| | Bucket Size | YD$^3$ | | 0.50 | 0.75 | 1.00 | 1.50 | 2.00 | 3.00 |
| | | m$^3$ | | 0.38 | 0.57 | 0.76 | 1.14 | 1.53 | 2.30 |
| | Engine HP (Approx.) | | | 50 | 75 | 100 | 130 | 160 | 200 |
| 1. Face Shovel | Maximum Cutting Height | m | | 7.0 | 7.0 | 7.0 | 7.5 | 8.5 | 10.0 |
| | Ideal Output/Hour (Loose, easy dig) | Lm$^3$ | | 60 | 90 | 120 | 180 | 220 | 300 |
| 2. Backhoe | Maximum Digging Depth | m | | 5.0 | 6.5 | 7.5 | 8.0 | 9.0 | 9.0 |
| | Ideal Output/Hour (Loose, easy dig) | Lm$^3$ | | 48 | 72 | 96 | 144 | 176 | 240 |
| 3. Dragline | Maximum Boom Length | m | | 21 | 21 | 21-27 | 21-27 | 27-30 | 30-33 |
| | Ideal Output/Hour (Loose, easy dig) | Lm$^3$ | | 45 | 67 | 78 | 135 | 165 | 225 |
| 4. Camshell | Maximum Boom Length | m | | 21 | 21-27 | 21-27 | 21-27 | 27-30 | 30-33 |
| | Ideal Output/Hour (Loose, easy dig) | Lm$^3$ | | 24 | 36 | 48 | 72 | 88 | 120 |

❑ **Scrapper Ideal Output Per Hour In Bulk Volume In Easy To Scrap Soil**

*Ideal output of the towed scraper*

**Job Conditions.** Assumed loading, manoeuvering and dumping time as 3.0 mins, and speed (loaded) as 3 km/m and empty as 6 km/h

| Heaped Capacity | | | Output Per Hour in m³ | | | | Heaped Capacity |
|---|---|---|---|---|---|---|---|
| 21.4 m³ | 215 | 140 | 105 | 85 | 70 | 60 | 28 Yd³ |
| 18.4 m³ | 185 | 120 | 95 | 75 | 60 | 50 | 24 Yd³ |
| 13.8 m³ | 140 | 90 | 70 | 55 | 45 | 40 | 18 Yd³ |
| 10.7 m³ | 105 | 70 | 50 | 40 | 35 | 30 | 14 Yd³ |
| 6.9 m³ | 70 | 50 | 35 | 30 | 25 | 20 | 9 Yd³ |
| Distance m | 100 | 200 | 300 | 400 | 500 | 600 | One way |

Hauling Distance in Metres

### Ideal output of the motorised scraper

**Job Conditions.** Assumed loading, manoeuvring and dumping time as 2.0 mins. haul road is less than 5% and speed (loaded) as 20 km/h and empty as 40 km/h rolling resistance of

| Heaped Capacity | | | Output Per Hour in m³ | | | | | | | Heaped Capacity |
|---|---|---|---|---|---|---|---|---|---|---|
| 38.3 m³ | 600 | 410 | 350 | 310 | 250 | 225 | 210 | 190 | 170 | 150 | 50 Yd³ |
| 30.6 m³ | 485 | 325 | 230 | 250 | 200 | 180 | 170 | 150 | 135 | 120 | 40 Yd³ |
| 22.3 m³ | 360 | 245 | 210 | 185 | 150 | 135 | 125 | 115 | 100 | 90 | 30 Yd³ |
| 15.3 m³ | 240 | 165 | 140 | 125 | 100 | 90 | 85 | 75 | 65 | 60 | 20 Yd³ |
| Distance m | 400 | 800 | 1000 | 1200 | 1600 | 1800 | 2000 | 2200 | 2600 | 3000 | One way |

Hauling Distance in Metres

## ❑ Performance Factor

| Job Conditions | Management Conditions | | | |
|---|---|---|---|---|
| | Excellent | Good | Average | Poor |
| Favourable | 1.0 | 0.9 | 0.8 | 0.7 |
| Average | 0.9 | 0.8 | 0.7 | 0.6 |
| Unfavourable | 0.8 | 0.7 | 0.7 | 0.5 |

*Note:* (1) Management conditions, under control of management include operators' efficiency, equipment operation worthiness, equipment maintenance capability, planning and supervision effectiveness, client attitude etc.
(2) Job conditions, which affect eficiency but are beyond the control of management cover terrain, weather conditions, temperature etc.

## Common Correction Factors

1. Soil Factor, Multiply

   | Easy Dig | Medium Dig | Hard Dig |
   |---|---|---|
   | (loam, sand, gravel) | (common earth) | (Stiff, slay, soft rock) |
   | 1.00 | 0.85 | 0.67 |

2. Swell Factor for in-place volume convesion, divide

   | Common earth | Sand and gravel | Clay (dry) |
   |---|---|---|
   | 1.2 | 1.1 | 1.3 |

3. Altitude, reduce performance

   0-300 m,     300 m and above
   Nil          Performance reduction 1% per 100 m increase in altitude above 300 m

   Temperature derating effect, reduce performance

   | Temp C | 0 | 15 | 30 | 45 |
   |---|---|---|---|---|
   | Performance change % | + 3 | 0 | − 3 | − 5 |

4. Working Efficiency, Multiply

   | 60 Min. | 55 Min. | 50 Min/h | 45 Min. | 40 Min/h |
   |---|---|---|---|---|
   | 1.00 | 0.92 | 0.83 | 0.75 | 0.67 |

## Correction Factors Special For Bull Dozer

Blade Factor Multiply

| S Blade | A Blade or P Blade | U Blade (used only in loose soil) |
|---|---|---|
| 1.0 | 0.65 | 1.20 |

Transmission system Factor Multiply

| Power Shift | Direct drive |
|---|---|
| 1.0 | 0.8 |

Grade Factor (Approximate), Multiply

| Up Grade | Down Grade |
|---|---|
| $1 - \dfrac{2.5 \text{ Grade \%}}{100}$ | $1 + \dfrac{2.5 \text{ Grade \%}}{100}$ |

## Correction Factors Special for Excavators

Swing Factor

| Angle of swing (Degrees) | 45 | 60 | 75 | 90 | 120 | 150 | 180 |
|---|---|---|---|---|---|---|---|
| Factor | 1.25 | 1.15 | 1.05 | 1.0 | 0.90 | 0.80 | 0.70 |

Load Factor

    Side Casting         Loading in Vehicles
       1.0                         0.8

## Correction Factors Special For Scrapers

Maximium Load Carrying Capacity
        = Weight of volumetric capacity, or,
        Scaper pay load, which ever is less.

# CHAPTER 10

# Selecting Construction Equipment

The use of equipment for accomplishing construction tasks is increasing rapidly. Plant and equipment now constitute a substantial portion of the construction costs in a project. The cost component depends upon the nature of the project and the extent to which equipment is employed. In a mechanized building project, the equipment costs can vary from 5% to 10% of the direct costs, whereas in highway construction projects the plant and equipment costs may touch as much as 40% of the project direct costs.

To quote examples, the types of major construction equipment employed by two Indian managed contracting companies engaged in the construction of building complexes is tabulated in Exhibit 10.1. One of these companies was working on the construction of a township project costing over US $160 million in Iraq, and the other was engaged in executing multi-projects totalling about US $100 million spread over the United Arab Emirates. Each was handling a peak workload of around US $5.0 million per month.

Equipment purchase involves initial heavy investments. In the long run, equipment adds to the profitability by reducing the overall costs, provided the equipment is properly planned, technically scrutinized, economically procured and effectively managed. Poor selection and bad management of equipment are generally attributed to task mismatch, unplanned requirement forecasts, hasty purchase decisions, inadequate repairs and spares supply, and lack of preventive maintenance.

This chapter deals with factors influencing the selection of equipment. These are: task considerations for the selection of equipment, method of evaluation of equipment owning and operating costs, mechanical characteristics (which affect its selection), equipment acquisition options, and finally the considerations affecting the selection of the construction equipment covered in Chapters 9 and 10.

## Exhibit 10.1

### Housing Construction Project
### Major Plant and Equipment Owned by Contractors

|  |  | $160M Project | $110M Project |
|---|---|---|---|
| **I** | **Earthmoving Machinery** | | |
| | (1) Dozers | 2 | |
| | (2) Loaders Shovels | 7 | 5 |
| | (3) Excavators | 3 | 1 |
| | (4) Compressors | 8 | 3 |
| | (5) Soil compactors | 30 | 12 |
| **II** | **Concreting Machinery** | | |
| | (1) Batching plants 35 m$^3$ | 2 | 1 |
| | (2) Transit mixers 6 cm | 4 | 3 |
| | (3) Concrete pumps | 1 (Mob) | 3 (Stationary) |
| | (4) Concrete mixers 21/4 | 3 | 2 |
| | (5) Screed pumps | 4 | 1 |
| | (6) Cement bag cutters | 2 | 1 |
| **III** | **Erection and Handling Machinery** | | |
| | (1) Cranes 55 Tons | 4 | 1 |
| | (2) Cranes 20 to 35 tons | 4 | 3 |
| | (3) Cranes 6 to 10 tons | 3 | 2 |
| | (4) Forklifts | 12 | 7 |
| | (5) Tower cranes | | 17 |
| **IV** | **Transport Fleet** | | |
| | (1) Heavy duty tractors/tippers/dumpers/tankers | 35 | 30 |
| | (2) Dumpers 2 ton capacity | 16 | 7 |
| | (3) Form tractors with trailors | 5 | 4 |
| | (4) Water/fuel tankers | 3 | 2 |
| **V** | **Power Generation and Water Supply Machinery** | | |
| | (1) Generators 500 KVA | 1 | |
| | (2) Generators 175 KVA | 10 | |
| | (3) Generators 25 to 55 KVA | 6 | 12 |
| | (4) Pumps | 7 | 39 |
| **VI** | **Precast Factory Machinery** | | |
| | (1) Batching plant 100 m$^3$/hr | 1 | — |
| | (2) Gantry cranes | 10 | — |
| | (3) Steam boilers | 2 | — |
| | (4) Moulds—vibratory | 75 | — |
| | (5) Electric cars | 4 | — |
| | (6) Prime movers for trailors | 5 | — |
| | (7) 'A' frame trailors | 10 | — |
| | (8) Flat head trailors | 5 | |

*(Contd)*

| VII Manufacturing Machines | S 160 M Project | $110M Project |
|---|---|---|
| (1) Duct making | 10 | 2 |
| (2) Inserts manufacturing | 20 | |
| (3) Metal-work fabrication | 7 | 4 |
| (4) GRC manufacturing | 9 | |
| (5) Plastic moulding | 2 | |
| (6) Wood-work and carpenter | 15 | 36 |
| (7) Steel doors and windows | 13 | |
| (8) Rebar fabrication | 8 | 31 |
| (9) Block making | 1 | 1 |
| (10) Spraying and plastering | 6 | 7 |

*Notes:* The $160 million project involved turnkey construction of a residential complex containing 2000 dwelling units made of precast concrete, shopping and social activity buildings, and connected external utility services. On the other hand, the $110 million project consisted mostly of administration building complexes in various cities, and its earthwork and utility services were mostly executed through subcontracts. Plant and machinery employed on roadwork is not included in the above list.

## ❏ 10.1 TASK CONSIDERATIONS

The task objectives at construction sites are stated in terms of the nature of the task and the quantity of work to be accomplished economically, within specified time, and under given site conditions.

The nature of the task dictates the type of equipment needed, and the time allowed in the work schedule determines the rate of work. This rate of work indicates the output capability of the required equipment. The equipment productivity determines its cost effectiveness.

### 10.1.1 Nature of Work

The nature of production tasks in building construction projects, which can be performed with equipment, include excavating, hauling, transporting, filling, compacting, grading, fabricating, hoisting, concreting, precasting, block making, plastering, finishing, trenching, pipe–laying, cable–laying, road–making and so on. Generally, special purpose equipment is available for each of these tasks. Broad guidelines for the types available and selection of equipment for major tasks in a building construction project are covered in Chapter 9. In addition, the support equipment at the project site consists of generators, pumping sets, treatment plants and other utility services equipment.

### 10.1.2 Rate of Daily Output

The forecast of the quantity of work to be completed in a specified period conforming to the schedule of work, under given job conditions, defines the rate of daily output and the peak production level. Since, the primary purpose of having equipment is to achieve task objectives, the output of the equipment under site conditions will have to be equal to or more than the planned hourly rate at which the task is to be executed economically. In order to cater for occasional peak fluctuations, suitable means of expediting work such as overtime working or inducting hired machinery, will have to be examined.

### 10.1.3 Equipment Output Capability

The assessment of equipment performance needs experience. The equipment capability to perform an assigned task under a given site situation can best be determined from the on-site actual trials or it can be assessed from its past performance records of operation under similar site conditions. But at the equipment selection stage, the actual on-site trials may not be feasible, and the past performance data may not be always available or it may not be adequate as the site conditions vary from place to place and project to project. In the absence of reliable data, the equipment output norms can be derived from the performance data given in the manufacturer's manuals. These manuals outline the equipment's hourly output for a given task under ideal conditions. These ideal output norms can be suitably modified to conform to site conditions, by computing the performance efficiency factor.

Equipment standard hourly output
= Ideal output per hour × Performance efficiency factor × Correction factor

The equipment performance at the site of work depends upon many situational factors that influence the output. These situational factors may include the equipment serviceability conditions the effect of terrain, the accessibility to work site, working space restrictions, weather conditions, working conditions including timings, logistic and equipment vendor support, and the availability of local resources like operators, equipment renting facilities, power and water supply, fuel and lubricants, etc. It is neither feasible nor desirable to evaluate the resultant impact of each of these situational factors as, overall, only a few may matter, and the remaining may not. In order to simplify this evaluation, the prominent situational factors, other than those considered while computing equipment output norms, can broadly be grouped under two headings, viz. (a) controllable factors and (b) uncontrollable factors.

**(a) Controllable factors** These are the factors, the effect of which can be controlled by the site management. The prominent contributing factors include but are not limited to the following:

- Equipment operational worthiness.
- Operator's skill to operate the machine effectively for performing the given task.
- Available equipment repair and maintenance facilities.
- Planning and supervision effectiveness.
- Level of motivation.

It is difficult to quantify the effect of the above controllable factors on the operation of the equipment, but the resultant effect of these can be conceptualized by assessing percentage operating efficiency of each and then averaging these to evaluate the overall grade.

| Average(%) | Grade |
|---|---|
| 80–100 | Excellent |
| 70–79 | Good |
| 60–69 | Average |
| 50–59 | Poor |

To quote an illustration, consider the following assessment of the controllable factors indicated by an experienced plant engineer:

| | |
|---|---|
| Equipment worthiness | 90% |
| Operator's skill | 80% |
| Repair and maintenance facilities available | 60% |
| Supervisory effectiveness | 70% |
| Mean operating performance | 75% |

Therefore, the performance efficiency on account of controllable factors can be termed as 'Good'

**(b) Uncontrollable factors** These are the environmental factors over which the site management has no control. These factors include terrain, weather, prevailing temperature, etc. The expected performance efficiency for each of these causes can be assessed and the product of these can be taken to categorize the working environment as 'favourable', 'average', or 'unfavourable'.

| Environmental conditions | Efficiency |
|---|---|
| Favourable | 80 to 100% |
| Average | 60 to 79% |
| Unfavourable | 40 to 59% |

In particular, the effect of altitude and temperature on the performance of heavy equipment can be determined as under:

(a) **Effect of altitude on the performance of the engine** With the increase in altitude, the density of air reduces and consequently the quantity of oxygen available in a given volume of air becomes less. This affects the air-fuel ratio, and in turn the engine power is reduced. The extent of reduction in power with the rise in altitude is given in the manufacturer's engine performance specifications. In the absence of this, it can be assumed that for four-cycle diesel engines and all internal combustion engines, the engine efficiency and consequently the ideal output reduces at the rate of 1% for every 100 meters increase in altitude after 300 meters altitude above the sea level.

| Altitude | Reduction percentage |
|---|---|
| 0–300 m | No loss |
| Above 300 m | 1% per 100 m increase in altitude above 300 m |

*Example* Determine the resultant efficiency of a crawler tractor employed in cutting and levelling in an area at altitude of 2400 m.

$$\text{Efficiency at 2400 m attitude} = \left\{100 - \frac{2400 - 300}{100}\right\} = 79\%$$

(b) **Effect of temperature** Temperature at the place of work, changes the performance of a four-cycle diesel engine (specially the internal combustion petrol engine) from its standard conditions. This change can be assumed as under:

| Temperature (C°) | 0 | 15 | 30 | 45 |
|---|---|---|---|---|
| Performance change (%) | −3 | 0 | +3 | +5 |

**(C) Performance efficiency factor** The performance efficiency resulting from various controlled and uncontrolled factors can be determined as follows:

$$\text{Performance efficiency factor} = \text{Controllable Factor} \times \text{Uncontrollable Factor}$$

The approximate value of the performance efficiency factor can be determined from Table 10.1.

Table 10.1

**Performance Factor Matrix**

| Uncontrollable Factors | | Controllable factors | | | |
|---|---|---|---|---|---|
| | | Excellent | Good | Average | Poor |
| *Environment multiplier* | | 0.90 | 0.75 | 0.65 | 0.55 |
| Favourable | 0.90 | 0.80 | 0.70 | 0.60 | 0.50 |
| Average | 0.70 | 0.65 | 0.55 | 0.45 | 0.40 |
| Unfavourable | 0.50 | 0.45 | 0.40 | 0.35 | 0.30 |

The equipment efficiency thus determined can be either expressed as a fraction or percentage or it can be stated in terms of effective time in minutes per hour. For example, the efficiency factor of 0.6 can be stated as 60% or 36 minutes effective output of hourly optimum production rate.

It may be noted that the given piece of equipment does not operate in isolation. Generally it follows a sequence, i.e. one machine is followed by the next machine or related activity. Thus, the performance of each equipment influences the outcome of the subsequent equipment or activity. The standard output of the machine, therefore, has to be viewed in the light of the system and adjustments made if required, as any imbalances in related activity will adversely effect the overall output of the system.

### 10.1.4 Equipment Productivity

Equipment productivity is a measure of the performance of the equipment. It is expressed as the output achieved per equipment hour. The higher the output, the better is the productivity. A given piece of equipment's productivity is optimum when it is employed on the primary task for which it is designed. For example, a bulldozer is most productive when it is used for cutting earth and hauling by dozing action up to 60 metres. In case an equipment is to be used on secondary tasks, its optimum productivity will have to be multiplied by the Task efficiency factor, as illustrated for excavating machinery in Chapter 9.

### 10.1.5 Future Use of Equipment

If all expenses connected with the ownership and operation can be amortized on the project on which it is to be employed, there is no need to consider the future use of the equipment. However, if the equipment is to be utilized only for a part of its economic life in the project, the recovery of cost on its balance life will have to be considered in terms of future use or disposal after part use. This involves evaluation of the equipment owning and operating costs.

## 10.2 COST CONSIDERATIONS

The economic use of equipment is related to its employment cost. Hourly plant employment cost forms the basis for the cost estimation of work executed by the plant. The plant employment cost can be determined by computing plant owning and operating costs as follows:

$$\text{Equipment employment cost} = \text{Owning cost} + \text{Operating cost}.$$

There are many factors, determinate as well as indeterminate, which affect the plant owning and operating costs. Some of these factors include the state of the plant (old or new) and its capitalized cost, the source through which the capital is to be raised in case of a new purchase, the site delivered price, the implication on corporate taxes for the new purchase, the company's policy regarding capitalization, the economical plant life in years, the resale value after a useful life, the number of hours of operational employment contemplated in a year, the past performance records in the case of an old plant, the job conditions, the skill of the operator, and the repair and maintenance facilities including timely supply of spares. The main factors affecting the owning and operating costs are explained below. These are followed by a simplified approach with examples for estimating these costs. There is no substitute for experience while evaluating the plant employment costs. Therefore, the method of estimation of the hourly plant cost given in succeeding paragraphs should be taken as simplified guidelines to be modified by the experienced estimator according to the situation.

### 10.2.1 Equipment Owning Costs

It represents the cost of ownership of the equipment. These costs are incurred by the owner whether the equipment is used or not. The equipment owning costs include:

(a) Depreciation cost.
(b) Cost of capital invested.
(c) Taxes and insurance.

**Depreciation cost**  Depreciation is the loss in market value of the plant over a period of time, resulting from usage, wear and tear or age. There are several methods of calculating the annual depreciation that should be charged to the project to cover the plant capital cost. These include the straight line method, sinking fund method, declining fund method, sum of digit method and experience of owning and operating a similar plant. Exhibit 10.2 outlines various methods of determining depreciation. Depending upon the company policy, market trends and nature of usage, an appropriate method of depreciation can be adopted.

The straight line method is most commonly used for depreciation estimation. The information required is the delivered-at-site purchase cost including attachments, the residual or resale value after use, and the equipment's usage life period. The tyre replacement cost is not included in the depreciation estimation as it is dealt under operation costs.

$$\text{Annual depreciation} = \frac{\text{Delivered price} - \text{Residual value}}{\text{Ownership period in years}}$$

$$\text{Depreciation per usage hour} = \frac{\text{Annual depreciation}}{\text{Usage hour per year}}$$

Consider an example of a crawler tractor. Its purchase price is $100,000 and the assessed resale value after using for 5 years is 25% of the delivered price. This equipment is planned to operate 2000 hours per year.

Delivered price = $100,000.

Residual value = 25% of $100,000
= $25,000.

$$\text{Annual depreciation} = \frac{\$100{,}000 - \$25{,}000}{5 \text{ Years}}$$

= $15,000.

# Exhibit 10.2

## Standard Methods of Determining Depreciation

*Straight Line Method*

It pre–supposes that equipment value reduces at a uniform rate over its economical life period. For example, annual depreciation of an equipment with all-in cost of $100,000 having economic life of 5 years and the end salvage value of $10,000, can be worked out as under:

$$\text{Annual Depreciation} = \frac{\text{Equipment cost} - \text{Salvage value}}{\text{Economic life in years}}$$

$$= \frac{\$100,000 - \$10,000}{5 \text{ Years}} = 18,000$$

*Sum–Digit Method*

It enables changing high depreciation in the first year and reducing gradually, in subsequent years. Depreciation by this method, for the above referred equipment costing $100,000, can be evaluated as under:

| | | |
|---|---|---|
| Sum of digit in 5 years life | = 5 + 4 + 3 + 2 + 1 = 15 | |
| Depreciation first year | = 5/15 (100.000 – 10,000) = | $ 30,000 |
| Depreciation second year | = 4/15 (100.000 – 10,000) = | $ 24,000 |
| Depreciation third year | = $ 15,000 | $ 18,000 |
| Depreciation fourth year | = $ 10,000 | $ 12,000 |
| Depreciation fifth year | = $ 5,000 | $ 6,000 |
| | | $ 90,000 |

*Declining Balance Method*

This provides means of accelerating depreciation for tax purposes:

(a) For new equipment, annual depreciation $= \dfrac{2.0 \times \text{Remaining book value}}{\text{Economic life}}$

(b) For old equipment, annual depreciation $= \dfrac{1.5 \times \text{Remaining book value}}{\text{Economic life}}$

In the above formulae, the remaining book value = Original purchase price – Accumulated depreciation Using the previous example of new equipment costing $100,000/-,

First year depreciation $= \dfrac{2.0 \times 100000}{5} = \$40,000$

Second year depreciation $= \dfrac{2.0(100,000 - 40,000)}{5} = \$24,000$

Third year depreciation $= \dfrac{2.0(100,000 - 40,000 - 24,000)}{5} = \dfrac{2.0 \times 36,000}{5} = \$14,400$

Fourth year depreciation $= \dfrac{2.0(100,000 - 78,400)}{5} = \dfrac{2.0 \times 21600}{5} = \$8,640$

But book value at the end of 4th year = 100,000 – 78,400 – 8,640 = 14960 and salvage value at the end of 5 year is $ 10,000

Therefore, depreciation for 5th year = 100,000 – Book value at the end of 4 years
= 100,000 – 78,400 – 15,000 = $4960

And depreciation in 5th year = Nil, since full depreciation is already paid.

Hourly depreciation $= \dfrac{\text{Annual Depreciation}}{\text{Usage hours per year}}$

$= \$15000/2000$

$= \$7.50.$

The declining yearly depreciation and residual value of the equipment at the end of subsequent years works out as shown in Table 10.2.

### Table 10.2
**Declining Yearly Depreciation and Residual Value of Equipment**

| Period | Depreciation ($) | Residual book value ($) |
|---|---|---|
| On receipt | Nil | 100,000 |
| End of first year | 15,000 | 85,000 |
| End of second year | 15,000 | 70,000 |
| End of third year | 15,000 | 55,000 |
| End of fourth year | 15,000 | 40,000 |
| End of fifth year | 15,000 | 25,000 |

When assessing the value of resale after a given period, it is essential to consider the local conditions, and the physical condition of the equipment depending upon the types of job and operating conditions.

The economical life of the equipment is difficult to determine due to inherent variables affecting the operation of the plant. For example, a sound preventive maintenance programme can add to the life by a considerable amount. Generally, an indication about the life of the plant can be obtained from the manufacturers, and the these can be modified depending upon the job conditions as illustrated in Table 10.3.

### Table 10.3
**Assessment of Plant Life in Operating Hours**

| Type of plant | Favourable conditions | Average conditions | Unfavourable conditions |
|---|---|---|---|
| Crawler tractor | 15000 | 12000 | 10000 |
| Scraper | 16000 | 12000 | 8000 |
| Front-end-loader | 12000 | 10000 | 8000 |
| Dumper | 25000 | 20000 | 15000 |

**Investment costs** The costs cover interest on the money invested in equipment/plant, taxes of all types, insurances, licences and storage expenses. Rates for these costs vary with owners and locations. However, these can be estimated based on the prevailing rates at the project location.

$$\text{Hourly investment} = \frac{\text{Average investment} \times \text{Annual interest rate}}{\text{Annual usage hours}}$$

$$= \frac{(N+1)\,\text{Delivered price} \times i}{2N \times \text{Annual usage hours}}$$

where,
  $N$ = Ownership years
  $i$ = Rate of interest.

In the crawler tractor example mentioned above, consider the prevailing rates of interest as 16%, taxes 2% and other expenses 2%. The total effect of the investment costs in terms of equivalent prevailing interest rates works out to be 20%. Average hourly investment costs using straight line depreciation method can be calculated as under:

$$\text{Hourly Investment cost} = \frac{(N+1)\,\text{Delivered price} \times i}{2N \times \text{Annual usage hours}}$$

$$= \frac{(5+1) \times \$100{,}000 \times 20\%}{2 \times 5 \times 2000}$$

$$= \$6.00.$$

It is a common practice to consider insurance, taxes and storage expenses as a percentage of the yearly average investment and then calculate the investment expenses considering the cost of interests, insurances, taxes and storage as total percentage expenses of the average investment.

## 10.2.2 Equipment Operating Costs

The cost of operating the equipment/plant includes fuel costs, routine maintenance costs, major repair costs, operators' costs, tyre replacement costs, and overhead costs.

**Fuel costs** Most of the construction plants at project sites use combustion ignition engines as the prime mover. These engines require fuel. The requirement of fuel at full load can be approximately estimated from the engine fly wheel horsepower CHP rating.

Cost of fuel consumed in one hour
  = Cost per litre × Hourly fuel consumption.

Hourly fuel consumption
  = Hourly fuel consumption at full load × Operating factor.

The fuel price per litre, delivered at the site, is obtained from the local suppliers as it varies from place to place. The rate of consumption depends upon the type of engine (diesel or petrol), the state of the engine and the working conditions.

(a) Diesel engine fuel consumption per hour = 0.15 litres × rated HP × load factor.

(b) Petrol engine fuel consumption per hour = 0.22 litres × rated HP × load factor.

The load factor depends upon the operating conditions as the equipment does not continue working at full load for long. For example, a front-end-loader may operate at maximum power at the time of filling a dumper, say for 6 seconds out of a cycle time of 30 seconds. Further, a loader may work for an average of 50 minutes in one hour, and for the remaining time the operator may rest, load fuel, etc. These operating factors are determined from experience or from equipment manuals. Typical equipment operating factors under various operating conditions for some of the earth moving plants are shown in Table 10.4.

Table 10.4

**Load Factor**

| Equipment | Operating conditions | | |
|---|---|---|---|
| | Favourable | Average | Unfavourable |
| Crawler tractor | 60% | 70% | 80% |
| Scraper-self loader | 48% | 55% | 65% |
| Scraper-push loader | 40% | 50% | 60% |
| Front-end-loader | 35% | 45% | 55% |
| Bottom dumper | 30% | 40% | 50% |
| Hauler | 25% | 35% | 45% |

For example, the hourly fuel consumption of a crawler tractor rated with 250 flywheel HP, operating under average conditions (load factor 70% from Table 10.4) and diesel costing $ 0.3/litre, can be worked out as under:

Diesel consumption per hour = 0.15 × Rated flywheel HP × Load factor

= 0.15 × 250 × 0.7 litres

= 26.25 litres

Cost of hourly consumption = Diesel consumption × Rate of diesel per litre

= 26.25 litres × $0.3

= $7.88.

**Routine maintenance costs** Maintenance costs include the cost of lubricating oil, grease, filter, batteries, minor repairs, and the labour involved in performing maintenance. The quantity of lubricating oil required for lubrication can be calculated from the manufacturer's manual showing the number of hours after which the oil changing is needed. Depending upon the operating conditions, the oil changing generally varies from 50 to 200 engine running hours. Generally, the maintenance costs including service, labour (mechanic) cost and minor repairs vary with the type of equipment involved and the project environment, and these can be approximately calculated as proportion of hourly fuel cost as follows.

| Operating conditions | Hourly maintenance cost |
|---|---|
| Favourable | 1/4 Fuel cost |
| Average | 1/3 Fuel cost |
| Unfavourable | 1/2 Fuel cost |

**Major repair costs** These costs vary with the type of equipment, the condition of the plant, the prices of spare parts, the maintenance charges and the operating conditions. Generally, the cost of repairs including cost of spare parts and labour can be roughly taken as equal to the depreciation cost × repair factors. For special purpose equipment such as the rock-crushing plant, the wear and tear is more and needs detailed estimation. Similarly, for electrically operated plants such as the concrete weight-batching and mixing plant, the repair cost is less than the depreciation cost.

$$\text{Repair cost} = \text{Depreciation cost} \times \text{Repair factor.}$$

| Equipment type | Repair factor with operating conditions | | |
|---|---|---|---|
| | Favourable | Average | Unfavourable |
| Crawler equipment | 85 | 90 | 95 |
| Scraper | 85 | 90 | 105 |
| Wheeled equipment | 50 | 60 | 75 |

Repair costs vary appreciably, with the age of the equipment. The repair cost in the first year of acquiring the new equipment is far less than say in the fifth year of its operation. An approximate year-wise repair cost can be estimated using the following relationship:

$$\text{Repair cost during } n\text{th year} = \frac{n \times \text{Value to be depreciated}}{\text{Digit sum of equipment's life in years}}$$

For example, if the total value of depreciation of a wheeled equipment (repair factor = 0.75) works out as $75,000 and its life is 5 years, then the repair cost during each year of operation (working 2000 hours per year) can be estimated as under:

Total repair cost = Total depreciation × Repair factor
$\qquad\qquad\qquad$ = $75,000 × 0.75
$\qquad\qquad\qquad$ = $56,250.

| Operation year | Annual repair cost | Hourly repair cost |
|---|---|---|
| 1 | 56,250 × 1/1 + 2 + 3 + 4 + 5 = $3,750 | 3,750/2,000 = $1.875 |
| 2 | 56,250 × 2/1 + 2 + 3 + 4 + 5 = $7,500 | 7,500/2,000 = $3.750 |
| 3 | 56,250 × 3/1 + 2 + 3 + 4 + 5 = $11,250 | 11,250/2,000 = $5.625 |
| 4 | 56,250 × 4/1 + 2 + 3 + 4 + 5 = $15,000 | 15,000/2,000 = $7.500 |
| 5 | 56,250 × 5/1 + 2 + 3 + 4 + 5 = $18,750 | 18,750/2,000 = $9.375 |
| | $56,250 | |

**Manpower cost** An equipment requires operators, drivers and helpers for its operation. The equipment operators are highly skilled persons. The number of persons working on an equipment varies with the type of equipment. A dumper may have only one driven-cum-operator whereas a bulldozer will need an operator and a helper. Some companies employ operators on a regular basis as operators generally remain with the equipment even when it is idle. Depending upon the persons required per machine, the prevalent wage rates, and the facilities provided by the company, the hourly manpower costs can be calculated as shown in Table 11.2.

**Tyre costs for wheeled equipment** It is not easy to forecast the tyre life due to a large number of interacting variables. In fact there is no accurate method of determining tyre life. The tyre manufactures provide indication of tyre life but these should be taken as guidelines only. The tyre life should be assessed by experienced plant engineers. In the absence of such a facility, Table 10.5 following can be used to estimate tyre life:

Table 10.5

**Estimation of Tyre Life of Wheeled Equipment**

| Equipment | Favourable hours | Average hours | Unfavourable hours |
|---|---|---|---|
| Scraper (twin tractor) | 4000 | 3000 | 2500 |
| Scraper (single tractor) | 4000 | 3000 | 2500 |
| Scraper | 5500 | 3500 | 2500 |
| Loader | 4000 | 3000 | 2000 |
| Dumper | 4000 | 3000 | 2000 |

$$\text{Hourly tyre replacement cost} = \frac{1.15 \times \text{tyre price} \times \text{No. of tyres}}{\text{Tyre life in hours}}.$$

*Note:* (1) Reduce above costs to 80% when recapping of tyre is feasible.
(2) Above costs include about 15% for tyre repairs.

*Example* If the four tyres of an equipment, each costing $500, are replaced after 800 hours and the tyres can be recapped locally, then the hourly tyre cost can be calculated as follows:

$$= \frac{1.15 \times 4 \times \$500 \times 0.8}{800}$$

$$= \$2.3/\text{hr}.$$

## 10.2.3 Method of Estimation of Owning and Operating Costs

Hourly owning and operating cost of an equipment can be calculated, moving step by step, as listed in Exhibit No. 10.3. This Exhibit contains two solved examples.

The step-by-step approach followed is self explanatory.

### Exhibit 10.3
### Construction Equipment Costing
### Hourly Owning And Operating Cost Estimate

**Ownership Data**

| Machine Nomenclature | | Crawler Tractor | Dump Truck |
|---|---|---|---|
| A. Rated horsepower | | 250 | 215 |
| B. Ownership period (years) | | 5 | 8 |
| C. Estimated Usage (Hours/years) | | 2000 | 1500 |
| D. Ownership Usage (Total Hours) | | 10,000 | 12,000 |
| (Condition–Severe/Average/Moderate) | | Severe | Severe |

**Owning Costs**

| | | | | |
|---|---|---|---|---|
| E. Delivered Price | | | 100,000 | 80,000 |
| F. Tyres Original Cost | | | Nil | 4,000 |
| G. Delivered price less tyres (E − F) | | | 100,000 | 76,000 |
| H. Residual Value at Replacement (Expressed as % of G) | | 25% | 25,000 | 16,000 |
| I. Value to be Depreciated (G − H) | | | 75,000 | 60,000 |
| J. Depreciation per hour (I/D) | | | 7.50 | 5.00 |
| K. Interest Cost per hour $\dfrac{(B+1)}{2B} \times \dfrac{E \times \text{Rate}}{D(\text{annual})} = \dfrac{5+1}{5 \times 2} \times \dfrac{100000}{2000} \times 0.16$ | | | 4.80 | 4.56 |
| L. Taxes & Insurance per hour $\dfrac{(B+1)}{2B} \times \dfrac{E \times \text{Rate}}{D}$ | | | 1.20 | 1.14 |
| M. Owning Cost per hour (J + K + L) | | | 13.50 | 10.70 |

**Operating Costs**

| | Crawler Tractor | Dump Truck |
|---|---|---|
| N. Fule (Consumption diesel = 0.227 litres × A × Fuel factor) | 4.50 | 3.22 |
| O. Oil, Lubricant, Filters etc. (N × Service factor) | 2.25 | 1.61 |
| P. Tyre Replacement Cost (= F/tyre life) | Nil | 2.00 |
| Q. Repairs (J × Repair Factor) | 7.12 | 3.75 |
| R. Special Wears | Nil | Nil |
| S. Total Operating Cost per hour (Sum of N to R) | 13.87 | 10.58 |
| T. Total Owning and Operating Cost (M + S) | 27.37 | 21.28 |

**Manpower Costs**

| | Crawler Tractor | Dump Truck |
|---|---|---|
| U. Operator Costs per hour | 10.00 | 10.00 |
| V. Helpers Costs per hour | Nil | Nil |
| W. Total Crew Cost per hour | 10.00 | 10.00 |
| X. Total Owning & Operating Cost (T + W) | 37.37 | 31.28 |

The above includes the example of a dumper (engine rated HP 215), purchased for a delivered price of $80,000, with an assessed life of 8 years while working under severe operating conditions, at planned working of 1500 hours per year. The residual value at the end of 8 years is 20%. Depreciation is being charged on an annual basis. The overall equivalent annual expenses are interest (16%), taxes (2.0%) and other expenses (2.0%), all in terms of interest. Its tyre replacement cost is assessed as $4000. The owning and operating cost data of the crawler tractor in Exhibit 10.3 is also detailed with illustrations in Section 10.2.

## 10.3 EQUIPMENT ENGINEERING CONSIDERATIONS

Construction equipment is manufactured according to standard specifications. The manufacturer's specification sheets do enumerate equipment characteristics but these sheets only highlight aspects which the manufacturer wants the customer to know. These specification sheets hide more than what they reveal. In order to unfold hidden information, the manufacturers' manuals need to be studied critically prior to making a selection. This critical examination varies with the type of equipment. For example, guidelines given below can be followed for studying some of the typical features of a piece of equipment.

### 10.3.1 Equipment Components Specially of Earthmoring Plant

**Engine** It is the most important component of the equipment. Its special features include:

(a) *Horsepower rating* The engine flywheel HP rating provides a measure of the engine power available but this is not enough. The engine performance can best be analyzed by evaluating the available rimpull or drawbar power.
(b) *Performance curves* Since earth-moving equipment is subjected to heavy loads for short periods of time, the engine should be able to provide high torque at low engine speed (rpm). It is the flat portion of the torque curve that indicates its lugging ability.
(c) *Maintenance* In order to facilitate easy maintenance and repairs, the engine should be suitably located within the body to minimize interference with other parts. Its exterior should be clear of lines and clutters to enable easy access for servicing. Its exterior features should motivate operators to conduct routine maintenance tasks.
(d) *Warranty* The period and comprehensiveness of the manufacturers' warranty can be taken as an indicator of the soundness of quality. It is desirable that both the engine and equipment warranty should be for the same peirod, and their service is looked after by the same source.

**Transmission** Like the engine, transmission needs to be matched to the job requirement. Direct drive transmission comes in a variety of forms, starting from a simple gear mechanism to sophisticated full-range planetary power shift transmission. Direct drive is considered to be the most efficient.

**Brakes** These should be able to withstand repetitive use without much wear, and should be able to stop the equipment within a short distance. Hydraulically operated brakes are preferred to exposed brakes due to their smooth braking action, less wear and longer life.

**Steering** Power steering is preferred to manual or hydraulically-boosted manual steering due to the ease of operation. Power steering is particularly necessary for the wheeled loader and other wheeled equipment carrying heavy loads. Articulated power steering is now being employed to reduce turning circles (by literally bending the machine in the middle of long-wheel-base equipment such as motor graders,) so as to increase manoeuvrability and stability.

**Operator's cabin** Reduction in the operator's fatigue while at work can enhance his efficiency. Fatigue reduction can be achieved by making the operator comfortable with normal expenses. Some of the following operator's cabin features can improve the working conditions:

(i) Adequate cabin size with high-strength glazed and shatter-proof windows to permit unrestricted visibility, and fitted with air-conditioning devices to maintain a comfortable working temperature during all weathers.
(ii) Fully adjustable suspension seats.
(iii) Easily accessible and suitable separated control levers.
(iv) Comprehensive, promptly-readable monitoring panels, indicators, and instrument gauges.
(v) Skid-proof mounting arrangement and cabin surfaces to prevent slipping.

**Carrier** Equipment carriage mountings are of three types: crawler mounting, truck mounting, and wheel mounting. Crawler mounting is specially useful for weak pressure bearing soils. Crawler mounting exerts low ground pressure and can operate over soils having low-bearing capacity. Tracks can be made extra wide if required to overcome the special low-ground pressure condition, and its links can be treaded when increased traction is required. Because of their low speed, say 3 km/hour, crawler mounted equipment is transported on trailers. Short movements, say less then a kilometre, are possible on tracks, but highway travel is avoided to prevent damage to the pavement.

Truck mounting and wheel mounting use rubber tyres. These can move on wheels with speed. During movement they do not cause damage to the paved highway surfaces, but they cannot operate effectively over low ground pressure areas. The main difference between truck mounting and wheel mounting is that while the former requires separate engines for vehicular movement and equipment like crane operation, the latter uses the same engine for both purposes.

### 10.3.2 Standard Equipment

Standard equipment performs multipurpose tasks. Such items of equipment are manufactured by reputed firms, and are easily available in the market. They can be utilized in other projects, and can be sold easily when not required. They are also easily repairable. Unless a project justifies the purchase of a special purpose equipment, preference is given to selecting standard equipment.

## 10.3.3 Minor Equipment

Items of equipment and tradesmen's machinery each costing less than a value specified by the project management, say US $2000, can be considered as minor equipment. This includes plate compactors, impact vibrators, small pumps, power generators, workshop machinery like welding sets, tile cutting and polishing machines, plastering and spraying machines, concrete scrubbing and finishing equipment, light-duty tradesmen's tools and similar small equipment. Minor equipment frequently needs repairs. For minor equipment, stress is laid on standardization and preference in selection is given to those manufacturers who have locally established dealers for spares and service even if it amounts to paying a higher initial cost. If local service is not available, the need of having a stand-by should be given due weightage against the cost of stocking spares and remaining idle while awaiting repairs.

## 10.3.4 Repair and Maintenance Considerations

**After-sale service** Despite due care, the parts in an equipment are subject to failure. Unless immediately replaced, a broken part can delay the entire operation. It is therefore essential that after-sale service like spare parts availability repair facilities, and after-sale consultancy be ensured at the time of selection of the equipment by visiting the local dealer's/vendor's office, workshop and other service facilities. In particular, equipment manufactured by a reputed firm should be preferred.

**Standardization of equipment** If a contractor owns equipment of a particular make, and he is satisfied with its performance and dealer's service, induction of the same make equipment can facilitate reduction in spares inventory, ease of repairs and maintenance, and speedy deployment of equipment.

## 10.3.5 Safety Features

The equipment is generally manufactured to conform to the safety regulations of the country. These regulations specify the measures necessary to meet minimum safety requirements. However, some of the manufacturers do provide additional safety features. The extent of these mandatory and additional safety features vary with the types of equipment and the manufacturers, and these should be studied prior to making a selection of the equipment.

## ❏ 10.4 EQUIPMENT ACQUISITION OPTIONS

A project has multifarious activities where plant can be employed effectively and efficiently, but this does not justify purchasing plant to perform all these activities. Purchase of plant requires a heavy investment of capital, and no contractor can afford the luxury of owning all types of plant and machinery required in a project. Contractors have a number of options for acquiring plant. These include the following:

(a) Purchasing plant.
(b) Renting plant.
(c) Leasing and hire-purchase of plant.
(d) Replacing old plant.

There are many aspects which are considered while taking a decision regarding the mode of acquiring plant. These aspects are outlined in the following paragraphs:

### 10.4.1 Purchasing Plant/Equipment

Outright purchase of plant requires heavy initial investment, and is resorted to only when it can yield a rapid rate of return.

Any money spent on plant is considered as an investment, and like any other investment it must recover the capital invested along with profit. At least plant purchased must pay for its cost incurred in the project. As a general guideline, contractors own only items which are frequently required, have profit potential, yield quick adequate returns, and are absolutely necessary for project operations. Further, merely owning plant is not enough, it must be adequately backed up by spares, repairs and maintenance machinery.

There are two modes of payment for purchasing equipment, i.e. outright purchases by making full payment or credit purchases by making payments in agreed instalments. If the company has sufficient cash available, then an outright cash purchase saves interest and inconveniences of arranging sureties and guarantees. Credit purchase is less demanding on cash than outright purchase. To quote an example, a concrete pump with cash sale price in Saudi Riyals (SR) of SR 1.54 million was offered by the sales agency on credit purchase basis for down payment of SR 114,000 (SR) 114,000 at the time of delivery and the balance of SR 1,4000,000 (plus interest) in 59 equal monthly instalments of SR 33,634.

Credit payments are time related. Time is money, money yields interest. Consequently, the time and the amount of instalment payments are extremely important to determine the present value of the deal. The present value of the expected future payment is calculated by discounting these future cash in-flows using the following relationship:

$$PV = 1/(1 + k)^n$$

Where $PV$ = Present value of $1 received at the end of $n$ years at $k\%$ annual discounting rate.

For example, the present value of $1 received after two years from now, when discounted at 10% annum, is given by

$$PV = 1/(1 + 0.1)^2 = 1/1.21 = \$0.83$$

Proceeding similarly, the present value of each installment of the agreed mode of payment can be discounted to calculate the present value of the acquisition option. To quote an example, the present sale/purchase of an equipment at an agreed price of $250,000, with down payment of $100,000 and balance payment in three equal yearly instalments of $50,000 each, can be worked out as under:

$$\begin{aligned}\text{Present value} = \;&\text{Down payment} + \text{Present value of First year instalment}\\&+ \text{Present value of Second year instalment}\\&+ \text{Present value of Third year instalment}\end{aligned}$$

where,

| | | |
|---|---|---|
| Down payment | = | $100,000 |
| PV of first year instalment | = $\dfrac{\$\,50{,}000}{(1 + 0.1)^1}$ = | $45,500 |
| PV of second year instalment | = $\dfrac{\$\,50{,}000}{(1 + 0.1)^2}$ = | $41,500 |
| PV of third year instalment | = $\dfrac{\$\,50{,}000}{(1 + 0.1)^3}$ = | $37,500 |
| PV of the deal | | $224,500 |

The equipment holding of a construction company conveys its strength. Equipment after purchase becomes an asset of the company. Ownership implies better care and maintenance of the equipment and the company can exercise full control over its deployment according to its need at various project sites. The owner has the option to dispose off the equipment when not required after completion of the job. Purchase grants title of ownership to the acquiring company and it enables the company to claim various tax reliefs/benefits of capital purchases. These include investment allowances, depreciation charges and salvage values as applicable.

However, in addition to initial heavy investment, equipment ownership has certain inherent disadvantages, as well. If not fully utilized, it is more expensive than renting. With the rapid improvement in technology, the equipment may become obsolete in due course. Further, equipment repairs and maintenance costs increase with the passage of time and the continuous use of old equipment may affect the contractor's profitability and ability to compete with others having more efficient equipment.

## 10.4.2 Hiring Equipment

Increasing short-term requirement of equipment by contractors and the heavy investment needed for its purchase, has ushered in an era of equipment-hiring companies. These companies provide a wide range of equipment relieving contractors from the burden of stocking all the equipment and their spares. Their main purpose is to hold those items which have profit potential. Companies holding specialized equipment/generally take work on sub-contract rather than hiring out their machines. As a general rule, contractors hire mobile expensive equipment for short periods of time to boost output, as and when required. An economic analysis could be made initially, to decide weather to purchase or hire the equipment.

Consider, for example, a crawler tractor having 5 years' life with 2000 hours' employment capability per year and having the following associated costs:

(a) Fixed cost/hour          = $22 (Depreciation $17 + Other fixed $5)
(b) Operating variable cost/hour = $35
(c) Hire charges/hour        = $90 (including operator, repairs, maintenance, etc.).

If the equipment is utilized for '$n$' hours ($n < 2000$ hours) in the year, the contractor's yearly cost for either purchasing or hiring can be worked out as under:

Ownership cost = $22 \times 2000 + \$35 \times n$     (A).
Hiring Cost    = $90 n$     (B).

Therefore value of $n$ for equal expenses on ownership and hiring basis can be obtained by equating A = B or

$$22 \times 2000 + 35n = 90 n$$
or
$$n = 800 \text{ hours.}$$

This calculation shows that it is economical to own the equipment if the operational requirement exceeds 800 hours, and cheaper to hire the equipment if less than 800 hours. Further, if the contractor has used this machine for 600 hours in 8 months, and he contemplates full utilization in subsequent years, the maximum cost which he should be prepared to pay for owning it on hire-purchase offer, can be calculated as under:

Balance of useful life       = 10,000 hours–600 hours
                                        = 9,400 hours
Original depreciation/hour   = $17
Approximate Hire-purchase    = $17 \times 9400$
for balance amount
                                        = $159,800.

Hence, the contractor can purchase the equipment after renting it from the hiring company for eightmonths, provided the hiring company is willing to sell it for less than $159,800. Alternately, the contractor can negotiate a suitable hire-purchase offer at the time of taking the equipment on hire.

### 10.4.3 Leasing and Hire-purchase of Equipment

Both leasing and hire-purchase imply the payment of hire charges regularly for an agreed period, with the option to buy the equipment at a predetermined price after the specified period. Both the methods involve regular payments over an extended period of time but they are less demanding on the cash available than outright purchase.

When an equipment is acquired on a lease basis, the ownership title remains with the leasing company, and the acquiring company cannot get the tax and other benefit of owning the equipment. It only uses it on payment of rent. In short the lessor is the owner of the equipment and the lessee is its user. At times the leasing company provides finance for leased time (called primary period) to the equipment manufacturer, from whom then it is bought by the leasing company. Payments for the primary period is calculated by the leasing company after taking into consideration the capital cost of the equipment, less its resale value plus overheads and profit. The payment for the balance period, termed the secondary period are negotiated. They are usually small as the primary period generally, covers other costs and profits. In particular, the leasing company makes the leases agreement with the acquiring company in such a way that the acquiring company is unable to cancel the agreement during the primary period. These agreements also specify the responsibility for insurance, maintenance, servicing and repairs, so as to protect the leasing company's property during the primary period. The leasing company thus, acts as a financing company for the primary period. The quote an example, an offer given by a leasing company to a contractor for a new concrete pump costing Saudi Riyal (SR) 1.54 million is shown in Exhibit 10.4. The offer is for two alternative—one involving a monthly instalment, and the other a quarterly instalment. During both the primary and the secondary period, it has purchase offers commencing from the third year of leasing.

## Exhibit 10.4

### Plant Leasing Offer of a Concrete Pump

*Concrete Pump, PM Make, Model BSF 1409*
*Extracts From Leasing Offer By a Leasing Company*

1. Lessor: XYZ Equipment Leasing Enterprise.
2. Lessee: ABT Construction Company
3. Equipment Particulars: Concrete Pump, PM make, Model BSF 1409, Year of manufacture 1990, Boom 36 metres, performance specifications and accessories as per manufacturer's manual and supplier's quotation.
4. Purchase Price: SR 1,540,000.00
5. Lease Maturity: 3 Years starting from delivery of equipment.
6. Rental Options: Payable Monthly or Quarterly (two options)

| Payment option | No. of Instalments | Amount per Instalment |
|---|---|---|
| Monthly | 60 | SR 33,634 |
| Quarterly | 20 | SR 99,561 |

7. Purchase Options in-between leasing period:

| Purchase Date by lessee | Monthly Scheme | Quarterly Scheme |
|---|---|---|
| After 2 Years | SR 1,052,401 | SR 1,014,933 |
| After 3 Years | SR 767,568 | SR 750,568 |
| After 4 Years | SR 443,926 | SR 433,937 |
| After 5 Years | SR 77,000 | SR 77,000 |

8. Contract Other Terms: As mutually agreed.

To a contractor, leasing provides certain advantages. Leasing does not involve incurring of initial costs and it does not carry the risk of obsolescence. It is not affected with appreciation or depreciation of the prices as the contractor does not have to look for resale. It enables the contractor to pay back as the work progresses and brings in returns. Leasing is generally advantageous to the lessor also if its profit flow is comparatively small. It does not need tax exemption benefits of capital purchase. When the company's cash flow situation is unable to provide for the necessary funds or when the company is unable to arrange further borrowings for capital purchases, it is advantageous. Hire-purchase and leasing are similar as far as the regular rental payments are concerned but they differ in some ways. Generally, hiring companies provide operators, repair and spare services whereas the leasing companies do not. The hiring companies are equipment-holding companies whereas leasing companies are generally, financing companies.

## 10.4.4 Replacing Equipment

An equipment once purchased need not be kept till it becomes unserviceable. In its useful life, every equipment passes through a period of most economical operation, and there is also a period when it ceases to be economical. It is at this uneconomical point of time that an equipment should be considered for replacement. The replacement time is difficult to determine as it depends upon many cost factors such as depreciation cost, investment cost, operations cost, down-time cost, obsolescence cost, inflation and the new equipment purchase cost. Some of these cost computations require in-house records and equipment marketing experience. A replacement decision involves analysis of mathematical models incorporating a large number of variables. This analysis aims at determining the optimum time in equipment life at which the equipment should be replaced for maximizing profits or minimizing operating costs. There are a number of methods of analysing the economics of equipment replacement. A simple approach is to consider the resultant effect of replacement costs during each year of operation and identify the time which corresponds to lowest cumulative cost per hour of operation. The typical replacement costs considered during the analysis are as follows:

(a) *Depreciation cost*  The basis and method of determining depreciation is covered above. This determination of depreciation, which generally conforms to statutory requirements, should be modified to meet real-life situations.
(b) *Investment costs*  This includes the costs of capital invested, and covers expenses like interest, taxes and insurance. These cost can be assessed, say, as 15% of average investment.
(c) *Down-time costs*  Generally, equipment breakdown increases with increase of equipment age. During the breakdown period, substitute equipment has to be hired to maintain the planned production. This additional cost, required to compensate for equipment breakdown time or poor performance, is termed down-time cost.
(d) *Obsolescence cost*  The sale price of an old equipment decreases with the induction of the latest versions reflecting an improved performance. The loss in value thus, suffered by a equipment is termed obsolescence cost. It is expressed as a percentage of the original purchase price. At times, the obsolescence cost gets offset by inflationary

tendencies and the differences between the original and resale value over a short period of time gets nullified.

(e) *Replacement cost* The replacement cost is the cost incurred for acquiring an equivalent new equipment and disposing off the old one. Generally, the cost of owning new equipment increases at a rate higher than the inflationary trend.

The method of determining replacement costs is illustrated with an example of a front-end loader costing $100,000. The equipment is assessed to have a useful life of 12,000 working hours, and generally works for about 2000 hours per year. Analysis of the hourly effect of various costs, each considered separately, leads to the economical-operation time at which the plant should be considered for replacement.

The data tabulated in Exhibit 10.5 illustrates the methodology adopted for evaluating various hourly costs affecting replacement decisions. These cost are depreciation, investment, down-time and obsolescence.

*Replacement decision*—The summarized effect of costs tabulated in Exhibit 10.5 indicates an approach to determine the most economical time when the equipment should be replaced. In the given Illustration, the cost analysis shows that the economical period for holding the equipment upto is the end of three years, and after this period, the old equipment can be considered for replacement.

## 10.5 SUMMARY OF EQUIPMENT SELECTION CONSIDERATIONS

Selection of an equipment or plant system to perform an assigned task depends upon many interrelated factors. These factors, mostly covered in Chapters 9 and 10, are outlined below:

### 10.5.1 Task Considerations

— Nature of task and specifications.
— Daily or hourly forecast of planned production.
— Quantity of work and time allowed for completion.
— Distribution of work at site.
— Interference expected and interdependence with other operations.

### 10.5.2 Site Constraints

— Accessibility to location.
— Manoeuvrability at site.
— Working space restrictions.
— Altitude and weather conditions.
— Working season and working hours.
— Availability of local resources of manpower, materials and equipment.
— Availability of land, power supply and water supply for workshop and camp.
— Availability of equipment hiring, repair and maintenance facilities, locally.
— Availability of fuel, oil and lubricants.

## Exhibit 10.5
## Equipment Replacement Decision Data

| Code | Basic Data | Unit | 1 | 2 | 3 | 4 | 5 |
|---|---|---|---|---|---|---|---|
| A | Predicted sale-value (end of year) | $ | 75000 | 60000 | 45000 | 30000 | 20000 |
| B | Assessed machine utilisation | hrs | 2000 | 2000 | 2000 | 2000 | 2000 |
| C | Cum machine utilisation | hrs | 2000 | 4000 | 6000 | 8000 | 10000 |
| | *Depreciation Cost* | | | | | | |
| D | Yearly depreciation | $ | 25000 | 15000 | 15000 | 15000 | 10000 |
| E | Cum depreciation | $ | 25000 | 40000 | 55000 | 70000 | 80000 |
| F | Depreciation/hour (E/C) | $/hr | 12.5 | 10.0 | 9.17 | 8.75 | 8.00 |
| | *Investment Cost* | | | | | | |
| G | Investment (beginning of year) | $ | 100,000 | 75,000 | 60,000 | 45,000 | 30,000 |
| H | Deduct depreciation | $ | 25000 | 15000 | 15000 | 15000 | 10000 |
| I | Investment (G − H) | $ | 75000 | 60000 | 45000 | 30000 | 20000 |
| J | Average investment $\left(\frac{G+I}{2}\right)$ (during year) | $ | 87500 | 67500 | 52500 | 37500 | 25000 |
| K | Investment cost (15% per year) | $ | 13125 | 10125 | 7875 | 5625 | 3750 |
| L | Cum investment cost | $ | 13125 | 23250 | 31125 | 36750 | 40500 |
| M | Cum investment cost/Hr (L/C) | $/hr | 6.56 | 5.81 | 5.19 | 4.59 | 4.05 |
| | *Down-time Costs* | | | | | | |
| N | Assessed availability | (%) | 97.5 | 95 | 92.5 | 90 | 87.5 |
| O | Machinery not available | (%) | 2.5 | 5 | 7.5 | 10 | 12.5 |
| P | Machinery non-utilisation | hrs | 50 | 100 | 150 | 200 | 250 |
| Q | Predicted hiring charges per hour | $/hr | 30 | 32.5 | 35 | 37.5 | 40 |
| R | Down-time cost | $ | 1500 | 3250 | 5250 | 7500 | 10000 |
| S | Cum-down-time cost | $ | 1500 | 4750 | 10000 | 17500 | 27500 |
| T | Down-time cost/hour (S/C) | $/hr | 0.75 | 1.19 | 1.67 | 2.19 | 2.75 |
| | *Cost of Obsolescence on Performance* | | | | | | |
| U | —Assessed obsolescence (i) | | — | 5 | 10 | 15 | 20 |
| V | —Shortfalls with respect to new model (T × B) | hr | — | 100 | 200 | 300 | 400 |
| W | —Hiring charges per hour | $ | — | 32.5 | 35 | 37.5 | 40 |
| X | —Obsolescence costs | $ | — | 3250 | 7000 | 11250 | 16000 |
| Y | —Cum obsolesence costs | $ | — | 3250 | 10250 | 21500 | 37500 |
| Z | —Obsolescence cost per hour (Y/C) | $/hr | — | 0.81 | 1.71 | 2.69 | 3.75 |
| | Total replacement costs/hr (F + M + T + Z) | $/hr | 19.81 | 17.81 | 17.74 | 18.22 | 18.55 |

### 10.5.3 Equipment Suitability

— Type of equipment considered suitable for the task.
— Make, models and sizes of special purpose, and general purpose equipment available that can handle the task.
— Production capability, serviceability condition and delivery time of each equipment available.
— Equipment already owned by the contractor.
— Usefulness of the suitable equipment available for other and future tasks.

### 10.5.4 Operating Reliability

— Manufacturer's reputation.
— Equipment components, engine-transmission, brakes, steering operator's cabin.
— Use of standard components.
— Warranties and guarantees.
— Vendor's after-sale service.
— Operator's acceptability, adaptability and training requirements.
— Structural design.
— Preventive maintenance programme.
— Safety features.
— Availability of fuel, oil and lubricants.

### 10.5.5 Maintainability

— Ease of repair and maintenance.
— Vendor's after-sale service, repairs, spares and maintenance.
— Availability of spare parts.
— Standardization consideration.

### 10.5.6 Economic considerations

— Owning costs.
— Operating costs.
— Re-sale or residual value after use.
— Replacement costs of existing equipment.

### 10.5.7 Commercial Considerations

— Buy second-hand or new equipment.
— Rent equipment.
— Hire-purchase equipment.
— Purchase on lease.

Equipment selection analysis considers various factors but not necessarily limited to the above. It leads to alternative choices for acquiring the required equipment. It is then for the management to make a selection decision of the equipment after careful consideration of all the facts. It may be noted that in most cases, the final equipment selection decision is likely to be a compromise between what is ideally required and what can actually be obtained economically.

# CHAPTER 11

# Planning Construction Costs

Cost accounting and financial accounting systems make use of the same income and expenditure data, but there is a basic difference between them. Cost accounting is an internal accounting system designed for managing costs in an organization. It provides information for controlling costs whereas financial accounting is a method of presentation of the financial status of the organization to the shareholders, legal authorities or financial institutions who are not directly involved in the day-to-day running of the organization. Cost planning forms a part of the cost accounting system.

Construction cost planning encompasses planning judgement, costing techniques and accounting discipline for developing standard costs, financial forecasts, project budget, and cost control measures with the ultimate goal of achieving project profit/cost objectives. It uses standard cost concepts for costing work-packages, work-items or activities. The work–packages' standard costs facilitate planning and controlling of costs. Financial forecasts indicate the trends of expected sales, production expenses, profit and cash flow at specified intervals of time. Project budget quantifies the project plan in monetary terms and outlines the financial plan for implementation.

This chapter describes the cost classification and nature of production costs. It explains the methodology for establishing resource costing standards, work-package standard cost and standard sale price. It outlines the 'S' curve forecasting technique. The approach for making a budget is outlined in Chapter 12, and the methodology for controlling cost is covered in Chapter 15.

## ❑ 11.1 CLASSIFICATION OF CONSTRUCTION COSTS

The cost of a work-unit which may be an activity, a work-item or a work-package is composed of one or more cost elements. These cost elements include labour costs, material costs, plant and machinery costs, administration costs and other expenses. The process of cost estimation (termed costing) would be simple if it were possible to directly correlate various cost elements to the activity that incurs them. These costs can then provide a clear picture of the construction costs and thus simplify planning, forecasting, accounting and controlling costs. But it is not always possible to precisely define various cost elements activity-wise. In order to identify the costs associated with an activity, construction costs generally referred to as production costs are categorized into 'Direct costs' and 'Indirect costs' or 'Overheads'.

$$\text{Production cost} = \text{Direct cost} + \text{Indirect cost}$$

Direct costs are costs that can be correlated to a specific activity or a work-item which is being done or produced. All other costs that are incurred to accomplish the activity or the work-item but cannot be correlated directly, fall in the category of indirect costs.

The breakdown of the construction cost elements and their interrelationship is shown in Fig. 11.1. These costs are built up as follows:

Figure 11.1

**Construction Costs Breakdown**

| Direct Costs Breakdown | | Indirect Costs Breakdown | | Total Costs Breakdown |
|---|---|---|---|---|
| Direct Materials Cost | + | Indirect Materials Cost | = | Materials Costs |
| + | | + | | + |
| Direct Labour Cost | + | Indirect Labour Cost | = | Production/Labour Cost |
| + | | + | | + |
| Direct Expenses' | + | Indirect other Expenses | = | Other Expenses |
| = | | = | | = |
| Direct Costs | + | Indirect Costs | = | Total Costs |

| Cost Elements | Amount |
|---|---|
| (i) Direct material costs | A |
| (ii) Direct labour costs | B |
| (iii) Direct other expenses | C |
| (iv) Direct Costs (A + B + C) | D |
| (v) Indirect Costs | E |
| (vi) Total Production Costs (D + E) | F |

Production costs are initially estimated for each item of work as stated in the scope of the project work. These are listed under bill of quantities, and can be combined or split up to determine the cost of each work-package, using the technique described earlier in Chapter 3.

### 11.1.1 Direct Costs

These are costs of materials, labour and other expenses which can be identified with the execution of an item of work or activity.

Direct cost of permanent work item = Direct materials cost + Direct labour cost
+ Other direct expenses

**Direct materials cost** These cover all costs connected with materials which become a permanent part of the project. These can be measured and costed item-wise. For example, materials used in concrete work of a specified concrete mix can be both measured, and its cost allocated to the concreting activity in terms of costs of cement, sand, aggregate, admixture and water, per cubic meter of ready-mix concrete. The direct materials cost generally includes the following:

- Purchase costs, ex-factory or specified delivery location.
- Transportation costs including freight by rail, road, ocean, custom clearance, insurance and handling charges till arrival at site, as applicable.
- Site manufacturing and fabrication costs to transform raw materials into products for use in permanent works. Examples of such items are—doors and windows fabrication, steel reinforcement fabrication, cement tiles and manufacturing hollow blocks. In order to make a comparison with the rates of these materials prevalent in local markets, their site overheads can also be included into direct manufacturing and fabricating costs.

It is not necessary to have detailed costing of all types of materials that go into the production of an item of work or activity. Minor material items like screws, nails and trademen's tools can best be grouped under one head titled 'minor materials and tools' under the indirect costs.

**Direct labour costs** It covers net expenses for procurement, maintenance, and wages of foremen and all category of workers employed at the work site for the execution of an item of project. These expenses include:

- Basic wages.
- Overtime and allowances.
- Procurement expenses including recruitment and conveyance at site.
- Benefits and statutory regulation compensation expenses such as earned leave, provident funds, gratuity, bonus, insurance, medical, etc. It also covers expenditure on accommodation and mess amenities if these are not covered under overheads.

Another method for evaluating direct labour cost is to cover only salary and wages under direct cost and consider the balance expenses under indirect labour costs.

**Other direct expenses** These include all other expenses on account of services rendered, which can be directly attributed to and clearly identified with the execution of an activity or work-item. Examples of such expenses are:

- Special purpose plant and machinery costs, such as owning and operating costs of ready-mix concrete production, transportation and placing equipment.
- Sub-contracted activities.
- Hired resources costs for execution of specified permanent work, like excavator for trenches.
- Temporary activity required for a specific work like erecting a scaffolding platform for plaster work.
- Special technical consultant services for architecture, designing, investigation, etc. when these are designated as separate activities.
- Investigation/trials necessary to establish procedures for undertaking the construction of a given work or activity, such as making concrete circular wall for a water treatment plant, or driving of foundation piles.

## 11.1.2 Indirect Costs

Indirect costs include all costs which are attributable to a given project but cannot be identified with the performance of a specific activity or a work-package. In other words, all costs other than direct costs are covered under indirect costs.

In construction projects, indirect costs or overheads constitute a significant amount when compared to the direct costs. The range of indirect costs, depending upon the nature of the project, may vary from 7.5% to 35% of the total costs. To quote an example, the indirect costs of a typical small-size building construction project are outlined in Table 11.1.

Table 11.1

**Indirect Costs of a Typical Small-size Building Construction Project**

| Sl. No. | Types of Indirect Costs (Other than Direct Costs) | Percentage Mark up of Direct Cost |
|---|---|---|
| 1. | Project supervisor and other indirect labour including management costs | 5% |
| 2. | Project office expenses | 3% |
| 3. | Design and drawing costs | 2% |
| 4. | General purpose plant and machinery cost | 3% |
| 5. | Finance, risk management and contingencies | 4% |
| 6. | Accommodation, utility services and furnishing | 4% |
| 7. | Tools and minor equipment | 2% |
| 8. | Home office overheads and public liabilities | 3% |
|  |  | 26% |

The indirect costs cover a wide range of items. To quote an illustration, the items grouped under indirect costs of a multinational construction company are listed in Exhibit 11.1. The items of indirect costs depend upon the type and size of the project. A typical breakdown of these costs grouped on a functional basis is shown in Exhibit 11.2. In general, from a performance consideration indirect costs can be broadly divided as follows:

**(a) Production overheads** These include all indirect manpower, indirect materials and other indirect expenses incurred by each production responsibility centre.

| Nature of costs | Examples |
| --- | --- |
| (1) Indirect manpower costs | Salary and wages of supervisors and other indirect workers. |
| (2) Indirect material costs | Tradesmen's tools, minor equipments and consumable materials. |
| (3) Indirect other expenses | General purpose plant hiring costs. |

**(b) External support services costs** These cover all indirect manpower, indirect materials and other expenses of the functional set-ups concerned with providing technical and logistic support to the production centres. Examples are as follows:

(1) Technical design and quality control services.
(2) Materials-at-site manufacturing services.
(3) Equipment supply services.
(4) Personnel and security services.
(5) General services including temporary works and camp utility services.

**(c) Administration overheads** These contain indirect manpower, indirect materials and other expenses incurred by the project management for the direction, control and administration of the project. The costs covered under this head include:

(1) Office management costs.
(2) Planning and coordination management costs.
(3) Technical management costs.
(4) Marketing, costing and contract management costs.
(5) Resources management costs.
(6) Finance and risk management costs.

**(d) Home office overheads** These overheads represent the expenses relating to the operations and services rendered by the home-office. These costs include the consultant's fee, legal expenses, licensing charges, visits, entertainment taxes, insurances and a share of the home-office running expenses. Home-office overheads are specified by the corporate management.

The above functional grouping and its breakdown are not rigid. These are guidelines and can be suitably modified in line with corporate policy and project characteristics.

### 11.1.3 Indirect Costs Behaviour

An estimator, at the time of costing, computes all the indirect costs in detail or evaluates by using predetermined company norms. The estimator adds these indirect costs to the direct costs for calculating the final production cost. But this is not adequate for planning, budgeting and controlling costs. In order to analyze the cost behaviour, a planner or the cost accountant further splits up each item of indirect cost into three broad categories, i.e. variable costs, fixed costs and semi-variable costs.

(a) Variable costs tend to vary directly with the volume of production, i.e. work done or output. No production means no cost. Cost rises as the volume of production increases. These costs change at a constant rate (assumed) to changes in the volume of production as shown in below:

**Nature of Variable Indirect Costs**

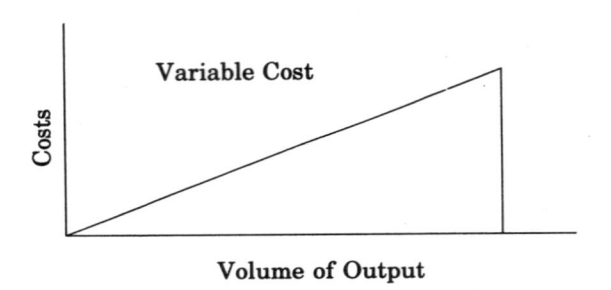

Examples of indirect variable costs are telephone running expenses, camp messing expenses and office stationery expenses.

(b) Fixed costs do not show any appreciable fluctuations with changes in production levels. These costs are either one-time costs like the camp construction cost or periodic costs such as supervisor's salary for a period of six months, or are monthly recurring expenses like monthly rent for project office and monthly depreciation for project construction equipment.

**Nature of Fixed Indirect Costs**

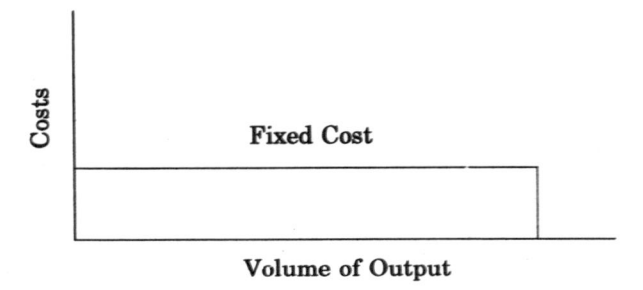

## Exhibit 11.1

**Typical Indirect Costs Classification of a Multinational Construction Company**

1. *Supervisor*—It includes construction management and related staff.
2. *Indirect personnel*—It includes logistics, clerks, security, site cleaning, warehousing, maintenance of equipment, (except personnel involved in temporary facilities construction, operation, maintenance and dismantling).
3. *Temporary site facilities*—It includes supply, installation (Including labour) and dismentalling of temporary facilities such as, but not limited to;

    — Furnished offices to be installed at the job site.
    — Fencig of equipment, warehouse and storage areas.
    — Shops for fabrication or maintenance purposes.
    — Installation of temporary utility services network (electrical, industrial water potable water sewer, telecommunication & air).
    — Sanitary facilities.
    — First aid facilities.
    — Construction of temporary roads, fences, car parks. Necessary storage facilities for fuel, water.
    — Safety materials.

4. *General field expenses*—It consists of operating costs associated with temporary facilities such as but not limited to;

    — Supply of stationary, documentation, photography, cleaning products, pharmaceutical products.
    — Communication (Phone, telex, postage).
    — Utilities consumption.
    — Administrative permits, medical checks.
    — Other field office expenses.

5. *Equipment costs*—It covers costs associated (except transportation cost) with constructional equipment, vehicles, cars, spare parts, in the entire duration of project.
6. *Small tools & consumables*—It includes costs of fuel, labricants, small tools, wearing parts and consumables.
7. *Housing costs*—It covers supply, istallation and dismantalling of camp and related facilities (kitchen, temporary roads, utility materials.)
8. *Catering costs*— It includes catering lundeing and camp operating costs.
9. *Mobilisation and demobilisation*—It caters for personnel equipment, temporary facility item, small tools, consumables, camp structure and other facilities.
10. *Other facilities*—Overhead and Profit:

    — Expenses such as company taxes, insurances, home-office services, overhead related to contract/field.
    — Contingency margin and profit.

## Exhibit 11.2

### Indirect Costs: Functional Breakdown
### (Where not covered under direct costs)

1. *Client consultant requirements*—Manpower, accommodation, furniture and fittings, telephone, stationery, equipment, operating and maintenance, survey equipment, photography, transport, incidental expenses.

2. *Head office expenses—Connected with project work*—Planning and co-ordinating, consultancy services, visits, entertainments, bank gurantees, bank service charges, taxes and incidental expenses.

3. *Project office expenses*—Accommodation, furniture and fittings, telephone, stationery, equipment, operation and maintenance.

4. *Establishments expenses*—Field supervisors, technical staff and workers, materials management staff and workers, plant and machinery management staff and workers, administration staff, workers and managers.

5. *Personnel management costs*—Mobilisation and demobilisation, stationery expenses, medical, missing, camp maintenance, personnel carriers, security, amenities and welfare, entertainment, insurances, incidental and protective clothing.

6. *Technical management costs*—Designs and drawings, project consultancy, data processing, site laboratory and testing, technical library, sub-contracted workers expenses, site surveying, incentive scheme, tie crashing, formwork, drawing office equipment, after completion maintenance, site clearance.

7. *Materials management costs*—Inventroy holding costs, site materials handling costs, tradesment tools and minor equipment costs, minor materials costs, losses/wastages costs, load carriers expenses, dumarages/breakages, insurance and demobilisation.

8. *Plant and machinery management*—(deduct for costs catered elsewhere)—Mobilisation costs, owning costs, operating costs, fuel/oil/lubricant costs, repairs costs, spare inventory costs, operators and drivers costs, statutory expenses, personnel carriers expenses and demobilisation.

9. *Finance and risk management costs*—Bid bond, performance bond, work insurance, social security, contribution, unforeseen fines and penalties, excalation, bank service charges, bank gurantees, local taxes.

10. *Temporary work and services*—Office accommodation, camp accommodation, external utility services (installations and running expenses), roads and fencing, furniture and fittings, kitchen equipment and utencials, messing and lodging, sign boards and traffic signs, site cleaning and wastages disposal, indirect site works and services and dismentalling and demobilisation.

(c) Semi-variable costs are partly fixed and partly variable in nature. Examples of these are telephone expenses which consist of fixed installation expenses, and variable operating expenses which vary with the volume of work or production activities:

**Nature of Semi-variable Indirect Costs**

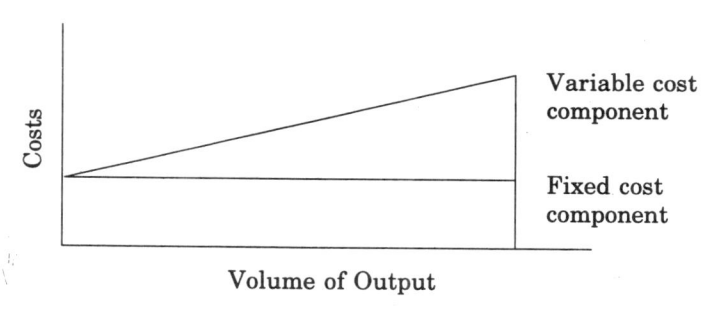

It is not always feasible to clearly demarcate indirect costs into variable and fixed categories as many cost behaviour patterns are possible. There are indirect costs which may display rising mixed behaviour patterns. For example, when material prices get discounted with an increase in the order quantity. But for apportioning indirect costs, it is necessary to divide each item of indirect cost broadly into production-related variable indirect costs and periodic or time-related fixed indirect costs.

## ❏ 11.2 UNIT-RATE COSTING STANDARDS OF RESOURCES

The term 'costing' stands for the method of estimation of production costs. Barring a few exceptions, for estimating direct and indirect costs of a work-package or work-item, the resources of men, equipment and materials are computed as under:

Labour cost = Labour effort in man-hours × Standard labour hourly rate.

Equipment utilization cost = Equipment utilization hour × Standard equipment hourly rate.

Materials cost = Materials consumption quantity × Standard materials unit price.

Methodology for determining labour productivity standards, equipment output standards and materials consumption standards is covered in Chapters 7 to 10. The technique for developing a standard labour hourly rate, equipment hourly rate and materials unit price is covered in subsequent paragraphs.

### 11.2.1 Labour Standard Hourly Rate

Direct labour, employed on monthly or daily wages, is costed on an hourly rate basis. Complete labour hourly standard rate includes net expenses incurred on procurement, wages, benefits and statutory costs. The labour hourly standard rate is determined for each category of direct labour employed at the site of production work. For costing purposes, direct labour is categorized into foremen/supervisors, highly skilled, skilled, semi-skilled and unskilled. In some firms, semi-skilled and unskilled are treated at par, and both are grouped into the category of general helpers. The method of calculation of labour hourly standard rate involves the determination of annual labour estimated cost and the number of productive hours worked in the year.

$$\text{Labour hourly standard cost} = \frac{\text{Annual estimated labour cost}}{\text{Annual productive hours}}$$

To quote an example, consider the case of an Indian expatriate skilled worker employed in Saudi Arabia on a monthly wage of Saudi Riyal (SR) 750 who is being provided free accommodation, food and medical aid. This labourer is employed on two years' contract; he gets leave at the rate of 15 days per year after the completion of his contract and his gratuity and other entitlements are governed by the Saudi Labour Law. The hourly standard rate for this worker can be calculated as follows:

### (a) Estimating annual productive hour

| | | |
|---|---|---|
| Calendar days in a year | = | 365 |
| Less: Weekly holidays on Friday at the rate of one per week | = | 52 |
| : Public holidays as per Saudi Labour Law excluding Friday | = | 10 |
| : Reduced working time during Ramadan month at 2 hours per day for 24 days (assessed) i.e. $\frac{2 \text{ hours}}{8 \text{ hours}} \times 24$ days | = | 6 |
| : Unproductive time during bad weather (assumed) | = | 17 |
| : Casual leave/sickness (assumed) | = | 10 |
| Net working days in a year | = | 270 days |
| Therefore, annual productive working hours at 8 hours per working day (8 × 270) | = | 2160 hours |

### (b) Estimating Total annual expenses

| | | |
|---|---|---|
| A. Annual wage at SR 750 for 12 months | = | 9000 |
| B. 50% of recruitment expenses at SR 500 for two years (0.5 × 500) | = | 250 |
| C. Airfare one way (first year mobilization and second year de-mobilization on completion of contract) | = | 1,250 |
| D. Messing at SR 300 per month | = | 3,600 |
| E. Medical (assessed from past statistics) | = | 450 |
| F. Accommodation at SR 100 per month | = | 1,200 |
| G. Annual leave equivalent ½ month's wage | = | 375 |

## Planning Construction Costs

| | | |
|---|---|---|
| H. Gratuity equivalent ½ month's wage | = | 375 |
| I. Insurance and social security contribution | = | 600 |
| J. Other expenses like sports, entertainment, etc. | = | 1,200 |
| Total expenses | | =18,300 |

Therefore, labour hourly standard rate

$$= \frac{\text{Annual estimate cost}}{\text{Annual productive hours}}$$

$$= \frac{\text{SR } 18,300}{2160 \text{ hours}}$$

= SR 8.45 per hour; say SR 8.50 per hour.

Proceeding similarly, the hourly labour rate of various categories can be computed easily by using an hourly labour rate as shown in Table 11.2. Then labour rates can be expressed in different forms as under:

$A$ = Hourly labour rate of a crew

$B$ = Average hourly labour rate per worker of a crew

$B = \frac{A}{N}$

Where $A$ = Hourly labour rate of the crew
and $N$ = Number of workers of the crew

$C$ = Crew cost per unit of work

$C = \frac{A}{Q}$

Where $A$ = Hourly Labour rate of the crew
and $Q$ = Quantity of work done in one hour.

For example, if a crew consisting of two carpenters and one helper can fix 10 square meters of slab form work in 8 hours, and the labour hourly rate of a carpenter is SR 8.50 and a helper is SR 6.95, then

$A$ = Hourly labour rate of the crew
 = 2 × 8.50 + 1 × 6.95
 = SR 23.95.

$B$ = Average hourly rate per worker of the crew
 = $\frac{A}{N}$
 = $\frac{23.95}{3}$
 = SR 7.98.

### Table 11.2

### Hourly Labour Rate Calculation Sheet

| Serial Code | Cost Head | Foreman | Highly Skilled | Skilled | Unskilled |
|---|---|---|---|---|---|
| | | \multicolumn{4}{c}{Personnel Category — Annual Expenditure in Saudi Riyals} | | | |
| A | Annual wages | 18,000 | 12,000 | 9,000 | 6,000 |
| B | Recruitment expenses at SR 500 for two years employment contract. | 250 | 250 | 250 | 250 |
| C | Airfare one way (first year mobilisation and second year de-mobilisation) | 1,250 | 1,250 | 1,250 | 1,250 |
| D | Messing at SR 300 per month for 12 months | 3,600 | 3,600 | 3,600 | 3,600 |
| E | Medical assessed from past statistics | 450 | 450 | 450 | 450 |
| F | Accommodation at site | 2,400 | 1,200 | 1,200 | 1,200 |
| G | Annual leave equivalent half month wages | 750 | 500 | 375 | 250 |
| H | Severance pay equivalent half month wages | 750 | 500 | 375 | 250 |
| I | Insurance and social security | 750 | 600 | 600 | 600 |
| J | Other expenses such as sports, entertainment, incentive etc. | 1,500 | 1,200 | 1,200 | 1,200 |
| K | Total Annual Expenses (Sum of A to J) | 29,700 | 21,550 | 18,300 | 15,050 |
| L | Annual Productive Hours | 2,160 | 2,160 | 2,160 | 2,160 |
| M | Labour hour (K÷L) | 13.75 | 9.98 | 8.47 | 6.97 |
| | Standard rate (say) | 13.75 | 10.00 | 8.50 | 7.00 |

$$C = \text{Crew cost per unit of work} = \frac{\text{Labour rate per hour}}{\text{Output quantity per hour}}$$

$$= \frac{23.95}{10/8}$$

$$= \text{SR } 19.16/M2 \text{ of form-work.}$$

It may be noted that various cost heads listed in Table 11.2 provide a simplified approach. These cost heads and their corresponding basis for computing annual expenditure vary with the company accounting system and the prevalent statutory regulations at the project site. In some cases, where provisions are made for expenditures like overtime, tool cost, bonus, pension, insurance and taxes, the calculation of hourly labour rate becomes a laborious process. Further, it is not necessary to account for all expenses while calculating direct labour hourly rate. Some companies who employ labour supplied through sub-contractors, have predetermined hourly labour rates. Some other companies consider monthly salary and wages only under labour direct hourly rate and account expenditure like mobilization, housing and statutory benefits under indirect labour costs.

### 11.2.2 Equipment Hourly Standard Rate

The method of estimation of the equipment hourly rate is covered in Chapter 10. In brief, this involves the estimation of equipment owning and operation costs:

Equipment rate per hour = Owning cost per hour + operating cost per hour.
Where, Owning cost = Depreciation
and Operating cost = Fuel cost + Maintenance cost + Major repair cost + Operator's cost + Tyre replacement cost for rubber tyred equipment.

The above mathematical approach for determining the equipment hourly standard rate can at best be treated as a guideline as there are many factors, determinate as well as indeterminate, which affect the equipment owning and operating costs. These factors include the state of the equipment (old or new), corporate capitalization policy, sources of funding for the new purchase, site delivered price, purchase implication on corporate taxes, economical plant life in years, resale value, annual operational hours contemplated, past performance record in the case of old equipment, job conditions, skill of the operator and the repair and maintenance facilities available. Equipment utilization rate also depends upon its ownership. This rate will be different if it is taken from the client's own plant than if it is hired from the market. There is no substitute to the experience of the estimator. Therefore, while establishing hourly standards for an item of equipment, the mathematically estimated equipment utilization rate is suitably modified by the experienced estimator according to the situation.

### 11.2.3 Materials Standard Price

Materials standard price is defined as the estimated all-in price of the unit quantity of an item, delivered at the project site. This all-in price includes price at source, wastage costs, transportation costs up to site, and taxes involved. Site storage and handling costs from site warehouse to construction sites are covered under indirect costs.

The purchase price of each item can be ascertained by inviting quotations and then concluding a supply sub-contract with the selected supplier. Some items can be priced from standard price catalogues, commercial cost guides and past experience. Although, enquiries regarding the purchase price are made by the estimator at the tender stage, the prices vary from time to time. The purchase price depends upon many considerations such as quantity required, lot-size of each delivery, delivery dates, specifications, shelf-life and payment terms. The true picture of the purchase price can only be known after the quotations are received for each item, but this is time consuming and may not be feasible specially, when the standards are to be set up at the stage of project planning. Therefore, direct materials standard price can best be estimated by the project materials manager, who in due course is required to control these prices.

The following needs to be noted:
(a) The materials standard price is fixed and does not change with market fluctuations. These fixed price standards simplify the estimation, planning, budgeting and control of material costs. The difference between the standard price and the actual price is analyzed at the time of accounting costs.
(b) It is not necessary to evaluate the standard price of each item. The standard price should be established for major high value A and B categories of materials, the ABC materials classification system is covered in Chapter 8.
(c) Consumable materials like screws, nails, tools, etc. need not be individually priced. These can best be grouped under a separate accounting head of indirect materials, and charged at a predetermined percentage of labour cost, direct material cost, prime cost or direct cost.
(d) In the case of fixing the standard price for site manufactured or site fabricated materials like readymix concrete, fabricated steel enforcement, manufactured doors and windows, precast masonry blocks and other concrete elements, the standard price should also include site overheads so that the end product's price can be compared with the prevailing marketing prices. To quote an example, the pricing methodology for establishing the standard price for the site manufactured readymix concrete at break-even is depicted in Table 11.3. This technique is outlined in Section 11.2.4.

## 11.2.4 Break-even Analysis

The method of determining prices of services rendered will depend upon the nature of service rendered. For example, the service centre like a 'materials transporting centre' will have to go into service costing to calculate charges per km of the product transported, and the 'equipment supplying centre' will need to cost the owning and operating costs to determine the hiring charges.

The price of site manufactured materials can be determined by computing the break-even point. The break-even point (BEP) marks the lowest level at which the production cost and sale value of deliveries are equal, resulting in a no profit no loss situation, and it is the point at which the fixed costs are totally absorbed. Consider the example of the supply of readymix concrete by its production centre to the Foundation Construction Centre. The Readymix Concrete Production Centre is set up to supply 2500 m$^3$ per month working 10 hours per working day. The concrete production cost data for 2500 m$^3$ delivering is shown in Table 11.3. This cost consists of variable costs (V) and fixed costs (F), where

$V$ = Variable cost of one month production
   = Variable cost per m$^3$ × Quantity manufactured and delivered
   = $v \times q$

Planning Construction Costs 355

Table 11.3

## Site Manufactured Readymix Concrete
### Cost of Production of One Cubic Metre Concrete

A-*Material Cost*

| Mix-Design | kgs | Wastage | Quantity | Rates per kg | Cost (SR) per m³ | Variable per m³ | Fixed per month for 2500 m³ |
|---|---|---|---|---|---|---|---|
| 1. Cement | 350 | 1% | 353.5 | 0.230 | 81.30 | | |
| 2. 3/4" aggregate | 780 | 3% | 803.5 | 0.013 | 10.45 | | |
| 3. 3/4" aggregate | 360 | 3% | 371.0 | 0.013 | 4.80 | | |
| 4. Washed sand | 320 | 5% | 336.0 | 0.018 | 6.05 | | |
| 5. White sand | 335 | 5% | 352.0 | 0.012 | 4.20 | | |
| 6. Water | 211 | 15% | 243.0 | 0.005 | 1.20 | | |
| | | | | | 108.00 | 108.00 | |

B-*Manufacturing and Transportation Expenses*

| | | | |
|---|---|---|---|
| 1. Manpower costs (all permanent categories) | 17.30 | | 43350 |
| 2. Repair & maintenance (based on past records) | 10.05 | 10.05 | |
| 3. Oil, diesel & lubricant (based on past records) | 3.90 | 3.90 | |
| 4. Administration costs | 3.15 | | 7875 |
| 5. Insurance | 0.60 | | 900 |
| 6. Contingencies | 2.00 | | 5000 |
| 7. Depreciation | 5.00 | | 12500 |
| Cost of Production and transportation in SR | 150.00 per m³ | 121.95 per m³ | 69625 per month |

Note: The above costing is based on monthly supply of 2500 m³ concrete installed capacity, working 8 hours per working day, with other matching resources.

$F$ = Fixed cost per month
 = Monthly fixed expenditure on overheads including supervision, equipment depreciation, insurance, operators & drivers costs and other indirect expenses

$S$ = Sale value for one month production
 = sale price per m³ concrete × Quantity delivered
 = $p \times q$

Then, at break-even, say for 2500 m³ concrete supply,

$$S = V + F$$
$$\text{Or, } p \cdot q = v \cdot q + F$$
$$\text{Or, } p = v + \frac{F}{q}$$

Therefore, price/m³ ($p$) to break-even for monthly 2500 m³ delivery with variable cost of SR per m³ and fixed cost of SR per month is:

$$p = \text{Variable cost/m}^3 + \frac{\text{Fixed Costs}}{\text{Quantity delivered}}$$

$$= \text{SR } 150$$

Note that budgeted sale price is estimated for assumed most frequently occuring lowest level of deliveries. Higher volume of delivery can thus yield marginal profit to cater for contingencies.

Break-even analysis (Fig. 11.2) can also be used to establish a relationship among the three variables, i.e. sales price, production volume and profit and it can highlight the effect of changes in any of these parameters, but with certain limitations. These include:

(a) Break-even analysis assumes that all costs can be categorised into fixed and variable. This in practice is difficult. Further, the concept of variability varies with situation, the break-even analysis for a given situation may not hold good for another similar situation.
(b) Break-even analysis assumes that the fixed cost and the rate of variable cost of each unit of production remains constant even with the rise in production volume, though in practice this may not be true. Generally, these assumed linear relationships of various parameters may take the shape of curves instead of straight lines.
(c) Break-even analysis assumes one type of production, but in practice, each activity

Figure 11.2

**Break-even Analysis to Establish a Relationship Between Sales Price, Production Volume and Profit.**

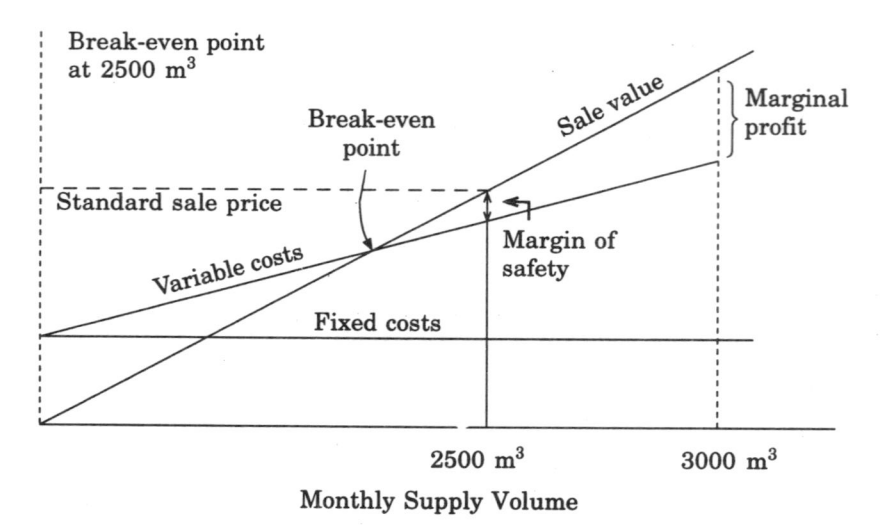

has a product-mix, and a construction project consists of wide and varied type of activities. In construction practices, break-even analysis should be viewed as guidelines for decision-making.

## ☐ 11.3 WORK–PACKAGE STANDARD COST

A work-package comprises activities. Each work-package contains identifiable, quantifiable, measurable and costable packages of work. In the process of plan development, each work–package is assigned its performance objectives generally stated in terms of its completion period, standard cost and standard sale price. The primary purpose of standardizing work–package cost is to:

- Freeze the expected production cost under operating conditions with normal facilities.
- Account the costs being incurred during the execution stage.
- Compare the actual cost with the budgeted cost for corrective action.
- Forecast the future costs.

Further, where feasible the standard costs should be developed jointly by the estimating, planning, financing and resources accounting staff, all working under the directions of the project manager. Ultimately it is the project manager who has to accept and live with these standards. The concept behind standardizing costs, and the method of determining the work–package standard cost and the standard sale price are outlined in subsequent paragraphs.

### 11.3.1 Standard Cost Concept

The standard cost of a work-package, a work-item or an activity represents its predetermined production cost objective. While the term cost relates to the production cost, the concept of 'standard' varies with the purpose for which the standard is established. The commonly used cost standards encountered in the construction industry are:

(a) *Basic cost standards (or norms)*—These are production cost standards developed by a firm using its past experiences or time and motion studies, with all–in costs being priced at the then prevailing rates. Some of the government construction agencies and established contracting firms publish their basic cost standards in the form of 'Standard schedule of rates'.
(b) *Currently attainable standards*—These are standards developed by updating basic cost standards so as to convert the basic production costs into currently attainable production costs standard.
(c) *Ideal cost standards*—These represent the estimated production costs for an activity, work–package or work–item assuming the most efficient use of present or planned resources and facilities.
(d) *Normal cost standards*—These standards reflect the general production costs valid for longer periods of time as compared to short-period costs defined by currently attainable standards.

Standard costs, on the other hand, stand for the expected average production cost of a work–package, activity or work–item of a specific project, assessed at the project planning stage, adopting a planned method of execution of work, using planned resources, allowing normal delays and wastage while operating efficiently under the prevailing working conditions. These become the cost objectives. It may be noted that the standard costing methodology is similar to the method of estimation of cost at the pre–contract stage. The main difference is that the tendered costs are estimated at the pre–contract stage by the estimator and the standard costs are established by the project management after the award of the contract by reviewing the earlier tendered costs, as it is based on the production method proposed to be adopted and not on the pre–contract stage assumed production method.

## 11.3.2 Standard Costing Methodology

The production cost of a work-package in a standard work–unit can be estimated using the following relationships:

| | |
|---|---|
| Production cost | = Direct cost + Indirect cost. |
| where: | |
| Direct cost | = Direct labour cost + Direct material costs + Direct equipment utilization cost + Other direct expenses. |
| Direct labour cost | = Work quantity × Workers' productivity standard × Labour standard hourly rate. |
| Direct materials cost | = Work quantity × Material consumption standard × Material standard unit price. |
| Direct equipment expenses | = Work quantity × equipment output standard × Equipment standard hourly employment costs. |
| Other direct expenses | = Remaining direct expenses not covered above. |
| Indirect costs | = Apportioned variable overheads + Apportioned fixed overheads. |

The expected average production costs of a work–package under operating conditions with facilities functioning normally is termed its standard cost. The standard cost of production of a work-package can preferably be determined in terms of its 'Work-unit', i.e. $m^3$ is taken as a work-unit for costing concreting activity. These work-units are the standards used for measuring the unit quantity of output or end product.

## 11.3.3 Estimating Standard Direct Cost

The estimation of the standard direct cost of a work–package thus involves:

(a) Estimation of the quantity of work to be executed in standard units of measurement.
(b) Setting up of the workers' productivity standard, materials consumption standard and equipment utilization standard. These are described in Chapters 7 to 10.

(c) Developing costing standards for labour hourly rate, material's unit price, equipment utilization hourly rate and evolving methodology for apportioning indirect costs and evaluating standard costs. These unit-rate costing standards for direct resource estimation are covered above.

To quote an example, consider the case of the 'foundation task' of a housing unit project. The labour costs and materials costs are derived for each work-package from the data reflected in Tables 2.7 and 2.8 and other direct expenses are tabulated in Table 11.4. The work–packages direct costs thus computed are shown against each.

Table 11.4

**2000 Housing Units Project**
**Standard Direct Cost in Dollars of One Foundation Module**
**(Actual Data Modified)**

| Sl No. | Work Package Description | Manpower Cost | Materials Cost | Other Costs | Total Direct Cost |
|---|---|---|---|---|---|
| 1. | Base Preparation | 613 | 2178 | 463 | 3254 |
| 2. | Raft | 820 | 13732 | 1701 | 16254 |
| 3. | Plinth Wall | 1637 | 5079 | 1163 | 7880 |
| 4. | Ground Floor | 363 | 3817 | 527 | 4705 |
| Total Direct Cost per Module | | 3433 | 24806 | 3854 | 32093 |

## 11.3.4 Sharing Indirect Costs

The indirect costs are detailed at the time of estimation of project costs. The estimators use various methods for absorbing these indirect costs into production costs. These costs can be charged (or added) to the direct costs on a proportionate basis. In some contracts, most of the indirect costs are priced under the preliminaries section of the bill of quantities and the balance is distributed proportionately in the remaining items of the Bill of Quantities (BOQ).

Another method is to divide the indirect costs under four heads, i.e. Indirect manpower costs, Indirect materials costs, Indirect equipment costs and Indirect other expenses, and then distribute these costs to the production direct costs using predetermined criteria. But the sharing of indirect cost for use in planning, budgeting and controlling is a complex process as it involves knowing what the costs are, who has incurred the costs, what was the nature of the costs, and how to share these indirect costs for evaluating work–package standard costs.

**What are the indirect costs involved?** The indirect costs considered are those costs which cannot be identified with the execution of the work packages pertaining to permanent works. The types of indirect costs encountered in a typical project are shown in Exhibits 11.1 and 11.2. The amount of money involved requires a detailed computation of the indirect costs, costing each item one by one and then aggregating them to determine the total indirect cost.

**Who incurs these costs?**  Indirect costs are incurred by various functional groups of the project employed to produce work, support production or administer production. These functional groups are called 'Responsibility or Cost centres'. Project responsibility centres, depending upon the task assigned, can be broadly divided into four categories:

(i) Production or profit responsibility centre.
(ii) Support services responsibility centre.
(iii) Administration responsibility centre.
(iv) Sales and contract administration centre.

The methodology for structuring cost centres is outlined in Chapter 12.

**What is the nature of indirect costs?**  Each item of indirect cost from the production point of view can be divided into two broad categories, i.e. variable overheads and fixed overheads. These can be grouped separately for each responsibility centre.

| *Responsibility centre* | *Variable overheads* | *Fixed overheads* |
|---|---|---|
| Production centre | xx | xx |
| Service centre | xx | xx |
| Administration centre | xx | xx |
| Sales and contract centre | — | xx |
| Project cost | xxx | xxx |

**How to share indirect costs?**  Since production centres produce permanent works grouped into work-packages, all overheads are finally charged to work-packages by allocating to them a predetermined part of all indirect costs (variable and fixed). The sharing process aims at the allocation of indirect costs to the work-packages, using a fair distribution policy so as to derive the work-package standard cost.

Work-package standard cost = Work-package standard direct Cost
+ Shared variable overheads
+ Shared fixed overheads.

There is no tailor-made solution for sharing of indirect costs. The sharing methods vary from company to company and project to project. Generally the method of sharing involves apportionment and absorption of indirect costs. Cost apportionment refers to the process of allocating project overheads among various responsibility centres, whereas overhead absorption stands for the process of allocating the overheads of the production centre within its work-packages. The sharing process can be divided into the following sequential stages.

(a) *Apportioning administrative overheads to production centre.*

(1) Apportion administration variable overhead costs to various production centres, using a fair distribution method. To quote an example, some typical costs considered under this head and their basis of distribution can be as under:

| *Administration variable overheads* | *Basis of cost distribution* |
| --- | --- |
| Accommodation rent | Floor area occupied by responsibility centres. |
| Building maintenance | Percentage of rent |
| Office running expenses | Manpower costs of each centre |
| Depreciation | Book value of equipment. |

Another method of administrative variable overhead costs is to distribute these to responsibility centres in proportion to sale value of the work entrusted.

(2) Apportion project fixed administration centre costs to all production responsibility centres in pro-rata percentage of their manpower costs or any other suitable criteria.

Apportioned administration fixed cost of a responsibility centre

$$= \frac{\text{Responsibility centre manpower costs} \times \text{Fixed administrative costs}}{\text{Project manpower costs}}$$

(b) *Apportion service centre costs to production centres*

All service responsibility centres' costs, including the allocation of administration centre costs, are finally apportioned among various direct production centres utilizing the respective service. It is done by pricing the service and then charging each production centre, as appropriate, for the services rendered. Some of the examples for apportioning service charges are as under:

(1) Technical service design costs on pro-rata basis are charged to appropriate work–packages/tasks for which the designs are prepared.
(2) Material services costs on pro rata basis can be charged to the cost of materials supplied.
(3) The price of concrete delivered can take into consideration all costs to be incurred by the concrete production and supply centre. The break-even prices can be adopted for calculating costs of concrete delivered, as illustrated in Table 11.3.
(4) The supply of construction equipment can be charged on a predetermined hourly rental basis.
(5) Transportation costs of materials can be measured in terms of the quantity transported per kilometre.

The purpose of pricing of services is twofold. It enables a fair distribution of services costs, and it enables a comparison of the internal services with similar services available outside the project boundaries. However, pricing of services should be limited to major items only. Otherwise accounting will become cumbersome.

(c) *Absorb production centres' overhead costs within its work–packages.*
The standard cost of each work–package of the production responsibility centre can thus be derived as under:

| | | |
|---|---|---|
| Direct labour cost | = | A |
| Direct material cost | = | B |
| Other direct expenses | = | C |
| Direct costs (A + B + C) | = | D |
| Share of production centre variable overheads | = | V |
| Share of production centre fixed costs overheads | = | F |
| Share of other centres apportioned overheads | = | O |
| Standard production cost of work–package (D + V + F + O) | = | S |

In the absorption costing technique, the variable and the fixed overheads are absorbed using predetermined absorption rates. The absorption rate varies with each of the above overhead categories, and these are developed using sophisticated accounting tools like dividing each of these overheads into three categories, i.e. indirect labour costs, indirect materials costs and other indirect expenses; and then developing a separate absorption rate for each category. However, a simplified (though less accurate) approach for computing the absorption rate is to distribute the total overheads in proportion to the direct cost of each work-package.

$$\text{Absorption Rate} = \frac{\text{Project overhead costs}}{\text{Project direct costs}}$$

Work-package indirect cost = Absorption rate × Work-package direct cost.

There will be some cases where taking a decision as to where to charge a particular indirect cost may appear difficult. In such cases, it is not worth wasting time on examining the merits and demerits of various options. A near appropriate course should be adopted to decide the basis for sharing.

In the marginal costing technique, only variable production costs are considered and the fixed costs are charged against the profit of the period in which they have accrued. This technique is an improvement over absorption costing and is of particular significance in cost control, where it separates the production–related variable costs and the time–related fixed costs. This enables the production centres to concentrate on the control of production's variable costs, and leave the administrators and accountants to analyze period costs.

## ❏ 11.4 STANDARD 'S' CURVE FORECASTING TOOL

### 11.4.1 'S' Curve Chart

The time-related cumulative forecasts of main input resources and outputs, in monetary value, when plotted graphically against the project time scale, follow the 'S' curve pattern.

Usually in 'S' curves, construction time is plotted along abscissa, and the item to be forecast is represented along the ordinate axis. Further, both the time and resources axes are divided into 100 units representing percentages. By doing this the trends of projects with different cost and completion periods can be compared with each other.

To quote an example, the standard 'S' curve forecasts for value of the work done and manpower requirements of a building construction project handled by the author in the Middle East are shown in Figure 11.3.

**Figure 11.3**

**2000 Housing Units Project**
**Typical Man-months Requirement and Earned Value S**
**Curve Forecast Cumulative in Percentage**
*S-Curve Forecasts*

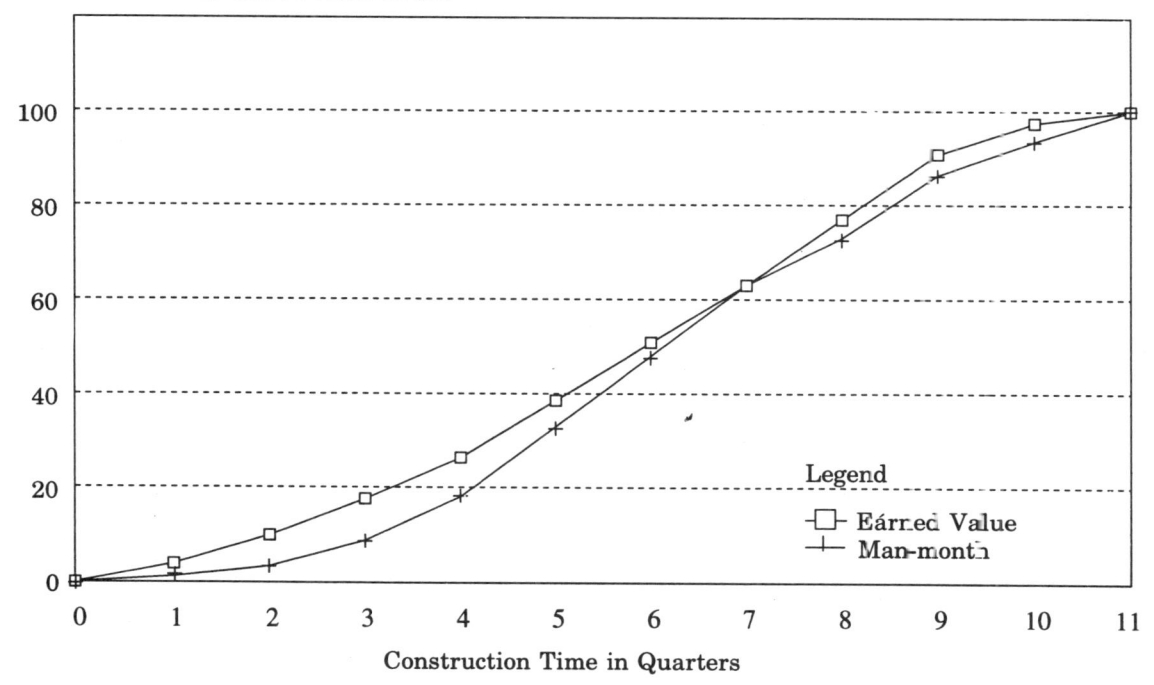

1. Man-months    Total Estimated   = 57,520
                                         = $160 million

## 11.4.2 'S' Curve Tool

The 'S' curve trends derived from analysis of large number of similar projects such as value of workdone, product costs, cash-in-flow, manpower requirement, commonly used materials like concrete, tend to follow near similar pattern. Figure 11.4 shows the actual 'S' curve patterns of workers employment in similar building projects.

**Figure 11.4**

**Typical Curve 'S' curve Forecasting Tool**
**Workers' Employment Trend**
**Percentage Man-months Utilised at a Given Time**

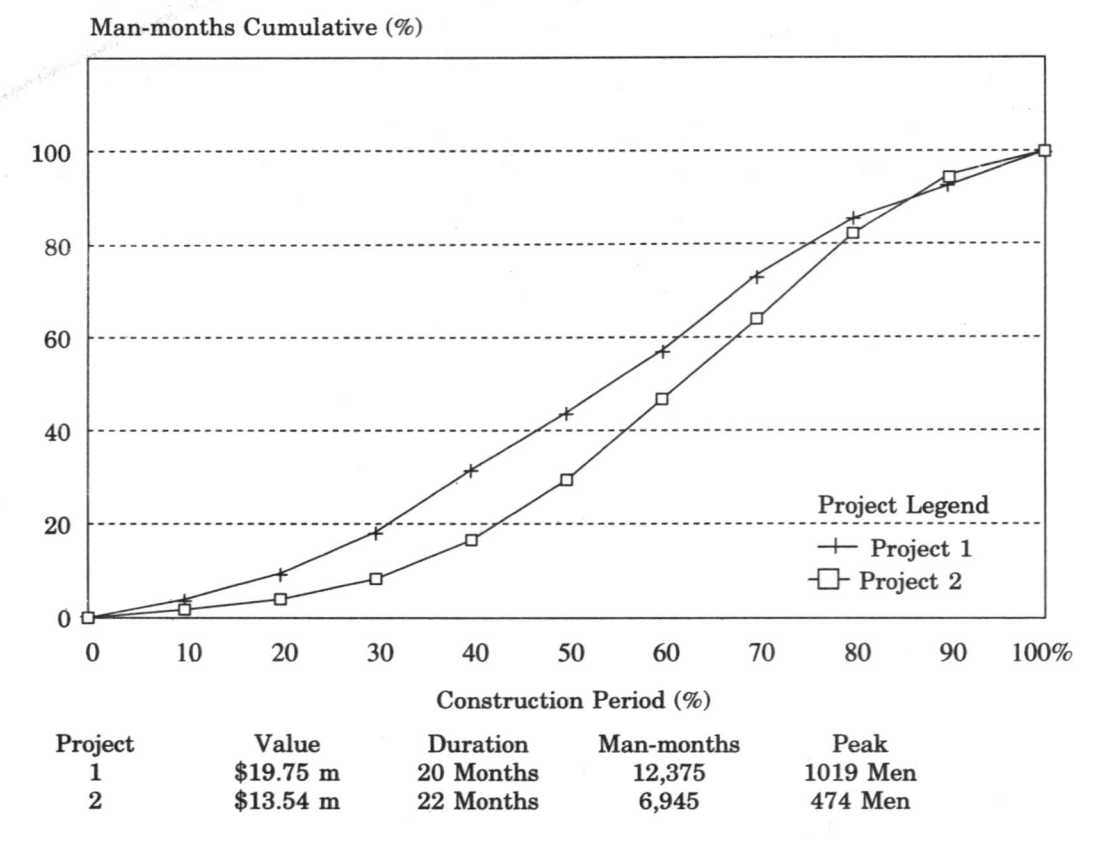

| Project | Value | Duration | Man-months | Peak |
|---------|---------|-----------|------------|----------|
| 1 | $19.75 m | 20 Months | 12,375 | 1019 Men |
| 2 | $13.54 m | 22 Months | 6,945 | 474 Men |

The 'S' curve forecasts thus distilled from the past performance of similar type of project, say group housing construction, proven in practice, can thus be viewed as management tools to conceptualize resources and financial forecasts at feasibility stage. In the absence of planned forecasts, these 'S' curves can be used to conceptualize resource requirements and predict financial forecasts for formulating project objectives. In actual practice, these Standard 'S' curve forecasts may be out by 10% to 30%, but it is better to have some tool for indicating forecasts rather than basing forecasts on judgements or guess-work by individuals. It may be noted that the preparation of Standard 'S' curve forecasts is an art as well as a science. While the methodology outlined above provides a scientific approach, its application needs experts. It is again emphasized that this sophisticated 'S' curve forecasting device cannot be left in inexperienced hands and it should not be considered as mathematical jugglery. It needs competent planners for scrutinizing past performances, formulating variances during execution and reasoning variations from the Standard 'S' curve forecasts.

# CHAPTER 12

# Planning Construction Budgets

A Project budget reflects the financial plan of the operations, divided into responsibility centres, with specific goals clearly outlined along with the costs expected to be incurred. The primary purpose of having a budget is to assign financial targets and resources to each responsibility centre, to coordinate their activities, to form the basis for controlling performance, and to make the participant's cost consciousness instead of purposeless routine working.

The budget uses the language of accounting to state objectives and measure performance. The project budget integrates monetary objectives, responsibilities and allocated resources. The base of the budget is the project plan and its schedule of work. The project functional organization is structured into responsibility centres. Each responsibility centre is assigned goals in the form of the sales budget. It is allocated resources in the form of materials, labour, equipment and budgeted costs for the assigned goals. And, finally, the project financial plan is presented in the form of the master budget which summarizes all the budget information like profit and loss statements, balance sheets, capital expenditure budget, cash flow forecasts and performance indicators.

In a construction project, the client and the contractor have separate budgets. Although, the project schedule of work and work done value (or earned value) form the common baseline for developing these budgets, their purpose differs.

The client's construction budget is primarily a capital budget designed to formulate time-phased funds requirement and the sources from which these funds are to be provisioned. The client capital budget includes the expenditure on preliminaries, procurement of land, client supply resources, consultants fee, contractors payments and the cost of working capital.

On the other hand, a contractor's budget is resources-cost and sales-income oriented budget. It includes quarterly statements of income and expenditure and forecast of financial statements of projected balance sheet, cash flow, profit and loss and performance measuring baselines. The break up of a typical contractors budget is shown in Fig. 12.1.

The project budget making process goes through the following stages:

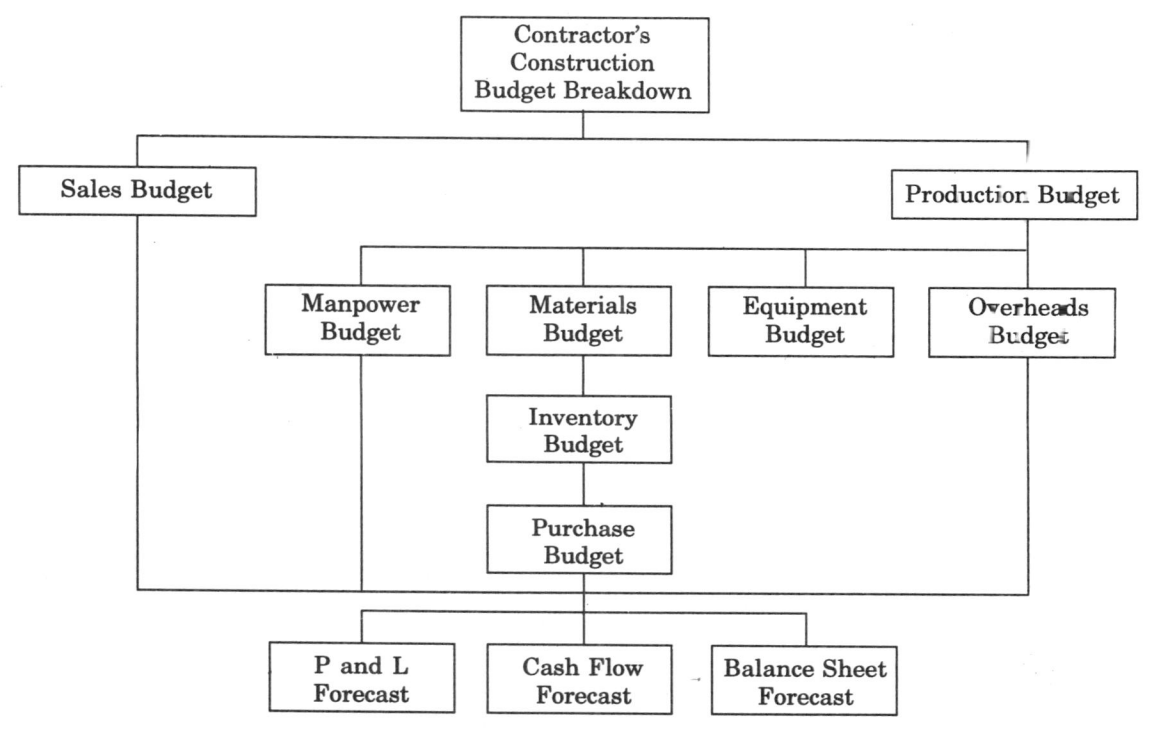

## Figure 12.1
### Contractor's Construction Budget Breakdown

```
                    Contractor's
                    Construction
                    Budget Breakdown
        ┌───────────────┴────────────────┐
   Sales Budget                    Production Budget
                ┌──────────┬──────────┬──────────┐
           Manpower    Materials  Equipment   Overheads
           Budget      Budget     Budget      Budget
                       Inventory
                       Budget
                       Purchase
                       Budget
        ┌──────────────┬──────────────┐
   P and L         Cash Flow      Balance Sheet
   Forecast        Forecast       Forecast
```

(a) Structuring responsibility centres.
(b) Budgeting sales and assigning a sales target to each responsibility centre.
(c) Budgeting production expenses necessary for the fulfilment of assigned tasks of each responsibility centre.
(d) Provisioning for inflation and escalation.
(e) Forecasting profit and loss, cash flow statement and balance sheet.
(f) Preparing a project master budget.

Salient features of each of the above stages are briefly described in subsequent paragraphs.

## ❏ 12.1 STRUCTURING RESPONSIBILITY CENTRES

Project objectives are linked with the performance of a number of result-oriented organizational units. These units are structured according to their task-responsiblity-reporting relationship, as can be seen in Exhibit 12.1 depicting the organizational chart of the housing units project. The number of organizational units depends upon the magnitude and complexity of the project. A simple project may have only a few organizational units whereas a large number of interacting organizational units are required for a large complex project. In a major project, each organizational unit is usually headed by a manager and it is referred as a 'responsibility centre'.

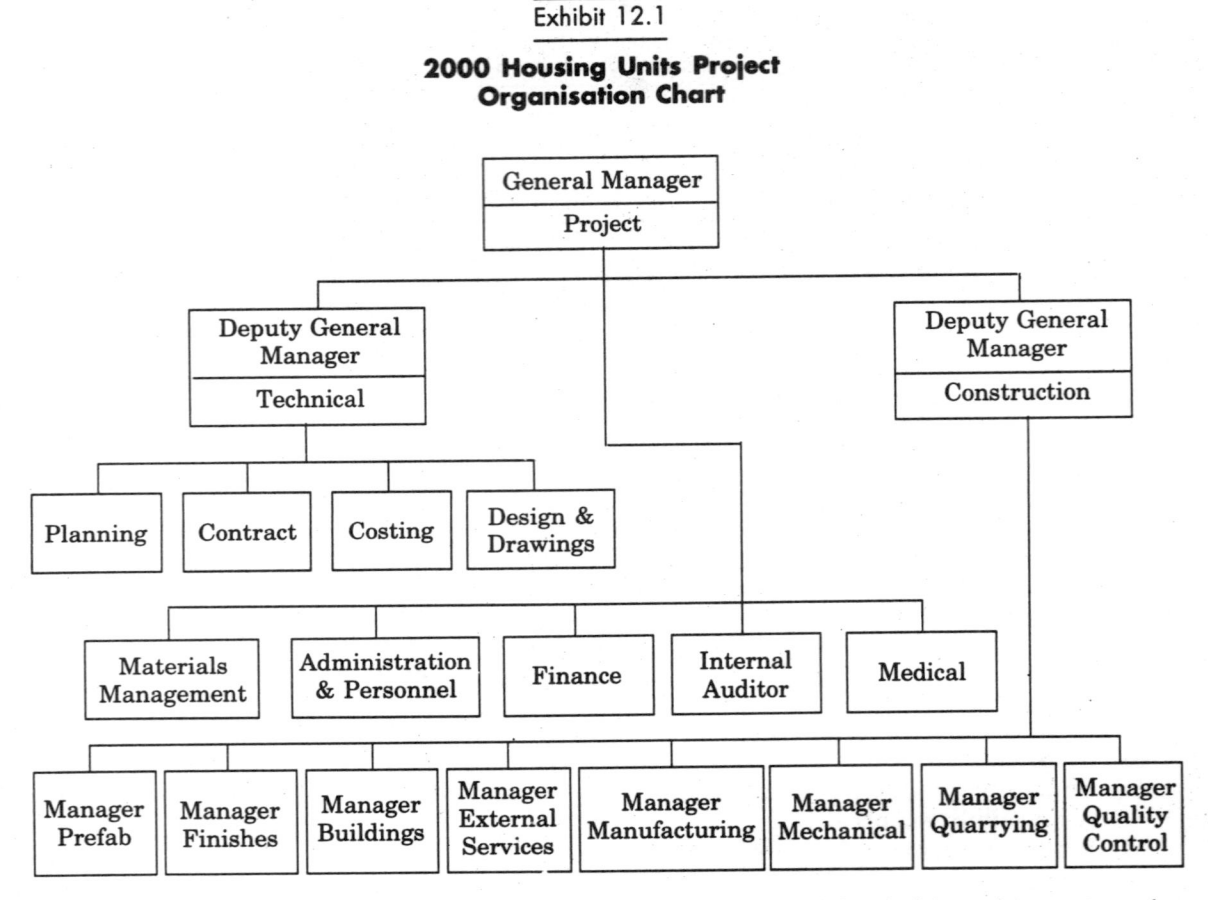

Exhibit 12.1

**2000 Housing Units Project Organisation Chart**

```
                          General Manager
                             Project
          ┌──────────────────────┴──────────────────────┐
   Deputy General                                Deputy General
      Manager                                       Manager
     Technical                                    Construction
   ┌────┬────┬────┐
Planning Contract Costing Design &
                          Drawings
   ┌────────┬──────────┬────────┬─────────┬────────┐
Materials  Administration  Finance  Internal  Medical
Management & Personnel             Auditor
   ┌──────┬──────┬──────┬──────┬──────┬──────┬──────┬──────┬──────┐
Manager Manager Manager Manager   Manager   Manager   Manager  Manager
Prefab Finishes Buildings External Manufacturing Mechanical Quarrying Quality
                         Services                                    Control
```

In construction projects, responsibility centres can be broadly divided into three categories viz. construction (or production) centres, support service centres, management and administration centres. (These are depicted in Exhibit 12.2)

## 12.1.1 Construction/Production Centres

A construction centre consists of one or more work centres. A work centre is entrusted with the execution of a group of activities constituting one or more work-packages. The work-packages in a work centre are identifiable, measurable and costable units. This concept makes it possible to express the input resources and expected performance of each work centre in physical and monetary terms.

### Exhibit 12.2

### 2000 Housing Units Project
### Task Responsibility Centres

**Project Management**

- **Construction Responsibility Centres**
  - Building Foundation Centre.
  - Building Finishes Centre.
  - Precast Erection Centre.
  - Public Building Centre.
  - Pavement Construction Centre.
  - Landscaping Centre.

- **Services Responsibility Centres**
  - Precast Concrete Production Factory
  - Readymix Concrete Production Plant.
  - Steel Fabrication Shop.
  - Quarrying Establishment.
  - Plant & Machinery Maintenance Unit.

- **Management and Administration Responsibility Centres**
  - Administration & Personnel Management.
  - Materials Management.
  - Plant & Machinery Management.
  - Finance Management.
  - Cost Management.
  - Engineering Services Management.
  - Contract Management.
  - Planning and Monitoring Cell.

Ideally, a work centre production budget should be prepared item-wise, as listed in the bill of quantities. Each work centre can then have a specified scope of work, unit of measurement, unit sale price, and performance objectives associated with it. But this is not always feasible. Despite various codification systems regarding the listing of work-items, the concept of determining the work-items vary, with the estimators. For example, in one contract all items relating to the foundation concrete work may be included as one work–item under 'concreting', whereas in another contract a similar foundation concrete work-may be found split into form-work, reinforcement and placing concrete. In fact, the CI/SfB system an internationally recognized construction indexing method can be used for developing and codifying building construction work centres and work-packages.

### 12.1.2 Service Centres

These centres support construction centres with technical, material, manpower equipment and general services like accommodation and temporary utility services. Examples of such investment-oriented centres are ready-mix concrete production plant, steel reinforcement fabrication workshop, GRC elements manufacturing factory, metallic doors and windows fabrication unit, and plant and machinery operation and maintenance establishment.

Service centres supply equipment and manufactured materials to construction centres at predetermined in-house prices which are usually-cheaper than the local market prices. In major projects, the divisions are set-up primarily to economize on costs and to ensure reliable quality and timely supply of selected items of plant, equipment and fabricated materials. Service centres or departments, based on their needs, incur costs and these costs are reflected in each service centre budget.

### 12.1.3 Administration Centre

This includes the project management, staff, workers and all types of resources needed for setting up and operating the project office which supports the project management. This centre is personally headed by the project manager.

## ❏ 12.2 SALES REVENUE BUDGET

The sales value of the work-in-progress yields revenue. This revenue in turn nourishes the growth of the project. Without regular sales revenue, a project cannot survive. It is the sales forecast that forms the base for the quantification of the entire production budget. Therefore, it is imperative that all those engaged in project management and specially, the functional heads of the production centres should take an active role in the formulation of the sales budget.

The first step in the sales budget preparation is to develop the monthly physical targets to be achieved. These physical targets are stated in the form of planned progress of work-packages. These targets are derived from the project schedule of work.

The sales forecast of the monthly value of work done can then be computed by assigning standard sales value for each work-package, and then aggregating these month-wise to derive the work done sales value. This process, described in Chapter 6, enables the preparation of a sales value forecast for the project.

The sales forecast is a prediction of the anticipated value of work planned, it may or may not come through. The sales forecast need not necessarily be the management's sales budget. The sales budget implies commitment. It lays down the sales revenue to be achieved. The committed monthly sales projections for each production centre are generally derived after critically examining the schedule of work and the connected sales forecast by taking into consideration the complexities and characteristics of the project and the terms and conditions for payment by the client.

A typical format used for the computation of the monthly sales budget is given below and its preparation method is explained in subsequent paragraphs.

**Typical Format for Computation of Monthly Sales Budget**

| | | |
|---|---|---|
| (A) | Stipulated receipts of sales value of work done | xx |
| (B) | Less retention as per contract | (xx) |
| (C) | Receipts from sales (A-B) | xx |
| (D) | Add for materials at site | xx |
| (E) | Add for extra work, if any | xx |
| (F) | Less pro rata recovery for advance | (xx) |
| (G) | Monthly amount payable by client | xx |
| (H) | Add other incomes (sales of scrap, etc. if any) | xx |
| (I) | Net monthly sales revenue projection | xx |

In practice, contractors are given on-account payments in the form of advance for work done and materials delivered on site at regular intervals of time according to the terms of contract, and the contractors do not have to wait for payment till the final completion of the contract. A typical 'Advance Payment Application' form, specified by a client for use by the contractor, is shown in Table 12.1.

Normally, the payments are made by the client on a monthly basis and the predetermined mode of payment is incorporated in the contract documents. The payment evaluation is generally carried out by measuring the work completed, the work-in-progress and the materials brought at the site by the contractor as per bill of quantities. In order to determine the value of work done, the measured quantities of work completed and work-in-progress are multiplied by the unit sale price for each work-item completed and split assessed sale price for work-in-progress:

| | | |
|---|---|---|
| Value of work done | = | Value of work completed + Value of work-in-progress. |
| Where, Value of work completed | = | Sum of product of unit sale price multiplied by respective quantity of work done. |
| Value of work-in-progress | = | Value of payable work-in-progress at assessed split rate of sale price. |

The advance for materials at the site are paid at a predetermined percentage (say 70%) of the materials' purchased price. Most of the contract conditions provide for the retention of a certain amount (say 5% of the value of work done) as a performance guarantee. Further, proportionate deductions are also made for the mobilization advance if paid by the client (according to the contract) prior to the commencement of the work. Finally, the sales budget for the value of work are plotted in the pattern of cumulative 'S' curve graphs as shown in Fig. 11.4, and the net payments receivable with its breakdown as per standard format are tabulated month-wise.

Table 12.1

## Monthly Interim Payment Application
## Typical Format

Client: (Name and Address)  
Contractor: (Name and Address)  
Contract No. & Description: ...............................  
Contract Amount: ................................................  Change Order Amount: ...........................  
Total Amount: .......................................................  (In words                                                                )  
Interim Payment No. ..........................................  Period: ..........................................................

|  | New Accumulated | Previous Accumulated | This Period |
|---|---|---|---|
| *Workdone* |  |  |  |
| Works contracted |  |  |  |
| Extra works |  |  |  |
| Total workdone |  |  |  |
| Less retention |  |  |  |
| A—Workdone Payable |  |  |  |
| *Materials-at-Site* |  |  |  |
| Value |  |  |  |
| B—Materials Payable |  |  |  |
| *Advance Payment* |  |  |  |
| Amount advanced |  |  |  |
| Less amount refunded |  |  |  |
| C—Advance Payable |  |  |  |
| *Payment Status* |  |  |  |
| Total amount payable (A + B + C) |  |  |  |
| Less Amount already paid |  |  |  |
| Balance Due |  | Amount in words |  |

Sign                                       Stamp of the                               Sign  
Contractor                               Contractor                                Approved by Client  
(Name and Status)                                                                  (Name & Status)  
Date:                                                                                       Date:

*Enclosure:* Back-up details of Original Works Valuation, Extra Workdone Statement and Materials-at-site sheet.

It may be noted that the stipulated date of receipt of the payment from the client against the sales invoice is a critical factor in the computation of the sales budget. Although the progressive monthly payment invoices do get scrutinized by the client within a week of submission by the contractor, depending upon the terms and conditions of the contract it may take anything from one week to three months for the payment to reach in the contractor's bank account. It is the date of receipt of the money which is considered in the cash-flow budget and not the date of the invoice for payment.

## 12.3 OPERATING EXPENSES BUDGET

Project operating expenses of accomplishing planned tasks in a given accounting period can be determined by summing up the standard costs of corresponding work-packages constituting the tasks. The standard costs are adequate for forecasting the expenditure and controlling the costs of work-packages, but these are not sufficient for budgeting resources with their cost breakdown for coordinating, communicating and controlling the tasks and overall resources assigned to the responsibility centres.

The project operating expense budget details the resources and costs planned for achieving phased objectives. In simple words, it can be termed as an 'expenditure budget'. While detailing, the expenditure is considered on a monthly basis. The accounting period while preparing the budget is generally taken as quarterly. The project accounting period is matched with the reporting period as well as the corporate accounting period so as to avoid duplication.

### 12.3.1 Types of Budgets and Schedules

Operating an expense budget comprises of a number of budgets and schedules as shown in Fig. 12.2.

Project expenditures can be broadly divided into two categories, i.e. production-related expenses and administration-related expenses. The production costs budget, which accounts for production-related expenses, includes budgets of each of the production responsibility centres and the services responsibility centres who support the production. The administration expenditure budget consists of the general administration budget, technical management budget, and temporary work and common facilities budget.

The basis of preparation of the budgets of production-related responsibility centres is the specified production physical and financial targets to be accomplished during each accounting period. These physical targets are stated in terms of work-packages to be completed, and in case of service centres, the physical targets quantify the services to be rendered. The physical targets are converted into sales targets at predetermined rates derived from the bill of quantities or specified service charges.

The administration-related expense budget accounts for the expenditure planned for the project command and control set-up, and the project temporary works and common facilities. These costs can be further divided into general administration expenses, technical management expenses and common facilities expenses.

**374** Construction Project Management

Figure 12.2

**Expense Budget Breakdown**

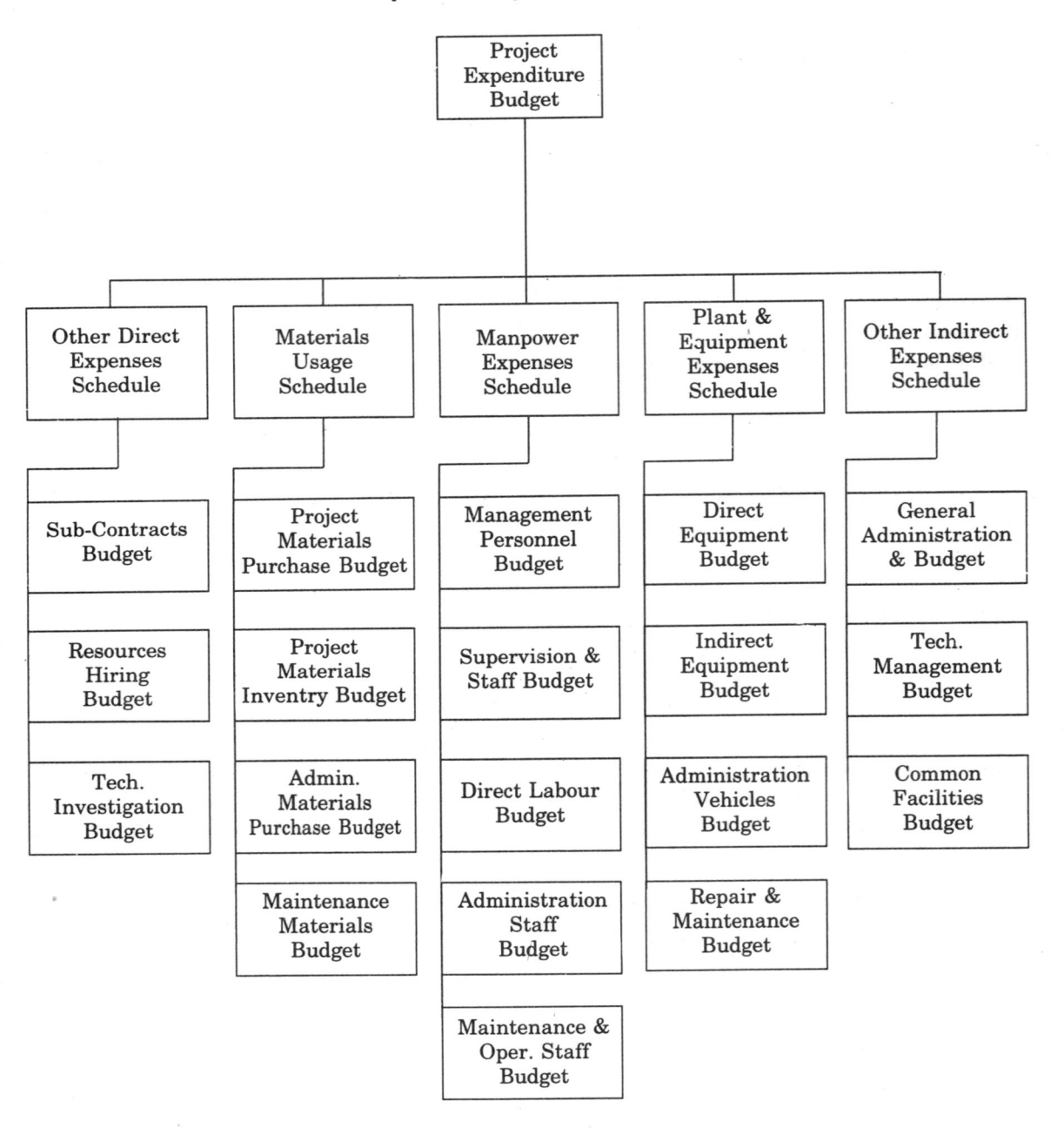

```
                          Project
                        Expenditure
                          Budget
```

| Other Direct Expenses Schedule | Materials Usage Schedule | Manpower Expenses Schedule | Plant & Equipment Expenses Schedule | Other Indirect Expenses Schedule |
|---|---|---|---|---|
| Sub-Contracts Budget | Project Materials Purchase Budget | Management Personnel Budget | Direct Equipment Budget | General Administration & Budget |
| Resources Hiring Budget | Project Materials Inventry Budget | Supervision & Staff Budget | Indirect Equipment Budget | Tech. Management Budget |
| Tech. Investigation Budget | Admin. Materials Purchase Budget | Direct Labour Budget | Administration Vehicles Budget | Common Facilities Budget |
|  | Maintenance Materials Budget | Administration Staff Budget | Repair & Maintenance Budget |  |
|  |  | Maintenance & Oper. Staff Budget |  |  |

The making of a project expenditure budget starts with the budgeting of resources for each service centre. Where feasible, the service centre's sale price or service charges are then incorporated while preparing the budget for each production centre. These production and service centres, budgets are then added up to the administration centre's budget to develop the project operating expense budget. The nature of budgets prepared at each responsibility centre are listed in Exhibit 12.3. Each responsibility centre as well as the combined project expenditure budget is reflected into schedules and sub-budgets. These schedules include the following:

(a) Manpower expenses schedule.
(b) Materials usage cost schedule.
(c) Plant and equipment expenses schedule.
(d) Other direct expenses schedule.
(e) General and administration expenses schedule.

Exhibit 12.3

### 2000 Housing Units Project Budgeting Data Source

| S. No. | Category of budget | Construction task forces ||||  Service centres |||||| Adm centre |
|---|---|---|---|---|---|---|---|---|---|---|---|---|
| | | Fndn. | Strc. | Fnsh. | Srvs. | Perso. Mgt. | Mtrl. Mgt. | Tech. Mgt. | Finc. Mgt. | P & M Mgt. | Fabn. Mtl | |
| 1. | Sales Budget | × | × | × | × | | | | | | × | |
| 2. | Direct Cost Budget | | | | | | | | | | | |
| | (a) Direct Labour | × | × | × | × | | | | | | × | |
| | (b) Materials | × | × | × | × | | | | | | × | |
| | (c) Other expenses | × | × | × | × | | | | | | | |
| 3. | Indirect expense Budget | | | | | | | | | | | |
| | (a) Indirect manpower | × | × | × | × | × | × | × | × | × | × | × |
| | (b) Indirect materials | × | × | × | × | × | × | | | × | × | × |
| | (c) Indirect plant & machines | × | × | × | × | × | × | | | × | × | |
| | (d) Administration expenses | | | | | | | | × | | × | |
| | (e) Depreciation | | | | | | | | × | | | |

## 12.3.2 Project Manpower Expenses Schedule

Project manpower expenses schedule represents the phased manpower costs of the entire project. This budget comprises of the manpower expenses sub-budgets of all responsibility centres. This schedule can be divided into the following categories:

(a) Management personnel budget—It includes the managers' salaries and their connected expenses.
(b) Supervisory and site staff budget—It represents the manpower costs of the technical supervisors and site staff employed in the production and service responsibility centres.

(c) **Direct labour budget**—It cover the direct labour costs of labour employed in the production centres and product manufacturing service centres. This manpower strength constitutes the majority of the personnel employed at the project site.

(d) **Equipment maintenance and operation staff and workers**—It covers all categories of manpower both direct and indirect, employed in the plant and equipment responsibility centre.

(e) **Administration staff budget**—It consists of the indirect manpower employed in the administration and resources management set-up, other than already covered by the management personnel, supervisory staff and equipment repair and maintenance manpower (if not catered separately). It includes the personnel administration staff, project office manpower, technical staff, and common utility services manpower.

A typical manpower schedule format is shown in Table 12.2.

Table 12.2

**Manpower And Connected Expenses Budget**
**Typical Format For Quarterly Summary**

Responsibility Centre                Quarter Ending:

| S No. | Manpower Category | Nos | Salary/Wages | Bonus/ Overtime | Connected Expenses | Total |
|---|---|---|---|---|---|---|
|  | *Establishment* |  |  |  |  |  |
| 1. | Manager |  |  |  |  |  |
| 2. | Senior engineers |  |  |  |  |  |
| 3. | Junior engineers |  |  |  |  |  |
| 4. | Staff grade 1 |  |  |  |  |  |
| 5. | Staff grade 2 |  |  |  |  |  |
| 6. | Staff grade 3 |  |  |  |  |  |
|  | *Direct Workers* |  |  |  |  |  |
| 7. | Foreman |  |  |  |  |  |
| 8. | Charge-hand |  |  |  |  |  |
| 9. | Specialists |  |  |  |  |  |
| 10. | Highly skilled |  |  |  |  |  |
| 11. | Skilled |  |  |  |  |  |
| 12. | Semi-skilled |  |  |  |  |  |
| 13. | General helpers |  |  |  |  |  |

(Quarter No)

*Notes*: Connected expenses breakdown include mobilisation costs, messing, medical, accommodation, conveyance leave entitlement, social and terminal benefits, welfare etc, as applicable.

### 12.3.3 Usage Schedule of Materials

The usage schedule of materials is compiled from usage requirements of materials projected by the responsibility centres. Based on these requirements, the following budgets are prepared:

(a) Project materials purchase budget.
(b) Project materials inventory budget.
(c) Administration materials budget.
(d) Maintenance materials budget.

In particular, the project materials purchase budget takes into account the materials' consumption as reflected in the materials' usage schedule and the planned materials inventory at the end of each accounting period. The typical format for developing materials budget is indicated in Table 12.3.

The materials' purchase budget indicates the time, quantity, and cost of materials to be purchased. The purchase budget is prepared after considering materials usage and inventory requirements, prevailing relevant market factors, the shelf life characteristics of the materials, and the warehouse capability. The materials' purchase budget is of great significance as materials constitute over 50% of the project expenses.

### 12.3.4 Plant and Equipment Budget

Plant and equipment budget includes all owning and operating costs of the plant and the equipment and vehicles employed at the project site. Generally, the manpower like mechanics, operators and drivers, and the spare parts, repair and maintenance materials are budgeted separately as their procurement is done by the personnel and materials departments. The plant and equipment budget can be broadly divided into the following categories:

(a) Direct plant and equipment budget.
(b) Indirect plant and equipment budget.
(c) Administrative vehicles budget.
(d) Repair and maintenance budget.

Typical format for developing plant and equipment budget is reflected in Table 12.4. For budgeting purposes, as far as feasible, the employment of each equipment should be accounted for in terms of predetermined hire charges for the period (in hours) it is physically employed at the site.

### 12.3.5 Other Direct Expenses Schedule

In addition to manpower, material and equipment costs, some responsibility centres also incur expenditure which can be identified with the execution of permanent works. The type

## Table 12.3
## Construction Materials Budget Summary: Typical Format

| Sl. No. | Type of Materials | | | Estimated Cost | | | Quarter No. 1 Cost | | | ..... | Last Quarter Cost | | | Remarks |
|---|---|---|---|---|---|---|---|---|---|---|---|---|---|---|
| | Name | Code | Unit | Quantity | Unit Rate | Amount | P | U | I | | P | U | I | |
| | Materials A | | | | | | | | | | | | | |
| | Materials B | | | | | | | | | | | | | |
| | Total | | | | | | | | | | | | | |

*Abbreviations:* P = Materials procurement planned amount  U = Material usage cost  I = Materials quarter ending inventory (Below stock value)

## Table 12.4
## Equipment Usage Budget Summary: Typical Format

| S. No. | Type of Equipment | | WDV | Expenditure basis | | | Quarter No.1 | | | | | ..... | Last quarter | | | | Remarks |
|---|---|---|---|---|---|---|---|---|---|---|---|---|---|---|---|---|---|
| | Nomenclature | Code | | Effort | Rate | Total | D | R | M | F | Total | | D | R | M | F | Total | |
| 1. | Equipment A | | | | | | | | | | | ..... | | | | | | |
| ... | ... | ... | ... | ... | ... | ... | ... | ... | ... | ... | ... | ..... | ... | ... | ... | ... | ... | |
| | Total | | | | | | | | | | | ..... | | | | | | |

*Abbreviation:* WDV = Work-Down Value/Purchase Price, D = Depreciation payable, R = Repairs/Spares/Replacement costs
M = Specific maintenance cost, F = Fuel, oil & lubricants.

of such expenses will vary from project to project. However, the following are some of the other direct expenses which need budgeting:

(a) Sub-contracted works.
(b) Resources of manpower and equipment which are planned to be hired from external sources.
(c) Technical studies like soil investigations.
(d) Professional fees for the preparation of designs, drawings, etc.

### 12.3.6 General and Administration Expenses Schedule

This schedule includes all other indirect expenses which are not included elsewhere during budgeting. Such indirect expenses, which mostly result from administrative functions, can be broadly divided into the following three main heads. Each of them can be budgeted separately:

(a) General administration expenses.
(b) Technical management expenses.
(c) Temporary works and common facilities expenses.

(a) General administration expenses cover management personnel costs, project office costs, computer system costs, and costs of resource managing departments like personnel, materials, plant and equipment, and finance.
(b) The technical management expenses comprise:

- Technical office staff including designers, quantity surveyors, draftsmen and certain special categories of workers.
- Technical office equipment, instruments, publications and special stationery.
- Contracts and sub-contacts preparation administration costs.
- Designs and drawings preparation expenses.
- Quality control costs.
- Project planning and controlling costs.

(c) Temporary works and common facilities include accommodation, utility services, HVAC, roads and fencing, messing, sports and recreation, etc.

In the case of small-size projects, cost heads listed in Table 12.5 can be used to develop the general and administration budget.

## ❏ 12.4 COST INFLATION, ESCALATION AND CONTINGENCIES

Inflation and escalation are two common terms that are often misunderstood. Inflation results in an increase in the prices of goods and services, and thus gradually, decreases the

### Table 12.5

### General and Administration Budget
### Quarterwise Summary: Typical Format

| Sl. No. | Expenses Category | | Amount |
|---|---|---|---|
| 1. | *Establishment (not covered elsewhere)*<br>(a) Salary/wages<br>(b) Bonus/overtime/incentive<br>(c) Connected manpower expenses<br>(d) Welfare and other expenses | | |
| 2. | *General Expenses*<br>(a) Office expenses<br>(b) Travelling<br>(c) Entertainment<br>(d) Audit fees<br>(e) Legal & other services<br>(f) Bank charges<br>(g) Bad debts<br>(h) Miscellaneous | | |
| 3. | *Period Expenses*<br>(a) Office rent, taxes etc.<br>(b) Insurance<br>(d) Depreciation | | |
| 4. | *Fixed Expenses*<br>Interest on loans & borrowings | | |
| | Total Quarter | | |

purchasing power of money. On the other hand, escalation in a project work can be taken as the difference between the original and the latest estimate of the final cost of the project. The term escalation also includes unforeseen costs which were not anticipated at the time of preparation of the original estimate. Generally, escalated costs include the effects of inflation as well as unforeseen expenditures and these are covered in project contingencies. In some construction contracts, provision for inflation is made in the contract clauses in terms of increase or decrease of a certain price index such as the consumer price index, wages price index or construction cost index. These indices are published regularly by Government and other autonomous organizations and federations. Some of the companies also develop the company cost indices for monitoring and forecasting cost changes, and pricing tenders to cater for inflationary tendencies, potential marketing trends and business environments. However, there is no hard and fast method to estimate the effect of inflation on the project costs as the variables involved are too many.

To quote an example, if the rate of inflationary trend is less than 5%, then it need not be considered as the contractors generally make allowances for contingencies (say up to 5% of the direct cost) to cater to such eventualities. It may be noted that the anticipated inflation gets compounded every year. For example, if the inflationary trend during the current year is 10% per annum, the forecast for the next year with the current trend of inflation at 10% will be 11%, with an average rate of increase in two years at 10.5% per year.

| | |
|---|---|
| Assumed current price | = 100 |
| Anticipated inflation during the current year | = 10% |
| Assessed price at the end of the current year | = $100 × (1 + 0.10) |
| | = $110 |
| Forecasted rate of inflation for the next year | = 10% |
| Assessed price at the end of the next year | = 121, i.e. 110 (1 + 0.10) |
| Therefore, the average price rise in two years form the current price level of $100 | = $\frac{121 - 100}{2}$ = 10.5% |
| Average price rise during the second year at the current price of $100 | = $(121 − 110) − 100 |
| | = $11.0 |

The inflationary trend can be reviewed at the time of the review of budget and the cashflow forecast can be modified by taking the then prevailing trends of prices.

## 12.5 BUDGETARY FORECASTS

### 12.5.1 Forecasting Profit

Business motive is to make profit. A business firm needs profit to cover its risks, to assist in its growth and to meet the financial needs of its shareholders, directors, staff and workers. A construction firm takes risks when it tenders for a project and, after winning the contract, it expects a reward in the form of calculated profit which is expected to be higher than what it can get through safe investments like bank fixed deposits and government bonds and securities. In this process, the construction firms also face the risk of losing money. Higher profit projects usually involve more risk and grater uncertainty.

While undertaking a construction project, the company estimates its profit and defines its profit objectives. These profit objectives lead to a more practical and systematic approach for making profit. On the contrary, the maximization of profit is generally not the objective of professional companies. Maximization concept is bound to go directly against the company's values as this may involve overlooking administrative policies, violating statutory regulations and adversely affecting the trade reputation. However, in construction business, it is not unusual for a contracting firm to make a bid without prospects of profit in an odd contract so as to prevent idling of resources and to maintain the continuity of business. On the whole, efficient management leads to profit whereas, losses can be viewed as a case of penalty for inefficient handling or incorrect estimation of profit objectives.

In accounting practices, gross operating profit (also referred to as net income) is computed as under:

1.0 Revenue
1.1 Sales value of work done                     xx
1.2 Other revenues                               xx
                                                 ———
                                                                xxx
2.0 *Less direct production cost of workdone*
2.1 Direct labour costs                          xx
2.2 Direct material costs                        xx
2.3 Other direct costs                           xx
                                                 ———
                                                              (xxx)

3.0 *Gross margin (Sl 2.0-Sl 1.0)*                             xx
4.0 *Less overhead expenses*
    Indirect variable costs                      xx
    Indirect fixed costs                         xx
                                                 ———
                                                              (xx)

5.0 *Gross operating profit or loss*                           xx
    *(Sl 3.0-Sl 4.0)*

Assuming that in project execution, non-operating income is negligible, the gross operating profit at a given point of time can be determined by evaluating the difference between the total sales and the total costs of sales at that point of time:

$$\text{Gross operating profit} = \text{Sales revenue} - \text{cost of sales}.$$

Generally the gross profit can be forecast by plotting the cumulative effect of Sales revenue and Production costs in the project time-related 'S' curve chart. In this chart, the project time duration is scaled along abscissa and the monetary values are scaled along the ordinate axis. The schedule of project work forms the basis for plotting 'S' curves representing the cumulative effect of sales revenue and the cumulative production costs. The method of plotting these 'S' curves is dealt with in Chapter 11.

A typical 'S' curve pattern graph of cumulative sales and cumulative production costs of a project are shown in Fig. 12.3. The extent of profit (or loss) at a given point of time can be estimated by measuring the vertical gap in monetary value between the cumulative sales and cumulative production cost curves.

The point of time at which the cumulative sales curve intersects with the cumulative production cost curve is termed the project break-even point and the time at which break-even occurs is called the project break-even time. The project break-even point shows the no-profit-no-loss situation, and after the break-even time, the project trend changes towards making profit.

In the initial stages of the project, till break-even is reached, the production costs are higher than the sales revenue. This period of cash loss or negative profit, which may stretch beyond half-life of the construction period, calls for the mobilization of cash resources to meet the inadequacy of funds.

It may be noted that the forecasting of profit is a touchy subject, which needs careful handling due to the inherent uncertainties and complexities in the nature of construction projects.

**384** Construction Project Management

Fig 12.3

## 'S' curve pattern graph of cumulative sales and cumulative production costs of a project

Financial Trends

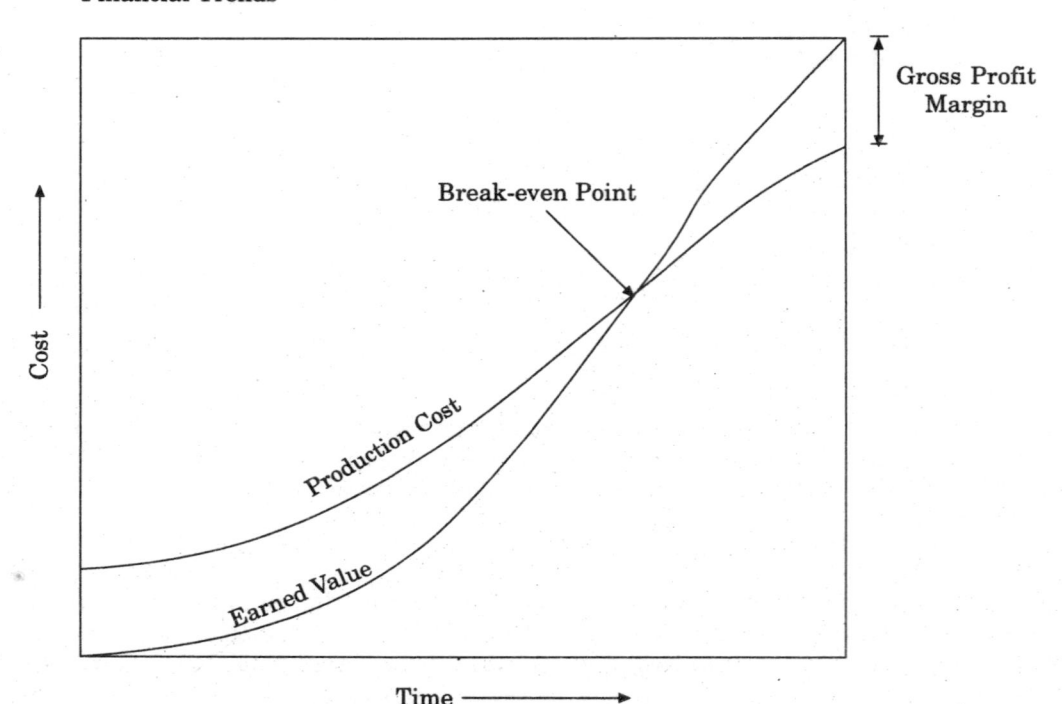

*[Graph showing Cost vs Time with Production Cost curve and Earned Value curve intersecting at Break-even Point, with Gross Profit Margin indicated on the right]*

Actual profit, if lower than the profits forecasted, can create unpleasant situations specially, when the profit reporting is carried out too frequently as fluctuations in forecasts can create conflict and confusion. Moreover, profit reporting has to be done and it cannot wait till the completion of the project. Further, it is not feasible to account for all factors, seen and unforeseen, at the time of forecasting profit. Under these circumstances, it is better to divide the profit reporting period on a half-yearly basis or at the most a quarterly basis (say in four to eight stages in the life of a project) using the following guidelines for adjusting profit:

| Sl. No. | Profit reporting stages | Nature of forecast |
|---|---|---|
| (1) | Initial stage | Profit assessed at the time of tendering be reviewed, and profit forecast re-assessed and theoretical forecasts derived from 'S' curves be reduced, say about 20% to 25% at each progressive intermediate stage, up to half-life of the project. |
| (2) | Intermediate stages | Compute actual profit, analyze reasons for variations and revise forecasts, if necessary. |

(3) Project completion stage    Profit sealed after making provision for known and unknown expenses during the maintenance period and demobilization of site.

(4) Final stage    Determine final net profit from the construction cost accounts after completion of maintenance period and demobilization from site.

It is worth noting that the profit computed in the cost accounting system (as outlined above) and the financial accounting system do differ. The differences mainly arise because of the following:

(a) Some expenses appear in financial accounting but are not considered in cost accounting, examples—discounts, profit on disposal of fixed assets, interest paid, fines and penalties and statutory expenses like income tax.
(b) Possible differences may occur in pay back amount on account of amortization and depreciation.
(c) Possible differences may arise due to methods of evaluation of stock inventory.

The differences in the profit and loss statement between cost accounting and financial accounting are reconciled at the end of the accounting period and posted in the accounting ledgers through a 'memorandum of reconciliation' statement.

## ❏ 12.5.2 Forecasting Cash Flow

Despite the progressive payment stipulations in the contracts, the client as well as the contractors do face liquidity problem. Shortage of funds affects the progress of the project and in the worst case it can lead to the stoppage of work. It is important that the necessary capital budget provision to meet the inadequacy of the project cash requirements be made well in advance.

The project funding pattern can be determined by making a cash flow forecast that predicts the monthly net effect of the cash inflow and outflow. Separate cash flow forecasts are made by the client and the contractor. The purpose of the client's cash-flow study is to forecast the extent of the funds required periodically for meeting payment commitments. On the other hand, the contractor's cash flow forecast is more detailed and complex as it has to cater for cash inflow as well as cash outflow.

While the contractor's cash in flow or project revenue receipts can be easily derived from the sales budget, the difficulty arises in determining cash outflow. Some of the aspects which need capital additions from time to time are:

(a) Working capital requirement.
(b) Major equipment purchase costs.
(c) Material inventory costs.
(d) Manpower mobilization costs.
(e) Temporary works and utility installations construction costs.

The detailed working of the month-wise cash outflow for each of the above items of expenditure is a tedious process. However, the cash outflow on account of the above expenditure can be determined with reasonable approximation by splitting up the expenditures into one-time costs and time-related costs and then preparing a monthly schedule of expenditure after taking into consideration the anticipated deferred payment facilities and the paying back of refunds spread over a long period in the form of retained profit/amortization of long-life fixed assets and depreciation of plant and equipment.

A typical format used for preparing the cash inflow and cash outflow statement is shown in Table 12.6.

Table 12.6

**Cash-Flow Chart: Typical format**

| Sl. No. | Cost Headings | Pre-start | Project Period Monthly Breakdown M-1 | M-2 | Post-completion |
|---|---|---|---|---|---|
| | *Budgeted Cash-in-Flow*  1. Net revenue | | | | |
| | *Budgeted Cash-out-Flow*  2. Manpower expenditure  3. Materials purchases  4. Plant & machinery operating expenses  5. Sub-contracted works and other direct expenses  6. Project administration & other expenses  7. Working capital | | | | |
| | 8. Total cash-outflow | | | | |
| | 9. Cash-flow status (1-8)  (a) Monthly  (b) Cumulative | | | | |

The difference between cash in flow and cash outflow, month-wise, gives the cash flow pattern.

The cumulative effect of the cash inflow and cash outflow, when plotted graphically against the project time, follows the 'S' curve pattern with the vertical difference between the two curves representing the cash resources status. For a long duration project the cash outflow will also have to be modified to cater for inflationary trends.

The negative cash flow experienced generally in the early stages of the project by the contractor calls for the mobilization of cash resources to meet the inadequacy of funds. The mode of financing can be divided into two categories, i.e. short-term and long-term financing.

The sources of short-term financing include contributions from the owner's equity, overdraft and loan facilities from commercial banks, deferred payment facilities from the suppliers, and short–term borrowing from financial institutions against guarantees. The long–term sources of funds are retaining profits, raising share capitals, bank loans, government loans, and loans from industrial and finance corporations. The extent of loan which a contractor can muster will depend upon many factors such as the financial position of the company, past performance of the company, project profitability, contractor's ability to provide guarantees, rate of refund of loans, and project cash-flow pattern.

### 12.5.3 Forecasting the Balance Sheet

The project balance sheet is the statement of assets and liabilities of a project on a particular date usually, the end of the specified accounting period. Balance sheets are compiled for each accounting period. Besides showing the assets and liabilities, the balance sheets also provide a link between the successive accounting periods. According to statutory requirements, all companies have to produce an yearly balance sheet to show the capital invested and how it has been employed in the business.

#### Typical format of a balance sheet

| | | |
|---|---|---|
| *Assets* | | |
| Current assets | xx | |
| fixed assets | xx | |
| | —— | xxx |
| *Less liabilities* | | |
| Current | xx | |
| Long-term | xx | |
| | —— | (xxx) |
| Shareholder's equity | | xxx |

Commonly used headings in balance sheets are standardized. These include the following:

(a) *Current assets*   These are sub-divided into debtors, (receivable) stock inventory, work in progress, short-term investments/advances and cash.
(b) *Fixed assets*   These cover land, building, plant and equipment, furniture and fixtures, all evaluated at their current value to the firm. Current value = Purchase value–Depreciation.
(c) *Short-term liabilities*   These include the creditors to whom the money is payable for the goods and services supplied by them and the other sources from where the short-term refundable funds are raised.
(d) *Long–term liabilities*   These consist of the loaned capital employed for running the project and employees' long-term benefit liabilities.
(e) *Shareholder's equity*   These are contributions by the shareholders in the form of capital, stock, other assets and retained earnings.

## 12.6 PROJECT MASTER BUDGET

### 12.6.1 Budget Manual

The project master budget integrates and summarizes the project functional budgets. At times, the master budget is also referred to as the finance budget or profit plan. The project master budget is prepared in the form of a manual. The text of a typical Project budget manual may summarize the following. The detailed working patterns are attached as schedules or appendices with the text:

(a) *Project planned objectives*   These are stated in physical and financial terms with the plan assumptions and the functional organization of work.
(b) *Organization of responsibility centres*   It highlights the division of the functional organization into responsibility centres (and their being further split up into work-centres where applicable) with the tasks and resources assigned to each responsibility centre.
(c) *Sales revenue budget*   It reflects the monthly or quarterly financial targets for the overall project and its breakdown for each production centre and other revenue earning sources.
(d) *Production cost budget*   It covers the production cost of goods sold, and it can be further split up into direct costs and indirect costs. These costs can be suitably arranged so as to bring out the production cost budget for each responsibility centre.
(e) *Project general and administration expense budget*   It represents the overall site office, administration, and head office expense budget, arranged in conformity with the finance heads of accounts and the functional needs.
(f) *Budgeted financial forecasts*   These include the profit and loss statement, cash flow forecast and forecast balance sheet.

### 12.6.2 Project Budget Preparation Guidelines

Budget preparation guidelines given below can go a long way to make a budget effective:

(a) The budget should be prepared after the project plan is crystallized. A financial budget document compiled at the time of quoting a tender, however detailed, can at best be termed a 'preliminary budget'.
(b) The budget should be prepared by a team and not by an individual, however efficient he may be. Specially, the preparation must not be left only to the accountants. Effective participation by the executives and heads of functional departments should be encouraged/ensured. This will safeguard the budget from becoming a mere paper exercise.
(c) The budget should be prepared, proceeding systematically using scientific techniques as applied in a given situation, and it should not be viewed merely as a mathematical, statistical or accounting exercise.

(d) The budget should be prepared in the format used for making the corporate budget, as far as possible, so that it can fit into the corporate financial accounting system.
(e) Budget should be prepared as a comprehensive total document. Piecemeal budgeting should be avoided as this can result in imbalances if not carefully integrated into the overall budget.
(f) The budget should be prepared keeping in mind that it has to be used for budgetary control. It is therefore necessary that a budget should specify the tools for measuring performances, and preferably incorporate the outline of the reporting system

Numerous problems are encountered while preparing a budget. In the fast changing environment, it is difficult to forecast sales. The production resource costs change frequently with the market trends. Future resource prices get affected with inflation but the sale value which is based on the agreed bill of quantities remains the same. There is a behavioural aspect to budgeting. It includes the tendency to inflate expenditure, and resistance to budgeting itself as the budget provides a tool to measure their performance.

It may be noted that the project budget can crash if it has unrealistic targets specially when it is thrust by the top hierarchy. A project budget is a financial plan based on certain assumptions and like the project plan, it needs to be reviewed regularly as it cannot take care of all eventualities and unforeseen circumstances. Further, a project budget provides a tool for effective management but it has to be handled carefully with the changing situations.

## 12.7 IMPORTANCE OF PROJECT BUDGET

The project budget is essentially, a planning document. It outlines the financial plan of the project. The project budget depicts the management's vision for the future, it aims at specifying the future financial course of action for steering the project. Budget quantifies in monetary terms the project cost objectives, it allocates responsibility for attaining these objectives, it reflects the resources earmarked, it pinpoints the results to be achieved by the responsibility. It provides a standard for measuring effectiveness and efficiency with which activities are to be performed.

A project budget is a financial commitment for actions, an instrument for delegation of responsibility, a means for communication, an aid for coordination, a tool for motivation, an authority for implementation and a device foe controlling performance.

A project without a budget is like a missile without a guidance system or a ship without navigational instruments. If there is no budget, there will be no means to measure performance. Working without quantified objectives and without commitments amounts to working aimlessly.

Budget and budgetary control are inseparable. Without a budget, there can be no budgetary control and without budgetary control, even the best formulated budget will serve no purpose. Budgetary control makes use of budget and budgetary reports to compare the actual with budgeted standards to bring out the extent of variations, it reasons out the causes for significant verifications, brings out actions necessary to achieve objectives and provides a base for its revision when necessary. Budgetary control methodology is described in Chapter 15.

# PART IV

# Planning Control System

- ❑ Project Control Methodology
- ❑ Resource Productivity Control
- ❑ Project Cost Control
- ❑ Project Time Control
- ❑ Codification of the Planning System
- ❑ Project Management Information System

# CHAPTER 13

# Project Control Methodology

An efficient control system generates information that can improve the productivity of men and materials; economize the employment of resources; enable understanding of time and cost behaviour; provide early warning signals of ensuing dangers; update resources planning and costing norms; prevent pilferages and frauds; and assist in formulating bonus/incentive schemes for motivating people.

Despite the well-recognized importance of controlling projects, experience shows that the controlling systems are rarely effectively implemented at the project sites. There could be many reasons for this slipshod attitude to the system. The inherent variables in the construction projects make it impossible to derive a tailor-made solution for developing and implementing a project control system. Further, managers and site engineers are generally hesitant to face predetermined performance evaluation measures specified in control systems. A control system involves interaction among managers, and the system collapses when there are conflicts and communication gaps. It is noticed that in the initial stages, the project management goes on debating the design and procedures of the control system, and in turn the implementation continues slipping thus losing valuable time and information. The problems and conflicts inherent in controlling projects can be minimized if the management has a clearly defined policy on how to organize a control system and each participant understands its methodology.

This Chapter outlines the project control methodology for controlling a time-bound, capital-intensive, high-cost construction project. It introduces the control system framework and identifies the parameters to be controlled for achieving specified objectives. It covers the methodology for accounting and monitoring performance and describes the salient features of the information communication process. Towards the end, it highlights the resulting benefits of an effective control system.

The methodology for resource productivity control, cost control and time control is described in Chapters 14 through 16. The guidelines for codification are outlined in Chapter 17. Project Management Information System (PMIS) and the application of computers in the planning and controlling of projects are described in Chapter 18. In fact, Chapter 18 should be read in continuation with this chapter.

**394** Construction Project Management

The contents of this Chapter should be viewed as guidelines. The system and methodology covered here should be suitably modified to conform to the varied nature of the construction projects, and to meet the needs of the client and corporate management.

## ❑ 13.1 CONTROL SYSTEM FRAMEWORK

### 13.1.1 Systems Approach

A system is a set of interrelated elements that work collectively to achieve common objectives. It is an assemblage or a combination of things or parts forming a complex or unitary whole. The system approach is viewed as a series of logical, interrelated steps/stages/processes that integrate all the necessary functions to achieve optimum performance.

Construction project management system (or systems in case of large project) comprises a number of logically related sub-systems. The key sub-systems include planning, organisation, project control and information communication. Planning sub-system consists of project plan, time schedule, manpower plan, materials procurement plan plant and machinery plan, cost plan, project budget, policy documents, procedures, programmes, targets, etc. all combined to give direction to the project. An organisation sub-system constitutes personnel policies, procedures and people grouped together to perform the work. Project control system collects, collates and processes data to extract and disseminate information on time, resources, costs and quality performance. The information communication sub-system (or Project Management Information System) deals with collection, dissemination, communication and retrievals of information for decision making. Project management system also includes an array of other sub-systems like finance management, materials management, estimation and contract management, safety management, etc. Generally, the systems/sub-systems in project conform to corporate system/policy, if necessary, they can be tailor-made.

### 13.1.2 Project Control System

The project control objectives are generally stated in terms of the specified completion time within predetermined costs and profitability. The project plan shows the path for achieving these objectives. But even with the best efforts, the probability of execution of a project exactly as per planning is negligible. There will be unpredictable resource limitations and unforeseen activity delays. Like the guidance system of a missile, a project needs an effective control system to continuously monitor the deviations from the planned paths, and to apply corrective measures.

Project control follows the systems concept. Each organisational unit in a project, usually referred to as a responsibility centre, can be viewed as a sub-system. These sub-systems are interdependent and interactive. Typical sub-systems encountered in a Housing Project are sketched in Exhibit 13.1.

Project Control Methodology **395**

Exhibit 13.1

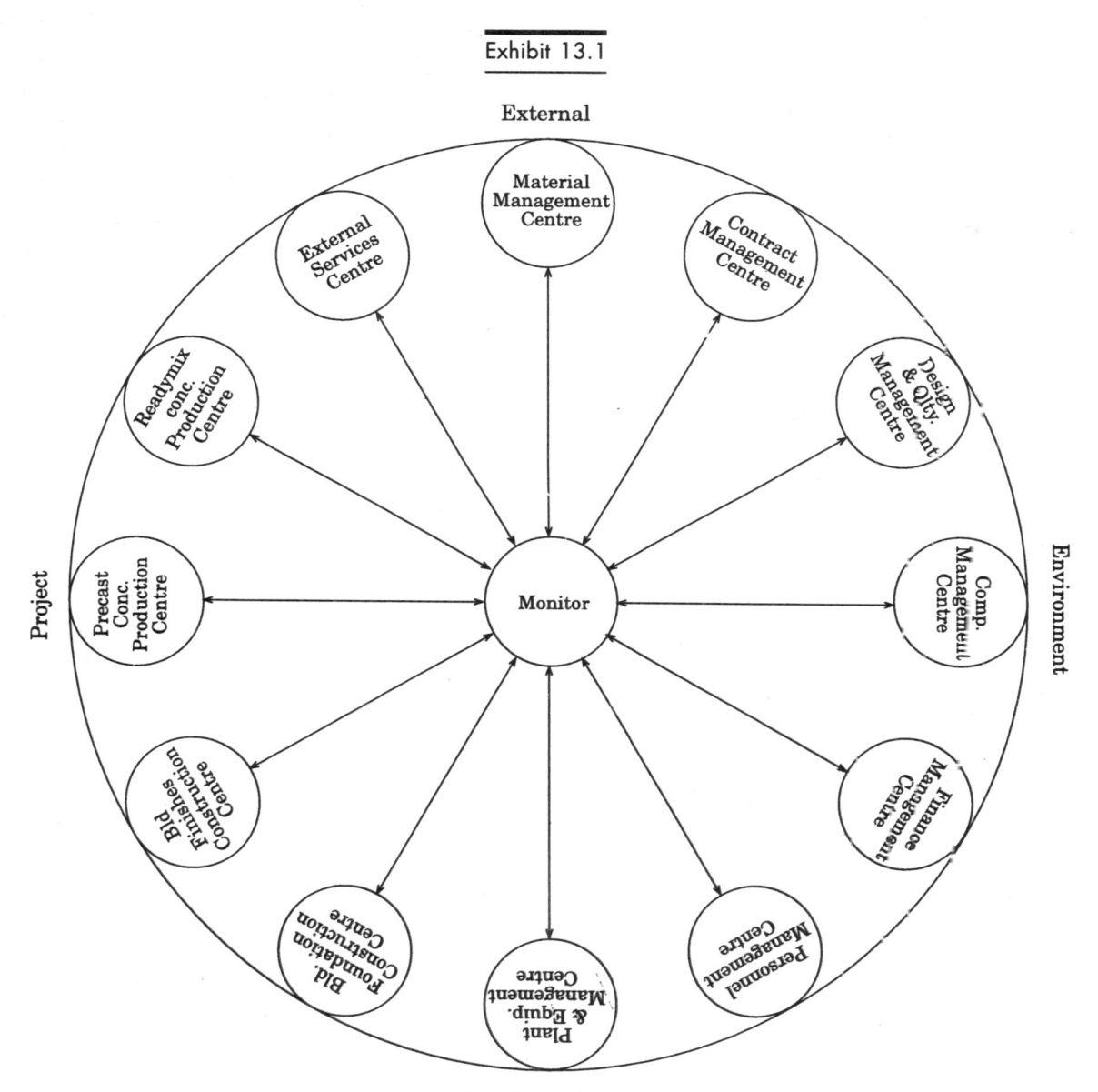

*External*

*Project* — *Environment*

Project Control System

## 13.1.3 Control Process

The performance objectives of a sub-system are stated in terms of parameters to be controlled. The typical parameters include time-progress targets, resources productivity standards, project sales, and standard costs. Each sub-system accounts for its performance, and transmits the actual performance and the deviations between the planned and the actual performance to the monitor. The project control system inputs are the actual performance accounting data generated by the sub-systems. This input data is processed in the project control system to extract and communicate information. The schematic diagram of a control process is shown in Fig. 13.1.

Figure 13.1

**Schematic Diagram of a Control Process**

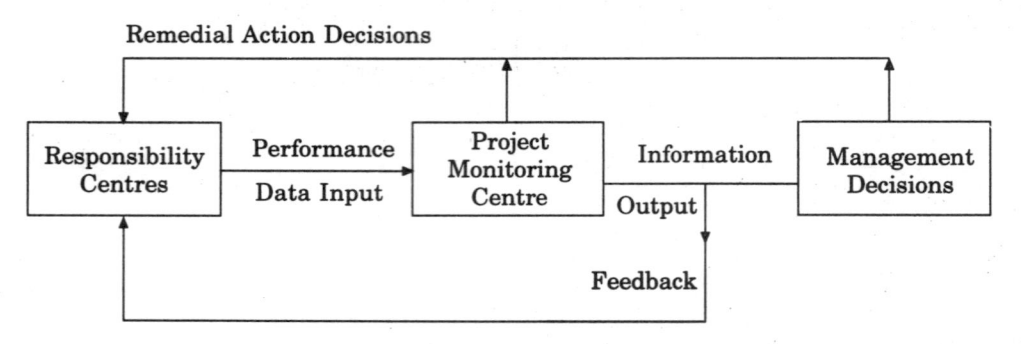

```
                    Remedial Action Decisions
         ┌──────────────────────────┬──────────────────────────┐
         │                          │                          │
         ↓                          │                          │
  ┌──────────────┐  Performance  ┌──────────┐  Information  ┌────────────┐
  │Responsibility│───────────────│ Project  │───────────────│ Management │
  │   Centres    │  Data Input   │Monitoring│   Output      │ Decisions  │
  │              │               │  Centre  │               │            │
  └──────────────┘               └──────────┘               └────────────┘
         ↑                            │
         │                         Feedback
         └────────────────────────────┘
```

The project control centre, manned by a monitor, is the heart of the system. The monitor processes the performance data received from the sub-systems. Monitoring involves tapping of reported data from various accounting sub-systems (i.e. responsibility centres), consolidating and analysing this data to extract information suggesting remedial courses of action for achieving project objectives. This information, when communicated at appropriate levels, for making decisions results in steering **the organisational efforts** towards the attainment of the project objectives.

Planning-Executing-Accounting-Monitoring-Re-planning (when necessary)-Communicating is a continuous controlling process, and goes on till the completion of the project. Steps in the control process are as under:

*Step* 1 : Define the parameters to be controlled.
*Step* 2 : Establish base lines for measuring performance.
*Step* 3 : Account performance by
- measuring performance
- recording performance
- reporting performance deviations.

*Step* 4 : Monitor performance by
- consolidating reported performance data.
- analysing performance variations
- forecasting performance trends.

*Step* 5 : Communicate information.
- feedback
- management report
- record keeping

The methodology of accounting, monitoring, and communicating information concerning the time, resources and the costs performance parameters to be controlled is outlined in subsequent paragraphs.

## 13.2 PERFORMANCE PARAMETERS TO BE CONTROLLED

Performance in simple words implies the degree of achievement. Parameters define the goals to be achieved. Each responsibility centre accounts for the performance of the assigned parameters, and transmits the deviations between the actual and planned performance to the monitor. In a construction project, the typical parameters that may be controlled are as follows:

**(a) Time progress control** It aims at the timely execution of the work as per the work programme and applying corrective measures in cases of deviation so as to achieve the project time objective. It involves:

- Measuring the project time progress.
- Analyzing the implications of deviation from the project time schedule.
- Formulating remedial measures including time crashing to achieve project time objectives.

**(b) Resource productivity control** It aims at the effective utilization of direct resources of men, materials, plant and machinery:

- Evaluating variances from resource productivity standards.
- Analyzing the causes of variations.
- Directing resource productivity improvement measures.
- Revising resource standards (if necessary).
- Modifying resources mobilization plan (if necessary).

**(c) Resource mobilization control** It aims at ensuring the timely availability of resources at the site as per plan:

- Updating the resource status and forecasting requirements.
- Analyzing the implications of variations from the original mobilization plan.
- Directing resource mobilization for timely completion.

**(d) Direct cost control** It aims at economizing operations by creating cost consciousness in the project environment. It involves:

- Analyzing causes for variances.
- Directing cost economizing measures.
- Developing unit rates of items of work for future tendering.
- Updating project cost status.

**(e) Budgeted cost control** It aims at forecasting trends from the budgeted cost plan by:

- Evaluating project cost status and its variations from the budget.
- Analyzing causes for variations.
- Forecasting production costs behaviour.
- Initiating cost reduction measures.

**(f) Work done sales or earned value control** It aims at work quantity and work done sales control by:

- Measuring work done as per bill of quantities, and stock taking of direct materials and other payable items at the site.
- Evaluating the monthly sales status of the project.
- Billing work done, work-in-progress and additional payable items.
- Forecasting cash-in-flow.
- Raising claims for deviations due to extra work.

The parameters required to be controlled, listed above, are indicative and not exhaustive. Depending upon the nature of the project, there can be additions and alterations in these parameters. For example, in a simple project, direct cost control can be combined with resource productivity control or budgeted cost control. In complex projects, new parameters such as investment control may have to be added to evaluate the economics of 'make or buy' and 'hire or purchase' decisions.

Further, in case of projects being executed in a foreign country, mobilization control becomes necessary so as to ensure the timely induction of resources.

The control parameters are not mutually exclusive. They are interrelated as well as interdependent (See Fig. 13.2). To quote an example, the work-progress time goals do get affected if the productivity adopted norms change or the resources are not inducted as per mobilization plan.

Similarly, the budget is interlinked with the outcomes of almost all other parameters. The weaknesses and deviations in each of these parameters resulting from non-fulfilment of planned targets, not only have their repercussions on the respective parameter goals but they affect the project as a whole.

## 13.3 PERFORMANCE BASE LINES

Performance is measured with respect to predetermined specified targets or standards termed 'performance base lines'. These base lines are devices used for measuring performance variations by comparing the originally planned performance with the actual performance to determine the deviations from the planned path. The purpose of establishing performance base lines is to assist the responsibility centres in measuring deviations in the actual performance from the planned standards. It is these deviations that serve as the early warning signals of ensuing dangers to the goal controllers.

Some of the goal measuring base lines or standards used for various controlled parameters are illustrated below:

### Figure 13.2

**Project Performance Control**

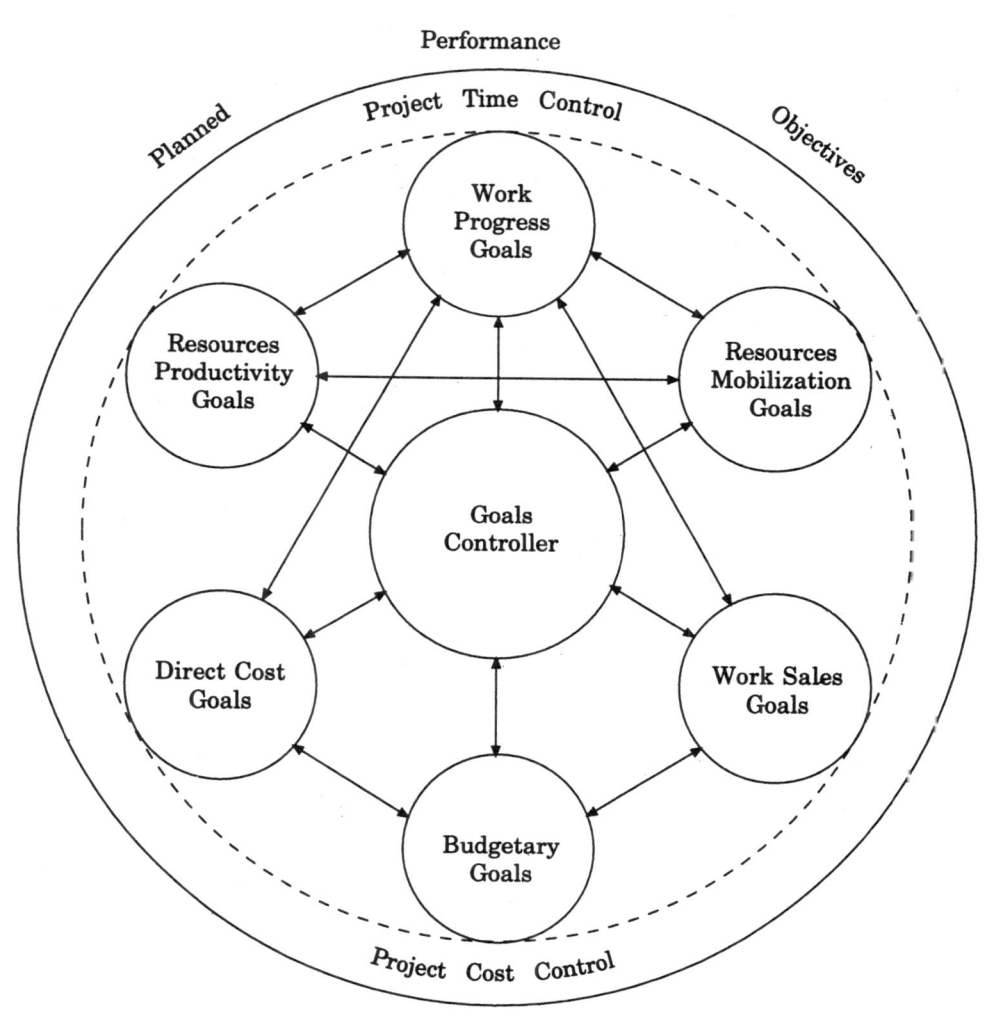

Interaction and interdependence of performance goals.

| S.No. | Control parameters | Performance base lines |
|---|---|---|
| (1) | Time progress | Project master time schedule |
| (2) | Resource productivity | Resource performance standards |
| (3) | Resource mobilization | Project resource induction plan |

(4)    Work-package direct cost    Standard direct cost
(5)    Project costs                Project budget
(6)    Sales income                 Sales budget

The base line for time control is the project master time schedule. This schedule, generally prepared as a bar chart, covers the entire scope of the project work and its execution plan. It depicts the time schedule for the commencement and completion of all work packages. It highlights the milestones and the contracts/subcontracts planned during the entire project life. It provides the yardstick for measuring the time progress. The project master time schedule is supported by part plans developed for sub-projects and construction tasks. These sub-projects and construction task plans are prepared using planning techniques like network analyses and line of balance techniques. In its summarized form, the master schedule is used for reporting progress to corporate authorities and forming the data base for engineering activities, resource mobilization and time saving.

Resource productivity base lines are defined in terms of productivity standards. These standards are used to measure deviations of the actual resource productivity from its base lines. It is these deviations that give the early warning of ensuing dangers to the goal controllers.

Project budget acts as the base line for measuring cost and sales performances. It is supplemented by standard cost and earned value estimates for each work package.

It may be noted that the base line or standard performance parameter of a work package are fixed (or frozen) till it is revised during the course of implementation of the project. These base lines are an assessment of the expected performance by the planners. It may not be equal to the performance estimated by the estimators at the time of tendering. Further, the planned performance reflects the average value over a period of time. Initially the actual performance may be lower due to the teething troubles. These performance base lines should be reviewed after 20–25% of the project has progressed.

An important point to remember is that a given task can be executed by different methods, but the actual performance is based on the method actually adopted for execution and not on what was considered at the time of planning.

## ❑ 13.4 PERFORMANCE ACCOUNTING PROCESS

The term 'accounting' covers measuring and recording actual performance, and reporting it to the appropriate authority. The accounting methodology depends upon the parameters being controlled.

### 13.4.1 Measuring and Recording Performance

Performance is measured in relation to the base line yard-sticks. Recording involves documenting facts about the actual progress of goals/targets/activities/resource utilization using established procedures or specified devices, and presenting these facts in a concise and comprehensive form for analysis. The performance measured is documented scientifically.

The recording of performance by a contractor at the project site can be divided into two groups, i.e. recording in contractual documents, and recording in contractor's own accounting documents.

**Project contractual documents** These documents are maintained by the contractor at the site to record the work progress, resource employment, and other progress related matters for the information of the client. In large-size projects, the contractor furnishes this information to the client in the form of reports. The client's engineer, after scrutiny, gives his remarks on the documents at the specified places. The types of documents vary from client to client and project to project. Some of the commonly used contractual documents for recording work related matters are listed below:

(a) Work schedule and work programmes.
(b) Work diary.
(c) Stage passing register.
(d) Work deviations order register.
(e) Work measurement books.
(f) Work progress reports.
(g) Materials sample approval register.
(h) Materials inspection register.
(i) Major equipment employment register.
(j) Equipment instruments calibration certificates.
(k) Equipment performance test report.
(l) Contract cost status.
(m) Minutes of site meetings.

In particular, it is the usual practice to maintain a works diary to daily record the weather, activities in progress, manpower engaged at the site, major materials received, equipment deployed, important events of the day, and comments of the visitors. This document is scrutinized daily and signed by the client's engineer with his remarks. Contractual documents are primarily used by the client to monitor the contractor's work progress, but these are not sufficient for the contractor to control his time, resources and cost objectives.

**Contractor's documents** At the project site the contractors design their own systems for accounting the project parameters. Generally, their functional heads maintain their project records centrally, but the physical performance data originates from the respective responsibility centres. Accordingly, each responsibility centre also maintains its respective documents to record the progress of the work and day-to-day employment of resources of men, materials and equipment. In particular, the typical activity performance sheet, shown in Table 14.3 can be used by the monitor and manager in charge of the responsibility centre to record the construction activities and connected resources. In addition to the work-package performance monitoring sheet, some of the documents used on the construction site for recording performance data are listed in Table 13.1.

### Table 13.1
### Documents Used for Recording Performance Data on the Construction Site

| Sl. No. | Control Parameter | Facts Recorded | Typical Recording Documents |
|---|---|---|---|
| (1) | Work progress | Actual starting and completion dates of each activity | Works diary, Daily work progress report, work-package performance sheet |
| (2) | Materials utilization | Receipts and issues | Materials ledgers |
| (3) | Manpower utilization | Daily workers' employment | Time-keeper's muster rolls register/sheet |
| (4) | Plant and machinery utilization | Hours utilized | Equipment operation log-books |
| (5) | Production costs | Actual costs | Construction accounts |
| (6) | Sales | Quantity and value of work done | Measurement books, Monthly invoices of work done and materials at site, Extra work statements |

#### 13.4.2 Reporting Performance by Responsibility Centres

A performance report is generally a written document that shows the up-to-date performance status of a task entrusted to a responsibility/accounting centre. Performance reports (Exhibit 13.3) transmit the performance data covering the actual achievements and deviations from standards, and highlight the reasons for such deviations in a standard format at a predetermined frequency to the specified monitoring centre. The frequency of reporting varies with the nature of the task being handled by the performance centre and the efforts required to compile it. The nature and frequency of these reports encountered in typical major housing construction projects are shown in Exhibit 13.2.

In a project, each Control Responsibility Centre generally accumulates data while accounting performance. This data, either spoken, verbal or written, is furnished from time to time by the subordinates operating at various levels to the respective manager incharge of the responsibility centre. All this data, if communicated to the monitor, can only clutter up his records and unnecessarily increase his work-load or even the vital data may get lost in the process. Out of this mass of accounting data, monitor needs relevant easy-to-analyze data that effects the assigned goals and objectives of the control centre. The desired input data can best be obtained by the monitor through suitably designed performance reports taking the following into consideration:

(a) What are the short-term goals and long-term objectives assigned to the Responsibility Centre?
(b) What is the data needed to monitor the performance of these goals and objectives?
(c) How should this data be obtained from the initiators, viz. in a verbal or a written form?
(d) What should be the nature, format and frequency of reports to be submitted by each control responsibility centre to the monitor?

## Exhibit 13.2
### 2000 Housing Units Project
### Typical Responsibility Centre Control Performance Reports

| Sl. No. | Responsibility Centre Designation | Purpose of Report |
|---|---|---|
| | *Central Batching Plant* | |
| 1. | Monthly concreting materials reconciliation report | (a) To assess wastage of materials<br>(b) To take stock of materials |
| 2. | Daily concrete production and delivery report | (a) To monitor the daily performance of the concrete production centre<br>(b) To determine excess concrete consumed—building-wise and activity-wise |
| | *Rebar Yard* | |
| 3. | Daily reinforcement fabrication report | To assess daily output for cutting, bending and transportation. |
| 4. | Weekly materials reconciliation report | (a) To assess wastage of materials<br>(b) To evaluate total fabrication work done |
| | *Construction Sites* | |
| 5. | Activity-wise progress report | To monitor daily physical and financial progress activity-wise |
| 6. | Labor Employment Report | (a) To assess manpower output activity-wise<br>(b) To control effectiveness of machines employment |
| | *Plant and Equipment Maintenance Centre* | |
| 7. | Machinery utilisation report | To monitor performance of machinery |
| | *Materials Department Reports* | |
| 8. | Daily cement, sand and aggregate receipt report | To record quantity of cement, sand and aggregate received from various sources |
| 9. | Daily imported materials and machinery received | To monitor mobilisation of materials and implication of the deviations from laid down stock levels |
| 10. | Weekly status of important construction materials | |
| | *Personnel Department Reports* | |
| 11. | Workers, daily employment report | To control distribution of workers with project |
| 12. | Workers arrival/departure report | To update manpower planning records |
| 13. | Weekly site staff allocation report | To control overall distribution of key project personnel |

*(Contd.)*

*(Contd.)*

| Sl. No. | Responsibility Centre Designation | Purpose of Report |
|---|---|---|
| | *Technical Department Reports—Design and Drawings* | |
| 14. | Approval of drawing status | To monitor the schedule of approval of drawings |
| | *Quantity Survey Section* | |
| 15. | Weekly status of quantities estimates. | To monitor the progress made in estimation of quantities. |
| 16. | Weekly materials sample approved status | To track the materials procurement plan |
| 17. | Monthly value of work executed | To monitor the value of the sales income from the workdone |
| | *Planning Cell* | |
| 18. | Weekly work progress materials monitoring report | To analyse the implications of deviations from the project plan |
| 19. | Weekly resource mobilisation monitoring report | |
| 20. | Monthly site report | As per the requirement of the client |
| 21. | Monthly management information report | To report performance and hold-ups/bottlenecks to corporate management |

(e) Is the data reported required for controlling the performance of other control centres? If so, who should be asked to initiate the report?

(f) How accurate should each report be? The degree of accuracy will depend upon the purpose of the report.

(g) Will the report initiator need additional assistance to submit the report? If so, what and how much? (In particular, the stationery and printing requirements should also be assessed.)

(h) Can the report under consideration be eliminated, substituted, combined, rearranged or simplified? This should be reexamined before finalization.

It is emphasized that there are no tailor-made formats for reporting the performance. Generally, the contents of a report should show the performance goals in the form of current and cumulative status. It should indicate variances from planned targets with reasons. It should identify bottlenecks in achieving goals, and it should highlight the aspects needing further action.

The reporting formats should conform to the monitor's specifications, organization's management information system (MIS), computer software requirements, and codification system. The format design should seek the participation of the performance controllers prior to finalization.

In particular, responsibility centres must not be loaded with paperwork. The reports should be designed in such a manner that it reduces the recording effort. To quote an example, the 'daily activities time progress' report format of the foundation responsibility centre of the housing units project is shown in Exhibit 13.3. This report served the following main purposes:

(a) It made the site supervisors pre-plan for the next day's work including the allocation of resources for each activity.
(b) It provided the following valuable data to the monitor and cost accountant in respect of each current activity:

   (i) State of time progress showing the dates of commencement and completion activity-wise.
   (ii) Correlation of activity with resources deployed and consumed such as man-days utilized for the completion of each activity and the corresponding productivity achieved.
   (iii) The earned value of the work done.
   (iv) Reasons for hold-ups or work stoppages.

When read with the time-keeper/foreman's activity-wise daily workers' employment report (see Table 14.3), the monitor can determine the workers' productivity in man-hours consumed for each completed activity. Further, by suitably designing the Demand and Delivery Note, the monitor can assess the wet concrete wastage for each concreting activity by comparing the actual concrete supplied with the theoretical quantity, after he receives the daily building-wise concrete delivery report from the ready-mix concrete centre.

Similarly, by comparing the ready-mix concrete responsibility centre's monthly stock consumed and concrete supplied report, the monitor can estimate the percentage wastage of cement, sand and aggregate. The format given in Table 13.2 will prove useful.

## ❏ 13.5 MONITORING PERFORMANCE

The performance monitoring process commences after the monitor receives the appropriate performance data through site reports, personal visits and discussions. The performance monitoring process can be divided into the following stages:

(a) Consolidating reported performance data.
(b) Analyzing performance variances.
(c) Forecasting performance trends.

### 13.5.1 Consolidating Data

The 'responsibility centres' performance reports generate ample tabulated data. This reported tabulated data, generally unorganized, needs consolidation and reorganization. The common types of charts used for control data consolidation can be divided into the following categories:

(a) **Network charts** These are used for time planning and controlling of projects. Examples are CPM, PERT, precedence network diagrams, and time-scaled Network charts.

## Exhibit 13.3

## Foundation Construction Sub-project

*Daily Progress Report*

Dated

| | | | | Foundation Tasks | | | |
|---|---|---|---|---|---|---|---|
| | | | | Modules | Building Nos. | | |
| S.No. | Activities per Module | Unit | Quantity | Completion Reported Earlier | Completed Previous Day | In Progress Today | Planned Next Day |
| 1. | Layout for excavation | — | — | | | | |
| 2. | Excavation with machine | CM | 400 | | | | |
| 3. | Base preparation | SM | 360 | | | | |
| 4. | Anti-termite at base | SM | 362 | | | | |
| 5. | Polythene sheeting | SM | 362 | | | | |
| 6. | Shuttering for blinding | RM | 90 | | | | |
| 7. | Placing concrete M-100 | CM | 18 | | | | |
| 8. | Layout for raft | — | — | | | | |
| 9. | Shuttering for raft | SM | 22.5 | | | | |
| 10. | Reinforcement for raft | MT | 6.066 | | | | |
| 11. | Raft concreting M-250 | CM | 88.14 | | | | |
| 12. | Curing raft | — | — | | | | |
| 13. | Bitumen coating raft sides | SM | 362 | | | | |
| 14. | Layout for plinth wall | — | — | | | | |
| 15. | Wall shuttering | SM | 485 | | | | |
| 16. | Wall concreting M-250 | CM | 43.78 | | | | |
| 17. | Deshuttering | — | — | | | | |
| 18. | Curing wall | — | — | | | | |
| 19. | Bitumen coating wall and raft | SM | 319 | | | | |
| 20. | Back filling | CM | 120 | | | | |
| 21. | Plinth filling | CM | 305 | | | | |
| 22. | Anti-termite under GF slab | SM | 172 | | | | |
| 23. | Polythene sheeting | SM | 225 | | | | |
| 24. | Shuttering for GF slab | SM | 11 | | | | |
| 25. | Weld mesh fixing | MT | 0.651 | | | | |
| 26. | GF concreting M-250 | CM | 28.34 | | | | |
| 27. | Curing GF slab | — | — | | | | |

**Table 13.2**

**Materials Wastage Control Report**
**Summary Ready-mix Concrete Monthly Stock Status**

|     |                                           | Cement | Sand  | Aggregate |
|-----|-------------------------------------------|--------|-------|-----------|
| (A) | Opening stock                             | x      | xx    | xxx       |
| (B) | Quantity received                         | xx     | xxx   | xxxx      |
| (C) | Closing stock                             | – (x)  | – (x) | –.(xx)    |
| (D) | Actual amount consumed (A + B – C)        | xx     | xxx   | xxxx      |
| (E) | Budgeted consumption for concrete supplied | xx     | xxx   | xxxx      |
|     | Wastage (E – D)                           | x      | x     | xx        |

**(b) XY charts** These indicate trends over a period of time. There are many varieties in the XY charts.

*Types*  |  *Examples*
XY Bar charts  |  Bar chart schedules
XY Line charts  |  Resource productivity control charts
XY Curve charts  |  'S' Curve forecasts. Cyclographs.

The main types of XY charts considered useful for consolidating data are listed in Table 13.3.

**(c) Tables** These are used to compile and compare data such as in financial statements and work-progress evaluation.

Various types of charts used for consolidating data have certain common features to enhance presentation and comprehension. These include:

**(a) Chart title and subtitle** The title identifies the chart and the subtitle emphasizes the central idea.

**(b) Footnotes and legends** These contain the explanatory portions of the charts.

**(c) X and Y axes** X axis is the horizontal axis and Y, the vertical. These axes are described with a brief text.

**(d) Scale** This represents the range of values assigned to the axes.

**(e) Grid lines** These are the graphic lines showing the intersections of data.

**(f) Border** It frames the chart and adds beauty to it.

## Table 13.3

**Typical XY Charts for Data Consolidation**

| S. No. | Type of charts | Application | Example |
|---|---|---|---|
| 1. | XY Horizontal bar | To show growth trend with time. | Work schedules |
| 2. | XY Stack bar | To demonstrate parts of a total, spread over a time period. | Month-wise workers forecast, LOB Control Chart |
| 3. | XY Stack bar cumulative | To depict increase over a time period in numbers or percentage. | Financial cumulative forecast month-wise |
| 4. | XY Paired bar (horizontal or vertical) | To compare planned and actual. | Double bar charts |
| 5. | XY Curves | To highlight changes in data over time. | Cumulative 'S' curves |
| 6. | XY Line (zigzag) | To illustrate sharp changes in trends. | Resources productivity charts |
| 7. | XY Deviation (line or bar) | To compare changes from the standards. | Range charts |
| 8. | XY Point chart | To establish co-relation. | Concrete wastage chart |
| 9. | XY Histograms | To depict frequency or probability distribution. | Risk probability distribution pattern |

Consolidated data displays in the form of graphs, charts, diagrams, tables and pictures have visual appeal. They are the best means of human communication. Visual displays help in understanding the complications and interrelated states of performance of various control centres at a glance and provide insights into the operations.

### 13.5.2 Analyzing Performance Variances

The term 'variance' stands for the difference between the planned and the actual. When associated with the parameter of a work-item or activity being controlled, variances represent differences in planned and actual performance of the controlled factors.

Performance variance = Planned performance − Actual performance.

For example,
Work quantity variance = Planned work quantity − Actual work quantity.
Activity duration variance = Planned activity duration − Actual activity duration.
Production cost variance = Standard production cost − Actual production cost.
Sales revenue variance = Budgeted value of sales revenue − Actual revenue from sales.

Variances when evaluated can be zero, plus or minus. Plus or zero value variances are called favourable, and the minus value variances are termed unfavourable.

Variance ≥ 0, Favourable (F).
Variance < 0, Unfavourable (U).

To quote an example, if the actual cost of a work-item is greater than the standard cost, the work-item has an unfavourable variance.

Further, a variance is said to be controllable if it is associated with the operational efficiency, say the responsibility of an executive or the performance of a work-centre. For example, variance due to wastage of concreting material more than the planned wastage is a controllable variance.

On the other hand, the causes of variance which are beyond the control of the management such as increase in labour wages due to labour legislation are called uncontrollable variances.

The primary purpose of introducing the variance concept is that it generates information for determining the causes of deviations from the planned approach. Variance analysis generally follows the questioning approach following:

(a) What is the extent of the variance?
(b) What are the controllable and the uncontrollable causes of variances?
(c) How to tackle controllable and uncontrollable variances and what are their implications?
(d) Will the uncontrollable variance occur again? If so, when and what will be its effect?

It may be noted that variance analysis presupposes that the work-item or activity being analyzed is identifiable and measurable and therefore, each variance can be considered an isolated item. But some of them may have interacting effects and in such cases they should be analyzed in conjunction with others.

## 13.5.3 Trends Forecasting

Performance variance analysis reveals the extent and causes of variances. On the other hand, performance efficiency, when read in conjunction with variance analysis, indicates the implications of the past performance on future trends.

$$\text{Performance variance} = \text{Planned performance} - \text{Actual performance}$$

$$\text{Performance efficiency} = \frac{\text{Actual output performance}}{\text{Planned input performance}}, \text{ e.g. } \frac{\text{Workdone per man-day}}{\text{Work planned per man-day}}.$$

Performance efficiency (or index) determines how efficiently the task was done; performance efficiency greater than 1 shows better performance than planned and vice versa. See the following:

$$\text{Performance efficiency} \quad \begin{aligned} &> 1, \text{ Performance better than planned.} \\ &= 1, \text{ Performance equal to planned.} \\ &< 1, \text{ Performance less than planned.} \end{aligned}$$

Performance efficiency is a trend indicator. It provides the tool for forecasting future requirements of resources.

A simple method of forecasting trends is to calculate the performance efficiency and to proportionately increase or decrease the resources for the remaining work. For example, consider a masonry wall construction activity with planned and actual performance as follows:

|  | *Planned Performance* | *Actual Performance* |
|---|---|---|
| Scope of masonry work | 1200 m$^2$ | 1200 m$^2$ |
| Crew size | 8 men | 8 men |
| Construction time | 15 days | 18 days. |

Labour performance efficiency for the given task can be calculated as under:

Planned labour performance = 8 men × 15 days = 120 man-days

Actual labour performance = 8 men × 18 days = 144 man-days

$$\text{Labour performance efficiency} = \frac{\text{Workdone per Man-day}}{\text{Work planned per Man-days}} = \frac{W/144}{W/120} = \frac{120}{144} = \frac{5}{6}$$

Therefore, a simple approach for determining the resources for future similar works to be completed during the specified period of 15 days (disregarding improvements in efficiency due to the learning process) will be to increase the labour crew size in proportion to the recorded actual labour performance efficiency = 8 × 6/5, say 10 men.

This simple approach for forecasting future labour requirement trends based on performance efficiency is not enough. This performance efficiency should be studied along with performance variances to determine what caused the low performance and whether these causes will be repeated or not, and what is the possibility of improvement by adopting alternate construction methods, through, better organization or with the learning process, or a combination of all these factors.

Understanding of some of the techniques and concepts given below can help in producing a realistic forecast of future performance. There are no hard and fast rules to state as to which technique will be used, when and where:

(a) **Time forecasting techniques** Network analysis, and line-of-balance technique.

(b) **Statistical analysis and operations research methods** Data analysis, forecasting, regression analysis, statistical control charts (similar to statistical quality control) and analytical decision-making techniques.

(c) **Management accounting technique** Cost accounting, cost control, working capital management, cost–benefit analysis, break-even analysis, and performance audit.

(d) **Management concepts** Management principles, behaviour science, personnel management, materials management, plant management, finance management, contract management, and quality management.

The methods of forecasting the performance can be broadly divided into three categories, i.e. resource performance forecasting, time performance forecasting, and cost performance forecasting. Trend forecasting methods are outlined in Chapters 15 and 16.

### 13.5.4 Monitoring Frequency

It is a debatable point as to what should be the frequency of performance monitoring. One school of thought lays stress on economizing monitoring costs. Another school of thought advocates site reporting and monitoring at regular preplanned intervals of time.

It is felt that depending upon the importance and complexity of the project, the status evaluation of controlled parameters should be carried out immediately on receipt of the concerned performance reports whereas the trend analysis based on the current plan can be performed at weekly/fortnightly intervals. Replanning is a time-and-effort consuming process and it should be undertaken only when necessary.

It is important to note that effective monitoring depends upon the accurate and timely reporting of the input data. Delays or distorted data lead to incorrect analyses. Similarly, monitoring has no meaning if the feedback by the monitor is not given on time to the site executives. Team spirit coupled with a sense of responsibility of all the participants can go a long way to make monitoring effective.

## ❏ 13.6 INFORMATION COMMUNICATION

Information is the crucial ingredient of the decision-making process. Timely, relevant and accurate information is necessary for making quantitative analyses of the feasible courses of action for achieving goals and deciding the most suitable one for implementation. The greater the size and complexity of the project, the greater is the need for information pertaining to the project resources and their performance behaviour within the framework of stipulations made in the project plan.

The project control system aims at economically collecting the right information in the right form through the right means at the right time from the right place and communicating it to the right person on time for taking the right action. The project monitor, who taps data from various sources and processes it to extract information, is assigned the task of data record keeping, data processing and timely communication of the performance feedback to the project teams and the information report to the top management.

### 13.6.1 Data Record Keeping

The project data bank, manned by the monitor, can be set up at each site to hold the following up-to-date records for ready reference:

(a) Contract documents including terms and conditions, drawings, specifications, bill of quantities, and activity-wise costs and sale prices.
(b) Project models, layout pictures, tabulated scope and progress-of-work statements, and photographs depicting work progress.
(c) Project plans and connected charts, networks, planning assumptions including productivity standards.
(d) Statistics of various reports and returns handled in the project and pictorial displays.

(e) Records of minutes of all meetings, conferences, policies and important correspondence.
(f) Control charts showing progress-of-work, mobilization status of resources, contract cost status and the 'S' curve forecasts.
(g) Updated unit rates and resource cost planning data.

It is ideal to have a project control room at site office where all updated monitoring information is displayed. The executives should be encouraged to regularly visit this room and read the feedback.

## 13.6.2 Feedback Communication

Feedback conveys information to the responsibility centres pertaining to their performance and its implications on assigned goals. It may reveal what was achieved, what was targeted for accomplishment, what is the extent of deviations in performance, what caused these deviations and what are the remedial courses of action possible.

Feedback can be communicated in many ways. It can be transmitted verbally, in the form of brief feedback reports or as briefings during regular planning meetings. In these planning meetings, the monitor can highlight deviations in the planned performances and stress the subsequent performance targets and the measures contemplated by the project manager. Where considered necessary, minutes of the formal planning meetings can be recorded and distributed to all concerned. As far as possible, writing lengthy memoranda and notes should be avoided.

It is important that feedback is given in time as delayed feedback may not serve the purpose. For example, it is no use telling a site engineer a week after the completion of an activity that its productivity was 20% lower than the standard rate. Timely feedback creates prompt awareness and enables initiation of timely remedial actions.

It is not necessary for the monitor to feedback the analyzed data down to each supervisor. He should feedback only relevant information to each level. Too much information can overshadow the vital information, whereas, too little may not convince the receiver about the reliability of the information.

In some projects, contractors do not encourage feedback. According to them, it can reveal business secrets and jeopardize their security of information. These contractors wish to conceal their estimates and performance figures for bidding future works, and to support their financial claims. In such cases the remedy lies not in withholding the feedback, but in suitably codifying the feedback. This codification can be achieved by giving feedback data in the form of percentages of standards instead of actual numbers, by graphical representations of performance or by other suitable methods. It is better to trust the executives as most of them remain loyal to the organization in which they serve.

With the right feedback, the site executives can analyze their performance and take remedial measures where necessary. In fact all executives need feedback to effect improvements. It is unfortunate that at some sites, executives rarely come to know of their performance because of a lack of monitoring or non-appreciation of the importance of feedback. It is difficult to change the behaviour of people but the feedback does effect changes in the behaviour of the recipient with the least cost.

It may be noted that the monitor diagnoses the deviations and formulates suggested remedial options but he cannot implement these himself. It is the site executives who are responsible for processing the work as per project plan and correcting deviations from the planned path.

### 13.6.3 Project Management Information Report

The corporate management or the board of directors are primarily concerned with the progress, profitability, cash flow, and capital investment needed for achieving the objectives. The project report, submitted by the contractors' project manager to the corporate management at a predetermined frequencies (generally monthly), provides an overview of the project status. It outlines the present performance and the future targets. It focuses on actual and potential deviations from the planned path and the possible remedial actions suggested to overcome adverse situations. This report enables the top management to exercise an effective control over the project.

The contents of the project management information report can be broadly divided into six parts as given below:

(a) **Project particulars** It shows the report title, number and date of report, project name, code number, location, client's details, and site address.

(b) **Project objectives status** It includes information relating to:

- Original contract amount, amount of work deviation, and percentage of financial progress.
- Contract starting date, current week numbers, balance of original completion period (in weeks), extended completion period (in weeks), total completion period (in weeks) and final completion date.
- Suspensions or hold ups during the reporting period.
- Client's extended completion date.
- Expected completion date as per current plan.

(c) **Project parameters' performance** Performance of parameters to be reported depends upon corporate policy. The selected parameters can vary from a few like billing status, work progress and budget status to a detailed report on performance of targets of each responsiblity centre. Formats designed for furnishing performance information in a housing project, in respect of the following parameters are shown in Exhibit 13.4.

- Work done value billing status.
- Work progress summary.
- Project budget status.

(d) **Project resources mobilization forecasts for the next quarter** It outlines the near-future resource requirements at the site for achieving planned targets. These forecasts include the following:

## Exhibit 13.4

### Formats for Reporting Selected Project Parameters Performance

**1.0 Monthly Billing Status Report**

| Item Code | Contracted Work ||||  Contract Amount | Billing Amount | Progess Percentage |
|---|---|---|---|---|---|---|---|
| | Description | Unit | Qty | Rate | | | |
| | | | | | | | |

**2.0 Progress Work Done Residential Building**

| Building Identity ||| This Period Value |||| To date Value |||| Reasons for this period deviation |
|---|---|---|---|---|---|---|---|---|---|---|---|
| Code | Building Description | Value | Target | Actual | Deviation Amt. | % | Target | Actual | Deviation Amt. | % | |
| | | | | | | | | | | | |

**3.0 Project Budget Variances Report**

| Expense Head || Budgeted | Actual || Deviation || Remarks |
|---|---|---|---|---|---|---|---|
| Code | Description | | This period | To date | This period | To date | |
| | | | | | | | |

- Site staff status and forecasts of requirements (See Exhibit 13.5).
- Workers' status and forecasts of requirements.
- Materials sample approval status and scheduled approvals.
- Major materials procurement status and scheduled requirements.
- Equipment status and induction schedule for balance required.

(e) **Gist of important site meetings** These include meetings with client's representatives, sub-contractors, suppliers and other connected agencies. It is in addition to the recorded minutes of meetings which are submitted to the top management.

(f) **Concluding remarks** The concluding paragraph of the report summarizes the overall performance and highlights the actions requested from the top management.

Exhibit 13.5

**Site Staff Mobilization Status and Forecasts**

**Strength Statement**

| Serial No. | Category | Strength last month | Strength on date | Forecast next month | Remarks |
|---|---|---|---|---|---|
| 1 | Managers | | | | |
| 2 | Engineers | | | | |
| 3 | Quantity surveyor | | | | |
| 4 | Foreman | | | | |
| 5 | Charge-hand | | | | |
| 6 | Store keepers | | | | |
| 7 | Draftsmen | | | | |

**Names of Site Staff Added/Deleted**

| Serial | Name | Appointment | Transferred | Added | Remarks |
|---|---|---|---|---|---|
| | | | | | |

In addition, up-to-date graphs showing the performance of selected parameters can be attached with the report.

The project management information report generally, does not include classified information such as controversial issues, actual expenditure details, profitability status, and financial matters. These are dealt with separately.

The project report must be concise and meaningful. It should indicate variances from the planned targets with reasons. It should restrict the report to essentials, making the report exception oriented by focusing attention on critical areas. Its contents should contain more of statistics, graphs, charts and other details having visual appeal. Narration as far as possible should be kept to the minimum. It should highlight potential bottlenecks and aspects needing action at the top-management level. It should avoid duplication of effort by suitably designing the reporting format to conform to the site reports, computer software requirements, and codification system.

## ❑ 13.7 CONTROL BENEFITS

The control system aids the management at various levels to perform their functions efficiently and effectively for achieving overall project objectives. The illustration given below shows the typical pyramidal management structure with the nature of control exercised at each level.

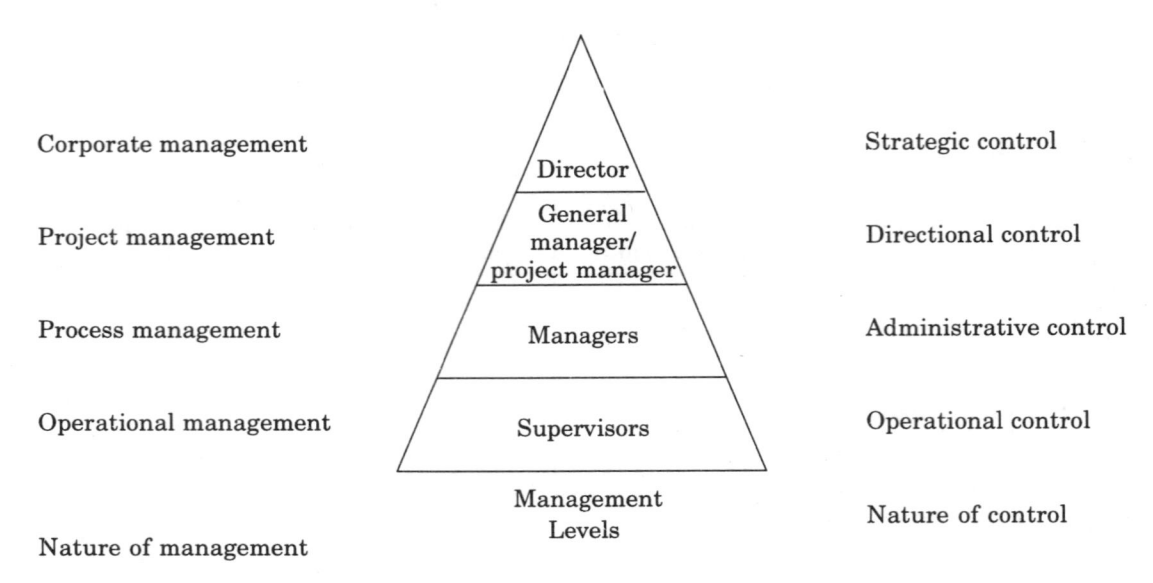

| Nature of management | Management Levels | Nature of control |
|---|---|---|
| Corporate management | Director | Strategic control |
| Project management | General manager/ project manager | Directional control |
| Process management | Managers | Administrative control |
| Operational management | Supervisors | Operational control |

The benefits which can be derived at each level of management through an effective control system are outlined below:

**(a) Operational control at supervisory level**  It improves productivity by:

- Minimizing unproductive manhours.
- Preventing wastage of materials.
- Economizing plant and machinery utilization.
- Reducing activity execution time.

**(b) Administrative control at managerial level**  It assists in ensuring project organizational efficiency and effectiveness by:

- Updating the work quantities status and determining the balance scope of work.
- Analyzing project time status and its implications on project-time objectives.
- Reviewing resources mobilization status and their forecast of requirements based on revised resources planning norms.
- Evaluating production cost status and forecasting future trends.
- Calculating income status and forecasting cash flow.
- Computing budget status and analyzing the implications of variances on future expenditure.

**(c) Directional control at general manager's/project manager's level**  It helps in formulating and directing policies for achievement of project objectives by:

- Analyzing project time-cost behaviour and making decisions on time-saving when required.

- Reviewing project costs and profitability, and making profitability improvement decisions concerning wastage reduction through rigorous cost control, cost reduction using value engineering techniques, and cost-benefit analysis by introducing measures such as incentive schemes and alternate methods of construction which cost less.
- Auditing management's performance.

**(d) Strategic control at corporate level** It provides information concerning corporate goals and assistance in formulating corporate strategies by:

- Determining overall profitability.
- Budgeting and allocating funds and resources.
- Updating the company's planning norms and unit rates for securing future works.

## 13.8 PREREQUISITES OF CONTROL EFFECTIVENESS

The effectiveness of the project control system, to a great extent, depends upon the foundation on which the system is built. As a prerequisite, the system must be backed up with a realistically developed time, manpower, materials, machinery, mobilization and cost plans of the project. The system should operate under conflict-free, healthy and harmonious working environments with the monitor playing the key role, and the management committed to make the system a success.

Control is a personalized activity as all control functions are exercised through people. Knowledge, ability and motivational skills may differ from man to man. Behavioural scientists have brought out abundant literature on control theory. However, it is an established principle that no one can be held responsible for an activity over, which he has no control. For example, in the execution of a construction activity at the site a construction supervisor is responsible for materials consumed. He cannot be asked to account for the prices of materials incorporated into the works, as it is the materials manager who has to account for these prices. Efficient and effective achievement of the goals depend upon the contribution of the persons controlling the goals. In order to make the system effective, it is imperative that in a control system, the accounting responsibilities of persons at each control point be clearly defined.

A typical performance control responsibility matrix showing the responsibilities of various managers is given in Exhibit 13.6.

It addition, the controlling tools and techniques employed for processing the data covered in Chapter 14 through 16 should be understood at appropriate levels

Exhibit 13.6

## Typical Performance Control Responsibility Matrix for a Medium-size Housing Project

| Sl. No. | Control Responsibility | Time Control | Resources Control | Cost Control |
|---|---|---|---|---|
| 1. | Operational Control by Construction Supervisor | Activity scheduled time | Wastage in resource utilisation | — |
| 2. | Administrative Control by Managers | | | |
| | — Design Manager | Timely supply of drawings | Drawing effort and project laboratory | Design costs |
| | — Construction Manager | Time targets and Milestones | Resources productivity safety and forecasting resources | Work package/Activity direct cost and earned value |
| | — Contract Manager | Contract time and quantity estimates | Variations from original works | Earned value and extra works claims |
| | — Plant Manager | Timely supply of equipment | Plant and equipment maintenance and utilisation productivity | Plant and equipment operation costs |
| | — Materials Manager | Timely supply of materials | Materials procurement safety and security | Materials costs |
| | — Personnel Manager | Timely provisioning of manpower | Manpower mobilization, welfare and security | Manpower indirect costs and project administration costs |
| | — Finance Manager | Provisioning funds | Resources budget | Cash-flow, expenses and budgeted costs, budgetary control |
| 3. | Directional Control by Project Manager assisted by Planning, Cost, and Finance Manager. | Project time objectives | Resources performance and mobilization | Cost control and Profitability |

# CHAPTER 14

# Resource Productivity Control

Resource inputs at the project site include men, materials, machinery, and money. These inputs produce outputs in the form of work. The success of a project depends upon the performance of these input resources. Productivity provides the scale to measure the performance of these input resources.

The term 'productivity' as commonly understood, implies the ratio of output to input. But productivity conveys different meanings to different people. Some regard productivity and production capability as synonymous terms. Many link productivity to mean workers' output capability; they express productivity as work quantity produced per man-hours of input. Productivity is also defined as dollars of output per man-hour of input. Some consider productivity as performance output in dollars for every dollar of input. In the narrower sense of controlling project resources, the productivity concept is used to measure the performance of resources. In this chapter, various terms connected with productivity imply the following:

(1) Workers' productivity

   = Quantity of work done per man-hour

   = $\dfrac{\text{Work units}}{\text{Man-hours}}$

(2) Material productivity

   = Quantity of work done per unit of materials

   = $\dfrac{\text{Work units}}{\text{Material quantity}}$

(3) Equipment productivity

= Quantity of work done per equipment hour

$$= \frac{\text{Work units}}{\text{Equipment hour}}$$

As can be seen from the above, more work done with the same input implies higher productivity, and less work done shows lower productivity than estimated.

The various productivity parameters which need to be controlled in construction projects are labour productivity, equipment productivity, and material productivity.

Productivity control aims at ensuring the efficient utilization of the input resources of men, materials, and equipment, and forecasting changes in productivity of these direct resources. The efficient utilization of resources is accomplished by identifying causes of their wastage at the project site with a view to minimize these wastages. The causes of wastage are located by analyzing variances between standard and on-site actual productivity:

Resource productivity variance

= Standard productivity − Actual productivity.

Resource performance index

$$= \frac{\text{Standard performance}}{\text{Actual performance}}$$

The methodology used for controlling each of the productivity parameters is similar. It can be divided into four stages, i.e. defining the control purpose, measuring the actual performance, computing productivity performance variances, and identifying causes for these variances, and applying corrective measures as necessary.

## 14.1 LABOUR PRODUCTIVITY CONTROL

Labour productivity achieved at the site for a given work provides a measure of the labourer's efficiency. It shows the total time for which the labourer was employed at work, the time he was productive on work and the time he remained unproductive. Studies carried out at construction sites reveal that the labourer's productive work time varies from 50 to 70% of his total employment time, and the remaining time is wasted for various reasons such as idle waiting, unnecessary travelling, late starting, early quitting, unscheduled breaks, and delays in the receipt of tools, materials and work instructions. Labour productivity can be improved by cutting down such unproductive time of the labourers. The control process involves accounting of actual productivity, comparing the actual with the standard, analyzing the causes for variations between actual and standard, and finally taking remedial measures to improve productivity.

### 14.1.1 Labour Productivity Accounting Methodology

The project labour accounting system is designed to serve many purposes. It enables the computation of accurate payment to the labourers. It provides data for the evaluation of labour productivity for various tasks and it facilitates the estimation of labour costs of works executed.

Labour accounting system provides the information and record keeping needs of all the project departments, especially those of personnel, accounting, costing and planning. A typical labour accounting system can be modelled as shown in Fig. 14.1.

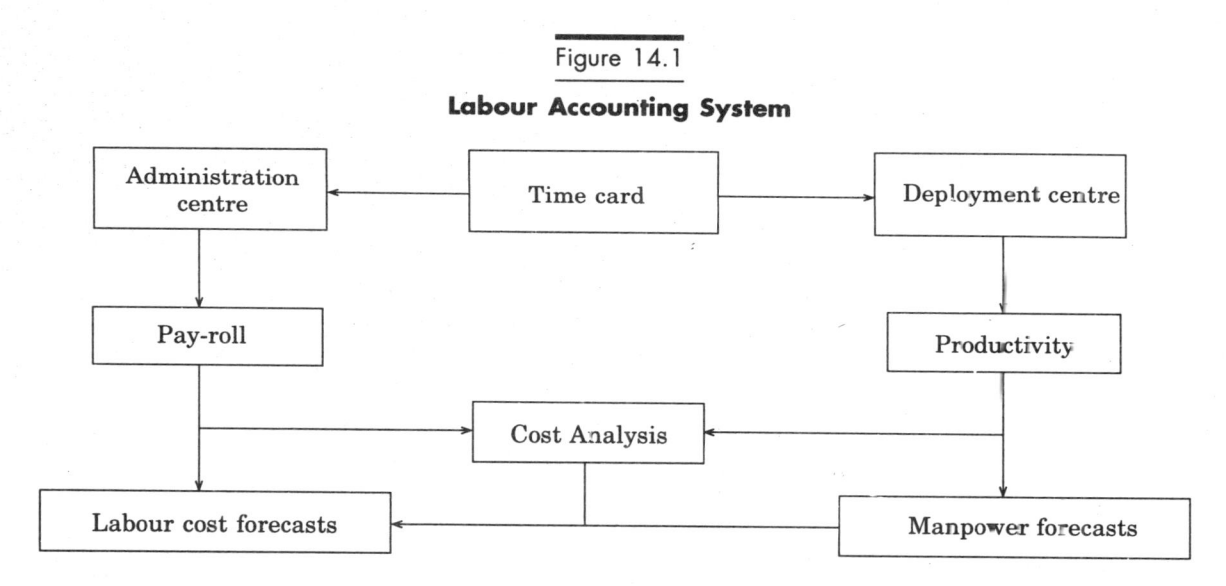

Figure 14.1
**Labour Accounting System**

```
┌──────────────┐     ┌──────────┐     ┌──────────────────┐
│Administration│◄────│ Time card│────►│ Deployment centre│
│    centre    │     └──────────┘     └──────────────────┘
└──────┬───────┘                              │
       │                                      ▼
       ▼                               ┌──────────────┐
┌──────────────┐                       │ Productivity │
│   Pay-roll   │                       └──────┬───────┘
└──────┬───────┘                              │
       │         ┌──────────────┐             │
       └────────►│ Cost Analysis│◄────────────┤
                 └──────┬───────┘             │
       ┌────────────────┘                     │
       ▼                                      ▼
┌──────────────────────┐           ┌─────────────────────┐
│ Labour cost forecasts│◄──────────│  Manpower forecasts │
└──────────────────────┘           └─────────────────────┘
```

The input necessary for labour productivity accounting are the time-keeper's daily time records for the labourer, and the foreman/supervisor's daily labour employment record.

This data is processed by the labour administration centre to determine the actual labour productivity, the labour forecast and the labour costs.

### 14.1.2 Time-Keeper's Time Record

The first step in productivity evaluation is to record payable time. The labour's time account is maintained by the time-keeper, and the basic document used for this purpose is the time-card. A time-card records the daily attendance time of the worker. It contains details of his trade category and possibly, the task in which he is employed. The design of the time-card depends upon the requirements of the information system. A specimen is shown in Table 14.1.

Workers' time-card showing daily attendance data in the form of time-in and time-out, duly completed, is submitted by the time-keeper to the personnel department at specified intervals for making pay-rolls. It is important to remember that the labour force's attendance time record affects every worker at the project site as it forms the basis of wage calculation.

## Table 14.1

**Typical Labour Time Cards**
**(Card size as per time recording machine specifications)**

*Attendance Time–Card*                                                                 Week Ending...

| No. | Category | Name | | | | |
|---|---|---|---|---|---|---|
| Work Centre/Dept./Work Package | | | | | Cost Code | |
| | Normal Working Time | | | | | Overtime |
| Date | IN | OUT | IN | OUT | Hours | Hours |
| | | | | | | |
| | | TOTAL | | | | |

| For use by Accountant | | | |
|---|---|---|---|
| Normal wages | Overtime wages | | Total |
| Deductions | | | |
| Amount payable | | | |

Time-card data ensures that a worker is paid exactly what is due to him. Accounting for time and wages has to be accurate and timely so as to avoid human relation problems, and any temptation for overpayment or fraud.

### 14.1.3 Foreman's Daily Labour Employment Report

The time-card data is then transmitted by the time-keeper in the form of the daily work attendance statement (specimen Table 14.2) to the concerned supervisor or foreman for incorporating the daily work progress and the employment time distribution. The foreman's daily labour employment statement, at the end of the day, is forwarded by the foreman through his construction manager/project engineer to the monitor. This statement reveals the time, activity-wise, for which a labourer (or crew member) was employed on construction work or productive work, and it highlights the labour idle time breakdown with causes. In this statement the work done quantities can be inserted on a daily basis or as and when the work-item or activity is completed. This employment statement can be maintained on a ledger and need not be prepared on a separate sheet, as a copy (photocopy or duplicate) of the ledger sheet can be forwarded to all concerned.

## 14.1.4 Construction/Planning Engineer's Weekly Labour Productivity Report

The data reflected in the foreman's daily labour employment statements is used to determine the unproductive time and identify its controllable causes for the remedial action. This data, after scrutiny, is transferred by the project engineer or planning engineer into the weekly labour productivity report, a typical format of which is shown in Table 14.3 The reporting engineer can compile the weekly labour productivity report for each item of work separately, or combine them suitably in one report. The labour productivity report is of great value as it can be used to monitor labour performance and evaluate labour cost for each item of work. It provides a device to compare the operating efficiencies of different teams working at the project site for creating a competitive spirit. It helps to forecast the labour work force required for remaining similar works, and it can form the basis for developing labour productivity norms for use in future similar works.

## 14.1.5 Analysing Labour Productivity Performance

Labour productivity variances are determined by comparing the actual with the standard. Labour productivity variance

$$= \text{Labour productivity standard} - \text{Labour actual productivity}.$$

In order to consolidate the actual data, the value of labour productivity achieved is suitably plotted graphically on mean (X) and range (R) chart, where $x$ represents the expected standard value and range indicates the variation trend from the standards.

To quote an example, Exhibit 14.1 shows the actual productivity data in respect of steel fixing of the raft of each foundation module of a project, involving the construction of several similar size foundations. The standard productivity of steel fixing including cutting and bending was estimated as 90 kg/man-day, having eight working hours per day. The actual reinforcement fixing productivity data, plotted in the sequence of the completion of building foundation modules, shows the trend of productivity variation. Particularly in the initial six weeks, the actual productivity ranged from 50 kg/man-day to 70 kg/man-day which is lower than the standard productivity of 90 kg/man-day of eight hour and it gradually improved with the learning process till it records a near steady state level of 80 kg/man-day after 5 weeks stretched over to about 12 weeks. Thereafter, it showed a further jump to around 110 kg/man-day of eight hours after a job based incentive scheme with work measure as 90 kg steel fixing for first eight hours. Overtime at the rate of one hour for every subsequent 10 kg output was introduced, where workers got one to two hours' over time on each working day though they physically worked for eight hours per day.

## 14.1.6 Typical Causes of Low Labour Productivity

There can be many assignable causes for variations in actual productivity from the standard productivity. It is the moving average of actual productivity that indicates the extent of variations from the standard productivity. One of the causes of variations between actual

## Table 14.2
## Foreman's Labour Employment Statement
## Daily Man-Hour Report

Foreman's Name
Crew Nos. and Productivity Standard
Work Centre/Responsibility Centre

Dated:

| Sl No | Workers' Names/Code | Productive Man-Hour ||||||| Daily Grand Total (Hrs) | Non-Productive Man-Hours ||||||||
|---|---|---|---|---|---|---|---|---|---|---|---|---|---|---|---|
| | | Act. A | Act. B | Act. C | Work P Item | Work Q Item | Total (Hrs) | | Sick | Def. work | Work | Instruction | Waiting for |||| Other duty | Total |
| | | | | | | | | | | | | | Equipment | Materials | Bad weather | Interruption | | |

Current total

Previous employment

Total employment

Work Done: Qty | Unit

Productivity Work/MH(OQW)

Note: Work done quantity can be entered when the work is completed.

### Table 14.3

**Weekly Activity Productivity Report**

Activity — Block Work in Superstructure    Code:    Unit Sq. m.

| Date | Crew mix ||  Actual MH on date | Actual MH cumulative | Quantity work ||  Productivity actual | Productivity standard |
|------|-------|----------|------------|------------|-----------|-----------|------------|------------|
|      | Skill | Unskilled |           |            | Completed | Cumulative |           |            |
|      |       |          |            |            |           |            |           |            |
|      |       |          |            |            |           |            |           |            |
|      |       |          |            |            |           |            |           |            |
|      |       |          |            |            |           |            |           |            |
|      |       |          |            |            |           |            |           |            |
|      |       |          |            |            |           |            |           |            |
|      |       |          |            |            |           |            |           |            |
|      |       |          |            |            |           |            |           |            |
|      |       |          |            |            |           |            |           |            |
|      |       |          |            |            |           |            |           |            |

and standard productivity may be due to the incorrect estimation of standard productivity. However, low productivity at the steady state level can be broadly attributed to the low morale of the workers, poor pre-work preparation by the supervisors, and the directional failure of the project management.

**(A) Workers' low moral**  This can result from:

- Non-fulfilment of employment terms and conditions by the management.
- Insecurity of employment.
- Sub-standard working conditions.
- Frequent transfers.
- Frequent changes in the scope of work and work methodology.
- Conflicts between supervisors and workers.

**(B) Poor pre-work preparation by supervisors**  The lack of preparation for the execution of the assigned work prior to commencement can result in inefficient handling of resources due to:

- Excess workers employed for the task.
- Insufficient instructions for the execution of work.
- Incorrect sequencing of work activities.

### Exhibit 14.1

**Labour Productivity Control Chart
Steel Reinforcement Fixing Output
in Kilograms per 8-hour Man-day**

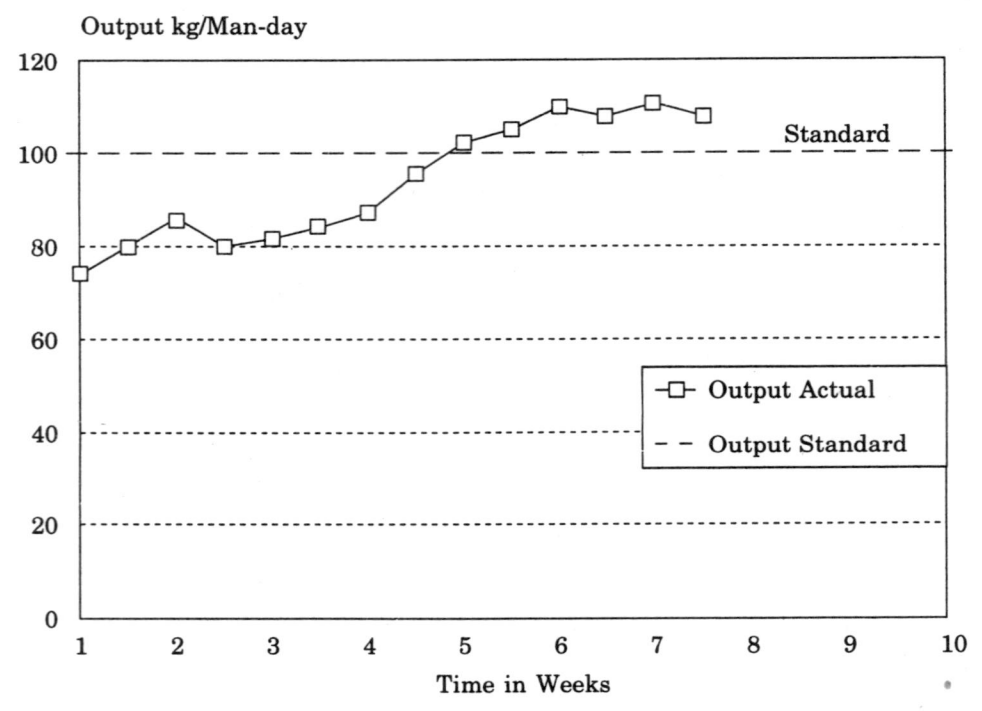

*Note*: Output increased gradually after Job-incentive Scheme Introduced in 4th Week

- Shortage of tools and materials at the site.
- Wastage resulted from unnecessary frequent shifting of materials, and making and breaking of poor quality/defective work.

### (C) Directional failures of the project management   These include:

- Failure to set performance targets.
- Failure to make provision for timely resource support.
- Failure to provide feedback.
- Failure to motivate workers.

It is never feasible to eliminate all the causes resulting in low productivity. Mere increase of labour may result in increase in production but it may not necessarily improve productivity.

Workers' productivity can be increased in many ways. Some of the typical down-to-earth approaches are given below:

(a) Reduce unproductive time by constantly reviewing and minimizing causes contributing to unproductive time.
(b) Replace labour by appropriate equipment where economically feasible.
(c) Substitute inefficient working tools by appropriate efficient tools.
(d) Improve method of executing work remembering that there is always a better way of doing a task.
(e) Improve working conditions.
(f) Employ competent supervisors.

Experience shows that most of the factors that affect the workers' productivity adversely can be minimized by good management following guidelines listed under the role of the construction manager in improving productivity.

The next stage of monitoring labour productivity is to forecast its trends for executing balance work. This is done by revising labour productivity (if required) by critically examining all the causes affecting low labour productivity, devising remedial measures to improve productivity, and evaluating the implications on existing productivity standards. The revised productivity standards can then be used to forecast the workers' requirements for balanced work.

It may be noted that it is not necessary to conduct analyses of labour productivity of all work-items or activities. Labour productivity analyses should be carried out on a selective basis only for those work-items or activities which consume a major portion of the total manpower.

## 14.2 EQUIPMENT PRODUCTIVITY CONTROL

In construction, some tasks are labour intensive, some predominantly employ equipment, and some use a combination of both, i.e. labour and equipment. While the actual work done and the associated labour is accounted for by the foreman concerned, the equipment productivity control is undertaken to determine its employment time, the output achieved, and its productivity at site. The main purpose of equipment productivity control is to minimize wastage in utilization.

### 14.2.1 Accounting Equipment Productivity

In equipment accounting, stress is laid on tracing the employment time, expenditure and corresponding quantity of work accomplished for each major item of equipment. This accounting approach can enable a contractor to account for each equipment's expenditure as direct cost, and to evaluate its productivity and profitability. Then decisions regarding owning or hiring an individual piece of equipment can be taken.

The following paragraphs outline the basic approach for accounting the productivity of capital equipment. The method is similar to labour accounting. Two accounting documents of interest to the planning cell are the daily equipment employment account and weekly equipment productivity account.

**Daily equipment employment accounting** Equipment time-card is the basic document for accounting each equipment's employment time and the corresponding work performance. For each equipment, the time-card format generally follows the layout of the labour time-card, and each card can be suitably modified where necessary to meet the information requirement. Specimens of typical daily equipment employment cards are shown in Table 14.4. This time-card remains with the operator of the equipment, and it is filled up by the respective foreman/supervisor employing the equipment for work. The 'quantity of work executed' column provides important information for computing productivity data, and if quantity measurement takes time, the 'work-quantity' column can be filled up later on after the completion of activity by the respective foreman. Further for cycle-time calculation, if necessary, either the time-card can be modified or an additional suitably-designed time sheet can be used for collecting cycle-time data.

Table 14.4

**Typical Daily Equipment Employment Card**

Equipment No....................... Operator ............................. Date

Type ...................... Make and Model .......................

| Working Time ||||| Total Employment Time | Unproductive Time (Hrs) |||
|---|---|---|---|---|---|---|---|---|
| From | To | Nature of Work | Qty | Hrs | | Waiting Time | Repair Time | Misc Time |
|  |  |  |  |  |  |  |  |  |

1. Engine Operating hours    Reading Start ...............    End .........
2. Received on date  Fuel ............ Oil ................... Lubricant ...............
   in Litres
3. *Repairs carried out*

The daily equipment time-card, at the end of the work shift, is handed over by the equipment operator to the equipment cost centre. In particular, the fuel consumption is generally calculated by measuring the quantity needed to fill the fuel tank.

If the equipment starts work with full tank, then

Fuel consumption  = Additional fuel needed to fill the tank.

= Fuel tank capacity − balance fuel in tank.

**Weekly equipment productivity sheet** The equipment productivity sheet shown in Table 14.5 provides information about the actual productivity of each equipment for a given job. It shows the equipment's particulars, nature of work done, booking time, waiting time, repair time, and the serviceability condition of the equipment. The time lost when the equipment is not utilized is shown under waiting time of serviceable equipment, and under repair in case of breakdown of equipment at the site of work. The waiting time can be further subdivided into avoidable waiting time and unavoidable waiting time, and the reasons for waiting can be written on the reverse of the time-card. The equipment productivity can then be summarized, at the end of each week, in the form of the weekly equipment productivity sheet.

Table 14.5

**Weekly Equipment Productivity Report**

| Sl No. | Equipment Particulars ||  Work Details || Productivity | Time Account ||||
|---|---|---|---|---|---|---|---|---|---|---|
| | No. | Type | Nature of Work | Qty | Qty ÷ Hrs | Total Hrs | Work Hrs | Waiting Hrs | Repair Hrs | Misc. Hrs |
| | | | | | | | | | | |

In order to make the construction site cost conscicous, and to assess the unit rate for various items of work, the equipment utilized by the sites can be charged by the equipment cost centre at a standard hourly rate. The usage cost accounting takes into consideration the owning and operating costs of each equipment. The details of these are covered in Chapter 10. These costs can be determined by maintaining the following records for each equipment in the form of log-book:

(a) Equipment ownership data including identification numbers, make, and model: purchase particulars such as date and purchase cost: and replacement costs of major components.
(b) History sheet of equipment's major repairs.
(c) Equipment's periodical maintenance record.
(d) Equipment's employment history since purchase and monthly operating hours and fuel consumption record.
(e) Operators' record.
(f) Do's and don'ts for equipment operation.

The method of working out hourly owning and operating costs is given in Chapter 10.

It is stressed that the equipment productivity accounting and its costing need not be carried out for all pieces of equipment. Minor items of equipment like welding sets, compressors or even small capacity generators need not be accounted for while estimating the ownership costs, all such equipment is budgeted to last for the project duration. Their ownership costs are distributed proportionately throughout the life of the project. It is only the major items of equipment having long life that are included for evaluation of hourly equipment performance costs.

The standard hourly rate can be reviewed once a month/quarter' if necessary. Preferably, the standard hourly rate should be fixed close to no-profit-no-loss basis, so as to enable the accurate calculation of equipment unit cost for various items of work. The equipment operator hourly cost can be included in the standard equipment hourly cost, or it can be accounted separately. In addition to controlling productivity, it is also necessary to keep an account of the serviceability, and utilization time of each equipment, so as to optimize their use. For this purpose, the daily equipment employment schedule can be prepared by the plant cost centre and it is distributed to all concerned at least a day prior to the date of utilization. In case of equipment which operates under the instructions of construction sites, the utilization schedule is prepared by the site and a copy of this is given to the planning and plant cost centres so as to enable these centres to monitor equipment availability and performance.

## 14.2.2 Equipment Productivity Analysis

Generally, the equipment productivity at site differs from the standard productivity. In the initial stages, actual productivity is less than the standard productivity. It gradually improves provided the equipment remains in serviceable condition. However, the equipment performance depends upon many inherent variables. These include equipment serviceability condition, effect of terrain. access to work site, working space restrictions, weather conditions, working conditions, working timings, logistic and equipment vendor support, and so on. Some of the controllable factors which effect equipment productivity adversely are as follows.

(a) Insufficient preparation.
(b) Lack of continuity of task.
(c) Inadequate operator's skill.
(d) Lack of effective supervision.
(e) Non-availability of maintenance, repair facilities and spares.
(f) Poor equipment management, specially, lack of preventive maintenance measures.
(g) Accidents.

Equipment productivity can be improved by suitably matching machines with the job, employing experienced operators and competent maintenance staff, adopting correct methods for work execution, employing service-worthy machines, enforcing proper maintenance measures, and having an effective plant manager.

## ❑ 14.3 MATERIALS PRODUCTIVITY CONTROL

Wastage of materials can take place during the procurement process, storage, and during utilization.

Wastage during procurement can result from one or more of the following main causes:

(a) Buying materials of wrong specifications.
(b) Buying more than the actual requirements.
(c) Unnecessary buying of items to cater for unrealistic and unforeseen eventualities.
(d) Untimely buying of short-life materials.
(e) Improper and unnecessary handling of materials.
(f) Wastage in transportation.

Wastage during storage can occur due to the followings reasons:

(a) Damages and breakages during handling.
(b) Deterioration due to incorrect storage, incorrect maintenance and short-shelf life.
(c) Losses due to fire, thefts and exposure to extreme climatic conditions.

Some unavoidable wastage is inherent during utilization, but it is the excessive wastage which is of concern to the management. Excessive wastage during the utilization stage affects the productivity adversely, and consequently results in extra costs. Productivity control aims at minimizing wastage in usage. Productivity control at the construction responsibility centre level can be broadly divided into accounting for materials, analyzing usage variances to determine the causes of wastage and implementing measures to minimize wastage.

### 14.3.1 Accounting for Construction Materials

Materials accounting system documents the materials data. It provides the materials procurement status. It shows the holding of materials inventory for the incoming works. It identifies and quantifies issues of materials to the site and it reveals the materials costs. Project planners are specially concerned with materials-flow data for ensuring the timely procurement of materials, and site availability of materials of right quantity and quality at the required time and place. They also aim at minimizing wastage during usage, evaluating implications of variations from the acceptable wastage standard, updating costs estimates and expenditures of materials, and formulating materials costing norms for future works.

The materials accounting process from the demand initiation till its consumption stage involves maintenance of up-to-date records of receipts and issues at the project central store, monthly stock checking of materials in the store and at the work site, and the return of the unused materials after completion of the intended job.

### 14.3.2 Materials Stock Accounting

Stock accounting is the clerical process of recording the movement of materials in and out of the stores. The basis of the stock accounting method is the stock record card (also called bin card), which provides an up to date record of the stock of materials. The stock record card (specimen shown in Table 14.6) is the main source of information on the availability of materials and other connected data. A suitably designed stock record card can show stock code, description, unit of specification, stock location, stock levels (i.e. minimum, maximum and re-order levels), source of supply, lead time for procurement, sequential data-wise record of receipt and issue quantities, balances at any point of time and other connected information as required. In particular, the stock levels set on the stock record card regulate the inflow and the outflow of materials, and sound a timely warning for commencing stock replenishment. An effective stock acccunting system can assist in controlling materials stocks by ensuring that:

Table 14.6

**Typical Materials Stock Control Bin Card**

| Code No. Description | | | Bin No. Stores Ledger No. | | |
|---|---|---|---|---|---|
| | Receipts | | Issues | | Stock Balance |
| Date | GRN No. | Qty | REQ No. | Qty | Qty |
| | Balance B/F | | | | |

A bin card shows level of stock of an item in a bin at a particular store location.

(a) Materials of the right quantity and quality are available in the stores at the right time.
(b) The stock levels are kept as low as feasible so as to minimize the investment or inventory holding costs on the materials and to avoid occupying of excessive storage space resulting in high overheads.
(c) Stock quantities can be easily verified thus preventing pilfering, theft and wastage.

On the whole, the stock record card if properly maintained, can serve as the main source of information on materials to the materials department, planning department, costing department and finance accounting department.

### 14.3.3 Materials Issues and Returns Accounting

The construction materials are obtained by the construction supervisors from the project control stores, or the materials are directly delivered at the place of work. In both cases, the construction supervisors, on behalf of the construction manager, sends a materials requisition note for the materials required by him to the project central store. The specimen of the materials requisition note is shown in Table 14.7. The store in-charge on the authority of this note issues these materials. In case of non-availability of materials in the project central store, the store in-charge passes this note to the materials controller for procurement and delivery at the central stores or at the place of work.

Table 14.7

**Typical Materials Requisition and Issue Control**

**Materials Requisition and Issue Note**

| Name | Responsibility Centre | | Centre Code | | |
|---|---|---|---|---|---|
| Description | Work Package/Activity | | Code | | |
| S. No. | Materials | | Unit | Quantity | |
| | Code | Nomenclature | | Reqd. | Issd. |
| | | | | | |
| | | | | | |

Indenting Supervisor                           Issuing Storekeeper

Date and Signature                              Date and Signature

If the materials are delivered directly at the construction site, a goods received note (GRN) is signed by the site supervisor receiving the materials, and the GRN duly signed is sent by him to the project materials controller for accounting and payment through the accounting department.

Generally, there is a tendency on the part of the site supervisors to demand more materials than required for avoiding the risk of shortage at the time of execution. The surplus materials are eventually either returned along with the materials return note specimen shown in Table 14.8 or they get wasted at the site.

### Table 14.8

### Typical Materials Return Control

**Materials Return Note**

| Name | Responsibility Centre | | Centre Code | |
|---|---|---|---|---|
| S. No. | Item Code | Description | Qty | Remarks |
|  |  |  |  |  |
|  |  |  |  |  |

Returning Supervisor  
Date and Signature

Receiving Storekeeper  
Date and Signature

### 14.3.4 Monthly Stock Taking of Selected Materials

Stock taking is the process of accounting physically the stock-in-hand and verifying this with the balances shown in materials accounting document at predetermined intervals (See Table 14.9). The monthly stock taking enables cost evaluation of materials for billing the materials-at-site advance, costing materials inventory, and controlling materials mobilization status, and reconciling stock discrepancies. Possible causes of discrepancies between physical stock and storekeepe's records can be due to the following:

(a) Materials received of different types and qualities than those shown on goods received notes (GRN) and site materials requisition notes (REQ).
(b) Quantity of stock issued to construction centre is different than the quantity shown on the requisition note.
(c) Surplus materials held in the construction centres are transferred or returned without documentation.
(d) Breakages, damages and losses at the construction centres are not accounted for during stock taking.
(e) Clerical errors in accounting.

## Table 14.9

### Typical Stores Accounting Ledger Sheet

| Code No.<br>Description<br>Location<br>Quantity Required | | | | | | | Max Stock Level<br>Min Stock Level<br>Re-order Level<br>Re-order Quantity | | | |
|---|---|---|---|---|---|---|---|---|---|---|
| | Ordered | | | Receipts | | Issues | | Stock Balance Qty | Ordered Qty |
| Date | S.O. No. | Qty | GRN No. | Qty | Req No. | Qty | | | |

*Stores ledger sheet contains entire stock information of a particular item Depending upon the company policy, an additional column showing price can be included.

The discrepancies are reconciled every month or quarter, and the adjustments are made in materials cost, or these are written off from the profit and loss account.

### 14.3.5 Materials Wastage Analysis

The first step in materials wastage analysis is to quantify standard quantity and type of direct materials needed for each work item.

The actual materials consumed for each work-item can be complied from the material issues and return notes transacted between supervisors and stockholders. In case of materials delivered directly to the construction sites by the supplier, such as ready-mix concrete from site batching plant or fabricated steel for reinforcement from the site steel yard, or aggregate from a crusher, the supplier's delivery note along with the materials' return note (if any) can be used to determine the quantity consumed for a given work-item. These issue slips and delivery notes, when consolidated from the start to completion of the work-item/activity, can give the quantities of materials consumed. The difference between the standard materials' requirement and the materials actually consumed indicates the excess (if any) from the accepted materials wastage standard prepared at the time of estimation.

Materials usage variance
= Standard acceptable materials wastage − Actual materials wastage.

### 14.3.6 Causes of Excessive Wastage

The main reasons for excessive materials wastage during usage can be attributed to one or more of the following:

(a) Excess quantity estimation.
(b) Shortage in delivery.
(c) Theft and pilferage.
(d) Breakages and damages during handling.
(e) Lack of pre-work preparation and coordination.
(f) Inferior quality of materials.
(g) Improper accounting and poor storekeeping.
(h) Negligent and careless attitude of the supervisor.
(i) Unforeseen circumstances like accidents, fire, etc.
(j) High rate of deterioration due to long storage at the place of work.
(k) Over–issues from the central stores and failures to return unused surplus materials.

Some of the preventive measures to minimize wastage include the use of proper handling and transportation of equipment, minimizing unnecessary shifting, setting up of proper and secure storage areas, correct accounting of materials, fire precautions, improvements in the process of construction, and the education and training of staff and workers to ensure productivity improvement.

## ❑ 14.4 ROLE OF CONSTRUCTION MANAGERS IN IMPROVING PRODUCTIVITY

Productivity control is the primary function of the construction manager employing the resources. The planning cell assists the construction manager in exercising productivity control.

The construction manager can play the most vital role in exercising resources productivity control by ensuring the following.

### 14.4.1 Setting Targets and Monitoring Performance by Ensuring that

(a) Supervisors participate in setting future weekly targets, understand the method of their accomplishment and know the resources standards specified for achieving these targets.
(b) All workers know their job-oriented productivity standards and the connected incentive schemes.
(c) Supervisors prepare and conduct briefings to workers a day prior to the day of starting the activity.
(d) The project planning team is effectively monitoring the performance of resources, and is getting cooperation from all concerned.

### 14.4.2 Providing Resources Support by Ensuring that

(a) Materials in right quantity and quality from the right source are ordered and their supply is closely followed up so that the materials are delivered to the sites at the right time. In case of anticipated delays in deliveries, the work plans are rescheduled well in time, and all concerned are informed accordingly.
(b) The suitable manpower is identified in time, and it possesses the right skills and experience needed to perform the job.
(c) The type and capacity of equipment and tools provided at the work site can perform the task assigned, that the equipment operators possess the necessary skill, that there is necessary maintenance support and that preventive maintenance is carried out.

### 14.4.3 Communicating Feedback by Ensuring that

(a) Each week he meets the supervisors to review the actual progress with targets, and analyzes the causes for changes from planned progress and standards.
(b) Each week after the review meeting, he verbally communicates information on the performance to each supervisor.
(c) Each week, every supervisor knows the job progress of the previous week, the resources productivity he achieved, the causes for changes in productivity and the expected target and productivity for the current week.

### 14.4.4 Motivating the Work Force by Ensuring that

(a) The personal policies are well formulated and properly implemented so that workers get what they are assured according to the terms and conditions of their employment. In particular, ensure that their salaries and wages are given on time.
(b) Safety rules and security measures formulated are properly enforced, so as to prevent accidents and pilferage.

(c) Workers are protected against adverse weather conditions and environmental health hazards, so as to minimize the health risks.
(d) The performance of supervisors who perform well is acknowledged.
(e) The engineers, supervisors and workers feel they are making a valuable contribution.
(f) Good performance is rewarded by providing non-monetary recognition, giving monetary benefits through job-related incentive schemes and other morale raising and work motivating measures.

# CHAPTER 15

# Project Cost Control

Project cost control aims at controlling changes to the project budget. It provides management with cost related information for making decisions with a view to complete the project with specified quality, on time and within budgeted costs. This information, extracted from performance data and other sources, is used to minimize waste, update current budget estimates forecast cost trends, and make decisions about the future. Cost control involves processing of cost accounting reports received from various responsibility centres or operating divisions, relating the cost incurred with standards, analyzing the reasons for variances, and presenting the results of monitoring to the project management for making decisions for the future and not of the past.

In construction projects, generally, there are two parties whose investments are involved—the clients and the contractors. The cost control objectives of the involved parties differ.

Client investment starts with his decision to go ahead with the project. His expenses continue during design, execution and commissioning stages. After taking into consideration the contract commitments, escalation and contingencies, he formulates his cost budget for the project. He plans his cash flow on the basis of the progress pattern forecast prepared during the engineering stage. He employs an individual or a small group to monitor costs, so as to keep the costs within budgeted limits and to meet the cash-flow requirement of the project. Through his limited cost control set-up, which is more like finance control, he keeps a constant vigil on the project activities to prevent cost escalations and not let costs expand without purpose. He tries to reduce his budgeted costs by various measures such as economizing the scope of work by using value analysis techniques and offering incentives to contractors for early completion, which may yield him early revenue from the project than the originally planned completion time.

On the other hand, it is the contractor who executes contracted works and it is he who bears the cost of input resources employed by him for the execution of the work. These input resources and site expenses include the cost of men, materials, machinery and capital. He also incurs expenditure on interest on loans, statutory payments, insurance, depreciation and so on. In addition, like the client, he has also to control his finances to meet the cash requirements from time to time. His motto is to maximize profits by effective cost control.

Considering the above modes of cost control, it is evident that the contractor working needs special emphasis on controlling costs. And the cost control methodology covered in this chapter has been developed keeping the contractors' needs in view.

This chapter describes the methodology for performing the cost control function by the project monitoring team including cost accountant, headed by the chief planner. After outlining the cost control preliminaries, the subject covered deals with methodology for controlling direct costs, controlling budget, forecasting trends and it ends up with the cost control responsibility. Cost control principles described in this chapter are applicable to any project, except that the level of details and the tools chosen vary from project to project.

Cost codification system, which is a pre-requisite for effective cost control system, is described in Chapter 17. Resources productivity control and project cost control are inseparable and, therefore, this chapter can be considered as a continuation of the previous chapter.

## 15.1 COST CONTROL PRELIMINARIES

### 15.1.1 Cost Control Approach

A project cost control system for effective implementation, as far as feasible, should be easy to understand and simple to implement, without creating any interdepartmental and interpersonnel conflicts. The system should have least response time, thus enabling quick monitoring and prompt decisions based on simple cost reports initiated at regular frequency by cost incurring centres and a monthly cost control report compiled by the cost accountant.

Numerous types of cost control systems for construction projects are available in the libraries of management scientists and computer software dealers. Some of these systems are based on the profit and loss accounting method, standard costing method and the PERT/COST method. But there is no tailor made system which can suit projects of all types and sizes.

Since, maximization of profits (through professional and ethical means) is generally the main motto of the contractors, the contractors cost control system can be designed to control each stage of accounting operations that contribute to profit. These stages are shown below:

| Stages in Profit Computation | Nature of Control |
|---|---|
| A. Sales income | Sales control |
| B. Less direct cost | Direct cost control |
| C. Gross margin (A – B) | |
| D. Less variable overheads | Variable overheads control |
| E. Contribution (C – D) | Contribution control |
| F. Less fixed overheads | Fixed overhead control |
| G. Operating profit (E – F) | Budgetary control |

In practice, the responsibility for sales control rests with the Construction Responsibility Centres. Direct Cost Control methodology can be used for controlling work-package costs at construction centre level. Contribution control can be viewed with regard to what the responsibility centres can contribute towards overall profit and fixed costs, whereas project profitability as a whole can best be monitored through Budgetary Control. And all these methods make use of the concept of Variance Analysis to reason out the variances.

### 15.1.2 Control Estimates

The feasibility study during the inception stage outlines the approximate cost of the project. For cost control, it is necessary to have a master control estimate for establishing the philosophy for overall cost control. This master control estimate is prepared during the project planning stage. It is made up of direct costs, indirect cost and funds earmarked for contingencies and escalation. The approved original master control estimate remains unchanged throughout the life of the project. However, during the execution stage, master control estimate is revised at a predetermined frequency (say half yearly), and in its approved revision, is called current control estimate. Generally, expenditure is incurred at various levels/departments after it is approved by the cost controller/authorised manager.

### 15.1.3 Cost Planning

Cost breakdown generally follows the hierarchy pattern of work-breakdown structure. The cost breakdown levels can be divided as under:

| Level | Scope | Cost Control Responsibility |
|---|---|---|
| 0 | Total project cost | Cost accountant |
| 1 | Sub-project cost | Cost accountant |
| 2 | Task/logistics | Respective managers/contractors/functional heads |
| 3 | Work-package costs | Cost centres |

The costs, at each level, may be divided into the following cost elements:

(a) Direct manpower costs—salary, wages, and other costs.
(b) Direct material at-site delivered costs.
(c) Direct equipment, plant and services costs.
(d) Sub-contract costs.
(e) Indirect on-site costs—variable, fixed.
(f) Indirect external costs—head office overheads, management related and commercial—fixed and variable costs.

The cost element files should have the standard rates established for estimating work packages. The actual rates of the resources get determined as the work progresses. These rates should be updated at the time of revision of the control estimate. Cost breakdowns are related to the individuals responsible for their accomplishment. The individuals may include connected engineering staff, supervisory in-house persons, the sub-contractors and vendors as applicable. The cost breakdown is generally coded at various levels of detail. These codes enable organization of the vast project-cost data. The cost codes within the project should be specific for each work package.

### 15.1.4 Budgeting Costs

Budget relates the costs with time progress. Each work package is budgeted with its data base containing the scope of work, resource, cost quality, time, and performance responsibility. Commonly used project cost budget monitoring parameters are:

- *Budget Cost of Work Scheduled (BCWS)*: It represents a time phased schedule of the budget.
- *Budgeted Cost of Work Performed (BCWP)*: It shows the approved cost of the work performed on data date.
- *Actual Cost for the Work Performed (ACWP)*. Cost incurred on accomplishing a work on data date.

Cost variance = BCWP − ACWP
Schedule variance = BCWP − BCWS
Cost performance index = BCWP/ACWP
Schedule performance index = BCWP/BCWS

There is a fundamental difference in the use of the terms budget, standard, commitment and value, with respect to a work package.

(a) Budget reflects expected costs of performance under prevailing conditions.
(b) Standard stands for the costs achievable under efficient operating conditions.
(c) Commitment marks the booked cost of resources utilized/consumed or expected.
(d) Value of work performed implies the monetary value of work completed. In contracted projects, it is equal to the value of work done at contract rates.
(e) Earned value analysis is the method for measuring project performance.

### 15.1.5 Measurement of Cost Performance

Project earned value, depending upon the nature of the project, can be measured in one or more of the three parameters, i.e. cost, work hours and quantity of work done. Its progress is expressed in percentage. For example, the cost performance of a project can be determined as:

$$\text{Project progress (\%)} = \frac{\text{Budgeted cost of work performed}}{\text{Budgeted cost of total project}} \times 100$$

Budgeted cost of work performed is equal to the sum of the approved costs of completed works. The percentage progress of completed works can be calculated by tabulating and updating the work progress data, work-package wise, as shown in Table 15.1.

### Table 15.1
### Evaluation of Financial Progress

| Particulars | Work Package ($) | | Progress (%) | | |
|---|---|---|---|---|---|
| | Budget | Work Done | Work Package | Task | Project |
| Task L | B | W | W ÷ B | W ÷ L | W ÷ P |
| Code 126 | 15000 | 15000 | 100.00 | 18.75 | 3.00 |
| 127 | 20000 | 16000 | 80.00 | 20.00 | 3.20 |
| 128 | 45000 | 9000 | 20.00 | 11.25 | 1.80 |
| Total L | 80000 | 40000 | — | 50.00 | 8.00 |
| Task M | | | | | |
| Task N | | | | | |
| Project P | 500000 | 75000 | — | — | 15.00 |

The evaluation of project progress in percentage, needs two inputs for each work package, i.e. budget cost and work done cost. The method of measurement of up-to-date work done cost varies with the nature of work. The various methods of measuring progress of the different types of work packages can be categorized as under:

1. *Ratio method* In most of the construction tasks, the performance of work is measured as proportionate to a predominant parameter like excavated quantity in earthwork, concrete placed in mass concreting of a dam, actual cost of work done, and man-hours of effort spent in formwork. In all such cases, the percentage progress can be calculated as under:

$$\text{Percentage progress} = \frac{\text{Progress accomplished in units of predominant parameter} \times 100}{\text{Total estimate at completion}}$$

For example, if 25 m³ of earth is excavated out of a total of 200 m³, then excavation progress = $\frac{25}{200} \times 100 = 12.5\%$.

Similarly, the progress of formwork for roofing can be determined either on area erected basis or man-hours of effort spent. To quote another case, in a lube-oil refinery project, the progress of RCC foundations work was calculated as under:

$$\text{Percentage progress of RCC foundation work} = \frac{\text{Quantity concreted} \times 100}{\text{Total concrete quantity}}$$

2. *Repetitive-type work packages* In repetitive activities (or work package) say in a building project, each activity becomes the unit of measure.

$$\text{Percentage progress} = \frac{\text{Units completed}}{\text{Total number of units}} \times 100$$

3. *Non-repetitive complex construction work packages* Generally, work packages of a complex multi-activities work package can be grouped into a chain of broad sequential stages. Thereafter, each stage in the chain can be assigned a predetermined percentage of budget catered for the work package. The overall progress of the work package at a given point of time can then be estimated by totalling the percentages of the stages completed.

4. *Start/Finish method* In certain tasks such as preparation of drawings, procurement of materials, planning of project, investigation of soil, the start and completion are well defined, but the progress of intermediate stages is difficult to estimate. For such tasks, an arbitrary percentage can be assigned to mark the start, and the balance can be considered after the task is completed.

## 15.1.6 Cost Reports

Cost reports are generally initiated at the level of responsibility centres (cost centre). The cost data should relate the same period physical data at the time of reporting. Preferably, cost reports should be initiated monthly and their frequency can be increased in the early stages of the project. The cost reports of construction/production centres should reflect a comparison of standard and actual costs. In case of functional departments, cost comparison should be made between budgeted/actual costs.

The project cost controller monitors the responsibility centre cost reports. He updates the project budgeted costs, changes order, keeps track of variations in control estimates, and forecasts the trends pertaining to the remaining project costs. A specimen of cost-time progress charting is drawn in Fig. 15.1.

## 15.1.7 Management Role in Cost Control

Cost control can be called effective if the management:

- Implements efficient cost control procedures and systems.
- Develops and updates the control estimates.
- Analyses cost trends to discover potential cost problems and takes remedial measure to control cost.
- Encourages a cost conscience and time conscience attitude.
- Continuously examines methods of execution with an object of total project cost reductions.

**Figure 15.1**

**Integrated Time-cost Performance Chart (Performance be scheduled)**

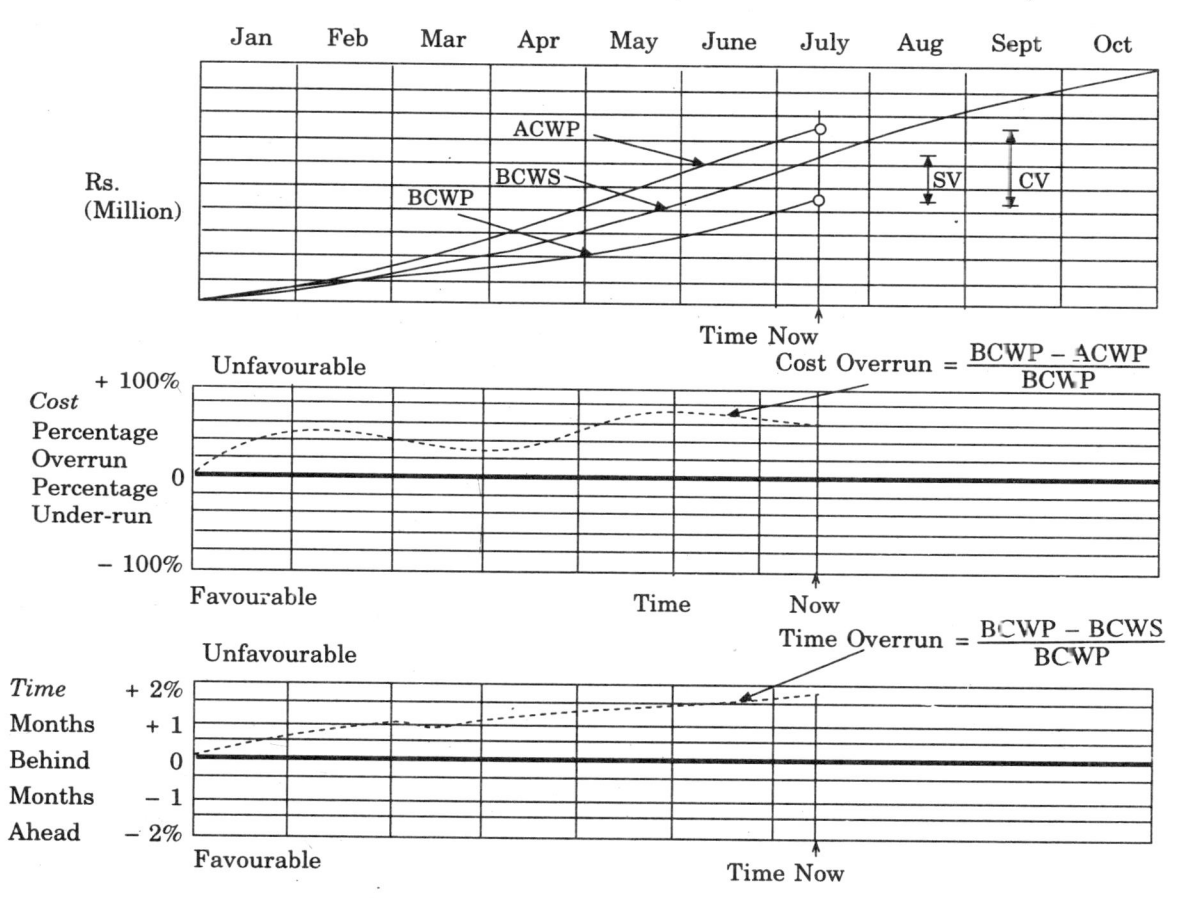

$$\text{Cost Overrun} = \frac{BCWP - ACWP}{BCWP}$$

$$\text{Time Overrun} = \frac{BCWP - BCWS}{BCWP}$$

## ☐ 15.2 REVENUE OR SALES CONTROL

Sales revenue, at the project site, is made up of the value of work done at predetermined prices, the cost of site materials inventory to be paid at an agreed percentage of the purchased cost and the value of work changes (over contracted quantities).

Revenue control aims at the analysis of variances for the work executed. These variances can be computed as under:

|  |  | Original Work | Materials at Site | Work Change Order |
|---|---|---|---|---|
| (A) | Budget forecasts cumulative | XXXX | XXX | XX |
| (B) | Contract value of work done | | | |
| | (a) Up to previous month | XXX | XX | XX |
| | (b) During current month | XX | X | X |
| | Cumulative (B) | XXXX | XXX | XX |
| (C) | Actual approved (cumulative) | XXX | XX | XX |
| (D) | Work done value or quantity Variance (A − B) | XX | XX | X |
| (E) | Price variance (B − C) | XX | X | X |
| (F) | Budget variance (A − C) | XXX | XX | XX |

The budgeted revenue variance can be accounted by:

(a) Measuring quantities of work done and its value at the sale price generally given in the bill of quantities.
(b) Stock taking of direct materials and other payable items at the site.
(c) Evaluating change orders (deviations from the original contract).
(d) Estimating and billing all payable items at the site.
(e) Comparing the revenue actually approved and the revenue planned as per budget and analyzing the causes for variations.

### 15.2.1 Accounting Work Progress

Sale or earned value of work done at predetermined standard prices or contract rate, stated in the bill of quantities, is assessed by measuring the quantity of work done, recording the details of these measurements in the measurement books, and then evaluating the value of work done for each item of work:

Value of work done = Contract price × Actual quantity of work done

The value of the work progress is then compiled, item-wise, in the prescribed manner. The format used for consolidating values of work progress varies from project to project, and depends on the financial and accounting methodology devised by the client. A typical format is shown in Table 12.1. It may be noted that the value of work done during the month is calculated by evaluating the cumulative work done at the end of the month and then subtracting the cumulative value of work done approved in the previous month.

### 15.2.2 Accounting Direct Materials Inventory

The evaluation of direct materials-at-site inventory involves stock taking of materials lying at site and then multiplying these with their unit prices, generally as shown in the materials purchase invoices. The admissible advance for the value of materials-at-site is then computed by multiplying the total purchased value of these materials with the mutually agreed percentage, as incorporated in the terms of the contract. It may be noted that the value (and quantity) of materials-at-site consumed during the month can be determined as under:

Value of materials-at-site consumed during the month
= Value of opening stock of the month + Value of materials inducted during the month
  − Value of closing stock at the end of the month.

### ❑ 15.2.3 Accounting Work Changes Orders

In construction projects work changes through deviations in orders are inevitable. In some projects such deviations may run into hundreds. The cost of extra works can be determined by any of the following mutually or contractually agreed methods:

(a) Pro rata assessment based on elemental unit rates given in the bill of quantities.
(b) Lump sum price for each work change order.
(c) Actual cost plus fixed percentage to cater for contractor's overheads and profits.
(d) Actual cost or guaranteed maximum price, whichever is greater.

For accounting purposes, each change order for extra work is allotted a serial number; it is documented and resources employed for its execution are properly accounted. The revenue accrued from a deviation order is not added to the revenue from sales of items of the original work progress, and each is treated separately.

### 15.2.4 Revenue Variance

Budget revenue variance encountered in construction projects is made up of (a) sale price variances and (b) work done quantity variances. These are explained below:

(a) **Work done quantity variance** determines the changes in the quantity of work done from the budgeted quantities of work. It is the general practice to analyze the original work progress, materials at the site, and work changes separately.

(b) **Sale price variance** shows the changes between the standard sale price and the actual selling price. In contracted projects, unless the work completed is defective, the sale price is fixed and it is reflected in the bill of quantities. Accordingly, in original contracted works the sale price variance can only arise as a result of deductions made from the standard price due to defective or incomplete work.

## 15.3 DIRECT COST CONTROL

Direct cost control aims at improving productivity by minimizing the wastage of input resources, developing standards for costing future works, and accounting all direct costs for 'contribution control' and 'budgetary control'. Direct costs constitute over 60% of the total project costs. Direct cost control (with predetermined labour rates and materials purchase prices) can best be exercised at the lowest organizational level at the production centre or even work-centre, where cost is actually incurred.

### 15.3.1 Approach

The basic concept behind controlling direct costs is that each work package for which the standard cost is established, is identifiable, measurable, and costable. Direct cost control is exercised by comparing the actual direct costs with the standard direct costs, analyzing the reasons for variations, and applying corrective measures to improve the performance. A prerequisite for controlling direct costs is that the standards must be expressed in terms of the physical and monetary value of each item of resource needed for accomplishing the work package.

| Type of resources | Physical measure | Monetary value example |
|---|---|---|
| Direct labour | Man-hours (MH) | Labour employment cost |
| Direct materials | Unit quantity | Materials usage cost |
| Direct equipment | Equipment hours (EH) | Equipment utilization cost |
| Direct other expenses | — | Other direct costs. |

Likewise, the actual direct cost being compared with the standard direct cost must aim at measuring the actual quantity and cost of the resources in the same unit as that of the standard.

The resource utilization records, covered in Chapter 14, form the basis for accounting resources. Time-cards provide data for computing the wages and salaries for each direct labourer and the foreman's daily employment report helps in tracing the labour cost for accomplishing a given work-package.

Equipment employment records make it possible to account for direct equipment costs. Storekeepers' stock cards show the quantity of stores issued to the responsibility centres against their requisitions. In addition, other direct expenses connected with a work package or a sub-contract can be easily found. This direct resources data can enable evaluation of the actual costs incurred for accomplishing each work package. Direct resources performance data, when converted into money value, generates cost data for exercising standard direct cost control.

The primary purpose of introducing standard direct costs is to generate information by comparing actual performance against the standards and to analyze variance.

Direct cost variance = Standard direct cost − Actual direct cost.
If variance ≥ 0, it is favourable (F).
If variance < 0, it is unfavourable (U).

Direct cost control involves the evaluation and analysis of the following variances:

(a) Direct cost variance.
(b) Direct materials cost variance.
(c) Direct labour cost variances.
(d) Direct equipment cost variance.
(e) Other direct expenses variance.

Further, breakdown of the direct cost variances is shown in Fig. 15.2 and the sequence in which production cost variances are generally analyzed is reflected in Fig. 15.3.

The methodology used for analyzing cost variances at the production centre level, is illustrated below with a simple example from the case of a foundation construction task force of a housing units construction project. The concrete placing team has been assigned the task of placing ready-mix concrete in the rafts of the building foundations. Each module of the raft measures 80 cubic metre (CM). During a particular week, the placing team concreted four rafts, using 330 CM of concrete. It procured ready-mix concrete from the project central batching plant at SR 145 per CM delivered at site. It completed placing the concrete in 14 hours, using a concrete pump hired at the rate of SR 120 per hour. The concrete placing team consisting of one foreman, four masons, and eight helpers was employed at the work site for 40 hours to prepare shuttering, rebar steel fixing, concreting, deshuttering and curing. Average man-hour rate for this team works out as SR 7.90 per man-hour.

At the time of planning standard costs for placing concrete, the concrete price for delivery at the site of work was taken at (SR) 150 per cubic metre. The concrete pumping charges were assessed at SR 100 per hour, with pumping rate of about 20 $m^3$ per hour. The concrete wastage at the site during placing was considered as 2%. The concreting team composition was taken as one foreman six masons and seven helpers with an average rate of SR 8.125 per man-hour with production capacity of laying one raft of 80 cubic metre, five hours. The steel shuttering used for the raft is to be charged at SR 400 per set per raft shuttering.

The standard and actual cost data for concreting four raft foundations, is tabulated in Table 15.2. It is summarized below:

| Cost Category | Standard Cost (SR) | Actual Cost (SR) |
|---|---|---|
| Direct materials | 48,960 | 47,850 |
| Direct labour | 3,640 | 4,108 |
| Direct equipment | 1,600 | 1,680 |
| Shuttering | 1,600 | 1,600 |
| | 55,800 | 55,238 |

## Figure 15.2

**Main Cost Variances Breakdown**

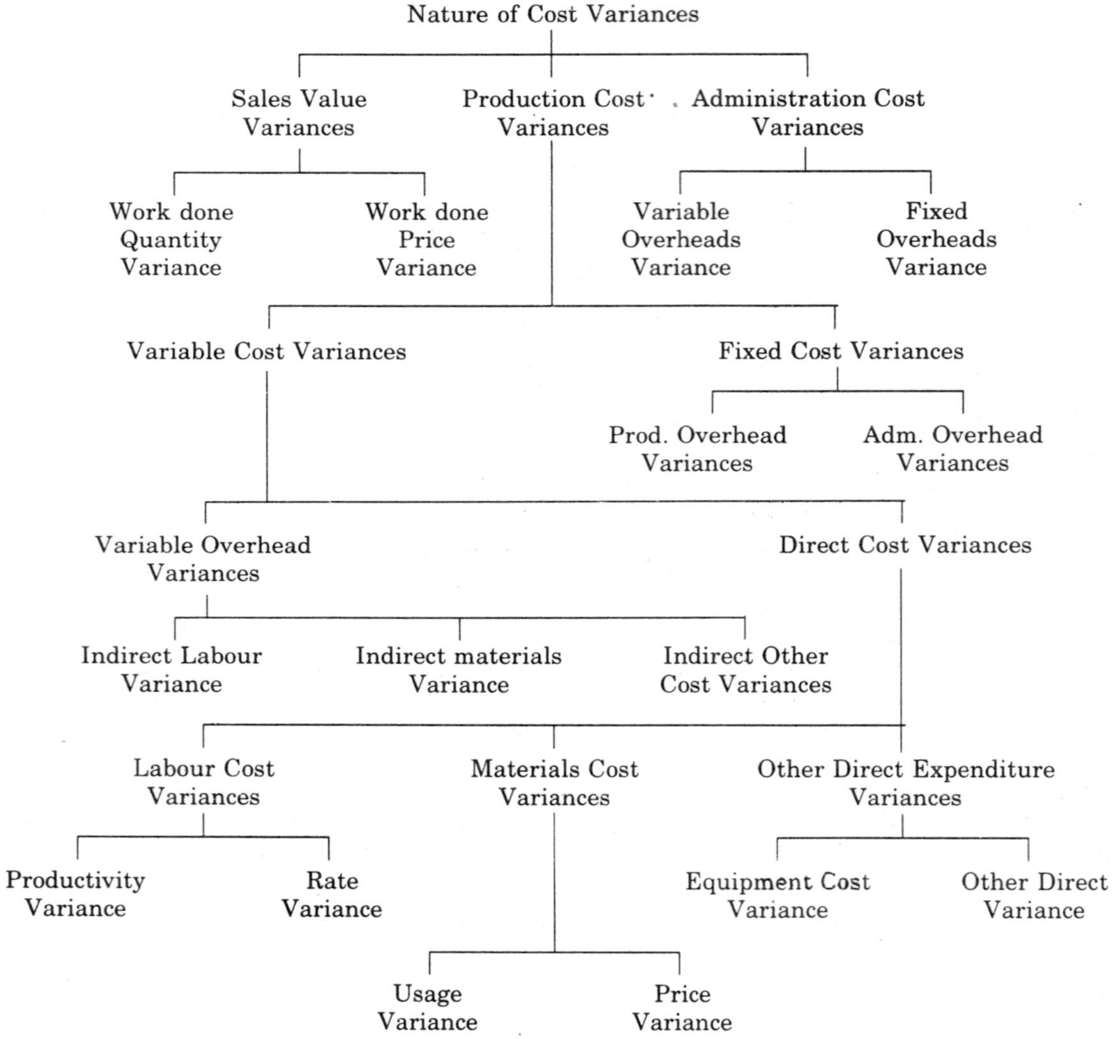

```
                        Nature of Cost Variances
         ┌──────────────────────┼──────────────────────┐
    Sales Value            Production Cost       Administration Cost
    Variances              Variances             Variances
    ┌────┴────┐                                  ┌────┴────┐
Work done   Work done                       Variable      Fixed
Quantity    Price                           Overheads     Overheads
Variance    Variance                        Variance      Variance
                   ┌──────────────────────────────┴──────┐
            Variable Cost Variances              Fixed Cost Variances
                   │                              ┌──────┴──────┐
                   │                         Prod. Overhead  Adm. Overhead
                   │                         Variances       Variances
         ┌─────────┴──────────────────────────┐
   Variable Overhead                    Direct Cost Variances
   Variances
   ┌───────┼────────────┐
Indirect   Indirect      Indirect Other
Labour     materials     Cost Variances
Variance   Variance
         ┌──────────────┼──────────────────────┐
    Labour Cost     Materials Cost        Other Direct Expenditure
    Variances       Variances             Variances
    ┌────┴────┐                           ┌────────┴────────┐
Productivity  Rate                    Equipment Cost   Other Direct
Variance      Variance                Variance         Variance
                    ┌────┴────┐
                 Usage      Price
                 Variance   Variance
```

### 15.3.2 Direct Cost Variance

Direct cost variance is the difference between the standard direct cost of the output desired and the actual direct cost incurred to accomplish it.

In the above example of concreting 320 m$^3$ of 4 rafts foundation.

Direct cost variance = Standard direct cost − Actual direct cost

## Figure 15.3

**Sequence of Production Cost Variances Analysis**

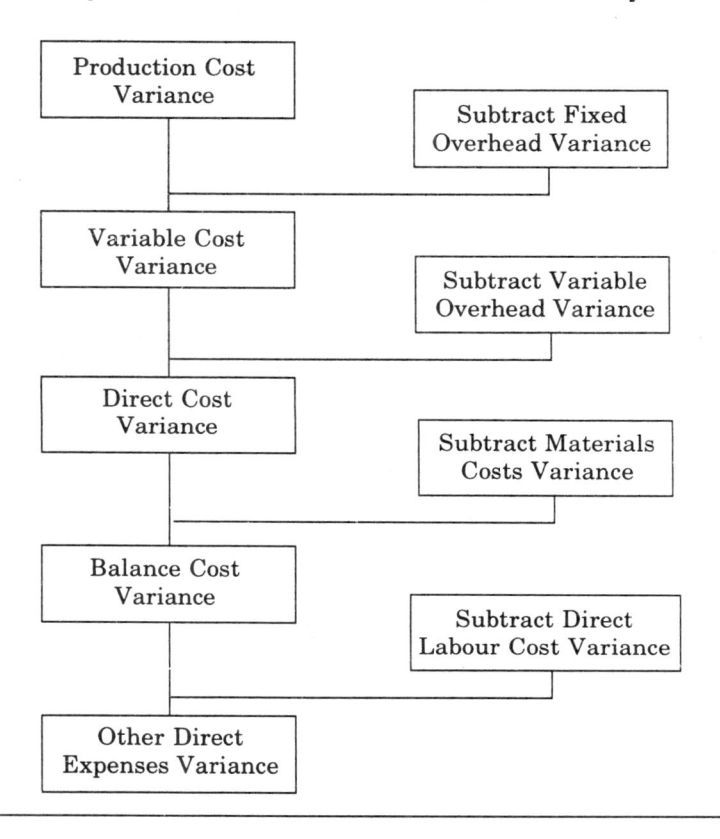

```
┌─────────────────┐
│ Production Cost │
│    Variance     │
└────────┬────────┘         ┌──────────────────┐
         │                  │  Subtract Fixed  │
         │←─────────────────│ Overhead Variance│
         │                  └──────────────────┘
┌────────┴────────┐
│  Variable Cost  │
│    Variance     │         ┌──────────────────┐
└────────┬────────┘         │ Subtract Variable│
         │←─────────────────│ Overhead Variance│
         │                  └──────────────────┘
┌────────┴────────┐
│   Direct Cost   │
│    Variance     │         ┌──────────────────┐
└────────┬────────┘         │Subtract Materials│
         │←─────────────────│  Costs Variance  │
         │                  └──────────────────┘
┌────────┴────────┐
│  Balance Cost   │
│    Variance     │         ┌──────────────────┐
└────────┬────────┘         │ Subtract Direct  │
         │←─────────────────│Labour Cost Variance
         │                  └──────────────────┘
┌────────┴────────┐
│   Other Direct  │
│Expenses Variance│
└─────────────────┘
```

Now, Standard direct cost = 55,800
Actual direct cost = 55,238
∴ Direct cost variance = 55,800 − 55,238
= (+) 562 (Favourable).

Even if the value of direct cost variance is small, the process of analysis should be continued, as explained below.

## 15.3.3 Direct Materials Cost Variance

This is the difference between the standard direct materials cost and the actual materials cost for the same output.

## Table 15.2
### Cost Data of Concreting Four Rafts

| Costs for 4 Rafts | Unit | Standard Rates for one Raft (SR) | | Standard Costs for four Rafts (SR) | | Actual Costs for four Rafts (SR) |
|---|---|---|---|---|---|---|
| | | | Qty | | Qty | |
| 1. Direct materials costs | M$^3$ | 150.00 | 326.4 | 48,960.00 | 330 | 47,850.00 |
| 2. Direct labour costs | MH | 8.125 | 448 | 3,640.00 | 520 | 4,108.00 |
| 3. Direct equipment costs | EH | 100.00 | 16 | 1,600.00 | 14 | 1,680.00 |
| 4. Depreciation of shuttering | Set | 400.00 | 4 | 1600 | 4 | 1,600.00 |
| 5. Total direct costs | | | | 55,800.00 | | 55,238.00 |

Standard concrete quantity of 4 rafts, each 80 m$^3$ plus 2% wastage
= 4 × 80 × 1.02 = 326.4 m$^3$
Price/rates are in SR (Saudi Riyal is currency of Saudi Arabia)

Direct materials cost variance = Standard materials cost − Actual materials cost
= 48960 − 47850
= 1110 (Favourable)     (A)

The direct materials cost variance is made up of materials usage variance and materials price variance. These variances and their further breakdown can be evaluated using a generalized materials variances analysis model sketched in Fig. 15.4. This model also shows the relationship among various components of materials cost variances. Taking the raft concreting example,

Materials cost variance = Materials usage variance + Materials price variance

where,

1. Materials usage variance = Standard rate (Standard quantity − Actual quantity)
= 150 (326.4 × − 330) (from Table 15.2)
= (−) 540 Unfavourable)     (B)

Unfavourable materials usage variance reveals that the wastage has been greater than the expected standard wastage and it needs to be controlled in future similar works.

2. Materials price variance = Actual quantity (Standard rate − Actual rate)
= 330 (150 − 145) (from Table 15.2)
= 1650 (Favourable)     (C)

Favourable materials price variance shows the saving on account of discounting of prices from the prices considered at the time of estimation of standards.

## Figure 15.4
## Direct Materials Cost Variances

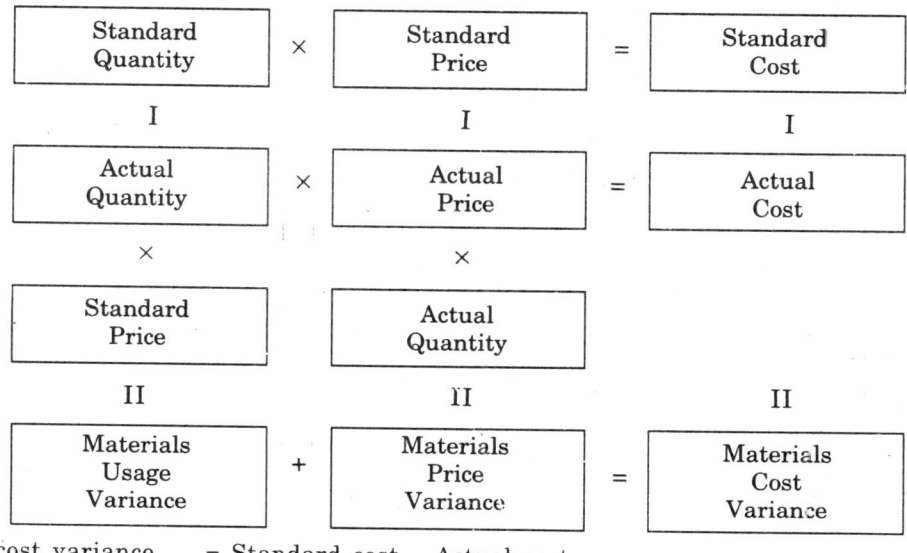

```
┌──────────┐     ┌──────────┐     ┌──────────┐
│ Standard │  ×  │ Standard │  =  │ Standard │
│ Quantity │     │  Price   │     │   Cost   │
└──────────┘     └──────────┘     └──────────┘
      I                I                I
┌──────────┐     ┌──────────┐     ┌──────────┐
│  Actual  │  ×  │  Actual  │  =  │  Actual  │
│ Quantity │     │  Price   │     │   Cost   │
└──────────┘     └──────────┘     └──────────┘
      ×                ×
┌──────────┐     ┌──────────┐
│ Standard │     │  Actual  │
│  Price   │     │ Quantity │
└──────────┘     └──────────┘
      II               II               II
┌──────────┐     ┌──────────┐     ┌──────────┐
│ Materials│     │ Materials│     │ Materials│
│  Usage   │  +  │  Price   │  =  │   Cost   │
│ Variance │     │ Variance │     │ Variance │
└──────────┘     └──────────┘     └──────────┘
```

Materials cost variance = Standard cost − Actual cost
= Materials usage variance + Materials price variance
Materials usage variance = Standard rate (Standard quantity − Actual quantity)
Materials price variance = Actual quantity (Standard rate − Actual rate)

---

3. Therefore, direct materials cost variance = B + C
   = − 540 + 1650
   = 1110 (Favourable).

   (It is same as A above)

4. Materials productivity variance (%) = Standard wastage % − Actual wastage %

   $= 2\% - \dfrac{(330 - 320)}{320} \times 100$

   = (2% − 3.125%) of 4 rafts concrete quantity of 80 m³ each. (i.e. total 320 m³ concrete)

   = (−) 1.125% (Unfavourable).

   $= \dfrac{-1.125 \times 320 \times 150}{100}$

   = − SR 540. (It is same as B above)

In case of materials like concrete manufacturing, the materials usage variance analysis can be further extended to cover mix variance and yield variance:

Materials mix variance
= Standard rate × Standard yield (Standard mix – Actual mix).

Materials yield variance
= Standard rate × Standard mix (Standard yield – Actual yield).

### 15.3.4 Direct Labour Cost Variance

This is the difference between the standard labour and the actual labour cost for performing the same output.

In the given example,

Direct labour cost variance = Standard labour cost – Actual labour cost
= 3640 – 4108
= (–) 468 (Unfavourable)

The labour cost variance can be further analyzed using the generalized labour cost variance model shown in Fig. 15.5. The two components of the labour cost variance are:

Figure 15.5

**Direct Labour Cost Variances**

| Standard Time | × | Standard Rate | = | Standard Cost |
|---|---|---|---|---|
| I | | I | | I |
| Actual Time | × | Actual Rate | = | Actual Cost |
| × | | × | | |
| Standard Rate | | Actual Time | | |
| II | | II | | II |
| Labour Operating Variance | + | Labour Rate Variance | = | Labour Cost Variance |

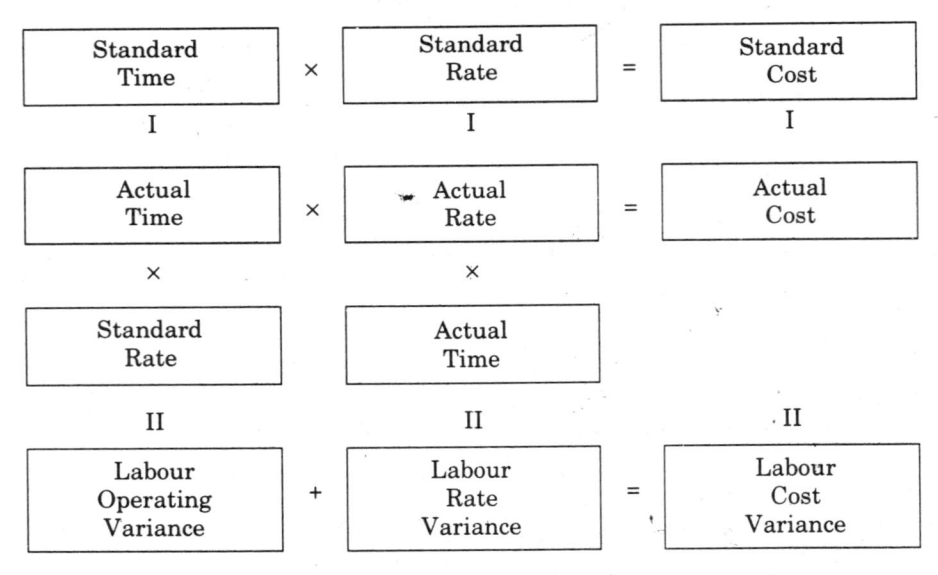

1. Labour operating variance = Standard rate (Standard time – Actual time)
2. Labour rate variance = Actual time (Standard rate – Actual rate)
3. Labour cost variance = Labour operating variance + Labour rate variance.

Labour operating or productivity cost variance
= Standard rate (Standard time − Actual time)
= 8.125 (14 × 8 × 4 − 13 × 40) (from Table 15.2)
= 8.125 (448 − 520)
= (−) 585 (Unfavourable).

Labour rate variance = Actual time (Standard rate − Actual rate)
= 40 × 13 (8.125 − 7.9)
= 117 (Favourable).

*Note*: The sum of labour operating variance and labour rate variance, calculated above is equal to direct labour cost variance i.e.

Labour operating variance + Labour rate variance = − 585 + 117
= (−) 468
= Direct labour cost variance.

### 15.3.5 Equipment Variance

This is the difference between the standard equipment cost and actual equipment cost for accomplishing the same output. The Equipment variance analysis model is similar to that of the labour variance analysis. Proceeding similarly:

Equipment cost variance = Standard equipment cost − Actual equipment cost
= 400 × 4 − 1680 (from Table 15.2)
= (−) 80 (Unfavourable).

This equipment cost variance be further split up into:

Equipment operating (or productivity) cost variance
= Standard rate (Standard time − Actual time)
= 100 (4 × 4 − 14) (from Table 15.2)
= 200 (Favourable).

Equipment rate variance = Actual time (Standard rate − Actual rate)
= 14 (100 − 120) (from Table 15.2)
= (−) 280 (Unfavourable).

### 15.3.6 Summary of Direct Cost Variances

All the variances evaluated for concreting 4 rafts can be summarized as follows:

(1) Direct cost variance                                                     (+) 562 (Favourable)

(2) Direct materials variance
    (a) Materials usage variance      (−) 540 (Unfavourable)
    (b) Materials price variance      (+) 1650 (Favourable)

(3) Direct labour variance
    (a) Labour operating variance      (−) 585 (Unfavourable)
    (b) Labour rate variance      (+) 117 (Favourable)

(4) Direct equipment variance
    (a) Equipment operating variance      (+) 200 (Favourable)
    (b) Equipment rate variance      (−) 280 (Unfavourable)

    562 (Favourable)      562 (Favourable)

## 15.3.7 Causes of Unfavourable Direct Cost Variances

Direct cost control and resources productivity control are inseparable. The object of direct cost control is to minimize expenditure through cost variance analysis, and this mainly depends upon minimizing wastage in the employment of resources.

Cost variance can result from many causes. Some of the main causes for unfavourable variances are given below. This list is indicative and not comprehensive:

**(a) Material price variance**    Increased prices, unplanned purchases.

**(b) Materials usage variance**    Sub-standard materials, excessive wastage, other reasons resulting in low materials productivity.

**(c) Labour rate variance**    Wage increases, labour associated costs increases, unforeseen social security legislations.

**(d) Labour operating variance**    Sub-standard materials used, inappropriate labour skills, lack of work preparation, other reasons resulting in low productivity.

**(e) Equipment rate variance**    Higher hiring charges, incorrect matching of machine with the job.

**(f) Equipment operating variance**    Rise in fuel prices, excessive repairs, unplanned idle time, other reasons resulting in low productivity.

**(g) Other common reasons**    Unrealistic standards, higher resource procurement costs, higher sub-contract costs, mismanagement of resources.

There is a difference between direct cost control and direct cost reduction. Direct cost control prevents wastage within the existing environment. On the other hand, cost reduction is a creative process which aims at reducing resources expenditure using techniques like value analysis, work study, automation, quality improvement, and other innovative approaches.

## 15.4 INDIRECT COST CONTROL

Production cost constitutes direct costs and indirect costs. Direct cost control methodology is covered earlier in this chapter. Direct cost items account for the major portion, say 70%, of the production costs. Indirect costs are numerous, accounting for a comparatively lesser percentage (say 30%) of the production costs. In the current competitive market where the profit margin varies from 3.5 to 15% of the production costs, it is important that indirect costs should be controlled to prevent overruns.

As already mentioned in Chapter 11, the indirect cost of each responsibility centre can be broadly divided into two categories, i.e. production-related variable overheads and time-related periodic fixed overheads. Theoretically, no production implies no variable overheads. In reality, fixed overheads are incurred independent of the level of production.

Production-related variable overheads are incurred by almost all the responsibility centres. Construction centres have production overheads on what they produce. Similarly, service centres incur expenditure on what they serve and this expenditure gets apportioned as service centres' variable overheads on construction centres. Even in the administration centre, there is a component of variable overheads.

Since, all the fixed overheads in the project are generally ordered, accounted for and controlled by the administrative responsibility centre, the project indirect costs for accounting and control purposes can be categorized as under:

(a) Construction centre variable overheads.
(b) Services centre variable overheads.
(c) Administration centre variable overheads.
(d) Project fixed overheads.

Each of the above heads can be divided into indirect manpower costs, indirect material costs, indirect equipment costs, and other indirect expenses.

The indirect cost control brings out variances, and the reasons for variances between the budgeted and actual, in respect of the above variable and fixed overheads. For accounting purposes, the fixed costs are charged to the profit as in the case of marginal costing techniques then the balance overheads are all variable in nature. This concept is at the root of contribution control methodology covered under budgetary control.

## 15.5 PROJECT BUDGETARY CONTROL

The project budget is the well coordinated and management approved financial plan of operations, indicating the amounts required for achieving assigned targets, and the expected receipts from sales or the value of work done. The project budget includes budgets at each responsibility centre.

Budgetary control is the process by which the managers of responsibility centres exercise control over their budgeted costs through continuous appraisals of actual expenditure and income with the budgeted costs and revenue receipts. The budgetary control process lays emphasis on the identification of areas of responsibility of the individual managers, and regular comparisons of their actual achievements with the budgeted targets.

### 15.5.1 Accounting Budgeted Costs

The first step in the budgetary control process is to establish a system for accounting income, costs and finances, generally conforming to the pattern adopted while developing the budget. This calls for a suitably designed integrated finance and cost accounting system.

Broadly, these accounting areas can be divided into the following heads of accounts:

**(a) Sales revenue accounting**
- Original works progress.
- Materials-at-site inventory.
- Works change orders.

**(b) Production costs accounting**
- Materials costs.
- Manpower costs.
- Equipment costs.
- Other production costs.

**(c) General and administration costs**

**(d) General financial adjustment accounts**
- Non-operating incomes like interests on deposits, short-term investments, discounts, etc.
- Non-operating expenses such as taxes and dividends paid.

**(e) Profit and loss accounting**
- Fixed budget contribution concept.
- Flexible budgetary control concept.

Finance cost and accounting heads encountered in a medium size building project are listed in Fig. 15.6. General financial adjustment accounts are maintained to carry out financial adjustments in profit and loss accounts, and these are not considered for cost control purpose.

Contribution and flexible budget concepts are the tools used for exercising costs and profits control.

### 15.5.2 Contribution Control

Profitability of the project and cost performance can best be controlled by using the 'contribution control' methodology.

Contribution is defined as the difference between the sale value and the variable cost of these sales. Variable cost of the sales represent the production-related variable component of production cost. It excludes the fixed overheads.

Project Cost Control 459

## Figure 15.6
### Finance and Cost Accounting Interface for Contribution Accounting

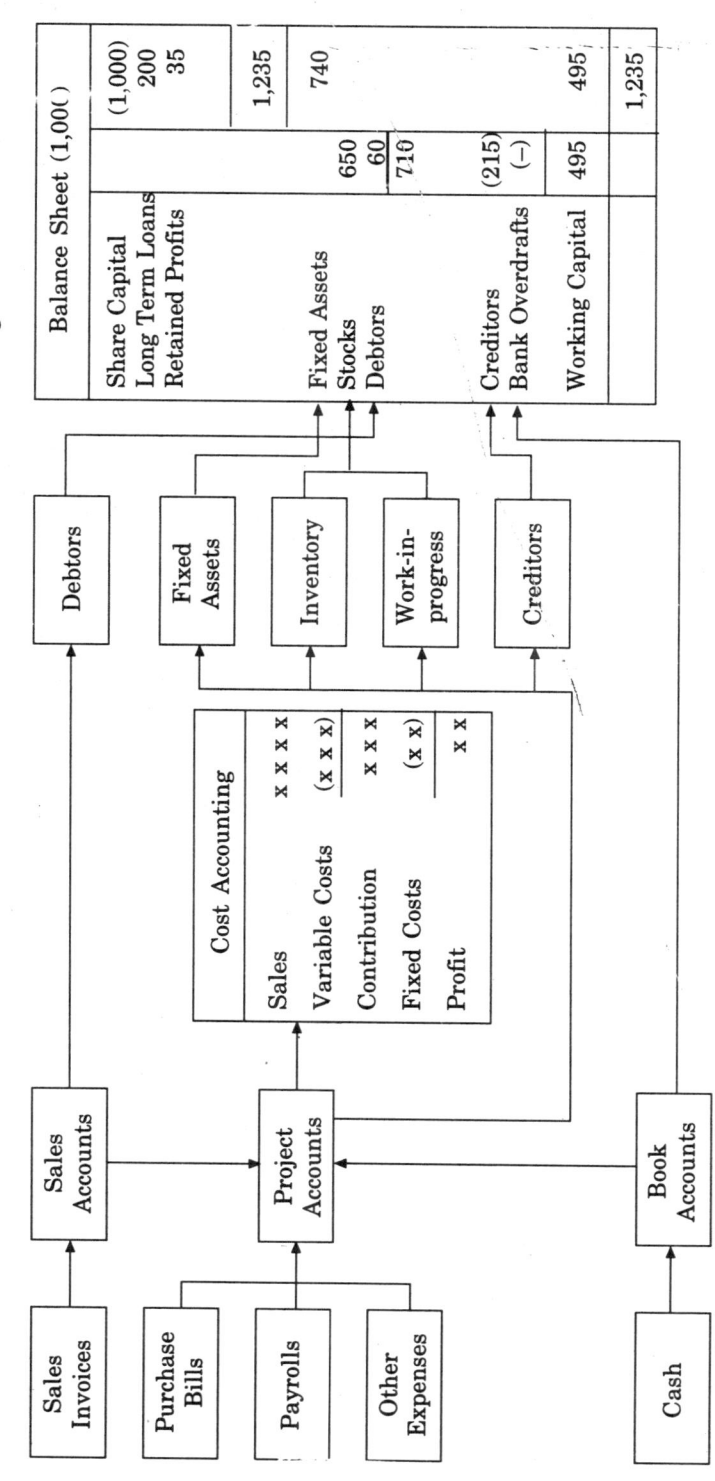

| Balance Sheet (1,000) | | |
|---|---|---|
| Share Capital | | (1,000) |
| Long Term Loans | | 200 |
| Retained Profits | | 35 |
| | | 1,235 |
| Fixed Assets | | 740 |
| Stocks | 650 | |
| Debtors | 60 | |
| | 710 | |
| Creditors | (215) | |
| Bank Overdrafts | (—) | |
| Working Capital | 495 | 495 |
| | | 1,235 |

Cost Accounting

| | |
|---|---|
| Sales | x x x x |
| Variable Costs | (x x x) |
| Contribution | x x x |
| Fixed Costs | (x x) |
| Profit | x x |

Flow: Sales Invoices → Sales Accounts → Debtors → (Balance Sheet: Debtors)

Purchase Bills, Payrolls, Other Expenses → Project Accounts → Cost Accounting → Fixed Assets, Inventory, Work-in-progress → (Balance Sheet)

Project Accounts → Creditors → (Balance Sheet: Creditors)

Cash → Book Accounts → (Balance Sheet: Working Capital)

Contribution = Sales − Variable costs  (A)
But, profit = Sales − Production costs
= Sales − Variable costs − Fixed overheads  (B)

From A and B above,

Contribution = Profit + Fixed overheads.

It shows that:

(a) If the contribution exceeds fixed costs, a profit is made.
(b) If the contribution equals fixed costs, break-even results.
(c) If the contribution is less than fixed costs, the projects is running at a loss.

Contribution can be viewed as the contribution of the responsibility centres towards the profits and fixed overheads of the project, and it is taken as a measure to judge the cost performance of the centre. For example, if at the end of the month, a construction responsibility centre executes works worth $1,000,000 (payable), and its corresponding expenditure on its direct costs and its variable overheads is $900,000, then its contribution to the project = Sales − Variable costs = $1,000,000 − $900,000 = $100,000.

Contribution is evaluated generally in terms of work packages sold, or for sold work units as listed in bill of quantities. It is preferable to have the work package as the data base for computing contribution as each work package has a specified scope of work with a fixed sale price. It has its predetermined production cost objectives, expressed as standard variable cost, consisting of direct cost and variable overheads, and standard rate of absorption for fixed overheads.

The concept of variability of cost varies with the level of project hierarchy:

(a) At the corporate level, barring a few exceptions like depreciation on equipment and the management costs, all the project costs, which can be identified with the execution of the project, can be considered as variable.
(b) At the project level, all the overhead costs being incurred by a responsibility centre, except the administration responsibility centre, can be considered as variable.
(c) Similarly, at the construction centre level, all production related costs can be considered as variable; and those which are periodic in nature, like supervisor's salary, can be treated as fixed costs, to be accounted for by the project management.

Contribution control makes use of the variance analysis technique to trace the causes of sales variance and variable cost variance. A generalized model depicting the relationships among the components of contribution variances is shown in Fig. 15.7.

### 15.5.3 Flexible Budgetary Control Concept

The contribution control process raises one main issue in the case of projects specially those involving uncertainties. What if the planned volume of production is not achieved? Will the

## Figure 15.7
### Contribution Variance Analysis

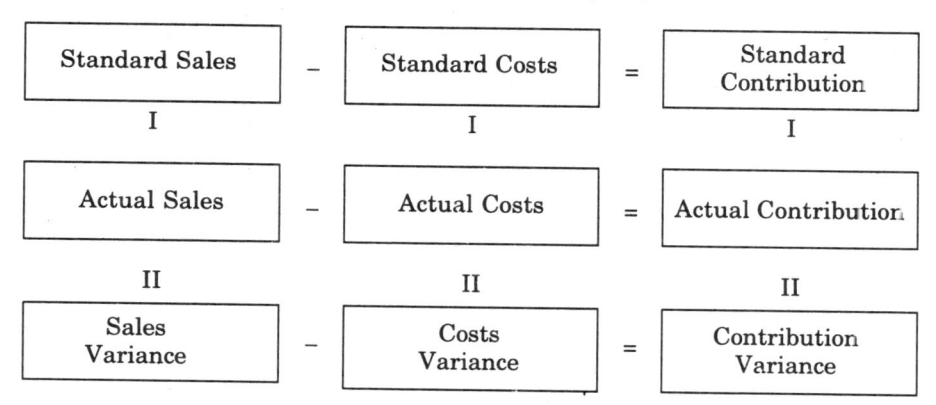

| Standard Sales | − | Standard Costs | = | Standard Contribution |
|---|---|---|---|---|
| I | | I | | I |
| Actual Sales | − | Actual Costs | = | Actual Contribution |
| II | | II | | II |
| Sales Variance | − | Costs Variance | = | Contribution Variance |

comparison between the actual profit and budgeted profit provide meaningful control information? Obviously, this comparison is of little use as there is bound to be the effect of changed volume of production, specially, as the fixed costs remain practically unchanged, irrespective of the change in the volume of productions. In construction projects, appreciable variations in the planned output can therefore, influence the budgeted costs. Wherever such substantial changes occur frequently, it is necessary to reckon the effect of such changes by reviewing the budget regularly, say every quarter, where the budget can be assumed to be fixed in a period of three months. Or a flexible budget can be prepared in which the allocations in the budgets are established separately for various levels of outputs at regular intervals of time and in which the fixed overheads are dealt with separately for the combined project. In particular, the variable costs are separated from fixed costs as it is the variable (production-related costs) which are affected with change.

It is important to note that project environments are dynamic. The fixed budget generally cannot provide directions with changing situations as the fast changing situations call for regular reviews of the budget. On the other hand, a loose budget is as dangerous as is an over tight budget. What is required to be achieved is the project's overall objectives and not mere rigid adherence to a fixed budget allocations. A budget plan in itself is not an end. Therefore, any construction project's fixed level annual budget, due to uncertainties and complexities, can only be considered fixed for the initial short duration and needs to be constantly reviewed.

### 15.5.4 Budgeted Costs Analysis

Cost analysis aims to predict future costs. These cost forecasts serve two main purposes:

(a) To apprise the project management of the possible cost over-run or under-run for taking timely corrective actions such as modifying cash flow, and updating financial forecasts and project profitability expectations.

(b) To update key personnel on anticipated cost changes in their field of responsibility, so as to create cost consciousness for exploring means of minimising wastage and reducing costs.

Cost analysis involves the following steps:

- Evaluation of cost variances by comparing actual costs with budgeted costs, to determine cost overrun/under-run,
- Computing schedule variances by comparing budgeted costs of work schedule and work performed, to determine deviations from the schedule. The time over-run/under-run reveals the cost and time the project is behind or ahead of schedule.
- Estimate project cost at completion.

Budget relates the costs with time progress. Commonly used budget monitoring parameters, already covered in section, 15.1.4 are:

- Budget Cost of Work Scheduled (BCWS) which represents time-phased cost projections made in the budget. It shows what is planned for execution.
- Budgeted Cost for Work Performed (BCWP), which shows the cost budgeted for the work performed to date.
- Actual Cost for the Work Performed (ACWP), which is obtained by summing up the actual cost incurred to date in progressing work packages.

Variances relating to cost parameters are defined as under:

Cost variance = BCWP − ACWP, Schedule variance = BCWP − BCWS
Cost Performance Index = BCWP/ACWP
Schedule Performance Index = BCWP/BCWS

BCWS, when plotted graphically against the time scale, resembles the 'S' curve pattern. Graphical representation of the BCWS function along with actual performance for two typical projects, one with favourable and the other with unfavourable variances, are shown in Fig. 15.8.

**Cost Variances** Cost variance is computed by comparing actual performance (ACWP) with the budgeted cost of work performed (BCWP).

$$\text{Cost variance} = \text{BCWP} - \text{ACWP}$$

If the cost variance is positive, then the project has a cost under-run, i.e. the cost incurred is less than the planned or budgeted cost.

If the cost variance is negative, then there is a cost overrun, i.e. the cost incurred is more than the planned or budgeted cost.

If the cost variance is zero, then the project is proceeding according to the budgeted cost.

Cost overrun and cost under-run are usually expressed in percentage. These can be represented graphically as shown in Fig. 15.1 and 15.8. Each point of cost overrun (or under-run) is derived using the following relationship.

## Cost and Schedule Variances

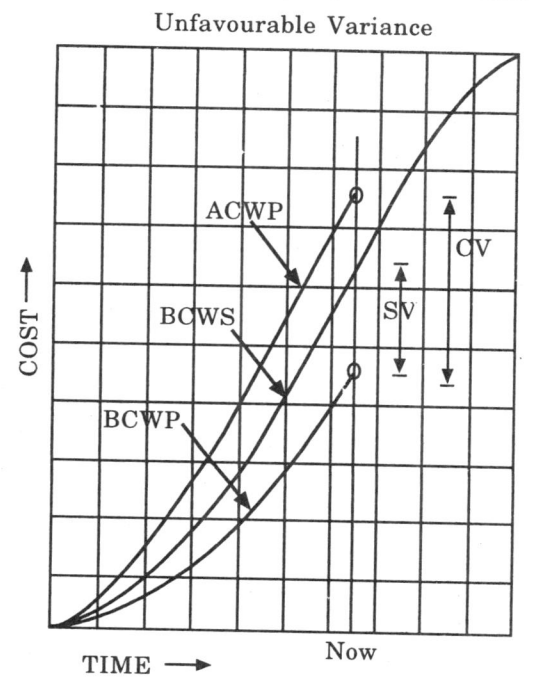

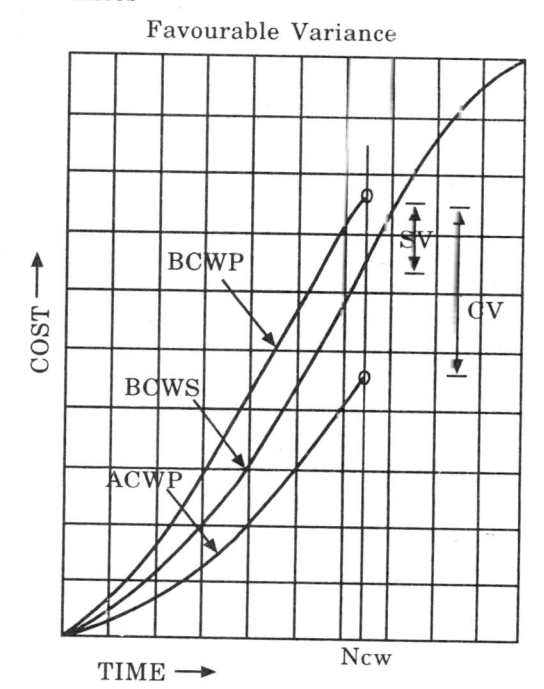

**Unfavourable Variance** — **Favourable Variance**

(Graphs showing COST vs TIME with curves ACWP, BCWS, BCWP, indicating SV and CV at "Now")

Scheduled Variance (SV) = (Earned work hours or value) − (Budgeted work hours or value)

$$SV = BCWP - BCWS$$

$$\text{Schedule Variance (\%)} = \frac{SV}{BCWS} \times 100$$

$$\text{Schedule Performance Index (SPI)} = \frac{\text{(Earned work hours or Value)}}{\text{(Budgeted work hours or Value)}}$$

$$= \frac{BCWP}{BCWS}$$

Cost Variance (CV) = (Earned work hours or value) − (Actual work hours or value)

$$CV = BCWP - ACWP$$

$$\text{Cost Variance (\%)} = \frac{CV}{BCWP} \times 100$$

$$\text{Cost Performance Index (CPI)} = \frac{\text{(Earned work hours or value)}}{\text{(Actual work hours or value)}}$$

$$= \frac{BCWP}{ACWP}$$

$$\text{Cost overrun (or under-run)} = \frac{\text{BCWP} - \text{ACWP}}{\text{BCWP}} \times 100$$

**Schedule variances** Schedule variance is computed by comparing budgeted cost of work performed (BCWP) with the budgeted cost of work scheduled (BCWS).

$$\text{Schedule variance} = \text{BCWP} - \text{BCWS}$$

If schedule variance is positive, then the project is ahead of its planned cost, i.e. earned value of the work performed is higher than the planned or scheduled earned value.

If scheduled variance is negative, then the project is behind its planned cost, i.e. earned value of work performed is less than the planned or scheduled earned value.

If scheduled variance is zero, then the project is proceeding according to the planned schedule.

When the project is behind schedule, there is a time overrun. Similarly, there is a time under-run, if the project is ahead of schedule. Time overrun (or under-run) is equal to the period the project is behind or ahead of the schedule.

Time overrun and time under-run are usually expressed in terms of units of time, say month. These can be represented graphically as shown in Fig. 15.1. The graphs in Fig. 15.1, which provide information about cost and time—budgeted or actual—in one sheet of paper on a common time scale, are useful devices for monitoring and controlling costs.

**Cost trends/forecasts** Variance analysis reveals the extent and causes of variances. On the other hand, performance efficiency determines how efficiently the task was done and what its implications will be on the future trends. The future trends in productivity, cost and time performance can be predicted as under:

Cost Performance Index     = BCWP/ACWP
Schedule Performance Index = BCWP/BCWS

$$\text{Task Productivity Index} = \frac{\text{Estimated unit rate}}{\text{Actual unit rate}}$$

An index of 1.0 or greater indicates a favourable performance and less than 1.0 implies an unfavourable trend.

Performance indices vary during the execution of a project. Minor variations are normal, but the significant changes in indices call for forecasting of the probable performance on completion. These forecasts can be prepared by extrapolating the past data to produce the best fit curve, and thereafter extending the same for predicting performance on completion as under:

(a) Assuming the future trend at the originally planned rate,
Probable completion value = (ACWP − BCWP) + (planned BCWS on completion)

(b) Assuming that the future rate of progress will continue at the present trend,

$$\text{Probable completion value} = \frac{\text{Planned BCWS on completion}}{\text{Performance index or trend}}$$

There can be situations where the originally specified time and cost objective are revised. For example, the original completion time of the project is extended, or the agreed contract amount is increased. In such cases, forecasts corresponding to various situations can be worked out using methods given above.

*Example*

Consider the data reported below at the end of the 10th week of the Site Development Project, which is scheduled for completion at the end of 20th week; BAC is the budgeted cost at completion:

| Activity | Progress(%) Planned | Progress(%) Actual | BAC | BCWS | BCWP | ACWP |
|---|---|---|---|---|---|---|
| a | b | c | d | b × d | c × d | e |
| C | 100 | 100 | 6 | 6 | 6 | 8 |
| H | 45 | 40 | 34 | 15.3 | 13.6 | 15 |
| B | 100 | 100 | 4 | 4 | 4 | 5 |
| G | 100 | 100 | 8 | 8 | 8 | 7 |
| L | 56 | 20 | 21 | 11.8 | 4.2 | 8 |
| E | 100 | 100 | 8 | 8 | 8 | 8 |
| J | 70 | 60 | 16 | 12 | 9.6 | 10 |
| F | — | — | 6 | — | — | — |
| K | — | — | 12 | — | — | — |
| D | 100 | 100 | 15 | 15 | 15 | 13 |
| I | 100 | 100 | 12 | 12 | 12 | 12 |
| A | — | — | 18 | — | — | — |
|  |  |  | 160 | 92.1 | 80.4 | 90 |

*Note*: Network and the original schedule of work of Site Development Project are shown in Exhibits 5.8 and 6.4. Cost data listed above is in thousand dollars. Progress is expressed in percentage of budgeted cost of work. The expected project cost at the end of 10th week, for different situations, can be assessed as under:

*Case 1*: Assuming that the remaining work shall progress at planned rates.

Cost forecast at completion = ACWP + (BAC − BCWP)
= 90 + (160 − 80.4)
= 169.6

*Case 2*: Assuming that the remaining work shall progress at prevailing trend.

Cost forecast at completion = (BAC)/CPI,
= (BAC) × ACWP/BCWP
= 160 × 90/80.4
= 179.1

where Cost Performance Index = BCWP/ACWP

*Case 3*: Assuming remaining work shall progress at assessed crashing costs amounting to 8 units

$$\text{Cost forecast at completion} = \text{ACWP} + (\text{BAC} - \text{BCWP}) + \text{Crashing cost}$$
$$= 90 + (160 - 80.4) + 8$$
$$= 177.6$$

## 15.6 RISK COST MANAGEMENT

Forecasts, at best, are educated guesses based on assumptions and expectations derived from the present knowledge of the future. Business decisions are based on future predictions about environments. Construction projects are subject to fast changing environments. The stability of the project environment is affected by numerous external and internal factors. The resulting instability causes uncertainty. Uncertainties bring in an element of risk.

Risk, in general, signifies situations where the actual outcome of an activity or event is likely to deviate from the estimated or forecast value.

Risk management aims at controlling risk costs which might affect the performance of the project. It uses tools of risk analysis.

Risk analysis is the process of dealing with risks and uncertainties in a structured manner. It involves the following stages:

(a) Identifying risks.
(b) Quantifying risks.
(c) Categorizing risks.
(d) Controlling risks.

### 15.6.1 Identifying Risks

Construction projects encounter unlimited uncertainties. Some of these uncertainties may arise from the following:

(a) Changes in the external environment caused by unstable political, economic, and financial, conditions, natural disasters like fires and floods, and man-made catastrophes like burglary and fraud.
(b) Changes in the internal environment concerning quality considerations, commercial dealings, internal safety and security of resources, accidents, errors in estimations, design alterations, labour strikes, materials wastage, equipment breakdown, project management internal conflicts, client holds, client-contractor disputes, corruption, and so on.

The first step in risk analysis is to identify the nature of risks. Most of the risks can be identified if the project is broken down into the manageable level of details. This breakdown can enable estimators to recognize the nature of each risk. Once a risk is established, it can be suitably priced and a methodology can be developed to cope with it.

## 15.6.2 Quantifying Risks

A risk is mathematically quantified by multiplying risk consequences with the probability of its occurrence.

Risk cost = Probability of occurrence of risk × Risk consequences.

Risk assessment involves breaking down the project into types of risks like investment risks, operational risks, sales or income risks and other related activities. These risks are further split up into risk elements.

Quantifying for risks starts with the estimation of the probability of occurrence and the cost of risk consequences of each risk element. The risk cost probability differs with each risk element. The elemental probability distributions may be normal or binomial or may have other patterns.

Probability distribution and the cost consequences of each manageable risk are assessed corresponding to 50% probability of occurrence and the resulting probability is then evaluated statistically. A typical probability distribution for project costs risk is shown in Fig. 15.9.

## 15.6.3 Categorizing Risks

In general, risks can be classified as under:

|   | Probability of Occurrence | Cost impact |
|---|---|---|
| 1. | High | High |
| 2. | Low | High |
| 3. | High | Low |
| 4. | Low | Low |

The impact can be positive or negative. Further, some of the low probability and low cost risks may carry a marginal cost impact. However, in the initial stages, all types of risks are considered, as some may have a high cost impact at a later stage.

Depending upon the nature of environment, risks can be broadly divided into two categories: the manageable risks and the non-manageable risks.

(a) *Manageable risks* These include risks arising from changes in the internal environment of the project and foreseeable high probability risk prone occurrences. These manageable risks can be covered by various means such as forward business dealings, rate running material contracts, risk transferring to sub-contractors and other methods.

Astute estimators can skillfully develop cost estimates to cover such manageable risks.

(b) *Non-manageable risks* These result from an unstable external environment of the project and unforeseen internal changes. These include political upheavals, unusual

### Figure 15.9

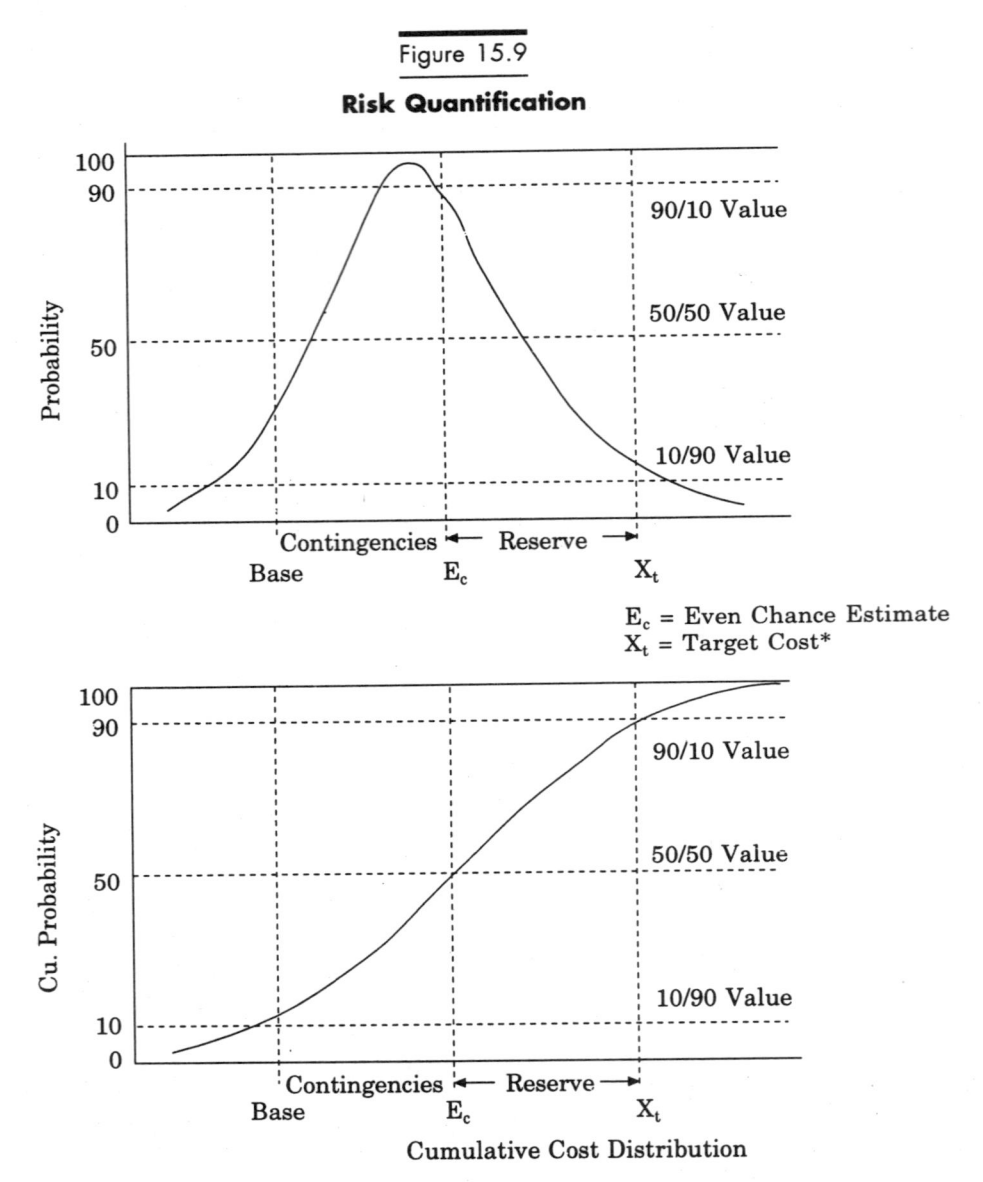

**Risk Quantification**

[Upper chart: Probability distribution curve with x-axis labeled Base, $E_c$, $X_t$, showing Contingencies and Reserve ranges; y-axis Probability 0–100. Reference lines at 90/10 Value, 50/50 Value, 10/90 Value.]

$E_c$ = Even Chance Estimate
$X_t$ = Target Cost*

[Lower chart: Cumulative probability S-curve with same x-axis (Base, $E_c$, $X_t$) and y-axis Cu. Probability 0–100. Reference lines at 90/10 Value, 50/50 Value, 10/90 Value.]

Cumulative Cost Distribution

\* Target Cost = Base Estimate + 50/50 Contingencies Estimate + Project Reserves

escalations, unpredictable resource behaviour, unforeseen losses, abnormal price fluctuations, and subsequently, promulgated statutory requirements. Generally, such risks have a low probability of occurrence.

The evaluation of manageable risks in terms of monetary value is done by the quantity surveyors at the estimation stage and it is included in project 'contingency'. The amount covered under contingency includes minor changes within the scope of work and estimating uncertainties. Contingency excludes major unforeseen risks resulting from unusual political, geographical, economic and natural changes. The project contingency corresponds to the difference between the mean of the overall project risk distribution and the base estimate. The base estimate can be kept at 10% confidence level.

The amount assessed for unmanageable risks generally form part of 'project reserve'. It is earmarked to cover special uncertainties, currency exchange rate fluctuations, abnormal changes in market prices, cost of major losses, unforeseen environmental changes etc. Project reserve are funds in addition to the contingency. The project reserve does not form part of control estimates, as it is the client reserve for the total project.

Risk cost equals the sum of contingency and project reserve. Contingency and project reserve represent the amount earmarked to overcome the risks.

### 15.6.4 Controlling Risks

In construction projects, both the client and the contractor face risky situations. Both aim to minimize their risks.

A client may resort to a lump-sum type contract to overcome resource fluctuations, cost inflation and quantity variation risks. The client may also opt for a turnkey contract approach to prevent design risks and incorporate penalty clauses in the contract to compensate for damages resulting from time delay risks.

Similarly, a contractor may decide to go in for insurance to quantify safety and security risks, book forward supplies of costly materials on the stock market, enter into back-to-back agreements with his sub-contractor and suppliers, and incorporate suitable escalations and other safeguards as part of the contract agreement.

Despite various strategies of the client and the contractor to prevent risks, some risks are unavoidable. These vary from project to project. In business, risks are taken, they are priced and the estimated risk costs are controlled.

Risk control aims at controlling deviations to cut down risk costs and maximize project value. The periodically measured risk cost deviations demonstrate the difference between the estimated and the actual expenditure of risk costs, and the reasons for these deviations are analysed to determine risk forecasts for the remaining project.

There are no ready-made solutions to minimize risks, but the following remedial measures can assist in controlling them:

(a) Adjust plans, scope of work and estimates to counter risk implications.
(b) Evolve alternate plans to manage foreseeable risks.
(c) Keep all concerned informed about the possible risks.

At the project site, it is the planners who are primarily concerned with uncertainties and risks analysis for evaluating future trends. In case of complex high-tech projects, it may be beneficial to use specialist risk consultants, if necessary.

# CHAPTER 16

# Project Time Control

Construction projects are time bound and all project activities are directed towards the achievement of project time objectives. In a complex project, where a large number of activities are performed at different places by different agencies or task forces, with each having its own scheduled targets, a small delay in a critical activity can affect many schedules. Delays can alter the planned level of resources and their mobilization. Time over runs increase overheads, reduce planned revenue from sales and create cash inflow problems. Delays in contracted projects can result in penalties, and adversely affect the reputation of the company. Delays cause confusion and conflicts.

Project time control aims at the timely execution of work according to the project planned schedule and applies corrective measures in cases of time deviations. In its broader sense, time control implies the control of the entire planning system as time is directly or indirectly related with all activities and project functions.

Time control hinges on time performance and the sequence of execution of activities. The basis of measuring activity time progress is the project master schedule of work. Time control monitoring starts with measuring of time status of completed, in-progress and non-starter balance activities. It uses time plan updating techniques to depict progress pictorially. The updated time analyzed plan indicates the assessed project completion period for the balance work. A what-if analysis highlights the implications of imposed constraints on the balance work. Time compression and time crashing (by trading time with cost) techniques are employed to reduce time overruns. The review of project work progress, at predetermined time intervals, reduces the communication between the project management and executing agencies.

In this chapter, coverage of time control is limited to the following:

(a) Time progress monitoring methodology
(b) What-if Analysis
(c) Time reduction techniques
(d) Guidelines for reviewing work progress

## 16.1 TIME PROGRESS MONITORING METHODOLOGY

The baseline for time monitoring is the Project Master Construction Schedule (PMCS). It is generally drawn in a bar chart format. These bars may also show the extent of total float and free float available against each work package. The Bar Chart Master Construction Schedule is easy to read, understand and communicate. Time monitoring of simple projects can be carried out by directly reflecting the time progress of activities on the project master schedule and then analyzing the implications of deviations from the schedules. But in the case of complex projects, a critical examination of the project master schedule is only feasible after sub-project plans of the work-in-progress are analyzed, as the bar chart master schedule generally does not reflect the logical relationship of activities. Accordingly, time monitoring of complex projects can broadly be divided into the following three stages:

(a) Measuring the progress of current activities
(b) Updating sub-project plans
(c) Updating the project master schedule

## 16.1.1 Measuring Time Progress of Current Activities

At any point of time, activities can be classified into completed activities, in-progress activities, and still-to-start activities. The state of activities is measured by comparing their actual progress against the monthly or quarterly bar chart work programme and/or the sub-networks.

While the completed and the non-starter activities can be easily identified, the measurement of in-progress activities is considered from two angles, i.e. time performance and physical performance (or work done quantity performance):

(a) The in-progress time performance of an activity indicates the time lapsed since its commencement and the time required for completion of the balance activities. Both these aspects are expressed in terms of time units or in calendar dates.
(b) The in-progress performance shows the workdone quantity (or value), and the remaining quantity (or value). Generally, physical performance is expressed in percentage of work done or earned value. For example, the performance of an in-progress activity 'concreting roof slab', which includes formwork, reinforcement fixing and concrete placing, which requires a duration of 13 days. When ready for placing concrete (one day's task), it shall be measured and reported as under:

| Activity | Scheduled dates | | Progress as on 15/10/1992 | | |
| --- | --- | --- | --- | --- | --- |
| | Start | Finish | Start | Work done | Remaining duration |
| Concreting root slab | 2/10/92 | 14/10/92 | 01/10/92 | 10% | 12 |

The format for reporting/compiling of progress varies with the nature of the tasks, i.e. repetitive task and non-repetitive tasks. The stress in reporting on repetitive type of tasks is on the number of activities. In non-repetitive types of projects, progress is measured activity-wise in terms of time performance, and percentage quantity or value of work done.

## 16.1.2 Updating Sub-project Plan

A project is be said to be proceeding smoothly as long as the activities are being performed as per schedule. But at times, deviations from the schedule do occur. Some of the reasons for the delay could be inaccurate estimation of the duration of completed activities, unforeseen climatic conditions, non-supply of materials on time, effect of changes in the scope of work, inadequate employment of resources and labour strikes. On the other hand, some of the activities may need less time than planned. These time changes can be measured activity-wise from the sub-project current schedule of work, and these changes are recorded in the work progress reports. These reports include the actual data regarding the completed activities, the in-progress activities and the future planning for the balance activities. In the case of activity delays, the progress reports may also indicate the extent of delay and the availability of activity floats.

A progress report does not make much sense unless it is depicted pictorially on a network and a schedule in a comprehensive form. The method used for displaying progress of activities on the planning charts, corresponding to a given time is called updating. The procedure of updating and the symbols used vary with the technique adopted for planning projects. These updating methods are explained in subsequent paragraphs.

## 16.1.3 CPM/PERT Network Progress Updating Method

The three states of activities in the network can be depicted as under:

(a) For completed activities, delete the duration and draw wiggly line, preferably on the horizontal portion of the arrow. Completed activities and completed events can be represented as:

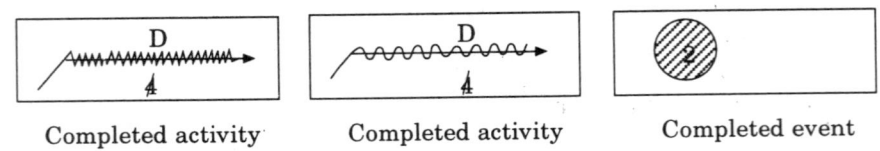

    Completed activity    Completed activity    Completed event

(b) For partially completed activities, delete the existing duration and insert the expected duration for balance work. Preferably, draw a wiggly line on the horizontal part of the arrow in proportion to the work done. In-progress activity is represented as:

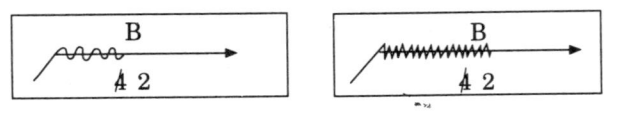

    Partially completed activity

(c) For the remaining activities, examine their duration reflected in the network. Delete the original durations and insert the revised durations if it needs to be changed. The revised duration of still-to-start activity is shown thus:

Project Time Control  **473**

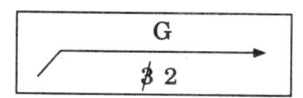

Still-to-start activity

(d) New activities visualized as a result of changes in the scope of work, should be incorporated logically into the network, and their durations written.
(e) Compute the Earliest Finish Time (EFT) of the network to determine the minimum time required for the completion of the remaining work.
(f) Set the Latest Finish Time (LET) equal project time objective in the network. Time analyze the updated network.

*Example* The progress of work of a project at the end of 6th week is tabulated in Table 16.1.

Table 16.1

**Progress of Work of a Project at the end of the 6th Week**

| Sl. No. | Activity Code | Activity Description | Duration Original | Duration Balance of Work | Work Done Value (in 1000$) Total | Work Done Value (in 1000$) Percent |
|---|---|---|---|---|---|---|
| 1 | 0–1 | D | 5 | 2 | 100 | 60% |
| 2 | 1–6 | E | 2 | 2 | 10 | Nil |
| 3 | 6–8 | F | 1 | 1 | 5 | Nil |
| 4 | 5–8 | G | 3 | 3 | 15 | Nil |
| 5 | 0–2 | A | 4 | 0 | 20 | 100% |
| 6 | 2–4 | B | 3 | 2 | 30 | 33% |
| 7 | 0–3 | C | 2 | 0 | 20 | 100% |
| 8 | 3–7 | H | 3 | 3 | 45 | Nil |
| 9 | 7–8 | J | 2 | 2 | 15 | Nil |
|  |  |  |  | Total | 260 | 42.3% |

The above progress of work can be transferred on to the network using conventional symbols. The original and updated networks are shown in Fig. 16.1.

## 16.1.4 Precedence Network Progress Updating Method

**In precedence networks** The activity box of the completed activity is double crossed and that of in-progress activity is shown with a single line across. The completed activities' durations are deleted by double, crossing activity boxes; 'in-progress activities' original duration is deleted and the expected duration for balance work is inserted; and for 'non-starter remaining activities' the revised duration (where necessary) is substituted in place

## Figure 16.1

## CPM Updated Sub-network

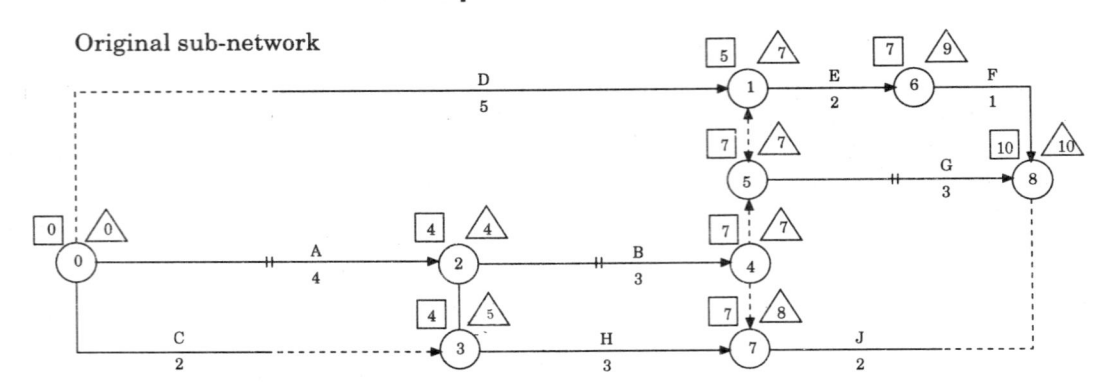

Original sub-network

**Updated Sub-network at the end of 6th Week the Completion Balance Activities of Takes upto 5 Weeks**

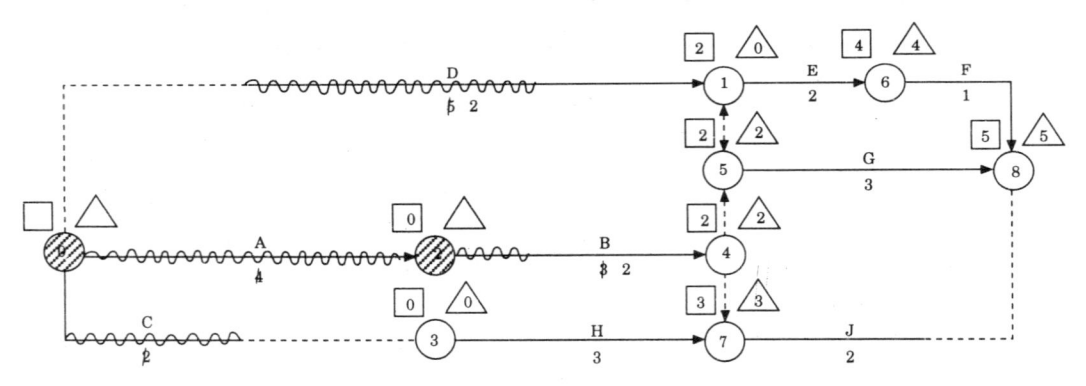

of the original duration. Thereafter, new activities resulting from change orders are incorporated into the network.

But that is not enough. Unlike CPM/PERT networks, the precedence (constraints) relationship also changes as time progresses. Therefore, in precedence networks, activity earliest start time, duration and its precedence relationships are scrutinised and the network is updated, accordingly.

The precedence relationship updating can take many forms. Some of these for in-progress, partially completed activities are given below. The activity box is coded as:

| Description Resource |||
|---|---|---|
| EST | d | EFT |

where  EST is earliest start time
EFT is earliest finish time
d is duration

## Updating finish-to-start (FS) Relationship
Typical cases encountered are as follows:

(1) At the end of the 7th week, progress on 'A' activity and no progress on its succeeding week with no change in original duration of activities or sequencing of work.

Original sub-network

| A | | | FS 2 | B | | |
|---|---|---|---|---|---|---|
| 0 | 10 | 10 | | 12 | 6 | 18 |

Updated sub-network end of the 7th week

| A | | | FS 2 | B | | |
|---|---|---|---|---|---|---|
| ~~0~~ | ~~10~~ | ~~10~~ | | ~~12~~ | 6 | ~~18~~ |
| | 3 | 3 | | 5 | | 11 |

*Note*: Updated sub-network shows that the balance duration of Activity 'A' after the 7th week is 3 (i.e. = 10 – 7) and Activity 'B' completion will take the 11th week.

(2) Case of progress on both 'C' activity and 'D' activity
Original sub-network

| C | | | FS 5 | D | | |
|---|---|---|---|---|---|---|
| 0 | 12 | 12 | | 17 | 7 | 24 |

Updated sub-network at the end of the 10th week with balance reassessed durations of C and D activities as 3 and 6 respectively and FS changed to 4.

| C | | | FS 4 | D | | |
|---|---|---|---|---|---|---|
| ~~0~~ | ~~12~~ | ~~12~~ | | ~~17~~ | ~~7~~ | ~~24~~ |
| | 3 | 3 | | 7 | 6 | 13 |

## Updating start-to-start (SS) relationship
Typical cases can be updated as under:

(1) Case of progress on 'A' activity is less than the overlap value of 'B' activity.

Original sub-network updated at the end of the 4th week:

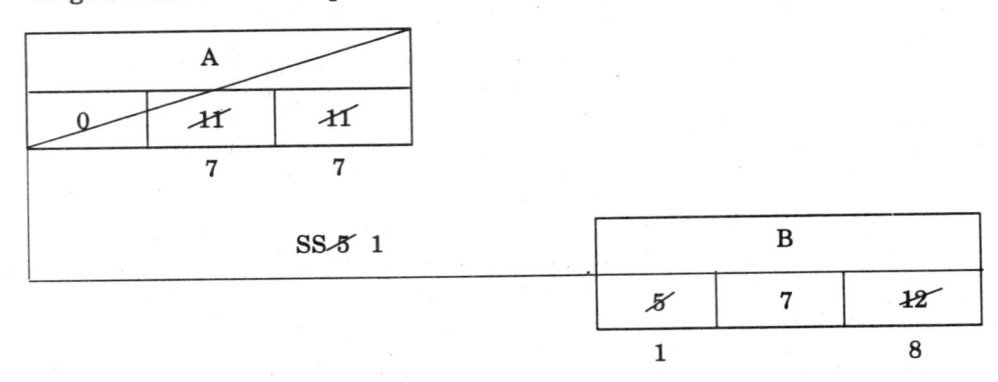

```
|        A        |
| 0 | ~~11~~  | ~~11~~ |
|   |   7    |   7   |
```

SS ~~5~~ 1

```
|        B        |
| ~~5~~ |  7  | ~~12~~ |
|   1   |     |   8    |
```

(2) Case of progress of activity 'A' greater than or equal to overlap value:

Original sub-network updated at the end of the 8th week; with balance durations of A and B as shown.

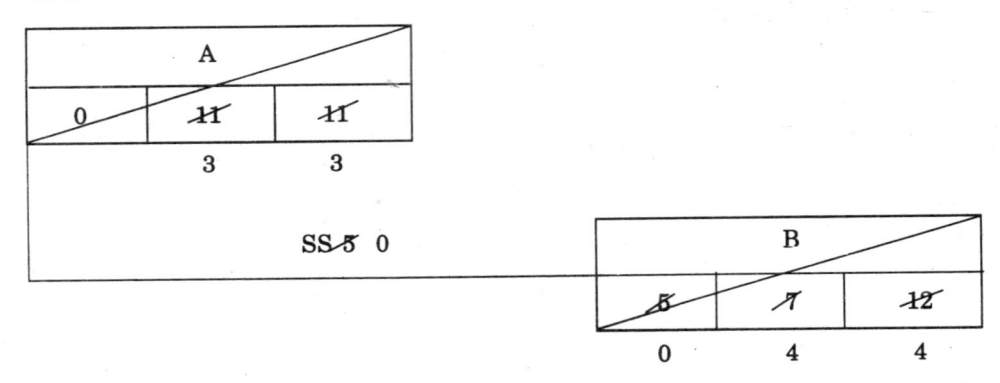

```
|        A        |
| 0 | ~~11~~ | ~~11~~ |
|   |   3   |   3    |
```

SS ~~5~~ 0

```
|        B        |
| ~~5~~ | ~~7~~ | ~~12~~ |
|   0   |   4   |   4    |
```

**Finish-to-finish (FF) relationship** Some typical cases of such relationships are as follows:

(1) Case of progress after 12 weeks of start of project. Balance completion time of Activity 'A' is 7, but there is no change on duration of Activity 'B'.

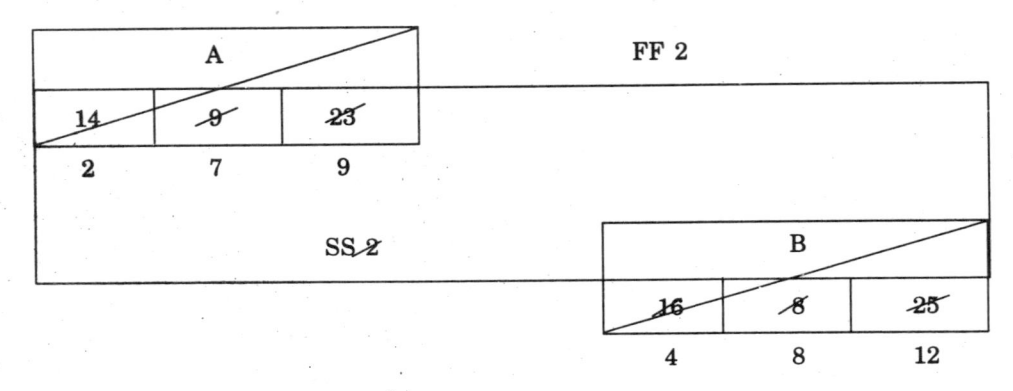

```
|           A           |    FF 2
| 14 | ~~9~~ | ~~23~~ |
|  2 |  7   |   9     |
```

SS ~~2~~

```
|        B        |
| ~~16~~ | ~~8~~ | ~~25~~ |
|   4    |   8   |   12   |
```

*Note*: Activity 'B' is no longer dependent on the start of Activity 'A'.

(2) Case when Activity 'A' is completed, but Activity 'B' has just started:

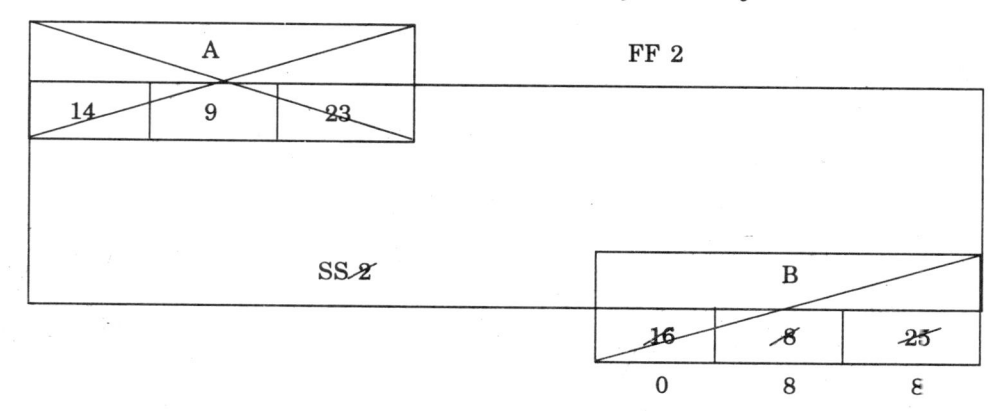

*Note*: Activity 'B' is no longer dependent on the completion of Activity 'A'.

*Example* Updating of primary school precedence network

The status of the in-progress work packages, reported at the end of the 20th week from the start of construction, is shown in Table 16.2.

Table 16.2

**Status of In-progress Work Packages at the End of 20th Week**

| Code | Status | Duration for balance work | Precedence logic/Remarks |
|------|--------|---------------------------|--------------------------|
| FW | Completed | — | — |
| FP | Completed | — | — |
| SG | In progress | 2 | Logic no change |
| SW | In progress | 3 | Logic no change |
| BP | Started in areas | 7 | Delete predecessor constraint 2FS |
| CJ | Still to start | 5 | Can start 2 weeks prior to completion of TP activity, i.e. tiling and painting activity |

The updated time-analyzed network incorporating the above changes, is shown in Exhibit 16.1

## 16.1.5 Line-of-Balance (LOB) Charts Updating Method

Repetitive type construction projects, like multi-housing complexes, are planned and scheduled using LOB technique. The main purpose of using LOB techniques is to optimize the

## Exhibit 16.1

**Primary School Construction: Updated Summary Precedence Network (Showing Progress at the end of the 20th Week)**

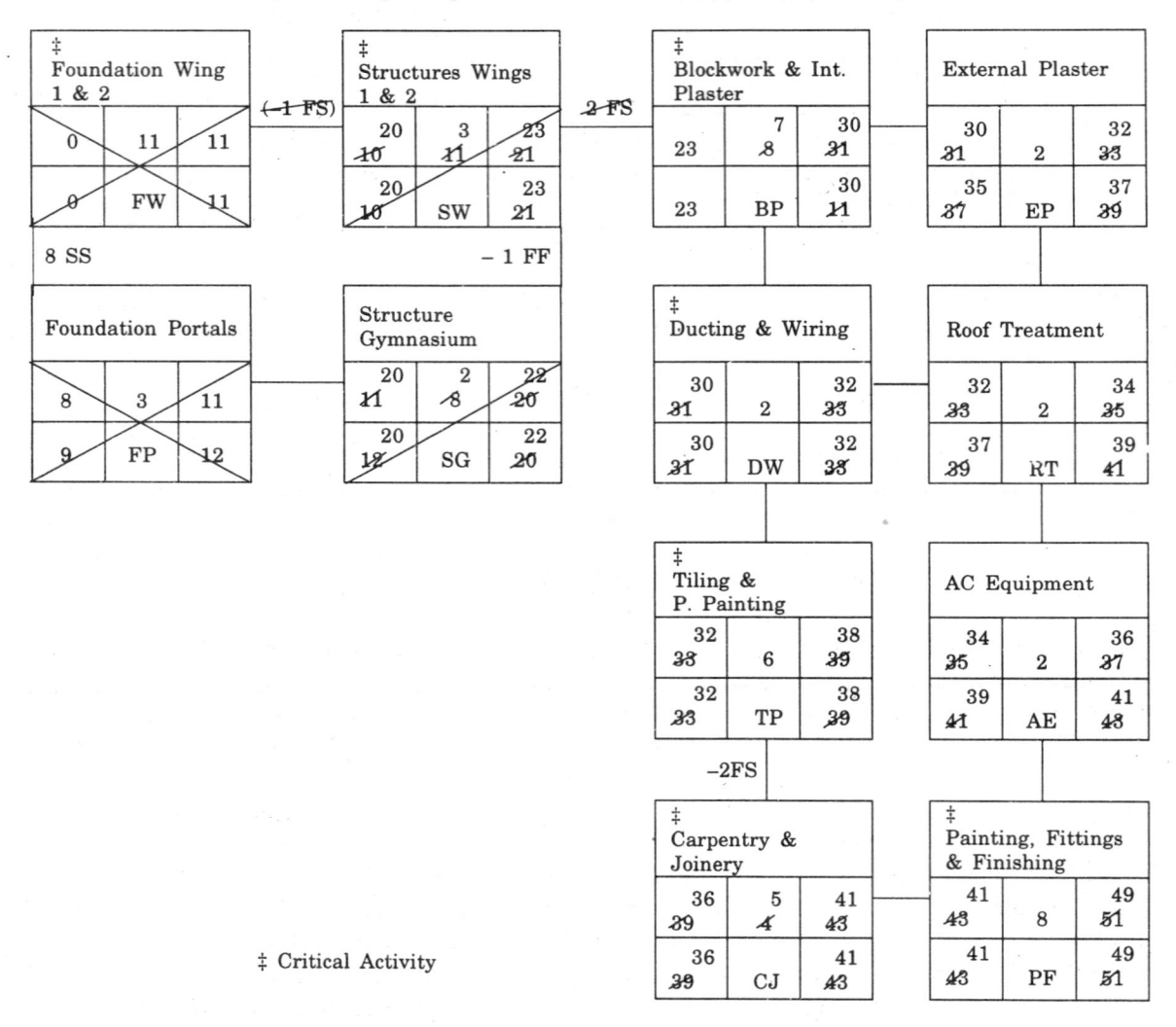

```
‡ Foundation Wing          ‡ Structures Wings              ‡ Blockwork & Int.         External Plaster
  1 & 2                      1 & 2                           Plaster
                                      (-1 FS)                              -2 FS
┌────┬──────┬────┐        ┌────┬──────┬────┐              ┌────┬──────┬────┐      ┌────┬──────┬────┐
│ 0  │  11  │ 11 │        │ 20 │  3   │ 23 │              │ 23 │  7   │ 30 │      │ 30 │  2   │ 32 │
│    │      │    │        │ 10 │  11  │ 21 │              │    │  8   │ 31 │      │ 31 │      │ 33 │
├────┼──────┼────┤        ├────┼──────┼────┤              ├────┼──────┼────┤      ├────┼──────┼────┤
│ 0  │  FW  │ 11 │        │ 20 │  SW  │ 23 │              │ 23 │  BP  │ 30 │      │ 35 │  EP  │ 37 │
│    │      │    │        │ 10 │      │ 21 │              │    │      │ 31 │      │ 37 │      │ 39 │
└────┴──────┴────┘        └────┴──────┴────┘              └────┴──────┴────┘      └────┴──────┴────┘
  8 SS                                 -1 FF

  Foundation Portals        Structure                      ‡ Ducting & Wiring         Roof Treatment
                            Gymnasium
┌────┬──────┬────┐        ┌────┬──────┬────┐              ┌────┬──────┬────┐      ┌────┬──────┬────┐
│ 8  │  3   │ 11 │        │ 20 │  2   │ 22 │              │ 30 │  2   │ 32 │      │ 32 │  2   │ 34 │
│    │      │    │        │ 11 │  8   │ 20 │              │ 31 │      │ 33 │      │ 33 │      │ 35 │
├────┼──────┼────┤        ├────┼──────┼────┤              ├────┼──────┼────┤      ├────┼──────┼────┤
│ 9  │  FP  │ 12 │        │ 20 │  SG  │ 22 │              │ 30 │  DW  │ 32 │      │ 37 │  RT  │ 39 │
│    │      │    │        │ 12 │      │ 20 │              │ 31 │      │ 33 │      │ 39 │      │ 41 │
└────┴──────┴────┘        └────┴──────┴────┘              └────┴──────┴────┘      └────┴──────┴────┘

                                                           ‡ Tiling &                 AC Equipment
                                                             P. Painting
                                                          ┌────┬──────┬────┐      ┌────┬──────┬────┐
                                                          │ 32 │  6   │ 38 │      │ 34 │  2   │ 36 │
                                                          │ 33 │      │ 39 │      │ 35 │      │ 37 │
                                                          ├────┼──────┼────┤      ├────┼──────┼────┤
                                                          │ 32 │  TP  │ 38 │      │ 39 │  AE  │ 41 │
                                                          │ 33 │      │ 39 │      │ 41 │      │ 43 │
                                                          └────┴──────┴────┘      └────┴──────┴────┘
                                                                  -2FS

                                                           ‡ Carpentry &            ‡ Painting, Fittings
                                                             Joinery                  & Finishing
                                                          ┌────┬──────┬────┐      ┌────┬──────┬────┐
                                                          │ 36 │  5   │ 41 │      │ 41 │  8   │ 49 │
                                                          │ 39 │  4   │ 43 │      │ 43 │      │ 51 │
       ‡ Critical Activity                                ├────┼──────┼────┤      ├────┼──────┼────┤
                                                          │ 36 │  CJ  │ 41 │      │ 41 │  PF  │ 49 │
                                                          │ 39 │      │ 43 │      │ 43 │      │ 51 │
                                                          └────┴──────┴────┘      └────┴──────┴────┘
```

employment of resources, and avoid interference in the progress of activities. This scheduling technique is covered in Chapter 6.

The LOB schedules are easily updated by plotting cumulative physical progress lines on the activity schedule and LOB control chart (see Exhibit 16.2). The actual progress lines thus formed, can indicate the following with respect to each activity:

(a) Planned versus actual progress in terms of the number of units completed.
(b) Planned versus actual rate of progress.

Project Time Control  479

## Exhibit 16.2
### Updated Line-of-balance Chart of a Residential Building Finishes Plan
### (Derived Using Line-of-balance Technique)
### (In Units of Modules)

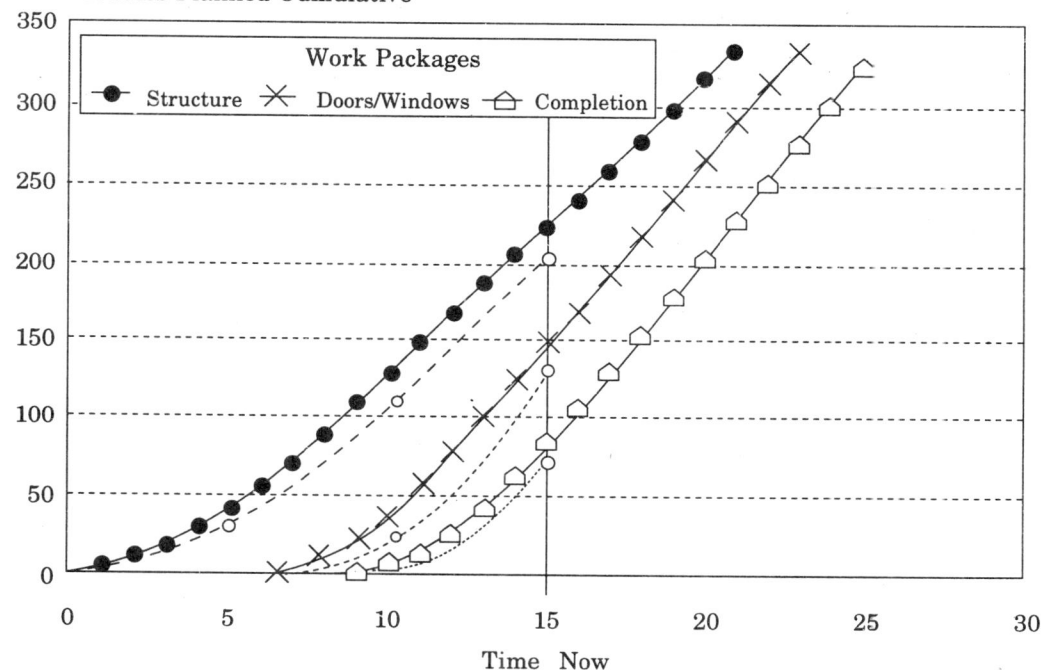

Modules Planned Cumulative

Work Packages: ●—Structure  ×—Doors/Windows  ⬠—Completion

Time Now

Time in Months

**Planned completion**

| | 1 | 2 | 3 | 4 | 5 | 6 | 7 | 8 | 9 | 10 | 11 | 12 | 13 | 14 | 15 | 16 | 17 | 18 | 19 | 20 | 21 | 22 | 23 | 24 | 25 | 26 | 27 | 28 | 29 | 30 |
|---|---|---|---|---|---|---|---|---|---|---|---|---|---|---|---|---|---|---|---|---|---|---|---|---|---|---|---|---|---|---|
| Structure | 4 | 6 | 8 | 10 | 12 | 14 | 16 | 18 | 20 | 20 | 19 | 20 | 19 | 19 | 18 | 17 | 18 | 19 | 20 | 19 | 18 | | | | | | | | | |
| Doors/Windows | | | | | | | 2 | 6 | 10 | 14 | 18 | 25 | 24 | 24 | 23 | 20 | 25 | 24 | 25 | 24 | 25 | 25 | 20 | | | | | | | |
| Completion | | | | | | | | | 0 | 4 | 8 | 12 | 16 | 20 | 23 | 20 | 25 | 24 | 25 | 24 | 25 | 25 | 24 | 25 | 24 | | | | | |

**Actual progress**

| | | | | | | |
|---|---|---|---|---|---|---|
| Structure | 28 | 110 | 205 | | | |
| Doors/Windows | 0 | 28 | 135 | | | |
| Completion | 0 | 0 | 70 | | | |

(c) Risks of interference in progressing work of interdependent activities.
(d) Forecast rate of progress for executing activities, within the specified time targets.

In case of work-packages with longer durations, say exceeding four weeks, the LOB chart can also show date-wise commencement and completion of these activities. But it is preferable to plot activities completed so as to avoid congestion.

### 16.1.6 Bar Chart Schedule Updating Method

Bar chart schedules are easy to construct, understand, communicate and update. Bar charts are widely used for depicting schedule of construction works. For simple projects, the bar chart schedules can be easily drawn, but for complex projects, these schedules are developed using network analysis techniques. The method of scheduling work is covered in Chapter 6.

The updating of a typical bar chart schedule involves the following steps:

(a) Draw time scaled second bar, below the scheduled activity.
(b) Depict its date of commencement, and its time status.
(c) Show the physical progress of activities as percentage of work completed, either below/above the end of the progress bar. It can also be depicted graphically as shown in Exhibit 16.3.

Note that the commonly used bar charts (other than time-scaled network plan) do not show an interdependent relationship among activities. Therefore, as a planning and controlling tool, it has limited use. However, it is commonly used at all levels for measuring and reporting progress.

### 16.1.7 Updating to Determine Contract Time Extension

The conventional methods do not provide a scientific way to determine the extension of the original contract time due to unforeseen delays and extra work deviation orders. Generally the tendency is to total up delays. In certain cases, the claims of the contractor for delays due to reasons beyond his control may be accepted, but no extension is awarded and no logical reasons are assigned to it. In the network based contract system, the Master Network and its schedule provide an index to assess the delays, and analyze its effects on the completion of the project. Since, the network logic and durations of activities are well established between both the parties, the implications of delays in the completion of critical/non-critical activities can be determined more accurately. For example, a delay in the commencement of a non-critical activity, which is completed before its latest finish time (may be due to any reasons), does not entitle a contractor to claim for extension of time. But delay in critical activities due to non-supply of the materials under the client's supply, or due to reasons beyond the contractor's control, need consideration for the extension of time.

The procedure given below can form a reasonable basis for determining the extension of time:

**Step 1** List the delayed activities. Add acceptable period of delays (for causes beyond contractor's control) to the original period of affected activities.

Project Time Control  **481**

## Exhibit 16.3

## Updated Bar Chart Schedules of a Site Development Project
## (Work Progress at the end of the 10th Week)

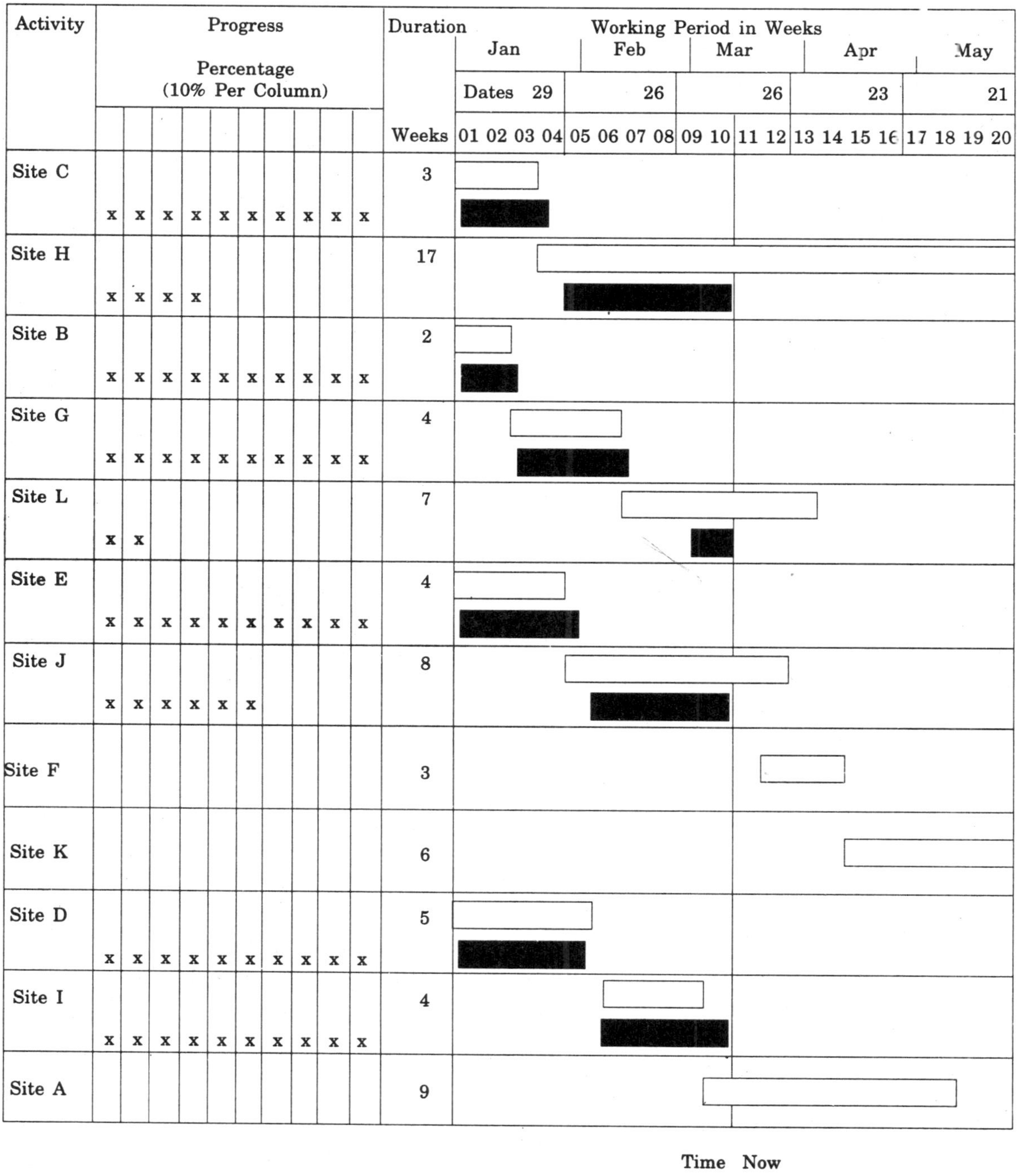

| Activity | Progress Percentage (10% Per Column) | Duration | Working Period in Weeks |
|---|---|---|---|
| | | | Jan 29 / Feb 26 / Mar 26 / Apr 23 / May 21 |
| | | | Weeks 01–20 |
| Site C | x x x x x x x x x x | 3 | |
| Site H | x x x x | 17 | |
| Site B | x x x x x x x x x x | 2 | |
| Site G | x x x x x x x x x x | 4 | |
| Site L | x x | 7 | |
| Site E | x x x x x x x x x x | 4 | |
| Site J | x x x x x x | 8 | |
| Site F | | 3 | |
| Site K | | 6 | |
| Site D | x x x x x x x x x x | 5 | |
| Site I | x x x x x x x x x | 4 | |
| Site A | | 9 | |

Time Now

**Step II** List out additional work as a result of changes in activities, and assess their duration, taking into consideration the reasonable lead time involved for the procurement of additional resources.

**Step III** Update the original network by incorporating additional activities arising as a result of change orders, where applicable, in a logical manner and change the duration of delayed Activities as mentioned under Step I.

**Step IV** Analyze the modified network to determine the minimum period required for the completion of the project.

**Step V** Extension period can now be determined by computing the difference in project completion time between the modified and the original network.

Consider the case of the pumping station project. The master network of this project is given in Exhibit 16.4. The original contract period was 35 weeks. During the 34th week, the contractor's claim for extension of time was discussed. The client accepted the delays on account of the following reasons (details omitted) beyond the contractor's control for extension of time:

### Extension on account of original work deviation

| Activity code | Description | Original duration | Actual duration |
|---|---|---|---|
| 0–1 | Excavation | 2 | 3 |
| 5–7 | Office electrification | 1 | 2 |
| 0–11 | Procurement of pumps | 20 | 25 |
| 12–13 | Installation of pumping sets | 1 | 2 |

**Extension due to additional work ordered as deviation** The list of activities added/amended on account of deviation orders in the pumping station project were as follows:

(a) *Office roofing activity 3–4*: Duration to be changed from 1 week to 3 weeks.
(b) *Excavation for pipe*: Duration 2 weeks. The work can commence in the 31st week (the date of ordering work). Logic dictates that this should be undertaken after fixing suction and delivery pipes (Activity 13–14).
(c) *Connecting rising mains including laying of pipe-line*: Duration 3 weeks. Work to commence after fixing suction and delivery pipes and procurement of pipes.
(d) *Procurement of pipe*: Duration 7 weeks. It can commence at the time of ordering the extra work in the 31st week.

**Update original network** The revised updated network of the pumping station project incorporating delays and deviation orders in a logical manner is shown in Exhibit 16.5. In the updated network, the revised project completion works out to be 41 weeks.

Project Time Control   **483**

Exhibit 16.4
**Master Network of Pumping Station Project**

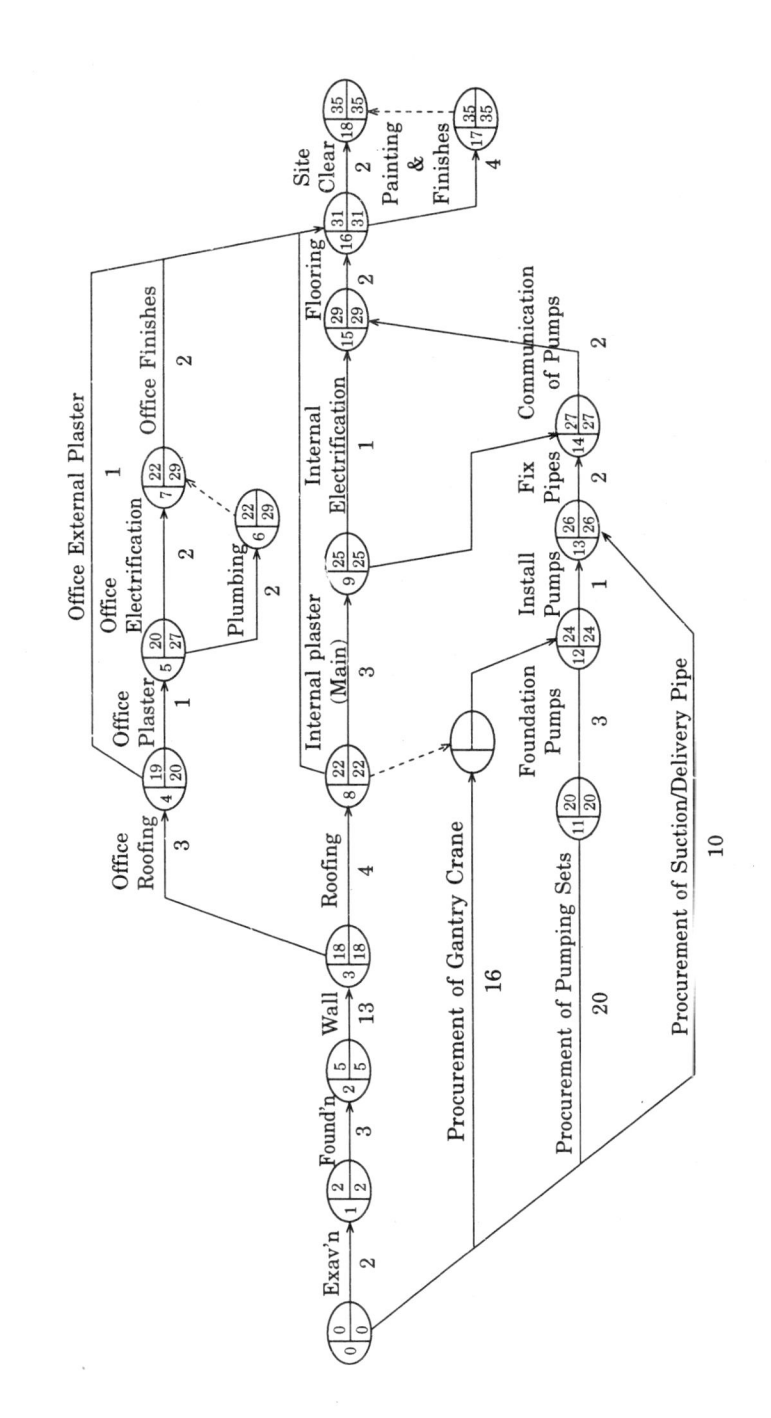

**484** Construction Projects Management

Exhibit 16.5
**Pumping Station Project
Modified Network Incorporating Changes**

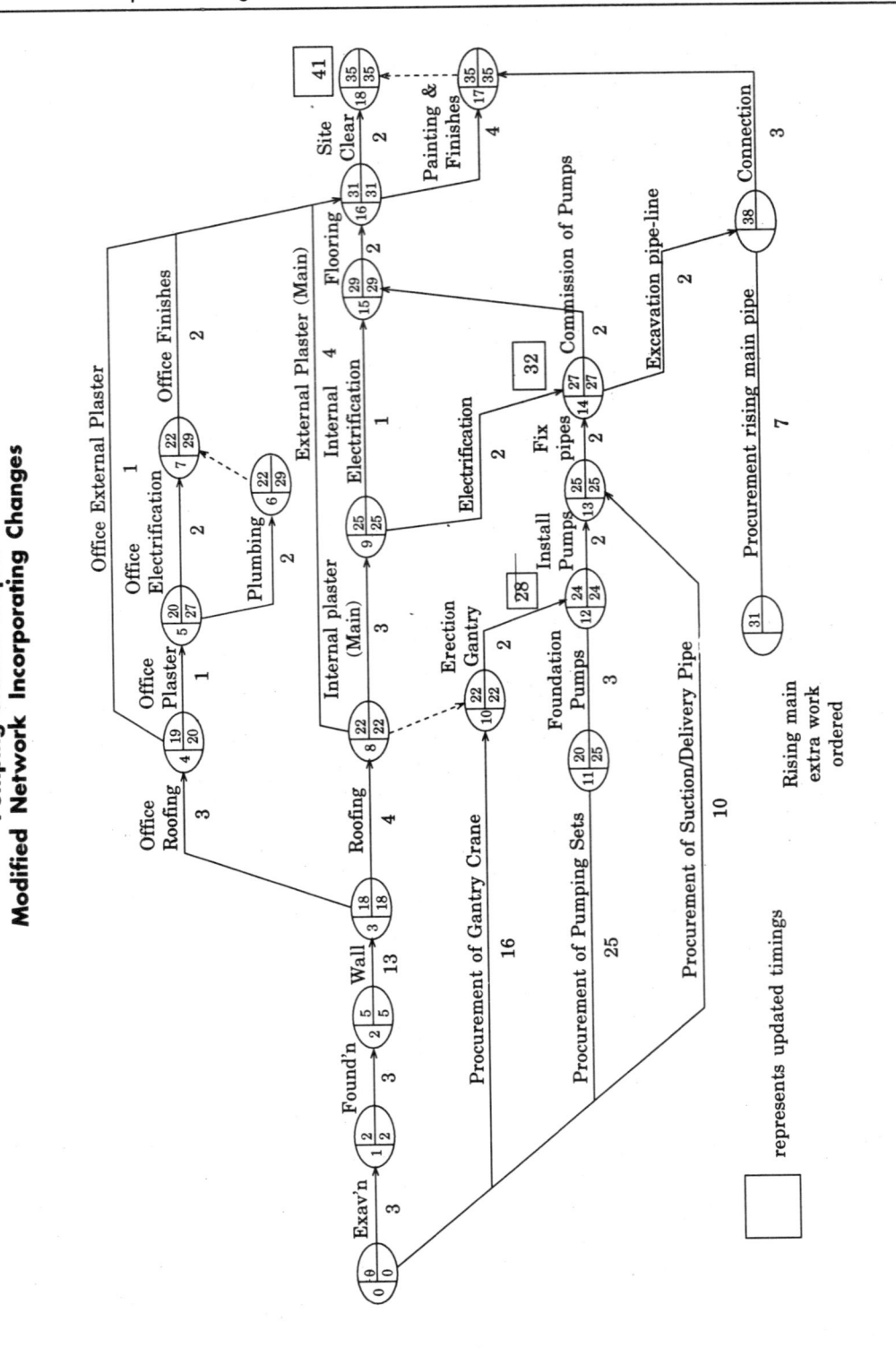

## Compute extension permissible

The estimated extension period = Revised completion period of contract
− Original contract period
= 41 weeks − 35 weeks
= 6 weeks.

## ❑ 16.2 'WHAT-IF' ANALYSIS

In the fast changing dynamic environments, specially, in case of complex projects, a project faces situations which tend to divert the project from its planned path. There may also be instances when the project management wants to alter the planned schedules for various reasons. During project review, questions may also be raised to devise courses of action for achieving certain specific targets. All such cases start with the question 'what-if' and they follow it up by possible constraints with the aim of deriving feasible alternate options to overcome time delays and its cost implications.

'What if' analysis aims at exploring alternative approaches to meet imposed/anticipated/desired constraints, with a view to provide information for making decisions regarding the incorporation of changes in the current schedule of work. The project constraints needing 'what-if' analysis can be broadly divided as under:

(a) Time constrained 'what if' analysis.
(b) Resources constrained 'what if' analysis.

### 16.2.1 Time Constrained 'What-if' Analysis

There are times when the scheduled dates get affected due to actual/anticipated situations like weather conditions, resources supply breakdown, equipment delivery schedule changes, or other reasons. Such cases impose time constraints of the following types:

- Start not later than ...
- Finish not later than ...
- Start not earlier than ...
- Finish not earlier than ...
- Mandatory start on ...
- Mandatory finish by ...
- Schedule within the activity total float (zero total float or latest start time constraint)
  ...
- Schedule within activity free float (zero free float constraints) ...
- Schedule activities at the earliest start time ...

The implications of imposing time constraints can be studied by updating, and time analyzing the project network, and re-scheduling activities. In case of activities having negative floats, the time compressions and/or the time crashing will have to be resorted to for accomplishing the balance tasks within the scheduled time.

## 16.2.2 Resources Constrained 'What-if' Analysis

During work scheduling, vital resources are generally levelled to allow the normal build up at the beginning of the connected tasks; a constant level of employment during the major period of execution; and the normal tapering-off towards the end of the operation. These schedules also assume that resources when required shall be available. But in actual practice, costly resources are mostly limited. These impose constraints on their availability. Constraints imposed on resources can be grouped as follows:

(a) **Time limited resource availability** These are situations when sufficient resources are available during a limited period of time. In such cases, the work schedule may have to be revised to execute affected activities during the availability period of resources.

(b) **Resources limited conditions** Such situations occur when there are insufficient resources to meet the scheduled work requirements. Such situations call for rescheduling the work within limited resource constraints. The method of creating the work schedule under resource constraints is covered in Chapter 6.

## ❏ 16.3 TIME REDUCTION TECHNIQUES

The two commonly used techniques for reducing time overruns are 'compressing the critical path' and 'trading time with cost'.

### 16.3.1 Time Compression of Critical Path

Time compression is the process of reduction of the project completion time without any appreciable change in the cost of activities. It involves splitting (where feasible) of the critical activities into smaller activities, either by using different methods of execution without any appreciable change in resources, or by changing to lower levels of activity details. Some of these smaller activities may form a chain of activities and the others may be parallel. Generally, it is the paralled component of the critical activity that compresses the project completion time.

*Example of time compression* Consider the critical activity 5–10 of 'Electrification of pumping station sub-project original network' drawn in Exhibit 16.6. It includes internal electrification and external power supply works. Power is essential for testing of pumping sets, but it is desirable that both internal electrification and power supply must be completed prior to the commencement of flooring.

Resolving of activity 5–10 into two parallel components (see Fig. 16.2) each of two weeks duration, without any appreciable increase in cost, will result in cutting down the project completion period by two weeks.

## Figure 16.2
## Part of Network Showing Significance of Resolving an Activity 5-10 into two Parallel Activities

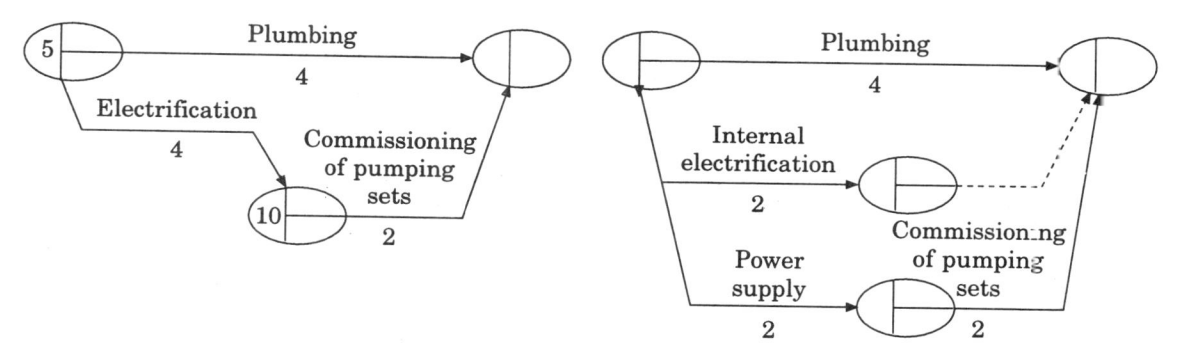

Take the critical activity 3–4, representing the roofing of pump house and office building. In the network, roofing of both the rooms is combined into a single activity (assuming that roofing of the pump house building and office building will be taken up simultaneously). This activity can be conveniently split into two parallel activities, i.e office roofing and pump house building roofing. Similar is the case with the internal plastering activity 4–5, flooring activity 11–12, and finishes activity 12–13. The network showing time compression of critical activities reduces the project duration from 41 weeks to 35 weeks, and the new critical paths resulting from time compression is shown in Exhibit 16.6.

### 16.3.2 Time-cost Trade off Technique

Project time and cost are interrelated. The project cost function shows the relationship of the cost versus the completion time. Its ordinate represents the cost and the abscissa has a time scale. In the formulation of the project cost function, the direct and indirect costs and the financial gains resulting from early completion are considered. The project time corresponding to the minimum value of the cost function gives the most economical duration of the project. The project cost curve also gives the minimum cost of reducing the project duration from its optimum (economical) completion time. But the project cost function varies from project to project and it is not easy to formulate the time-cost relationship.

The basic concept behind the formulation of a project time-cost function is that the normal time duration of an activity is based on considerations of normal cost using an efficient or desired method of performance of the activity. Each activity is considered in isolation while working out its normal time and normal cost. The reduction in duration below the normal time by a changed method of execution implies an increase in cost. There will also be a stage beyond which the activity duration cannot be further reduced. The lower limit, up to which an activity time can be reduced is called crash time, and the corresponding cost is referred to as crash cost.

The difference between the normal time and crash time of an activity indicates its

**488** Construction Projects Management

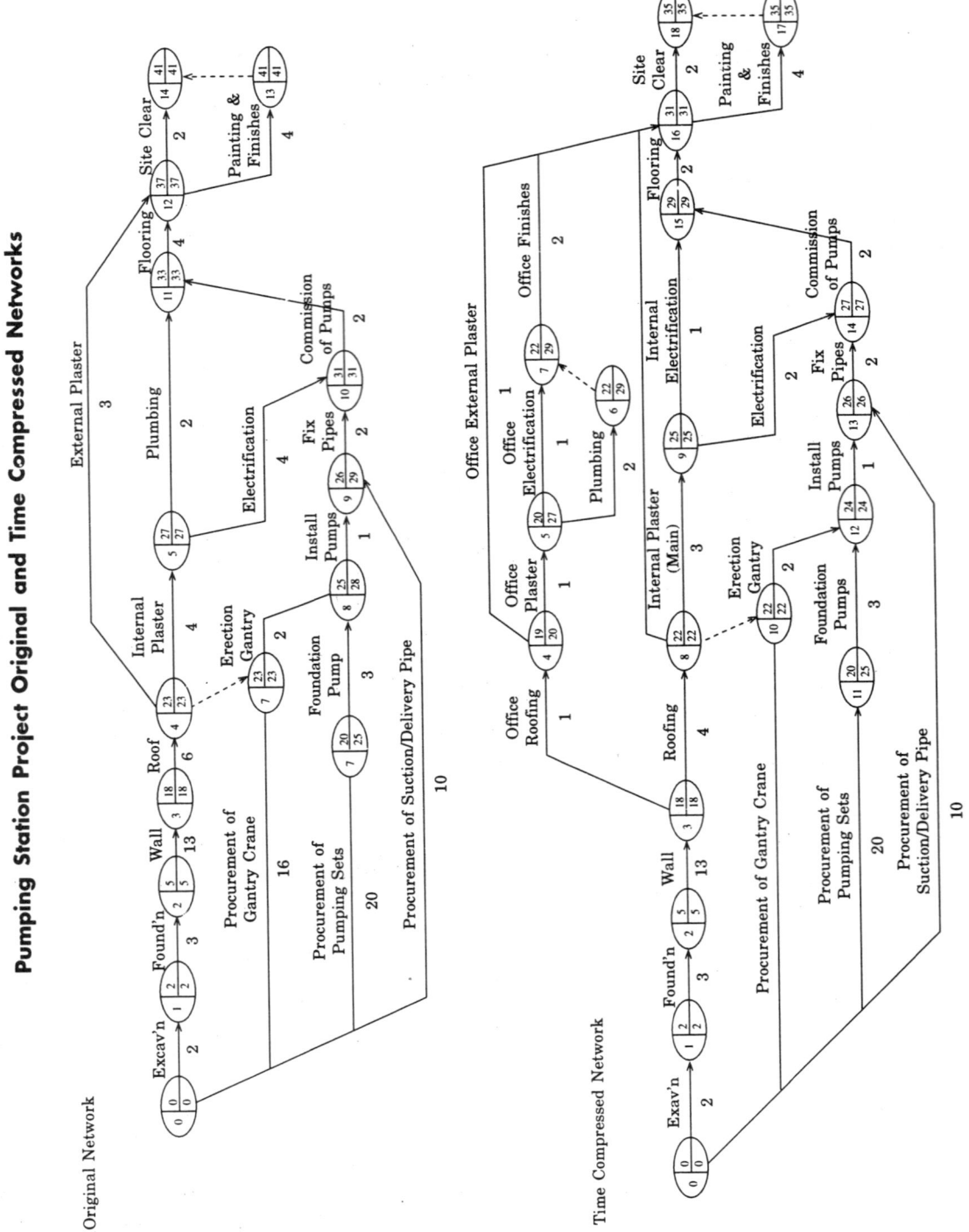

### Exhibit 16.6
### Pumping Station Project Original and Time Compressed Networks

potential to undergo crashing. The slope of the activity cost function shows the rate of increase of cost, with the reduction in time for the activity.

Crashing potential of an activity = Normal time − Crash time.

$$\text{Rate of crashing} = \frac{\text{Crash cost} - \text{Normal cost}}{\text{Normal time} - \text{Crash time}}$$

There are a number of ways of reducing the activity duration from normal time and these will depend upon the activity under consideration. The most common methods of time reduction are as follows:

(a) Increase the resources allotted and/or work overtime.
(b) Change the mode of execution/performance of an activity, say from the manual method to the mechanical method.

In rare cases, the use of several methods of performance of an activity may give a non-linear relation between activity time and cost, but with a view to simplify calculations in the formulation of the project cost function, it is assumed that the portion of the curve between the normal point and the crash point is linear.

To quote an example, the project cost function of a project drawn in the following page shows that the least cost of this project is $2,35,000, and the corresponding optimum completion time is 33 weeks. The project cost curve is shown in Fig. 16.3.

The procedure of preparation of the least cost schedule is illustrated with the example of a simple project, the network for which is drawn in Fig. 16.4.

Formulation of a project cost function involves the following stages. These are listed in Table 16.3.

**Determination of activity cost** Production costs of an activity are classified into two categories. These categories are—direct cost and indirect cost. Direct cost is the cost that can be traced to a specific activity or a work-item which is being done or produced. All other associate costs that are incurred to accomplish the activity or the work-item but cannot be traced directly, fall in the category of indirect costs. The method of estimation of production costs is given in Chapter 11.

In the given example the direct (normal) cost data of each activity of the project under consideration is reflected on the network. The indirect cost of the project for which the least cost network plan is to be prepared, is taken as $500 per week. The anticipated gains in terms of revenue for early completion are assessed as $800 per week. In practice, activity time-cost data can be recorded as shown in Table 16.4.

**Estimation of activity crashing potential** The assessed crashed costs and their crashing potential for the project are as shown in Table 16.5.

**Determination of the rate of crashing** The slope of the activity cost curve gives the rate of increase of the activity with reduction of activity completion time.

$$\text{Rate of crashing} = \frac{\text{Crash cost} - \text{Normal cost}}{\text{Time crashing potential}}$$

Figure 16.3

**Project Time Crashing Curve Showing Cost of Crashing per Week (In thousand dollars)**

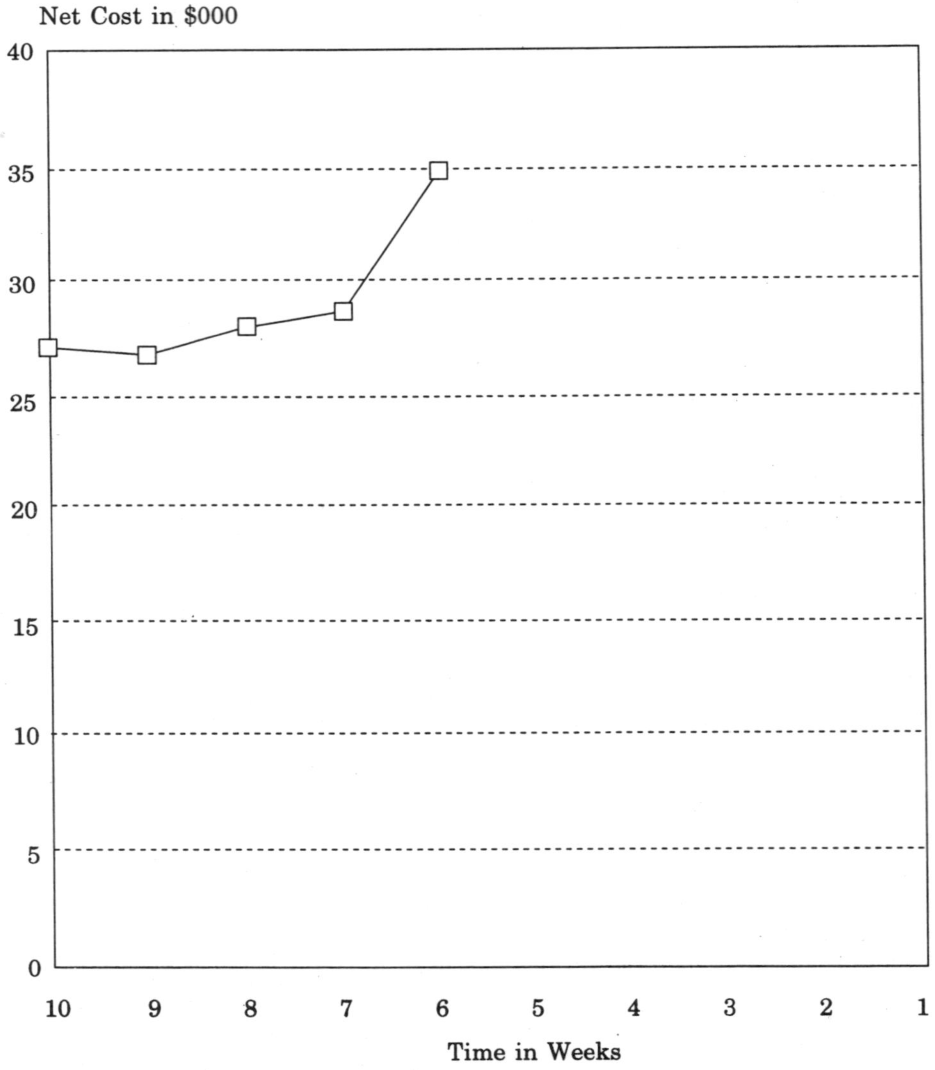
Net Cost in $000
40
35
30
25
20
15
10
5
0
10
9
8
7
6
5
4
3
2
1
Time in Weeks

The increase in the cost of crashing per week for the activities under consideration is listed in Table 16.6.

**Crashing critical activities** Project completion time can be decreased by crashing the duration of selected critical activities. This successive crashing implies minimum increase

## Figure 16.4

### Network of a Project to be Time Crashed Schedule

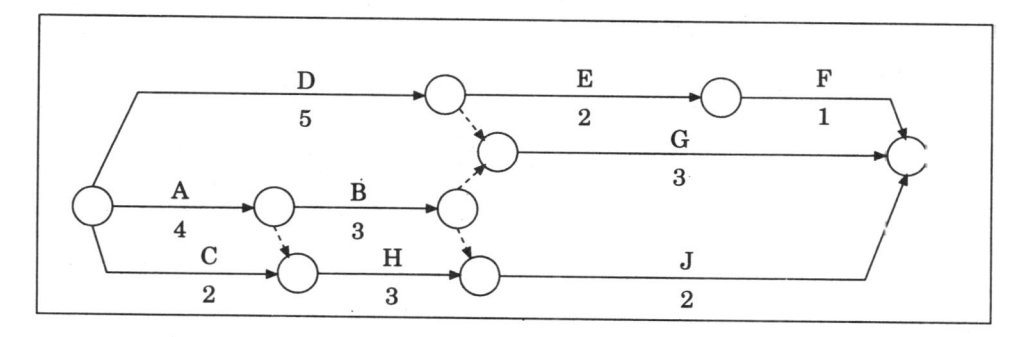

## Table 16.3

### Procedure for Plotting Project Cost-Time Function

1. Time analyse the network and determine the critical path.
2. Tabulate normal and crash duration, and normal and crash cost for all the activities.
3. Estimate activity crashing potential for each activity.
4. Determine the rate of crashing of all the activities.
5. Crash critical activities beginning with the activity having the least rate of crashing. Each activity is shortened until its crashing potential is exhausted, or a new critical path is formed.
6. If a new critical path is formed, reduce the combination of critical activities having the combined lowest rate of crashing, and continue till there is no more scope for crashing.
7. At each crashing incorporates the cost implication in a table.
8. Add direct cost date-wise, and then tabulate its cumulative effect.
9. Assess indirect cost and saving for early completion, date-wise, and tabulate their commulative effect.
10. Aggregate cumulative effects of direct and indirect costs and the savings for early completion.
11. Plot the data thus obtained, by selecting suitable scale with time along the abcissa and cost along the ordinate axis.
12. The lowest point of the project cost curve indicates the lowest cost and the corresponding optimum completion time.

in the cost of the project for reduction of project duration each time by one week. Consider the example of networks shown in Fig. 16.5.

(a) *First crashing* Examination of Fig. 16.5 shows that there is one critical path. The critical activities are A, B and G. Activity B has the least rate of crashing and its potential for crashing is one week. Therefore, reduce the duration for Activity B by one week. The

## Table 16.4
### Project Time Crashing Potential Data

| Sl No. | Activity | Duration in Weeks Normal | Duration in Weeks Crash | Cost in $ Normal | Cost in $ Crash | Reduction Possible | Rate of Crashing | No Crash | First Crash | Second Crash | Third Crash | Fourth Crash | |
|---|---|---|---|---|---|---|---|---|---|---|---|---|---|
| 1 | 2 | 3 | 4 | 5 | 6 | 7 | 8 | 9 | 10 | 11 | 12 | 13 | |
| 1. | A | 4 | 2 | 4000 | 7000 | 2 | 1500 | | | 1500 | 1500 | | 1 |
| 2. | B | 3 | 2 | 3000 | 4000 | 1 | 1000 | | 1000 | | | | 2 |
| 3. | C | 2 | 2 | 2000 | 2000 | — | — | | | | | | 3 |
| 4. | D | 5 | 3 | 2000 | 5000 | 2 | 1500 | | | | 1500 | 1500 | 4 |
| 5. | E | 2 | 1 | 2000 | 4000 | 1 | 2000 | | | | | | 5 |
| 6. | F | 1 | 1 | 1000 | 1000 | — | — | | | | | | 6 |
| 7. | G | 3 | 2 | 3000 | 8000 | 1 | 5000 | | | | | 5000 | 7 |
| 8. | H | 3 | 2 | 3000 | 5000 | 1 | 2000 | | | | | | 8 |
| 9. | J | 2 | 1 | 2000 | 3000 | 1 | 1000 | | | | | 1000 | 9 |
| 10. | Crashing cost | | | | | | | | 1000 | 1500 | 3000 | 7500 | 10 |
| 11. | Cumulative crashing cost | | | | | | | | 1000 | 2500 | 5500 | 13000 | 11 |
| 12. | Normal cost | | | | | | | 22000 | 22000 | 22000 | 22000 | 22000 | 12 |
| 13. | Indirect cost | | | | | | | 5000 | 4500 | 4000 | 3500 | 3000 | 13 |
| 14. | Total cost | | | | | | | 27000 | 27500 | 28500 | 31000 | 38000 | 4 |
| 15. | Gains for early completion | | | | | | | | 800 | 1600 | 2400 | 3200 | 15 |
| 16. | Net financial effect | | | | | | | 27000 | 26700 | 26900 | 28600 | 34800 | 16 |
| | Crashed project duration in weeks | | | | | | | 10 | 9 | 8 | 7 | 6 | |

## Table 16.5

**The Assessed Crashed Costs and the Crashing Potential for a Project**

| S. No. | Activity | Duration in Weeks Normal | Duration in Weeks Crash | Cost in $ Normal | Cost in $ Crash | Crashing Potential in weeks |
|---|---|---|---|---|---|---|
| 1 | A | 4 | 2 | 4000 | 7000 | 2 |
| 2 | B | 3 | 2 | 3000 | 4000 | 1 |
| 3 | C | 2 | 2 | 2000 | 2000 | X |
| 4 | D | 5 | 3 | 2000 | 5000 | 2 |
| 5 | E | 2 | 1 | 2000 | 4000 | 1 |
| 6 | F | 1 | 1 | 1000 | 1000 | X |
| 7 | G | 3 | 2 | 3000 | 8000 | 1 |
| 8 | H | 3 | 2 | 3000 | 5000 | 1 |
| 9 | I | 2 | 1 | 2000 | 3000 | 1 |

## Table 16.6

**Determination of the Rate of Crashing**

| S. No. | Activity | Crashing potential | Rate of crashing in $ |
|---|---|---|---|
| 1 | A | 2 | 1500 |
| 2 | B | 1 | 1000 |
| 3 | C | X | X |
| 4 | D | 2 | 1500 |
| 5 | E | 1 | 2000 |
| 6 | F | X | X |
| 7 | G | 1 | 5000 |
| 8 | H | 1 | 2000 |
| 9 | I | 1 | 1000 |

cost of the project increases by $1000 and the revised project duration works out to be 9 weeks.

*(b) Second crashing* Scrutiny of network after first crashing reveals that there are two critical paths. Further, reduction means that the sum of durations of critical activities along each critical path be reduced by one week. It can be easily verified that critical Activity A is common to all the critical paths and its rate of crashing is the cheapest. Therefore, further crashing of Activity A reduces the project duration to 8 weeks. The total increase in the cost for crashing the project duration from 10 weeks to 8 weeks is $2500, i.e. cost of crashing Activities A and B each by one week.

*(c) Third crashing* The number of critical paths increase after the second crashing. The various ways of reducing the project time during the third crashing are as under:

## Figure 16.5
## Networks After Time Crashing

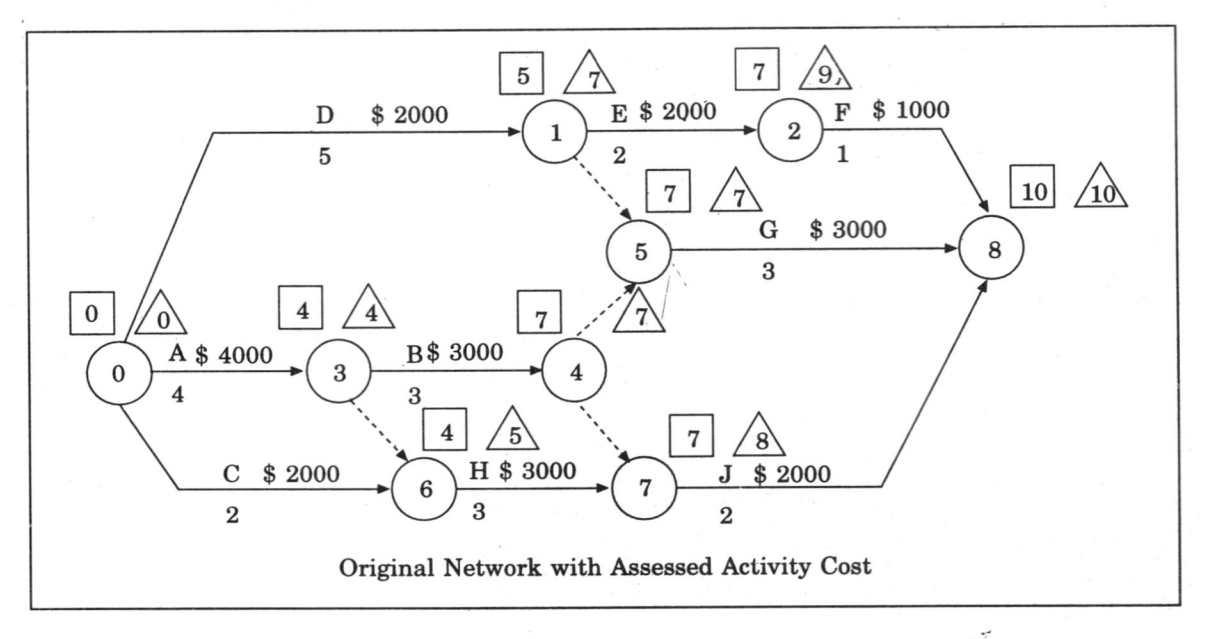

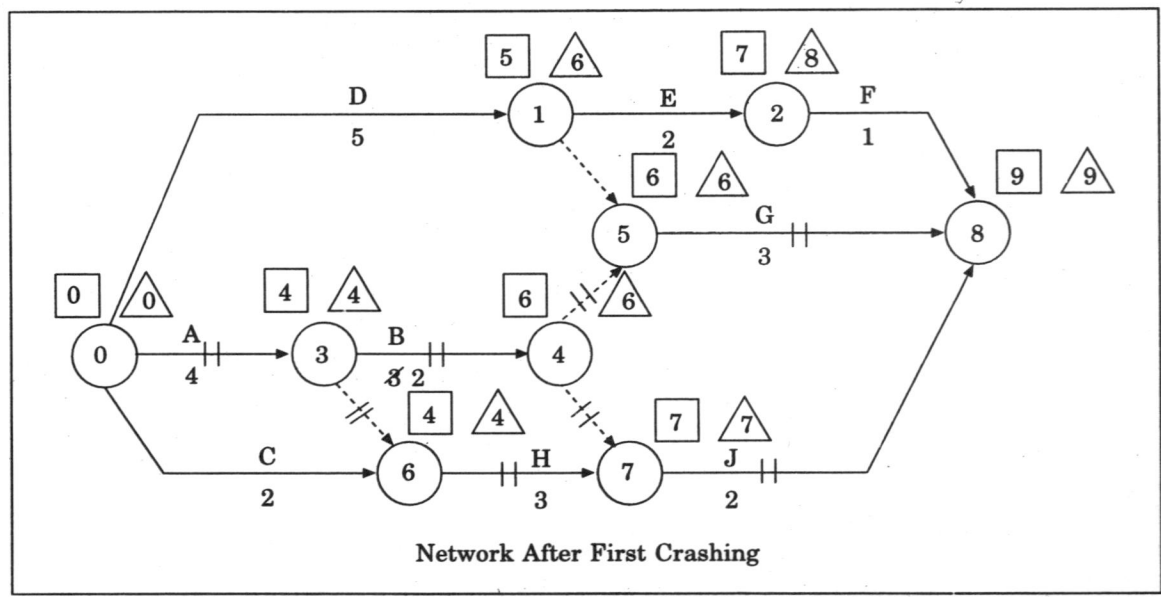

*Original Network with Assessed Activity Cost*

*Network After First Crashing*

*(Contd.)*

*(Contd.)*

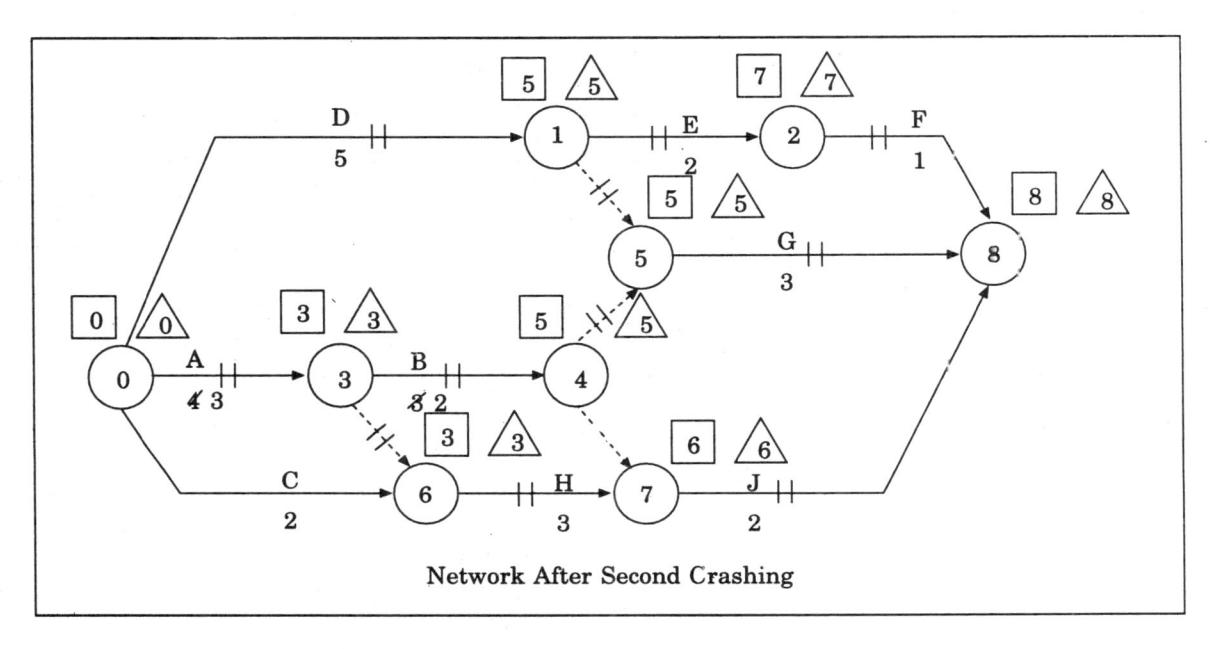

**Network After Second Crashing**

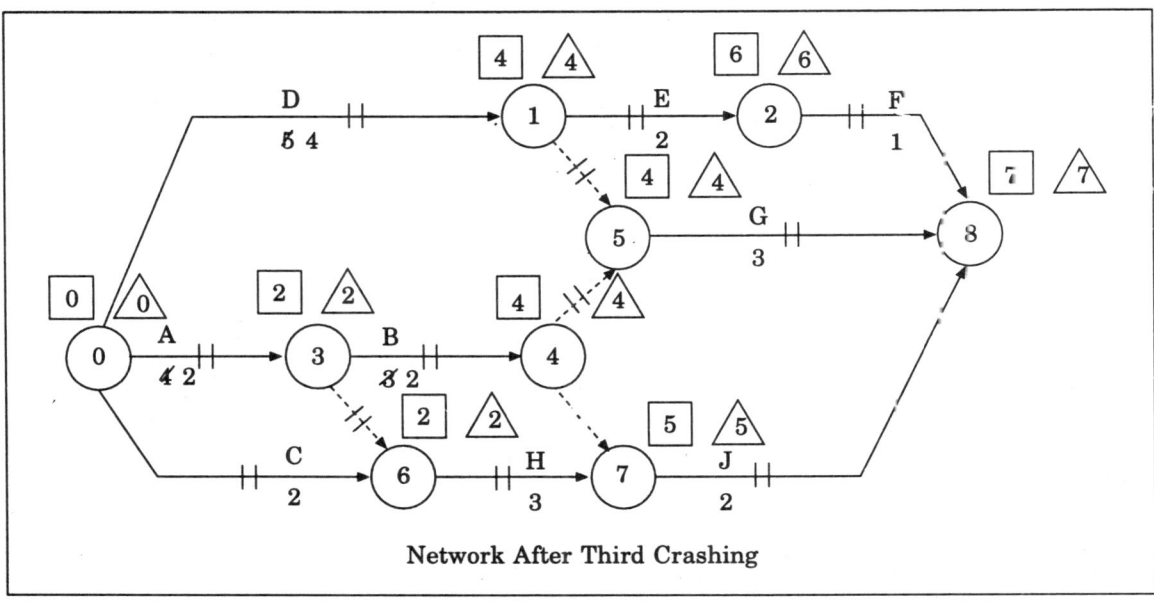

**Network After Third Crashing**

*(Contd.)*

*(Contd.)*

Network After Fourth Crashing

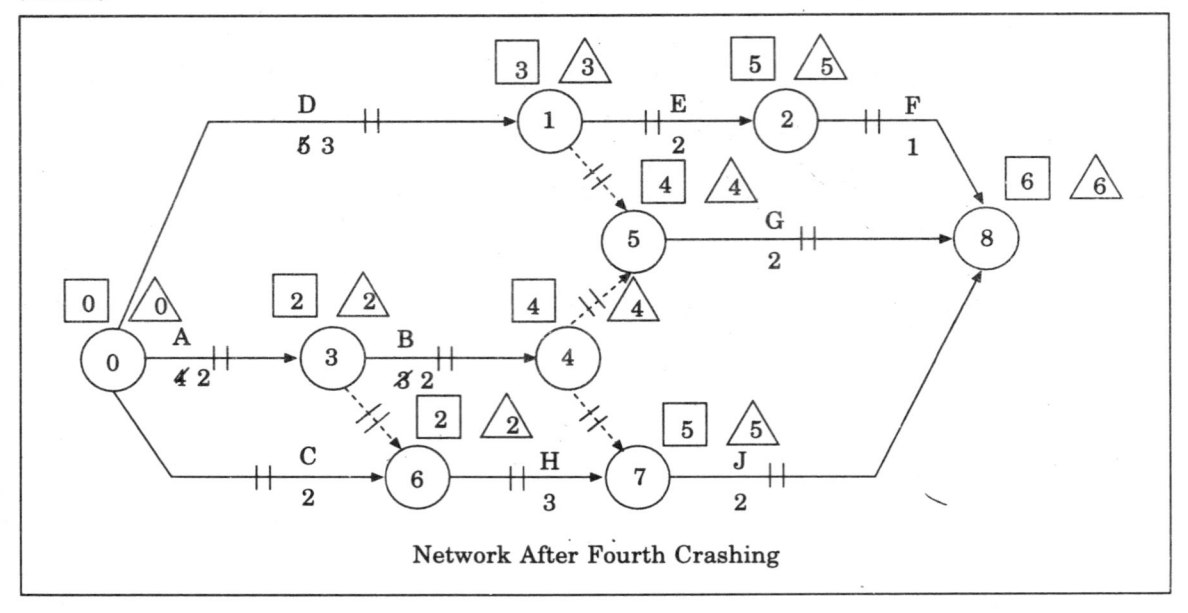

## Table 16.7

**Methods of Reducing Project Time During Third Crashing**

| Possible Courses | Affected Activities | Cost of Crashing in $ |
|---|---|---|
| 1 | A & D       | 1500 + 1500        = 3000 |
| 2 | E, G & J    | 2000 + 5000 + 1000 = 8000 |
| 3 | E, G & H    | 2000 + 5000 + 2000 = 9000 |
| 4 | A, E & G    | 1500 + 2000 + 5000 = 8500 |
| 5 | D, G & J    | 1500 + 5000 + 1000 = 7500 |

Therefore, the third crashing can be achieved by reducing the duration of critical Activities A and D by one week, each with further increase in the cost of the project by $3000. The revised duration of activities for 7 week's completion time are given in the network drawn in Fig. 16.5.

*(d) Fourth crashing* Proceeding similarly, it can be easily verified that although all activities are critical, there is still room for crashing. The fourth crashing is possible by reducing the duration for critical Activities D, G and J. Further, increase in the cost is $7500 and the revised network is reflected in Fig. 16.5.

It may be noted that after the fourth crashing, although activities E and H can be reduced, further crashing of all the critical paths is not possible. Therefore, the fourth crashing becomes the final crashing.

*Plotting cost function* The project cost function data for the example under consideration is tabulated in Table 16.4. The breakdown of overall costs have been worked out as follows:

(a) *Direct cost* It is the sum of the normal cost and crash cost. For example, the direct cost for reducing the project duration by two weeks is $24,500.
(b) *Indirect cost* This can be calculated from various overheads. In the given example, it has been taken as $500 per week.
(c) *Gain* It has been assumed that the project, when completed, will provide a revenue of $800 per week.

From the data given in serial and of the cost function, the cost curve can be plotted graphically, point by point, by the suitable selection of scales. The time is represented along the abcissa (being the independent variable) and the cost (dependent variable) along the ordinate axis. The project curve is shown in Fig. 16.3, and the corresponding time crashed networks are drawn in Fig. 16.5.

**Least cost schedule** The project cost-time function generally takes the shape of a concave curve as shown above. The ordinate of the lowest point in the curve gives the most economical cost of the project, and the time corresponding to the least value ordinate gives the optimum duration of the project.

The optimum duration for the project under consideration comes out to be 9 weeks and its optimum cost works out to be $267,000.

The network after its first crashing shows the duration of the crashed activities, and depicts the network plan of the least cost of the project.

### 16.3.3 Time Crashing

Normally a project should be planned for the completion period determined from the network. The question of increasing the project duration beyond optimum completion time does not arise as it will add to the project cost. But some of the circumstances given below, may compel to set the project completion time objectives lesser than the analyzed completion time:

(a) To meet the management's needs for the early completion of the project with acceptable cost to be paid for gaining time.
(b) To avoid delays which may attract heavy penalty or loss of goodwill.
(c) To venture on another project.
(d) To earn bonus for early completion, if found feasible.
(e) To transfer the resources needed elsewhere.
(f) To conform to a given resource's availability schedule.

The method of time crashing in network analysis aims at keeping the increase in cost of speeding up the project from its optimum completion period to its minimum. In other words, it means buying time with the least price. Unlike traditional methods, where crashing implies speeding up all works, in networks analysis, crashing is carried out for selected activities at least increase in project cost.

The project cost curve, which shows the pattern of cost variation with time, provides the ready-reckoner for assessing the increase in cost for the given project duration. All crash-point corresponds to the maximum time crashing possible.

The crashing cost can be determined from the project cost curves. In addition, the tabulated data gives the information regarding the corresponding critical activities and their revised durations.

The quote an example, the implications of completing the project as shown in Fig. 16.5 in 7 weeks are given below:

(a) The increase in cost for the optimum completion period is given as:

Estimation economical cost for 9 weeks completion = $26,700.00.
Assessed cost for 7 weeks completion = $28,600.00.
Increase in cost due to crashing by 2 weeks = $1,900.00.

(b) The revised durations of critical activities are shown in the network drawn after third crashing, and the increase in the cost of affected activities are as follows:

| Critical activity | Increase in cost in $ |
|---|---|
| A | 3,000.00 |
| B | 1,000.00 |
| D | 3,000 |
| G | 5,000.00 |
| J | 1,000.00 |

(c) The revised network shows that all the activities have become critical. This implies stricter control during the execution.

Since all activities are on the critical path, the optimization of sources during scheduling also becomes difficult.

### 16.3.4 A Word of Caution

There are many gains which can be achieved by the early completion of the project. The early project completion can yield added revenue, early release of capital and facilities, and, in some cases, can save idle time expenses of machinery. The non-financial gains can be earning goodwill, boosting of reputation, and raising of morale.

But the technique of minimizing cost by crashing of activities, although mathematically feasible as explained, has a great many inherent practical difficulties. One of the main reasons is that it is not possible to predict activity cost-time data accurately. In addition, the advantage gained by economizing the project cost is nullified by the fact that optimization of resources becomes extremely difficult, resulting in increased cost, and idle resources.

## 16.4 WORK PROGRESS REVIEWING PROCEDURE

Activity duration and logic are not rigid. Some odd activities may be completed earlier than the scheduled dates, whereas few others may be delayed. There is inherent overlapping in the logic of activities, and in some rare cases, succeeding activities may start earlier than the preceding activities. The updating methodology, covered above, brings out the deviations from the current project master schedule. The extent and implications of deviations are considered under 'review', carried out jointly by the project manager with the executing agencies at pre determined time intervals during the project execution phase.

### 16.4.1 Aim of Review

Review involves the critical examination of the work progress with a view to make decisions for achieving specified objectives. The review process looks ahead rather than getting bogged down in conducting postmortems of past occurrences. A project review acts as an effective tool for coordinating and controlling the common objectives between the client and the executing agencies.

The scope of the review process can vary from a mere time progress updating exercise to the other extreme of performance analysis of the time, cost and quality objectives. Generally, the review should be confined to the time performance monitoring and related problems of resources and cost changes necessary to achieve the pre-determined agreed objectives.

### 16.4.2 Stages in Review

Reviewing of the work progress can proceed along the following lines:

1. Presenting updated current work programme and sub-networks (as applicable) showing completed, in-progress and still-to-start activities, together with start and completion dates.
2. Comparing the actual work-package progress with its base line schedule and costs, as per the project master plan.
3. Examining what can be done to neutralize time and cost overruns. Some of the options open are:

    (a) Time compress schedule without any appreciable increase in cost to shorten time by:

    - Increasing resources of long duration critical activities.
    - Splitting up sequential critical activities into parallel components.

    (b) Time crash the critical path to reduce balance completion period by using alternate methods of construction, involving minimum increase in overall-project cost.

    (c) Explore new methods of reducing costs within agreed specifications and time constraints.

4. Replanning and rescheduling balance works, if necessary, to ensure completion of the project on time.
5. Studying the emerging critical and near critical activities to anticipate problems and device means to overcome them.

6. Checking the resources at site to see if adequate resources are available to execute the scheduled work; and to verify that additional resources, when required, shall arrive on time.
7. Evaluating the project cost status and updating forecasts for the future resources and costs for the remaining works.
8. Verifying the health, safety and security measures to prevent mishaps.

Frequency of updating and reviewing will depend upon a number of factors such as degree of control, purpose of the project, magnitude of work, phasing of work and so on. There can be no rigid rules laying down the period after which the network and schedule should be updated and reviewed. Frequency of updating and the review can be specified either as a percentage of project completion time or in terms of regular interval of time. As a thumb rule, for medium-sized construction projects, the following can be taken as a guide:

(a) Frequency of updating—weekly.
(b) Frequency of review—monthly.

A review enables the project manager to make decisions concerning the actions to be taken to overcome the anticipated time and cost overruns. Some of the decisions can be made on the spot, during the review meeting, while others may need further time to analyse the implications.

It is emphasized that during the review, the project manager is to produce a workable solution for future course of actions. This solution must take into consideration the varying interests of the executing agencies and the action plan should be acceptable to them. The review should look ahead to explore alternate ways of executing work to save time and costs, rather than diagnosing historical mistakes resulting in delays. The project manager should avoid discussions regarding responsibility for time and cost overruns, as these lead to conflicts and contractual disputes.

# CHAPTER 17

# Codification of the Planning System

A major turnkey construction project has two organizations at the site, i.e. the client's organization and the contractor's organization. Each one of these has architects, designers, estimators, planners, accountants and construction engineers with interrelated functions for managing the project. In addition, the contractor's organization (which manages the execution of project work) also has managers in charge of planning materials, plant and equipment, personnel and finance. Each one of these functional heads has his/her own requirements of information, and some of them process common data. Left to themselves, each manager/functional head will have to develop his own codes to identify, sort out and process data. If this is allowed, it may lead to confusion and duplication of efforts. In fact, an organized control of a major project is not possible without the proper codification of project data. Codes enable identification, classification and quick retrieval of data. These codes abbreviate data and expressions used in natural language. Short-length data code reduces storage space and costs.

In construction projects, the codes used can be broadly divided into two categories, i.e. project interfacing codes or simply referred as project codes, and department specialized codes.

**Project interfacing codes** These are the common codes used for developing an interdepartmental data base. To quote an example, a project code for the foundation of a building is needed by the designer for indexing foundation drawings; the estimator for splitting up the foundation into items of the bill of quantities; the planners for developing codes for activities constituting the foundation work package; the materials manager for codifying foundation materials; the cost accountant for relating foundation production costs; and so on.

**Departmental specialized codes** These codes are developed by the departmental heads for their use. Examples of this category are the codes used for indicating the location of materials in-site warehouses, indexing working drawings, designating day-to-day operations or processes necessary to execute a construction activity, and so on. Such codes, when required, can best be developed by the departmental heads. Departmental specialized codes are not covered in this Chapter.

This Chapter highlights the various ways of codifying data and describes the methodology for developing project interfacing codes. It covers the methodology for codification of project work components such as group tasks, work packages, and related activities. It introduces cost-accounting codes and outlines resources and finance codification methods. Also, it describes specifications, drawings, and bill of quantities codification approach. The subject covered is illustrated with a medium-sized building construction project.

## 17.1 CODIFICATION APPROACH

### 17.1.1 Purpose

A project organization handles large varieties of data. This data includes activities, resources, costs and documents. A simple approach to describe these items is to assign suitable names. This process may result in several different names being assigned to each item by different persons handling the same item. It is therefore essential to develop a code to identify each frequently occurring item. The item code is built up by using alphabets, numerals, symbols, or a combination of these. It may be noted that a code consists of a string of alphanumeric characters and that these are not the arithmetic numbers or functions used for making calculations. The project management system is codified primarily to serve a four-fold purpose:

(a) To identify the data connected with each work package, as work packages form the data base for managing various project functions.
(b) To aid in the organisation of data from the very detailed to the very broad levels.
(c) To enable the processing, sorting, and extraction of information required at various levels of management and functional units.
(d) To computerize the data processing system.

### 17.1.2 Data Needing Codification

There is no end to the demand for the codification of data from the various departments within a project. But unnecessary codes can create confusion and may defeat the very purpose for which they are designed. Some of the aspects which may need codification are listed below:

(A) Activity, work package, sub-group and group identification.
(B) Bill of quantities.
(C) Cost accounting system.
(D) Drawings and specifications.
(E) Equipment identification.
(F) Finance accounting system.

(G) General and administrative accounts.
(H) Head office expenses.
(I) Indexing system.
(J) Jobs, sub contracts.
(K) 'K' to represent kiloes and thousands, in large-sized numerical data.
(L) Labour categories.
(M) Material types.
(N) Numbering activities, areas, building locations etc.
(O) Overhead Categories.
(P) Projects codes.

The project interfacing codes, composed of a number of divisions or components, can be broadly grouped into work package and connected activities identification codes, resource codes, cost and sales accounting codes, and technical document codes.

To quote an example of an activity identification code in a building construction project, consider the steel reinforcement fixing activity of wall foundation work package of residential building No. 13 under the foundation responsibility centre. This activity can be represented by the code "RB130110FD" where

RB represents the type of building, say residential building.
13 indicates building location, i.e. building number.
01 identifies wall foundation work package.
10 stands for steel reinforcement fixing activity of wall foundation work package.
FD is the code for foundation responsibility centre.

The alphabets and numerals used in the above illustration are not assigned at random but they follow a systematic labelling approach, as explained later in this chapter.

## 17.1.3 Labelling Approach

**Label types** Codes can be labelled using alphabets or numerals or a combination of both.

*(a) Alphabet codes* Alphabet letters, A to Z, single or combined, can be used to represent a code. An alphabet (capital or small) in a single character-space can represent 26 variations as compared to numerals 0 to 9, which can depict maximum of 10 variations. In some cases, codes can best be represented by abbreviating them, for example carpenter can be coded as CARP.

*(b) Numerical codes* It is the most important form of coding. In numerical codes, each character can be represented by a numeral varying from 0 to 9. These numerals, when used in combination, can generate a large number of variations. Numerical codes are easy to comprehend, and as such are extensively used for codification specially those requiring analysis by computers. Some codes omit the number '13'.

*(c) Alphanumeric codes* It uses a combination of alphabets and numerals to develop a code. Each character in an alphanumeric code can represent up to 36 distinct variables e.g. 0 to 9, and A to Z.

**Importance of 'zero' in a code**  In some codification systems, "0" (zero) has a special significance. Zeroes, when used on the right side of a non-zero character, indicate summary level information. For example:

| | |
|---|---|
| 81 00 00 | Stands for all residential buildings. |
| 81 13 00 | Represents the residential building number 13. |
| 81 13 0I | Indicates the foundation work-package of building number 13. |

This concept of 'zeroes' in a codification system aids in building up the code level's pyramidal structure, which enables the summarizing of detailed data for meeting the information requirements at the higher levels of management. In some codes, 'Zero' is used to it represent 'not applicable'.

**Code labelling approach**  In the construction industry, there are a number of labelling systems in vogue. Some of these are designed for specific applications. These systems include universal decimal classification system (UDC), Computer based project management and costing system (CBC), and Construction index/Samarbetskommitten for Byggnadsfragor system (CI/SfB).

The CI/SfB system originated in Sweden in 1947, and it is internationally recognized. The CI/SfB Construction Index Manual, published initially in 1976 by RIBA Publications Limited (66 Portland Place, London, WIN 4AD, England) is primarily designed for use in project information and related general information with a guide to its use for project data coordination applications.

The CI/SfB makes use of alphanumeric labels listed in five basic tables of the CI/SfB manual. These tables are numbered 0, 1, 2, 3, and 4. Table no. 0 and 1 can be used for labelling project titles, types of facilities, work-packages and activities. Table no. 2 and 3 are used for indexing construction materials, and Table no. 4 contains the code for documenting administrative and accounting functions, and plant and equipment. Typical contents from these tables are listed in Table 17.1.

### 17.1.4 Significant Code

A code is termed significant if it can be easily understood by applying certain sets of simple rules to each of its components. For example, if a code is based on mnemonic features, it can help the user to memorize the code. Further, accounting becomes simple if the code includes numerical digits. Generally, significant codes consist of two or more alphanumeric components. For example, BW 013, representing activity block work of building number 13, can be termed as significant code where,

BW = Block work.
013 = Building number.

Exhibit 17.1 shows the two character alphabetic component of the significant code adopted for representing various types of work in the 2000 Housing Units Project. The alphabetic two-character code adopted for various construction activities in a primary school construction project is listed in Exhibit 3.7.

## Table 17.1

## CI/SfB Manual
## Main Contents With Codes

*CI/SfB Table 0: Physical environment*

1. Utilities, civil engineering facilities
2. Industrial facilities
3. Administrative, commercial, protective service facilities
4. Health, welfare facilities
5. Recreational facilities
6. Religious facilities
7. Educational, scientific, information facilities
8. Residential facilities
   - 81  Housing
   - 87  Temporary, mobile residential facilities

*CI/SfB Table 1: Building elements*

(1–) **Ground, substructure**
- (11)    Ground
- (13)    Floor beds
- (16)    Retaining walls, foundations

(2–) **Structure, primary elements, carcass**
- (21)    Walls, external walls
- (22)    Internal walls, partitions
- (23)    Floors, galleries
- (24)    Stairs, ladders
- (27)    Roofs
- (28)    Building frames, other primary elements
- (28.8)  Chimneys
- (29)    Parts, accessories, etc.

(3–) **Secondary elements, completion of structure**
- (31)    Secondary elements to walls, external walls
- (31.4)  Windows
- (31.5)  Doors, doorsets, frames
- (35)    Suspended ceilings
- (37.4)  Rooflights
- (38)    Balustrades, barriers

(4–) **Finishes to structure**
- (41)    Wall finishes, external
- (42)    Wall finishes, internal
- (43)    Floor finishes
- (45)    Ceiling finishes
- (47)    Roof finishes
- (48)    Other finishes to structure
- (49)    Parts, accessories, etc. special to finishes to structure elements

(5–) **Services, mainly piped, ducted**
- (52)    Waste disposal, drainage
- (52.1)  Refuse disposal
- (52.5)  Rain water, surface water drainage
- (52.6)  Internal drainage, above ground drainage
- (52.7)  Below ground drainage
- (53)    Liquids supply
- (53.1)  Cold water supply
- (53.3)  Hot water supply
- (54)    Gases supply
- (54.1)  Fuel gas supply
- (54.2)  Vapour supply
- (54.4)  Medical, industrial gas supply
- (55)    Space cooling
- (56)    Space heating
- (56.4)  Central heating: hot water, steam distribution
- (56.5)  Central heating: warm air distribution
- (56.6)  Central heating: electrical distribution
- (56.8)  Local heating
- (57)    Air conditioning, ventilation
- (59)    Parts, accessories, etc, special to piped, ducted service elements

(6–) **Services, mainly electrical**
- (61)    Electrical supply
- (62)    Power
- (63)    Lighting services
- (64)    Communications
- (66)    Transport

*(Contd.)*

*(Contd.)*

|  |  |  |
|---|---|---|
| | (68) | Security, control, other services |
| | (68.2) | Security services |
| | (68.5) | Fire protection services |
| | (68.6) | Lightening protection |
| **(7–)** | **Fittings** | |
| | (71) | Circulation fittings |
| | (71.1) | Notice boards, signs |
| | (71.3) | Doormats |
| | (73) | Culinary fittings |
| | (74) | Sanitary, hygiene fittings |
| | (75) | Cleaning, maintenance fittings |
| | (76) | Storage, screening fittings |
| | (76.7) | Blinds |
| **(8–)** | **Loose furniture** | |
| | (84) | Sanitary loose equipment |
| **(90)** | **External elements, other elements** | |

### CI/SfB Table 2: Constructions, forms

- **F** Blockwork and brickwork
- **G** Large block, panel work
- **H** Section work
- **J** Wire work, mesh work
- **L** Flexible sheet work (proofing)
- **N** Rigid sheet overlapwork
- **R** Rigid sheet work
- **S** Rigid tile work
- **T** Flexible sheet work
- **W** Planning work
- **X** Work with components
- **Z** Joints

### CI/SfB Table 3: Materials

- **e** Natural stone
- **f** Precast with binder
- **g** Clay (dried, fired)
- **h** Metal
- **i** Wood
- **j** Vegetable and animal materials
- **n** Rubber, plastics, etc.
- **o** Glass
- **p** Aggregated, loose fills
- **q** Lime and cement binders, mortars, concretes
- **r** Clay, gypsum, magnesia and plastics binders, mortars
- **s** Bituminous materials
- **t** Fixing and jointing materials
- **u** Protective and process/property modifying materials
- **v** Paints
- **w** Ancillary materials

### CI/SfB Table 4: Activities, requirements

- **(A)** Administration and management activities, aids
- **(B)** Construction plant, tools
  - (B1) Protection, plant
  - (B1c) Protective clothing, etc.
  - (B2) Temporary (non-protective) works
  - (B3) Transport plant
  - (B4) Manufacture, screening, storage plant
  - (B5) Treatment plant
  - (B6) Placing, pavement, compaction plant
  - (B7) Hand tools
- **(D)** Construction operations
- **(F)** Shape, size, etc.
- **(G)** Appearance, etc.
- **(H)** Context, environment
- **(J)** Mechanics
- **(K)** Fire, explosion
- **(L)** Matter
- **(M)** Heat, cold
- **(N)** Light, dark
- **(P)** Sound, quiet
- **(Q)** Electricity, magnetism, radiation
- **(R)** Energy, other physical factors
- **(U)** Users, resources
- **(W)** Operation, maintenance factors

## Exhibit 17.1
### 2000 Housing Units Project Work Codes

| Code | Nature of Work | Code | Nature of Work |
|---|---|---|---|
| HU | Housing unit | WT | Water tank |
| PS | Primary school | WP | Water pump house |
| HS | High school | SW | Sewage pump house |
| KG | KG school | BH | Boiler house |
| NR | Nursery | EL | Electrical services |
| SO | Social centre | UW | Unfiltered water supply |
| SC | Shopping complex | FW | Filtered water supply intake |
| SS | Sub-shopping complex | FD | Filtered water distribution |
| YC | Youth centre | HW | Hot water supply |
| HC | Health centre | SD | Sewage drainage system |
| BP | Baath party | SW | Sewage collection & pumping system |
| PL | Police station | | |
| HM | Hammam | ST | Storm water drain system |
| MQ | Mosque | SM | Storm water collection & pumping system |
| SP | Swimming pool | | |
| PF | Post office | GS | Gas supply |
| RS | Receiving station | LS | Landscaping |
| SB | Sub-station | RD | Road walkways and pathways |

Significant codes can be assigned at the corporate level as well as the project level. For example, an earth-moving equipment like the bulldozer can be given the code BD012 at the corporate level, representing the company's bulldozer number 12. But at the project site where there is one bulldozer employed primarily for earth work for the formation of a road, it can be coded as DZ01. In general, the codes assigned at the project level are preferred to the corporate codes because they can be made comparatively more significant with less characters.

It is not necessary that all codes should be significant in nature. Generally, all numeric codes are non-significant.

## 17.2 WORK PACKAGE AND ACTIVITIES IDENTIFICATION CODE

### 17.2.1 Code Composition

There are many ways of identifying a work package. In simple projects, work package abbreviation can be used to identify a work package. For a major project, work package abbreviation is not sufficient.

To quote an example, it may be sufficient to abbreviate 'excavation' as 'excv' in a small project involving the construction of only a few buildings, but in a major housing construction project having numerous different types of buildings, the work-package abbreviation/number may need certain prefixes and suffixes for proper identification. The prefixes/suffixes may include codes of the project and sub-projects to which the work-package belongs. The suffixes may be added to specify the activity, functional unit or name of the person responsible for its execution.

The types of sub groups associated with a work package will depend upon many factors such as the size and nature of the project. Further, various alternative arrangements for prefixing and suffixing of the sub groups can be considered while formulating a work-package code. Two extreme examples are given below:

| Work Package and Activity Identification Code ||||
|---|---|---|---|
| Sub-project code | Work-package code | Activity No. | Other related code |

Alternate Arrangement

| Activity and Work Package Identification Code ||||
|---|---|---|---|
| Activity code | Work-package code | Sub-project code | Other related code |

In general, each of these sub-groups can occupy 2 to 3 character-spaces, but the overall aim should be to restrict the number of alphanumeric characters code to a minimum.

### 17.2.2 Sub-project Code

A project can be divided into a number of sub-projects or group-tasks or facilities. These sub-projects can be coded using alphabets or numerals.

The alphabet character code, derived by abbreviating the sub-project, has an advantage over the numerical code as the abbreviated sub-project can be easily identified. For example, some of the buildings encountered in a housing complex can be coded as under:

| Type of buildings | Codes |
|---|---|
| Residential Building | RB |
| Public Building | PB |
| Education Building | EB |

The CI/SfB Table '0' can be used to label the sub-project using numerals. For a project having a number of sub-projects or facilities, a four-digit code can be derived from this table to represent each sub-project. Some of the typical examples illustrating the codification of various facilities in the housing units complex project No. 05 and using headings of Table '0' of CI/SfB are given in Table 17.2.

### 17.2.3 Work Package, Work-items and Related Activities Codes

Building construction elements, shown in CI/SfB Table 1 (original table marginally modified), produced as Table 3.2 in Chapter 3, represent the overall process of project construction,

### Table 17.2

**Sub-project codes**

| S. no. | Work component | Facility code |
|---|---|---|
| (1) | Dwelling units | 0581 |
| (2) | Education buildings | 0571 |
| (3) | Shopping centre | 0534 |
| (4) | Hospital | 0541 |
| (5) | Mosque | 0565 |
| (6) | Sports grounds | 0556 |
| (7) | External utility services | 0510 |

beginning with site development and proceeding vertically down to the external utility services. In this Table, the primary divisions are vertically divided as shown in Table 17.3.

### Table 17.3

**Primary Divisions of CI/SfB Table I (Modified) of Building Construction Elements**

| Code No. | Primary division | Basis of grouping within the division |
|---|---|---|
| (00) | Site development | Information relating to external site development and paving works. |
| (10) | Sub-structures | Foundation work below grade. |
| (20) | Superstructure primary elements | Load-bearing structural elements above grades. |
| (30) | Superstructure secondary elements | Non-load bearing elements. |
| (40) | Finishes | Exposed surface treatment. |
| (50) | Mechanical services | Mostly piping and ducting systems including materials and equipment. |
| (60) | Electrical services | Mostly wired systems, materials and equipment. |
| (70) | Fixed equipment | All fixed equipment components and fixtures in a building. |
| (80) | Moveable equipment | All moveable equipment components and furnishings in a building. |
| (90) | External utility services | All services, not within the enclosed limits of the buildings. |

Table 17.4 matrix depicts primary divisions in the first column, and the corresponding subdivisions of the primary division are reflected horizontally against each primary divison. Project work packages can be identified with the primary division or subdivision or combination of subdivisions. For example, 21 (Table 17.4) represents external wall (load-bearing) and 43 stands for floor finishes. There are vacant positions for incorporating additional subdivisions when necessary.

Generally, each primary division can represent a work package of small projects, whereas for large projects each subdivision or its further breakdown may be used to denote a work package. If in a particular situation, a work package comprises two or more sub divisions within a primary division, then the code of the primary division or the first occurring subdivision is used to represent the work package. In a major building construction project, each of these subdivisions (after modifications, if necessary) can be considered as a work package.

In order to provide further breakdown of subdivisions, Table 3.4 also details sub-heading for each of the subdivisions. For example, roof (27) is broken into flat roof (27.1), pitched roof (27.2), folded plate roof (27.4), etc. Such breakdown of subdivisions can be used to derive the related activities of the work package.

### 17.2.4 Activity Identification Code

An activity number is assigned to identify an activity. It can be an alphanumeric code or it can be derived from the project network or schedule or work.

In CPM and PERT Networks, activities are numbered using (i–j) events whereas, Precedence Networks have a specific numerical or alphanumerical label. The numbering methods are covered in Chapter 4.

Activity numbers are primarily used by the planners. These numbers correlate network logic, activity description and activity sub-group codes. Various options for developing identification code for work packages and activities are given below:

#### CPM/PERT Even–oriented Activity Identification Code

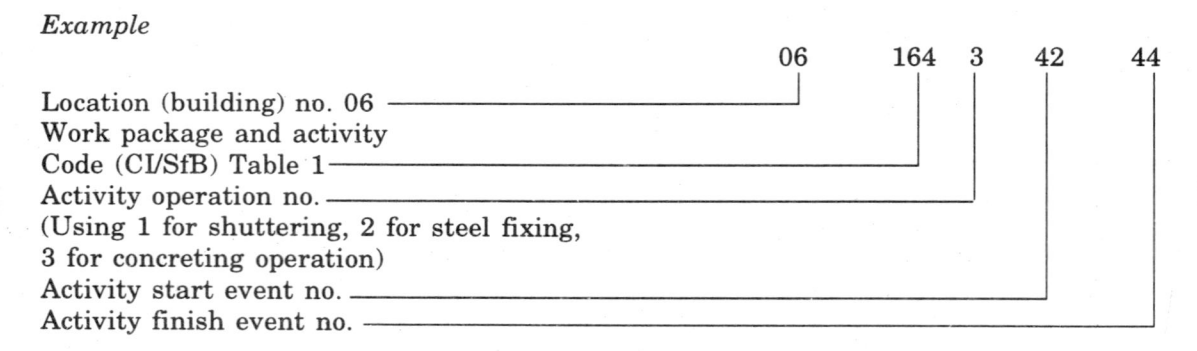

*Example*

```
                              06    164   3   42   44
Location (building) no. 06 ─────────┘     │   │    │
Work package and activity                 │   │    │
Code (CI/SfB) Table 1 ────────────────────┘   │    │
Activity operation no. ───────────────────────┘    │
(Using 1 for shuttering, 2 for steel fixing,       │
3 for concreting operation)                        │
Activity start event no. ──────────────────────────┘
Activity finish event no. ─────────────────────────
```

#### Precedence Network Number Related Activity Identification Code

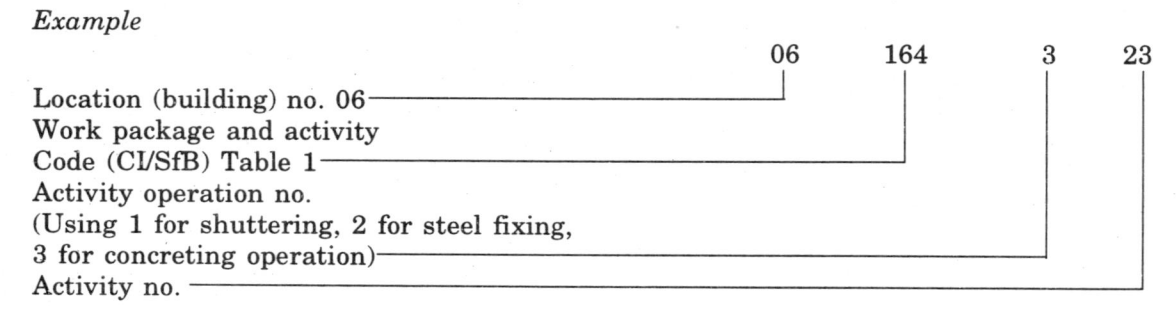

*Example*

```
                              06    164      3    23
Location (building) no. 06 ─────────┘        │     │
Work package and activity                    │     │
Code (CI/SfB) Table 1 ───────────────────────┘     │
Activity operation no.                             │
(Using 1 for shuttering, 2 for steel fixing,       │
3 for concreting operation) ───────────────────────┘
Activity no. ──────────────────────────────────────
```

Codification of the Planning System 511

## Responsibility-oriented Activity Code

*Example*

```
                                          397    164    06    FD
Activity number ─────────────────────────────┘     │     │     │
Work package and activity                          │     │     │
Code (CI/SfB Table 1) ─────────────────────────────┘     │     │
Building no. 6 ──────────────────────────────────────────┘     │
Foundation responsibility centre ──────────────────────────────┘
```

## Bill of Quantities-oriented Activity Code

*Example*

```
                                          RB    A16    164    235
Residential building ────────────────────────┘    │      │     │
Bill of quantities ref. no. ─────────────────────┘      │     │
Work-package related operation ─────────────────────────┘     │
Activity no. ─────────────────────────────────────────────────┘
```

## Location-oriented Activity Code

*Example*

```
                                          1306    134    314
Cluster no. 13, building no. 6 ───────────────┘      │     │
Work-package and related activity code ──────────────┘     │
Activity no. ──────────────────────────────────────────────┘
```

## Work Package and Activity Identification Code

*Example* Foundation work package and activity code of 2000 Housing Unit Project residential building designed for computerisation are listed in Exhibit 17.2.

## ❏ 17.3 RESOURCES CODES

Generally, well established construction companies do identify their resources by assigning certain codes in documents like materials master manual, personal record documents, and plant and machinary accounting books, but these may not be enough. Resources codification at the project site is necessary to identify, locate, account and monitor each item of resource from the moment it is indented to the time it is finally disposed off.

## Exhibit 17.2

### Work Packages & Activity Identification Codes
### Foundation Work of 2000 Housing Units Project

| *Base Preparation* | FD 010 | *Plinth Wall Construction* | FD 030 |
|---|---|---|---|
| 1. Layout for excavation | FD 011 | 14. Layout for plinth wall | FD 031 |
| 2. Excavation with machine | FD 012 | 15. Wall shuttering | FD 032 |
| 3. Base preparation | FD 013 | 16. Wall concreting M-250 | FD 033 |
| 4. Anti-termite at base | FD 014 | 17. Deshuttering | FD 034 |
| 5. Polythene sheeting | FD 015 | 18. Curing wall | FD 035 |
| 6. Shuttering for blinding | FD 016 | 19. Bitumen coating wall & raft | FD 036 |
| 7. Placing concrete M-100 | FD 017 | *Ground Floor Construction* | FD 040 |
| *Raft Construction* | FD 020 | 20. Back filling | FD 041 |
| 8. Layout for raft | FD 021 | 21. Plinth filling | FD 042 |
| 9. Shuttering for raft | FD 022 | 22. Anti-termite under GF Slab | FD 043 |
| 10. Reinforcement for raft | FD 023 | 23. Polythene sheeting | FD 044 |
| 11. Raft concreting M-250 | FD 024 | 24. Shuttering for GF Slab | FD 045 |
| 12. Curing raft | FD 025 | 25. Weld mesh fixing | FD 046 |
| 13. Bitumen coating raft slab | FD 026 | 26. GF Concreting M-250 | FD 047 |
| | | 27. Curing GF Slab | FD 048 |

*Note* Last character of all work packages is 'zero', and the activities within a work package are serially numbered.

The resources can be identified using a four-numerical digit code as under:

| *Resource* | *Resource Group* (2 characters) | *Resource Category* (2 characters) |
|---|---|---|
| Manpower | × × | × × |
| Materials | × × | × × |
| Equipment | × × | × × |
| Others direct resources | × × | × × |

The above resources code can have suitable suffixes and/or prefixes to further identify the associated codes like work package, responsibility centre, cost categories and so on, as illustrated below; resources cost codes are covered in Section 17.4.

## 17.3.1 Construction Manpower Code

Manpower is planned, indented, accounted and controlled by categories. A 4-digit numerical/alphabet code can be developed to represent manpower categories and their further sub-divisions. For example, a typical 4-character code manpower can be structured as under:

## Table 17.4

### Typical Two-character Construction Materials Group Identification Code
### (Excludes consumeables and minor materials)

| Primary Division | Sub-Division | | | | | | | | | |
|---|---|---|---|---|---|---|---|---|---|---|
| (1–) Substructure Bulk Materials | (11) Soil Treatment | (12) Filling | (13) Sand | (14) Aggregate | (15) Cement | (16) Blocks | (17) Steel Bar | (18) Steel Fabric | (19) Other | |
| (2–) Superstructures/Precast Elements | (21) Exterior Wall Bearings | (22) Interior Wall Bearings | (23) Floors | (24) Stairs/Ramps | (25) Balcony | (26) Parapet | (27) Roofs | (28) Structural Frames | (29) Inserts & Lifting | |
| (3–) Superstructure/Secondary Elements | (31) Metallic Wall Openings | (32) Wooden Wall Openings | (33) Floor Openings | (34) Railings | (35) Suspended Ceilings | (36) Wall Bearings | (37) Roof Openings skylights | (38) Insulation | (39) Fixing A Jointing | |
| (4–) Finishes | (41) Exterior Wall Finishes | (42) Interior Wall Finishes | (43) Floor Finishes | (44) Stairs Finishes | (45) Ceiling Finishes | (46) Surface Protection | (47) Roof Finishes | (48) Special Finishes | (49) Other Finishes | |
| (5–) Mechanical Services | (51) Refuse Disposal | (52) Drainage/ Waste Disposal | (53) Water Supply | (54) Gas Supply | (55) Refrigeration/Space | (56) Space/ Systems | (57) NVAC/ Systems | (58) Special Services | (59) other Services | |
| (6–) Electrical Services | (61) Electrical Power Supply | (62) Power Distribution | (63) Lighting | (64) Communication Audio/Visual | (65) | (66) Elevations/ Escalators Conveyors | (67) | (68) Security, Fire Protection System | (69) Other | |
| (7–) Fixed Equipment | (71) Sign Display | (72) General Room Furniture | (73) Cooking/ Eating | (74) Plumbing Fixtures | (75) Cleanings Maintenance | (76) Storage | (77) Special Activity | (78) Others | (79) | |
| (8–) Moveable Equipment | (81) Circulation Furniture | (82) General Room Furniture | (83) Cooking/ Eating | (84) Sanitary | (85) Cleaning & maintenance | (86) Storage | (87) Special Activity | (88) Other | (89) | |
| (9–) Site External Works | (91) Site Development | (92) Site Structure | (93) Site Enclosures | (94) Roads, Paths and Pavings | (95) Mechanical Services | (96) Electrical Services | (97) Fixed Equipment | (98) Moveable Equipment | (99) Landscape | |

*Note:* Each material group can be further divided into Subdivisions (01 to 99).

### Table 17.5

**Materials Codification Based on Type and Shape of Work and Materials Tables 2 and 3 SfB (Modified) for 2000 Housing Units Project**

| Type of Materials | a | b | c | d | e | f | g | h | i | j | k | l | m | n | o | p | q | r | s | t | u | v | w | x | y | z |
|---|---|---|---|---|---|---|---|---|---|---|---|---|---|---|---|---|---|---|---|---|---|---|---|---|---|---|
| | Aministration materials | Capital Plants & Equipments | Labour Requirements | Trades Tools & Machinery | Natural Stone | Precast/Composite | Clay | Metal | Wood | Natural Fibres | | Mineral Fibres | Rubber, Plastics | Glass | Loose Aggregates | Mortars/Cement Mix | Gypsum/Clay Binders | Bituminous Materials | Fixing & Fastening Materials | Protective Materials/Admixtures | Paints | Other Materials | Plant | Composite Materials | Substances |

*Type of Work*

A
B Demolition/Shoring
C Excavation/Filling
D
E Cast in Place
F Bricks, Blocks
G Large Structural Units
H Sections, Bars
I Pipe Conduit
J Wire/Wire Mesh
K Insulation/Quilts
L Vapour Barrier/Membranes
M Malleable/Formed Sheets
N Rigid Overlapping Sheets
O
P Thick Coating
Q Rigid Sheets
R Rigid Tiles
S Flexible Sheets
T Carpeting
U
V Thin Coatings/
W Planting/Landscaping
X Prefabricated
Y Solids/Liquids
Z Joints

The matrix shown above is arranged to show Table 2 (Type and shape of work) vertically and Table 3 (Types of materials and equipment) horizontally. Table 2 and Table 3 when cross referred, can define a two-character materials group.

Codification of the Planning System **515**

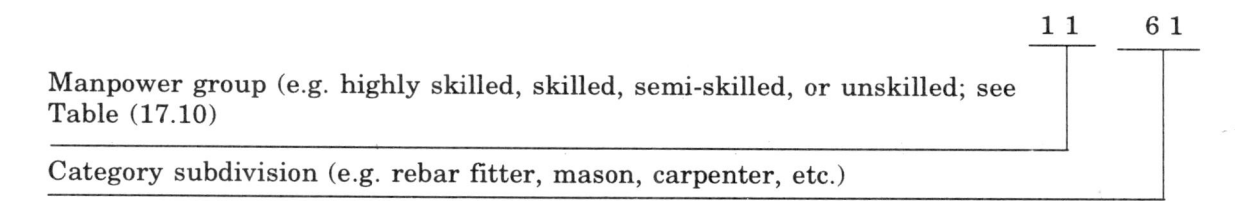

```
                                            1 1    6 1
Manpower group (e.g. highly skilled, skilled, semi-skilled, or unskilled; see
Table (17.10)

Category subdivision (e.g. rebar fitter, mason, carpenter, etc.)
```

Manpower at project site can be grouped under various heads. These include management group, technical staff, administration staff, supervisors, highly skilled workers, skilled workers, semi-skilled workers, helpers and others. Construction workers can be further categorised according to their trade skills as shown in Table 7.2.

### 17.3.2 Construction Materials Code

Project inventory of bulk stores, finishing materials, electrical and mechanical components, etc. run into thousands of items. These materials vary in many ways such as use and purpose, supply source, stocking methodology, procurement date, location in warehouse, site requirement date, and so on. A common practice is to identify the materials by individual names. But these material names or descriptions go on changing, while passing through various processes, departments or transit agencies. It is therefore, necessary, that all concerned use the same unique label to identify and describe materials.

Ideally, the materials code should describe the type of material, material specifications, and its location in warehouse. All this will make the material code lengthy and cumbersome. Further, it is not necessary to code all materials. Generally, the codification can be restricted to A and B category materials. In practice, the materials code to describe the type of materials can be limited to the 4 characters with a 3-character extension for departmental code. The extreme left two characters can depict the material group and the remaining 2 can represent the material category A typical material code can be composed as given below:

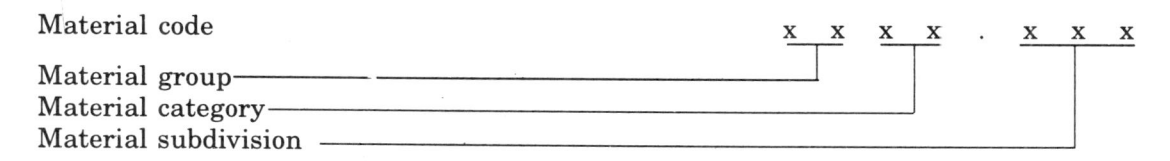

```
Material code                       x x x x . x x x
Material group—————————————————————|   |   |
Material category—————————————————————————|   |
Material subdivision ——————————————————————————|
```

**Material group**  The project materials can be grouped using 2-character code in many ways such as:

(a) Using main division labels of CI/SfB Tables 1, 2 or 3 or their combinations, as shown in Tables 17.1, 17.4 and 17.5.
(b) Using divisions of standard specifications. See Table 17.6.
(c) Using classifications of materials into main divisions like fast moving bulk materials, repetitive materials, one-time use materials, equipment related materials, maintenance related materials, office related materials, utility service materials, and so on.

## Table 17.6
### Construction Specifications Grouping

| Primary Division | Subdivision | | | | | | | | | |
|---|---|---|---|---|---|---|---|---|---|---|
| | 000 | 100 | 200 | 300 | 400 | 500 | 600 | 700 | 800 | 900 |
| General Requirements 0100 | Summary of Work 01010 | Special Project 01100 | Project Meetings 01200 | Submittals 01300 | Quality Control 01400 | Construction Facilities 01500 | Materials & Equipment 01600 | Contract Close-out 01700 | Maintenance 01800 | |
| Site Work 02000 | Surface Investigation 02010 | Site Preparation 02100 | Earthwork 02200 | Tunneling 02300 | | Paving & Surfacing 02500 | Utility Piping 02600 | | Site Improvements 02800 | Landscaping 02900 |
| Concrete | | Concrete Formwork 03100 | Concrete Reinforcement 03200 | Concrete-in-place Concrete 03300 | Precast Concrete 03400 | Cementation Decks & Toppings 03500 | Grout 03600 | Concrete Restoration 03700 | Mass Concrete 03800 | |
| 03000 | | | | | | | | | | |
| Masonry | | Mortar & Masonry Grout 04100 | Unit Masonry 04200 | | Stone 04400 | Masonry Restoration & Cleaning 04500 | Corrosion Resistance Masonry 04600 | Simulated Masonry 04700 | | |
| 04000 | | | | | | | | | | |
| Metal | Metal Materials 05010 | Structural Metal Framing 05100 | Metal Joints 05200 | Metal Decking 05300 | Cold Framed Metal Framing 05400 | Metal Fabrication 05500 | | Ornamental Metal 05700 | Expansion Control 05800 | Hydraulic Structures 05900 |
| 05000 | | | | | | | | | | |
| Statistic | Fasteners & Adhesive 6050 | Rough Carpentry 06100 | Finish Carpentry 06200 | Wood Treatment 06300 | Architectural Woodwork 06400 | Structural Plastics 06500 | Plastic Fabrications 06600 | | | |
| 06000 | | | | | | | | | | |
| Thermal & Moisture Protection 07000 | | Water Proofing 07100 | Insulation 07200 | Shingles & Roofing 07300 | Manufactures Roofing & Sidings 07400 | Membrane Roofing 07500 | Flashing & Sheet Metal 07600 | Roof Specialities & Accessories 07700 | Skylights 07800 | Joint Sealers 07900 |
| Doors & Windows 08000 | | Metal Doors & Frames 08100 | Wood & Plastic Doors 08200 | Special Doors 08300 | Entrance & Store Fronts 08400 | Metal Windows 08500 | Wood & Plastic Windows 08600 | Hardware 08700 | Glazing 08800 | Glazed Curtain Walls 08900 |
| Finishes 09000 | | Metal Support System 09100 | Lath & Plaster 09200 | Tile 09300 | Terrazzo 09400 | Accoustic Treatment 09500 | Stone Flooring 09600 | Special Flooring 09700 | Special Coatings 09800 | Painting 09900 |

*(Contd.)*

## Codification of the Planning System

*(Contd.)*

| Primary Division | \<br\>000 | 100 | 200 | 300 | 400 | Subdivision\<br\>500 | 600 | 700 | 800 | 900 |
|---|---|---|---|---|---|---|---|---|---|---|
| Specialities\<br\>10000 | | Visual Display Boards\<br\>10100 | Louvers & Vents\<br\>10200 | Fireplaces & Stoves\<br\>10300 | Identifying Devices\<br\>10400 | Lockers\<br\>10500 | Partitions\<br\>10600 | Exterior Protection Opening devices\<br\>10700 | Toilet & Bath Accessories\<br\>10800 | Wardrobe & Closet Specialities\<br\>10900 |
| Equipment\<br\>11000 | Special Purpose Equipment\<br\>11010 to 11100 | | Water Supply & Treatment Equipment\<br\>11200 | Fluid Waste Equipment\<br\>11300 | Food Service Equipment\<br\>11400 | Industrial & Process Equipment\<br\>11500 | Laboratory Equipment\<br\>11600 | Medical Equipment\<br\>11700 | Navigational Equipment\<br\>11850 | Equipment\<br\>11870 |
| Furnishings\<br\>12000 | Fabrics\<br\>12050 | Artwork\<br\>12100 | | Manufactured Case Work\<br\>12300 | | Window Treatment\<br\>12500 | Furniture & Accessories\<br\>12600 | Multiple Seating\<br\>12700 | Interior Plant & Planters\<br\>12800 | 12900 |
| Special Construction\<br\>13000 | Air Supported Structures\<br\>13010 | Nuclear Reactors\<br\>13100 | Liquid & Gas Storage Tanks\<br\>13200 | Utility Control Systems\<br\>13300 | Industrial & Process Control\<br\>13400 | Recording Instrumenta-tion\<br\>13500 | Solar Energy System\<br\>13600 | Wind Energy Systems\<br\>13700 | Building Automation Systems\<br\>13800 | Fire Suppression & Supervisory System\<br\>13900 |
| Conveying Systems\<br\>14000 | | Dumb Waiters\<br\>14100 | Elevators\<br\>14200 | Escalators & Moving walks 14300 | Lifts\<br\>14400 | Material Handling systems 14500 | Hoists & Cranes 11600 | Turntables\<br\>11700 | Scaffolding\<br\>11800 | Transportation Systems\<br\>11900 |
| Mechanical\<br\>15000 | Basic Mech-anical Materials & Methods\<br\>15050 | Valves\<br\>15100 | Mechanical Insulation\<br\>15200 | Fire Protection\<br\>15300 | Plumbing\<br\>15400 | HVAC\<br\>15500 | Refrigeration\<br\>15650 | Heat Transfer\<br\>15750 | Air Handling\<br\>15850 | Controls, Testing Adjustment & Balancing\<br\>15900 |
| Electrical\<br\>16000 | Basic Electrical Materials & Methods\<br\>16050 to 16195 | | Power Generation Systems\<br\>16200 | Medium Voltage Distribution\<br\>16300 | Service Distribution\<br\>16400 | Lighting\<br\>16500 | Special Systems\<br\>16600 | Communica-tions\<br\>16700 | Electric Resistance Heating\<br\>16800 | Controls\<br\>16900 |

*Note*: Each subdivision is further divided into number of subdivisions and sections, these are omitted due to printing difficulties/space.

(d) Using four-digit numerical group 0001 to 9999 to label materials in sequence of requirement, indenting, receipt or as planned in bill of materials.
(e) Grouping of materials, needed for building works in sequence of construction as shown in Exhibit 8.2 for 2000 Housing Units Project. This Exhibit contains 20 groups of materials.

**Materials category** These show further split up of the group of materials like cement into types (ordinary or sulphate resistance) and its further sub-divisions can be bulk cement or bagged cement. Exhibit 8.2 lists 92 items of materials used for construction of residential buildings.

Further, codes to identify the location of materials can be developed by the materials department.

### 17.3.3 Equipment Code

An equipment is a high-cost long life item of machinery. Equipment is a fixed asset, and it is capitalized for accounting purposes. Generally, its performance is measured in terms of hours utilized. Plant and equipment is codified to facilitate its identification for recording purchase costs and depreciation value, locating and procuring spares, updating maintenance and repairs documents, monitoring performance and accounting operating costs.

Equipment generally carry codes assigned at the corporate level. The equipment code can be structured as follows:

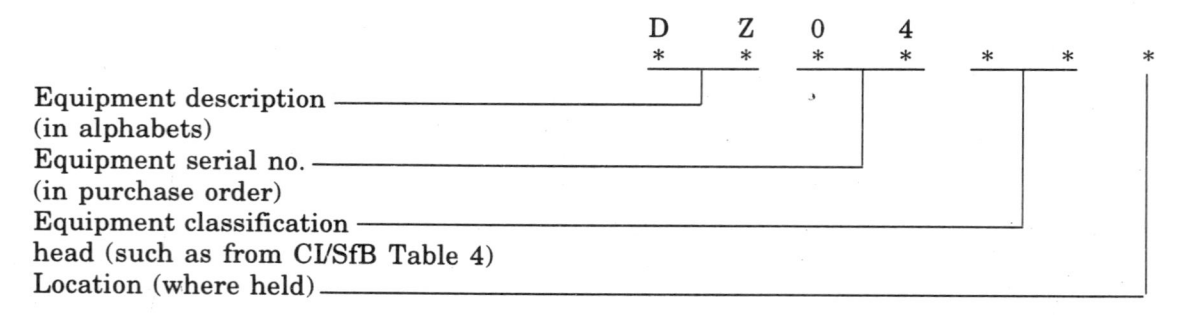

```
                    D   Z   0   4
                    *   *   *   *   *   *   *
Equipment description ──────────────┘
(in alphabets)
Equipment serial no. ───────────────────
(in purchase order)
Equipment classification ───────────────────────────────
head (such as from CI/SfB Table 4)
Location (where held) ──────────────────────────────────────
```

At project site, equipment group can use 2-digit code and each equipment item can be described by using two alphabets from its nomenclature. For example, excavator can be coded as 'EX' and dozer can be described as 'DZ'. A typical project-equipment-code structure is given in Table 17.7.

### 17.3.4 Other Expenses Code

In addition to manpower costs, materials costs and equipment costs, numerous miscellaneous expenses are incurred during the execution of a project. Some of them are directly or indirectly related to the work package. These expenses include costs relating to designs and drawings, investigation and trials, sub-contracts, equipment hiring, and share of indirect costs. In some projects, direct equipment costs are also covered under other expenses. For codification these expenses can be assigned a 4-character space, two each for expense group and expense category, similar to other resources codes.

Table 17.7

**Typical Construction Equipment Group Identification Codes**

| Equipment Group No. | Equipment Group Description | Equipment Item | Item Identification Code |
|---|---|---|---|
| 01 | Earth-moving Plant | Dozers | DR |
|  |  | Loaders | LR |
|  |  | Excavators | XR |
|  |  | Scrappers | SR |
| 02 | Concreting Equipment | Batching Plant | BP |
|  |  | Concrete Pump | CP |
|  |  | Transit Mixer | TM |
|  |  | Concrete Mixers | CM |
| 03 | Materials Handling Equipment | Mobile cranes | MC |
|  |  | Tower cranes | TC |
|  |  | Gantry cranes | GC |
|  |  | Overhead cranes | OC |
|  |  | Forklifts | FL |
| 04 | Transportation Fleet | Tippers | TR |
|  |  | Dumpers | TR |
|  |  | Water tankers | WT |
|  |  | Fuel tankers | FT |
| 05 | Utility Services Equipment | Power supply Equipment | PS |
|  |  | Water supply Equipment | WS |
|  |  | Sewage disposal Equipment | SD |
|  |  | HVAC equipment | HC |

*Notes*
1. Codes given above are for project site equipment. In addition, this equipment may also have associated corporate code as per the company's Equipment Master List.
2. Each equipment is assigned a unique identification and accounting code as each equipment is capitalised.
3. Generally, each equipment has a basic data card and a log book. The log book is used to record operating history including repairs and maintenance.

4. The basic data card contains the following information, as applicable.

| | | | |
|---|---|---|---|
| *Identification Code* | *Description* | | |
| *Registeration No.* | *Model No.* | *Chassis No.* | *Engine No.* |
| *Purchase Price* | *Capitalised amount* | | *Depreciation/Month* |
| *Purchase Order No.* | *GRN No.* | | *L/C No.* |

Supplier :
Customer Declaration Particulars :
Current Insurance Particulars :
Final Disposal Particulars

## ❏ 17.4 COST AND FINANCE ACCOUNTING CODES

### 17.4.1 Cost Accounting Code

A cost accountant mans the cost management information system of the project and accounts for all the costs. These costs include standard or budgeted costs, actual costs, and future costs. His database is work package. He develops each work package construction costs. He identifies the nature and type of each transaction involving indirect costs and classifies them into fixed overheads and variable overheads. He generally splits up each work package production cost into the following elemental costs:

(a) Direct labour costs
(b) Direct materials costs
(c) Direct equipment costs
(d) Direct other expenses
(e) Indirect apportioned variable overheads
(f) Indirect apportioned fixed overheads
(g) Production cost
(h) Production direct cost
(i) Production indirect cost
(j) Earned value

A cost accountant computes the above costs, by work packages or jobs, for each responsibility centre. He compares the work package actual costs incurred with the standard or budgeted costs. He analyses variances and identifies possible causes for the variances. He accounts for network package costs, project cost status as well as predicts future costs.

In order to identify, account and control different types of costs in the cost management system; it is necessary to label the essential characteristics of each cost, so as to build up its composite structure. These characteristics are:

| Cost Characteristics | Code Requirement |
|---|---|
| Who incurred? | Responsibility centre code. |
| To accomplish what? | Work package code. |
| On what account? | Resources code. |
| What type of costs? | Cost category code |
| How to account cost? | Cost and finance accounting codes. |
| What are returns? | Bill-of-quantity code. |

A typical 12-character cost accounting code, conforming to characters' space earmarked in some of the project management software, is outlined below:

## Cost accounting code

- Responsibility centre code
- Work package code
- Manpower group code
- Materials group code
- Other expenses group code
- Cost category code

*Notes*

(a) Responsibility centre executing the work package can be depicted by two-character spaces, alphabet or numerical code. This code can be prefixed or suffixed to work package code.

(b) Work package can be assigned a 3-character alpha-numerical code, as explained under work-package identification code.

(c) Resources group codes are generally used for manpower, materials and other expenses. These codes are outlined in section 17.3. Resources codes vary from project to project and can be suitably designed.

(d) Types of cost can be coded using a single alphabet. For example, in a building construction project, the cost accountant code for work package 040 of Foundation Responsibility Centre which is executed by employing a construction workers crew code (21), and needing materials listed in group code (12) and equipment group code (04), can be represented with 12-character code as FD 040 21 12 04 X, where X represents different cost categories as illustrated in Table 17.3.

## Table 17.8

**Cost Accountant Work Package Cost Codes**

| Type of Cost | Cost Category Code |
|---|---|
| (a) Direct labour costs | FD 040 21 — L |
| (b) Direct materials costs | FD 040 — 12 — M |
| (c) Direct equipment and other expenses | FD 040 — 04 E |
| (d) Indirect apportioned variable overheads | FD 040 — V |
| (e) Indirect apportioned fixed overheads | FD 040 — F |
| (f) Production cost | FD 040 21 12 04 P |
| (g) Production direct cost | FD 040 21 12 04 D |
| (h) Production indirect cost | FD 040 — I |
| (i) Workdone value | FD 040 — V |

*Notes*

1. Dash (—) represents the empty space and is added to illustrate code development.
2. Zeros can be used to sum up various heads of accounts. For example, FD 000 00 00 00 P, can represent the production cost of work in Foundation Responsibility Centre.
3. The above procedure can also be used to develop activity cost code.

### 17.4.2 Sales or Earned Value Accounting Code

The cost accountant correlated the work-package sale value with its production cost. For this purpose, he splits up each work package into work-items as listed in bill of quantities (BOQ). He generally adopts the bill of quantities sequential code to account for the sale value of each saleable item. By this way he correlates costs with sales of each work–package, as well as each item of BOQ. A typical sales accounting code structure, showing the cost accountant's work–package code and its split up into BOQ items and corresponding elemental cost/activity codes, is depicted below:

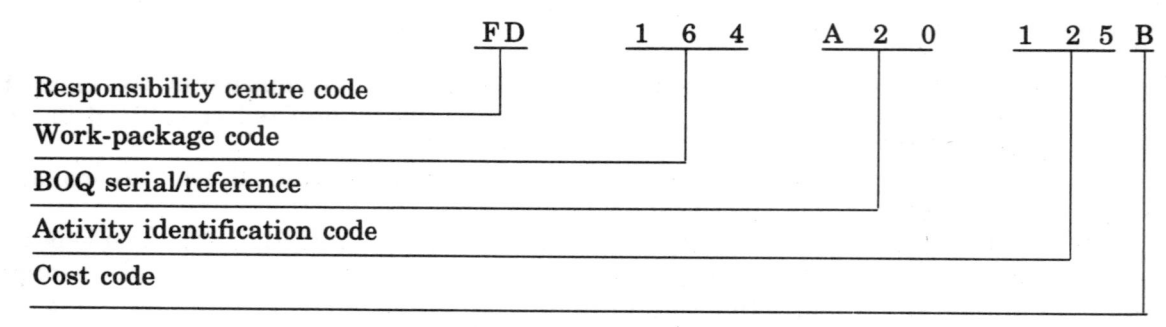

```
                    FD    164    A20    125 B
Responsibility centre code  ─┘     │     │    │
Work-package code ────────────────┘     │    │
BOQ serial/reference ───────────────────┘    │
Activity identification code ───────────────┘
Cost code
```

The above code represents the work done value of activity 125 of Work package no. 164, which is priced in BOQ serial A20.

### 17.4.3 Finance Accounting Code

Finance accounting accounts the expenses and revenue with their debtors and creditors, generally conforming to the corporate policy which is formulated in line with the statutory requirements. An integrated finance and resources accounting code which correlated with the cost accounting code can be composed as shown in Table 17.9.

Table 17.9

**Integrated Finance and Resources Accounting Code**

| | Finance Accounting Head | Code Label |
|---|---|---|
| 1. | Revenue account heads | 0001 to 0999 |
| 2. | Manpower expenses | 1000 to 1999 |
| 3. | Materials expenses | 2000 to 2999 |
| 4. | Equipment expenses | 3000 to 3999 |
| 5. | Other production expenses | 4000 to 4999 |
| 6. | General and administration cost of project | 5000 to 5999 |
| 7. | Fixed assets account | 6000 to 6999 |
| 8. | Individual debtors' accounts | 7000 to 7999 |
| 9. | Individual creditors' accounts | 8000 to 8999 |
| 10. | Balance sheets heads of accounts | 9000 to 9999 |

For example, manpower costs can be split up into the following nine resource categories— management, administrative staff, technical staff, site supervisors, equipment operators, drivers, highly skilled labour, skilled labour, and unskilled labour. Each of these manpower categories can be further split into separate account heads (up to 99) conforming to information required for costing manpower. These account heads are shown in Table 17.10. Cost and finance accounts directories are available in computerised accounting packages.

## 17.5 TECHNICAL DOCUMENTS CODE

### 17.5.1 Drawings Code

There are two approaches to handling the drawing preparations. These are the traditional unstructured approach and the structured systematic approach.

In the traditional unstructured approach, drawings are divided into two categories, i.e. general arrangement drawings and the detailed working drawings, with each showing the whole building or its parts in plan, elevation and sections. The traditional group of drawings are numbered serially in the group, as they are produced.

### Table 17.10
**Typical Two-character Manpower Group Finance Accounting Codes**

| Gp No. | Manpower Categories | All-in Total cost | Salary/ Wages | Over-time | Medical | Convey-ance | Accomo-dation | Leave Salary | Terminal Benefits | Bonus | Others |
|---|---|---|---|---|---|---|---|---|---|---|---|
| | **Direct Manpower** | | | | | | | | | | |
| 1. | Highly Skilled | 10 | 11 | 12 | 13 | 14 | 15 | 16 | 17 | 18 | 19 |
| 2. | Skilled | 20 | 21 | 22 | 23 | 24 | 25 | 26 | 27 | 28 | 29 |
| 3. | Semi-skilled | 30 | 31 | 32 | 33 | 34 | 35 | 36 | 37 | 38 | 39 |
| 4. | Helpers | 40 | 41 | 42 | 43 | 44 | 45 | 46 | 47 | 48 | 49 |
| | **Indirect Manpower** | | | | | | | | | | |
| 5. | Managers | 50 | 51 | 52 | 53 | 54 | 55 | 56 | 57 | 58 | 59 |
| 6. | Senior Engineers/ Equivalent | 60 | 61 | 62 | 63 | 64 | 65 | 66 | 67 | 68 | 69 |
| 7. | Junior Engineers/ Equivalent | 70 | 71 | 72 | 73 | 74 | 75 | 76 | 77 | 78 | 79 |
| 8. | Foreman/ Equivalent | 80 | 81 | 82 | 83 | 84 | 85 | 86 | 87 | 88 | 89 |
| 9. | Other Categories | 90 | 91 | 92 | 93 | 94 | 95 | 96 | 97 | 98 | 99 |

The structured or systematic approach divides the drawings into four categories:

**(a) Location drawings (L series)** These are unique to each project. These drawings show the position and arrangement of works by means of plan elevations and sections of sites/buildings/external works. Location drawings may show names, room numbers, window and door numbers. These drawings include references to schedules, specifications and other location drawings. These drawings are meant for use in particular project.

**(b) Assembly drawing (A series)** These show as to how the components are fixed (constructed) at the site. They show the shapes and dimensions of the components and locate them during assembly. Generally, some of the information on assembly drawings can be reused on future projects.

**(c) Components drawings (C series)** These show the shapes and sizes of unfixed components, prior to installation. Component drawings can be reused on future projects without much alteration.

**(d) Schedules (S series)** These are the matrix tables showing the repetitive elements and the references of their frequency of use with locations on drawings and references of their specifications.

In the 2000 Housing Units Project, the drawings were labelled using a five to six-character code.

An example illustrating the drawing required for the construction of a health centre with a five-character code is shown in Exhibit 17.3.

## 17.5.2 Specifications Code

Specifications describe the types characteristics and methods of installation of materials and equipment as per drawings and schedules. Project specifications are covered in the text of the contract documents and these can be generally extracted from specification standards such as Bureau of Indian Standards, other national building specifications (NBS) like British Standard Specifications.

The code used for labelling specifications such as, Construction Specifications Institute (CSI), Washington, DC, and British Standard Specifications can also provide the guidelines for developing own specification codes by the construction consultants.

**Bills-of-quantity (BOQ) code** Bills of quantity (BOQ) itemize the quantity of work and the contracted costs to complete the project. BOQ links the scope of work with drawings and specification to facilitate pricing.

Element headings and subdivision codes of the CI/SfB Table 1 can enable the systematic preparation of BOQ. This enables a direct cross reference between the work-item and specifications. There are occasions when the work under two or more elements in Table 1 such as drainage disposal services (52) and connected builders' work (16), are to be listed under one head. In such cases, the principle is to use the dominant work code (i.e. drainage disposal), and include the minor works (without code) under the dominant work-head.

### Exhibit 17.3

## Labelled List of Drawings for a Health Centre Building

| SfB Div. | Drawing Code | Drawing Title | SfB Div. | Drawing code | Drawing Title |
|---|---|---|---|---|---|
| (00) | (00)1 | Title sheet | | (—)22, 37 | Toilet rooms, plans & elevations |
| | (00)2 | SfB instructions | | (—)38 – 34 | Stairs, plans & sections |
| | (00)3 | Drawings list | | (—)44 – 999 | Not used |
| | (00)4 | Symbols and abbreviations | | (3-)1 – 100 | Not used |
| (1-) | *Substructure* | | | (3-)101 – 200 | Window types & frame types |
| | (1-)1 | General notes and abbreviations | | (3-)201 – 300 | Not used |
| | (1-)2 | Foundation and floor plan | | (3-)301 – 370 | Door types & details |
| | (1-)3 – 99 | Not used | | (3-)371 – 400 | Not used |
| | (10) – (15) | Not used | | (3-)401 | Door schedule |
| | (16)1 – 500 | Not used | | (3-)402 | Door schedule |
| | (16)501 – 510.1 | Foundation details | | (3-)403 – 500 | Not used |
| | (16)511 – 519 | Foundation details | | (3-)501 – 506 | Door details |
| | (16)520 – 999 | Not used | | (3-)507 – 518 | Door details |
| (2-) | *Primary Elements* | | | (3-)519 – 530 | Door details |
| | (2-)1 | First floor framing plan | | (3-)531 – 600 | Not used |
| | (2-)2 | Roof framing plan | | (3-)601 – 608 | Window details |
| | (2-)3 – 400 | Not used | | (3-)609 – 620 | Window details |
| | (2-)401 | Beam and slab schedules | | (3-)621 – 626 | Window details |
| | | | | (3-)627 – 628 | Window details |
| | (2-)402 – 999 | Beam and slab schedules | | (3-)639 – 999 | Not used |
| | | | | (30) | Not used |
| | (20) – (22) | Not used | | (31)1 – 21 | Exterior door numbers |
| | | | | (31)22 – 999 | Not used |
| | (24)501 | Stair details | | (32)1 – 42 | Interior door numbers |
| | (28)1 – 500 | Not used | | (3-)43 – 104 | Interior door numbers |
| | (28)517 – 516 | Superstructure details | | (3-)105 – 999 | Not used |
| | (28)517 – 523 | Superstructure details | | (33) – (37) | Not used |
| | (28)524 – 999 | Not used | | (38)1 | Screen types |
| (3-) | *Secondary Elements* | | | (38)2 – 20 | Not used |
| | (—)1 | Ground floor plan | | (38)21 – 24 | Trellis details |
| | (—)2 | First floor plan | | (38)25 – 500 | Not used |
| | (—)3, 4 | Exterior elevations | | (38)501 – 506 | Screen details |
| | (—)5, 6 | Exterior elevations | | (38)507 – 570 | Not used |
| | (—)7, 8 | Sections | | (38)571 – 576 | Trollis details |
| | (—) 9 | Roof plan | | (38)577 – 999 | Not used |
| | (—)10 | Reflected ceiling plan, ground floor | (4 – ) | *Finishes* | |
| | | | | (4-)1 – 400 | Not used |
| | (—)11 | Reflected ceiling plan, first floor | | (4-)401 | Finish schedule |
| | | | | (4-)402 | Finish schedule |
| | (—)12, 13 | Exterior wall sections | | (4-)403 | Finish schedule |
| | (—)14, 15 | Exterior wall sections | | (4-)404 | Finish schedule |
| | (—)16, 17, 18 | Exterior wall sections | | (4-)405 – 500 | Not used |
| | (—)19, 20, 21 | Exterior wall sections | | (4-)501 – 512 | Finish details |

*(Contd.)*

*(Contd.)*

| SfB Div. | Drawing code | Drawing Title | SfB Div. | Drawing code | Drawing Title |
|---|---|---|---|---|---|
| | (4-)513 – 524 | Finish details | | (57)501, (5-)501 | Details plumbing |
| | (4-)525 – 999 | Not used | | (57)501 – 4 | Control diagram—HVAC |
| | (41)1 – 10 | Exterior wall finish number | | (57)505 | Flow diagram—HVAC |
| | (41)11 – 999 | Not used | | (57)505 – 18 | Details — HVAC |
| | (42)1 – 14 | Interior wall finish numbers | | (57)519 – 24 | Details — HVAC |
| | | | | (57)525 – 29 | Details — HVAC |
| | (42)15 – 500 | Not used | (6-) | *Electrical* | |
| | (42)501 – 999 | Not used | | (6-)1 | General notes and legend |
| | (43)1 – 14 | Floor finish numbers | | | |
| | (43)15 – 999 | Not used | | (6-)101, (6-)104, | Ground floor plan auxiliary systems |
| | (44)1 – 7 | Stair finish numbers | | | |
| | (44)8 – 500 | Not used | | (6-)102 | First floor plan power & auxiliary systems |
| | (44)501 – 504 | Stair finish numbers | | | |
| | (44)505 – 999 | Not used | | (6-)103 | Clinical labs power systems |
| | (45)1 – 12 | Ceiling finish numbers | | | |
| | (45)13 – 999 | Not used | | (6-)401 to 406 | Risers and schedules |
| | (46)1 – 999 | Not used | | (6-)501 | |
| | (47)1 – 4 | Roof finish numbers | | (6-)407, (62)408 | Riser and schedules |
| | (47)5 – 500 | Not used | | (6-)501 – 514, 541 542 | Fixture details |
| | (47)501 – 507 | Roof details | | | |
| | (47)508 – 509 | Roof details | | (6-)515 – 530 | Fixture details |
| | (47)510 – 999 | Not used | | (6-)531 – 540 | Fixture details |
| | (48)1 – 500 | Not used | | (6-)543 – 554 | Fixture details |
| | (48)501 – 512 | Special equipment details | (7-) | *Fixed Equipment* | |
| | | | | (7-)1 – 44 | Clinical labs and equipment |
| | (48)513 – 530 | Special equipment details | | (7-)45 – 53 | Treatment rooms and equipment |
| | (48)531 – 999 | Not used | | (7-)54 – 60 | Dental room and equipment |
| (5-) | *Mechanical* | | | | |
| | (5-)1 | Logend—HVAC | | (7-)61 – 83 | Pharmacy and equipment |
| | (5-)51 | Legend—Plumbing | | | |
| | (5-)101 | Ground floor plan | | (7-)84 – 87 | Isolation room and equipment |
| | (5-)102 | First floor plan | | | |
| | (5-)103 – 5 | Mechanical room—Health centre | | (7-)88 | Pediatrics—Partial plan |
| | (5-)201 | Ground floor plan | | | |
| | (5-)202 | First floor plan | | (7-)89 – 96 | Pediatrics—Interior elevation |
| | (5-)203 | Clinical labs, Part plan | | | |
| | | | | (73)1 | Plumbing fixture item number floor plan ground floor |
| | (5-)401 – 4 | Schedules—HVAC | | | |
| | (5-)405, 6 | Schedules—HVAC | | | |
| | (5-)407 – 13 | Schedules—HVAC | | (73)2 | Plumbing fixture numbers floor plan first floor |
| | (5-)451 | Schedules—Plumbing | | | |
| | (5-)501 | Flow diagram | | | |
| | (5-)1, 401, 50 | Site utilities plan | | | |

BOQ contents vary with each contract, but out of all the contract documents, BOQ is referred most frequently. It is therefore, desirable to follow an elemental oriented pattern for listing BOQ items.

## 17.6 CODIFICATION EFFECTIVENESS CRITERIA

For a codification system to be effective, it should fulfil the following requirements:

(a) Comprehensive enough to interface the varying needs of all concerned.
(b) Concise enough not to get lost in voluminous elaborations.
(c) Flexible enough to accommodate new items.
(d) Significant enough to be easily recognized, like abbreviations of the letters to be codified.
(e) Logical enough that its composition follows a systematic building-up approach.
(f) Simple enough that any non-technical person can understand it.
(g) Compatible enough to be programmed for computer application.
(h) Short enough to fit into the character-space earmarked in the software.
(i) Publicized enough so as not to become a mere paper exercise.

It is not possible to have a perfect codification system for a given construction project. But a suitably designed workable codification system is indispensable. The CI/SfB and other codification systems are merely means to an end, not an end in itself. Above all, these systems should be used in a simple way appropriate to the desired purpose.

# CHAPTER 18

# Project Management Information System

Project management attempts to achieve project mission objectives within specified constraints. It needs information to make decisions. Information plays an important role in binding the building blocks of modern multidivision, multilocation and multinational organizations.

Some people use the terms data and information synonymously. But technically they are different. Data refers to raw, unsummarised and unanalysed inputs. Managers do not need loads of input data generated in the control process. It is the information extracted from the data that helps the managers in performing their functions efficiently and effectively. The following characteristics are associated with information:

(a) Information is what human mind has perceived to be of use, after analysing the data.
(b) Information reduces uncertainty about a situation thus minimising risks while making decisions.
(c) Information quality shows the degree of accuracy with which reality is represented. Incorrect information can mislead managers.
(d) Information must be reliable, comprehensive, error free, precise, clear, consistent and understandable by those who need it.
(e) Information should be available on time, when needed.
(f) Information should be sufficient to support the situation warranting decision.
(g) Information should be adequate, excess information causes overload and money, while insufficient information can frustrate the decision-maker.
(h) Information furnished to a manager should be relevant to his area of responsibility.
(i) Information should be presented to make it comprehensive by using appropriate graphs, and highlighting critical factors.

An information system is a set of interrelated parts operating together to provide appropriate feedback to the decision-makers. The greater the size and complexity of the project, the greater is the need for information. Without automated processing, it is almost impossible to isolate trends or causes of problems quickly while they still exist. Construction projects need an information system for making appropriate decisions speedily. A suitably designed and effectively implemented Project Management Information System can improve managerial efficiency and effectiveness in construction projects.

The project Management Information System (PMIS) aims at collecting economically, the right data, in the right form, through right means, at the right time, in the right place; and communicating the extracted information to the right person on time, for making decisions.

The PMIS covers wide areas. The contents of this chapter are limited to its functions, related primarily to project time, cost and resources control. It is divided under the following heads:

(a) PMIS concept
(b) PMIS framework
(c) Computerbased system applications
(d) Specifications for developing information system
(e) System acquisition
(f) Problems in Information System Management
(g) Benefits of Computerised Information System.

## 18.1 PMIS CONCEPT

### 18.1.1 PMIS Functions

Project Management Information System (PMIS) is an integrated user-machine system that provides information to support operations, management and decision making functions relating to planning and control of project objectives. Its main functions are:

1. To set standards against which to measure and compare progress and costs. These standards include project time schedules, project control budgets, material schedules, labour schedules, productivity standards, quality control specifications and construction drawings.
2. To organise efficient means of measuring, collecting, verifying and quantifying data reflecting performance with respect to time, cost, resources and quality.
3. To manage means of converting data from operations into information.
4. To report the correct and necessary information in a form which can best be interpreted by management, and at a level of detail most appropriate for the individual managers or supervisors who will be using it.
5. To provide management 'exception reports' to highlight critical factors.
6. To deliver the information on time for consideration and decision making for remedial corrective action.

*Notes:*

1. PMIS is a broad concept rather than a rigid system. Its design varies with the nature and type of the project.
2. PMIS deals with structured information that is systematically and routinely collected. It does not include informal and unstructured information like significant information that might sometimes be collected, say, at the bridge table or on a golf course.
3. PMIS provides formal information for making planning and control decisions at various levels. It does not include information to be provided to other outside agencies like government departments.
4. PMIS includes means to provide information that sub serves managers in making planning and control decisions. Such information comes by comparing the historical data and current status with the originally established database. This database is an essential component of the PMIS.

### 18.1.2 PMIS Components

PMIS components comprise hardware, software, database, procedures, operators and documents.

**Hardware** The term hardware covers all the electronics and electro-mechanical equipment used in computerized data processing systems. This equipment consists of the Central Processing Unit (CPU) and its peripherals. Peripherals are the externally connected devices of the computer such as input devices, storage disks and output devices. The hardware components of a computerized system are shown in Fig. 18.1.

**Software** Computer hardware needs proper instructions to perform specified operations. These instructions are communicated to the computer by the programmer (or user) in the form of a programme. These source programmes are written for a particular purpose in a predetermined manner using an appropriate computer language. These programmes are then translated by the computer's in-built system into object programmes or a set of instructions expressed in the machine's language. The CPU understands and processes these instructions with the operating systems to perform specified functions. All these operating procedures and instructions in a computerized system are grouped under the term 'software'. Broadly, the term software covers whatever is necessary to generate instructions with a view to operate the system's hardware as per the programmer's requirements.

A schematic diagram showing further subdivisions of the types of softwares is shown in Fig. 18.2.

**Database** The database contains all data utilized by models and application softwares. An individual set of stored data is often referred to as a file.

**Procedure** Formal operating procedures are physical components because they exist in a physical form such as a manual or an instruction booklet.

### Figure 18.1
**Hardware Components of a Computerised System**

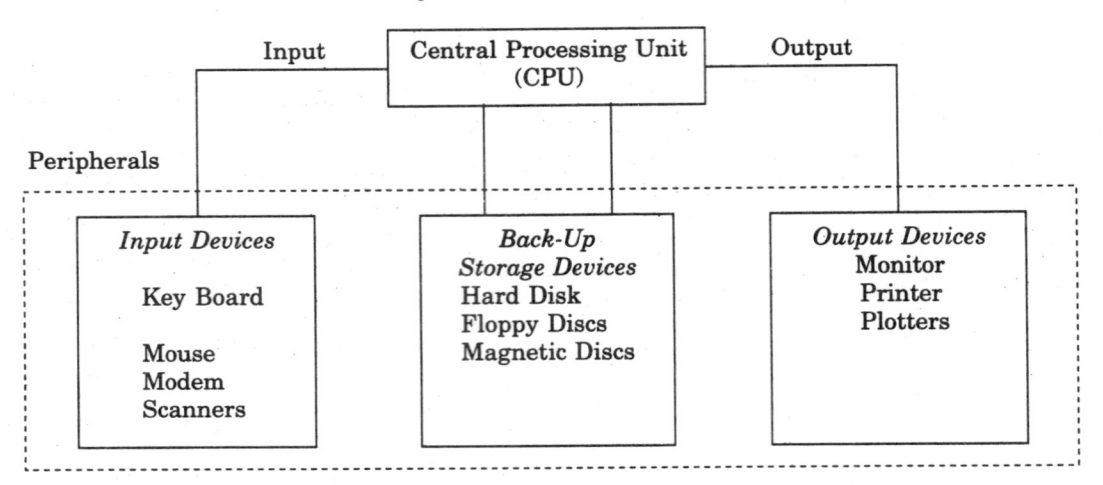

```
                    Input    Central Processing Unit    Output
                             (CPU)
Peripherals
    ┌──────────────────────────────────────────────────────────────┐
    │  Input Devices          Back-Up              Output Devices  │
    │                         Storage Devices      Monitor         │
    │  Key Board              Hard Disk            Printer         │
    │                         Floppy Discs         Plotters        │
    │  Mouse                  Magnetic Discs                       │
    │  Modem                                                       │
    │  Scanners                                                    │
    └──────────────────────────────────────────────────────────────┘
```

**Operators** These include computer operators, system analysts, programmers, data preparation personnel, information system management, data administrators, etc.

**Documents** These consist of processing transactions, master files, reports, process enquiries, output, etc.

### 18.1.3 The Structure of PMIS

PMIS can be structured according to information needs of managerial planning and control activities, or these can be based on organizational functions or a combination of both.

The areas of managerial planning and control activities can be divided into three categories, i.e. strategic planning, management control and operational control. Strategic planning is the process of deciding the long term plan for achieving the project objectives. Management control is the process by which managers ensure that the assigned resources are used efficiently and effectively to accomplish the assigned targets. Operational control aims to minimize wastage in resource utilization. The PMIS structure for managing planning and control activities resembles a pyramid. The information System aims to provide appropriate information at various levels of management for managing the assigned functions. The bottom level contains information pertaining to transaction processing at the operation level, like the activity progress status or its resource productivity. The second level consists of information necessary at the responsibility centre/managerial level for operational planning, decision making and controlling assigned objectives. The top level consists of information necessary to support strategic planning at the project/corporate level (top management level). It may be noted that information generated at the lower level is processed to derive information for the next higher level. Managerial planning and controlling activity levels are depicted in Fig. 18.3.

## Figure 18.2
### Software Classification

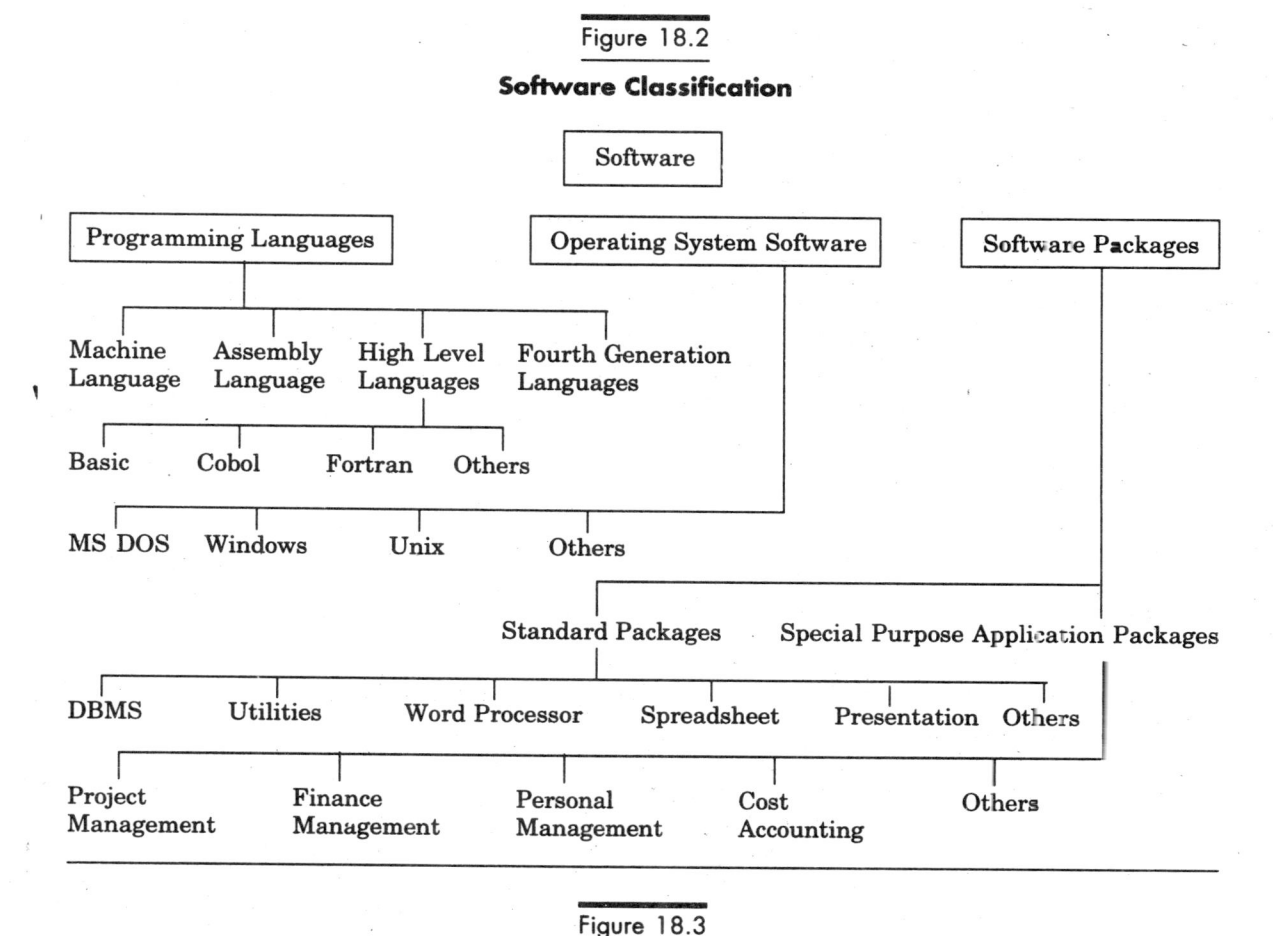

```
                              Software
          ┌──────────────────────┼──────────────────────┐
Programming Languages    Operating System Software   Software Packages
```

- Programming Languages:
  - Machine Language
  - Assembly Language
  - High Level Languages
  - Fourth Generation Languages

- High Level Languages: Basic, Cobol, Fortran, Others

- Operating System Software: MS DOS, Windows, Unix, Others

- Software Packages:
  - Standard Packages
  - Special Purpose Application Packages

- Standard Packages: DBMS, Utilities, Word Processor, Spreadsheet, Presentation, Others

- Special Purpose Application Packages: Project Management, Finance Management, Personal Management, Cost Accounting, Others

## Figure 18.3
### PMIS Control Information Pyramid

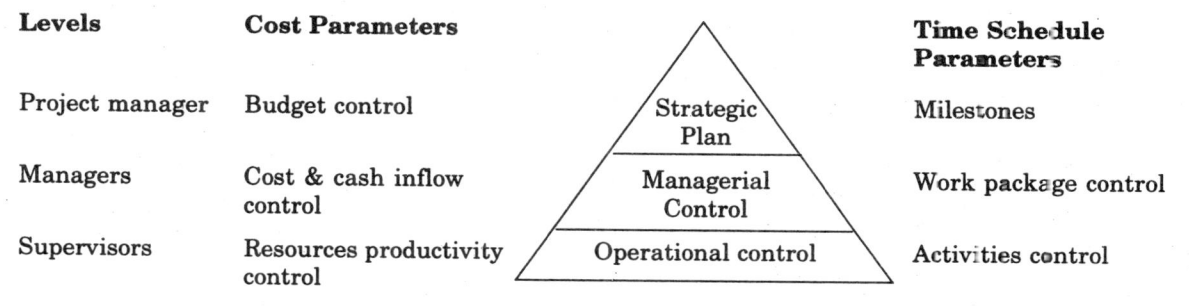

| Levels | Cost Parameters | | Time Schedule Parameters |
|---|---|---|---|
| Project manager | Budget control | Strategic Plan | Milestones |
| Managers | Cost & cash inflow control | Managerial Control | Work package control |
| Supervisors | Resources productivity control | Operational control | Activities control |

PMIS can also be viewed as a group of information sub-systems, one for each major organisational function. These sub-systems interact with each other through information channels (see Exhibit 13.1).

## 18.2 PMIS FRAMEWORK

The information system supporting project management can be broadly categorised into five subsystems. These are:

(a) Data processing system for operation and managerial levels.
(b) Decision support system for managerial and top level.
(c) Office information system for office and general purpose applications.
(d) Artificial intelligence based system for top level.
(e) Communication system for coordination at all levels.

The above classification is not rigid and these subsystems blend together in providing information. Further, a system may be composed of any one or a combination of the above five subsystems.

### 18.2.1 Data Processing System

Using computers, the data processing system, speedily performs the three main accounting functions—book-keeping, issuance and control reports.

(a) Book keeping including gathering and recording data.
(b) Issuance of routine documents such as invoices, pay cheques and reminders. The process includes sorting, comparing, storing, retrieving, displaying and printing.
(c) Control reports of operations are by-products of routine transactions. Control reports provide pre-formatted type of information, generally used for structured types of decisions. Its focus is to supply relevant information to decision-makers on pre-formatted hard copy schedule reports, exception reports and on-demand reports. It also retrieves information as and when required.

Data control process inputs are the data captured from transactions in responsibility centres. The input data is either processed periodically as a batch or is updated on real-time occurrence. Data is stored in files and control report is given to the appropriate person. It helps in running the project smoothly by automatically processing voluminous data. Its output is in the form of documents such as pay cheques, invoices, periodic reports, reminders and the management control reports.

For example, in the 2000 Housing Units Project, typical reports initiated by responsibility centres with the purpose of each report are shown in Exhibit 13.2. Further, Project Control Methodology covered in Chapter 13 is similar to data processing system.

### 18.2.2 Decision Support Systems

Decision Support System presents information in such a way that managers can conveniently use to take structured decisions. With the rapid advancements in interactive technology, microcomputing, and menu driven application software, the information technology has now provided complete solutions to the managerial decision-making needs in semi-structured situations. The Decision Support Systems provide a support to the managers to extend their decision-making capabilities.

```
┌──────────┐                    ┌────────────┐
│ DATABASE │                    │ MODEL BASE │
└────┬─────┘                    └──────┬─────┘
     │    ┌──────────────────────┐     │
     └────┤    USER INTERFACE    ├─────┘
          └──────────────────────┘
```

Elements of a DSS

The major elements of a DSS are database model, problem model base and user dialogue system. For example, take the case of appraisal of a project feasibility. The decision to accept or reject depends upon the return on investment, which in turn is related to inflow and outflow of cash. The project investment database model of this project can be build using standard spreadsheet software. However, cash flow model base will depend upon several parameters, some of which may be uncertain. A decision maker (user) in such uncertain situations, using sensitivity analysis can predict range of cash flow forecasts, to develop the corresponding several rates of return options.

The DSS considers all the important aspects of a situation systematically and provides an orderly means of recording and presenting information to the decision-maker.

The Executive Support System (ESS) is similar to DSS and is designed to meet the strategic planning information needs of top executives in the organization hierarchy.

## 18.2.3 Office Information Systems

The primary purpose of office information systems is to facilitate speedy communication within the project and between project office and corporate office. An office information system includes many types of computer-based technologies. These include office documentation management system, message handling system, teleconferencing system and office support system. The technologies used in these systems are tabulated below:

*Document management systems:*   Word processing
                                 Desktop publishing
                                 Photocopiers
                                 Projectors
                                 Archival storage
*Message transmission system:*   Electronic mail
                                 Telephones
                                 Facsimile
*Teleconferencing system:*       Audio conferencing
                                 Video conferencing
                                 Computer conferencing

*Office support system:*      Desktop organizer
　　　　　　　　　　　　　　Computer-aided design
　　　　　　　　　　　　　　Presentation graphics
　　　　　　　　　　　　　　Close circuit television

### 18.2.4 Artificial Intelligence Systems

The capability of a computerised system to provide information that reflects human-like intelligence is commonly referred to as artificial intelligence. The five main areas of application of artificial intelligence systems are in expert systems, natural language interface, vision systems, robotics and neural network. Expert systems software imitates the reasoning process of experts and provides decision makers with advice on similar problem solving. Natural language systems use computers to communicate with users in different languages. Vision systems use computers to perform tasks, like updating 3-dimensional images, which can only be done through the use of human eye. Robot-based computerised systems use devices that mimic the motor activity of human beings. Neural networks are like a knowledge-based computer system that emulates the human brain for activities such as detection of fraud, risks and trends. Artificial intelligence systems are undergoing extensive research.

Expert systems do find some application at project sites. These provide decision support to inexperienced managers through structured problem solving approach. The Expert System captures the possible solutions to a problem from experts and offers these as advice when referred to.

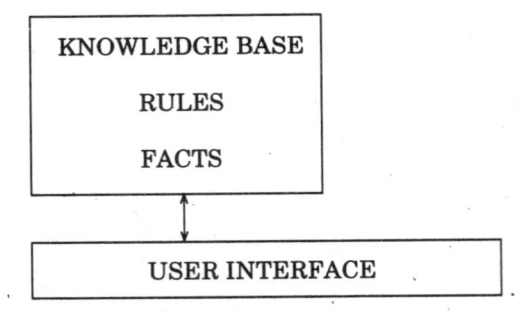

```
          ┌─────────────────┐
          │  KNOWLEDGE BASE │
          │      RULES      │
          │      FACTS      │
          └────────┬────────┘
                   ↕
          ┌─────────────────┐
          │  USER INTERFACE │
          └─────────────────┘
```

Elements of an Expert System

The 'knowledge engineers' capture the knowledge from experts to create a knowledge base and build inference mechanism, which leads from the problem input parameters to the solutions using the existing knowledge base. These systems not only give solutions but can also like an expert give reasoning for the solution.

### 18.2.5 Information Communication

Telecommunications and information technology is fast reducing communication barriers. Managers can have relatively faster access to the databases, whether centralised or distributed. Not only is information access faster, but everyone can obtain up-to-date data, and post their own inputs for others to use without delay.

Information can be shared among various groups working at the same geographical site by LAN (Local Area Network). The data may be maintained on a central computer (Server) and accessed and updated by users from different terminals (Clients). Terminals at different sites may be connected to the LAN through modems and communication lines. This makes the information accessible and easy-to-update from remote locations.

LAN's at different sites may be connected with each other through WAN's (Wide Area Networks). In such systems, part of the information may be held centrally and part may be handled only at the LAN at site. Internet, a large area network with open distribution system now offers facilities for disseminating information over geographically dispersed areas. It is basically being used for the following:

- Electronic mail
- Group discussions—Users networking
- Long distance programming and data access
- File transfers

## 18.3 INFORMATION SYSTEM COMPUTERISATION

Computers prove an invaluable tool for managing construction projects. Computer applications in project management include project planning and control management, computer aided design and drafting, estimating and costing, resources management, finance and cost accounting, word processing and office operations management. It can assist project management in meeting their informational and functional requirements. The main requirements at project site are shown in Table 18.1.

In order to meet the informational and functional requirements, the first step is to decide whether to make or buy application software.

Making in-house software involves conducting feasibility studies, preparation of flow diagrams, designing of system, installing the system and implementing it. All this is a time consuming process.

However at the project site, a microcomputer network with a selected application package can serve the needs of the project management.

Off-the-shelf pre-packaged application packages are designed to meet specific requirements. Such packages are known for quality. They can be installed rapidly and carry low risks. They are reasonably priced when compared to the cost of in-house program development. On the other hand, application software may not meet all the needs of project management.

Project management application software packages contain the programme written for specific purposes, i.e. Planning, scheduling, and controlling of project time, resources and costs. In most of the softwares, the activation of the package for creating the project plan and controlling the preformance can proceed in a sequential manner using software menus and data sheets. The computerised system based on suitably matching application software can aid in creating projects and reporting information. The facilities available and operating features of a typical project management package are outlined in the following section.

## Table 18.1
## Project Management Functional Areas: Typical Software Requirements

| Main Functions | Some Examples of Software Needs |
|---|---|
| **1. Planning Manager**<br>• Formulating Planning Systems<br>• Making Project Plan<br>• Monitoring Scheduled Progress<br>• Mobilising and Controlling Resources<br>• Controlling Costs and Sales.<br>• Establishing Planning Database<br>• Communicating Preformance.<br>• Maintaining Information Centre. | *Project Management Software for*<br>Creating Project Plan<br>Updated Networks<br>Time Schedule Report<br>Cost Control Reports<br>Resources Status and Trend Forecasting<br>What-if Analysis<br>Materials Wastage Reports<br>Labour Productivity Reports<br>Equipment Utilisation Report |
| **2. Technical Manager**<br>• Design and Drawing Preparation<br>• Testing Building Materials for Suitability<br>• Progressing Designs and Drawings Approvals<br>• Writing Construction Methods Statements<br>• Controlling Quality of Work<br>• Co-ordinating with External Agencies<br>• Managing Materials Testing Laboratory | *Computer-Aided Design and Drafting*<br>General Purpose Packages for<br>Data Management<br>Office Management<br>Special Purpose Construction Specification Software |
| **3. Cost and Finance Manager(s)**<br>• Accounting Direct Costs<br>• Establishing Standard Costs<br>• Monitoring Cost Variance<br>• Maintaining Project Cost Status<br>• Minimising Resources Wastage<br>• Managing Funds<br>• Compiling Financial Statements | *Cost and Finance Management Software for*<br>Accounts Payable<br>Accounts Receivable<br>Budgetary Control<br>Fixed Asset Control<br>Financial Statements<br>Cost Control Software |
| **4. Contract Manager**<br>• Estimating Work Quantities and Materials<br>• Billing Contract Running Payments<br>• Maintaining Contract Cost Status<br>• Dealing with Contract Disputes and Claims<br>• Accounting Extra Works/Change Orders<br>• Administering Contract | *Special Purpose Quantity Surveying Software for*<br>Billing<br>Cost Tracking<br>Quantity Estimation<br>Standard Rate Schedule<br>General Purpose Software |
| **5. Materials Manager**<br>• Planning and Procuring Materials<br>• Inventory Control<br>• Storekeeping and Warehousing<br>• Handling and Transportation<br>• Codification and Standardisation<br>• Disposal of Surpluses | *Materials Management Packages for*<br>Purchase Management<br>Inventory Management<br>Warehousing<br>Materials Flow Monitoring<br>Materials Budgetary Control |
| **6. Plant and Equipment Manager**<br>• Identifying Equipment Requirements<br>• Procuring Equipment<br>• Deploying Equipment Efficiently and Effectively<br>• Controlling Equipment Costs<br>• Maintaining Equipment<br>• Insuring and Operator Safety | *Equipment Master File*<br>Special Purpose Equipment Management Packages<br>General Purpose Office Management Software |
| **7. Personnel Manager**<br>• Exploring Local Manpower Availability<br>• Formulating Pay Scales and Service Conditions<br>• Recruiting and Inducting Manpower<br>• Training and Development<br>• Welfare, Health, Morale and Motivation<br>• Safety and Security<br>• Maintaing Harmonious Industrial Relations | *Personnel Management Software for*<br>Attendance Reporting<br>Manpower Status and Trend Forecast<br>Payroll<br>Manpower Budget<br>Applicant Tracking<br>Construction Safety Management<br>General Purpose Office Management Software |

## 18.3.1 Plan Creating Facilities

After the necessary inputs, the computer can print the following typical graphs:

(a) Networks.
(b) Activity schedule matrix.
(c) Project bar chart schedule.
(d) Time-scaled network.
(e) Histogram of resources category-wise.
(f) Forecast of inputs and outputs.

## 18.3.2 Project Control Facilities

By feeding project performance data and executing appropriate commands, computers provide the solution in no time. This easy-to-read, on-the-spot information can be seen on the screen or printed as hard copies. Typical performance reports generated by computers include the following:

(a) *Time control report*

- Actual vs planned bar chart schedules and time analysed network reports.
- Activity status reports with early and scheduled starting and completion dates, for current and balance activities and floats.
- Activity reports generated by departments, resources, costs, and sales.

(b) *Resource control reports*

- Actual vs planned resources by activity, work package, resources (men, materials and equipment), departments.
- Resource productivity analyses report by activities, work packages, resources, departments.
- Histograms of resources and forecasts for planned, actual and balance work.
- Optimum schedules of resources by varying resource availability patterns.

(c) *Cost control reports*

- Actual and budgeted cost variances by activity, work item, work package, resources, department.
- Cost performance analyses by activity, work package, resources, departments.
- Sales value of work done and balance work by activity, work package, bill-of-quantities, departments.
- Planned vs actual costs and sales forecasts and future trends.
- Monthly progress payment invoices.

(d) *Project data records*

- Men, materials and equipment status report.
- Financial status reports.
- Project costs status reports.

### 18.3.3 Salient Operating Facilities

The latest project management packages have most of the following operating features:

- They can handle practically unlimited activities with activity associated resources, costs and sales value.
- They have an in-built graphic capability to generate all types of networks, bar charts, various types of schedules, resources and cost profiles, and 'S' curve cumulative resource forecasts.
- They can add activities, define relationships and modify activity data, and update the work progress by clicking with the mouse.
- The allow a user to add, modify and delete activities and resources on screen.
- They allow interface with other application packages like Lotus 1-2-3, Auto CAD, dBASE, Windows and so on.
- They provide multiuser operating facilities that enable a number of users to work at the same time.
- They are user friendly and their output can be reviewed on the screen prior to printing.
- They are easy to learn and operate as they are menu driven and do not need any specialized training or knowledge.
- They are not very expensive—a reasonable package generally costs less than US $5000.

### 18.3.4 Criteria to Computerize Planning and Control System

With all its beneficial characteristics, the first step in developing a computerized system is to examine its necessity. British Standards BS 6046: Part 3: 1992 stipulate certain guidelines to determine the choice between manual and computer application in network based projects. In short, the guidelines affecting the choice between manual and computer based project management system are as under:

**Network size and complexity** Simple projects containing less than 200 activities, unless required to be frequently monitored, do not need a computerized system. Use of computerised system is desirable for projects having more than 200 activities.

**Duration time-unit of activities** Generally, activities having a duration time unit greater than 'weeks' can be handled manually unless the project life span is spread over a number of years, say more than three years.

**Frequency of updating** In case of complex projects, considering that each work package duration is normally not less than 1% of total project duration and the projects are to be monitored weekly or where the information is required continuously at random, then the computerization of project management system is advisable. In particular projects, which are monitored quarterly (or rarely) need not be computerized.

**Other considerations** It is advisable to consider computerization of the planning and control systems of complex projects if:

(a) Progress is to be frequently updated (at least once a week) to analyze the what-if and what-then implications.
(b) Management frequently requires updated information at random as well as on a continuous basis.
(c) Resources need frequent analyses to determine their mobilization status, productivity, and costs.
(d) Outputs are to be frequently printed to furnish information to the client and concerned persons.
(e) Reliable system computerization facilities are available at a reasonable cost.

## ❏ 18.4 USER'S SYSTEM SPECIFICATIONS DEVELOPMENT

After installing the system, it is not uncommon for the user to realize that the system purchased does not fully meet the requirements. There can be many reasons for it, but such situations can be minimized if the users communicate to the system dealer or the potential supplier what they want.

The system specifications outline the user's or the purchaser's requirements. This can be expressed in the form of written system specifications. These enable the system houses to apply their mind for developing the solution, and prepare their price quotations, accordingly. It is not necessary to prepare elaborate system requirements for a small project personal computer network. But for a major project, the salient points to be included in the requirement oriented system specification are as under:

(a) Nature of the functional areas to be computerized or, in other words, what the client wants the system to do.
(b) Volume of data involved in outline for each function. If could be stated in terms of A3 or A4 size pages of data to be stored in the project life-cycle, and the number of pages of data to be processed at any peak time and average per day.
(c) Desired methods for recording data and reporting information for each functional area. These methods should bring out the specimen input formats, desired output with format and frequency of reporting and possibly data processing flow diagram depicting the interrelationship among the functional areas, and highlighting the common data such as work-package with associated resources.
(d) Available data processing equipment, including hardware, software, telex, fax, word processor, photocopier, etc.

(e) Future system development plans as, at a later date, it is difficult to mix and match hardware components and software packages from different sources. However, in a construction project, generally all the system equipment is installed at one time and rarely expansion is undertaken with in the same project.
(f) Number of persons going to utilize the facility. How often, for how long, and for the same job or different areas. What are their training needs?
(g) The staff earmarked for operating the system with their functional responsibility, educational qualifications, professional attainments and data processing experience.
(h) Outline architectural, utility services and furniture layout drawings of the accommodation earmarked.
(i) The completion period from the date of placing order.

It is important that the system specifications should be developed on a requirement basis as the purpose of specifications is to tell the system supplier the user's needs. Specifications where possible should avoid suggesting details of hardware and software. This should be left to the system houses to propose along with their priced proposals. But in case the user has a system which he wants to improve, he must give full details of the existing system in the specifications to the potential supplier. Detailed guidelines for software requirements, and specifications are given in many standard publications including The Institute of Electrical and Electronics Engineers (USA, New York).

## 18.5 ACQUIRING A SYSTEM

The procurement process involves choosing software, matching the hardware, analyzing training needs, evaluating system costs and finalizing the supplier.

### 18.5.1 Choosing Software

One may choose to procure an existing software package available in the market with or without the option of having it customized; or have it tailor-made, i.e. developed as per specific requirements.

Software packages available 'off-shelf' may not cater to 100% of the job requirements. They often require the user to adapt and make compromises on their needs. They however, have an advantage of the shortest lead time, are better tested and developed to be competitive both technically and commercially.

Packages developed exclusively for a specific requirement may meet 100% of the job requirements, with their user interfaces, outputs and presentation, tailored to the exact needs of the user. However, they have a long lead time and may continue to throw up problems for a considerable period of time. There may be software companies who have developed the packages and offer it with customisation to the specific needs of the user. This is the best compromise between the above two options, but may not always be available easily.

**Package preview** Software selection is a time-consuming process, and each software package may take about half a day's time to go through. The aim of previewing is to shortlist two to three out of available software packages which come close to the user's specifications. This shortlist is prepared by reading through the software specifications.

**Operations evaluation** The shortlisted software packages are evaluated for their operational features to find the best fit. This evaluation is based on a critical examination of the following essential features; other features mentioned by the supplier can be considered on merits.

(a) How far it meets the user's specifications, and in particular what it cannot do? A package may perform 90% of the job requirements but it is essential to analyze as to what are the 10% exceptions? How can these be overcome?
(b) Can it handle the size of files required and can it interface these files with other application packages.
(c) Which operating system is needed to operate the package and how much internal memory does it need for its operations?
(d) Are there any user's references, and if so, what is their opinion about the package.
(e) Is software package manufacturer a reputed firm? If so, how many packages have been sold by the firm? What was the original date of marketing and how many revisions has it undergone since its issue?
(f) What is the speed of operations? The speed demonstrated by the supplier is likely to be misleading as the system in this case will be operating under ideal conditions. Verify speed from actual users or by operating the system on realistic files data.
(g) Check the machine's manuals for adequacy. These should be comprehensive and easy to read. Manuals are indispensable as they cover much more than what appears to be the operational capability of the system at first review.
(h) Examine the file access and security system offered by the package.

**Demonstrations** At the selection stage, the demonstration of the package, preferably using the proposed hardware, can give a fair idea of the working of the system and its capabilities. These demonstrations can be arranged by the supplier at his location or at a place where the software has already been installed by the supplier.

### 18.5.2 Matching Hardware with Software

Softwares are the products of highly skilled brains. They undergo constant improvements at a pace faster than the development of micro-electronic technology of the computers. The choice of hardware is invariable tied up with software. It is the software that dictates the type of hardware required. For example, a package will not work if the basic software parameters such as language operating system, internal memory or file handling capacity, do not fit.

**Scrutinizing processor capability** The computer processor contains a number of specially designed chips to perform various jobs. These include control chips, memory chips, operating system chips, and other software chips. These chips determine the processors ability, specially that of word-length processing, speed of input-output operations and size of internal memory. The processor's performance capability for a particular application depends upon the balanced combination of various types and sizes of chips.

The international chips manufacturing firms distinguish their products by assigning certain codes to describe different chips, for example 'Intel' microprocessor chips are labelled as 80386, 80486 and pentium.

The control processor generally has a single chip. Additional support chips or co-processors are incorporated to manage memory, to run different operating systems, and to perform a particular operation like the maths co-processor. The speed of the processor is measured in MHz, i.e. millions of cycles per second. Processor chips have different speeds. The higher the speed the quicker is the performance.

Memory chips provide the RAM and ROM memories. It is the software package that will specify RAM and ROM memory needs, but generally in-built RAM memory of 640 KB and extended to 16MB is considered adequate for most of the project management packages. ROM memory may also contain sets of starting-up routines and operating systems, interpreters and assemblers.

**Video display units (VDU)** The selection of displaying units should take into consideration their size, colour, character design, and clarity:

(a) *Size* It depends upon the viewing distance. A screen size of 12 inches is preferred for desk-tops and 5 inches is generally used for portable computers.

(b) *Colour* Multi-coloured facilities and combinations are available for screen displays. These colours can be adjusted to suit the preferences of the user.

(c) *Character design for normal viewing distance* The characters should be at least 3 mm high and the following should be clearly distinguishable between alphabets and digits:

| Alphabets | Digits |
|---|---|
| i, I | 1 |
| o, O, Q | 0 |
| B | 8 |
| S | 5 |
| Z | 2 |

(d) *Clarity* The clarity of the picture depends upon the density of tiny dots called pixels or picture elements on the screen. Each character requires at least a block of pixels containing 5 wide and 7 deep. 7 by 9 is a preferred arrangement. Graphics need 9 by 11 arrangement. Quality of display on screen is generally related to the number of pixels present on the screen area. A common pattern is 500 × 500. Graphics need 2000 × 2000 array of pixels.

**Keyboards** These are similar to typewriter keyboards but have additional keys to cater for special functions such as shifting data, cursor shift, etc.

**Input/output (I/Os) ports** I/O ports provide plug-in facilities to connect various peripherals. The number of ports required should be at least one more than the total number of peripherals so as to avoid the use of multi-pin plugs. Additional ports may be considered for future expansion, if contemplated.

**Options** All systems do provide a range of options. These options include:

(a) Provision for various drives of hard and floppy disks.
(b) Provision of expansion slots for future expansion.
(c) Provision for extra memory, modem, mouse, network interface, etc.

**Power requirement** Generally, the local power supply voltage is 110/120 V or 220/240 V and its frequency is either 60 HZ or 50 HZ. It is imperative that the system should be compatible with the local power supply and its tolerance preferably being within ± 10 per cent.

**Back-up storage capacity** Selection of back-up storage equipment will depend upon the quantity to be stored, which in turn is dictated by the software package equipments and the number and size of files.

The file storage requirement will depend upon the nature of information, i.e. text or picture. To quote an example, A4 size paper having 80 characters in a line and 60 lines per page, can hold theoretically 4.8 KB of text characters but in actual practice after leaving space for margin and space for paragraphs, the requirement for a text page may vary from 2 KB to 3 KB. Similarly, the storage requirement of A4 size page picture is around 35 KB.

**Choosing printers** The selection of a printer is influenced by the quality of print, quantity of printed output and the speed of printing. This is explained below:

(a) *Quality of print* Laser and ink-jet printers give better quality, but matrix printers need less maintenance.

(b) *Quantity of daily printed output* The quantity to be printed per day can be estimated in a manner similar to that of the storage space calculation at the rate of 3 KB per A4 page.

(c) *Speed of printing*

$$\text{Speed} = \frac{\text{Quantity of daily printing}}{\text{Time available for printing}}$$

In the above equation, the critical factor is the time available for printing. Generally, printers work for 20 to 40% of the daily working hours, and during the remaining time they are idle because processors are employed on work other than printing, specially, when no spool or buffer facilities are available.

(d) *Nature of printing work*

   (i) For graphic work, the choice of printers will have to be restricted to those which can use graphic software.
   (ii) Special stationary and typescript requirements do slow down printing.
   (iii) Some printers may not be able to print multiple copies.

The ultimate choice of a printer, after evaluating the above factors, is a matter of preference by the user.

### 18.5.3 Training

Computer suppliers may claim that their system is easy to use by saying that it is fully menu driven and it provides on-line helps. It is that an intelligent person, with technical background and some knowledge of computer functioning, may be able to start and run a microcomputer with about one hour's briefing, but this is not enough. Both the user and the computer staff responsible for routine operations need orientation and training before they are assigned on specific computing tasks. These tasks vary with the person using the computer and their training needs will differ accordingly. For example, a computer operator should be able to use software, operate and maintain hardware, and rectify minor operation faults, but he need not be trained in the repair of computers. Similarly, a user manager's training may be limited to equipment and software familiarization, retrieval information and report generation. Although computer suppliers do provide easily understandable manuals and instructional materials for training computer staff, what is needed is a job oriented training.

Some of the main criteria for evaluating the supplier's training support are summarized below:

(a) What opportunities for training do the suppliers offer?
(b) Are the suppliers' training aids and facilities adequate to meet the demands of Job-oriented training?
(c) For how long have the suppliers been conducting training and are there supporting references available?
(d) Are the suppliers' instructors experienced practitioners?

### 18.5.4 Systems Costs

Systems costs are analyzed by comparing the offers received from the systems suppliers. In general, the system costs can be grouped into equipment purchase costs, installation costs, operating costs, and computer furnishing and accommodation costs. Costing of the system to determine the hourly rental rate is similar to the calculation of equipment owning and operating costs, covered in Chapter 10.

**Equipment costs** These are one-time costs and include costs of purchasing hardware, software and the media. Suppliers quote prices separately for each of these items. In some cases the supplier's price may include mark-up to cater for demonstration, training, and other support facilities. In addition, for a major project, it may also cover the consultancy fee for analysis and design for the multi-tasks, multi-network computerized system. It is difficult to compare the quoted prices on a one-to-one basis as is done for commodity purchases, because the success of the system, to a great extent, depends upon the supplier's support. A reputed supplier is always better than the unknown starter and is far better than the clearance sale supplier who is trying to close his business. Further, one should avoid purchasing second-hand equipment as the computer technology is accelerating rapidly. Apart from many other disadvantages, the second-hand equipment may need additional peripherals, software facilities, and maintenance support.

**Installation costs** These are the one-time costs of setting up the equipment at the site. It includes on-site utility connections, recording and storage of past data, and training of the staff.

**Operating costs** These are the recurring costs of operating the system. This includes the equipment maintenance and repair costs, software updating or rental costs, storage media costs, utility services costs, insurance costs, stationery costs, and operator's cost. All these costs will vary from case to case and place to place. However, as a rule-of-thumb maintenance costs can be taken as 10 to 15% of the equipment purchase cost, and the overall annual running costs (less manpower costs) may fall in the range of 25 to 40% of the equipment costs.

**Computer room costs** These costs may include the following:

(a) Accommodation with renovations to meet system requirements.
(b) Laying cables and connections for power supply.
(c) Computer office equipment and special furniture such as disk storage cabinet, etc.
(d) Air-conditioning.

### 18.5.5 Selecting the Supplier

While purchasing the system, it is important to examine the track record of the supplier so as to evaluate his competence and support capabilities. The track record can be assessed by knowing about the organizations where the supplier has installed such systems, finding out how these systems have functioned, and ascertaining what is his reputation with his old customers. In particular, answers to the following questions can give a fair idea about the supplier:

(a) Does the supplier provide support for the software? Has he got the expertise to modify the software at a later date?
(b) Does the supplier have adequate technical staff and facilities for installing the system and training the users?

(c) Is he prepared to conclude a support contract?
(d) Can the supplier give references where he has installed similar systems?
(e) How has the supplier responded to the specifications given to him? Has he covered all the requirements? Is he willing to set up a demonstration?

## ❏ 18.6 PROBLEMS IN INFORMATION SYSTEM MANAGEMENT

### 18.6.1 System Organization Problems

The major information problems existing in most of the organizations can be classified as:

1. **Managers do not know what they need**  The information needs of managers varies with the level at which they are operating and the function within which they are operating. Very few organizations have made a conscious and deliberate effort to identify specific information needs of various managerial positions. Generally, there exists a gap between what information a manager thinks should be made available to him and what is actually made available to him. Consequently, there is a tendency to store every element of data, in many media like photocopy, hard copy, floppies, magnetic tapes, compact disks, optical disks, hard disks and microfilms. Unless properly controlled, acquiring and storing large amount of information is a costly process.

2. **Information is not easily retrieveable**  Some projects do generate useful and necessary data, but often in a form or location that makes it uneconomical and unfeasible to retrieve. This might lead to a wastage of effort, if such information cannot be accessed. Information can go out of control when it is held in different media, using different softwares. These could be from different sources and of various levels, and languages, and stored at different locations.

3. **Information can get misinterpreted**  This problem arises due to different sources within the organization or due to excessive pressure on the source to collect information.
   It leads to poor and ineffective decision making, specially when information is not read in the proper context. Misunderstood information can have a negative effect.

4. **Information 'accumulation' is common**  This is caused due to a system having grown with the growth and diversification of the organization. At times, people tend to make extra copies just in case it gets lost. This duplication adds to the costs of producing, filing, storing and retrieving information. The sheer volume of data makes it impossible to be consistently accurate and reliable. Overloads cause major communication problems.

5. **Some people hide information**  They are reluctant to share it with others so as to remain indispensable.

6. **There is a resistance to change**  Some people do not easily shed old methods and keep face with fast-changing new technology. Some are reluctant to witness the obsolescence of their skills.

7. **Information delays are common**  There is a time-lag between the occurrence of an event and the information reaching the concerned person. At times, data is not moved and processed fast enough to allow enough time for managers to react quickly and in time. Several times, data are no longer of any value when they are made available to them.

8. **Information systems are of little use to construction man**  In practice the paper work at site level does not change. Further, the site managers manage construction by walking around rather than siting with a desktop. PMIS and the PC's may help the functional managers but do not prove very useful for the construction managers who can see most of the relevant information on ground with naked eye. This may lead to an unnecessary conflict between the site mannager and the MIS personnel.

9. **Information systems cost money**  But most of the time, the installed equipment is not fully utilised. Moreover, with the rapid advancement in information technology, money spent on equipment which soon becomes obsolete is often questioned.

If projects are not to be bogged down by these problems, it is imperative that the project management make a deliberate and conscious effort to manage their information by setting up an effective PMIS.

### 18.6.2 System Acquisition and Implemention Problems

The procurement and installation of a computerised system is not trouble free. The system procurement poses problems and the installation too has teething troubles. However, the following guidelines can minimise these difficulties:

- Acquiring a computerised system needs extra effort and is a time-consuming process. It should be treated as a project in itself.
- People do not know what they want until they get what they do not want. It is therefore necessary that the functional requirements of the computerised system be crystallized at the feasibility stage.
- Success of the system depends upon the suppliers' support. Therefore, the supplier should be chosen after a thorough scrutiny.
- Scrutinize the system carefully before purchasing. The end results should not be that the patient died but the operation was successful.
- The initial 90 per cent of system-installation costs are incurred within 10 per cent of the time of installation but it is the last 10 per cent of installation and commissioning that becomes tricky and time consuming.
- Do not give up if the system does not function properly, in the beginning. If anything can go wrong, it will. There will be problems and a few problems are not the same thing as failure.
- Job training on the installed system will instill confidence. Detailed study of manuals may reveal the extra facilities, which the trainee may not have thought of earlier.

- Test the system thoroughly after installation by running it with known inputs and outputs. It will lead confidence in the machine and may reveal hither-to-unnoticed exceptions in the system.
- Keep all concerned informed about the progress of computerization at regular intervals, before, during and after the system is installed. This will save your time in answering frequent enquiries from people.

### 18.6.3 Management Role in Problem Solving

1. Management should treat information as a resource requiring proper management, like money, manpower, machinery and materials.
2. Management should appoint a monitor for information system.
3. The monitor should be assigned specific responsibility for planning and coordination, if not direct control, of the use of the following:

    - Information handling skills
    - Information technology
    - Information sources and stores.

4. All expenditure on information systems and resources should be centrally coordinated.
5. The monitor should keep abreast with new developments that can contribute to the better management of information resources.

## ❏ 18.7 BENEFITS OF COMPUTERISED INFORMATION SYSTEM

Salient features of the project management package, covered above, highlight many benefits of computerized project planning and control system. In particular, the computerized system indicates the plan-making sequence, removes data voids, clearly defines the tasks involved, speedily works out answers to the resource constraints, and generates implications of their changes. The computer possesses the ability to analyze large networks of complex projects speedily, economically and accurately. Its speed of making resource profiles coupled with its interactive ability to speedily generate the alternatives on the screen, enables the speedy optimization of resources and preparation of resources limited schedule. Computer can promptly provide answers to 'what if' in the form of alternate project plans. Computer printers and plotters can quickly produce reports, graphs, bar charts, histograms, and pictorial diagrams including updated network models, both on the screen as well as the hard copy print-outs. Computers can store historic networks, past-planning data, actual performance, and current-planning information on hard disks and floppies, doing away with bulky paper records. This back-up information can be recalled when required. One of the prime merits of using computers in the planning fields is that they follow instructions faithfully. Computerized system errors are practically non-existent whereas the manual operations are liable to human errors.

The information generated by a computerised system provides an invaluable tool for managing projects. Traditionally, transaction-processing systems have been employed by the lower level managers to improve efficiency and productivity. The management reporting systems are mostly designed for middle-level managers to make them functionally effective by providing information for better decision-making process. The information systems today are meeting the information needs of strategic planners.

A computerized system provides a project manager the information to fulfil his various roles which are as follows:

(a) **Interpersonal role of figurehead, leader and liaison** It gets enhanced using office information systems including information technologies such as audio conferencing, satellite communication, video teleconferencing, electronic mail, Internet, graphic presentation, etc.

(b) **Informational role of monitoring, disseminator and spokesperson** Information generated by transaction process, management reporting systems, decision support system, office automation, and electronic mail can support this role.

(c) **Decisional role of entrepreneur, disturbance handler, resource allocator and negotiation** It gets speeded up by using decision support systems, knowledge-base expert systems, office automation systems and the artificial intelligence.

However, the computer cannot replace the planning engineer. It can only increase his productivity and performance at an additional cost. The computer is not indispensable. The manual methods have their own merits. The computer cannot help in work break-down and in developing logic of network models. This has to be done manually by the planning experts. Experienced planning engineers can generally compute the critical path of the project network faster then even the time required to feed the relevant data into the computer. Manual scheduling of work and forecasting of resources consume time. But it is worthwhile to make the first draft manually as the manual method gives insight into the working of a project which the computer cannot provide. The manual process with its step-by-step manipulation recognizes the effects of changes on the connected activities and carried out adjustments accordingly. The manual method has obvious added advantages specially when those adjustments are carried out by the person who is to execute it. On the whole, it can be said that for the complex important projects, which are to be frequently monitored, the computer is an invaluable tool for efficiently and effectively managing the planning function, but the planning engineer is indispensable.

# Bibliography

ACCA Study Text, *Cost and Management Accounting 1,* BPP Publishing Ltd., 1988.
Adrian, James J. *CM: The Construction Management Process;* Reston Publishing Company, INC (A Prentice-Hall Company), Virginia, 1981.
Adrian, James J., *Construction Estimating*: *An Accounting and Productivity Approach,* Prentice-Hall Reston Publishing Co., Virginia, 1982.
Ahuja, H.N., *Project Management: Techniques in Planning and Controlling Projects,* John Wiley & Sons, New York, 1984.
Al-Sedairy, Salmani, *Large-Scale Construction Projects—Management, Design and Execution,* Batsford Academic and Educational, London, 1985.
Alfeld, Louis Edward, *Construction Productivity*: *On-Site Measurement and Management,* McGraw-Hill Book Company, New York, 1988.
Anderson, S.D., Woodhead, *RW Project Manpower Management,* John Wiley & Sons, 1981.
Austen, A.D., *Management Construction Projects,* I.L.O Publications, Geneva, 1984.
Bennett, John, *Construction Project Management,* Butterworths, London, 1985.
Bent, James A., Albert, Thumam, *Project Management for Engineering & Construction,* The Fairmont Press, Lilburn, 1989.
Bingham, John, *Data Processing,* Macmillan Publishing, London, 1989.
British Standard Institute—Use of Network Technique in Project Management,' BS6046:

| | | |
|---|---|---|
| Part-1 | 1984 | *Guide to the use of Management, Planning, Review and Reporting Procedures* |
| Part-2 | 1992 | *Guide to the use of Graphical and Estimating* |
| Part-3 | 1992 | *Guide to the use of Computers.* |
| Part-4 | 1992 | *Guide to Resource Analysis and Cost Control.* |

Caterpillar Performance Handbook, CAT Publication, Illinois, USA, 1988.
Choudhury, S., *Project Management,* Tata McGraw-Hill Publishing Company Limited, New Delhi, 1988.
Cronin, Blaise, *Information Management,* Aslib, 1985.
Cushman, Robert E. and Others, *Construction Management Form Book,* John Wiley, 1994.
Fisher, Norman, *Marketing for the Construction Industry,* Longman Scientific and Technical, Longman Group Ltd., Essex, England, 1986.
Fisher, Norman, Shen Li Yin, *Information Management in a Contract,* Thomas Telford, London, 1992.
Harris, Frank, and Mecaffer Ronald, *Modern Construction Management,* Granda Publishing Ltd., London, 1983.
Harris, Frank, *Construction Plant,* Granda, 1981.
Havers, J.A. and F.W. Stubbs, *Handbook of Heavy Construction Equipment,* McGraw-Hill, N.Y, USA, 1977.

Hellarrd, R.B., *Total Quality in Construction Projects,* Thomas Telford, London, 1993.

Jackson, Michael J., *CM: Computers in Construction Planning and Control,* Allen & Unwin, 1986.

Jones, Charles, *The Computer Handbook—A Businessmen's Guide to Choosing and Using a Computer System,* Macmillan Education Ltd., London, 1986.

Kerzner Harold, *Project Management: A Systems Approach to Planning, Scheduling and Controlling,* 6/ed, Van Nostrand Rem hold, New York, 1998.

Kharb, K.S., *'A Guide for Quantity Surveyors, Engineers, Architects and Builders,'* Vols 1-4, published by author.

> Volume 1 *Taking-off Quantites, Abstracting and Billing.*
> Volume 2 *Valuation of Properties and Analysis and Prices,* 1989.
> Volume 3 *Cost Planning and Cost Control for Building Projects, Professional Practice and Procedure, Arbitration and Report Writing* 1990.
> Volume 4 *Project Management, Quality Assurance, Design Process and Construction Technology,* 1992.

Kharbanda, O.B. and Others, *Project Control in Action,* Gower Publishing Co., Hampshire, England, 1980.

Makridakiis, S.G., *Forecasting, Planning and Strategy for the 21$^{st}$ Century,* The Free Press (A Division of Macmillan, Inc), New York, 1990.

Neale, R.H., and D.E. Neale, *Construction Planning,* Thomas Telford, London, 1989.

Neil, James, M., *Construction Cost Estimating for Project Control,* Prentice-Hall 1982.

Nunnally, S.W., *Managing Construction Equipment,* Prentice-Hall, USA, 1977.

Nunnally, S.W., *Construction Methods and Management,* Prentice-Hall, New Jersey.

O' Brien, J.J. and R.G. Zilly, *Contractor's Management Handbook,* McGraw Hill New York, 1971.

Peters, Glen, *Project Management and Construction Control,* Construction Press, London, 1981.

Peurifoy R.L., *Construction Planning Equipment, and Methods,* McGraw-Hill International Book Company, 1979.

Prasanna Chandra, *Projects: Preparation, Appraisal, Budgeting and Implementation,* Tata McGraw-Hill Publishing Company Limited, New Delhi, 1993.

Project Management Institute, *A Guide to the Project Management Body of Knowledge,* Upper Darby, PA, OSA, 1996.

Raina, V.K., *Construction Management Practice: The Inside Story,* Tata McGraw-Hill Publishing Company Limited, New Delhi, 1993.

Ray, Alan, and others, *CI/SfB Construction Indexing Manual,* RIBF Publication Limited, 1976.

Soichiro, Nagashima, *100 Management Charts,* Asian Productivity Organisation, Tokyo, 1973.

Walker, Anthony, *Project Management in Construction,* Granda, 1984.

# Index

Activities level 75
Activity
   code 510
   costs 92
   definition 104
   direct cost 93
   indirect cost 93
   production cost 93
   duration 86
   earned value 93
   numbering 153
   sale value 93
   timings 116
Actual cost of work performed (ACWP) 442
Administrative control 62
Architect-engineering associates 7
Area under the normal curve 143
Artificial intelligence systems 536
Bar chart method 181
Benefits of computerisation of information system 537, 550

Bill of quantity (BOQ) code 525
Budget at completion (BAC) 465
Budgeted
   cost trends/forecasts 465
   cost of work performed (BCWP) 442
   cost of work scheduled (BCWS) 442
   cost variances 462
   schedule variances 464
Budgeting
   general and administration expenses 380
   manpower expenses 375
   material usage 377
   operating expenses 373
   other direct expenses 377
   plant and equipment 377
   sales revenue 370
Building workers trade categories 222

Cantonment project
   work-breakdown approach 95, 96
   skeleton network 103
   work-breakdown structure 101
   CPM skeleton network 99
Causes of
   excessive materials wastage 436
   labour low productivity 423

   unfavourable direct cost variances 456
Functions of chief planner 63
CI/SfB manual 83
Code labelling approach 503
Codification
   applications of CI/SfB 505, 509
   effectiveness criteria 528
   purpose 502
Codifying information 59
Common earth compacting equipment 293
Commonly used time planning techniques 47
Concrete
   batching and mixing equipment 298
   hauling and placing concrete 304
   transportation equipment 303
Construction
   business promoters or client 7
   contractors 8
   costs breakdown 342
   equipment cost estimation 328
   home market 4
   international market 5
   input suppliers 7
   management consultants 7
   manpower code 512
   materials code 513
   participants 6
   project concept 8
   projects classification 10
Contract master schedule 216
Contractors construction budget breakdown 368
Contribution variance analysis 461
Control effectiveness prerequisites 417
Control system framework 394
Controlling costs 440, 441
Controlling
   resources productivity 58
   time 59
Cost accounting code 31
   budgeting 442
Cost
   estimation failures 31
   performance index (CPI) 464
   performance measurement 442
   planning 441
   reports 444
   variance (CV) 462
   classification 92

Index **555**

contingencies   380
CPM network analysis procedure   120
Criteria for selection of network technique   43
Criteria to computerise planning and control system   540
Critical activities   117, 119
   path   118, 119
   events   115
Critical Path Method (CPM)   173
Equipment employment card   428

Data needing codification   502
   processing system   534
   record-keeping   411
Decision support systems   534
Designing site organisations   242
   workers financial incentive schemes   243
Detailed network   167
Activities identification   77
Direct cost   62
   control approach   448
   variance   450
   equipment cost variance   455
   labour cost variance   454
   labour costs   343
   material cost variance   450
   materials cost   451, 453
   other expenses   344
Directional control   62
Drawings code   523
Dummy activity   106
Duration
   estimation basis   88
   estimation methods   89
   estimation procedure   91

Earlier start time (EST)   116
Earliest event time (EET)   113, 118
Earliest finish time (EFT)   116
Earned value   92
Earth
   compacting equipment   292
   cutting and hauling equipment   285
   excavating equipment   280
   factors in earthwork   276
   grading equipment   296
   hauling equipment   291
Education buildings activities matrix   84
Equipment acquisition options   331
   classification   276
   hire purchase option   334
   hiring option   333
   leasing with purchase option   334
   operating costs   324
   output determining procedure   284
   output planning data   279, 282, 295, 307, 309
   owning costs   321

productivity analysis   430
productivity control   430
replacement decisions calculations   338
replacement option   336
Equipment selection criteria   331
   commercial considerations   331
   cost considerations   320, 337
   engineering considerations   329, 337
   safety considerations   331
   summary   337
   task considerations   316, 337
Estimating
   break-even analysis   354
   equipment hourly standard rate   353
   indirect cost   359
   labour standard hourly rate   349
   materials standard price   353
   standard direct cost   358
   work package standard cost   357
   owning and operating costs   327
Event timings   113
Events   106
Excavator output adjustment factors for secondary tasks   283

Factors affecting
   acquiring of a computer system   542
   inventory cost   263
   production efficiency   229
   work scheduling   208
Factory project
   task matrix   82
Fast track approach   20
Feedback communication   412
Finance & costs accounting interface   459
Finance accounting code   523
Float or total float (TF)   116
Forecasting
   cash flow   385
   indirect manpower   239
   input and output   46
   inputs   209, 211
   outputs   209, 213
   profit   382
   rate of work   213
   forecasting the balance sheet   387
Foreman's daily labour employment report   424
Foundation construction
   sub-project major materials estimate   56
   activity-wise labour estimate   56

Hammock activity   162
Hardware components of a computerised system   532
Hourly labour rate calculation sheet   352
Housing units project   237
   organisation chart   237
   major plant & equipment planned   53

# 556  Index

forecast of manpower and earned value  48
organisation chart  368
scope of work  40
summary schedule of construction tasks  44
task responsibility centres  369
typical 'S' curve forecast  363
workers' requirement forecast  235
works code  507
standard direct cost of foundation module  359

Indirect cost
   control  457
   functional breakdown  348
   behaviour  346
   pattern of a multinational company  347
Information
   communication systems  536
   system computerisation  537
Integrated time-cost performance chart  445
Inventory replenishment model  265
Drawings codes or a health centre building  526

Labour accounting system  421
   productivity control  420
   productivity control chart  426
   productivity performance analysis  423
   time cards  422
Latest event time (LET)  114, 118
Latest finish time (LFT)  116
LOB technique  195, 203
LOB control chart  206

Major compacting equipment  299
   salient features  299
Major concreting equipment  301
Causes of management failures  33
Management team  26
Materials
   ABC classification  246
   hoisting equipment  305, 306
   inventory  259
   procurement monitoring sheet  258
   productivity control  431
   provisioning process  254
   requisition, issue and return notes  433
   stock control : bin card  432
   usage standards  253
   wastages analysis  435
Minor materials mobilisation stock  270
Modelling and analysing networks  42
Monitoring frequency  411

Network
   analysis fundamentals  104
   analysis procedure  42
   preparation  108
   techniques limitations  179

classification  169
Numbering events  111

Object of scheduling  43
Scheduling procedure  43
Office information systems  535
Operation level  75
Operational control  62

Performance
   accounting process  400
   base lines  398
   monitoring  405
   parameters  397
   reporting  402
PERT critical path  134
PERT network analysis procedure  130
PERT network modelling  130
PERT network of pumping station  126
PERT versus CPM  146
Plan development process  35
Planning construction
   equipment  49
   materials  49
   standard costs  54
   work force  49
Planning
   inventory of minor materials  270
   inventory of non-repetitive one-time purchase materials  269
   inventory of repetitive materials  265
   materials inventory  259
Plant leasing offer of a concrete pump  335
PMIS
   components  531
   concept  530
   framework  534
   functions  530
   structure  42, 532
PNA
   network presentation  172
   versus CPM common features  173
   versus CPM major differences  177
Precedence
   diagramming method (PDM) same as PNA
   network activity representation  150
   network analysis (PNA)  147
   network of four rafts foundation construction  156
   network of a raft foundation construction  148
   network raw water clarifier tank  167
Primary school construction
   precedence network  162
Problems in information system management  548
Procedure for
   ploting project cost—time function  491
   scheduling network—based plan  45

# Index

scheduling repetitive projects using LOB technique   45
Production cost variance breakdown   451
Production efficiency factor   231
Project
   budgetary control   457
   construction equipment classification   277
   construction plan   39
   control methodology   57
   control process outline   55
   development process   14
   environment   12
   execution stage   18
   feasibility   16
   feasibility plan   37
   inception stage   16
   life cycle   15
Project management   21
   matrix organisation   29
   functions   25
   information system, see PMIS
   organisation and staffing   28
   manpower grouping   236
   master budget   388
   mission   10
   mobilisation stage   17
   network   155
   objectives   11
   phase, see project life cycle
   planning benefits   60
   planning scope   25
   preliminary plan   38
   preparation stage   17
   summary network   169
   time crashing potential data   492
   work-breakdown   41
      levels   71
      salient features   72
   control benefits   62
   scheduling benefits   61
Pumping Station Project
   original and modified master networks   488
   time compressed network   488
   updated cpm network   474
   work break-down structure   80
   time analysis CPM network   105

Raw water clarifier construction project   161
Raw water clarifier plant sketch   165
Repetitive works network   155
Resource planning process   46
Resources code   511
Resources constrained what-if analysis   486
Responsibility centre work schedule   216
Revenue or sales control   466
Risk cost management   466
Risks
   categorising   467

response control   469
identification   466
quantifying   467
Role of
   chief planner   64
   construction manager in improving productivity   436
   management in cost control   445
   management in information system problem solving   550
   project manager   29

Sales accounting code   522
Schedule hierarchy   214
Scheduling
   construction site workers   232
   direct workers   233
   indirect workers   236, 239
   networks of repetitive projects   145
   repetitive projects using LOB technique   195
   network plan   182
   within resources constraints   195
Significant codes   504
Site Development Project
   CPM and PNA Analysis   170
   resources-limited schedule   196
   time-limited schedule   193
   forecasts of input   214
Site manufactured readymix concrete production cost   355
Skeleton network   169
Slack   114
Software classification   63
Specifications code   525
Standard
   'S' curve forecasting tool   363
   cost concept   357
   costing methodology   358
   methods of determining depreciation   822
Stores accounting ledger sheet   435
Strategic control   63
Structuring responsibility centres   367
Sub-project code   507
Sub-project level   73
Summary precedence network
   of educational buildings   164
   of primary school   163
Summary schedule of educational buildings   197
Supervisors work programme   216
Schedule variance (SV)
   computerised information   549
   system organisation problems   548

Task
   level   73
   matrix for repetitive works   81
   matrix   81
Technical documents codes   523

Time compression of critical path 486
Time constrained what-if analysis 485
Time crashing 497
    a word of caution 498
Time planning
    process 39
    techniques 46
Time reduction techniques 486
Types of
    project plans 37
Typical
    construction workers planning data 225
    equipment group identification codes 519
    expense budget breakdown 375
    format of construction materials budget summary 379
    format of equipment budget 329
    format of general and administration budget 381
    construction materials group identification codes 381
    manpower group identification codes 524

Use of connectors to link precedence sub-networks 172

User's system specifications development 157

Validating project time objectives 157

Work breakdown for repetitive works 81
Work breakdown structure of
    primary school 83
    cantonment construction project 101
    foundation work 76
    pumping station project 80
    residential buildings 75
Work breakdown at upto sub-project level of housing units project 74
Work package level 73
Work
    scheduling process 43
    scheduling purpose 181
    break-down structure 77
Workers
    production planning norms 221
    productivity standards 220
    trades skills 221
Work-item sale value 93

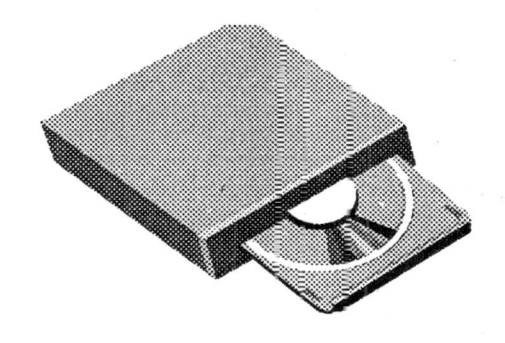

## *CPMT Plus*

## Construction Project Management Techniques and Practice

Auto-Run Starts CPMT Plus with screen opening-

**Introduction** in CPMT covers learning and operating features. It starts with 'Foreword' by Mr G V Ramakrishna, Chairman, Construction Industry Development Council(CIDC) of India.

**Main Menu** is the road map that leads to the Knowledge Areas covered in the **CPMT Plus**. There are eighteen lessons covering 36 topics, having over 1000 Self Assessment Quiz-type Questionnaire (SAQ) placed in Study Mode and Exam Mode, with over 200 practical Exercises. Text of each lesson is in question – answer form. It is illustrated with real life cases. Glossary includes definitions of about 250 keywords commonly used in Project Management.

Click on **Primavera** takes you to demo / working models of the world famous 'Primavera Project Planner' P3. vers 3.0 and Sure Trak.3.0. These contain tutorial with limited activity practice models, instructional manuals and sample projects.

**CPMT Plus** supports and supplements the book on **Construction Project Management: Planning, Scheduling and Controlling.** CD-ROM contains book references at appropriate places and it includes additional material.

### Who will Benefit and How?
- **Construction Industry**. The CD-ROM can form part of the project manuals of the construction enterprises thus facilitating policy formulation and standardizing knowledge areas. glossary of terms and practices on construction project management techniques and related subjects.

- **Project managers and their team members**. It will enable these busy professionals to browse the subject speedily and independently so as to form the common basis of understanding among the project team.

- **Academician, trainers and trainees connected with project management**. It will speed up online knowledge transfer, economically and in large volumes, especially by conducting internet-based education and training.

- **Professionals**. It will provide rapid learning tool to upgrade project management skills to professionals like consultants, architects, engineers, quantity surveyors, accountants and other managers associated with projects.

**Engineering students**. The question-answer interactive approach in the CPMT plus will help the students in faster learning of online updated Knowledge and it will provide ready-made material for examination preparation.